Rules for Predicate Logic

Rule UI: $(u)(\ldots u \ldots) / \therefore (\ldots w \ldots)$

Provided:

1. $(\ldots w \ldots)$ results from replacing each occurrence o
   u free in $(\ldots w \ldots)$ with a w that is free in $(\ldots w \ldots$
   (making no other changes).

Rule EI: $(\exists u)(\ldots u \ldots) / \therefore (\ldots w \ldots)$

Provided:

1. w is not a constant.
2. w does not occur free previously in the proof.
3. $(\ldots w \ldots)$ results from replacing each occurrence o
   u free in $(\ldots u \ldots)$ with a w that is free in $(\ldots w \ldots)$
   (making no other changes).

Rule UG: $(\ldots u \ldots) / \therefore (w)(\ldots w \ldots)$

Provided:

1. u is not a constant.
2. u does not occur free previously in a line obtained
   by **EI**.
3. u does not occur free previously in an assumed
   premise that has not yet been discharged.
4. $(\ldots w \ldots)$ results from replacing each occurrence o
   u free in $(\ldots u \ldots)$ with a w that is free in $(\ldots w \ldots)$
   (making no other changes) and there are no addi-
   tional occurrences of w already contained in
   $(\ldots w \ldots)$.

Rule EG: $(\ldots u \ldots) / \therefore (\exists w)(\ldots w \ldots)$

Provided:

1. $(\ldots w \ldots)$ results from replacing **at least one** occurrence of u free in $(\ldots u \ldots)$ with a w that is free
   in $(\ldots w \ldots)$ (making no other changes) and there
   are no additional occurrences of w already contained in $(\ldots w \ldots)$.

Rule QN: $(u)(\ldots u \ldots) :: \sim (\exists u) \sim (\ldots u \ldots)$

$(\exists u)(\ldots u \ldots) :: \sim (u) \sim (\ldots u \ldots)$

$(u) \sim (\ldots u \ldots) :: \sim (\exists u)(\ldots u \ldots)$

$(\exists u) \sim (\ldots u \ldots) :: \sim (u)(\ldots u \ldots)$

Rule ID: $(\ldots u \ldots)$ $\qquad\qquad$ $(\ldots u \ldots)$

$u = w / \therefore (\ldots w \ldots)$ $\qquad$ $w = u / \therefore (\ldots w \ldots)$

Rule IR: $/ \therefore (x)(x = x)$

Logic and Philosophy
A Modern Introduction
Eighth Edition

Logic and Philosophy
A Modern Introduction
Eighth Edition

Paul Tidman

Mount Union College

Howard Kahane

University of Maryland
Baltimore County

Wadsworth Publishing Company
I(T)P® An International Thomson Publishing Company

Belmont, CA • Albany, NY • Boston • Cincinnati • Johannesburg • London • Madrid • Melbourne
Mexico City • New York • Pacific Grove, CA • Scottsdale, AZ • Singapore • Tokyo • Toronto

Philosophy Editor: Peter Adams
Assistant Editor: Kerri Abdinoor
Editorial Assistant: Kelly Bush
Marketing Manager: Dave Garrison
Production Editor: Hal Lockwood
Accuracy Checker: Patricia Blanchette
Print Buyer: Stacey Weinberger
Permissions Editor: Robert Kauser
Interior Designer: Paula Goldstein
Copy Editor: Jennifer Gordon
Cover Designer: Jeanne Calabrese
Cover Photo: Steve McAlister/Image Bank
Compositor: Thompson Type
Printer: Maple-Vail Press

*This book is printed on
acid-free, recycled paper.*

Printed in the United States of America
1 2 3 4 5 6 7 8 9 10

For more information, contact Wadsworth Publishing Company, 10 Davis Drive, Belmont, CA 94002,
or electronically at http://www.wadsworth.com

International Thomson Publishing Europe
Berkshire House
168-173 High Holborn
London, WC1V 7AA, United Kingdom

International Thomson Editores
Seneca, 53
Colonia Polanco
11560 México D.F. México

Nelson ITP, Australia
102 Dodds Street
South Melbourne
Victoria 3205 Australia

International Thomson Publishing Asia
60 Albert Street #15-01
Albert Complex
Singapore 189969

Nelson Canada
1120 Birchmount Road
Scarborough, Ontario
Canada M1K 5G4

International Thomson Publishing Japan
Hirakawa-cho Kyowa Building, 3F
2-2-1 Hirakawa-cho, Chiyoda-ku
Tokyo 102, Japan

International Thomson Publishing Southern Africa
Building 18, Constantia Square
138 Sixteenth Road, P.O. Box 2459
Halfway House, 1685 South Africa

Library of Congress Cataloging-in-Publication Data

Tidman, Paul
    Logic and philosophy: a modern introduction / Paul Tidman, Howard
Kahane.—8th ed.
        p.   cm.
    Includes blibliographical references and index.
    ISBN 0-534-52614-4
    1. Logic.   I. Tidman, Paul.   II. Title.
BC108.K3   1998
160—dc21   98-13674

To my Dad, who always taught me that logic can be fun.

—Paul Tidman

To Art, Betsy, Charles, Don, Edward, Frank, George, Harry, and . . . Nancy.

—Howard Kahane

Contents

Preface to the Eighth Edition

This new edition of *Logic and Philosophy* is designed to build on the strengths that have made the book one of the most widely used formal logic texts in the discipline for nearly thirty years. Three strengths are especially notable:

1. Clean, accurate exposition coupled with well-designed examples and a wide array of exercises
2. Rules for predicate logic that are both technically rigorous and accessible to the beginning student
3. Comprehensive coverage that goes beyond a bare-bones treatment of sentential and predicate logic, allowing instructors maximum flexibility in course design

The purpose of this book, as in previous editions, is to provide students with a clear and comprehensible introduction to a complete system for sentential and first-order predicate logic and other systems of logic.

- **Help for the Logic-Averse:** This edition is designed to be useful for those students who struggle with logic. There are predictable stumbling points in the typical logic course. For example, in sentential logic students commonly have difficulties with forms, with complex translations involving connectives like "unless," and "only if," and with proofs that require the use of distribution, addition, or assumed premises. Special attention has been paid to these trouble spots. Explanations have been expanded, there are more examples and more basic-level exercises, and the discussion of strategy has been substantially increased.
- **"Walk-Through" Sections:** For crucial exercises there are "how-to" sections, where the student is walked step by step through a moderately difficult sample problem.
- **Organization:** Each chapter is devoted to one basic theme. Related material is not spread out over several chapters.
- **Expanded Coverage of Basic Concepts:** Beginning with the first chapter, more attention is paid to the topic of consistency. The fundamental concept of an interpretation is used to provide a unified explanation of such basic concepts as validity, consistency, logical equivalence, and logical implication in both sentential and predicate logic.
- **Error Checking:** The eighth edition has undergone rigorous error checking throughout

development and during the production process. We've been especially cognizant of the difficulties that errors can cause in the classroom, and we hope you'll find this edition to be a vast improvement.

Changes in the Eighth Edition

The changes we have introduced attempt to preserve prior-edition strengths while making the text even more user-friendly. These changes have been motivated by classroom experiences gained while teaching the basic course in formal logic at the University of Delaware and Mount Union College, and from the comments of colleagues and reviewers. Here are some highlights:

Part One

The discussion of sentence forms and substitution instances has been expanded, and a new exercise on this topic has been added. Forms are now introduced at the end of Chapter 3, after truth tables and just before the discussion of argument forms in Chapter 4. The short truth table technique is now introduced in the chapter on truth tables (Chapter 3) instead of following the discussion of proofs in Chapter 5, where it seemed a bit out of place.

In Chapter 4 the exercises on proofs have been carefully reordered so as to move more gradually from the easiest to the most difficult. A new exercise has been added to this chapter in which students must supply mission premises and lines of the proof by working backwards from the last lines of the proof.

There are also a few helpful new diagrams. There is one in the first chapter that explains how any test of consistency can be modified to test for validity as well. In Chapter 5 there are diagrams that label the essential parts of proofs that make use of assumptions and the rules of Conditional Proof (**CP**) and Indirect Proof (**IP**).

Finally, there is a new section that briefly introduces a few of the basic concepts of metatheory, including the distinction between syntax and semantics and an explanation of what makes a logical system like sentential logic both sound and complete. This discussion sets up an improved explanation of how the truth conditions for the horseshoe are constrained by accepting Modus Ponens (**MP**) as a valid inference rule.

Part Two

There are fewer changes to Part Two of the book. We altered the order of the chapters so that the chapter that reviews the rationale for the predicate logic rules now immediately follows the chapter on relational predicate logic. The exercises on showing invalidity and consistency in predicate logic have been expanded, and we wrote a new discussion of invalidity in relational predicate logic. In Chapter 7 a new exercise lets students get their feet wet with predicate logic proofs before having to master all of the restrictions that follow. The treatment of predicate logic truth trees has been changed so that each individual step is now numbered, making these trees much easier to read.

Part Three

As in the seventh edition, the changes to Part Three have largely consisted of cutting and consolidating in order to keep the size (and thus the cost) of the text within bounds. The chapter on informal fallacies has been eliminated entirely, and the chapters on inductive logic and probability have been consolidated into a single chapter. We found that the chapter on fallacies was rarely used, and there are many excellent, inexpensive paperback treatments of the subject. It is very hard for textbook authors to eliminate large sections. Thus many textbooks grow larger and larger with each progressive edition and students are left to shoulder the burden (both literally and figuratively!). By contrast, this eighth edition of *Logic and Philosophy,* like the seventh, substantially expands the treatment of sentential and predicate logic while at the same time reducing the total number of pages.

In addition to these more general changes, there are many small changes throughout the book. Individual passages have been clarified. There are many new exercise items. As mentioned above, the text has undergone the most careful error checking in the book's history. Any errors found will be posted on the website http://www.muc.edu/-tidmanpa/.

Nelson Pole's LogicCoach software is now bundled with the book. An expanded study guide with many additional practice exercises is also available. The end result, hopefully, is a text genuinely more useful to both students and their instructors.

We would like to thank the reviewers of this eighth edition—Sidney Luckenbach, California State University, Northridge; Dr. Gilbert T. Null, University of Wisconsin, Green Bay; Robert Weingard, Rutgers, The State University of New Jersey, New Brunswick; and Jon Wulff, Bellevue Community College—as well as the prerevision reviewers: Harold Baldwin, University of South Alabama; John David Eatman, Xavier University of Louisiana; Robert Weingard, Rutgers, The State University of New Jersey; Roderick M. Stewart, Austin College; Walter H. O'Briant, University of Georgia; Nancy A. Stanlick, University of South Florida; Katherine Shamey, Santa Monica College; and Vincente Medina, Seton Hall University. We also want to thank our proof checker: Patricia Blanchette, University of Notre Dame.

We would also like to thank many students at the University of Delaware and Mount Union College for all of their suggestions.

1 *The Elements of an Argument*

Consider the following simple example of reasoning:

> Identical twins often have different IQ test scores. Yet such twins inherit the same genes. So environment must play some part in determining IQ.

Logicians call this kind of reasoning an *argument.* (But they don't have in mind shouting or fighting. Rather, their concern is *arguing for* or presenting reasons for a conclusion.) In this case, the argument consists of three statements:

1.　Identical twins often have different IQ test scores.
2.　Identical twins inherit the same genes.
3.　So environment must play some part in determining IQ.

The first two statements in this argument give *reasons* for accepting the third. In logic talk, they are said to be **premises** of the argument, and the third statement is called the argument's **conclusion.** An **argument** can be defined as a series of statements, one of which is the conclusion (the thing argued for) and the others are the premises (reasons for accepting the conclusion).

In everyday life, few of us bother to explicitly label premises or conclusions. We usually don't even bother to distinguish one argument from another. But good writing provides clues that signal the presence of an argument. Such words as *because, since, and for* usually indicate that what follows is a premise. And words like *therefore, hence, consequently,* and *so* usually signal a conclusion. Similarly, certain expressions like "It has been observed that . . . ," "In support of this . . . ," and "The relevant data . . ." generally introduce premises, whereas other expressions such as "It follows that . . . ," "The result is . . . ," "The point of all this is . . . ," and "The implication is . . ." usually signal conclusions. Here is a simple example:

> *Since* it's wrong to kill a human being, *it follows that* abortion is wrong, *because* abortion takes the life of (kills) a human being.

In this example, the words *since* and *because* signal premises offered in support of the conclusion signaled by the phrase "it follows that." Put into textbook form, the argument reads:

1. It's wrong to kill a human being.
2. Abortion takes the life of (kills) a human being.
∴ 3. Abortion is wrong.

The symbol "∴" represents the word *therefore* and indicates that what follows is a conclusion. This particular argument has two premises, but an argument may have any number of premises and may be surrounded by or embedded in other arguments.

Not just any group of sentences makes an argument. The sentences in an argument must express statements, that is, say something that is either true or false. Many sentences are used for other purposes: to ask questions, to issue commands, or to give vent to emotions. In ordinary contexts none of the following express statements:

Open the door. *(command)*
Who's the boss here? *(question)*
Thank goodness! *(expression of emotion)*

Of course, sometimes nondeclarative sentences are indeed used to make statements. "Who's the boss here?" *can* be used to make a statement, particularly if it is the boss who is talking. In this case the boss is not really asking a question at all, but rather is saying "*I am the boss here,*" thus declaring a fact under the guise of asking a question.

But even if every sentence in a group of sentences expresses a statement, the result is not necessarily an argument. The statements must be related to one another in the appropriate way. There must be something argued for (the conclusion), and there must be reasons for accepting the conclusion. Thus, mere bald assertions are not arguments, anecdotes generally are not arguments, nor are most other forms of exposition or explanation. It's important to understand the difference between rhetoric that is primarily expository or explanatory and rhetoric that is basically argumentative. A passage that contains only exposition gives us no reason to accept the "facts" in it other than the authority of the writer or speaker, whereas passages that contain arguments give reasons for some of their claims (conclusions) and call for a different sort of evaluation than merely an evaluation of the authority of the writer.

Examples

Only two of the following groups of statements constitute arguments. These examples also illustrate that although the words "therefore" and "because" usually signal the presence of an argument, this is not always the case.

1. I believe in God because that is how I was raised. (This is biography, not an argument. "Because" is used here to cite the cause of the speaker's belief—to give an explanation—not to signal a premise.)

2. I believe in God because life has meaning. If there is no God, life would be meaningless. (This is an argument. The speaker is advancing a reason to believe that God exists.) Here is the argument put into textbook form:
   1. Life has meaning.
   2. If there were no God, life would be meaningless.
   ∴ 3. God exists

   (Notice that in this case the word "because" does signal that a premise is to follow.)
3. Biff was obviously afraid of making a commitment to a long-term relationship. Therefore, Susie was not surprised when they eventually broke up. (This is not an argument. This is an explanation of why Susie was not surprised.)
4. We'll get a tax break if we marry before the end of the year. Therefore, I think we should move our wedding date up and not wait until January. (This is an argument):
   1. We'll get a tax break if we marry before the end of the year.
   ∴ 2. We should move our wedding date up and not wait until January.

Exercise 1-1

Here are twelve passages (the first six are from student papers and exams, modestly edited). Determine which contain arguments and which do not. Label the premises and conclusions of those that do, and explain your answers. Paraphrase if that makes things clearer. (The answers for even-numbered items in most exercise sets are provided at the back of the book.)

1. I don't like big-time college football. I don't like pro football on TV either. In fact, I don't like sports, period.
2. My summer vacation was spent working in Las Vegas. I worked as a waitress at the Desert Inn and made tons of money. But I guess I got addicted to the slots and didn't save too much. Next summer my friend Hal and I are going to work in Reno, if we can find jobs there.
3. Well, I have a special reason for believing in big-time college football. After all, I wouldn't have come here if Ohio State's football team hadn't gone to the Rose Bowl, because that's how I heard about this place to begin with.
4. At the present rate of consumption, the oil will be used up in 20 to 25 years. And we're sure not going to reduce consumption in the near future. So we'd better start developing solar power, windmills, and other "alternative energy sources" pretty soon.
5. The abortion issue is blown all out of proportion. How come we don't hear nearly as much about the evils of the Pill? After all, a lot more potential people are "killed" by the Pill than by abortion.
6. I've often wondered how they make lead pencils. Of course, they don't use lead— they use graphite. But, I mean, how do they get the graphite into the wood? That's my problem. The only thing I can think of is maybe they cut the lead into long round strips and then cut holes in the wood and slip the lead in.

7. Punishment, when speedy and specific, may suppress undesirable behavior, but it cannot teach or encourage desirable alternatives. Therefore, it is crucial to use positive techniques to model and reinforce appropriate behavior that the person can use in place of the unacceptable response that has to be suppressed. (Walter and Harriet Mischel, *Essentials of Psychology*)

8. There was no European language that Ruth could not speak at least a little bit. She passed the time in the concentration camp, waiting for death, by getting other prisoners to teach her languages she did not know. Thus did she become fluent in Romany, the tongue of the gypsies. (Kurt Vonnegut, *Jailbird*)

9. The death of my brother was another instance in which I realized the inadequacy of the superstition of progress in regard to life. A good, intelligent, serious man, he was still young when he fell ill. He suffered for over a year and died an agonizing death without ever understanding why he lived and understanding even less why he was dying. No theories could provide any answers to these questions, either for him or for me, during his slow and painful death. (Leo Tolstoy, *Confession*)

10. To be sustained under the Eighth Amendment, the death penalty must "[comport] with the basic concept of human dignity at the core of the Amendment"; the objective in imposing it must be "[consistent] with our respect for the dignity of [other] men." Under these standards, the taking of life "because the wrongdoer deserves it" surely must fail, for such a punishment has as its very basis the total denial of the wrongdoer's dignity and worth. (Justice Thurgood Marshall, dissenting opinion in *Gregg v. Georgia*)

11. If God were all good he would want his creatures to always be happy. If God were all powerful he would be able to accomplish anything he wants. Therefore, God must be lacking in either power or goodness or both.

12. Every event must have a cause. Since an infinite series of causes is impossible, there must be a first uncaused cause of everything: God.

2   *Deduction and Induction*

Deduction and induction are commonly thought to be the cornerstones of good reasoning. The fundamental logical property of a deductively **valid argument** is this: If all of its premises are true, then its conclusion must be true. In other words, *an argument is valid just in case it is impossible for all of its premises to be true and yet its conclusion be false.* The truth of the premises of a valid argument guarantees the truth of its conclusion.

In order to determine whether or not an argument is valid, one must ask whether there are any possible circumstances under which the premises could all be true and yet the conclusion be false. If not, the argument is valid. If it is possible for the premise to be true and the conclusion false, the argument is invalid. An **invalid argument** is simply an argument that is not valid.

The question naturally arises as to why it is impossible for the conclusion of a valid argument to be false if all of its premises are true. Why do its premises, if true, "guarantee" the truth of its conclusion? Unfortunately, there are no simple or generally accepted answers to questions of this kind. However, it is revealing to notice that in a typical case the information contained in the conclusion of a deductively valid argument is already "contained" in its premises. We tend not to notice this fact because it is usually contained in the premises implicitly (along with other information not contained in the conclusion). Indeed, cases in which the conclusion is explicitly mentioned in a premise tend to be rather trivial.

Examples

Here is an example of a deductively valid argument whose conclusion is implicitly contained in its premises:

1. All wars are started by miscalculation.
2. The Korean conflict was a war.
∴ 3. The Korean conflict was started by miscalculation.

Having said in the first premise that all wars are started by miscalculation and in the second that the Korean conflict was a war, we have implicitly said that the Korean conflict was started by miscalculation. And this is what is asserted by the argument's conclusion.

Here is another example:

1. If Bonny has had her appendix taken out, then she doesn't have to worry about getting appendicitis.
2. She has had her appendix taken out.
∴ 3. She doesn't have to worry about getting appendicitis.

The first premise states that if Bonny has had her appendix out, then she doesn't have to worry about appendicitis, and the second, that she has in fact had her appendix out, which implicitly asserts the conclusion that she doesn't have to worry about appendicitis.

And here is a trivial case in which the conclusion is explicitly stated in the argument's premise:

1. Shakespeare wrote *Othello,* and Chaucer wrote *The Canterbury Tales.*
∴ 2. Shakespeare wrote *Othello.*

In addition to deductive arguments, there are also **inductive arguments.** Arguments of this kind differ from deductively valid arguments in having conclusions that go beyond what is contained in their premises. Good inductive arguments are said to be **inductively strong.** The crucial difference between inductive strength and deductive validity is that it is possible for the premises of a strong inductive argument to be true and yet the conclusion be false. Whereas true premises in a valid argument *guarantee* the truth of the conclusion, true premises in a strong inductive argument make the conclusion *likely* or *probable.* The basic idea behind inductive reasoning is that of *learning from experience.* We notice *patterns, resemblances,* or other kinds of *regularities* in our experiences, some quite simple (sugar sweetens coffee), some very complicated (objects move according to Newton's laws), and project them onto other cases.

We use inductive reasoning so frequently in everyday life that the inductive nature of this kind of conclusion drawing generally goes unnoticed. It's a bit like being told that we've been speaking prose all our lives only to discover that we've been drawing perfectly good inductive inferences (and some stinkers) since an early age. By the age of five, the use of induction has taught us a great many of the basic truths that guide everyday behavior. We have learned, for instance, that some foods taste good and some don't, the sun is going to rise tomorrow morning and every morning after that, very hot things burn the skin, some people are good and some aren't, you can't hold your breath for more than a minute or two, and so on. Our reasoning to the belief that the sun will rise tomorrow, as an example, can be expressed in this way:

   1.   The sun has always risen every morning so far.
∴. 2.   The sun will rise tomorrow (or every morning).

The great virtue of inductive reasoning is that it provides us with a way of reasoning to genuinely new beliefs, and not just to psychologically new ones that were implicit in what we already knew, as in the case of valid deductions. However, this benefit is purchased at the cost of an increase in the possibility of error. The truth of the premises of a deductively valid argument guarantees the truth of its conclusion, but a strong induction may contain all true premises and yet have a false conclusion. Even the best "inductive leap" may lead us astray, because the pattern noticed in our experiences may not turn out to be true in other cases. For example, in 1986 after the success of the *Star Wars* movies, it was a pretty safe bet that the next film produced by George Lucas would be a box office hit. So moviegoers in 1986 could have constructed the following inductively strong argument:

   1.   All of the movies produced in recent years by George Lucas have been successful.
∴. 2.   The latest film produced by Lucas will be successful.

Unfortunately, the film turned out to be *Howard the Duck*.

Although an inductively strong argument does not guarantee that if its premises are true then its conclusion also will be true, it does make its conclusion more probable (one reason why the expression "probability argument" is sometimes applied to inductive arguments). And, of course, the more and the better the evidence, the higher the probability that its conclusion will in fact turn out to be true. Unlike validity, inductive strength comes in degrees. It makes no sense to speak of one argument as being more valid than another. All arguments are either valid or invalid. But it does make sense to describe one argument as being inductively stronger than another. This fact alone makes inductive logic much more complex and controversial. Induction is treated in greater detail in Chapter 14.

3   *Argument Forms*

Consider the following argument:

   1.   Art is an Abadab or he's a Glubphlab.
   2.   It's not true that Art is an Abadab.
∴. 3.   He's a Glubphlab.

In this argument, if premises 1 and 2 are both true, then the conclusion must be true also. But are both premises true? We have no way of knowing, since, presumably, we don't know anything about Abadabs or Glubphlabs and consequently don't know whether Art is or is not an Abadab. But in spite of this, it is clear that if the premises are true (that is, if Art is either an Abadab or a Glubphlab, but he's not an Abadab) then the conclusion must be true (that is, Art must be a Glubphlab). We know this because of the **form** of the argument and not because of its content; its form makes this argument a valid argument.* Any argument having the same form—that is, any argument of the form

1. _____ or _____ .
2. It's not true that _____ .
∴ 3. _____ .

where each pair of similar lines (solid lines, dashed lines) is filled in with the same expression—is deductively valid. (Of course, there are many other valid argument forms.)

Examples

Arguments (1) through (4) all have the same form. So do arguments (5) through (8), but the form they share is different from that of (1) through (4):

(1) 1. It will rain or it will snow.
    2. It's not true that it will rain.
∴ 3. It will snow.

(2) 1. A Democrat will win or a Republican will win.
    2. It's not true that a Democrat will win.
∴ 3. A Republican will win.

(3) 1. There's a devil or there's a God.
    2. It's not true that there's a devil.
∴ 3. There's a God.

(4) 1. There's complete justice, or there's a devil.
    2. It's not true that there's complete justice.
∴ 3. There's a devil.

(5) 1. If Art is an Abadab, then he's a Glubphlab.
    2. Art is an Abadab.
∴ 3. He's a Glubphlab.

(6) 1. If a Republican wins, then a Democrat loses.
    2. A Republican wins.
∴ 3. A Democrat loses.

---

*We shall see later that, in general, arguments have several forms; a valid argument is one that has at least one valid form.

(7) 1. If a Democrat wins, then a liar wins.
     2. A Democrat wins.
∴ 3. A liar wins.

(8) 1. If a Republican wins, then a thief wins.
     2. A Republican wins.
∴ 3. A thief wins.

Logic is concerned primarily with argument forms and only secondarily with arguments, for all arguments that have a valid argument form are valid. It is the form, not the content, of the above arguments that makes it impossible for them to have all true premises and a false conclusion. Thus, the principal task of deductive logic is to provide a method for distinguishing valid argument forms from invalid argument forms.

4   *Truth and Validity*

It is important to realize that a deductively valid argument can have a false conclusion if one or more of its premises are false. On the other hand, an invalid argument can have both true premises and a true conclusion. In fact, every combination of validity–invalidity and truth–falsehood can occur, except one: *A valid argument with true premises cannot have a false conclusion.* The question of validity is the question of whether the conclusion follows from the premises, that is, whether it is *possible* for the premises to all be true and the conclusion false. So if all you know about an argument is that it is valid, that alone tells you nothing about whether the premises or the conclusion are in fact true.

Examples

Valid Arguments

(1) True premises and true conclusion:
     1. If Ali beat Frazier, then Ali was heavyweight champion of the world.
     2. Ali beat Frazier.
∴ 3. Ali was heavyweight champion of the world.

(2) True premises and false conclusion: (This cannot occur; an argument with true premises and a false conclusion must be invalid.)

(3) False premises and true conclusion:
     1. Bill Clinton is a politician, and he once won a gold medal in the Olympics for the 200-meter hurdles.
∴ 2. Bill Clinton is a politician.

(4) False premises and false conclusion:
1. The moon is made of green cheese, and the planet Mars is made of milk chocolate.
∴ 2. The moon is made of green cheese.

Invalid Arguments

It is very easy to produce invalid arguments having any combination of truth and falsity with respect to premises and conclusion. Simply produce true or false statements that have no connection whatsoever to one another, such as the following:

(5) True premises and true conclusion:
1. Africa is a continent.
2. George Washington crossed the Delaware.
∴ 3. Broccoli is a vegetable.

Obviously, no one is going to be fooled by this argument. But there is an important point behind this example. *From the mere fact that an argument is invalid, you can draw no conclusion whatsoever about the truth or falsity of the premises or the conclusion.*

To make things more interesting, the remaining arguments will at least resemble valid arguments. Here's another invalid argument with both true premises and a true conclusion that at least looks like a valid argument:

1. If you are reading this book, then you are not asleep.
2. You are not asleep.
∴ 3. You are reading this book.

(6) True premises and false conclusion:
1. If Rhode Island is a small island in the South Pacific, then it is smaller than Texas.
2. Rhode Island is smaller than Texas.
∴ 3. Rhode Island is a small island in the South Pacific.

(7) False premises and true conclusion:
1. If the duckbill platypus is a mammal, then the duckbill platypus does not lay eggs.
2. The duckbill platypus does not lay eggs.
∴ 3. The duckbill platypus is a mammal.

(8) False premises and false conclusion:
1. Either Dianne Feinstein is a senator representing the state of New York, or Hillary Rodham Clinton is governor of Ohio.
2. Hillary Rodham Clinton is governor of Ohio.
∴ 3. Dianne Feinstein is a senator representing the state of New York.

Note that although all of these examples have either all true premises or all false premises, it is also possible to produce both valid and invalid arguments that have a mix of some true and some false premises. Here are two examples:

(9) Valid:
  1. Either Newt Gingrich is a Republican or he's a Southerner. (*true*)
  2. It is false that Newt Gingrich is a Republican. (*false*)
∴ 3. Newt Gingrich is a Southerner. (*true*)

(10) Invalid:
  1. If the oboe is a brass instrument, then some brass instruments are played with a double reed. (*true*)
  2. Some brass instruments are played with a double reed. (*false*)
∴ 3. The oboe is a brass instrument. (*false*)

The only combination of truth and falsity it is impossible to produce is argument that is valid and has all true premises and a false conclusion.

Although we can sensibly speak of valid and invalid arguments and argument forms, it makes no sense to speak of valid or invalid statements, premises, or conclusions. Nor does it make any sense to call an argument true or false. Validity and invalidity are properties of arguments; truth and falsity are properties of statements.

Exercise 1-2

1. Produce your own example of an argument that has the form

      1. _____ or _____ .
      2. It's not true that _____ .
    ∴ 3. _____ .

    and whose conclusion is obviously false.
2. Produce an argument with the same form but whose conclusion is obviously true.
3. Produce your own example of an argument that has the form

      1. If _____ then _____ .
      2. It's not true that _____ .
    ∴ 3. _____ .

    and whose conclusion is obviously false.
4. Produce an argument with the same form but whose conclusion is obviously true.
5. Is it possible to produce an example of argument having the first form that also has premises that are all obviously true and a conclusion that is obviously false? If so, produce such an argument.
6. Is it possible to produce an example of argument having the second form that has premises that are all obviously true and a conclusion that is obviously false? If so, produce such an argument.
7. Which of your arguments are valid and which are invalid? Explain.

5   *Soundness*

Obviously, an argument can be valid but still be a bad argument because it has one or more false premises. Such arguments are said to be valid, but not **sound.** In order to be sound an argument must meet two conditions: it must (a) be valid and (b) have all true premises. An **unsound** argument is any argument that fails to meet one or both of these two conditions. Thus, example (1) on page 8 is sound because it is valid and has true premises; the other examples are all unsound because they are invalid, have a false premise, or both.

In general, logic is not concerned with the soundness of arguments because, with one exception, logic alone cannot determine whether the premises of an argument are true or false. (The one exception concerns premises that are logically true or false. See the discussion of tautologies in Chapter 3.)

Examples

(1)   A sound argument:
  1. Either a majority voted for Clinton in 1992, or he received more votes than any other candidate.
  2. It's not true that a majority voted for Clinton in 1992.
  ∴ 3. Clinton received more votes than any other candidate.

(2)   An argument that is valid but clearly not sound:
  1. If grapefruits are fruits, then grapefruits grow on trees.
  2. It's false that grapefruits grow on trees.
  ∴ 2. It's false that grapefruits are fruits.

(3)   A valid argument. The soundness of the argument is a question that falls outside the scope of logic:
  1. Either an uncaused being exists, or an endless chain of beings has always existed.
  2. It is false that an endless chain of beings has always existed.
  ∴ 3. An uncaused being exists.

---

6   *Consistency*

Logic can be used for other purposes than the evaluation of arguments. In particular, logic can be used to determine whether a set of statements is consistent. A set of statements is **consistent** if it is possible for all of the statements to be true. If it is impossible for them all to be true, the set is **inconsistent.** No one wants to be guilty of inconsistency. Indeed, it is an interesting philosophical question (not to be pursued here) whether it is even psychologically possible for humans to knowingly believe explicitly inconsistent statements.

Examples

Perhaps the most obvious examples of inconsistent statements are pairs of statements that explicitly contradict one another.

1. Ronald Reagan was one of our country's greatest presidents.
2. Ronald Reagan was not one of our country's greatest presidents.

Unfortunately, sometimes inconsistency is not so obvious. The inconsistency in the following is a little less obvious:

1. John F. Kennedy was a man of great moral character.
2. John F. Kennedy regularly committed adultery.
3. No one who regularly commits adultery has great moral character.

Here is a famous example of an inconsistency that is not at all obvious:

1. Harry, the barber, shaves only those who do not shave themselves.
2. Harry, the barber, shaves all of those who do not shave themselves.

(*Hint:* Does Harry shave himself?)

If you have inconsistent statements, at least one of those statements must be false. Just as logic usually cannot tell us whether to accept the premises or conclusion of a valid argument, so too logic is typically silent on which statements of an inconsistent set are in fact false. (Again, the exception is sentences that are logically true or false.) As we saw with validity, the question of whether a set of sentences is consistent does not depend on the actual truth value of those sentences. A set of sentences can be consistent and all of its members be true, and a set can be consistent but all of its members be false. The only possibility that is ruled out is a set of sentences that is inconsistent and whose members are all true. (Just as with validity, where the only possibility that can be ruled out is an argument with all true premises and a false conclusion.) All of the other possible combinations of truth and falsity, consistency and inconsistency are possible.

7   *Consistency and Validity Compared*

Consistency, like validity, is a matter of logical form. Surprisingly, validity and *in*consistency have a lot in common. To say that an argument is valid is to say that something is impossible—it is to say that it is impossible for the premises of the argument all to be true and the conclusion false. Likewise, to say that a group of sentences is inconsistent is also to say something is impossible—in this case, it is to say that it is impossible for the sentences all to be true. Just as the form of a valid argument guarantees that it is not possible for the premises to be true and the conclusion false, so the form of a set of inconsistent sentences guarantees that they cannot all be true.

We will explore the relationship between consistency and validity in some detail in the chapters that follow. For now we can summarize the relationship as follows: *An argument is valid if and only if it is inconsistent to say that all of its premises are true and its con-*

clusion is false. This is a very useful relationship. It means that any procedure that can be used to test for inconsistency can be slightly modified and used as a test for validity (and vice versa). For example, suppose you had a computer program that could scan any group of sentences and tell you whether or not they were consistent. To use this program to check an argument for validity, simply attach the words "It is false that . . ." to the beginning of the conclusion and then scan the resulting statement along with the argument's premises. If the program informs you that these sentences are *consistent,* then the original argument is invalid (because this shows it is possible for the premises to be true and the conclusion false). On the other hand, if these sentences are *inconsistent,* then the argument in question is valid.

How to Use a "Consistency Checker" to Determine Whether an Argument Is Valid

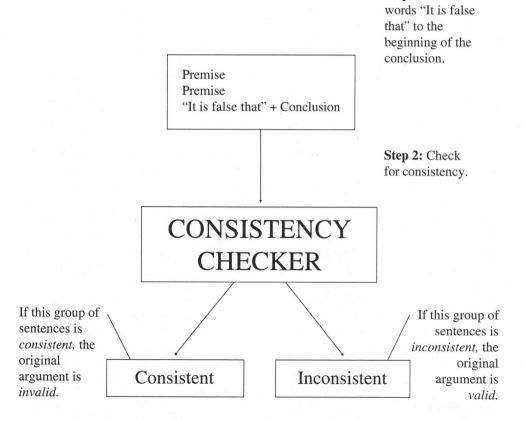

Step 1: Add the words "It is false that" to the beginning of the conclusion.

Premise
Premise
"It is false that" + Conclusion

Step 2: Check for consistency.

CONSISTENCY CHECKER

If this group of sentences is *consistent,* the original argument is *invalid.*

Consistent

Inconsistent

If this group of sentences is *inconsistent,* the original argument is *valid.*

Why this is so: If the premises together with the claim that the conclusion is false form a consistent set, then it is possible for the premises to all be true and the original conclusion false. Thus the argument is invalid. On the other hand, if the premises and modified conclusion are inconsistent, then it is impossible for the premises to be true and the conclusion false, and the argument is valid.

> **Example**
>
> The argument
>
> 1. If capital punishment is not a better deterrent than life imprisonment, it should be abolished.
> 2. Capital punishment is not a better deterrent than life imprisonment.
> ∴ 3. Capital punishment should be abolished.
>
> is valid if and only if the following three sentences are inconsistent:
>
> 1. If capital punishment is not a better deterrent than life imprisonment, it should be abolished.
> 2. Capital punishment is not a better deterrent than life imprisonment.
> 3. *It is false that* capital punishment should be abolished.

8   *Contexts of Discovery and Justification*

When someone states that something is true, two important kinds of questions can be asked: First, what psychological factors led that person to think of such a conclusion; and second, what reasons are offered for accepting it as true? Questions of the first kind are said to be in the area or context of **discovery**; those of the second kind are in the area or context of **justification.**

In general, logic does not deal with the context of discovery. The mental processes used in thinking of hypotheses or conclusions are of interest to the psychologist, not the logician. The logician is interested in reasons that are, or might be, presented in support of conclusions. In other words, the logician is interested in the context of justification.

The difference between discovery and justification is illustrated by the difference between the sometimes agonizing thought processes necessary to figure out solutions to difficult problems and the arguments we then present in their defense. The discovery process, the figuring out, often is long and involved, whereas the argument presented to justify the conclusion arrived at by this long process is elegantly simple.

For instance, a scientist may first think of a scientific theory in a dream. But the arguments presented to fellow scientists to support the theory would not refer to the dream. The dream and its contents are part of the process of discovering the theory, not part of the process of justifying it. (Of course, sometimes the processes of discovery and justification overlap.)

Exercise 1-3

1. Can an argument have all true premises and a true conclusion and yet not be deductively valid?
2. Can an inductively strong argument have all true premises and a false conclusion?
3. Can a deductively valid argument have false premises?

4. Can a deductively valid argument have a false conclusion?
5. Can a deductively invalid argument have a true conclusion?
6. Can a deductively valid argument have all true premises and a false conclusion?
7. Can an argument be sound but not valid?
8. Can a deductively valid argument be sound and yet have a false conclusion?
9. Have we proved that the conclusion of a deductively valid argument is true when we have established that its premises are all true?
10. Can all of the members of a consistent set of sentences be false?
11. Can some of the members of an inconsistent set of sentences be true?
12. Can all of the members of an inconsistent set of sentences be true?
13. List two English words that commonly signal premises of arguments.
14. List two English words that commonly signal conclusions of arguments.
15. What is the difference between the context of discovery and the context of justification? Which one is the concern of logic?

Key terms

argument: A series of sentences, one of which (the conclusion) is claimed to be supported by the others (the premises).

argument form: Informally, the logical structure of an argument.

conclusion: The sentence in an argument that is argued for on the basis of the argument's premises.

consistent: A set of statements is consistent if and only if it is possible for any of the statements to be true.

deductively valid argument: (See *valid argument*.)

deductively invalid argument: (See *invalid argument*.)

discovery, context of: The thought processes or psychological processes that may lead to the finding of new conclusions or theories. (See also *justification*.)

inconsistent: A set of statements is inconsistent if and only if it is impossible for all of the statements to be true.

inductive argument: An argument that is not deductively valid but whose premises provide some measure of support for its conclusion.

inductively strong argument: An inductive argument such that if its premises are all true its conclusion is *probably* true.

invalid argument: An argument that is not valid. An argument is invalid just in case it is possible for the premises of the argument to all be true and the conclusion false.

justification, context of: The context in which we try to justify conclusions by means of rational argument. (See also *discovery*.)

premises: The reasons given in support of an argument's conclusion.

sound argument: An argument that is valid and has all true premises.

unsound argument: Any argument that is either invalid or does not have all true premises.

valid argument: An argument is valid if and only if it is not possible for all of its premises to be true and its conclusion false. If all premises of a valid argument are true, then its conclusion *must* be true also. The conclusion of a valid argument follows logically from the premises.

Chapter Two

Truth-Functions

---

1   *Atomic and Compound Sentences*

It is a familiar fact about the English language that longer sentences can be built up out of shorter sentences. One way we do this is to use **sentence connectives** such as "and" and "or."

Examples

1. Reagan won in 1980, *and* he also won in 1984.
2. God's on our side, *or* He's on their side.
3. *If* we don't reduce the birthrate, *then* soon there won't be any room to sit down.

Sentences built from shorter sentences by means of sentence connectives, like "and" or "or," are called **compound sentences.** All others are said to be **atomic sentences.** Thus, the two sentences "God's in his heaven" and "All's right with the world" are atomic, whereas "God's in his heaven and all's right with the world" is compound. (Note, however, that an atomic sentence may be quite long, as is the atomic sentence "On the 23rd of September, 1945, the jazz singer Maurice Klotzman filed a name-changing petition in Los Angeles Superior Court before Judge Bonny Robbins.")

Chapters 2 through 5 of this text are concerned with the part of logic that can be developed without considering the interior structure of atomic sentences, the part that's called **sentential logic.** (Sentential logic, along with the predicate logic to be discussed in Part Two of this text, forms what is often called **symbolic logic,** to distinguish it from the older, Aristotelian system discussed in Chapter 13.)

2   *Truth-Functions*

The key to mastering sentential logic is to grasp the idea of a **truth-function.** To help you understand what a truth-function is, consider how functions work in mathematics. Mathematical functions operate like number transforming machines. The 2× function, for example, might be pictured as a black box that automatically transforms any number dropped into it into a number that is twice as large. Drop in a 2, out pops a 4. Drop in 54, out pops 108, and so forth. No matter what number you input, the output is determined—it is a function of the number you put in.

For a familiar use of functions, consider a simple hand-held calculator. The typical calculator has two kinds of keys: number keys and function keys. The function keys are used to perform various mathematical operations on numbers that are entered by the number keys. Some function keys, such as the square root key, take one number as their input; others, such as the multiplication key, take two. But the point to keep in mind is that the output produced by pressing these keys is automatic and determined by the input.

Now let's consider what a truth-functional calculator would be like. Here things are much simpler. Instead of the infinitely many numerical inputs that are possible in mathematics, with truth-functions we only have two **truth-values**—either true or false. Likewise, the output of a truth-function can only be one of these two values. Sentential logic is sometimes called "the logic of truth-functions" in that every compound sentence in sentential logic has a definite truth-value (it is either true or false), and that truth-value is determined by—is a function of—the truth-values of the atomic sentences it contains.

We use symbols such as "+" and "÷" to represent common mathematical functions. These symbols are called "operators." Likewise, in our system of logic there are five **truth-functional operators.** One operator, "~" (not), takes only one input; the other four, "·" (and), "∨" (or), "⊃" (if . . . then), and "≡" (if and only if), take two.

As we shall see, the logical form of sentences in ordinary English can be represented symbolically by means of the five truth-functional operators we are about to discuss.

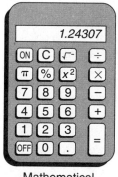

Mathematical
Calculator

Truth-Functional
Calculator

3   *Conjunctions*

Compound sentences formed by use of the sentence connective "and" are called **conjunctions,** and the two sentences joined together by the "and" are called **conjuncts** of the conjunction.

   Let's abbreviate the sentence "Art went to the show" by the capital letter *A,* the sentence "Betsy went to the show" by the capital letter *B,* and the connective "and" by the **dot** "·". Then the sentence "Art went to the show and Betsy went to the show" can be symbolized as $A \cdot B$. Now consider all of the possible truth-values of the two conjuncts of this sentence. First, if *A* and *B* both are true (that is if Art and Betsy both went to the show), then it is obvious that the compound sentence $A \cdot B$ is true. Second, if *A* is true and *B* is false, then $A \cdot B$ is false. Third, if *A* is false and *B* is true, then $A \cdot B$ is false. And finally, if *A* and *B* both are false, then $A \cdot B$ is false. There are no other possible combinations of truth-values for the sentences *A* and *B.* We have thus characterized the truth-functional meaning of the connective "·", because we've shown how the truth-values of the compound sentences formed by its use are uniquely determined by the truth-values of their two conjuncts. Anyone who is given the actual truth-values of *A* and *B* can "figure out" the truth-value of the compound sentence $A \cdot B,$ because (as was just illustrated) the truth-value of that compound sentence is determined by (is a function of) the truth-values of its component parts.

   The information about the compound sentence $A \cdot B$ contained in the above paragraph can be put into the form of a table, called a **truth table,** as follows:

A	B	A · B
True **(T)**	True **(T)**	True **(T)**
True **(T)**	False **(F)**	False **(F)**
False **(F)**	True **(T)**	False **(F)**
False **(F)**	False **(F)**	False **(F)**

Line 1 of this truth table indicates that if *A* and *B* both are true, then $A \cdot B$ is true. Line 2 indicates that if *A* is true and *B* false, then $A \cdot B$ is false, and so on.

   Not all uses of the word "and" are to be symbolized by the dot symbol. It would be wrong, for instance, to symbolize the sentence "Art and Betsy are lovers" as $A \cdot B,$ for that would say that Art is a lover and Betsy is a lover, but not that they love each other. Similarly, it would be wrong to symbolize the sentence "Babe Ruth and Lou Gehrig were teammates" as $R \cdot G,$ for that would say that Ruth was a teammate and Gehrig was a teammate, but not that they were teammates of each other.

   However, some sentences that look like the two we have just considered are logically quite different. For instance, the sentence "Art and Betsy are intelligent" looks just like "Art and Betsy are lovers," and indeed it has the same grammatical structure. But it does not have the same logical structure. The sentence "Art and Betsy are intelligent" does say the same thing as "Art is intelligent and Betsy is intelligent," and thus can be correctly symbolized as $A \cdot B$.

It is essential to understand that the objection to translating a sentence like "Art and Betsy are lovers" as $A \cdot B$ is *not* merely that this would leave out some information. As we shall see, this is often the case. Rather, the problem is that the truth-value of this particular complex sentence *is not a function* of the truth-value of the sentences "Art is a lover" and "Betsy is lover." If you know the truth-value of these two atomic sentences, you may still be in the dark about whether the sentence being symbolized is true. One can imagine possible circumstances where these two sentences are true and the longer sentence is clearly true, but one can also imagine circumstances where these two sentences are true and the longer sentence is clearly false (Art is a lover and Betsy is a lover, but Art and Betsy absolutely detest each other).

The fact that A and B could both be true even though the sentence "Art and Betsy are lovers" is false shows that it would not be accurate to symbolize this sentence as a conjunction using the dot truth-functional operator. But more fundamentally, the fact that one can imagine circumstances where A and B are both true and this sentence is clearly true, and other circumstances where A and B are both true and this sentence is clearly false shows that *no* truth-functional operator can be used to correctly symbolize this sentence as a compound of A and B. The truth-value of this sentence is simply not a function of the truth-values of A and B.

Our discussion has brought to light a useful way to test a proposed symbolization. Try to imagine circumstances where the two sentences—the English sentence and the symbolic sentence—clearly would have different truth-values. *If it is possible for your proposed symbolization to be true and the English sentence false, or the symbolization to be false and the English sentence true, the proposed symbolization is not an adequate symbolization.*

Several other common English words often are used to connect sentences in the same truth-functional way as the word "and." Thus, the word "but" often means "and on the contrary" or "and on the other hand." For example, the word "but" in the compound sentence "Art is smart but he's a poor athlete" informs the reader that the information to follow is significantly different from what came before. In this case, the information preceding the word "but" is favorable to Art; so this use of that word prepares us for contrasting information to follow. When the word "but" is symbolized by the dot, the part of its meaning that signals a switch of this kind is lost. However, only the truth-functional part of its meaning is important for sentential logic and that part is accurately captured by the dot symbol. Therefore, in this case, symbolization of the word "but" by the dot is acceptable for our purposes.

In addition to "and" and "but," the terms "however," "yet," "on the other hand," "still," "although," "despite the fact that," and many others usually are correctly symbolized by the dot when they are used to join two sentences together to form a larger compound sentence.

Examples

All of the following sentences might be symbolized as the conjunction $B \cdot L$ (letting $B =$ "many fought bravely"; $L =$ "some lost their lives").

1.   Many fought bravely, *and* some lost their lives.
2.   *Both* many fought bravely, *and* some lost their lives.
3.   Many fought bravely, *but* some lost their lives.
4.   Many fought bravely, *despite the fact that* some lost their lives.
5.   *Although* many fought bravely, some lost their lives.
6.   *While* many fought bravely, some lost their lives.
7.   Many fought bravely; *also* some lost their lives.

Exercise 2-1

Which of the following are truth-functional compound sentences that can be correctly symbolized using the dot? Explain.

1.   Paul McCartney went one way, and Ringo Starr went another way.
2.   A large star is large, but a large flea is small.
3.   Bonny and Eugene were classmates.
4.   Beth is a top student, not to mention being a great athlete.
5.   We'll always have death and taxes.
6.   In the '20s alcohol was prohibited, but now pot is.
7.   Beethoven and Mozart were great composers.
8.   Two and two are four.
9.   Though she loved him, she left him.
10.   Everything that's great fun is illegal, immoral, and fattening.
11.   All sound arguments are valid, and they have true premises as well.
12.   Both the right front fender and the passenger side door were damaged as a result of the accident.

4   *Variables and Constants*

The truth table on page 18 concerns the sentences *A, B,* and *A · B*. But clearly, what it says about these sentences is equally true of any two sentences connected by the dot. For example, we can construct a similar truth table for the sentences *C* ("Charles is a logician"), *D* ("Donna is a mathematician"), and *C · D,* as follows:

C	*D*	*C · D*
T	T	T
T	F	F
F	T	F
F	F	F

Obviously, the truth table for any two sentences and their conjunction will be just like the two truth tables already presented. This fact can be expressed in the form of a general truth table in the following way:

——— - - - - - -	——— · - - - - - -
T T	T
T F	F
F T	F
F F	F

In each use of this truth table, the blanks are to be filled in by any sentences, atomic or compound, provided only that whatever sentence is placed in the first solid line blank is also placed in the second, and whatever sentence is placed in the first dashed line blank is also placed in the second.

It is customary, however, to use letters instead of solid and dashed lines. Thus, the above truth table would normally be written as follows:

p *q*	*p* · *q*
T T	T
T F	F
F T	F
F F	F

This truth table indicates that given any two sentences *p* and *q*:

1. If *p* and *q* both are true, then their conjunction, *p* · *q*, is true.
2. If *p* is true and *q* false, then their conjunction, *p* · *q*, is false.
3. If *p* is false and *q* true, then their conjunction, *p* · *q*, is false.
4. If *p* and *q* both are false, then their conjunction, *p* · *q*, is false.

Since this truth table specifies the truth-value of any conjunction, given the truth-values of its two conjuncts, it can be said to define or specify the meaning of the dot symbol. We can summarize the content of this table with a single sentence, as follows: *A conjunction is true if both conjuncts are true, otherwise it is false.*

It is important to understand that in the above truth table, the small letters *p* and *q* are *not abbreviations for specific sentences.* Rather they serve as place holders. It is only when we replace them with capital letters (abbreviations for specific sentences) that we get expressions that are sentences. Place holders such as *p* and *q* are called *variables,* in this case **sentence variables** (because they are to be replaced by abbreviations for sentences).

In the remainder of our discussion of sentential logic, we shall conform to the convention that the small letters *p*, *q*, *r*, and so on are to be used as sentence variables, and the capital letters *A*, *B*, *C*, and so on as sentence abbreviations, referred to as **sentence constants.**

5   *Negations*

The dot sentence connective is a kind of operator. It operates on two sentences, say, *A* and *B*, to produce a third—the compound sentence *A* · *B*. But some logical operators generate a new sentence out of just one starting sentence. For instance, the operator "It is well known that" operates on the sentence "Ronald Reagan was a movie star" to produce the compound "It's well known that Ronald Reagan was a movie star."

Only one operator of this kind, **negation,** is used in standard sentential logic (practically all of the others are non-truth-functional—as is the operator "It is well known that"). Negation is the easiest of the truth-functional operators to learn because it operates only on individual sentences, and it works just as you would expect. If you negate a true sentence, you get a false sentence, and if you negate a false sentence, you get a true one. We will use the **tilde** symbol "~" to symbolize negations. Then we can symbolize, say, the statement "It's not the case that Jesse Jackson was a movie star" or, more colloquially, "Jesse Jackson was not a movie star," as ~ J (where J = "Jesse Jackson was a movie star"). For the sake of convenience, we will follow the common practice of referring to "~" as a connective, although it does not literally connect two sentences.

Now let's consider the possible truth-values for compound sentences formed by adding a negation sign. Unlike the case for conjunctions, there are only two possibilities. Take the sentence "Art is smart," abbreviated as A. Either A is true, in which case ~ A is false, or A is false, in which case ~ A is true. Of course, we again can generalize because the truth table for any sentence and its negation will be just like the one for A and ~ A. We can express this general fact by constructing a truth table using the variable p, as follows:

p	~ p
T	F
F	T

This truth table succinctly illustrates how the negation truth-function operates. Since this function operates on single sentences, there are only two possible cases, and the truth table shows the truth-value that results given any sentence p:

1. If p is true, then its negation is false.
2. If p is false, then its negation is true.

Again, we can summarize these results with a single sentence: *A negation is false if the sentence being negated is true, and true if the sentence being negated is false.*

Examples

Here are a few of the several ways of expressing a negation. All of the following are correctly symbolized as ~ T (where T = "tomatoes are vegetables"):

1. Tomatoes are *not* vegetables.
2. Tomatoes are*n't* vegetables.
3. It's *not true* that tomatoes are vegetables.
4. It's *not the case* that tomatoes are vegetables.
5. It is *false* to claim that tomatoes are vegetables.

6 *Parentheses and Brackets*

Consider the mathematical expression $6 \div 3 \times 2 = 1$. Is this expression true or false? If it states that 6 divided by the result of multiplying 3 times 2 (that is, 6 divided by 6) equals 1, then it is true. But if it states that 6 divided by 3 (which equals 2) multiplied by 2 equals 1, then it is false. As it stands, the expression is ambiguous (has more than one distinct meaning). In mathematics, ambiguity of this kind is removed by using parentheses and brackets. Thus, $(6 \div 3) \times 2 = 4$, whereas $6 \div (3 \times 2) = 1$.

Similarly, parentheses, "(" and ")", brackets, "[" and "]", and braces, "{" and "}", are used to remove ambiguity in logic. Consider once again the sentences "Art went to the show," A, and "Betsy went to the show," B. To deny A and assert B, we can write $\sim A \cdot B$. To deny A and deny B, we can write $\sim A \cdot \sim B$. But to deny the combination (the conjunction) $A \cdot B$, we need to use parentheses and write $\sim (A \cdot B)$, using the parentheses to indicate that it is the combination or conjunction of A and B that is being denied.

The sentence $\sim A \cdot B$ thus asserts that Art did not go to the show, but Betsy did. The sentence $\sim A \cdot \sim B$ asserts that Art did not go and Betsy didn't either (that is, neither Art nor Betsy went). And the sentence $\sim (A \cdot B)$ asserts that it is false that both Art and Betsy went. Notice that the sentences $\sim A \cdot \sim B$ and $\sim (A \cdot B)$ are not equivalent, as proved by the fact that if Art went to the show but Betsy didn't, then the sentence $\sim A \cdot \sim B$ is false whereas the sentence $\sim (A \cdot B)$ is true.

By using parentheses we can build up complex sentences out of shorter sentences. Thus the sentence $\sim (A \cdot B)$ can be combined with the sentence $C \equiv D$ using the connective "$\vee$" to form the longer sentence $\sim (A \cdot B) \vee (C \equiv D)$.

Let's call the shorter sentences that are combined to make longer sentences **component sentences.** Parentheses are used to indicate the **scope** of each logical operator in any well-formed sentence. The scope of an operator is the component sentence or sentences that the operator operates on. The negation operator "$\sim$" operates on a single component sentence. All of the other operators operate on two component sentences.

An important concept to be introduced at this point is that of the main connective of a sentence. The **main connective** of a sentence is the truth-functional connective whose scope encompasses the entire remainder of the sentence. (Remember we are calling the negation operator a connective even though it does not literally *connect* two sentences.) It is crucial that you develop the ability to pick out the main connective of any sentence. If you think of building up a sentence by starting with atomic sentences and forming larger and larger sentences, the main operator would be the last operator to be put in place. No sentence is well formed unless it is clear which operator is the main operator for the sentence and for each component sentence contained within the sentence. For example, the sentence $A \vee B \supset C$ is not well formed because it is not clear whether "$\vee$" or "$\supset$" is the main connective. We can use parentheses to transform this string of symbols into a well-formed sentence. The main connective of the sentence $A \vee (B \supset C)$ is "$\vee$" and the main connective of the sentence $(A \vee B) \supset C$ is "$\supset$".

Two conventions help to eliminate unnecessary parentheses. First, it is not necessary to place an outermost pair of parentheses entirely surrounding a sentence—we can write $A \supset (B \vee C)$ instead of $[A \supset (B \vee C)]$. Second, the scope of the "$\sim$" operator is always the shortest complete sentence that follows it: We can write $\sim A \vee B$ instead of $(\sim A) \vee B$.

When symbolizing complicated compound sentences, more than a single pair of parentheses may be needed, as in the sentence $\sim ((A \cdot (B \cdot \sim C)) \vee D)$. We will alternate parentheses, brackets, and braces to make it visually easier to see how parentheses are paired. For example, instead of $\sim ((A \cdot (B \cdot \sim C)) \vee D)$, we will write $\sim \{[A \cdot (B \cdot \sim C)] \vee D\}$. This is just a way to make our sentences a bit easier to read. There is no difference whatsoever in the logical function of the three varieties of parentheses.

Examples

Sentence	Main Connective	Component Sentence(s)
$\sim B \supset C$	$\supset$	$\sim B, C$
$\sim [(A \vee B) \supset C]$	$\sim$	$(A \vee B) \supset C$
$(A \vee B) \cdot \sim (D \supset R)$	$\cdot$	$A \vee B, \sim (D \supset R)$
$\sim [(A \vee B) \equiv (\sim B \supset C)]$	$\sim$ (the first one)	$(A \vee B) \equiv (\sim B \supset C)$
$\sim (A \vee B) \equiv (\sim B \supset C)$	$\equiv$	$\sim (A \vee B), \sim B \supset C$

Exercise 2-2

For each of the following sentences, identify the main connective and the component sentence(s) operated on by that connective:

1. $(A \vee B) \supset C$
2. $\sim (A \vee B) \supset C$
3. $\sim [(A \vee B) \supset C]$
4. $\sim [\sim (A \vee B) \supset C]$
5. $\sim \sim (A \vee B) \supset C$
6. $\sim [(A \vee B) \supset C] \supset D$
7. $\sim [(A \vee B) \vee (C \supset D)]$
8. $[\sim A \vee (B \supset C)] \equiv \sim D$
9. $\{[\sim (A \supset B) \vee C)] \equiv \sim D\} \vee L$
10. $[(\sim A \supset B) \vee C)] \equiv \sim (D \cdot R)$

7   *Disjunctions*

Another frequently used sentence connective is the English word "or" (and its variants, particularly "either . . . or"). Two sentences connected by the word "or" form a compound sentence called a **disjunction,** and the two sentences so connected are called **disjuncts** of the disjunction.

There are two different senses of the connective "or" in common use. One, the **exclusive** sense, is illustrated by the sentence "Art took the makeup exam on Tuesday or on Wednesday." Ordinarily the implication of this sentence is that Art took the makeup exam on Tuesday or on Wednesday, but not on both Tuesday and Wednesday. The other sense of the term "or" is called its **inclusive** sense, or sometimes its nonexclusive sense. If a football coach exclaims, "We'll beat either Penn State or Army," his assertion is not false if the team wins both of these games. The coach means to say that either we'll beat Penn State, or we'll beat Army, or we'll beat both Penn State and Army.

The inclusive sense of the term "or" sometimes is expressed by the phrase "and/or"— especially in legal documents. Thus, a contract may state that "Repairs will be made by the landlord and/or his agent," meaning that repairs will be made by one or the other, or both.

The symbol "∨", called **vel,** is introduced to symbolize the inclusive sense of the word "or" and, like the dot, "∨" is a truth-functional connective. Abbreviating the sentence "We'll beat Penn State" by the capital letter P and the sentence "We'll beat Army" by the capital letter A, we can symbolize the sentence "We'll beat Penn State or Army" as $P \vee A$.

Now let's consider all of the possible combinations of truth-values of P and A. First, if P and A both are true, then $P \vee A$ is true. Second, if P is true and A false, then $P \vee A$ is true. Third, if P is false and A true, then $P \vee A$ is true. Finally, if both P and A are false, then $P \vee A$ is false. Again this pattern will be true for any two sentences connected by "∨". The following truth table summarizes our findings:

p	q	$p \vee q$
T	T	T
T	F	T
F	T	T
F	F	F

This truth table indicates that given any two sentences p and q, their disjunction $p \vee q$ is false only when both p and q are false; otherwise, it is true.

In everyday English, disjunctions are usually signaled by means of the terms "or" or "either . . . or" (as in this very sentence). But not always. For example, the inclusive disjunction "Either Perot or Clinton spent over $50 million on their presidential campaigns" can also be expressed by saying "At least one of the two candidates, Perot and Clinton, spent over $50 million on his campaign," a statement not containing the word "or."

A sentence whose major connective is an exclusive "or" asserts more than it would if the "or" were inclusive. It says that (1) at least one of its disjuncts is true (which is all it would say if it were the inclusive "or"); and (2) at least one disjunct is false. Thus, there is a sense in which the whole meaning of the inclusive "or" is only part of the meaning of the exclusive "or." So if we symbolize an exclusive use of the word "or" by "∨", we lose part of its meaning. Surprisingly, in many arguments in which the exclusive "or" is used, no harm is done if we symbolize the "or" by "∨". The validity of these arguments depends on the part of the meaning of the exclusive "∨" that it shares with the inclusive "or," namely, the part that asserts at least one disjunct is true.

But there are some arguments for which this is not the case. An example is the argument

1. Art took the makeup exam on Tuesday or Wednesday (T or W).
2. Art took the makeup exam on Tuesday (T).
∴ 3. Art did not take the makeup exam on Wednesday ($\sim W$).

If the inclusive "or" is used to symbolize the "or" in the first premise of this argument, then the resulting argument will be invalid, since it will state that

1. Art took the makeup exam on Tuesday, or Art took the makeup exam on Wednesday, or Art took the makeup exam on Tuesday and on Wednesday.
2. Art took the makeup exam on Tuesday.
∴ 3. Art did not take the makeup exam on Wednesday.

But the original argument is valid if the "or" in the first premise is understood in the exclusive sense. This time the additional claim made by the exclusive "or" cannot be omitted and the validity of the argument preserved. We must not only assert that Art took the makeup exam on at least one of the two days, stated in symbols as $T \lor W$, but also *deny* that he took the exam on both days, stated in symbols as $\sim (T \cdot W)$. So we should symbolize the whole of the first premise as $(T \lor W) \cdot \sim (T \cdot W)$.

What should you do then when you encounter a sentence like "Art took the makeup exam on Tuesday or Wednesday"? You need to ask whether the sentence clearly conveys an exclusive disjunction. One way to test if this is the case is to ask whether the sentence would be false if both disjuncts were true. If Art took the makeup on both days would the sentence be false? In ordinary contexts, it would be reasonable to take the sentence as expressing just this, and so it is natural to symbolize this particular sentence as exclusive.

Unfortunately, taken in isolation, many "or" sentences are just ambiguous. A father might say to his daughter, "We'll either play ball, or go fishing this weekend" and intend to communicate an exclusive disjunction. Don't be surprised if the daughter hears the sentence differently. In our example, Dad will probably clarify. But the sentence by itself could be legitimately interpreted either way. When faced with such ambiguity, seek clarification. If none is available, the rule to follow is this: When in doubt, symbolize an "or" sentence as inclusive. So our practice will be to symbolize disjunctions as inclusive unless the exclusive interpretation is clearly intended.

Examples

Disjunctions are commonly expressed using "either . . . or" or just plain "or." Here are two sentences that might be properly symbolized as the disjunction $R \lor E$ ($R =$ "we will reduce the deficit"; $E =$ "the economy will collapse").

1. *Either* we will reduce the deficit, *or* the economy will collapse.
2. We will reduce the deficit, *or* the economy will collapse.

LC Exercise 2-3

Symbolize the following so as to reveal as much structure as possible. (Specify the abbreviations you use.)

1. Either the deficit will be reduced soon, or the income tax rate will be raised.
2. The greatest basketball player to ever play the game is either Michael Jordan or Kareem Abdul-Jabaar.
3. Pete Rose bet on Reds games, or he didn't.
4. It's going to snow on Christmas Eve or on New Year's Eve.

5. They're either going to play Mozart's Piano Concerto No. 22 or Haydn's Symphony No. 94.
6. Either this sentence is true, or it's false.
7. At least one of the two major political parties (the Democrats and the Republicans) supports an anti-flag-desecration amendment.
8. The A's are going to win the World Series this year; otherwise it'll be (at last) the Cleveland Indians!
9. Anita Hill or Clarence Thomas lied before the congressional committee.
10. Anita Hill either told the truth about Clarence Thomas, or the lie detector test is totally unreliable.
11. Abortion is either murder, or it's a harmless form of birth control.
12. The gunman must have been insane, or perhaps he was experiencing a severe emotional disturbance.

8 *"Not Both" and "Neither . . . Nor"*

Many English sentences contain more than one logical operator. For example, consider the sentence "Mary went to the movie, and she didn't like it." This sentence is a conjunction that contains a negation as one of its components—the claim that Mary did *not* like the movie. So it should be symbolized as $M \cdot \sim L$. Likewise, the sentence "Henry was either not driving very carefully, or the officer was not in a very good mood that day" is a disjunction of two negations and could be symbolized $\sim C \vee \sim G$.

In symbolizing sentences with more than one operator, it is essential to pay attention to the scope of each operator. Compare the following two sentences:

1. It will not rain, and it will snow.
2. It will not both rain and snow.

The crucial difference is the scope of the negation operator "not." In the first sentence "not" negates the atomic claim that it will rain. The main connective of this sentence is the word "and." So this sentence might be symbolized $\sim R \cdot S$. In the second sentence what is negated is a conjunction—the claim that it will *both* rain *and* snow—and is correctly symbolized $\sim (R \cdot S)$. An equivalent and equally acceptable way of translating this sentence is $\sim R \vee \sim S$. The bottom line is that all that it takes to make a "not both" sentence true is for at least one of the two atomic components to be false.

Now consider sentences built around the English connective "neither . . . nor" such as, "It will neither rain nor snow tomorrow." It is tempting to think that these sentences should be symbolized as disjunctions, but this is a mistake. Someone who asserts that neither A nor B is true is not merely saying that either A or B is not true; rather, what is being said is that *both* A and B are not true. For neither A nor B to be true, it must be the case that A is not true and it must be the case that B is not true. So for the sentence "It will neither rain nor snow tomorrow" to be true, it must both not rain and not snow tomorrow. Likewise, consider the sentence "Neither Clinton nor Dole received a majority of the vote." If $C =$ "Clinton received a majority of the vote," and $D =$ "Dole received a majority of the vote," then the correct symbolization of this sentence is $\sim C \cdot \sim D$. This sentence is only correct if Clinton did not receive a majority *and* Dole did not receive a majority. It would also be correct to symbolize the sentence as $\sim (D \vee C)$. These sentences say the same thing in two different ways, namely, that Clinton did not receive a majority and Dole did not receive a majority. On the other hand, it would not be correct to symbolize this sentence as $\sim D \vee \sim C$ because that sentence would be true even if only one of its two disjuncts were true, say if Dole didn't receive a majority of the vote but Clinton did.

Examples

Not Both

1. Bush did not both end the war quickly and guarantee the overthrow of Saddam Hussein. (Q = "Bush ended the war quickly"; G = "Bush guaranteed the overthrow of Saddam Hussein"):

   $\sim (Q \cdot G)$ or $\sim Q \vee \sim G$

Neither . . . Nor

2. Neither Saddam nor his generals displayed military genius. (S = "Saddam displayed military genius"; G = "Saddam's generals displayed military genius"):

   $\sim (S \vee G)$ or $\sim S \cdot \sim G$

LC Exercise 2-4

Symbolize the following sentences, using the indicated abbreviations.

1. Anthony will not both start at quarterback and miss practice this afternoon. (S = "Anthony will start at quarterback"; M = "Anthony misses practice this afternoon")
2. Anthony will neither start at quarterback nor attend practice. (A = "Anthony attends practice")
3. Although Anthony will not start at quarterback, he will attend practice.
4. Dennis neither completed his homework on time, nor did he participate in class. (H = "Dennis completed his homework on time"; P = "Dennis participated in class")
5. Samantha doesn't exercise or count calories. (E = "Samantha exercises"; C = "Samantha counts calories")
6. Although Samantha neither exercises nor counts calories, she still isn't overweight. (O = "Samantha is overweight")
7. Alex will either not be on time, or he won't have all of the equipment with him. (T = "Alex will be on time"; E = "Alex will have all of the equipment with him")
8. We will either go to the movies or dinner tonight, but not both. (M = "we go to the movies tonight"; D = "we go to dinner tonight")
9. My client may have had a motive, but he had neither the means nor the opportunity to commit the crime. (C = "my client had a motive to commit the crime"; M = "my

client had the means to commit the crime"; $O =$ "my client had the opportunity to commit the crime")

10. Neither Dennis nor Harry received an A on the final, but both actively participated in class. ($D =$ "Dennis received an A on the final"; $H =$ "Harry received an A on the final"; $P =$ Dennis actively participated in class"; $C =$ "Harry actively participated in class")

11. Sally received an A, although she neither studied nor participated in class. ($A =$ "Sally received an A"; $S =$ "Sally studied"; $P =$ "Sally participated in class")

12. Either unemployment and inflation both remain low or the stock market undergoes a major correction. ($U =$ "unemployment remains low"; $I =$ "inflation remains low"; $C =$ "the stock market undergoes a major correction")

13. Neither stocks nor bonds provide an absolutely risk-free investment opportunity. ($S =$ "stocks provide an absolutely risk-free investment opportunity"; $B =$ "bonds provide an absolutely risk-free investment opportunity")

14. Dick invests in both stocks and bonds although neither provides an absolutely risk-free investment opportunity. ($D =$ "Dick invests in stocks"; $I =$ "Dick invests in bonds")

9 *Material Conditionals*

Consider the sentence "If Clinton won in 1996, then a Democrat won." This compound sentence contains two atomic sentences, namely, "Clinton won in 1996" and "A democrat won," joined by the sentence connective "If _____ then _____ ." A compound sentence of this kind is called a **conditional,** or **hypothetical.** The sentence between the "if" and the "then" is called its **antecedent,** and the sentence after the "then" its **consequent.** The general form of a conditional sentence thus is "If (antecedent) then (consequent)."

In English, there are many other ways of expressing conditionals. For instance, the above conditional might be stated as "A Democrat won in 1996, if Clinton did," "Assuming Clinton won in 1996, a Democrat won," and so on.

Conditionals differ with respect to the kinds of connections they express between antecedent and consequent. For example, in the sentence "If Art or Betsy will go, then Betsy or Art will go" the connection is *logical,* whereas in the sentence "If Art goes, then Betsy will go" it is *factual.*

But perhaps the most important way in which conditionals differ is with respect to *truth-functionality.* Although a few of the conditionals uttered in daily life are truth-functional, the vast majority are not. Take the conditional sentence (1): "If Art went to the show, then Betsy went also," partially symbolized as "If A then B." Suppose Charles bets that this sentence is true, Donna that it is false. Clearly, if Art did go but Betsy didn't, so that A is true and B false, then sentence (1) is false and Donna wins the bet. So the second line of the truth table for sentence (1) must contain an **F.**

Suppose, however, that neither Art nor Betsy went to the show, so that both A and B are false. Then it is not clear whether sentence (1) is true, or if it is false, and thus not clear who should win the bet. Surely Charles would be foolish to agree that sentence (1) is false and that Donna thus wins the bet. For he could argue that although Betsy didn't go, sentence (1) doesn't assert that she did, only that she did *if Art did.* Since Art didn't go, sentence (1) is not necessarily false.

Donna, however, would be equally foolish to agree that sentence (1) is true, and hence that Charles wins the bet. For she could argue that although Betsy didn't go, sentence (1) doesn't assert that she did, but only that she did *if Art did.* Since Art didn't go, we can't say that sentence (1) is true.

It would seem, then, that if both the antecedent and consequent of sentence (1) are false, then its truth value is not determined by the truth values of its component sentences. Thus sentence (1) contains a *non*-truth-functional use of the connective "If _____ then _____". This causes little difficulty in betting situations (Charles and Donna, for example, could agree that if A turns out to be false, then the bet is off), but it creates serious problems for logic (discussed further later).

The example about Charles and Donna illustrates the difficulty that arises when both the antecedent and consequent of a conditional are false, thus illustrating the difficulty in filling in the fourth line of the truth table for "If _____ then _____ " sentences. Obviously, the same problem arises with respect to the third line, and it even sometimes arises with respect to the first.

Take the conditional sentence (2): "If Smith puts off her operation, then she'll be dead within six months," pronounced by a doctor about a particular cancer patient. Suppose Smith does put off her operation and then, unluckily, is killed crossing the street two weeks later, so that both the antecedent and consequent of sentence (2) are true. Clearly, this does not make sentence (2) true, for the consequent of (2) would be true *accidentally,* not because the antecedent turned out to be true. But the doctor meant to assert not simply that Smith would be dead within six months if she were not operated on, rather that if not operated on, *her cancerous condition would cause her death* (if nothing else did first). So we are not justified in placing a **T** on the first line of the truth table for sentence (2). But we aren't justified in placing an **F** there either, because Smith might indeed have died of cancer within six months if she hadn't been killed in an auto accident. So the use of "If _____ then _____ " in sentence (2) is not truth-functional.

However, our main concern here is not how conditionals differ one from another but how they all are alike, because we want to take the meaning common to all uses of the connective "If _____ then _____ " as the *entire* meaning of our truth-functional conditional sentence connective. It turns out that for a conditional sentence, truth-functional or non-truth-functional, *if its antecedent is true and its consequent false, then the whole conditional sentence is false.* Therefore, part of what we do in asserting a sentence of the form "If *p* then *q* is to *deny* the conjunction of its antecedent with the negation of its consequent; that is, we deny ($p \cdot \sim q$) and thus assert $\sim (p \cdot \sim q)$. We use this partial meaning shared by all conditional sentences as the *total* meaning of what is called a **material conditional,** or a **material implication.**

To signify material implication, we use the horseshoe sign, "$\supset$". (The arrow symbol, "$\rightarrow$", also is common.) Thus, a sentence having the form $p \supset q$ is taken to mean the same thing as, and hence to be equivalent to, a sentence having the form $\sim (p \cdot \sim q)$. Consequently, the truth table for a sentence having the form $p \supset q$ must be the same as the truth table for an analogous sentence having the form $\sim (p \cdot \sim q)$.

Methods for determining the truth values of compound sentences are discussed in Chapter 3. Let's anticipate a bit here and provide the truth table for sentences having the form $\sim (p \cdot \sim q)$, and thus for sentences having the form $p \supset q$:

p	q	~(p · ~q)	p ⊃ q
T	T	T	T
T	F	F	F
F	T	T	T
F	F	T	T

We take this truth table to provide a *definition* or a *specification of meaning* for the truth-functional horseshoe symbol.*

When symbolizing conditional sentences of everyday English, it must be remembered that most everyday conditionals are not truth-functional. Thus, when they are symbolized by "⊃", only part of their meaning is captured (namely, the part they share with all conditionals), the other part being lost. Usually, the part captured by material implication is all that is needed to solve problems containing everyday implications. But this is not always the case, so that translating non-truth-functional implications by means of the truth-functional connective "⊃" sometimes leads to problems and risks (to be discussed further in Chapter 10, Sections 5 and 6).

Examples

There are many different ways in which conditionals can be expressed. Here are some examples, all correctly symbolized as $M \supset R$ (letting M = "Mark McGwire breaks Roger Maris's record," and R = "Mark McGwire breaks Babe Ruth's record"):

1. If Mark McGwire breaks Roger Maris's home run record, then he'll break Babe Ruth's record also.
2. If McGwire breaks Maris's record, he'll break Ruth's record also.
3. McGwire will break Ruth's record, if he breaks Maris's.
4. In case McGwire breaks Maris's record, he'll have broken Ruth's also.
5. McGwire will break Ruth's record, should he break Maris's.
6. McGwire's breaking Maris's record means he'll also have broken Ruth's.

10 Material Biconditionals

Two sentences are said to be *materially equivalent* when they have the same truth-value. We introduce the symbol "≡" to stand for material equivalence. Thus, to assert that "Art went to the show" (A) is materially equivalent to "Betsy went to the show" (B), we can write "A is materially equivalent to B," or simply $A \equiv B$ (pronounced "A if and only if B"). Obviously, the sentence $A \equiv B$ is true if and only if A and B have the same truth-value, and in general a sentence of the form $p \equiv q$ is true if and only if p and q have the same truth-value. Hence, the truth table for material equivalence must be:

---

*Some other reasons for defining "⊃" in this way are explained in Chapter 5, Section 9.

p q	p ≡ q
T T	T
T F	F
F T	F
F F	T

We take this truth table to provide a definition or specification of meaning for the symbol "≡".

Compound statements formed by the symbol "≡" sometimes are called **material equivalences,** because they are true just in case they join together two smaller statements that have the same (equivalent) truth-values. But these compounds are more frequently referred to as **material biconditionals,** or simply **biconditionals,** because they are themselves equivalent to two-directional material conditionals. For instance, the material biconditional "Art went to the show if and only if Betsy went to the show," in symbols $A \equiv B$, is equivalent to the two-directional conditional "If Art went to the show, then Betsy went to the show, and if Betsy went to the show, then Art went to the show," in symbols $(A \supset B) \cdot (B \supset A)$.

The same problem concerning truth-functionality that arises for conditionals arises also for biconditionals.* In general, the question as to when equivalences can be symbolized by "≡" is answered in the same way. Once again, the material biconditional captures only the minimal truth-functional content of English biconditionals. The material biconditional does not imply any connection between the two component sentences. It simply states that the two components have the same truth-value.

Examples

Unlike conditionals, equivalences are fairly uncommon in everyday English, and indeed there are only a few standard ways to express them (some quite stilted). The two most common are "just in case" and "if and only if," illustrated by the following:

1. Bill Clinton kept warm at his inauguration if and only if he wore thermal underwear.
2. Bill Clinton kept warm at his inauguration just in case he wore thermal underwear.

We have now introduced each of our truth-functional connectives. The definitions of these connectives can each be precisely stated by means of their standard truth tables.

---

*Indeed, it arises for disjunctions also. Consider the disjunction "Either we operate or the patient dies." In this case, the truth of the left disjunct "We operate" does not guarantee the truth of the whole compound sentence, "Either we operate or the patient dies," even if the patient does not die, because it may be that the patient wouldn't have died even if we had not operated.

p	$\sim p$
T	F
F	T

p	q	$p \lor q$
T	T	T
T	F	T
F	T	T
F	F	F

p	q	$p \cdot q$
T	T	T
T	F	F
F	T	F
F	F	F

p	q	$p \supset q$
T	T	T
T	F	F
F	T	T
F	F	T

p	q	$p \equiv q$
T	T	T
T	F	F
F	T	F
F	F	T

You should memorize these tables and be able to reproduce them on your own without hesitation. *You cannot master sentential logic without mastering these tables.* You must know for every line of each of the tables what the appropriate truth-value is for that line. If the task of memorizing these tables seems daunting, here is a little help. The truth conditions for each connective can be summarized in a single sentence, so you can memorize the contents of the standard tables by memorizing the following five sentences:

1. *Negations* change *true* sentences to false and *false* sentences to true.
2. A *conjunction* is *true* if both conjuncts are true; otherwise, it is false.
3. A *disjunction* is *false* if both disjuncts are false; otherwise, it is true.
4. A *material conditional* is *false* if its antecedent is true and its consequent is false; otherwise, it is true.
5. A *material biconditional* is *true* if both component sentences have the same truth-value; otherwise, it is false.

11   *"Only If" and "Unless"*

"Only if" sentences are like "if" sentences turned around. So, whereas the sentence "You will pass the course if you pay attention in class" might be symbolized $A \supset C$, the sentence "You will pass the course only if you pay attention in class" should be symbolized $C \supset A$. The two sentences say something quite different. If you pay attention but don't pass, the first sentence is definitely false, but the second sentence may still be true. All the second sentence says is that paying attention is what philosophers call a *necessary condition* of passing the course, not a sufficient condition. That is, it might be true that in order to pass the course it is necessary to pay attention, but that alone may not be sufficient to guarantee passing—you may need to do some other things as well, such as performing well on your exams. Saying that you will pass the course only if you pay attention *doesn't* tell you that if you pay attention you will pass, but it *does* tell you this: If you do not pay attention, you will not pass. So another standard way of translating English sentences of the form "*p* only if *q*" is $\sim q \supset \sim p$.

Consider the sentence, "You will fail this course unless you study." One way to symbolize this sentence is to treat "unless" as synonymous with "if not" and so symbolize the sentence as $\sim S \supset F$. A slightly less intuitive but even simpler way of translating these sentences is simply to treat "unless" sentences as "or" sentences, thus translating the sentence $F \vee S$.

As was the case with "or," "only if" and "unless" may sometimes be interpreted more strongly than our standard symbolizations indicate. Consider the following two sentences:

I will play golf with you tomorrow, only if it doesn't rain.
I will play golf with you tomorrow, unless it rains.

According to the guidelines just given, we would standardly symbolize the first of these sentences as $G \supset \sim R$. But someone might be intending to say more with this sentence. They might be saying not only that if they golf it won't be raining, but also that if it doesn't rain they will be golfing. If this is the meaning of the sentence, the correct symbolization would be $G \equiv \sim R$. Likewise the second sentence could be symbolized according to the guidelines given above as $\sim R \supset G$ (or equivalently as $G \vee R$). The question to ask about the second sentence is this: Would it be false if the person plays even if it rains? In some contexts perhaps so. If so, the sentence may be symbolized, once again, $G \equiv \sim R$ (or $\sim R \equiv G$, or $(G \vee R) \cdot \sim (G \cdot R)$—these are all logically equivalent.) The situation here is precisely analogous to what we had with "or." "Unless" like "or" has both an inclusive and exclusive usage in English. (It is no coincidence that both can be symbolized with "$\vee$".)

Fortunately, clear-cut examples of these usages are even more rare than exclusive disjunctions. The guidelines are the same. Symbolize in the standard way unless the stronger meaning is clearly intended.

Examples

Only If

1. Peace will be gained in the Middle East only if Saddam is toppled from power. (P = "peace is gained in the Middle East"; T = "Saddam is toppled from power"):

   $P \supset T$

Unless

2. The war with Iraq was not a success unless Kuwait becomes more democratic. (S = "the war with Iraq was a success"; K = "Kuwait becomes more democratic"):

   $\sim K \supset S$ or $S \vee K$

LC Exercise 2-5

Symbolize the following sentences that feature the connectives "unless" and "only if":

1. Harry will run (for class office) only if Janet runs also. (H = "Harry will run"; J = "Janet will run")

2. Harry won't run unless Janet runs.
3. Unless Harry runs, Janet won't.
4. Neither the Russians nor the Americans will reduce their nuclear arsenals. (R = "the Russians will reduce their nuclear arsenal"; A = "the Americans will reduce their nuclear arsenal")
5. The Russians will not reduce their arsenals unless the Americans do the same.
6. The Russians will reduce their arsenals only if the Americans reduce theirs.
7. Only if the Russians will not reduce their arsenals will the Americans reduce theirs.
8. Anthony is not the starting quarterback unless he is at practice this afternoon. (A = "Anthony is the starting quarterback"; P = "Anthony is at practice this afternoon")
9. Anthony is the starting quarterback, unless Chris recovers from his shoulder injury. (C = "Chris recovers from his shoulder injury")
10. Anthony will start at quarterback only if he doesn't skip practice this afternoon. (S = "Anthony skips practice this afternoon")

12 *Symbolizing Complex Sentences*

The grammatical structure of a sentence often mirrors its logical structure. So many sentences are correctly symbolized simply by following grammatical structure, replacing grammatical connectives such as "or" and "if . . . then" by their logical counterparts "$\lor$" and "$\supset$".

Here is a list of sentences containing common English connectives and grouped according to the truth-functional connective that should typically be used to symbolize them.

Examples

Negations

1.	Susan is *not* at home.	$\sim S$
2.	Money does*n't* grow on trees.	$\sim M$
3.	It's *not true* that all Republicans are wealthy.	$\sim R$
4.	It's *not the case* that water is lighter than oil.	$\sim L$
5.	It is *false* to claim that happiness is the only intrinsic good.	$\sim H$

Conjunctions

6.	Woody Allen *and* Steve Martin were philosophy majors.	$A \cdot M$
7.	*Both* Perot *and* Clinton focused on the economy.	$P \cdot C$
8.	Bush was a strong leader, *but* Quayle was a liability.	$B \cdot Q$
9.	Bush almost won, *in spite of the fact that* the media was against him.	$B \cdot M$
10.	*Although* I liked Perot the best, I voted for Clinton.	$P \cdot C$
11.	*While* Perot had some great ideas, he was too unpredictable.	$G \cdot U$

Disjunctions

12. Rick is *either* a fast learner, *or* he's very lucky. $F \lor L$
13. It will rain *or* snow tomorrow morning. $R \lor S$

Conditionals

14. *If* anyone has a better plan, *then* I am all ears. $B \supset E$
15. You will pass this course, *if* you pass the final. $F \supset C$

Biconditionals

16. The liquid is an acid, *if and only if* the litmus paper is blue. $A \equiv B$
17. Today's lunch is nutritious *just in case* it is well balanced. $N \equiv W$

In addition we have discussed four very common but less straightforward sentence patterns you should learn to handle routinely. These include sentences with the following English connectives: "not both," "neither . . . nor," "only if," and "unless." Let's discuss each of these in turn.

Not Both

18. It will *not both* rain and snow. $\sim (R \cdot S)$

Neither . . . Nor

19. Candy bars are *neither* nutritious *nor* a good source for quick
     energy. $\sim (N \lor E)$
20. John isn't being considered for the position, *nor* is he even
     interested. $\sim (C \lor I)$

Only If

21. The deficit goes down *only if* taxes go up. $D \supset T$
22. *Only if* an eyewitness comes forward will the prosecution be
     able to prove its case. $P \supset E$

Unless

23. The stock market is due for a major correction, *unless* our
     expert's predictions are based on faulty assumptions. $\sim A \supset C$
24. *Unless* you are accompanied by an adult, you are not permitted
     to enter. $\sim A \supset \sim P$

The first step in symbolizing more complicated sentences is to identify the main connective of the sentence. Take the sentence (1): "Either Art and Betsy will go to the show or else Art and Jane will go." Its correct symbolization is $(A \cdot B) \lor (A \cdot J)$, because its main connective is "or." Compare that with the case for sentence (2): "Either Art or Betsy will go to the show, but Jane is not going to go." Its correct symbolization is $(A \lor B) \cdot \sim J$, because its main connective is "but" (which is truth-functionally equivalent to "and").

Here are some tips for identifying the main connective of English sentences. Sometimes the first word of the sentence is a dead giveaway. If, for example, your sentence begins with the word "if," you likely should symbolize with "$\supset$" as the main connective. Similarly, if the sentence begins with "either," the main connective will usually be "$\lor$". So pay attention to the first word. On the other hand, transitional words or phrases at the beginning of a sentence like "but," "however," "surely," "of course," and so on usually have no truth-functional meaning and can simply be ignored when translating. (On the other hand, remember that in the middle of a sentence "but" and "however" are commonly truth-functionally equivalent to "and").

The second thing you should look for is punctuation. Parentheses often mirror commas and semicolons. A single comma or semicolon often breaks a sentence into the same two parts you will place on each side of the main connective.

Once you have identified the main connective, you can then focus on translating each component sentence separately. Again start by identifying the main connective of these component sentences. In this manner you can break down the task of translating a very complex compound sentence into manageable portions. Divide and conquer!

In particular, *be careful to determine the correct scope of negations.* That is, make sure you pay attention to the question of how much of a sentence is negated by a negative term or expression. For instance, the scope of the negative expression in sentence (3): "Art will go, but it's not the case that Betsy will go" (colloquially, "Art will go but Betsy won't"*) is just the atomic sentence "Betsy will go." So sentence (3) is correctly symbolized as $A \cdot \sim B$, where "$\sim$" negates just B. But the negative expression in sentence (4), "It won't happen both that Art will go and Betsy will go" (colloquially, "Art and Betsy won't both go"), is the whole remainder of that compound sentence. So sentence (4) is correctly symbolized as $\sim (A \cdot B)$, where "$\sim$" negates all of $(A \cdot B)$.

To avoid mistakes resulting from overly mechanical symbolization, we have to pay close attention to the meanings particular English sentences convey in specific contexts, realizing that natural languages are flexible both in grammatical construction and in their use of grammatical connectives. The same expressions can mean different things in different contexts. So in each case, we have to figure out what the sentence says and try to construct a symbolization that says the same (relevant) thing. And this takes a bit of practice. (Since we already know what these sentences mean, learning how to symbolize them correctly involves the odd-sounding but crucial knack of getting clear about what it is that we understand when we understand the meaning of a particular sentence in a natural language.)

In this vein, it is always a good idea to double-check your answer. You can do this by forgetting about the original sentence for a moment and translating your proposed sentential logic sentence back into English. Compare the result with the original sentence. Do the

---

*We don't want to be too fussy translating everyday talk into symbols. We don't want to require that all the sentences symbolized by a single letter be exactly alike. We'll count "Betsy won't go," "Betsy isn't going to go," and "She won't go" (when it's clear that the she referred to is Betsy) as enough alike to all be symbolized by the same letter. If we don't allow this shorthand, we're going to have to say that intuitively valid arguments like "If Clinton won, then Bush lost. Clinton was the winner. So Bush lost" are invalid.

two sentences say basically the same thing? Do they have the same truth conditions? If not, you need to amend your symbolization so that it can pass this test.

Examples

Here are a few relatively simple symbolizations (letting A = "Art watched 'General Hospital' "; B = "Betsy watched 'General Hospital' "; F = "Betsy flunked chemistry"; and M = "a miracle occurred").

1. Art watched "General Hospital," but Betsy didn't. $A \cdot \sim B$
2. If Art watched "General Hospital," then Betsy didn't. $A \supset \sim B$
3. If Betsy watched "General Hospital," either she flunked her chemistry exam or a miracle occurred. $B \supset (F \vee M)$
4. If Betsy watched "General Hospital" and no miracle occurred, then she flunked her chemistry exam. $(B \cdot \sim M) \supset F$
5. Either Betsy watched "General Hospital" and a miracle occurred, or she flunked her chemistry exam. $(B \cdot M) \vee F$

Here are a few examples that are a bit more complicated:

6. If Melissa graduates with a strong academic record, she gets a good job and makes lots of money. (G = "Melissa graduates with a strong academic record"; J = "Melissa gets a good job"; L = "Melissa makes lots of money") $G \supset (J \cdot L)$
7. If Melissa graduates with a strong academic record, she gets a good job and makes lots of money—if she doesn't pursue other goals. (O = "Melissa pursues other goals")
   $$(G \cdot \sim O) \supset (J \cdot M)$$
   or
   $$G \supset [\sim O \supset (J \cdot M)]$$
8. If Melissa doesn't make lots of money, then either she doesn't graduate with a strong academic record, or she doesn't get a good job, or she pursues other goals. $\sim M \supset [(\sim G \vee \sim J) \vee O]$
9. Melissa doesn't make lots of money or pursue other goals, but she does graduate with a strong academic record and she gets a good job. $(\sim M \cdot \sim O) \cdot (G \cdot J)$
10. If we don't control the money supply and break the power of OPEC, we won't control inflation. (M = "we control the money supply"; O = "we break the power of OPEC"; I = "we control inflation") $\sim (M \cdot O) \supset \sim I$

11. Either we control the money supply and break the power of OPEC, or we won't control inflation and the economy will collapse. (*E* = "the economy will collapse")

$(M \cdot O) \vee (\sim I \cdot E)$

12. If the economy collapses, we'll know that we didn't break the power of OPEC or perhaps didn't control the money supply—or maybe it'll be because of some international economic debacle. (*D* = "there is an international economic debacle")

$E \supset [(\sim O \vee \sim M) \vee D]$

LC Exercise 2-6

1. If nothing is perfect, then I can't be blamed for my mistakes. (*N* = "nothing is perfect"; *B* = "I can be blamed for my mistakes")
2. If it's not true that everything is perfect, then I can't be blamed for my mistakes. (*E* = "everything is perfect")
3. No, if nothing is perfect and I make mistakes, then I can be blamed for them. (*M* = "I make mistakes")
4. I can be blamed for my mistakes only if I make mistakes and someone discovers them. (*S* = "someone discovers my mistakes")
5. But if everything is perfect, I neither make mistakes nor can I be blamed for them.
6. So if I either make a mistake or can be blamed for my mistakes, then it is not true that everything is perfect.
7. If a meteor caused the extinction of the dinosaurs, then a meteor could cause the extinction of the human race. (*M* = "a meteor caused the extinction of the dinosaurs"; *H* = "a meteor could cause the extinction of the human race")
8. If the extinction of the dinosaurs was not caused by a meteor, it was the spread of disease that did it. (*D* = "the spread of disease caused the extinction of the dinosaurs")
9. Dinosaurs can be cloned only if scientists can fill in the missing gaps in dinosaur DNA. (*D* = "dinosaurs can be cloned"; *G* = "scientists can fill in the missing gaps in dinosaur DNA")
10. Dinosaurs cannot be cloned unless scientists can fill in the missing gaps in dinosaur DNA.
11. Dinosaurs cannot be cloned unless scientists can both obtain samples of dinosaur DNA and fill in the missing gaps. (*S* = "scientists can obtain samples of dinosaur DNA")
12. Dinosaurs were neither cold-blooded nor were they like big lizards. (*C* = "dinosaurs were cold-blooded"; *L* = "dinosaurs were like big lizards")
13. If dinosaurs were not cold-blooded, they were like birds, not big lizards. (*B* = "dinosaurs were like birds")
14. You missed your appointment and the boss is not happy, but it is not my fault. (*M* = "you missed your appointment"; *B* = "the boss is happy"; *F* = "it is my fault")

15. You missed your appointment, but the boss is happy if you made the sale. (*S* = "you made the sale")
16. Even if you didn't miss your appointment and made the sale, the boss is still not happy.
17. If you made the sale, the boss is happy, unless she has a headache. (*H* = "the boss has a headache")
18. If you didn't miss your appointment and the boss is still not happy, then either you didn't make the sale or its my fault.
19. Bob will not win the election unless a miracle occurs, yet he is the best candidate. (*W* = "Bob will win the election"; *M* = "a miracle occurs"; *B* = "Bob is the best candidate")
20. Bob may be the best candidate, but he won't win the election unless he outspends his opponent on advertising. (*O* = "Bob outspends his opponent")
21. Bob will win the election if and only if he is the best candidate and outspends his opponent on advertising.
22. If Art neither diets nor exercises, he will gain weight. (*D* = "Art diets"; *E* = "Art exercises"; *G* = "Art gains weight")
23. If Art doesn't gain weight, then he either diets or exercises.
24. Art neither diets nor exercises, but he still does not gain weight.
25. The deficit will be reduced only if we raise taxes and eliminate wasteful government spending. (*D* = "the deficit will be reduced"; *T* = "we raise taxes"; *S* = "we eliminate wasteful government spending")
26. Either we raise taxes and eliminate wasteful government spending, or the deficit will not be reduced.
27. If we raise taxes, the deficit will not be reduced unless we also eliminate wasteful government spending.
28. If we raise taxes and eliminate wasteful government spending, the deficit still will not be reduced if there is a natural catastrophe. (*N* = "there is a natural catastrophe")
29. If we raise taxes and eliminate wasteful government spending, then unless there is a natural catastrophe the deficit will be reduced.
30. Neither rain, nor snow, nor gloom of night will prevent your postal carrier from delivering the mail. (*R* = "rain will prevent your postal carrier from delivering the mail"; *S* = "snow will prevent your postal carrier from delivering the mail"; *G* = "gloom of night will prevent your postal carrier from delivering the mail")

L C Exercise 2-7

Symbolize the following into more or less colloquial English sentences (trying not to mask logical structure). Let *R* = "Sheila likes 'Ren N Stimpy'"; *J* = "Sheila likes Jay Leno"; *D* = "Sheila likes David Letterman"; *S* = "Sheila likes 'The Three Stooges'"; *P* = "Sheila is a pacifist"; *T* = Sheila has a twisted sense of humor"; *B* = "Sheila is boring."

1. $R \cdot \sim J$
2. $\sim (J \cdot D)$
3. $\sim (J \vee D)$
4. $\sim J \cdot \sim D$

5. $\sim R \vee \sim S$
6. $R \supset \sim P$
7. $\sim D \supset B$
8. $(R \cdot S) \supset \sim P$

9. $(R \vee S) \supset \sim P$ 11. $[(\sim R \cdot \sim D) \cdot \sim S] \supset B$
10. $P \supset \sim (R \vee S)$ 12. $[(R \vee S) \cdot P] \supset T$

Now let B = "you should buy bonds"; R = "you should buy real estate"; S = "you should buy common stocks"; M = "you should invest in a mutual fund"; L = "interest rates are low"; D = "demand is high"; E = "the economy is in a recession"; K = "you are a knowledgeable investor"; and P = "you are a psychic."

13. $(D \cdot L) \supset \sim E$ 19. $\sim (K \vee P) \supset (E \supset \sim S)$
14. $E \supset \sim (R \vee S)$ 20. $\sim K \supset [\sim (S \vee B) \cdot M]$
15. $\sim E \supset (R \cdot S)$ 21. $[(E \cdot L) \cdot \sim K] \supset M$
16. $(D \cdot L) \supset (\sim K \supset R)$ 22. $\sim K \supset [\sim P \supset \sim (S \vee B)]$
17. $S \equiv (K \cdot \sim E)$ 23. $K \supset [(S \cdot B) \cdot R]$
18. $(S \vee B) \equiv [(K \vee P) \cdot \sim E]$ 24. $\{[(E \cdot L) \cdot \sim (K \vee P)]\} \supset R$

Exercise 2-8

1. What's wrong with abbreviating the sentence "George Plimpton is a known public figure" by the letter p?
2. What are the two principal meanings of the term "or" when that term is used as a sentence connective? Include at least one original example of each.
3. Why isn't the expression "It is well known that . . ." truth-functional?
4. What common words, other than "and," are sometimes correctly symbolized by means of "·"? Use each of them in a sentence (original if possible).
5. Is the sentence "Archie Leach and Cary Grant are well-known public figures" atomic or compound?
6. What about the sentence "Archie Leach is not a well-known public figure"?
7. And how about "Archie Leach and Cary Grant have been lifelong best friends"?
8. Or, "George Burns is not now, never has been, and never will be God"?
9. Why do we place a **T** on the last two lines of the truth table for "$\supset$"?

Key terms

antecedent: The part that follows "if" in an "*if . . . then*" sentence. In sentential logic, component sentence to the left of the "$\supset$" in a conditional sentence (or sentence form).

atomic sentence: A sentence that contains no sentence connectives.

biconditional: A compound sentence that expresses an "if and only if" relationship between two component sentences. In sentential logic, a sentence having "$\equiv$" as its main connective.

component sentence: The sentence or sentences operated upon by a truth-functional operator.

compound sentence: A sentence containing at least one sentence connective. Example: "Art is handsome, and Betsy is smart."

conditional: A compound sentence that expresses an "if . . . then" relationship between its component sentences. In sentential logic, a sentence having "$\supset$" as its main connective.

conjunct: One of the sentences joined together by "and," "·", and so on. Example: "Art is smart" is a conjunct of the compound "Art is smart, but he's lazy."

conjunction: A compound sentence whose main connective is "and," "but," or a similar term. In sentential logic, a sentence (or sentence form) having "·" as its main connective.

consequent: The part that follows "then" in an "if . . . then" sentence. In sentential logic, the component sentence to the right of the "$\supset$" in a conditional sentence (or sentence form).

disjunct: Either of the component sentences in a disjunction.

disjunction: A compound English sentence whose main connective is an "or." In sentential logic, a compound sentence (or sentence form) whose main connective is "∨".

dot: The symbol "·".

exclusive disjunction: A compound English sentence whose main connective is an exclusive "or."

exclusive "or": The English word "or" used in this sense implies that one and only one of the two disjuncts are true, not both.

horseshoe: The symbol "⊃".

inclusive disjunction: A compound sentence whose main connective is inclusive "or." The sentential logic symbol "∨."

inclusive "or": The sense of the English word "or" correctly symbolized as "∨". "Or," used in its inclusive sense, implies only that at least one of the two disjuncts is true but leaves open the possibility that both disjuncts are true.

main connective: The connective that has the greatest scope.

material biconditional: (See *material equivalence.*)

material conditional: A compound statement whose main connective is "⊃". Synonym: *material implication.*

material equivalence: Statement whose main sentence connective is "≡".

material implication: (See *material conditional.*)

negation: A sentence whose main connective is "∼", "not," "no," or a similar term. (See also *tilde.*)

scope: The scope of an operator is the component sentence or sentences that the operator operates on. The negation operator "∼" operates on a single component sentence. All of the other operators operate on two component sentences.

sentence connective: A term or phrase used to make a larger sentence from two smaller ones. Example: "It's raining, and it's cold." Also, the term *not* and its variations, when used to negate a sentence. Example: the word *not* in "Fred will not win at poker tonight."

sentence constant: A capital letter abbreviating an English sentence, atomic or compound.

sentence variable: A lowercase letter *p* through *z* used as place holders for sentences.

sentential logic: The logic that deals with relationships holding between sentences, atomic or compound, without dealing with the interior structure of atomic sentences. The logic of truth-functions. Synonyms: *logic of truth-functions, propositional logic.*

symbolic logic: The modern logic that includes sentential logic as a part (as well as the predicate logic to be discussed later).

tilde: The symbol "∼".

truth-function: A function that takes one or more truth-values as its input and returns a single truth-value as its output.

truth-functional operator: An operator is truth-functional if the truth-values of the sentences formed by its use are determined by the truth-values of the sentences within its scope. Similarly, sentences constructed by means of truth-functional sentence operators are such that the truth-values of their substitution instances are determined by the truth-values of their component sentences.

truth table: A table giving the truth-values of all possible substitution instances of a given sentence form, in terms of the possible truth-values of the component sentences of these substitution instances. (Analogously, we can also speak of the truth table of a sentence.)

truth-value: There are two truth-values, namely, true and false. Every sentence in sentential logic has a truth-value, and the truth-value of every compound sentence is a function of the truth-value of its component sentences.

vel: The symbol "∨".

Chapter Three

Truth Tables

---

1   *Computing Truth-Values*

In Chapter 2, truth table definitions were introduced for our five truth-functional sentence connectives. Here once again are the standard truth tables for these connectives.

p	$\sim p$
T	F
F	T

p	q	$p \vee q$
T	T	T
T	F	T
F	T	T
F	F	F

p	q	$p \cdot q$
T	T	T
T	F	F
F	T	F
F	F	F

p	q	$p \supset q$
T	T	T
T	F	F
F	T	T
F	F	T

p	q	$p \equiv q$
T	T	T
T	F	F
F	T	F
F	F	T

With this information available to us, we can determine the truth-value of any simple compound sentence containing one of these truth-functional connectives, when provided with the truth-values of the sentences they connect, simply by looking at the appropriate line in the truth tables and noting whether there is a **T** or an **F** at the appropriate spot.

Obviously, this method can be used to determine the truth-values of more complicated sentences also. Suppose Art and Betsy are running for class president and consider the sentence "It's not the case either that Art and Betsy will run or that Betsy won't run," symbolized as $\sim [(A \cdot B) \vee \sim B]$. Assume we are told that Art and Betsy both will run, so that A and B both are true. Then we can figure out the truth-value of $\sim [(A \cdot B) \vee \sim B]$ as follows: Since A and B both are true, $A \cdot B$ must be true, by line 1 of the truth table for "$\cdot$". And since B is true, $\sim B$ must be false, by line 1 of the truth table for "$\sim$". Hence, $[(A \cdot B) \vee \sim B]$ must be true, by line 2 of the truth table for "$\vee$". And finally, since $[(A \cdot B) \vee \sim B]$ is true, its negation $\sim [(A \cdot B) \vee \sim B]$ must be false, by line 1 of the truth table for "$\sim$".

The following diagram illustrates this process of truth table analysis as it was carried out on the sentence $\sim [(A \cdot B) \vee \sim B]$:

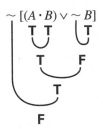

Notice that the process starts with the smallest units of the sentence and proceeds to larger and larger units, until the last loop determines the truth-value of the sentence as a whole.

This procedure, called **truth table analysis,** can be used to determine the truth-value of any compound sentence from the truth-values of its component sentences.

The loop method just introduced is very graphic, and so many students find it to be the best method to use when first learning to compute the truth-values of a sentence. But as soon as you've grasped the basic idea, you should move on to the more common, and more compact, way of computing truth-values that we will refer to as the *tabular method.* The tabular method is just the loop method without the loops. Instead, the truth-values are placed immediately beneath the main connectives of each component sentence. Thus, the truth-value of the sentence is the truth-value under the sentence's main connective. Here's what the sentence above looks like using the tabular method:

$$\downarrow$$
$$\sim [(A \cdot B) \vee \sim B]$$
$$\mathbf{F} \quad \mathbf{T T T} \ \mathbf{T F T}$$

Notice we have used an arrow to indicate the main connective.

🏃 Walk-Through: Computing Truth-Values

Having symbolized a compound sentence, the first step in determining its truth-value, when you know the truth-values of its atomic components, is to place the appropriate truth-value, **T** or **F,** directly beneath each atomic letter. Suppose our sentence is $(D \vee \sim B) \equiv \sim (C \cdot \sim D)$, and we are told that B and C are true and D is false. The first step will look like this on either the loop or tabular methods:

$$(D \vee \sim B) \equiv \sim (C \cdot \sim D)$$
$$\ \mathbf{F} \quad\ \ \mathbf{T} \qquad\ \ \mathbf{T} \quad\ \ \mathbf{F}$$

The second step is to assign truth-values below any negation signs that negate just one atomic letter. In our example, since *B* is true, we place an **F** under the first negation sign, thus indicating that $\sim B$ is false. Also, since *D* is false, $\sim D$ must be true—so we place a **T** under the third tilde.

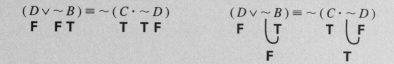

The third step is to look for connectives that have the next largest scopes and place the appropriate truth-values under them. In our example, we can at this stage place an **F** under the vel in $(D \vee \sim B)$ since both disjuncts are false and a **T** under the "·" in the conjunction $(C \cdot \sim D)$, since both conjuncts are true.

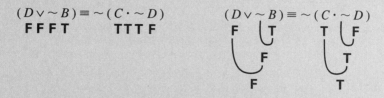

By repeated applications of the procedure described in step 3—finding connectives that have the next larger scope and placing the appropriate truth-value beneath them— we can compute the truth-value of any sentential logic sentence, no matter how complicated. The truth-value for the entire sentence will be the last truth-value assigned and will be placed below the main connective of the sentence. In our example, we first determine the truth-value of $\sim (C \cdot \sim D)$, which must be false since $C \cdot \sim D$ is true (justifying placing an **F** under the tilde), and finally that the whole statement must be true because both components of the biconditional have the same truth-value (justifying placing a **T** under the tribar). So our completed analysis looks like this:

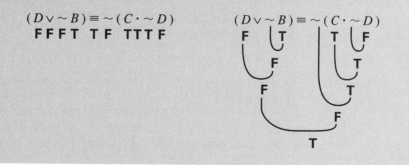

Once again, we illustrate both methods in this section, but you should learn the tabular method since we will employ this method later in the chapter to construct more complex truth tables.

Examples

In these examples, assume *A*, *B*, and *C* are true, and *D*, *E*, and *F* are false.

Tabular Method   *Loop Method*

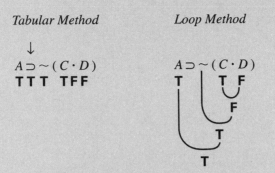

Notice that the negation sign negates the whole compound sentence (*C* · *D*) and therefore is treated after the truth-value of (*C* · *D*) is determined.

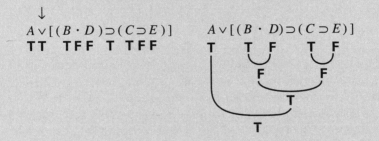

Notice that the major connective in this sentence is "∨" and that therefore it would be possible to determine the truth-value of this sentence without knowing the truth-value of any of the sentences in the right-hand disjunct, because the left-hand disjunct—namely *A*—is true, and consequently the whole sentence is true.

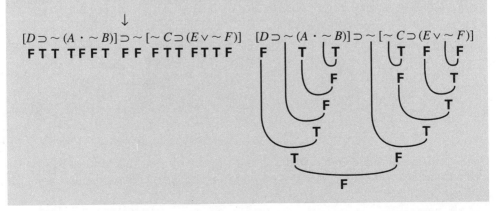

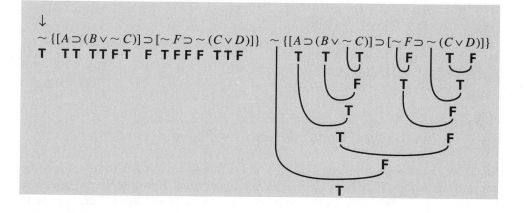

LC Exercise 3-1

If A and B are true, and C, D, and E are false, what are the truth-values of the following compound sentences?

1. $(A \lor D) \supset E$
2. $A \equiv (C \lor B)$
3. $B \supset (A \supset C)$
4. $\sim [C \lor (D \lor E)]$
5. $(A \equiv B) \equiv (D \equiv E)$
6. $\sim [(A \cdot \sim B) \supset (C \cdot \sim D)]$
7. $\sim (A \lor B) \lor \sim (\sim A \lor \sim B)$
8. $\sim (C \cdot D) \lor \sim (\sim C \cdot \sim D)$
9. $[(A \cdot B) \cdot C] \lor [(A \cdot C) \lor (A \cdot D)]$
10. $A \supset [(B \supset C) \supset (D \supset E)]$
11. $[(A \cdot B) \equiv (C \cdot D)] \supset E$
12. $[(A \supset \sim B) \lor (C \cdot \sim D)] \equiv [\sim (A \supset D) \lor (\sim C \lor E)]$
13. $[(\sim A \cdot \sim B) \supset C] \lor (A \supset B)$
14. $[A \supset (\sim A \lor A)] \cdot \sim [(A \cdot A) \supset (A \cdot A)]$
15. $[(E \lor \sim D) \cdot \sim A] \supset \{(\sim A \cdot \sim B) \cdot [(C \cdot D) \cdot E]\}$

LC Exercise 3-2

Knowing that A and B are true and C and D are false, but not knowing the truth-values of Q and R, what can we tell, if anything, about the truth-values of the following compounds?

1. $Q \supset (C \supset D)$
2. $B \supset (Q \lor \sim C)$
3. $\sim C \supset (D \supset Q)$
4. $R \equiv \sim R$
5. $\sim [\sim R \equiv R]$
6. $\sim [R \supset (\sim A \supset D)]$
7. $\sim [(\sim D \lor Q) \supset R]$

8. $[(C \supset Q) \supset \sim R] \supset Q$
9. $\sim (A \lor R) \lor \sim (\sim A \lor \sim R)$
10. $\sim (C \cdot R) \lor \sim (\sim C \cdot \sim R)$
11. $(A \cdot C) \supset [(D \cdot Q) \supset (\sim A \cdot R)]$
12. $[(D \supset R) \supset (D \supset Q)] \supset C$

2   *Tautologies, Contradictions, and Contingent Sentences*

So far we have seen how to determine the truth-value of a particular sentence when we know the truth-value of some or all of its atomic components. However, we can determine the truth-value of some sentences by logic alone, without needing such information. Truth tables provide a mechanical way of examining all of the possible truth-values of a sentence. Each line of a truth table represents what is known as an **interpretation** of a sentence. An interpretation is just a particular assignment of truth-values to the atomic constituents of the sentence.

A completed truth table displays *every* possible interpretation of a sentence. So if it is possible to make a sentence true, there will be at least one line of its truth table with a **T** under its main connective. Likewise, if it is possible to make the sentence false, there will be one or more lines with an **F** under the main connective. A sentence is a **contradiction** just in case there is no interpretation—no line of the truth table—on which it is true. A sentence is a **tautology** if and only if there is no interpretation on which it is false. A sentence that is neither a contradiction nor a tautology is said to be a **contingent sentence,** because its truth-value is not determined by logic alone but is contingent upon the state of the world. A sentence is contingent when on some interpretations it is true and on others it is false.

Thus, we can use a truth table to determine whether a sentence is a contradiction, a tautology, or contingent. Simply scan the truth table. If there are only **T**'s under the main connective, it's a tautology. If there are only **F**'s, it's a contradiction. And if there are both **T**'s and **F**'s, the sentence is contingent.

Some tables are quite simple. If a sentence only contains one atomic letter—even if that letter occurs in the sentence several times—there are only two possible interpretations of the sentence: one on which the atomic letter is true and one on which it is false. So, for example, there are only two interpretations of the sentence $A \cdot \sim A$, and on both of these interpretations the sentence is false, as is shown by the following truth table:

A	$\overset{\downarrow}{A \cdot \sim A}$
T	T F F T
F	F F T F

Since there is no interpretation that makes this sentence true, the truth table proves that this sentence is a contradiction. On the other hand, the sentence $A \lor \sim A$ is a tautology, as is shown by thē following truth table:

	↓
A	$A \lor \sim A$
T	T T F T
F	F T T F

Notice that each line of these truth tables corresponds precisely to what you produced in the last unit using the tabular method.

What if a sentence has two different atomic constituents, $A \supset (B \supset A)$, for example? Here there are four, and only four, possible interpretations: A and B could both be true, A could be true and B false, A could be false and B true, or both A and B could be false. Let's talk about each of these interpretations in turn.

If A and B are both true, the truth table analysis for the sentence is as follows:

$$\overset{\downarrow}{A \supset (B \supset A)}$$
$$\text{T T T T T}$$

Next, consider the interpretation of $A \supset (B \supset A)$ on which A is true and B is false:

$$\overset{\downarrow}{A \supset (B \supset A)}$$
$$\text{T T F T T}$$

On the third possible interpretation, A is false and B is true:

$$\overset{\downarrow}{A \supset (B \supset A)}$$
$$\text{F T T F F}$$

Finally, consider the fourth and last possible interpretation of $A \supset (B \supset A)$, where both A and B are false. The truth table analysis for our sentence under this interpretation is:

$$\overset{\downarrow}{A \supset (B \supset A)}$$
$$\text{F T F T F}$$

Putting these interpretations together yields the following truth table:

		↓					
A	B	A	$\supset$	(B	$\supset$	A	)
T	T	T	T	T	T	T	
T	F	T	T	F	T	T	
F	T	F	T	T	F	F	
F	F	F	T	F	T	F	

Notice that on every possible interpretation $A \supset (B \supset A)$ is a true sentence, no matter what the truth-values of its component sentences. So this sentence is a tautology. The form or structure of this sentence guarantees that it is true, no matter what the truth-values of its component sentences.

Finally, consider a third sentence, namely $(A \supset B) \supset B$. Here is its truth table:

A B	$(A \supset B) \supset B$
T T	T T T **T** T
T F	T F F **T** F
F T	F T T **T** T
F F	F T F **F** F

Notice that there is at least one **T** and one **F** in the column below the main connective in this truth table. This means that the sentence is contingent. We cannot determine the truth-value of this sentence without knowing the truth-value of its component sentences, since on some interpretations the sentence is true and on some it is false.

🏃 Walk-Through: How to Construct a Truth Table

1. The first step in constructing a truth table is to determine the total number of lines needed. This depends on how many different atomic letters are contained in a sentence. As we have seen a sentence with only one atomic letter needs only two lines. A sentence with two letters needs twice as many lines—four. A sentence with three different letters needs twice as many again—namely, eight; four atomic letters requires a sixteen-line table, and so on. For the mathematically inclined, the number of lines needed to construct a truth table for a sentence with n different atomic constituents is 2^n.

2. The second step is to systematically list each of the possible ways of assigning truth-values to the atomic letters of the sentence. The right-most column below the atomic letters always merely alternates truth-values every other line.

M R L	$(M \cdot \sim R) \supset [(M \lor L) \lor \sim L]$
T	
F	
T	
F	
T	
F	
T	
F	

The next column to the left alternates truth-values every two lines, the next alternates every four, and so on. So an easy way to construct truth-values is to proceed from right to left in this manner until the table is complete.

M R L	(M · ~ R) ⊃ [(M v L) v ~ L]
T T T	
T T F	
T F T	
T F F	
F T T	
F T F	
F F T	
F F F	

3. Now we are ready to begin computing the truth-value of the sentence itself. Basically we proceed in the same order used in computing single lines only completing entire columns at a time. (We could proceed by rows instead of columns but this would go much slower.) First we place truth-values in columns directly below the atomic letters. This amounts to merely repeating the relevant column already displayed on the right-hand portion of the line.

M R L	(M	· ~	R) ⊃ [(M	v L)	v ~	L]
T T T	T		T	T	T	T
T T F	T		T	T	F	F
T F T	T		F	T	T	T
T F F	T		F	T	F	F
F T T	F		T	F	T	T
F T F	F		T	F	F	F
F F T	F		F	F	T	T
F F F	F		F	F	F	F

4. The next step is to begin computing the truth-value of the compound components of the sentence. We begin with negated atomic letters.

M R L	(M	· ~ R) ⊃ [(M	v L)	v ~ L]
T T T	T	F T	T T	F T
T T F	T	F T	T F	T F
T F T	T	T F	T T	F T
T F F	T	T F	T F	T F
F T T	F	F T	F T	F T
F T F	F	F T	F F	T F
F F T	F	T F	F T	F T
F F F	F	T F	F F	T F

We continue by computing the truth-values of connectives with greater and greater scope.

M R L	(M · ~ R) ⊃ [(M ∨ L) ∨ ~ L]
T T T	T F F T T T T T F T
T T F	T F F T T T F T T F
T F T	T T T F T T T T F T
T F F	T T T F T T F T T F
F T T	F F F T F T T T F T
F T F	F F F T F F F T T F
F F T	F F T F F T T T F T
F F F	F F T F F F F T T F

5. The truth table is complete when we have completed the column below the sentence's main connective. Again, to make the table easier to read, we indicate the main connective with an arrow.

M R L	↓ (M · ~ R) ⊃ [(M ∨ L) ∨ ~ L]
T T T	T F F T T T T T T F T
T T F	T F F T T T T F T T F
T F T	T T T F T T T T T F T
T F F	T T T F T T T F T T F
F T T	F F F T T F T T T F T
F T F	F F F T T F F F T T F
F F T	F F T F T F T T T F T
F F F	F F T F T F F F T T F

   The division of sentences into tautologies, contradictions, and contingent sentences is of fundamental importance. In the first place, there is an important relationship between tautologies and valid arguments. For to every valid argument there corresponds a tautologous conditional sentence whose antecedent is the conjunction of the premises and whose consequent is the conclusion. And in the second place, the truth-values of all tautologies and contradictions can be determined by logic alone, without appeal to experience or to any kind of empirical test, although this is not the case for contingent sentences. Thus, the division into tautologies, contradictions, and contingent sentences is pertinent to basic philosophical questions about the ways in which knowledge can be acquired.

🔲 Exercise 3-3

Determine which of the following sentences are tautologies, which contradictions, and which contingent.

   1.   ~ (A · ~ A)
   2.   ~ (A ≡ ~ A)

3. $\sim [A \vee (A \supset B)]$
4. $A \supset (A \vee B)$
5. $A \equiv (B \vee \sim B)$
6. $A \equiv (B \vee A)$
7. $(A \cdot B) \supset (\sim A \supset \sim B)$
8. $(B \supset A) \supset (A \supset B)$
9. $(A \equiv B) \equiv (A \supset B)$
10. $(B \vee A) \supset (A \supset B)$
11. $(A \supset B) \supset (B \supset C)$
12. $A \supset [B \supset (A \supset C)]$
13. $[(A \cdot B) \cdot C] \vee [(A \cdot C) \vee (A \cdot B)]$
14. $\{A \supset [(B \vee C) \vee (D \vee \sim B)]\} \vee \sim A$
15. $\{(C \supset D) \supset [A \cdot (C \vee D)]\} \equiv [A \supset (D \supset C)]$

3   *Logical Equivalences and Conditionals*

Having explained the differences between tautologous, contradictory, and contingent sentences, we now can distinguish between two basic kinds of equivalences and conditionals.

A *contingent sentence,* like $A \equiv B$, whose main connective is "$\equiv$", is said to be a *material equivalence.* An equivalence that is also a *tautology,* like $(A \vee B) \equiv (B \vee A)$, is said to be a **logical equivalence,** because, being a tautology, its truth-value is independent of the truth-values of its parts and so can be determined by logic alone.

Similarly, the conditionals $A \supset B$ and $(A \cdot B) \supset A$ are very different from one another. The first is a *contingent conditional* and so is called simply a *material conditional.* Its truth-value is contingent upon the truth-value of its component parts, A and B. But the second is a **logical conditional** because this conditional is a tautology. Again, its truth-value is independent of the truth-values of its components.

We can use analogous terms to characterize logical relationships that may obtain between pairs of sentences. Two sentences are *materially equivalent* if in fact they have the same truth-value. But to say that two sentences are **logically equivalent** is to say more than this. It is to say that *it is not possible* for the two sentences to have different truth-values.

Suppose, for example, we symbolize the sentence "Elvis Presley lives" as E and "Pigs can fly" as P. E is materially equivalent to P, since both happen to be false. P is not logically equivalent to E, however, since it is possible for one of these sentences to be true and the other false. The sentences $E \cdot P$ and $P \cdot E$, on the other hand, are logically equivalent, since it is not possible for these two sentences to have different truth-values. In general, if two sentences p and q are materially equivalent, then the biconditional $p \equiv q$ is a material equivalence, and if p and q are logically equivalent, the biconditional $p \equiv q$ is a logical equivalence.

We can use a truth table to conclusively determine whether or not two sentences are logically equivalent. Two sentences are logically equivalent if and only if there is no line of the truth table on which the two sentences have different truth-values.

Examples

A B	↓ A ⊃ B	↓ ~ A ∨ B
T T	T T T	F T T T
T F	T F F	F T F F
F T	F T T	T F T T
F F	F T F	T F T F

These two sentences are logically equivalent since there is no line of the table on which the two sentences have different truth-values. Note that if we connected these two sentences with "≡" the result would be a logical equivalence.

A B	↓ A ⊃ B	↓ ~ B ∨ A
T T	T T T	F T T T
T F	T F F	T F T T
F T	F T T	F T F F
F F	F T F	T F T F

These two sentences are not logically equivalent, because on lines 2 and 3 the two sentences have different truth-values.

We also can distinguish between pairs of sentences where one merely *materially* implies the other and pairs where one *logically* implies the other. Two sentences *materially imply* each other if, in fact, it is not the case that the first is true and the second false. Thus "Elvis Presley lives" materially implies "There is snow on Mount Kilimanjaro." But one sentence **logically implies** another if and only if it is not possible for the first to be true and the second false. So, for example, "Elvis Presley lives, and George Burns smokes cigars" logically implies "Elvis Presley lives." One sentence, *p*, logically implies another sentence, *q*, if and only if the sentence that results from connecting the two sentences with "⊃", $p ⊃ q$, is a logical implication.

Examples

A B	↓ A ≡ B	↓ B ⊃ A
T T	T T T	T T T
T F	T F F	F T T
F T	F F T	T F F
F F	F T F	T T F

The previous truth table demonstrates that $A \equiv B$ logically implies $B \supset A$ since there is no line of the table on which $A \equiv B$ is true and $B \supset A$ is false. On the other hand, $B \supset A$ does not logically imply $A \equiv B$ because on line 2 $B \supset A$ is true and $A \equiv B$ is false.

A B	$\downarrow$ $A \supset B$	$\downarrow$ $B \supset A$
T T	T T T	T T T
T F	T F F	F T T
F T	F T T	T F F
F F	F T F	F T F

This table shows that neither sentence implies the other, because on line 3 $A \supset B$ is true and $B \supset A$ is false, and on line 2 $B \supset A$ is true but $A \supset B$ is false.

LC Exercise 3-4

Use a truth table to determine which of the following pairs of sentences are logically equivalent. For those sentences that are not logically equivalent, state whether one of the two sentences logically implies the other. Explain your answers.

1. $A, A \cdot C$
2. $F \vee G, F$
3. $L, L \vee L$
4. $A, A \vee \sim A$
5. $F, \sim F \supset G$
6. $F \cdot \sim F, F \equiv \sim F$
7. $A \cdot \sim A, A \vee \sim A$
8. $A \vee \sim B, A \cdot \sim B$
9. $M \cdot \sim R, (M \vee L) \vee \sim L$
10. $L \supset \sim M, L \cdot M$
11. $\sim (M \supset \sim M), K \vee M$
12. $A \vee B, A \vee (B \supset B)$
13. $(M \vee \sim A) \cdot (M \vee A), M$
14. $(M \cdot \sim A) \supset (M \cdot A), M \cdot A$
15. $(M \cdot \sim A) \vee (M \vee A), M$
16. $A \supset (B \supset A), B \supset (A \supset B)$
17. $\sim (H \cdot \sim K), (\sim H \cdot K) \vee \sim K$
18. $\sim (H \cdot \sim K), (\sim H \cdot \sim K) \vee (H \vee K)$
19. $[(H \cdot K) \supset L] \cdot (K \supset \sim L), H \supset L$
20. $(H \cdot K) \vee (K \cdot L), (\sim H \cdot \sim K) \vee (\sim K \cdot \sim L)$

4   *Truth Table Test of Validity*

We can use truth tables to determine whether any argument in sentential logic is valid. Recall that an argument is valid if and only if it is not possible for its premises to all be true while its conclusion is false. Using the terminology introduced above, we can say that a sentential logic argument is valid if and only if there is no interpretation that makes all of the premises of the argument true and the conclusion false. Remember, a truth table displays all of the possible interpretations of an argument. So we can use a truth table to conclusively establish whether or not an argument is valid. If there is no line of the truth table on which all of the premises of an argument are true and the conclusion false, the argument is valid. If there is such a line the argument is invalid. An interpretation on which the premises are true and the conclusion is false is called a **counterexample of an argument.**

As noted above, there is an important relationship between valid arguments and tautologies. To flesh this out we need only to introduce the notion of an argument's corresponding conditional. The **corresponding conditional of an argument** is the conditional whose antecedent is the conjunction of the argument's premises (adding parentheses where appropriate) and whose consequent is the argument's conclusion. Thus the corresponding conditional for the argument

1. $A \supset B$
2. $B \supset C$
∴ 3. $A \supset C$

is the conditional $[(A \supset B) \cdot (B \supset C)] \supset (A \supset C)$. An argument is valid if and only if its corresponding conditional is a tautology—that is, if and only if its corresponding conditional is a logical conditional.

Examples

The argument

1. $A \supset B$
2. $B \supset C$
3. $\sim C$
∴ 4. $\sim A$

is proved to valid by truth table analysis as follows:

	↓	↓	↓	↓
A B C	$A \supset B$	$B \supset C$	$\sim C$	$\sim A$
T T T	T T T	T T T	F T	F T
T T F	T T T	T F F	T F	F T
T F T	T F F	F T T	F T	F T
T F F	T F F	F T F	T F	F T
F T T	F T T	T T T	F T	T F
F T F	F T T	T F F	T F	T F
F F T	F T F	F T T	F T	T F
F F F	F T F	F T F	T F	T F

The argument is valid because it has no counterexample. There is no line on which the premises are all true and the conclusion false. The only line where all of the premises are true is line eight and on that line the conclusion is true as well.

The following truth table shows that the argument

1. $A \supset B$
2. $B \vee C$
3. A
∴4. C

is invalid:

A B C	$A \supset B$	$B \vee C$	A	C
	↓	↓		
T T T	T T T	T T T	T	T
T T F	T T T	T T F	T	F
T F T	T F F	F T T	T	T
T F F	T F F	F F F	T	F
F T T	F T T	T T T	F	T
F T F	F T T	T T F	F	F
F F T	F T F	F T T	F	T
F F F	F T F	F F F	F	F

The second line constitutes a counterexample to this argument. This line shows that it is possible for the premises to be true and the conclusion false, hence the argument is invalid.

LC Exercise 3-5

Use a truth table to determine which of the following arguments is valid.*

(1) 1. $A \cdot B$
    2. $B \supset C$ /∴ C

(2) 1. $C \supset A$
    2. $A \supset (B \cdot C)$
    3. C /∴ B

(3) 1. $(A \cdot B) \supset C$
    2. A /∴ $B \supset C$

(4) 1. $(H \cdot K) \supset L$
    2. H /∴ $K \supset L$

(5) 1. $\sim D \vee \sim F$
    2. $G \supset (D \cdot F)$ /∴ $\sim G$

(6) 1. $A \supset B$
    2. $\sim (C \cdot B)$
    3. C /∴ $\sim A$

(7) 1. $\sim (D \vee \sim K)$
    2. $H \supset D$ /∴ $H \supset K$

(8) 1. $L \vee N$
    2. $L \supset \sim R$
    3. R /∴ $\sim N$

(9) 1. $A \equiv B$ /∴ $\sim B \vee A$

(10) 1. $(A \cdot B) \vee C$
    2. $\sim A$ /∴ C

---

*From now on we will write the conclusion of an argument to the right of the argument's last premise, preceded by a slash, "/", to keep the items separate.

(11) 1. $F \supset G$
         2. $(G \cdot H) \vee K / \therefore F$
(12) 1. $(A \cdot B) \vee C$
         2. $\sim (A \vee B) / \therefore C$
(13) 1. $M \supset N$
         2. $K \supset P$
         3. $N \vee K / \therefore M \vee P$
(14) 1. $A \vee (\sim B \cdot C)$
         2. $B \supset \sim A / \therefore \sim B$
(15) 1. $A \supset (A \supset A)$
         2. $B \supset (A \supset B)$
         3. $A \supset B / \therefore B$
(16) 1. $A \supset B$
         2. $C \supset D$
         3. $B \vee D / \therefore A \vee C$

(17) 1. $\sim (A \vee \sim B)$
         2. $C \supset A / \therefore C \supset D$
(18) 1. $A \supset B$
         2. $C \supset D$
         3. $B \vee C / \therefore A \vee D$
(19) 1. $L \supset M$
         2. $K \supset P$
         3. $(M \vee P) \supset Z$
         4. $\sim Z / \therefore \sim (L \vee K)$
(20) 1. $F \supset (G \supset H)$
             $/ \therefore (\sim H \cdot K) \supset (G \supset \sim F)$

5   *Truth Table Test of Consistency*

Just as we can use truth tables to check for validity, so also we can use truth tables to determine whether a set of sentences is consistent. In sentence logic, a set of sentences is consistent if and only if there is an interpretation that makes each sentence in the set true. To use a truth table to check for consistency, simply construct the table and look for a line on which all of the sentences are true. Since the truth table displays all of the possible interpretations of the set being tested, the set is consistent if and only if there is such a line.

Examples

$A\ B$	$\downarrow$ $A \supset B$	$\downarrow$ $A \vee B$	$\downarrow$ $\sim B$
T T	T T T	T T T	F T
T F	T F F	T T F	T F
F T	F T T	F T T	F T
F F	F T F	F F F	T F

The above truth table shows that the set of sentences

1. $A \supset B$
2. $A \vee B$
3. $\sim B$

is inconsistent, because there is no line on which all of these sentences are true. On the other hand, the set

1. $A \supset B$
2. $A \vee \sim B$
3. $\sim A$

is shown to be consistent by line 4 of the following truth table:

A B	$\downarrow$ $A \supset B$	$\downarrow$ $A \vee \sim B$	$\downarrow$ $\sim A$
T T	T T T	T T F T	F T
T F	T F F	T T T F	F T
F T	F T T	F F F T	T F
F F	F T F	F T T F	T F

LC Exercise 3-6

Use a truth table to show whether each of the following sets of sentences is consistent.

1. $A \equiv B, A \supset \sim B$
2. $A \equiv B, A \equiv \sim B$
3. $A \equiv B, B, \sim B \vee \sim A$
4. $A \supset B, \sim B \vee \sim C, C \cdot \sim A$
5. $R \supset S, T \supset R, \sim (T \supset S)$
6. $(K \cdot L) \supset M, K \supset M, L \supset M$
7. $A \equiv B, C, C \supset \sim B$
8. $A \equiv \sim B, A, B \vee C, \sim C$
9. $\sim (A \equiv B), A \equiv \sim B, A \vee B$
10. $(H \supset J) \vee (H \supset K), \sim (J \vee K), H$

6   *Validity and Consistency*

We are now ready to cash in a suggestion made in the first chapter: Any test of consistency can be used as a test of validity. To see why this is so, let's introduce the notion of an argument's **counterexample set.** The counterexample set of an argument consists of the premises of the argument together with the denial of the conclusion. For example, the counterexample set for the argument

1. $\sim A \supset \sim B$
2. $B \vee C / \therefore \sim A \supset C$

is the set consisting of the following three sentences:

1. $\sim A \supset \sim B$
2. $B \vee C$
3. $\sim [\sim A \supset C]$

We can now say that for an argument to be invalid is just the same as for its counterexample set to be consistent. Put in terms of validity, an argument is valid if and only if its counterexample set is inconsistent. Recall that a valid argument is defined as any argument such that it is not possible for its premises to be true and its conclusion false, which amounts to it not being possible for the premises of the argument and the denial of the conclusion all to be true.

Suppose we have an argument that has inconsistent premises. What conclusion can we draw about the validity of the argument? The answer is that all arguments with inconsistent premises are valid. Obviously, if it is not possible for even the premises to all be true, it is not possible for the premises to all be true *and* the denial of the conclusion to be true as well. This surprising result will be borne out if you think of testing such arguments for validity using a truth table. Consider, for example an argument that has *A* as one premise and ~ *A* as the other premise. The truth table for this argument is guaranteed not to have a line on which all of the premises are true and the conclusion false (no matter what its conclusion is), because there is not even a line where all of the premises are true.

Likewise, any argument whose conclusion is a tautology is also valid no matter what its premises. Since it is not possible to make a tautology false, it is not possible for the premises of the argument to be true and the conclusion false.

This leaves us with three varieties of valid arguments: the normal sort and two special cases. These different kinds of valid arguments correspond to three different ways the form of an argument can guarantee that it is not possible for the premises of the argument to be true and the conclusion to be false.

The normal case

1.   It is possible for the premises to all be true.
     It is possible for the conclusion to be false.
     It is not possible for the premises to all be true and the conclusion to be false.

Two special cases

2.   It is not possible for all of the premises to be true (the premises are inconsistent). Therefore, it is not possible for the premises to all be true and the conclusion to be false.
3.   It is not possible for the conclusion of the argument to be false (the conclusion is a tautology).
     Therefore, it is not possible for the premises to all be true and the conclusion to be false.

As a shorthand way of summarizing these last two cases remember that *anything follows from an inconsistency,* and *a tautology follows from anything.*

7   *The Short Truth Table Test for Invalidity*

We have seen how to use a truth table to demonstrate the *invalidity* of an argument. Fortuntately, we can also employ a shortcut that enables us to demonstrate invalidity without having to go through the tedium of producing an entire truth table. All that it takes to show that an argument is invalid is a single counterexample—a single interpretation on which the premises are all true and the conclusion false. It is often possible to produce such a counterexample in short order simply by reversing the process we used to construct truth tables. Instead of starting with the truth-values of the atomic constituents and working outward until we determine the truth-value of the entire sentence, we will start by assigning a truth-value to the entire sentence and then work inward in an attempt to find an appropriate assignment of truth-values to the atomic constituents.

It is easiest to see how this method works by working through a specific example. Suppose we wanted to prove that the following argument is invalid:

1. $A \supset B$
2. $B / \therefore A$

We begin by assigning a **T** to each of the premises and an **F** to the conclusion.

1. $A \supset B$
    T
2. $B / \therefore A$
    T   **F**

We have to be consistent in our assignments of truth-values, so once a truth-value is assigned to an atomic letter in one line we must assign the same truth-value to that letter on every other line on which it occurs. So we must make B in the first premise true (since we made B true in the second premise), and A in the first premise must be false (because we made A false in the conclusion).

1. $A \supset B$
    F T T
2. $B / \therefore A$
    T   **F**

We have thus, in very short order, produced a counterexample of the argument.

Let's take a more complicated argument:

1. $A \supset (B \supset D)$
2. $\sim C$
3. $(B \vee C) \supset D / \therefore A \supset B$

Again, we begin by assigning the desired truth-values:

1. $A \supset (B \supset D)$
    T
2. $\sim C$
    T
3. $(B \vee C) \supset D / \therefore A \supset B$
    T   **F**

When using the shortcut method, you should always be on the lookout for lines where you are forced to make a particular truth-value assignment. Obviously, anytime you have an atomic sentence you should immediately assign that sentence the desired truth-value.

Likewise, whenever you have a negated atomic sentence (such as our second premise), you can immediately assign the appropriate truth-value to the atomic sentence (in this case an **F**). Again, once we've determined the truth-value for a letter, we fill in that truth-value for that letter wherever else it occurs in the proof.

1. $A \supset (B \supset D)$
    T
2. $\sim C$
    T F
3. $(B \vee C) \supset D / \therefore A \supset B$
    F T   F

After you have assigned truth-values to any atomic sentences and negated atomic sentences that occur, you should look for other sentences that force your hand. In our example, it is unclear at this point how to deal with the first and third premises, but there is only one way to arrive at the desired truth-value for the conclusion. In order to make a conditional false, one must make the antecedent true and the consequent false. So we must assign a **T** to A and an **F** to B.

1. $A \supset (B \supset D)$
    T T F
2. $\sim C$
    T F
3. $(B \vee C) \supset D / \therefore A \supset B$
    F F F T   T F F

It turns out not to matter which truth-value is assigned to D in this case. There are two counterexamples to this particular argument: the interpretation that assigns **T** to A, **F** to B, **F** to C, and **T** to D, and the interpretation that assigns **T** to A, and **F** to B, C, and D. All that it takes to show that the argument is invalid is a single counterexample, so let's just make D true and produce our counterexample as follows:

1. $A \supset (B \supset D)$
    T T F T T
2. $\sim C$
    T F
3. $(B \vee C) \supset D / \therefore A \supset B$
    F F F T T   T F F

It is interesting to notice what happens when we try to prove a *valid* argument invalid by this method. Consider the valid argument:

1. $[(A \cdot B) \supset \sim C]$
2. A
3. $C / \therefore \sim B$

In this example, we must assign **T** to B, in order to falsify the conclusion, and a **T** to A, as well as to C, in order to render the second and third premises true. But notice that if we do so, then we falsify the first premise, as the following indicates:

1. $[(A \cdot B) \supset \sim C]$
   T T T F F T
2. A
   T
3. $C / \therefore \sim B$
   T   F T

Since the argument is valid, there is no way to falsify the conclusion and at the same time render *all* of the premises true. One shortcoming of the shortcut method is that it is not well suited for showing that an argument is valid. We've only produced one interpretation of the argument. To show that an argument is valid, one must show that there is *no* interpretation on which the premises are true and the conclusion false. Merely producing one interpretation on which this is not the case isn't enough. We must show that no assignment of **T**'s and **F**'s will make the premises true and the conclusion false. For some arguments it may be quite complicated to spell out all of this. We may as well produce a complete truth table. Fortunately, in future chapters we will learn much more economical methods of demonstrating validity.

LC Exercise 3-7

Use the short truth table method to show that the following arguments are invalid.

(1) 1. $H \supset K$
    2. $\sim H / \therefore \sim K$

(2) 1. $A \supset B$
    2. $B / \therefore A$

(3) 1. $(H \cdot K) \supset L / \therefore L \supset (K \cdot H)$

(4) 1. $R \vee N$
    2. $L \supset N$
    3. $R / \therefore \sim N$

(5) 1. $(\sim R \vee M) \supset N$
    2. $\sim N / \therefore \sim R$

(6) 1. $A \supset B$
    2. $(C \cdot B) \vee D / \therefore A$

(7) 1. $A \supset \sim B$
    2. $(B \cdot C) \vee A / \therefore \sim B$

(8) 1. $[A \supset (\sim A \supset A)] \supset \sim A / \therefore A$

(9) 1. $H \equiv (K \vee L)$
    2. $K \equiv (L \vee H)$
    3. $L \equiv (H \vee K)$
    4. $\sim H / \therefore H \vee (K \vee L)$

(10) 1. $[(A \supset B) \supset C] \supset D$
    2. $D \supset [C \supset (B \supset A)] / \therefore A \equiv D$

(11) 1. $P \supset Q$
    2. $R \supset S$
    3. $R \vee Q / \therefore P \vee S$

(12) 1. $(A \cdot B) \supset (C \vee D)$
    2. $C \supset A$
    3. $\sim C \vee \sim D$
    4. $B / \therefore A \supset D$

(13) 1. $A \supset (B \supset C)$
    2. $C \supset (D \supset E)$
    3. $A \supset B$
    4. $E \supset A / \therefore D \supset E$

(14) 1. $A \supset B$
    2. $\sim (B \vee C)$
    3. $D \supset (C \vee A)$
    4. $E \supset (D \vee F) / \therefore \sim E$

(15) 1. $(A \vee B) \supset C$
    2. $D \supset (\sim E \supset B)$
    3. $(E \supset A) \supset \sim F$
    4. $\sim C \vee (B \vee F) / \therefore B \equiv C$

(16) 1. $\sim [(R \cdot \sim L) \cdot (L \cdot \sim R)]$
    2. $\sim [(D \cdot \sim R) \cdot (R \vee \sim D)]$
    3. $\sim [(D \cdot \sim L) \vee (L \cdot \sim D)] / \therefore L$

(17) 1. $(R \vee S) \supset T$
    2. $T \supset [(S \cdot L) \vee V]$
    3. $(L \cdot \sim S) \vee (R \vee \sim S)$
    4. $\sim R \supset (V \vee \sim T)$
    $/ \therefore R \supset (L \supset \sim S)$

(18) 1. $A \supset (B \cdot C)$
2. $\sim D \vee \sim E$
3. $D \supset (A \vee F)$
4. $F \supset (C \supset E) / \therefore F \vee \sim D$

(19) 1. $(H \vee \sim R) \cdot (K \supset L)$
2. $S \supset (M \supset T)$
3. $R \supset (T \supset N)$
4. $K \vee R$
5. $(H \vee L) \supset (M \cdot S) / \therefore R$

(20) 1. $Q \supset W$
2. $\sim P \supset \sim W$
3. $\sim N$
4. $W \supset (P \vee Q)$
5. $R \supset (S \vee T)$
6. $S \supset (Q \vee N) / \therefore R \supset (\sim Q \supset W)$

8 *The Short Truth Table Test for Consistency*

All that it takes to show that a set of sentences is consistent is to produce a single interpretation that makes them all true. We can use the short truth table method introduced in the last section to do just this. Suppose, for example, we want to show that the premises of an argument are consistent. Here, instead of attempting to make premises true and conclusion false, we only need to find a way to make the premises true.

For example, suppose we want to show that the argument

1. $A \supset B$
2. $A \supset \sim B / \therefore \sim A$

has consistent premises. We begin by assigning a **T** to both sentences and work backward, as before, until we come up with a complete interpretation. The current example may take a little trial and error, but it is possible to produce such an interpretation as long as we make A false. So, for example, by producing the following interpretation, we show that these sentences are consistent:

1. $A \supset B$
    F T F

2. $A \supset \sim B / \therefore \sim A$
    F T T F

We could just as well have made B true.

⨎ Exercise 3-8

Use the short truth table method to show that the following sets of premises are consistent.

(1) 1. $B \supset A$
2. $C \supset B$
3. $\sim C \cdot A / \therefore A \supset C$

(2) 1. $\sim (F \equiv G)$
2. $\sim (F \supset H) / \therefore F$

(3)　1. $(D \supset E) \vee (D \supset C)$
　　　2. A
　　　3. $A \supset (C \supset D) / \therefore A \cdot D$

(4)　1. $F \equiv \sim G$
　　　2. $\sim (F \vee H)$
　　　3. $F \vee G / \therefore G$

(5)　1. $A \cdot \sim B$
　　　2. $B \vee \sim C$
　　　3. $\sim (\sim C \cdot B) / \therefore \sim B \cdot C$

(6)　1. $(A \vee B) \supset C$
　　　2. $C \supset A$
　　　3. $\sim (D \supset C) / \therefore \sim A$

(7)　1. $\sim [(A \vee B) \supset (C \vee D)]$
　　　2. $C \supset \sim A$
　　　3. $D \supset E / \therefore \sim (A \supset C)$

(8)　1. $A \supset (B \cdot \sim C)$
　　　2. $D \supset E$
　　　3. $\sim (\sim D \vee F)$
　　　4. $D \supset (A \vee C)$
　　　5. $C \supset (\sim F \supset \sim C) / \therefore B \cdot \sim F$

9 *Sentence Forms and Substitution Instances*

Expressions such as $p \cdot q$ containing only sentence variables and sentence connectives are called **sentence forms.** Of course, sentence forms are not sentences (and so are neither true nor false). But if we replace all of the variables in a sentence form by expressions (atomic or compound) that are sentences, then the resulting expression will be a sentence. For instance, if we replace the variables p and q in the sentence form $p \cdot q$ by the sentence constants A and B, respectively, then the resulting expression, $A \cdot B$, will be a sentence. The sentence $A \cdot B$ is said to be a **substitution instance** of the sentence form $p \cdot q$. (Of course, in replacing sentence variables with sentences, we must make sure that every occurrence of a given sentence variable is replaced by the same sentence. Thus, $A \cdot \sim (B \cdot A)$ and $\sim C \cdot \sim (B \cdot \sim C)$ are correct substitution instances of $p \cdot \sim (q \cdot p)$, but $A \cdot \sim (B \cdot C)$ and $\sim C \cdot \sim (B \cdot C)$ are not.)

It is important to notice that compound sentences are substitution instances of more than one sentence form. For instance, the sentence $A \cdot B$, which is a substitution instance of the sentence form $p \cdot q$, also is a substitution instance of the sentence form p (because replacement of p, the one variable in the sentence form p, by the compound sentence $A \cdot B$ results in the sentence $A \cdot B$).

Because sentence forms are not sentences, they are neither true nor false. But all of their substitution instances are sentences, and hence all of their substitution instances are either true or false.

Here is the important rule to keep in mind regarding sentence forms: *A sentence is a substitution instance of a form if and only if you can produce exactly that sentence by doing nothing other than replacing each variable in the form with a well-formed sentence.* So if there is any question about whether a sentence is a substitution instance of a form, take the form and show how one can get the sentence by plugging in a sentence for each variable in the form. For example, the sentence $\sim (\sim A \vee B)$, is a substitution instance of the form $\sim (p \vee q)$ because one can produce this sentence by replacing p with the sentence $\sim A$, and q with the sentence B. This sentence is not a substitution instance of $\sim p \vee q$, however, because there is no sentence one can substitute for the p and q in this form to get the original sentence. If we replace p with $\sim A$ and q with B, we get a different sentence, namely, $\sim \sim A \vee B$. The only way one could produce the original sentence from this form would be to replace the variables in the form with sentence fragments $\sim (\sim A$, and $B)$. But these are just sentence parts, they are not themselves well-formed sentences. Any time the only way to produce the original sentence is to substitute sentence fragments (rather than complete sentences) for variables, the sentence is not a substitution instance of the form.

A common mistake you should be on guard against is confusing *logical form* with *logical equivalence*. For example, it is easy to see that the sentences A and $\sim \sim A$ are logically equivalent. That is, they have exactly the same truth conditions. If one is true, so is the other. Yet despite being logically equivalent, these two sentences are not substitution instances of the same forms. A is only a substitution instance of the form p; whereas $\sim \sim A$ is a substitution instance of three forms: p, $\sim p$, and $\sim \sim p$. A is not a substitution instance of $\sim \sim p$ because there is no sentence that you can substitute for the variable p in this form that will yield the sentence A. No matter what sentence you replace p with, the result will not be an atomic sentence. It will be a double negation, that is, a sentence governed by two negation signs. This example also illustrates an important rule of thumb regarding forms: A sentence may have more logical structure than a form of which it is a substitution instance, but it can never have less.

Understanding the difference between sentences and sentence forms and between variables and constants is the key to understanding the correct use of the rules of logic.

☈ Walk-Through: Sentence Forms

Complex sentences are substitution instances of many forms. Let's see how to go about determining all of the forms for the sentence $\sim (A \vee B) \supset (C \cdot D)$. If you can list all of the forms for a sentence of this level of complexity you should have no trouble with the following exercises.

1. First, every sentence is a substitution instance of what we can refer to as the *atomic form*, namely, the form p.
2. Second, if a sentence is not atomic, it will be a substitution instance of one of the five forms that have only one logical connective. We might call this the *basic form* of a sentence:

    $\sim p$
    $p \cdot q$

$$p \lor q$$
$$p \supset q$$
$$p \equiv q$$

The basic form of a sentence is the form that consists only of the main connective of the sentence and atomic letters. It provides the answer to the question "What kind of sentence is this?" Our sentence is a conditional and thus has the basic form $p \supset q$. Here is a very useful rule of thumb: *Other than the atomic form, every correct form should have the same main connective as the sentence's basic form.* So after we are done listing our forms we can double-check. If any have some other main connective, they are wrong.

3.   Another helpful guideline is that every sentence is a substitution instance of what we might refer to as its *expanded form*. The expanded form is the form you get when you systematically replace each atomic letter in the sentence with a variable. In our example, the expanded form is $\sim (p \lor q) \supset (r \cdot s)$. The expanded form shows all of a sentence's logical form. *No sentence is a substitution instance of a form that contains more logical structure, or a different kind of logical structure than the sentence's expanded form.*

These guidelines allow you to automatically produce three forms for any complex sentence: the atomic form, p, the basic form ($p \supset q$ in our case), and the expanded form, $\sim (p \lor q) \supset (r \cdot s)$. If there are more forms than these three, they will have the same main connective as the basic form, they will be more complex than the basic form, and they will be less complex but otherwise have the same kind of form as the expanded form.

4.   To produce the remaining forms systematically, think about the sentences represented by the variables in the basic form. For each variable ask: What kind of sentence does this variable represent? In our basic form $p \supset q$, p represents a negation, namely, $\sim (A \lor B)$. This gives us the form $\sim p \supset q$. Likewise, q in the basic form represents a conjunction, $(C \cdot D)$, so we can represent this bit of logical structure with the form $p \supset (q \cdot r)$. We can show both of these bits of structure at once with the form $\sim p \supset (q \cdot r)$.

If we had a really complicated sentence, we would just repeat this procedure for the new forms we've produced, revealing any structure represented by atomic letters in these new forms. In our case the only additional bit of structure we can reveal gives us the expanded form. So here are all of the forms of which $\sim (A \lor B) \supset (C \cdot D)$ is a substitution instance:

p (the atomic form)
$p \supset q$ (the basic form)
$\sim p \supset q$
$p \supset (q \cdot r)$
$\sim p \supset (q \cdot r)$
$\sim (p \lor q) \supset r$
$\sim (p \lor q) \supset (q \cdot r)$ (the expanded form).

Examples

Here are a few compound sentences with sentence forms of which they are substitution instances:

Sentence	*Forms*
1. $\sim C$	p
	$\sim p$
2. $A \cdot C$	p
	$p \cdot q$
3. $\sim C \cdot R$	p
	$p \cdot q$
	$\sim p \cdot q$
4. $\sim M \equiv \sim N$	p
	$p \equiv q$
	$\sim p \equiv q$
	$p \equiv \sim q$
	$\sim p \equiv \sim q$
5. $C \cdot (D \cdot \sim S)$	p
	$p \cdot q$
	$p \cdot (q \cdot r)$
	$p \cdot (q \cdot \sim r)$
6. $\sim L \vee \sim (F \supset G)$	p
	$p \vee q$
	$\sim p \vee q$
	$p \vee \sim q$
	$\sim p \vee \sim q$
	$p \vee \sim (p \supset r)$
	$\sim p \vee \sim (p \supset r)$
7. $(A \supset B) \supset (C \supset D)$	p
	$p \supset q$
	$(p \supset q) \supset r$
	$p \supset (q \supset r)$
	$(p \supset q) \supset (r \supset s)$
8. $A \vee \sim [(B \cdot D) \vee F]$	p
	$p \vee q$
	$p \vee \sim q$
	$p \vee \sim (q \vee r)$
	$p \vee \sim [(q \cdot r) \vee s]$

Note that for each of the above forms it doesn't matter which variables are used. Instead of p we could have listed the form q, or r, and so on. These are all just different ways of writing the very same form. Likewise $p \cdot q$, $p \cdot r$, $r \cdot q$, $q \cdot r$, and so on, are all ways to write the same form. Remember the variables in sentence forms are just placeholders.

L⟨ Exercise 3-9

1. Which of the following sentences *are not* substitution instances of the form $p \supset q$?
   a. $A \supset B$ d. $A \supset \sim B$
   b. $\sim A \supset (B \supset C)$ e. $\sim A \supset \sim B$
   c. $A \vee (B \supset C)$ f. $(A \vee B) \supset C$

2. Which of the following sentences *are* substitution instances of the form $p \supset q$?
   a. $\sim (A \supset B)$ d. $A \vee B$
   b. $A \supset \sim B$ e. $\sim A \vee \sim B$
   c. A f. $(\sim A \vee \sim B) \supset C$

3. Which of the following sentences *are* substitution instances of the form $\sim p$?
   a. A d. $\sim A \vee \sim B$
   b. $\sim A$ e. $\sim A \supset B$
   c. $\sim \sim A$ f. $\sim (A \supset B)$

4. Which of the following sentences *are not* substitution instances of the form $\sim \sim p$?
   a. A d. $\sim \sim \sim A$
   b. $\sim (\sim A \supset B)$ e. $\sim \sim A \supset \sim B$
   c. $\sim \sim (A \supset B)$ f. $(A \vee B) \supset C$

5. $\sim A \supset (B \supset C)$ is a substitution instance of which of the following?
   a. p d. $\sim p \supset q$
   b. $\sim p$ e. $p \supset (q \supset r)$
   c. $p \supset q$ f. $(p \supset q) \supset r$

L⟨ Exercise 3-10

For each sentence on the left, determine the sentence forms on the right of which it is a substitution instance. (Remember that a sentence may be a substitution instance of several different sentence forms.)

1. A		a. p
2. $A \supset B$		b. $\sim p$
3. $(A \vee B) \supset C$		c. $p \vee q$
4. $A \vee (B \supset C)$		d. $p \supset q$
5. $(\sim A \vee B) \supset C$		e. $\sim p \vee q$
6. $\sim (A \vee B) \supset C$		f. $\sim p \supset q$
7. $\sim A \vee (B \supset C)$		g. $\sim p \supset \sim q$
8. $(A \vee B) \supset \sim C$		h. $\sim (p \vee q)$
9. $\sim [A \vee (B \supset C)]$		i. $\sim (p \supset q)$
10. $\sim (\sim A \vee B) \supset C$		j. $\sim (\sim p \supset q)$
11. $\sim [(A \vee B) \supset C]$		k. $(p \vee q) \supset r$
12. $\sim (A \vee B) \supset \sim C$		l. $p \vee (q \supset r)$
13. $\sim [\sim (A \vee B) \supset C]$		m. $(\sim p \vee q) \supset r$
14. $\sim [\sim (\sim A \vee B) \supset C]$		n. $\sim (p \vee q) \supset r$
15. $\sim [(\sim A \vee B) \supset C]$		o. $(p \vee q) \supset \sim r$
		p. $\sim [p \vee (q \supset r)]$
		q. $\sim [(p \vee q) \supset r]$
		r. $\sim (\sim p \vee q) \supset r$

LC Exercise 3-11

Determine the sentence forms of which the following are substitution instances. Example:
The sentence $A \supset \sim B$ is a substitution instance of p, $p \supset q$, and $p \supset \sim q$.

1. $A \cdot \sim B$
2. $\sim D \supset \sim F$
3. $L \vee (M \cdot N)$
4. $\sim (H \vee K)$
5. $\sim (\sim R \supset S)$
6. $(A \cdot B) \equiv \sim B$
7. $\sim A \supset (B \supset A)$
8. $\sim (A \equiv B) \supset C$
9. $(\sim A \equiv B) \supset C$
10. $\sim [(A \equiv B) \supset C]$
11. $\sim (B \cdot D) \supset (R \vee D)$
12. $\sim [(B \cdot D) \supset (R \vee D)]$

10 *Truth Tables and Forms*

Tautologies are true in virtue of their form. Likewise, it is the form of a contradiction that makes it impossible for it to be true. So, corresponding to tautologies, contradictions, and contingent sentences are three types of sentence forms. If a sentence is a tautology, it is a substitution instance of at least one **tautologous sentence form.** For example, the sentence $A \supset (B \supset A)$ is a substitution instance of the tautologous form $p \supset (q \supset p)$. A form is tautologous if and only if every substitution instance of the form is a tautology. Likewise, we can identify **contradictory sentence forms** and **contingent sentence forms.** A sentence form is contradictory if and only if every substitution instance of the form is contradictory. A sentence form is contingent just in case it is neither tautologous nor contradictory, that is, just in case it has at least one contingent substitution instance.

We can use truth tables to determine whether sentence forms are tautologous, contradictory, or contingent. For example, here is the truth table for the form $p \supset (\sim p \supset q)$:

$p\,q$	$\overset{\downarrow}{p \supset (\sim p \supset q)}$
T T	T T F T T T
T F	T T F T T F
F T	F T T F T T
F F	F T T F F F

This table demonstrates that this is a tautologous form. Obviously any substitution instance of this form is a tautology. No matter what sentences are substituted for p and q, having this form will always guarantee that the resulting sentence is true.

Notice that we cannot say that all substitution instances of contingent sentence forms are contingent sentences, since all sentences are substitution instances of some contingent sentence form or other. For instance, all sentences are substitution instances of the atomic sentence form p, which is a contingent sentence form.

LC Exercise 3-12

Determine which of the following sentence forms are tautologous, which contradictory, and which contingent.

1. $\sim [p \supset (p \vee \sim p)]$
2. $\sim [p \supset (p \cdot \sim p)]$
3. $(p \supset q) \supset p$
4. $p \vee (q \supset \sim p)$
5. $p \supset (p \vee q)$
6. $(p \cdot \sim p) \supset q$
7. $p \supset (q \vee \sim q)$
8. $(p \vee q) \vee \sim (p \cdot q)$
9. $[(p \vee q) \cdot \sim (p \cdot q)] \supset (p \equiv \sim q)$
10. $\{[p \cdot (q \vee r)] \supset p\} \equiv q$
11. $(p \supset q) \supset [(p \supset r) \vee (p \supset q)]$
12. $[(p \cdot q) \vee r] \equiv [(p \cdot q) \vee (p \cdot r)]$
13. $[p \supset (q \supset r)] \supset (p \supset r)$
14. $p \supset [q \supset (p \supset r)]$
15. $[(p \supset q) \cdot (q \supset r)] \equiv (p \supset r)$

Exercise 3-13

1. What is the difference between contingent sentences and contingent sentence forms? Include examples.
2. Can a sentence be a substitution instance of more than one sentence form? Explain, including an original example.
3. Some substitution instances of contingent sentence forms are not themselves contingent sentences. Do any substitution instances of tautologous sentence forms exist that are not themselves tautologous sentences?
4. According to the rule of Double Negation (to be introduced in Chapter 4), p is equivalent to $\sim \sim p$. Does it follow that any substitution instance of p is also a substitution instance of $\sim \sim p$?
5. If a sentence form contains four variables, how many lines must its complete truth table analysis have?
6. Suppose you know only that one of the premises of an argument is a contradiction. What if anything can you conclude about the argument's validity? Explain.
7. If the premises of a valid argument are consistent, is its conclusion necessarily true? Give an example.
8. Suppose you know that a particular argument is deductively valid and has a false conclusion. What, if anything, can you tell from this about its premises?

Key terms

contingent sentence: A sentence that is not a substitution instance of any tautologous or contradictory sentence form.

contingent sentence form: A sentence form that has at least one true and one false substitution instance.

contradiction: A sentence whose logical form guarantees that it is false. Every contradiction is a substitution instance of a contradictory sentence form.

contradictory sentence form: A sentence form all of whose substitution instances are false. (See also *contradiction*.)

corresponding conditional of an argument: The conditional whose antecedent is the conjunction of the argument's premises (adding parentheses where appropriate) and whose consequent is the argument's conclusion. An argument is valid if and only if its corresponding conditional is a tautology.

counterexample of an argument: An interpretation that makes the premises true and the conclusion false. A sentential logic argument is valid if and only if it has no counterexample.

counterexample set: The set consisting of the premises of an argument together with the denial of the argument's conclusion. An argument is valid if and only if its counterexample set is inconsistent.

interpretation: In sentential logic an interpretation is a particular assignment of truth values to each of the atomic constituents of a sentence or group of sentences. The lines of a truth table represent all of the possible interpretations of a sentence or group of sentences.

logical conditional: A tautology whose main connective is "⊃". A tautological conditional whose truth can be determined by means of logic alone. Synonyms: *logical implication, logical entailment, strict implication.*

logical equivalence: A tautology whose main connective is "≡". A tautological equivalence whose truth can be determined by means of logic alone.

logically equivalent: Two sentences are logically equivalent if and only if it is not possible for one to be true and the other false. A sentence p is logically equivalent to a sentence q if and only if $p \equiv q$ is a tautology.

logical implication: A tautology whose main connective is "⊃". A tautological conditional whose truth can be determined by means of logic alone. Synonyms: *logical conditional, logical entailment, strict implication.*

logically implies: A sentence p logically implies a sentence q if and only if it is not possible for p to be true and q false.

sentence form: An expression containing sentence variables such that if all of its sentence variables are replaced by sentences, the resulting expression is a sentence.

substitution instance: A sentence obtained from a sentence form by replacing all of the sentence variables in the sentence form by sentence constants, making sure that every occurrence of a given sentence variable is replaced by the same sentence constant.

tautologous sentence form: A sentence form all of whose substitution instances are true. (See also *tautology*.)

tautology: A sentence whose logical form guarantees that it is true. Every tautology is a substitution instance of a tautologous form.

truth table analysis: A method for determining the truth-value of a sentence from knowledge of the truth-values of its component sentences. Similarly, a method for determining whether a sentence form is tautologous, contradictory, or contingent by considering the truth-values of all possible substitution instances and for determining the validity of arguments in sentential logic.

Chapter Four

Proofs

---

1   *Argument Forms*

As stated in Chapter 1, an *argument* consists of a list of sentences—one of which (the conclusion) is claimed to be supported by the others (the premises). An **argument form** is a group of *sentence forms* such that all of its substitution instances are arguments. For example, all substitution instances of the form

1. $p \supset q$
2. $p \; / \therefore \; q$

are arguments, and hence that form is an argument form. (Of course, in substituting into an argument form, every occurrence of a given sentence variable must be replaced by the same sentence wherever that variable occurs in the argument form.) The order of the premises in an argument is irrelevant. Thus,

1. $A \supset B$
2. $A \; / \therefore \; B$ and   1. A
                                 2. $A \supset B \; / \therefore \; B$

both can be thought of as substitution instances of the above form.

Examples

The following arguments are substitution instances of the argument form:

1. $p \supset q$
2. $p \; / \therefore \; q$

(1)   1. $A \supset B$
      2. $A \; / \therefore \; B$

(2)   1. $H \supset \sim K$
      2. $H \; / \therefore \; \sim K$

(3) 1. $(A \lor B) \supset C$
2. $A \lor B / \therefore C$

(4) 1. $\sim (A \cdot B) \supset (C \lor D)$
2. $\sim (A \cdot B) / \therefore (C \lor D)$

If an argument form has no substitution instances that are invalid, it is said to be a **valid argument form.** Every valid argument is a substitution instance of at least one valid form. Of course, no substitution instances of a valid argument form could have all of its premises true and its conclusion false, or, to put this another way, an invalid argument cannot be a substitution instance of a valid argument form. An argument form that has even one invalid argument as a substitution instance is called an **invalid argument form.**

We can use truth table analysis to demonstrate the validity of any argument form. Take the argument form just mentioned.

(1) 1. $p \supset q$
2. $p / \therefore q$

The truth table analysis for this argument form is as follows:

$p\ q$	p	$\downarrow$ $p \supset q$	q
T T	T	T T T	T
T F	T	T F F	F
F T	F	F T T	T
F F	F	F T F	F

Notice that there is a **T** for both premises only on line 1 of this truth table and that there also is a **T** for the conclusion on that line. Hence, there is no substitution instance of this argument form having all of its premises true and its conclusion false. Therefore, this argument form is a valid argument form.

An example of a valid argument in English having this form is:

1. If it's fall, then winter can't be far away.
2. It's fall.
∴ 3. Winter can't be far away.

Or, in symbols:

1. $F \supset \sim W$
2. F
∴ 3. $\sim W$

Now consider the invalid argument form:

1. $p \supset q$
∴ 2. $\sim p / \therefore \sim q$

Its truth table analysis is as follows:

p q	~ p	↓ p ⊃ q	~ q
T T	F T	T T T	F T
T F	F T	T F F	T F
F T	T F	F T T	F T
F F	T F	F T F	T F

Both premises yield a **T** on lines 3 and 4 of this truth table. But although the conclusion yields a **T** on the fourth line, it yields an **F** on the third. Thus, line 3 of this truth table indicates that it is possible for a substitution instance of this argument form to have true premises and a false conclusion and therefore proves that the argument form is not deductively valid.

Here is an example of an invalid argument in English that has this form (with its symbolization to the right):

1. If it rained last night, then the streets are wet.
2. It did not rain last night.
∴ 3. The streets are not wet.

1. $R \supset W$
2. $\sim R$
∴ 3. $\sim W$

Clearly, this argument is invalid. If the street cleaner just came along, the streets may be wet even though both premises are true, so it is possible for this argument to have true premises and a false conclusion.

2 *Modus Ponens and Modus Tollens*

In Chapter 3 we used truth tables to demonstrate the validity of arguments. Truth tables have two major shortcomings, however. First, they can be quite tedious. If an argument contains, say, 8 different atomic letters a 256-line truth table is required! Second, truth tables can be used to demonstrate the validity of sentential logic arguments only. In this chapter we introduce a method of demonstrating validity that avoids both of these deficiencies: *proofs*. In proofs, we reason step by step from premises to conclusion. We will use valid argument forms in proofs to justify the individual steps in each proof.

The argument form just proved valid, namely,

$p \supset q$
$p / \therefore q$

is called **Modus Ponens** (abbreviated **MP**) and is the first of eighteen valid argument forms (plus variations) to be used as rules of inference in constructing proofs of arguments.

This form tells us that any time you have two lines of a proof, one of which has the form $p \supset q$ and the other of which has the form p, you can validly infer q. (Again, the order in which these lines occur is irrelevant.) For example, here is a proof that uses this argument form twice:*

1. $A \supset (B \vee C)$ p (premise)
2. $(B \vee C) \supset D$ p
3. A p
4. $B \vee C$ 1,3 **MP**
5. D 2,4 **MP**

Each line of a proof must be justified in virtue of being a substitution instance of the conclusion of a valid argument form. So a **proof** can be defined as *a list of sentences all of which are either premises of the argument or else follow from previous sentences on the list because they are substitution instances of the conclusions of valid argument forms, where the last sentence on the list is the conclusion of the argument.* You can think of each new line of a proof as the conclusion of a short argument whose premises are the lines cited to right of the new line.

Here is why the recognition of sentence forms is so important. You must be able to look, say, at the first premise above and see that it is a substitution instance of the form $p \supset q$, where for p we substitute A and for q we substitute $B \vee C$. (In using the eighteen valid argument forms, we may substitute any sentences, no matter how complex, provided we substitute consistently—that is, provided that whatever we substitute for one occurrence of a particular variable also is substituted for every occurrence of that variable in the given use of that argument form.) Because we already have the sentence substituted for p (namely, A) elsewhere in the proof (line 3), we can use **MP** to add the substitution instance of q (in this case, $B \vee C$) as our new line 4. We can then use **MP** with lines 2 and 4 to produce our conclusion as line 5. This time $B \vee C$ is substituted for p and D for q.

Another of the eighteen valid argument forms is **Modus Tollens (MT):**

$p \supset q$
$\sim q \, / \therefore \sim p$

Here is an example of a valid argument having this form (with its symbolization to the right):

1. If it's spring, then the birds are chirping.   1. $S \supset B$ p (premise)
2. The birds aren't chirping.   2. $\sim B$ p
$\therefore$ 3. It isn't spring. $\therefore$ 3. $\sim S$ 1,2 **MT**

Modus Ponens and Modus Tollens are rules that you will use over and over again in natural deduction proofs. Any time both a conditional and its antecedent are true, the consequent must also be true. If both a conditional and the negation of its consequent are true, it follows that the negation of the antecedent is true.

Do not confuse these forms with two invalid forms that resemble them. These invalid forms are so notorious that they too have traditional names:

Affirming the consequent (invalid)

$p \supset q$
$q \, / \therefore p$

---

*We use the letter p (not italic) to indicate the argument's premises.

Denying the antecedent (invalid)

$p \supset q$
$\sim p \, / \therefore \sim q$

We used a truth table to demonstrate the invalidity of Denying the Antecedent in the immediately preceding section. We could do the same for Affirming the Consequent. Here's a quicker way to make the point. If for p we substitute a false sentence and for q we substitute a sentence that is true, the result would be a substitution instance of Denying the Antecedent that has true premises and a false conclusion.

Examples

Here are two more examples of proofs using the valid argument forms **MP** and **MT**:

(1) 1. $M \supset \sim N$ p
     2. M p
     3. $H \supset N$ p
     4. $\sim N$ 1,2 **MP**
     5. $\sim H$ 3,4 **MT**

(2) 1. $(R \vee S) \supset (T \supset K)$ p
     2. $\sim K$ p
     3. $R \vee S$ p
     4. $T \supset K$ 1,3 **MP**
     5. $\sim T$ 2,4 **MT**

Notice that in using **MP** to obtain line 4, the compound sentence $R \vee S$ was substituted for p and the compound sentence $T \supset K$ was substituted for q.

3   *Disjunctive Syllogism and Hypothetical Syllogism*

Another of the eighteen valid argument forms is **Disjunctive Syllogism (DS)**, which has two forms:

$p \vee q$ and $p \vee q$
$\sim p \, / \therefore q$ $\sim q \, / \therefore p$

The validity of these forms is obvious. From the fact that at least one of two sentences is true, together with the fact that one of the sentences is definitely false, it follows that the other sentence must be true.

Now let's look at the valid argument form **Hypothetical Syllogism (HS)**:

$p \supset q$
$q \supset r \, / \therefore p \supset r$

What this form tells us is that material implication is transitive, like "greater than" in mathematics. If one statement materially implies a second statement and the second statement materially implies a third, it follows that the first statement materially implies the third.

Example

Here is a proof using both Hypothetical Syllogism and Disjunctive Syllogism (as well as Modus Tollens):

1.	$A \lor B$	p
2.	$C \supset D$	p
3.	$A \supset C$	p
4.	$\sim D$	p
5.	$A \supset D$	2,3 **HS**
6.	$\sim A$	4,5 **MT**
7.	B	1,6 **DS**

LG Exercise 4-1

For each line (other than premises) in the following proofs, state the previous line or lines from which it follows and the valid argument form (**MP, MT, DS,** or **HS**) used to obtain it. (The sample proof illustrates this procedure.)*

Sample proof

1.	$A \supset \sim B$	p (premise)
2.	$\sim \sim B$	p
3.	$\sim A$	1,2 **MT** (correct justification for line 3)

(1)				**(3)**		
	1. $A \supset B$	p			1. $A \lor (H \cdot K)$	p
	2. $A \lor C$	p			2. $A \supset (B \lor C)$	p
	3. $\sim B$	p			3. $\sim (B \lor C)$	p
	4. $\sim A$				4. $\sim A$	
	5. C				5. $H \cdot K$	

(2)				**(4)**		
	1. $A \supset B$	p			1. $(H \lor K) \supset L$	p
	2. $B \supset C$	p			2. $M \supset \sim L$	p
	3. $\sim C$	p			3. M	p
	4. $A \supset C$				4. $\sim L$	
	5. $\sim A$				5. $\sim (H \lor K)$	

---

*We use the letter p (not italic) to indicate the argument's premises.

(5) 1. $D \vee E$ p
     2. $D \supset \sim A$ p
     3. $\sim E$ p
     4. $A \vee B$ p
     5. D
     6. $\sim A$
     7. B

(6) 1. $\sim R$ p
     2. $\sim S \supset T$ p
     3. $(A \supset B) \supset \sim S$ p
     4. $\sim R \supset (A \supset B)$ p
     5. $\sim R \supset \sim S$
     6. $\sim R \supset T$
     7. T

(7) 1. $A \supset (B \supset C)$ p
     2. $H \supset A$ p
     3. $H \vee (A \vee B)$ p
     4. $\sim (B \supset C)$ p
     5. $\sim A$
     6. $\sim H$
     7. $A \vee B$
     8. B

(8) 1. $A \supset (B \supset C)$ p
     2. $\sim \sim F$ p
     3. $\sim D \supset A$ p
     4. $\sim C \vee \sim F$ p
     5. $\sim D$ p
     6. $\sim D \supset (B \supset C)$
     7. $B \supset C$
     8. $\sim C$
     9. $\sim B$

(9) 1. $(H \vee K) \supset R$ p
     2. $A \supset (\sim M \supset \sim R)$ p
     3. $\sim M$ p
     4. $A \vee M$ p
     5. A
     6. $\sim M \supset \sim R$
     7. $\sim R$
     8. $\sim (H \vee K)$

(10) 1. $F \supset (G \supset H)$ p
     2. G p
     3. $B \supset F$ p
     4. $R \supset B$ p
     5. R p
     6. $R \supset F$
     7. F
     8. $G \supset H$
     9. H

LC Exercise 4-2

Use **MP, MT, DS,** and **HS** to prove that the following arguments are valid.

(1) 1. $\sim R$
     2. $S \supset R / \therefore \sim S$

(2) 1. $A \cdot S$
     2. $(A \cdot S) \supset R / \therefore R$

(3) 1. $\sim (H \cdot K)$
     2. $R \vee (H \cdot K) / \therefore R$

(4) 1. $(P \vee Q) \supset (R \cdot W)$
     2. $L \supset (P \vee Q) / \therefore L \supset (R \cdot W)$

(5) 1. $R \supset S$
     2. $T \supset R$
     3. $\sim S / \therefore \sim T$

(6) 1. $\sim M$
     2. $N \supset G$
     3. $N \vee M / \therefore G$

(7) 1. $\sim D \supset E$
     2. $D \supset F$
     3. $\sim F / \therefore E$

(8) 1. $G \vee H$
     2. $\sim H \vee I$
     3. $\sim I / \therefore G$

(9) 1. $\sim G \supset (A \vee B)$
     2. $\sim B$
     3. $A \supset D$
     4. $\sim G /\therefore D$

(10) 1. $(A \supset B) \supset C$
     2. $\sim D \vee A$
     3. $\sim D \supset (A \supset B)$
     4. $\sim A /\therefore C$

(11) 1. $A \supset (B \supset C)$
     2. $\sim C$
     3. $\sim D \supset A$
     4. $C \vee \sim D /\therefore \sim B$

(12) 1. $\sim (D \cdot F)$
     2. $(L \vee M) \vee R$
     3. $\sim T \supset \sim (L \vee M)$
     4. $(D \cdot F) \vee \sim T /\therefore R$

(13) 1. $(A \vee B) \supset (B \vee C)$
     2. $(B \supset C) \vee A$
     3. $(B \supset C) \supset (A \vee B)$
     4. $\sim A /\therefore B \vee C$

(14) 1. $(P \cdot Q) \supset [R \vee \sim (T \cdot S)]$
     2. $(P \cdot Q) \supset [R \vee (T \cdot S)]$
     3. $(T \vee R) \supset (P \cdot Q)$
     4. $\sim (T \cdot S)$
     5. $T \vee R /\therefore R$

4   Simplification and Conjunction

Another of the eighteen valid argument forms is **Simplification (Simp),** which, like **DS,** has two forms:

$p \cdot q /\therefore p$ and $p \cdot q /\therefore q$

You should have no problem with this rule. Obviously, from the fact that two sentences are both true one can infer that one of the sentences is true. So any time you have a line of a proof that is a conjunction, you can use simplification to derive one of the conjuncts.

   Now let's look at the valid argument form **Conjunction (Conj):**

p
$q /\therefore p \cdot q$

This rule allows you to take any two lines of a proof and put them together to make a conjunction. You can think of Simplification as the rule you use to take apart conjunctions and Conjunction as the rule you use to put them together.

Example

Here is a proof that uses both **Simp** and **Conj:**

(1) 1. $A \cdot B$ p
     2. $B \supset C$ p
     3. B 1 Simp
     4. C 2,3 MP
     5. A 1 Simp
     6. $A \cdot C$ 4,5 Conj

5 *Addition and Constructive Dilemma*

Another of the eighteen valid argument forms is **Addition (Add):**

$p / \therefore p \lor q$

Remember that all that it takes to make a disjunction true is for *at least one* of the disjuncts to be true. So once you've proven a sentence true, it follows that *any* disjunction that contains this sentence as one of its disjuncts is also true.

Addition allows us to infer the sentence $A \lor B$ from the sentence A; it also lets us infer $A \lor \sim B$. Indeed, from A we can use addition to infer the sentence $A \lor \{ \sim [Z \equiv \sim (X \lor Y)] \supset R \}$. In short, you can add *any* sentence you like as the second disjunct, because you have already established that the first disjunct is true. This makes addition very useful. In particular, if the conclusion of your proof contains atomic constituents that are not found in any of your premises, you can use addition to introduce them to the proof. This is illustrated in the following proof:

1. $A \cdot C /$ p
2. A 1 **Simp**
3. C 1 **Simp**
4. $A \lor E$ 2 **Add**
5. $C \lor D$ 3 **Add**
6. $(A \lor E) \cdot (C \lor D)$ 4,5 **Conj**

The sentence E contained in the conclusion is not in the premise. Nor is the sentence D. Addition allows us to introduce E into the proof at line 4, and D at line 5.

Now, let's look at the valid argument form **Constructive Dilemma (CD):**

$p \lor q$
$p \supset r$
$q \supset s / \therefore r \lor s$

Constructive Dilemma is the only argument form in our system that requires you to cite *three* lines. To use constructive dilemma, you need a disjunction and two conditionals, where the antecedents of the two conditionals are the two disjuncts of the disjunction. Here is an example of an argument in English that has the form **CD:**

1. If a Democrat is elected, then taxes will go up.
2. But if a Republican is elected, then unemployment will go up.
3. A Democrat or a Republican will be elected.
∴ 4. Either taxes will go up or unemployment will go up.

In symbols, this reads:

1. $D \supset T$ p
2. $R \supset U$ p
3. $D \lor R$ p
4. $T \lor U$ 1,2,3 **CD**

Here are two very important restrictions on the use of the eight valid argument forms we have just introduced. First, these forms work in *one direction only.* They permit inference, for example, from $A \cdot B$ to A, by Simplification, but surely not from A to $A \cdot B$. One-directional argument forms are said to be **implicational argument forms.** Second, you can apply these forms to *entire lines only,* never to parts of a line. For example, you are not allowed to apply Simplification to $(A \cdot B) \supset C$ to get $A \supset C$. (These two restrictions are the chief differences between the eight valid argument forms just presented and the ten to be discussed next.)

Here is the complete list of eight valid implicational argument forms to be used as rules of inference in our system:

Valid Implicational Argument Forms (Rules of Inference)

1. Modus Ponens (**MP**):

   $p \supset q$
   $p \ / \therefore q$

2. Modus Tollens (**MT**):

   $p \supset q$
   $\sim q \ / \therefore \sim p$

3. Disjunctive Syllogism (**DS**):

   $p \vee q$
   $\sim p \ / \therefore q$
   $p \vee q$
   $\sim q \ / \therefore p$

4. Hypothetical Syllogism (**HS**):

   $p \supset q$
   $q \supset r \ / \therefore p \supset r$

5. Simplification (**Simp**):

   $p \cdot q \ / \therefore p$
   $p \cdot q \ / \therefore q$

6. Conjunction (**Conj**):

   p
   $q \ / \therefore p \cdot q$

7. Addition (**Add**):

   $p \ / \therefore p \vee r$

8. Constructive Dilemma (**CD**):

   $p \vee q$
   $p \supset r$
   $q \supset s \ / \therefore r \vee s$

LC Exercise 4-3

For each line (other than premises) in the following proofs, state the line or lines from which it follows and the valid implicational argument form on the above list used to obtain that line.

(1) 1. $D \cdot R$ p
        2. $(D \cdot R) \vee [A \vee (B \cdot D)]$

(2) 1. $[L \supset (B \supset A)] \cdot (L \vee M)$ p
        2. $L \supset (B \supset A)$

(3) 1. $C \vee D$ p
        2. $[A \supset (B \supset \sim C)]$ p
        3. $A \supset (B \supset \sim C)] \cdot (C \vee D)$

(4) 1. $(A \cdot B) \supset S$ p
        2. $(D \cdot C) \vee (A \cdot B)$ p
        3. $(D \cdot C) \supset L$ p
        4. $L \vee S$

(5) 1. $A \supset D$ p
        2. $(B \cdot C) \supset H$ p
        3. $D \supset (B \cdot C)$ p
        4. $A \supset (B \cdot C)$
        5. $A \supset H$

(6) 1. $A \supset (B \supset D)$ p
    2. $\sim D$ p
    3. $D \vee A$ p
    4. A
    5. $B \supset D$
    6. $\sim B$

(7) 1. $A \supset \sim B$ p
    2. $A \vee C$ p
    3. $\sim \sim B \cdot D$ p
    4. $\sim \sim B$
    5. $\sim A$
    6. C

(8) 1. $A \supset B$ p
    2. $A \cdot \sim D$ p
    3. $B \supset C$ p
    4. A
    5. $A \supset C$
    6. C
    7. $\sim D$
    8. $C \cdot \sim D$

(9) 1. C p
    2. $A \supset B$ p
    3. $C \supset D$ p
    4. $D \supset E$ p
    5. $C \supset E$
    6. $C \vee A$
    7. $E \vee B$

(10) 1. $(A \vee M) \supset R$ p
    2. $(L \supset R) \cdot \sim R$ p
    3. $\sim (C \cdot D) \vee (A \vee M)$ p
    4. $\sim R$
    5. $\sim (A \vee M)$
    6. $\sim (C \cdot D)$

(11) 1. $(H \cdot K) \supset L$ p
    2. $\sim R \cdot K$ p
    3. $K \supset (H \vee R)$ p
    4. K
    5. $H \vee R$
    6. $\sim R$
    7. H
    8. $H \cdot K$
    9. L

(12) 1. $(R \cdot S) \supset \sim (Q \vee T)$ p
    2. $\sim B$ p
    3. $(Q \vee T) \vee \sim (\sim B \cdot \sim A)$ p
    4. $(\sim B \vee A) \supset (R \cdot S)$ p
    5. $(\sim B \vee A) \supset \sim (Q \vee T)$
    6. $\sim B \vee A$
    7. $\sim (Q \vee T)$
    8. $\sim (\sim B \cdot \sim A)$
    9. $\sim (\sim B \cdot \sim A) \cdot \sim B$

(13) 1. $(D \vee \sim H) \supset [R \cdot (S \vee T)]$ p
    2. L p
    3. $(L \vee M) \supset (D \cdot E)$ p
    4. $L \vee M$
    5. $D \cdot E$
    6. D
    7. $D \vee \sim H$
    8. $R \cdot (S \vee T)$
    9. $S \vee T$
    10. $D \cdot (S \vee T)$

(14) 1. $C \supset B$ p
    2. $\sim D \cdot \sim B$ p
    3. $[A \supset (B \supset C)] \vee D$ p
    4. $A \vee C$ p
    5. $\sim D$
    6. $\sim B$
    7. $A \supset (B \supset C)$
    8. $(B \supset C) \vee B$
    9. $B \supset C$

6   *Principles of Strategy*

Books on chess and checkers often start out with a brief summary of the rules of the game, a list of rules indicating which kinds of moves are permitted. But the major part of a book of this kind discusses not permissive rules but what might be called *principles of strategy*.

The permissive rules usually allow more than one move. (For instance, there are twenty permitted opening moves in a game of chess.) But only a very few of these are likely to lead to winning positions. A good chess book helps the chess student to get the feel of good play and to become familiar with principles of good strategy, principles that in general lead to strong positions. (For example, in chess, other things being equal, it is good strategy to develop a piece into the center of the board rather than to one side.) Of course, as every chess tyro soon learns, strict adherence to conventional strategy may lead to disaster.

The analogy between the game of chess and the game of logic problem solving is very close. The eighteen valid argument forms (plus the rules to be added in the next chapter) correspond to the rules of chess. They determine which steps (moves) are permitted in an argument or proof. But generally they permit many steps at any given point in a proof, only a very few of which are likely to lead to "winning the game," that is, to deriving the conclusion of the argument. A good logic player is one who develops a feel for good play, perhaps by becoming familiar with good strategy principles. We will give you a few general suggestions here that you can put to use in the next exercise. We will add some more strategy hints later in the chapter after we introduce the remaining ten argument forms. Of course, principles useful to one person may not be useful to another, for psychological reasons. The few hints given below have proved useful to many students.

It should be remembered, however, that just as chess strategy principles are not part of the rules of chess, so logic strategy principles are not part of the rules of logic. In fact, logic strategy rules belong not to the context of justification, but rather to the context of discovery, since they do not justify moves in proofs, but rather help us to discover winning moves. The justification for the assertion of a line in a proof must always be a valid argument form or rule of inference.

Perhaps the most important strategy rule is to *look for forms that correspond to valid rules of inference.* Consider the following argument:

1. $[A \vee (\sim B \supset C)] \supset [\sim D \vee (C \cdot E)]$
2. $\sim [\sim D \vee (C \cdot E)] / \therefore \sim [A \vee (\sim B \supset C)]$

Beginners are likely to be overwhelmed by the large number of letters in this argument, or by the complexity of its premises, and thus be unable to discover a proof for it. But if they try to see the premises and conclusion in terms of their basic forms, they will discover that the proof is quite simple. Notice that the major connective of the premise on line 1 is an implication and that that premise has the form $p \supset q$. Now notice that the major connective of line 2 is a negation, and that line 2 has the form $\sim q$, since what is negated on line 2 is the consequent (q) of line 1. (So the first two lines of the proof have the forms $p \supset q$ and $\sim q$.) Clearly here is an opportunity to use the argument form Modus Tollens, to obtain $\sim p$, which in this case is $\sim [A \vee (\sim B \supset C)]$, the desired conclusion. So we have figured out a simple proof:

1. $[A \vee (\sim B \supset C)] \supset [\sim D \vee (C \cdot E)]$ p
2. $\sim [\sim D \vee (C \cdot E)]$ p /$\therefore \sim [A \vee (\sim B \supset C)]$
3. $\sim [A \vee (\sim B \supset C)]$ 1,2 **MT**

A simple proof indeed, once attention is paid to the basic forms of the sentences that make up the proof.

This proof illustrates another general rule of thumb: Whenever the same sentence occurs on two different lines, look for ways to apply **MP, MT, DS,** or **HS** using those two lines. These four rules are particularly useful. Pay attention to the main connective of your premises with these four rules in mind. If you have a premise that is a conditional, look to see if you have (or can easily get) another line that allows you to employ **MP, MT,** or **HS.** If you have a premise that is a disjunction, look for ways to apply **DS.** If you have a line that is a negation, see if you can use **MT** or **DS.**

Now for some more specific strategy hints. Keep in mind that *small sentences (especially atomic sentences or negated atomic sentences) are your friends.* If you have them, use them. If you can get them, do so. Consider the following argument:

1. $B \supset A$
2. $\sim D \vee B$
3. $\sim A$ $/ \therefore \sim D$

The place to start to work on this proof is with the third premise. We can use this premise to apply **MT** to the first premise to get $\sim B$, which we can then use to apply **DS** to the second premise to derive the conclusion:

4. $\sim B$ *1,3* **MT**
5. $\sim D$ 2,4 **DS**

Real proficiency in natural deduction requires more than merely memorizing the rules. You need to learn how to use them to get what you want. Keep the conclusion in mind. Once you've mastered the rules, *you will find completing many proofs much easier by working backward from the conclusion.* To do this you should begin by examining the logical structure of the conclusion and asking whether there is some line that together with premises could be used to derive the conclusion. Ask yourself, "Given my premises, what would it take to get my conclusion?" Consider, for example, the following proof:

1. $C \supset A$
2. $M \supset B$
3. $B \supset C$
4. M $/ \therefore A$

Eventually you should get to the place where you can work a proof like this one backward in your head (for longer proofs you may want to use a piece of scrap paper). You should be able to see that you can get the conclusion, A, from the first premise using **MP** if somehow you could derive C.

1. $C \supset A$
2. $M \supset B$
3. $B \supset C$
4. M $/ \therefore A$
    .
    .
    .
    C
    A 1, _ **MP**

But then, in the same manner, it should be obvious that you can get C if you can get B (using the third premise). So all that it takes to complete the proof is to see that you can, in fact, derive B by using **MP** on the second and fourth premises. Filling in the line numbers, the completed proof is as follows:

1. $C \supset A$
2. $M \supset B$
3. $B \supset C$
4. M $/\therefore A$
5. B 2,4 **MP**
6. C 3,5 **MP**
7. A 1,6 **MP**

Notice also that the letter A, which occurs in the conclusion, is connected to the letter C in one of the premises, and C to B, and B to M. Short of working the entire proof backward, it is often useful to *trace the connections between the letters occurring in an argument, starting with the letter (or letters) occurring in the conclusion.* And then, having done so, it is often good strategy to *begin the proof with the letter (or letters) most distant from those in the conclusion,* which in this case means beginning with the letter M.

This proof also illustrates the fact that usually it is not fruitful to use the same line in a proof over and over again. "Fresh information" (an untapped line in a proof) tends to be most useful. Thus, after line 6 has been written down, every premise has been used in the proof except premise 1. At this point, the information in premise 1 is untapped, unused, and the information on line 6 is fresh, in the sense that it is psychologically new information. This is a strong clue that it is time to use line 6 in conjunction with premise 1, as in fact it is used to obtain line 7.

Beginning logic students are often reluctant to use Addition. Don't be. Some proofs cannot be completed without using this rule. (In the next chapter, however, we will learn some new rules that will make this no longer true.) In particular, if the conclusion contains an atomic component that does not occur in any premise, you must use Addition to introduce this information into the proof. For example, notice that the letter D in the conclusion of the following proof:

1. $B \supset C$
2. $\sim C$
3. $\sim B \supset R$ $/\therefore (R \lor D) \cdot \sim B$

does not occur in any of the premises. This tips us off that we must at some point use addition to complete the proof. We start to work on this proof with the handy short second premise. This gives us half of our conclusion, $\sim B$, by using **MT** on the first premise. We can then use **MP** on the third premise to get R:

4. $\sim B$ 1,2 **MT**
5. R 3,4 **MP**

This is where some students get stuck. What do we do now? Simple—add the D. We can then finish the proof as follows:

6. $R \vee D$ 5 **Add**
7. $(R \vee D) \cdot \sim B$ 4,6 **Conj**

Notice that you won't know what to add, and probably won't even think of adding in the first place, if you are only looking at the premises and not the conclusion. *Pay attention to where you are going.*

    One final point. If you get stuck, don't be afraid to produce a line you end up not using. If there is some rule you can legitimately apply, do it—even though you can't see how it helps. That's much better than just not finishing the proof. There's nothing wrong with trial and error. When completely stuck, try something—anything—you haven't tried yet. Of course, we mean anything that is valid.

    That's enough strategy for now. Let's summarize some of the main hints offered in this section:

- Look for sentence portions that are repeated, with a view toward applying **DS, HS, MP,** or **MT.**
- Small sentences are extremely useful.
- Work backward from the conclusion.
- Tap into fresh information. Use unused premises.
- When the conclusion contains atomic sentences not found in any premise, use **Add** to introduce this information.
- If stuck, try anything (that's valid).

🚶 Walk-Through: Basic Proofs

Here is a proof as difficult as any you will find in the following exercise.

1. $(\sim A \vee B) \supset L$
2. $\sim B$
3. $A \supset B$
4. $L \supset (\sim R \vee D)$
5. $\sim D \cdot (R \vee F) / \therefore (L \vee G) \cdot \sim R$

One of the first things we should notice is the small sentence on line 2. We can use this right away, as follows:

6. $\sim A$ 2,3 **MT**

We can also go ahead and simplify line 5:

7. $\sim D$ 5 **Simp**
8. $R \vee F$ 5 **Simp**

Lines 1 and 4 invite us to use **HS:**

9. $(\sim A \vee B) \supset (\sim R \vee D)$ 1,4 **HS**

It's not very clear how to proceed. When this happens, we should check to see if we need to use **Add.** In this case using **Add** will let us apply **MP** to line 9:

10.	$\sim A \vee B$	6 **Add**
11.	$\sim R \vee D$	9,10 **MP**

Next, notice that the conclusion is a conjunction. Working backward, we can solve the proof using Conjunction if we can obtain $L \vee G$ on one line and $\sim R$ on another. Looking more carefully, we see that G is not in any premise. This tips us off that we will need to use **Add** again.

$\sim R$ is already at our fingertips:

12.	$\sim R$	7,11 **DS**

as is L:

13.	L	1,10 **MP**

This leaves us only the **Add** and **Conj** steps to complete the proof:

14.	$L \vee G$	13 **Add**
15.	$(L \vee G) \cdot \sim R$	12,14 **Conj**

As usual, there is more than one way of completing this particular proof. Indeed, it is possible to complete this proof using only 13 lines. Can you do it?

The best way for you to pick up strategy is to complete proofs on your own. We supply lots of basic exercises you can use to hone your skills, and there are more strategy hints at the end of the chapter.

LC Exercise 4-4

Supply the premises and lines that are missing from the following proofs.

(1) 1. $Q \supset R$ p
     2.   p
     3. R 1,2 **MP**

(2) 1. $A \equiv B$ p
     2.   p
     3. B 1,2 **MP**

(3) 1. $\sim (A \equiv B)$ p
     2.   p
     3. $\sim B$ 1,2 **MT**

(4) 1. $(\sim A \vee B) \vee C$ p
     2.   p

3.	p
4. $\sim A \vee B$	1,2 **DS**
5. $\sim A$	3,4 **DS**

(5)
1. $A \supset (\sim B \supset C)$	p
2. $D \supset (R \vee \sim W)$	p
3.	p
4.	p
5. $(R \vee \sim W) \vee (\sim B \supset C)$	1,2,3 **CD**
6. $\sim B \supset C$	4,5 **DS**

(6)
1. $A \supset B$	p
2.	p
3. $\sim D$	p
4.	2,3 **DS**
5. B	1,4 **MP**

(7)
1. $A \supset B$	p
2. $D \supset E$	p
3.	p
4.	p
5. $\sim D$	2,3 **MT**
6.	4,5 **DS**
7. $A \supset C$	1,6 **HS**

(8)
1.	p
2.	p
3. $G \supset L$	p
4. $(T \cdot S) \vee V$	1 **Add**
5. $\sim L$	2,4 **MP**
6.	3,5 **MT**
7.	1 **Simp**
8. $T \cdot \sim G$	6,7 **Conj**

Exercise 4-5

Use the eight implicational argument forms to prove that the following arguments are valid.

(1) 1. $(B \cdot M) \supset R$
  2. $L \supset (B \cdot M)$ /∴ $L \supset R$

(2) 1. $R \vee S$
  2. $(A \supset L) \cdot [(R \vee S) \supset T]$ /∴ $T \vee L$

(3) 1. $R \cdot S$
  2. T /∴ $(T \vee L) \cdot (R \cdot S)$

(4) 1. $A \cdot B$
  2. $B \supset C$ /∴ C

(5) 1. $A \supset (A \cdot B)$
  2. $C \supset A$ /∴ $[C \supset (A \cdot B)] \cdot (C \supset A)$

(6) 1. $A \supset B$
  2. $C \cdot A$ /∴ $B \vee D$

(7) 1. $C \supset A$
  2. $A \supset (B \cdot D)$
  3. C /∴ B

(8)   1. $A \supset (\sim B \cdot C)$
        2. $C \supset D$
        3. $E \vee B$
        4. $A /\therefore D \cdot E$

(9)   1. $(F \supset G) \vee H$
        2. $\sim G$
        3. $\sim H /\therefore \sim F$

(10)   1. L
        2. $T \vee \sim R$
        3. $(L \vee R) \supset \sim T /\therefore \sim R \vee B$

(11)   1. $R \vee \sim W$
        2. $\sim W \supset L$
        3. $R \supset T /\therefore T \vee L$

(12)   1. $(R \cdot A) \vee E$
        2. $(R \cdot A) \supset D$
        3. $\sim D /\therefore E \cdot \sim D$

(13)   1. $(A \cdot D) \supset \sim C$
        2. $(R \vee S) \supset (A \cdot D)$
        3. $\sim C \supset \sim (A \cdot D)$
        $/\therefore (R \vee S) \supset \sim (A \cdot D)$

(14)   1. A
        2. $(A \vee \sim D) \supset (R \cdot S) /\therefore (R \cdot S) \vee B$

(15)   1. $\sim A$
        2. $(C \vee A) \supset L$
        3. $A \vee D$
        4. $(D \vee U) \supset C /\therefore L$

(16)   1. $R \supset (\sim P \vee \sim M)$
        2. $\sim R \supset (\sim M \cdot \sim N)$
        3. $\sim (\sim P \vee \sim M)$
        4. $Z \vee R /\therefore (\sim M \cdot \sim N) \cdot Z$

(17)   1. A
        2. $(B \vee C) \supset D$
        3. $(A \vee E) \supset (B \cdot C) /\therefore D$

(18)   1. $A \vee B$
        2. $C \supset A$
        3. $(B \cdot \sim C) \supset (D \cdot \sim C)$
        4. $\sim A /\therefore D$

(19)   1. $(\sim A \cdot \sim B) \supset (C \supset B)$
        2. $B \supset A$
        3. $\sim A /\therefore \sim C$

(20)   1. $[\sim A \cdot \sim (D \cdot E)] \supset (B \supset \sim D)$
        2. $\sim (D \cdot E) \cdot \sim R$
        3. $E \supset F$
        4. $\sim A \vee (D \cdot E)$
        5. $\sim (D \cdot E) \supset (B \vee E) /\therefore \sim D \vee F$

7   *Double Negation and DeMorgan's Theorem*

We noted above that implicational argument forms are one-directional, and permit, for instance, inference from $A \cdot B$ to A, but not the reverse inference from A to $A \cdot B$. The sentence $A \cdot B$ *implies* the sentence A, but is *not equivalent* to it. (So the argument $A /\therefore A \cdot B$ is invalid.)

But now, consider the valid inference from A to $\sim \sim A$. In this case, we can reverse the process, that is, we can validly infer from $\sim \sim A$ to A. This reversibility is due to the fact that the sentence A not only implies the sentence $\sim \sim A$ but also is equivalent (indeed, logically equivalent) to it, and equivalent sentences imply each other. It follows then that both of the following argument forms are valid:

1. $p /\therefore \sim \sim p$
2. $\sim \sim p /\therefore p$

Since these two argument forms are just the reverse of each other, we can simplify matters by combining them into one two-directional argument form. Let's introduce the symbol ":::" and use it to indicate that an argument form is two-directional. Then we can combine the above two one-directional (implicational) forms into one two-directional (equivalence) form as follows:

$p :: \sim \sim p$

This equivalence argument form is called **Double Negation (DN).** It permits inferences from any substitution instance of p to the analogous substitution instance of $\sim \sim p$, and from any substitution instance of $\sim \sim p$ to the analogous substitution instance of p. Thus, it permits all of the inferences permitted by the two implicational argument forms $p / \therefore \sim \sim p$ and $\sim \sim p / \therefore p$.

Argument forms, such as Double Negation, that permit inferences in both directions are called **equivalence argument forms** (because they permit inferences from given statements to statements with which they are logically equivalent).

Now let's consider the pair of valid equivalence argument forms called **DeMorgan's Theorem (DeM):**

$\sim (p \cdot q) :: \sim p \vee \sim q$
$\sim (p \vee q) :: \sim p \cdot \sim q$

The first of these forms permits inferences from any substitution instance of $\sim (p \cdot q)$ to the analogous substitution instance of $\sim p \vee \sim q$, and from $\sim p \vee \sim q$ to the analogous substitution instance of $\sim (p \cdot q)$; the second permits similar substitutions in both directions.

DeMorgan's Theorem is intuitively valid. For instance, it permits the intuitively valid inferences from

1.   It's not true that Candice Bergen and Paula Jones both were invited to the Inaugural Ball.

in symbols $\sim (C \cdot P)$, to

2.   Either Candice Bergen or Paula Jones wasn't invited to the Inaugural Ball.

in symbols $\sim C \vee \sim P$, and from

3.   Alexander the Great wasn't so great, and neither was Bonaparte.

in symbols $\sim A \cdot \sim B$, to

4.   It's not true that either Alexander the Great or Bonaparte was great.

in symbols $\sim (A \vee B)$.

The intuitive validity of DeMorgan's Theorem is reflected in the standard ways we used to translate English sentences of the forms "not both ..." and "neither ... nor. ..." Recall that in Chapter 2 we said that a sentence like "It will not both rain and snow tomorrow" can be translated as $\sim (R \cdot S)$, or it can equally well be translated as $\sim R \vee \sim S$. Likewise, we learned that "It will neither rain nor snow tomorrow" can be translated by either $\sim (R \vee S)$ or $\sim R \cdot \sim S$. DeMorgan's is the natural deduction rule that certifies that these alternative translations are equivalent.

When we use an equivalence argument form, we move from a given expression to one that is logically equivalent to it. In Chapter 3 we showed how to use truth tables to demonstrate that sentences and sentence forms are equivalent. Two sentences (or sentence forms) are equivalent if and only if there is no line of the truth table on which the forms have different truth-values. So two sentences that are logically equivalent have exactly the same truth conditions—they say exactly the same thing. Hence, we can use equivalence argument forms on *parts of lines* without fear of changing truth-values and thus without fear of inferring from true premises to a false conclusion. Thus, we can use Double Negation to infer validly from $A \vee B$ to $\sim \sim A \vee B$, because A is equivalent to $\sim \sim A$ and hence $A \vee B$ is equivalent to $\sim \sim A \vee B$. This is a very important difference between equivalence and implicational argument forms: *Implicational argument forms must be used on whole lines only; equivalence forms may be used on parts of lines.*

LE Exercise 4-6

Complete the following proofs that emphasize the rules **DN** and **DeM:**

(1) 1. $A \supset \sim B$
    2. $B / \therefore \sim A$

(2) 1. $\sim T \vee S$
    2. $T / \therefore S$

(3) 1. $\sim (J \vee K) / \therefore \sim K$

(4) 1. $\sim (F \cdot G)$
    2. $F / \therefore \sim G$

(5) 1. $\sim (A \cdot B) \vee C$
    2. $\sim C$
    3. $B / \therefore \sim A$

(6) 1. $\sim W \supset \sim X$
    2. X
    3. $\sim (W \cdot \sim Z) / \therefore Z$

(7) 1. $\sim B \supset \sim C$
    2. $\sim (\sim A \vee B)$
    3. $C \vee D / \therefore D$

(8) 1. $\sim (\sim A \cdot \sim B)$
    2. $B \supset C$
    3. $\sim A$
    4. $\sim (C \cdot \sim D) / \therefore D$

8   *Commutation, Association, and Distribution*

Intuitively, the statement "Art will go or Betsy will go" $(A \vee B)$ is equivalent to the statement "Betsy will go or Art will go" $(B \vee A)$, and the statement "Art will go and Betsy will go" $(A \cdot B)$ is equivalent to the statement "Betsy will go and Art will go" $(B \cdot A)$. These intuitions are captured by the two equivalence forms called **Commutation (Comm):**

$p \vee q :: q \vee p$
$p \cdot q :: q \cdot p$

The import of these two Commutation principles is that reversing the order of statements connected by "·" or "∨" does not change the truth-values of the compound sentences they form. (Once again, you may prove by truth table analysis that both forms of Commutation are valid.)

Notice that Commutation does not hold for sentences connected by "⊃". For instance, the sentence "If you overcooked the potatoes, you spoiled the meal" $(O \supset S)$ is certainly not equivalent to the analogous statement "If you spoiled the meal, then you overcooked the potatoes" $(S \supset O)$, given all the other ways there are to spoil a meal.

Now consider the valid equivalence argument forms called **Association (Assoc):**

$$p \vee (q \vee r) :: (p \vee q) \vee r$$
$$p \cdot (q \cdot r) :: (p \cdot q) \cdot r$$

The point of these two argument forms is that the movement of parentheses in either of the ways specified does not change the truth-values of compound sentences in which they occur.

Notice that Association holds only for compounds formed by two occurrences of "∨" or two occurrences of "·". Thus, an inference from, say, $A \vee (B \cdot C)$ to $(A \vee B) \cdot C$ is *invalid*. Similarly, Association does not hold for compounds formed by two occurrences of "⊃". For instance, the inference from $A \supset (B \supset C)$ to $(A \supset B) \supset C$ is *invalid*. (You can use a truth table to prove that this is true.)

Next, let's look at the two valid equivalence argument forms called **Distribution (Dist):**

$$p \cdot (q \vee r) :: (p \cdot q) \vee (p \cdot r)$$
$$p \vee (q \cdot r) :: (p \vee q) \cdot (p \vee r)$$

Distribution is an extremely powerful rule. In order to apply Distribution, look for a conjunct that is a disjunction or a disjunct that is a conjunction. Notice that if you apply Distribution to a conjunction, the result should be a disjunction, and if you apply Distribution to a disjunction, the result should be a conjunction. This gives you a handy way of double-checking to see that you've applied Distribution correctly. Make sure you have replaced a conjunction with a disjunction or a disjunction with a conjunction.

9   *Contraposition, Implication, and Exportation*

The valid equivalence form **Contraposition (Contra)**

$$p \supset q :: \, \sim q \supset \, \sim p$$

is useful when dealing with conditional sentences, in particular in some uses of the rule of conditional proof (to be introduced in Chapter 5).

The valid equivalence form **Implication (Impl)**

$$p \supset q :: \, \sim p \vee q$$

also is useful, in this case when we need to replace a conditional sentence by its disjunctive equivalent or a disjunction by its conditional equivalent.

Contraposition is intuitively valid and indeed holds for all kinds of implicational sentences, truth-functional or non-truth-functional. But Implication holds only for truth-functional implications, that is, for material implications.

Next, let's look at the valid equivalence argument form called **Exportation (Exp):**

$$(p \cdot q) \supset r :: p \supset (q \supset r)$$

This rule captures the intuitive idea that if the conjunction of two sentences, $(p \cdot q)$, implies a third, then the first (p) implies that the second (q) implies the third (and vice versa). For instance, if it is true that if Fran is intelligent and works hard, then she'll get an A in her philosophy class (in symbols $(I \cdot H) \supset A$), then it follows that if she is intelligent, then if she works hard, she'll get an A (in symbols $I \supset (H \supset A)$).

10 *Tautology and Equivalence*

The two valid equivalence forms called **Tautology (Taut)**

$p :: p \cdot p$
$p :: p \vee p$

are used chiefly to get rid of redundant letters, as in the following proof:

1. $A \supset \sim A$ $/ \therefore \sim A$
2. $\sim A \vee \sim A$ 1 **Impl**
3. $\sim A$ 2 **Taut**

The two valid equivalence forms called **Equivalence (Equiv)**

$p \equiv q :: (p \supset q) \cdot (q \supset p)$
$p \equiv q :: (p \cdot q) \vee (\sim p \cdot \sim q)$

(the last of the eighteen valid forms to be introduced into our system) are needed to manipulate statements in which the symbol "$\equiv$" occurs, as in the following proof:

1. $A \equiv B$
2. B $/ \therefore A$
3. $(A \supset B) \cdot (B \supset A)$ 1 **Equiv**
4. $B \supset A$ 3 **Simp**
5. A 2,4 **MP**

Here is a list of the ten valid equivalence argument forms to be used along with the eight valid implicational forms listed on page 82 as rules of inference in our system (for handy reference, all eighteen rules are also printed on the inside front cover):

Valid Equivalence Argument Forms

9. Double Negation (**DN**):
    $p :: \sim \sim p$

10. DeMorgan's Theorem (**DeM**):
    $\sim (p \cdot q) :: \sim p \vee \sim q$
    $\sim (p \vee q) :: \sim p \cdot \sim q$

11. Commutation (**Comm**):
    $p \vee q :: q \vee r$
    $p \cdot q :: q \cdot r$

12. Association (**Assoc**):
    $p \vee (q \vee r) :: (p \vee q) \vee r$
    $p \cdot (q \cdot r) :: (p \cdot q) \cdot r$

13.	Distribution (**Dist**):	16.	Exportation (**Exp**):

13. Distribution (**Dist**):
    $p \cdot (q \vee r) :: (p \cdot q) \vee (p \cdot r)$
    $p \vee (q \cdot r) :: (p \vee q) \cdot (p \vee r)$

14. Contraposition (**Contra**):
    $p \supset q :: \sim q \supset \sim p$

15. Implication (**Impl**):
    $p \supset q :: \sim p \vee q$

16. Exportation (**Exp**):
    $(p \cdot q) \supset r :: p \supset (q \supset r)$

17. Tautology (**Taut**):
    $p :: p \cdot p$
    $p :: p \vee p$

18. Equivalence (**Equiv**):
    $p \equiv q :: (p \supset q) \cdot (q \supset p)$
    $p \equiv q :: (p \cdot q) \vee (\sim p \cdot \sim q)$

It may be asked why we have chosen just these eighteen valid argument forms. In the first place, there are an infinite number of valid argument forms, so we could not prove and list every one. On the other hand, we don't want to list only the minimum number of argument forms required for a complete sentential logic, for such a short list would make proofs quite difficult to construct and much longer than is desirable. The usual procedure is to strike a happy medium, proving and listing about ten to twenty of the commonly used valid argument forms, making sure that the system is *complete* (that is, making sure that every valid argument of sentential logic can be proved using the listed valid argument forms). Our list of eighteen valid argument forms contains most of the commonly used forms and at the same time is complete (or, rather, will be complete when the rule of Conditional Proof is introduced in the next chapter).

LC Exercise 4-7

For each line (other than premises) in the following proofs, state the line or lines from which it follows and the valid argument form used to obtain it.

(1)
1. $(B \cdot C) \vee D$ p
2. $\sim C$ p
3. $D \vee (B \cdot C)$
4. $(D \vee B) \cdot (D \vee C)$
5. $D \vee C$
6. D

(2)
1. R p
2. $(\sim C \vee \sim D) \vee S$ p
3. $\sim (D \cdot C) \supset \sim R$ p
4. $\sim \sim R$
5. $\sim (C \cdot D) \supset \sim R$
6. $\sim \sim (C \cdot D)$
7. $\sim (C \cdot D) \vee S$
8. S

(3)
1. $(A \cdot B) \vee C$ p
2. $\sim (A \vee \sim D)$ p
3. $C \vee (A \cdot B)$
4. $(C \vee A) \cdot (C \vee B)$
5. $C \vee A$
6. $\sim A \cdot \sim \sim D$
7. $\sim A$
8. C

(4)
1. $(A \vee B) \vee \sim C$ p
2. $(\sim A \cdot \sim C) \vee (\sim A \cdot D)$ p
3. $A \vee (B \vee \sim C)$
4. $\sim A \cdot (\sim C \vee D)$
5. $\sim A$
6. $\sim C \vee D$

7. $B \vee \sim C$
8. $\sim C \vee B$
9. $(\sim C \vee B) \cdot (\sim C \vee D)$
10. $\sim C \vee (B \cdot D)$

(5) 1. $\sim R \vee S$ p
2. $(A \vee B) \supset (R \cdot \sim S)$ p
3. $\sim R \vee \sim \sim S$
4. $\sim (R \cdot \sim S)$
5. $\sim (A \vee B)$
6. $\sim A \cdot \sim B$
7. $\sim A$
8. $\sim A \vee (\sim B \vee D)$
9. $(\sim A \vee \sim B) \vee D$
10. $D \vee (\sim A \vee \sim B)$
11. $D \vee \sim (A \cdot B)$

(6) 1. $E \equiv F$ p
2. $\sim E \vee \sim F$ p
3. $(E \cdot F) \vee (\sim E \cdot \sim F)$
4. $\sim (E \cdot F)$
5. $\sim (E \cdot F) \vee E$
6. $(E \cdot F) \supset E$
7. $E \supset \sim F$
8. $(E \cdot F) \supset \sim F$
9. $E \supset (F \supset \sim F)$
10. $E \supset (\sim F \vee \sim F)$
11. $E \supset \sim F$

(7) 1. $A \supset (\sim B \supset C)$ p
2. $\sim B$ p
3. $\sim C$ p
4. $\sim C \cdot \sim B$
5. $\sim (C \vee B)$
6. $A \supset (\sim B \supset \sim \sim C)$
7. $A \supset (\sim C \supset B)$
8. $A \supset (\sim \sim C \vee B)$
9. $A \supset (C \vee B)$
10. $\sim A$

(8) 1. $\sim H \supset \sim G$ p
2. $(R \vee \sim H) \vee K$ p
3. $(\sim H \vee R) \vee K$
4. $\sim H \vee (R \vee K)$
5. $H \supset (R \vee K)$
6. $G \supset H$
7. $G \supset (R \vee K)$

8. $\sim G \vee (R \vee K)$
9. $(\sim G \vee R) \vee K$
10. $K \vee (\sim G \vee R)$
11. $\sim \sim K \vee (\sim G \vee R)$
12. $\sim K \supset (\sim G \vee R)$
13. $\sim K \supset (G \supset R)$

(9) 1. $G \equiv (H \cdot K)$ p
2. $\sim G \supset H$ p
3. $K \vee G$ p
4. $[G \cdot (H \cdot K)] \vee [\sim G \cdot \sim (H \cdot K)]$
5. $\sim \sim G \vee H$
6. $G \vee H$
7. $G \vee K$
8. $(G \vee H) \cdot (G \vee K)$
9. $G \vee (H \cdot K)$
10. $\sim \sim G \vee (H \cdot K)$
11. $\sim \sim G \vee \sim \sim (H \cdot K)$
12. $\sim [\sim G \cdot \sim (H \cdot K)]$
13. $G \cdot (H \cdot K)$
14. G

(10) 1. $(R \equiv \sim S) \supset \sim R$ p
2. $\sim R \vee \sim S$ p
3. $[(R \supset \sim S) \cdot (\sim S \supset R)] \supset \sim R$
4. $\sim [(R \supset \sim S) \cdot (\sim S \supset R)] \vee \sim R$
5. $[\sim (R \supset \sim S) \vee \sim (\sim S \supset R)] \vee \sim R$
6. $[\sim (\sim R \vee \sim S) \vee \sim (\sim \sim S \vee R)] \vee \sim R$
7. $[\sim (\sim R \vee \sim S) \vee \sim (S \vee R)] \vee \sim R$
8. $[(\sim \sim R \cdot \sim \sim S) \vee (\sim S \cdot \sim R)] \vee \sim R$
9. $[(R \cdot S) \vee (\sim S \cdot \sim R)] \vee \sim R$
10. $(R \cdot S) \vee [(\sim S \cdot \sim R) \vee \sim R]$
11. $\sim (R \cdot S)$
12. $(\sim S \cdot \sim R) \vee \sim R$
13. $\sim R \vee (\sim S \cdot \sim R)$
14. $(\sim R \vee \sim S) \cdot (\sim R \vee \sim R)$
15. $\sim R \vee \sim R$
16. $\sim R$

LC Exercise 4-8

Using the eighteen valid argument forms, prove that the following arguments are valid. (These proofs are very basic. None requires more than six additional lines to complete.)

(1) 1. $(A \cdot B) \supset C$
    2. A /$\therefore$ $B \supset C$

(2) 1. $\sim R \lor \sim S$
    2. $A \supset (R \cdot S)$ /$\therefore$ $\sim A$

(3) 1. $\sim M \lor N$
    2. $\sim R \supset \sim N$ /$\therefore$ $M \supset R$

(4) 1. $A \supset B$
    2. $\sim (B \cdot \sim C)$ /$\therefore$ $A \supset C$

(5) 1. $\sim A \supset (B \cdot C)$
    2. $\sim C$ /$\therefore$ A

(6) 1. $F \supset G$
    2. $\sim (H \cdot G)$
    3. H /$\therefore$ $\sim F$

(7) 1. $\sim (H \lor \sim K)$
    2. $L \supset H$ /$\therefore$ $L \supset M$

(8) 1. $M \equiv N$ /$\therefore$ $\sim N \lor M$

(9) 1. $A \supset \sim A$
    2. $(\sim A \lor \sim B) \supset C$ /$\therefore$ $\sim A \cdot C$

(10) 1. $R \supset S$
    2. $R \supset T$ /$\therefore$ $R \supset (S \cdot T)$

(11) 1. $H \supset K$
    2. $C \equiv D$
    3. $\sim C \supset \sim K$ /$\therefore$ $H \supset D$

(12) 1. $A \cdot (B \supset C)$
    2. $\sim (C \cdot A)$ /$\therefore$ $\sim B$

(13) 1. $(A \cdot B) \lor (C \cdot D)$
    2. $\sim A$ /$\therefore$ C

(14) 1. $D \lor \sim A$
    2. $\sim (A \cdot \sim B) \supset \sim C$
    3. $\sim D$ /$\therefore$ $\sim C$

(15) 1. $(A \cdot B) \supset C$
    2. $A \cdot \sim C$ /$\therefore$ $\sim B$

11   *More Principles of Strategy*

We conclude this chapter with some additional strategy hints involving equivalence forms. Recall that we have already emphasized the usefulness of short sentences, especially atomic or negated atomic sentences. You can use equivalence forms to break sentences down. DeMorgan's Theorem is particularly useful in this respect. Any time you have a negated complex sentence you can use DeMorgan's to produce a simpler sentence, that will almost always be easier to work with.

Consider the following argument:

1. $(B \supset C) \supset A$
2. $\sim (D \lor A)$ /$\therefore$ B

The place to start to work on this proof is with the second premise. When you see a sentence like this, you should automatically be thinking of using DeMorgan's Theorem. Applying DeMorgan's to this sentence will give us a conjunction that we can then use Simplification on to get $\sim A$. Of course, this little sentence is very useful because we can use it to apply **MT** to the first premise.

3. $\sim D \cdot \sim A$	2 **DeM**
4. $\sim A$	3 **Simp**
5. $\sim (B \supset C)$	1,4 **MT**

With line 5 we have once again a negated complex sentence. This sentence should still make you think of DeMorgan's; it just takes an extra step to get in position to use this rule. Once you do this, the rest of the proof is obvious:

6. $\sim (\sim B \vee C)$	5 **Impl**
7. $\sim \sim B \cdot \sim C$	6 **DeM**
8. $\sim \sim B$	7 **Simp**
9. B	8 **DN**

This proof illustrates another useful strategy. Notice that the letter D does not occur in the conclusion and that it occurs in the premises only once. Obviously, the information its presence adds to premise 2 is not necessary in deriving the conclusion. *A letter that occurs only once in the premises of an argument and not at all in the conclusion usually is excess baggage, to be gotten rid of or (if possible) ignored.* In this case, we used DeMorgan's and then Simplification to get rid of the superfluous letter D by separating the information it contains (which is not needed to derive the conclusion) from the other information contained in premise 2 (which is needed to derive the conclusion).

It should be obvious that DeMorgan's Theorem is a very useful rule. Whenever you have a complex sentence governed by a negation, that sentence can be transformed so that DeMorgan's can be applied to it. Unless the sentence governed by the negation sign is repeated in another premise, using DeMorgan's to remove the negation sign will almost always give you a sentence that is easier to work with.

Here are some other moves you should make almost automatically when you are not sure how to proceed. Break apart any nonrepeated conjunctions using Simplification. Break down nonrepeated biconditionals using Equivalence (the form that gives you a conjunction of two conditionals).

If you have some premises that are disjunctions and some that are conditionals, it will usually help to either change the conditionals into disjunctions, or the disjunctions into conditionals, using Implication. Consider, for example, the following argument:

1. $A \vee B$	
2. $C \supset \sim A / \therefore C \supset B$	

Here you should change the disjunction into a conditional. In this case you must first use Double Negation on the first disjunct before you can apply Implication. You can then apply **HS** to complete the proof:

3. $\sim \sim A \vee B$	1 **DN**
4. $\sim A \supset B$	3 **Impl**
5. $C \supset B$	2,4 **HS**

The solution to other proofs may hinge on your changing the conditional to a disjunction, as the following proof illustrates:

1. $A \supset B$
2. $\sim A \lor C / \therefore A \supset (B \cdot C)$

In this case changing the second premise into a conditional is of no use. There is no obvious way to use the resulting conditional, $A \supset C$, in combination with the other premise. On the other hand, if we change the conditional into a disjunction, we can apply Distribution after we conjoin the two disjunctions:

3. $\sim A \lor B$ 1 **Impl**
4. $(\sim A \lor B) \cdot (\sim A \lor C)$ 2,3 **Conj**
5. $\sim A \lor (B \cdot C)$ 4 **Dist**
6. $A \supset (B \cdot C)$ 5 **Impl**

This proof illustrates a very common pattern. When all else fails, break down all of the conditionals (and biconditionals) so that you have lines equivalent to the premises, but now containing just the connectives "·", "∨", or "∼". Then look for ways to rearrange this information so that you can get a line that contains just the same sentences as the conclusion. Once you get to that point usually the proof can be completed in short order.

Now consider the following proof:

1. $A \supset (B \cdot C) / \therefore A \supset C$

Obviously, to solve this proof we need to dispense with the B in the premise, another case of excess baggage. We've already seen how to use DeMorgan's to dispense with unneeded information. The solution to this proof illustrates how Distribution can also be used for the same purpose:

2. $\sim A \lor (B \cdot C)$ 1 **Impl**
3. $(\sim A \lor B) \cdot (\sim A \lor C)$ 2 **Dist**
4. $\sim A \lor C$ 3 **Simp**
5. $A \supset C$ 4 **Impl**

In our earlier section on strategy, we stressed the usefulness of *working backward from the conclusion* as well as forward from the premises. If we work backward from the conclusion and find a sentence that appears derivable from the premises, then we have discovered an intermediate target to aim at and have divided a relatively difficult task into two easier ones. Equivalence argument forms provide us with many more ways to work backward. We can use them to produce lines equivalent to the conclusion we want to reach.

Consider the argument

1. $A \supset B$
2. $C \supset B$ $/ \therefore (A \lor C) \supset B$

We can work backward from the conclusion, as follows:

1. $A \supset B$
2. $C \supset B$ $/ \therefore (A \lor C) \supset B$

$(B \lor \sim A) \cdot (B \lor \sim C)$

$B \lor (\sim A \cdot \sim C)$	**Dist**
$(\sim A \cdot \sim C) \lor B$	**Comm**
$\sim (A \lor C) \lor B$	**DeM**
$(A \lor C) \supset B$	**Impl**

At this point, we have learned that the conclusion $(A \lor C) \supset B$ is equivalent to $(B \lor \sim A) \cdot (B \lor \sim C)$. So by working backward from the conclusion, we have learned that the problem can be solved by working forward from the premises toward the intermediate sentence $(B \lor \sim A) \cdot (B \lor \sim C)$. This turns out to be fairly easy to do, as the following illustrates:

1.	$A \supset B$	
2.	$C \supset B$	$/ \therefore (A \lor C) \supset B$
3.	$\sim A \lor B$	1 **Impl**
4.	$B \lor \sim A$	3 **Comm**
5.	$\sim C \lor B$	2 **Impl**
6.	$B \lor \sim C$	5 **Comm**
7.	$(B \lor \sim A) \cdot (B \lor \sim C)$	4,6 **Conj**

We are now ready to add on the final portion of the proof we have already worked out. This time we can supply the line numbers.

8.	$B \lor (\sim A \cdot \sim C)$	7 **Dist**
9.	$(\sim A \cdot \sim C) \lor B$	8 **Comm**
10.	$\sim (A \lor C) \lor B$	9 **DeM**
11.	$(A \lor C) \supset B$	10 **Impl**

So by working backward from the conclusion as well as forward from the premises, we were able to construct a proof that might otherwise have eluded us.

Let's summarize some of the most important of these strategy hints:

- Break down complex sentences with **DeM, Simp,** and **Equiv.**
- Use **DeM** and **Dist** to isolate "excess baggage."
- Use **Impl** when you have a mix of conditionals and disjunctions.
- Again, work backward from the conclusion.

LC Exercise 4-9

All of the following proofs have only one premise and can be completed in very few steps. We've indicated for each proof the minimum number of additional steps it takes to complete each proof. Although short, many of these proofs are fairly difficult. Each proof embodies a very useful pattern of inference. You will find longer proofs much easier if you have these basic moves at your fingertips.

(1)   1. $\sim A \supset B / \therefore A \lor B$ (2 steps)
(2)   1. $A \lor B / \therefore \sim A \supset B$ (2 steps)
(3)   1. $\sim A / \therefore A \supset B$ (2 steps)
(4)   1. $\sim A / \therefore \sim (A \cdot B)$ (2 steps)
(5)   1. $A \supset \sim B / \therefore \sim (A \cdot B)$ (2 steps)

(6) 1. ~ $(A \cdot B)$ /∴ $A \supset \; \sim B$ (2 steps)
(7) 1. ~ $(A \vee B)$ /∴ ~ B (2 steps)
(8) 1. ~ $(A \supset B)$ /∴ ~ B (3 steps)
(9) 1. ~ $(A \supset B)$ /∴ A (4 steps)
(10) 1. A /∴ ~ {~ $[L \vee (\sim M \equiv R)]$} $\vee A$ (2 steps)
(11) 1. $(\sim A \supset L)$ /∴ ~ $[L \vee (\sim M \equiv R)] \supset A$ (3 steps)
(12) 1. $A \supset \; \sim B$ /∴ $B \supset \; \sim A$ (2 steps)
(13) 1. ~ $A \supset B$ /∴ ~ $B \supset A$ (2 steps)
(14) 1. $A \supset (B \supset C)$ /∴ $B \supset (A \supset C)$ (3 steps)
(15) 1. $(A \cdot B) \vee (C \cdot D)$ /∴ $(A \cdot B) \vee D$ (2 steps)
(16) 1. $(A \cdot B) \vee (A \cdot C)$ /∴ $B \vee C$ (2 steps)
(17) 1. $A \vee (B \cdot C)$ /∴ $A \vee C$ (2 steps)
(18) 1. $(A \cdot B) \vee C$ /∴ $C \vee A$ (3 steps)
(19) 1. ~ $(A \equiv B)$ /∴ ~ $(A \cdot B)$ (3 steps)
(20) 1. $A \supset \; \sim A$ /∴ ~ A (2 steps)

12 Common Errors in Problem Solving

There are several kinds of mistakes that beginners are likely to make in deriving proofs for arguments.

Using implicational forms on parts of lines

The valid implicational forms (numbers 1 through 8) can be used on *complete lines only.* For instance, we cannot go from

$(A \cdot B) \supset C$

to

$(A \supset C)$

dropping the letter B by *Simplification.* The reason is that the form of this process, namely, $(p \cdot q) \supset r$ /∴ $(p \supset r)$, is *not* the form of Simplification, and, in fact, is an invalid argument form. (An example of an invalid argument that has this form is the following: If George drives an automobile 70 miles per hour and smashes into a reinforced concrete structure, then he will be killed. Therefore, if George drives an automobile 70 miles per hour, then he will be killed.)

Examples

Here is a *correct* use of the implicational argument form Simplification:

1. $(A \vee \; \sim B) \cdot (C \vee \; \sim A)$ /∴ $A \vee \; \sim B$
2. $A \vee \; \sim B$ 1 **Simp**

In this case, the "$\cdot$" in line 1 is the major connective. Thus the whole of line 1 has the form $(p \cdot q)$ required for the use of the valid argument form Simplification.

Here is another example of the correct use of implicational forms:

1. $A \supset (B \cdot C)$
2. $(B \cdot C) \supset D$
3. $A \supset D$ 1,2 **HS**

This is a correct use of the implicational form Hypothetical Syllogism (**HS**), because **HS** requires that one whole line in a proof have the form $(p \supset q)$ and another whole line have the form $(q \supset r)$, and this proof does have two such lines, namely, line 1, which has the form $(p \supset q)$, and line 2, which has the form $(q \supset r)$. Therefore **HS** permits the assertion of line 3, because that whole line has the required form $(p \supset r)$.

Remember that although the ten equivalence argument forms may be used on whole lines, just as the implicational forms, they also may be used on parts of lines, as in the following example:

1. $\sim (A \cdot B) \supset C$ $/\therefore (\sim A \lor \sim B) \supset C$
2. $(\sim A \lor \sim B) \supset C$ 1 **DeM**

The use of equivalence argument forms on parts of lines is justified because their use always leads from a given sentence to an equivalent sentence.

Reluctance to use addition

Even after proving that Addition is a valid argument form, some students are reluctant to use it because they believe that somehow it is cheating to be able to add letters to a line simply at will. But a little thought about the matter should convince the hesitant that no cheating is involved in the use of Addition. Consider this example:

Art committed the crime. Therefore, either Art committed the crime or Barbara did.

symbolized as

1. A $/\therefore A \lor B$
2. $A \lor B$ 1 **Add**

Although $A \lor B$ is a longer and more complicated formula than A alone, we should not be tempted into concluding that it therefore makes a stronger claim. The addition of B to A, to get $A \lor B$, doesn't strengthen or extend the claim made by A alone; it weakens, waters down, that claim. Notice, for instance, how much more useful it is to know that Art is the guilty one rather than just that either Art or Barbara committed the crime.

The following extreme case nicely illustrates the weakening effect of the use of Addition:

1. A	$/\therefore (A \vee \sim A)$
2. $A \vee \sim A$	1 **Add**

In this extreme case, the use of Addition leads to the weakest possible kind of assertion, namely, a tautology, which has no factual content whatever.

Reluctance to use distribution

In this case, the reluctance generally stems not from doubts as to its validity but rather from inability to spot places where its application will be useful. The following proof contains a typical useful application of Distribution:

1. $(A \vee B) \supset C$	$/\therefore A \supset C$
2. $\sim (A \vee B) \vee C$	1 **Impl**
3. $(\sim A \cdot \sim B) \vee C$	2 **DeM**
4. $C \vee (\sim A \cdot \sim B)$	3 **Comm**
5. $(C \vee \sim A) \cdot (C \vee \sim B)$	4 **Dist** (the crucial use of **Dist**)
6. $C \vee \sim A$	5 **Simp**
7. $\sim A \vee C$	6 **Comm**
8. $A \supset C$	7 **Impl**

Notice that the use of Distribution is crucial in getting rid of the unwanted letter B, which occurs in the premise but not in the conclusion. Notice also that the second of the two distributive equivalence forms was used and that it was used from left to right (that is, the move was from line 4, whose form $[p \vee (q \cdot r)]$ is that of the left side of the second distributive equivalence form, to line 5, whose form $[(p \vee q) \cdot (p \vee r)]$, is that of the right side). This is the most common use of Distribution, because the line obtained in this way always has a "·" as its major connective and thus has the form $(p \cdot q)$ necessary for the use of Simplification.

Trying to prove what cannot be proved

The number of mistakes of this kind is much too large to catalogue. We consider two such mistakes, committed perhaps because they are very similar to two valid procedures.

Consider the following four argument forms:

1. $(p \vee q) \supset r / \therefore p \supset r$
2. $(p \cdot q) \supset r / \therefore p \supset r$
3. $p \supset (q \vee r) / \therefore p \supset r$
4. $p \supset (q \cdot r) / \therefore p \supset r$

The first and fourth of these argument forms are valid. The second and third are *invalid*, as we can prove by truth table analysis.

The important point is not to waste time and effort trying to prove substitution instances of invalid forms. For example, in trying to prove the validity of the argument

1. $(A \cdot B) \supset C$
2. $\sim (\sim B \vee D)$
3. $(C \cdot \sim D) \supset E / \therefore A \supset E$

it is useless to try to derive the sentence $A \supset C$ from line 1 alone since the form of such an inference, namely, the form $[(p \cdot q) \supset r] / \therefore (p \supset r)$, is invalid. The sentence $A \supset C$ can be derived in this proof, but not from line 1 alone.

Similarly, it is useless to try to derive the sentence $A \supset B$ from the sentence $A \supset (B \vee C)$, since the form of such an inference, namely, the form $p \supset (q \vee r) / \therefore p \supset q$, is invalid.

Failure to notice the scope of a negation sign

A mistake of this kind is usually merely an oversight; however, it is quite common. In particular, negation signs that negate a whole sentence, or a large unit in a sentence, are misconstrued as negating only one letter. Thus, in a sentence such as $\sim (A \vee B)$ the negation sign sometimes is misconstrued as negating merely the letter A, instead of the whole unit $(A \vee B)$. The remedy for this kind of error is care, plus the realization that a negation sign before a unit set off by parentheses (or brackets) negates that entire unit.

🏃 Walk-Through: More Challenging Proofs

Here is a fairly difficult proof:

1. $(A \supset \sim B) \cdot \sim C$
2. $B \supset (\sim A \supset C)$ $/ \therefore \sim B$

Obviously, we can simplify the first line:

3. $A \supset \sim B$ 1 **Simp**
4. $\sim C$ 1 **Simp**

Looking for a way to use $\sim C$, we see we can perform Exportation on the second line:

5. $(B \cdot \sim A) \supset C$ 2 **Exp**

This lets us use **MT**. We can then use **DeM** and **DN** to simplify the result:

6. $\sim (B \cdot \sim A)$ 4,5 **MT**
7. $\sim B \vee \sim \sim A$ 6 **DeM**
8. $\sim B \vee A$ 7 **DN**

Here's where the proof grows more difficult. We want to get $\sim B$. It would be great if somehow we could get $\sim A$, but we can't. It's tempting to use **Impl** on line 3 to change $A \supset \sim B$ to $\sim A \vee B$. We could then conjoin this with line 8 and distribute. But this only gets us $\sim B \vee (A \cdot \sim A)$. Unfortunately, although this sort of distribution move often works, it doesn't help us here. A more obscure strategy is this: We can get $\sim B$ if we can get $B \supset \sim B$. To get this formula we use **Impl** in the other direction, changing the disjunction to a conditional. We then use **HS** on the two conditionals:

9. $B \supset A$ 8 Impl
10. $B \supset \sim B$ 3, 9 HS

To get $\sim B$, we use **Impl** again, and then **Taut**, completing the proof:

11. $\sim B \vee \sim B$ 10 Impl
12. $\sim B$ 11 Taut

LC Exercise 4-10

Prove that the following arguments are valid. These proofs especially emphasize Distribution, Commutation, and Association. This exercise is fairly challenging. Remember that
Dist, like all of our equivalence rules, works in *both directions*.

(1) 1. $A \vee (B \cdot C)$
    2. $\sim C / \therefore \sim A$

(2) 1. $(A \vee B) \vee C$
    2. $\sim (B \vee C) / \therefore \sim A$

(3) 1. $(A \vee B) \cdot C$
    2. $\sim (B \cdot C) / \therefore C \cdot A$

(4) 1. $(A \cdot B) \vee (C \cdot D)$
    2. $\sim C / \therefore A$

(5) 1. $(A \cdot B) \vee (C \cdot D) / \therefore (A \cdot B) \vee D$

(6) 1. $(A \cdot B) \vee (C \cdot D) / \therefore D \vee A$

(7) 1. $(A \cdot B) \vee (C \cdot D) / \therefore (C \cdot D) \vee A$

(8) 1. $(A \vee B) \cdot C$
    2. $\sim A \vee \sim C / \therefore C \cdot B$

(9) 1. $[(A \cdot B) \cdot D] \vee (C \cdot A) / \therefore A$

(10) 1. $(\sim R \cdot A) \vee \sim (Q \vee R) / \therefore \sim R$

(11) 1. $[(A \vee B) \cdot (D \cdot F)] \vee [(A \vee B) \cdot C]$
     $/ \therefore C \vee F$

(12) 1. $[(A \cdot B) \vee (D \cdot F)] \vee (B \cdot C)$
     2. $\sim (D \cdot F) / \therefore B$

LC Exercise 4-11

Prove valid using the eighteen valid argument forms. (These proofs are moderately difficult. They will require between 6 and 15 additional lines to complete).

(1) 1. $(A \cdot B) \supset R$
    2. A
    3. $C \supset \sim R / \therefore \sim (C \cdot B)$

(2) 1. $\sim A$
    2. $(A \vee B) \equiv C$
    3. $\sim B / \therefore \sim (C \cdot D)$

(3) 1. $(A \cdot H) \supset (M \cdot N) / \therefore (A \cdot H) \supset N$

(4) 1. $S \vee (\sim R \cdot T)$
    2. $R \supset \sim S / \therefore \sim R$

(5) 1. $H \supset K$
    2. $(K \cdot L) \supset M / \therefore L \supset (H \supset M)$

(6) 1. $A \supset B$
    2. $C \supset D$
    3. $(B \vee D) \supset E$
    4. $\sim E / \therefore \sim (A \vee C)$

(7) 1. $\sim H$
    2. $H \vee K$
    3. $L \supset H$
    4. $\sim (K \cdot \sim L) \vee (\sim L \cdot M) / \therefore M$

(8) 1. $(A \cdot B) \equiv C$
    2. $\sim (C \vee \sim A) / \therefore \sim B$

(9) 1. $(H \vee K) \supset (A \supset B)$
    2. $(H \vee M) \supset (C \supset D)$
    3. $(H \vee N) \supset (A \vee C)$
    4. $L \cdot H /\therefore B \vee D$

(10) 1. $W \equiv Y$
    2. $\sim W \vee \sim Y$
    3. $X \supset (Y \cdot Z) /\therefore \sim X$

(11) 1. $A \vee B$
    2. C
    3. $(A \cdot C) \supset D$
    4. $\sim (\sim F \cdot B) /\therefore D \vee F$

(12) 1. $P \supset R$
    2. $\sim P \supset (\sim R \supset S) /\therefore R \vee S$

(13) 1. $\sim (D \vee C)$
    2. $\sim C \supset (A \supset \sim B)$
    3. $A \equiv B /\therefore \sim A$

(14) 1. $\sim (C \vee A)$
    2. $B \supset (\sim A \supset C) /\therefore \sim B$

(15) 1. $\sim (A \cdot B) \equiv \sim C$
    2. $(D \vee E) \supset C /\therefore E \supset A$

LG Exercise 4-12

Prove valid using the eighteen valid argument forms. (These proofs are difficult and require between ten and twenty additional lines to complete.)

(1) 1. $R \supset (\sim A \cdot T)$
    2. $B \vee \sim S$
    3. $R \vee S /\therefore A \supset B$

(2) 1. $S \vee (\sim R \cdot T)$
    2. $R \supset \sim S /\therefore \sim R$

(3) 1. $A \vee B$
    2. C
    3. $(A \cdot C) \supset D /\therefore D \vee B$

(4) 1. $C \vee D$
    2. $C \supset B$
    3. $\sim C \supset \sim D /\therefore B$

(5) 1. $P \supset [(Q \cdot R) \vee S]$
    2. $(Q \cdot R) \supset \sim P$
    3. $T \supset \sim S /\therefore P \supset \sim T$

(6) 1. $D \supset B$
    2. $D \supset (B \supset W)$
    3. $B \supset (W \supset S) /\therefore D \supset S$

(7) 1. $A \supset B$
    2. $A \vee (B \cdot C) /\therefore B$

(8) 1. $K \supset [(L \vee M) \supset R]$
    2. $(R \vee S) \supset T /\therefore K \supset (M \supset T)$

(9) 1. $(P \vee R) \cdot (P \vee Q)$
    2. $(Q \cdot R) \supset (V \supset W)$

3. $\sim [(P \supset S) \supset \sim (S \supset W)]$
4. $\sim W /\therefore\ V \supset S$

(10) 1. $A \supset B$
2. $A \lor C$
3. $D \supset B$
4. $D \lor \sim C /\therefore\ B$

(11) 1. $(M \lor N) \supset (M \supset \sim N)$
2. $\sim (N \supset P) \supset \sim (M \supset \sim N)$
3. $M \lor N /\therefore\ M \lor P$

(12) 1. $(A \supset A) \supset (\sim A \supset \sim A) /\therefore\ A \lor \sim A$

(13) 1. $A \equiv B$
2. $\sim (A \cdot \sim R) \supset (A \cdot S) /\therefore\ \sim (B \cdot S) \supset \sim (A \cdot R)$

(14) 1. $A \supset B$
2. $C \supset D /\therefore\ (A \lor C) \supset (B \lor D)$

(15) 1. $\sim [D \cdot \sim (E \lor B)]$
2. $\sim (E \lor F)$
3. $C \supset (E \lor A) /\therefore\ \sim (\sim A \cdot \sim B) \lor \sim (C \lor D)$

Exercise 4-13

1. Why can't implicational argument forms be used on parts of lines in a proof? Give an example.
2. Why *can* equivalence argument forms be so used? Give an example.
3. Why are all substitution instances of a valid argument form valid arguments?
4. We said that all substitution instances of a valid argument form are thereby valid arguments. Why can't we say that all substitution instances of an invalid argument form are invalid arguments? Give an example.

Key terms

For the argument forms introduced in this chapter, see the charts on pages 82 and 94–95. All of the forms are also listed on the inside front cover.

argument form: A group of sentence forms, all of whose substitution instances are arguments.

equivalence argument form: A two-directional argument form. For example, Double Negation is a valid equivalence argument form.

implicational argument form: A one-directional argument form. For example, Modus Ponens is a valid implicational argument form.

invalid argument form: An argument form that has at least one invalid substitution instance.

proof of an argument: A series of sentences and/or sentence forms such that each member of the series is either a premise or else follows from a previous member of the series by a valid argument form, the last line being the argument's conclusion.

valid argument form: An argument form all of whose substitution instances are valid arguments.

Chapter Five

Conditional and Indirect Proofs

---

1   *Conditional Proofs*

Here is a very simple valid argument that so far cannot be proved valid in our system:

$A \supset B \ / \therefore A \supset (A \cdot B)$

To prove it valid, we can reason as follows: What would be the case *if A* were true? (We don't *know* that it is. It isn't given to us as a premise. But what *if* it were true?) If *A* were true, then clearly *B* also would be true, since by Modus Ponens we could move from $A \supset B$ (the given premise) and *A* (the assumed premise) to *B*. So if *A* were true, *B* also would be true, and thus *A · B* would be true (by Conjunction). We therefore have shown that *if A*, then (*A · B*), or in symbols, $A \supset (A \cdot B)$, which is the conclusion of the argument in question. Thus we have proved that the argument displayed above is valid.

A proof of this kind is called a **Conditional Proof,** and the rule permitting the crucial step is therefore called the rule of Conditional Proof. Once we add this rule, our natural deduction procedure for sentential logic is complete, meaning that now every valid argument in sentential logic can be shown to be valid by means of a proof.*

Now let's put this proof into symbols:

1.	$A \supset B$	$/\therefore A \supset (A \cdot B)$
2.	A	**assumed premise** (or simply **AP**)
3.	B	1,2 **MP**
4.	$A \cdot B$	2,3 **Conj**

What we have proved so far is that *if A then* (*A · B*). Replacing the expression "if . . . then . . ." by "$\supset$", we get

5.	$A \supset (A \cdot B)$	2–4 **Conditional Proof** (or **CP**)

---

*There remain, however, valid arguments whose validity cannot be demonstrated by means of sentential logic. For these arguments, we need more powerful systems of logic, such as predicate logic, to be introduced in Chapter 6.

The important point to notice is that the conclusion, line 5, depends only on the *original premise* and not on the assumed premise stated on line 2. If premise 1 is true, then line 5 must be true, whether A (the assumed premise) is true or false. Line 5 does not assert that $(A \cdot B)$ is the case, but only that $(A \cdot B)$ is the case *on the condition* that A is the case. The notation to the right of line 5 indicates that the technique used is that of Conditional Proof **(CP)** using an **assumed premise** (an assumption—something not stated as a premise in the original problem); it lists the line of the assumed premise as well as the last line that depends on the assumed premise.

To keep track of assumed premises and the lines that depend on them, let's use arrows and lines so that the proof we have been discussing will look like this:

1.	$A \supset B$	$/ \therefore A \supset (A \cdot B)$
2.	A	**assumed premise** (or simply **AP**)
3.	B	1,2 **MP**
4.	$A \cdot B$	2,3 **Conj**
5.	$A \supset (A \cdot B)$	2–4 **CP**

The arrow pointing at line 2 indicates that line 2 is an assumed premise not given as part of the original problem. The line drawn down from line 2 to below line 4 indicates that lines 2, 3, and 4 *depend on* line 2 (in addition perhaps to the original premise). Such lines are said to be within the *scope of the assumed premise.* The horizontal line drawn between lines 4 and 5 indicates that the lines to follow do not depend on line 2; that is, it indicates that the scope of this assumed premise ends with line 4. From this point onward the assumption is said to have been **discharged.**

Using the arrow and line notation just introduced, we can express the structure of the rule of conditional proof (or argument form) as follows:

$\rightarrow p$ **AP**

$\cdot$

$\cdot$

$\cdot$

q

$p \supset q$ **CP**

This indicates that a premise is assumed, other lines are derived from it, and then the assumed premise is discharged as a premise, being retained as the antecedent of the line $p \supset q$.

Another way to consider Conditional Proofs is this. In a sense, *every* valid argument is conditional, since the truth of the conclusion is conditional upon the truth of the premises on which the conclusion depends. What is different about a so-called Conditional Proof is simply that some lines in a Conditional Proof depend on a line (the assumed premise) on which the conclusion does not depend, a line that was not given as a premise in the original problem. It is as though a line is introduced as a premise, a conclusion is drawn from it (in conjunction with the other premises), and then that premise is discharged as premise (or taken back as a premise), being retained rather as a *condition on* the acceptance of the conclusion, that is, retained as the antecedent of a new conditional's conclusion.

It is important to note that once an assumed premise is discharged, we no longer can use it, or any line that depends on it, to derive additional lines. For instance, in the previous example, we cannot assert as line 6 the sentence $\sim \sim (A \cdot B)$, following from line 4 by **DN,** since we have already discharged line 2 as a premise. It may help you to think of the horizontal line as boxing off all of the lines between the arrow (the assumed premise) and the line just above the horizontal line. *In effect, all that you gain from a Conditional Proof is one line, a conditional, which will be the line just below the horizontal line.* Of course, that conditional may very well be the key to solving the proof, if not the conclusion itself.

Example

Every correct application of **CP** incorporates the following elements:

1. The sentence justified by **CP** must be a conditional.
2. The antecedent of that conditional must be the assumed premise.
3. The consequent of that conditional must be the sentence from the preceding line.
4. Lines are drawn indicating the scope of the assumed premise.

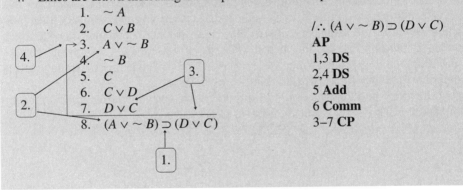

1.	$\sim A$	$/ \therefore (A \vee \sim B) \supset (D \vee C)$
2.	$C \vee B$	
3.	$A \vee \sim B$	**AP**
4.	$\sim B$	1,3 **DS**
5.	C	2,4 **DS**
6.	$C \vee D$	5 **Add**
7.	$D \vee C$	6 **Comm**
8.	$(A \vee \sim B) \supset (D \vee C)$	3–7 **CP**

One reason for introducing rule **CP** is to render our system complete, as we remarked earlier. But this goal of completeness could have been reached just as easily by introducing any one of several other rules. The one most frequently chosen, as a matter of fact, is Absorption: $p \supset q / \therefore p \supset (p \cdot q)$ (a generalization of the argument $A \supset B / \therefore A \supset (A \cdot B)$ discussed earlier). One reason to choose **CP** over Absorption is its tremendous power to shorten the proofs of many valid arguments and, in particular, to make proofs of a great many arguments a good deal easier to discover.

But the most important reason for introducing a rule like **CP** is that we want our system of rules to be a *natural deduction system*; that is, we want our rules to capture the sort of argumentation that goes on in, say, mathematics, or indeed in everyday life. Natural arguments like these commonly employ assumptions. A geometer may ask you to assume the existence of a given triangle in order to prove a general truth about all triangles. A lawyer may quite reasonably ask the jury to assume, for the moment, that her client is guilty in order to show what would follow from this assumption. "So you see, ladies and gentlemen, if my client is guilty as the prosecution says, their own star witness is not telling the truth about what happened that night." **CP** is designed to capture this natural way of deducing a conditional.

Rule **CP** turns out to be useful in almost any kind of case, but it tends to be most useful when we're dealing with arguments that have conditional conclusions or conclusions that can be translated into conditional form. Here is a classic example, with **CP** proof attached:

1.	$A \supset B$	
2.	$C \supset D$	$/\therefore (A \lor C) \supset (B \lor D)$
→ 3.	$A \lor C$	**AP**
4.	$B \lor D$	1, 2, 3 **CD**
5.	$(A \lor C) \supset (B \lor D)$	3–4 **CP**

Short and easily discovered, this **CP** proof contrasts starkly with proofs of the argument that do not use **CP**. Anyone who doubts that is invited to prove the argument valid using only the eighteen valid argument forms (toss in Absorption if you feel like it).

Notice that we chose the antecedent of the conditional conclusion as our assumed premise. When using CP, always assume the antecedent of the conditional you hope to justify via CP.

In the above example, only one assumed premise was used. But *any number* of assumptions can be introduced into a proof, provided that every one is eventually discharged, so that the conclusion of the argument depends only on the given premises. Proofs of equivalences commonly involve two separate subproofs, as the following proof illustrates:

1.	$A \supset \sim C$	
2.	$\sim B \supset C$	
3.	$A \lor \sim B$	$/\therefore A \equiv B$
→ 4.	A	**AP**
5.	$\sim C$	1,4 **MP**
6.	$\sim \sim B$	2,5 **MT**
7.	B	6 **DN**
8.	$A \supset B$	4–7 **CP**
→ 9.	B	**AP**
10.	$\sim \sim B$	9 **DN**
11.	A	3,10 **DS**
12.	$B \supset A$	9–11 **CP**
13.	$(A \supset B) \cdot (B \supset A)$	8,12 **Conj**
14.	$A \equiv B$	13 **Equiv**

Here is a different kind of case involving multiple assumptions:

1.	$C \supset D$	$/\therefore A \supset [B \supset (C \supset D)]$
→ 2.	A	**AP**
→ 3.	B	**AP**
→ 4.	C	**AP**
5.	D	1,4 **MP**
6.	$C \supset D$	4–5 **CP**
7.	$B \supset (C \supset D)$	3–6 **CP**
8.	$A \supset [B \supset (C \supset D)]$	2–7 **CP**

In this example, there are *three* assumed premises: A, B, and C. But the proof itself is really quite simple. Every step of this proof is automatic with the exception of line 5, an obvious **MP** step. There is no need to agonize over which rule to use. As a general rule of thumb, when you need to derive a line that is a conditional, assume the antecedent and try to derive the consequent, thereby allowing you to derive the entire conditional by **CP.** In this case, since we need to derive $A \supset [B \supset (C \supset D)]$, we assume A and try to get $B \supset (C \supset D)$. Once again we find ourselves needing to derive a conditional, so we assume B and work toward $C \supset D$. Of course, this is another conditional, so we assume C and try to derive D—leaving us needing only the obvious **MP** step to complete the proof.

There is a great deal of freedom that comes with **CP.** You can assume *anything*, provided that each assumption is eventually discharged properly. Our notation is designed to ensure that every assumption has been properly discharged. Every assumption should be marked by an arrow, each arrow must terminate in a horizontal line, and no two lines should intersect.

You can assume anything, but not all assumptions are profitable. Here is a very important rule of thumb: *In deciding what to assume, you should be guided by the conclusion or intermediate step you hope to reach, not by the premises.* For example, consider the following proof:

1. $A \supset B$
2. $(A \supset C) \supset D$ $/\therefore (B \supset C) \supset D$

Looking at the premises, you may be tempted to assume A or $A \supset C$ (so that you can apply **MP**). You can make these assumptions if you like, but whatever assumption you make must be discharged. So if you assume A, all that you eventually gain, after you discharge the assumption with **CP,** will be a conditional that has A as its antecedent. Likewise, assuming $A \supset C$ will eventually leave you with a conditional that has $A \supset C$ as its antecedent. Neither assumption gets you any closer to completing the proof.

What you *should* assume in this particular proof is the antecedent of the conclusion, as follows:

    1. $A \supset B$
    2. $(A \supset C) \supset D$ $/\therefore (B \supset C) \supset D$
    3. $B \supset C$ **AP**
    4. $A \supset C$ 1,3 **HS**
    5. D 2,4 **MP**
    6. $(B \supset C) \supset D$ 3–5 **CP**

Sometimes you can make a proof much shorter by working backward from the conclusion a bit before deciding what to assume, as the following example illustrates:

    1. $(E \cdot C) \supset B$
    2. $C \supset (D \cdot E)$ $/\therefore \sim B \supset \sim C$
    3. C **AP**
    4. $D \cdot E$ 2,3 **MP**
    5. E 4 **Simp**
    6. $E \cdot C$ 3,5 **Conj**
    7. B 1,6 **MP**
    8. $C \supset B$ 3–7 **CP**
    9. $\sim B \supset \sim C$ 8 **Contra**

What is assumed in this proof isn't the antecedent of the conclusion. Rather it is the antecedent of the contrapositive (obtained by Contraposition) of the conclusion. You can complete this proof by assuming $\sim B$, but it is a much more difficult proof. So keep in mind that it sometimes is useful to assume the antecedent of the contrapositive of a conditional rather than the antecedent of the conditional itself. (This strategy will be especially useful in completing predicate logic proofs as we will explain in Chapter 8.)

An assumption that falls within the scope of another assumption is called a *nested assumption*. We had an example just above of a proof with two nested assumptions. The thing to remember with nested assumptions is that you must discharge the nested assumption before you can discharge the original assumption. The lines that indicate the scope of your assumptions must never intersect.

You can avoid nesting assumptions, and make your proof a bit shorter, by working backward from your conclusion using Exportation. So here is a shorter proof of the same argument:

1.	$C \supset D$	$/\therefore A \supset [B \supset (C \supset D)]$
→ 2.	$(A \cdot B) \cdot C$	**AP**
3.	C	2 **Simp**
4.	D	1,3 **MP**
5.	$[(A \cdot B) \cdot C] \supset D$	2–4 **CP**
6.	$(A \cdot B) \supset (C \supset D)$	5 **Exp**
7.	$A \supset [B \supset (C \supset D)]$	6 **Exp**

Even if your conclusion is not a conditional, you may be able to use **CP**. If the conclusion is a disjunction, you can work backward using Implication to find a conditional that is equivalent to the conclusion and then use **CP** to obtain that conditional. If your conclusion is a biconditional, work backward using Equivalence to change the biconditional into a conjunction of two conditionals. You can use **CP** to separately prove each conditional. These two strategies are illustrated in the examples that follow.

🏃 Walk-Through: Using CP

Here's a proof that would be impossible without **CP**:

1.	$A \supset B$	
2.	$C \vee \sim B$	$/\therefore A \supset (A \cdot C)$

Looking at the conclusion, we assume the antecedent and work to derive the consequent:

→ 3.	A	**AP**
	.	
	.	
	.	
_.	$A \cdot C$	
_.	$A \supset (A \cdot C)$	_–_**CP**

Completing the rest of the proof is quite straightforward:

→ 3.	A	**AP**
4.	B	1,3 **MP**
5.	$\sim \sim B$	3 **DN**
6.	C	2,5 **DS**
7.	$A \cdot C$	3,6 **Conj**
8.	$A \supset (A \cdot C)$	3–7 **CP**

Once you get used to it, **CP** is really quite simple. When to use it is obvious: *Use it routinely whenever you need to derive a conditional.* Here is a slightly more complicated proof:

1.	$(M \vee N) \supset P$	$/\therefore [(P \vee Q) \supset R] \supset (M \supset R)$

Right away we assume our antecedent and pencil in the consequent as our next to last step:

1.	$(M \vee N) \supset P$	$/\therefore [(P \vee Q) \supset R] \supset (M \supset R)$
→ 2.	$(P \vee Q) \supset R$	**AP**
	.	
	.	
	.	
_.	$M \supset R$	
_.	$[(P \vee Q) \supset R] \supset (M \supset R)$	_–_ **CP**

We still need to derive a conditional, so let's use another assumption:

1.	$(M \vee N) \supset P$	$/\therefore [(P \vee Q) \supset R] \supset (M \supset R)$
→ 2.	$(P \vee Q) \supset R$	**AP**
→ 3.	M	**AP**
	.	
	.	
	.	
_.	R	
_.	$M \supset R$	_–_ **CP**
_.	$[(P \vee Q) \supset R] \supset (M \supset R)$	_–_ **CP**

Note that by using **CP** we have, in effect, taken a difficult one-premise proof and transformed it into a much simpler three-premise proof. Completing the proof now is simply a matter of making liberal use of Addition:

1.	$(M \vee N) \supset P$	$/\therefore [(P \vee Q) \supset R] \supset (M \supset R)$
→ 2.	$(P \vee Q) \supset R$	**AP**
→ 3.	M	**AP**
4.	$M \vee N$	3 **Add**
5.	P	1,4 **MP**
6.	$P \vee Q$	5 **Add**
7.	R	2,6 **MP**
8.	$M \supset R$	3–7 **CP**
9.	$[(P \vee Q) \supset R] \supset (M \supset R)$	2–8 **CP**

Examples

The following proofs contain correct uses of the rule of conditional proof:

(1)

1.	$(A \lor B) \supset (C \cdot D)$	
2.	$(D \lor E) \supset F$	$/ \therefore \sim A \lor F$
3.	A	AP
4.	$A \lor B$	3 **Add**
5.	$C \cdot D$	1,4 **MP**
6.	D	5 **Simp**
7.	$D \lor E$	6 **Add**
8.	F	2,7 **MP**
9.	$A \supset F$	3–8 **CP**
10.	$\sim A \lor F$	9 **Impl**

(2)

1.	$(Z \supset Y) \supset X$	
2.	$T \lor S$	
3.	$\sim (Z \cdot T)$	
4.	$\sim Y \supset \sim S$	$/ \therefore X$
5.	Z	AP
6.	$\sim Z \lor \sim T$	3 **DeM**
7.	$\sim \sim Z$	5 **DN**
8.	$\sim T$	6,7 **DS**
9.	S	2,8 **DS**
10.	$S \supset Y$	4 **Contra**
11.	Y	9,10 **MP**
12.	$Z \supset Y$	5–11 **CP**
13.	X	1,12 **MP**

(3)

1.	$A \supset C$	
2.	$B \supset D$	
3.	$(C \lor D) \supset A$	$/ \therefore (A \lor B) \equiv (C \lor D)$
4.	$A \lor B$	AP
5.	$C \lor D$	1,2,4 **CD**
6.	$(A \lor B) \supset (C \lor D)$	4–5 **CP**
7.	$C \lor D$	AP
8.	A	3,7 **MP**
9.	$A \lor B$	8 **Add**
10.	$(C \lor D) \supset (A \lor B)$	7–9 **CP**
11.	$[(A \lor B) \supset (C \lor D)] \cdot$ $[(C \lor D) \supset (A \lor B)]$	6,10 **Conj**
12.	$(A \lor B) \equiv (C \lor D)$	11 **Equiv**

ⅬⒸ Exercise 5-1

Prove valid using **CP** and the eighteen valid argument forms.

(1)   1. B /∴ $A \supset (A \cdot B)$

(2)   1. $A \supset (B \cdot C)$ /∴ $A \supset C$

(3)   1. $B \supset C$ /∴ $(A \supset B) \supset (A \supset C)$

(4)   1. $A \supset (B \supset C)$
    2. $\sim C$ /∴ $A \supset \sim B$

(5)   1. C /∴ $A \supset (B \supset C)$

(6)   1. $A \supset (B \supset C)$
    2. $A \supset B$ /∴ $A \supset C$

(7)   1. $A \supset B$
    2. $A \supset C$ /∴ $A \supset (B \cdot C)$

(8)   1. $(A \cdot B) \supset C$
    2. $(B \cdot C) \supset D$ /∴ $(A \cdot B) \supset D$

(9)   1. $R \supset (L \cdot S)$
    2. $(L \vee M) \supset P$ /∴ $\sim P \supset \sim R$

(10)   1. $A \supset (B \supset C)$
     2. $C \supset D$ /∴ $A \supset (B \supset D)$

(11)   1. $A \vee \sim (B \cdot C)$ /∴ $B \supset (C \supset A)$

(12)   1. $A \supset (B \cdot C)$
     2. $D \supset (E \cdot F)$
     3. $D \vee A$ /∴ $B \vee F$

(13)   1. $\sim H \vee \sim F$
     2. $\sim M \supset F$
     3. $(\sim H \vee M) \supset \sim F$
      /∴ $(H \supset M) \cdot \sim F$

(14)   1. $D \supset G$ /∴ $(D \cdot G) \equiv D$

(15)   1. $N \equiv P$ /∴ $(N \supset R) \equiv (P \supset R)$

ⅬⒸ Exercise 5-2

Use **CP** to prove arguments (1), (5), (6), (8), (13), and (14) in Exercise 4-12. Compare the length and difficulty of your answers to the ones you did in answering Exercise 4-12.

2 *Indirect Proofs*

A **contradiction,** or *contradictory sentence,* is any sentence that is inconsistent—any sentence that cannot possibly be true. Some contradictions are more obvious than others. An **explicit contradiction** is a sentence of the form $p \cdot \sim p$. Obviously such sentences cannot possibly be true; they are necessarily false. Logic alone guarantees the falsity of contradictions. Given the definition of a valid argument, a false sentence cannot be validly inferred from true premises. So if we infer validly to a contradiction, we have shown, without question, that at least one of our premises must be false.

Now consider, say, a four-premise argument, and assume we know that three of its four premises are true. If we derive a contradiction from that set of four premises, we have proved that the fourth premise in the set is false (since at least one member of the set is false, and we assume that the other three are true). So we also have proved that the negation of the fourth premise is true (since the negation of a false sentence is true). We have here the main ideas behind the rule of **Indirect Proof (IP).** (Indirect Proofs also are known as **reductio ad absurdum proofs,** because in an Indirect Proof an assumption is "reduced to absurdity" by showing that it implies a contradiction.)

Take the argument:

1. $A \supset B$
2. $B \supset C$
3. A $/\therefore C$

First, let's add the negation of the conclusion, namely, $\sim C$, to the above set of premises, to obtain the following set:

1. $A \supset B$
2. $B \supset C$
3. A
4. $\sim C$ **AP**

Then we can obtain a contradiction as follows:

5. $\sim B$ 2,4 **MT**
6. $\sim A$ 1,5 **MT**
7. $A \cdot \sim A$ 3,6 **Conj**

Obviously, if premises 1, 2, and 3 are true, then the added premise 4, $\sim C$, is false. And if the $\sim C$ is false, then C must be true. Using our new rule, **IP**, we can now discharge $\sim C$, having shown that that assumption implies a contradiction, and place the desired conclusion, C, on a new line.

8. C 4–7 **IP**

To sum up, by assuming $\sim C$ and then deriving a contradiction, we have shown that the argument

1. $A \supset B$
2. $B \supset C$
3. A $/\therefore C$

is valid, because we have shown that if its premises are true, then its conclusion, C, must be true (because $\sim C$ must be false).

The general method employed in an Indirect Proof, then, is to add the negation of the conclusion of an argument to its set of premises and derive a contradiction. If the conclusion is already a negation, you can just assume the conclusion minus the initial negation sign, instead of assuming a double negation. The following diagram illustrates these two versions of the rule.

$$\begin{array}{ll} \sim p & \textbf{AP} \\ \cdot & \\ \cdot & \\ \cdot & \\ q \cdot \sim q & \\ \hline p & \textbf{IP} \end{array} \qquad\qquad \begin{array}{ll} p & \textbf{AP} \\ \cdot & \\ \cdot & \\ \cdot & \\ q \cdot \sim q & \\ \hline \sim p & \textbf{IP} \end{array}$$

The derivation of the contradiction proves that if the original premises are true, then the *negation* of the added premise must be *true*. Since the negation of the added premise is the

the conclusion of the argument in question, the conclusion must be true and the argument valid.

Example

Every correct application of **IP** incorporates the following elements:

1. The sentence justified by **IP** must be the denial of the assumed premise (or vice versa).
2. The preceding line must be a substitution instance of the form $p \cdot \sim p$.
3. Lines are drawn indicating the scope of the assumed premise.

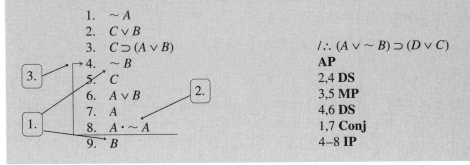

1.	$\sim A$	
2.	$C \vee B$	
3.	$C \supset (A \vee B)$	$/ \therefore (A \vee \sim B) \supset (D \vee C)$
4.	$\sim B$	**AP**
5.	C	2,4 **DS**
6.	$A \vee B$	3,5 **MP**
7.	A	4,6 **DS**
8.	$A \cdot \sim A$	1,7 **Conj**
9.	B	4–8 **IP**

Here is another example of an indirect proof (using arrows and lines as in Conditional Proofs to keep track of assumed premises and the lines that depend on them):

1.	$A \supset X$	
2.	$(C \vee \sim X) \supset A$	$/ \therefore X$
3.	$\sim X$	**AP** (the negation of the conclusion)
4.	$\sim A$	1,3 **MT**
5.	$\sim (C \vee \sim X)$	2,4 **MT**
6.	$\sim C \cdot \sim \sim X$	5 **DeM**
7.	$\sim C \cdot X$	6 **DN**
8.	X	7 **Simp**
9.	$X \cdot \sim X$	3,8 **Conj**
10.	X	3–9 **IP**

Notice that the contradiction obtained is simply the conjunction of the assumed premise and the conclusion. This is perfectly permissible: The derivation of any explicit contradiction is all that is required. Notice also that the proof does not stop with line 8. As with Conditional Proof, the assumption must be discharged. We could discharge the assumption with Conditional Proof, but that would only prove $\sim X \supset X$. But once the explicit contradiction is obtained, the rule of Indirect Proof permits the assertion of the conclusion independently of the assumed premise.

Another way to see that the rule of Indirect Proof is valid is to recognize that anything that can be proved by Indirect Proof can be proved by a slightly longer Conditional Proof. Consider the following skeleton of a typical Indirect Proof:

```
    1.  ?
    2.  ?                           /∴ A
 →  3.  ~ A                         AP
    4.  ?
    5.  ?
    6.  B · ~ B                     4,5 Conj
```

Every Indirect Proof begins by assuming the negation of the desired conclusion (here we've arbitrarily chosen *A* as our conclusion, but the point we are making will work with any conclusion) and deriving a contradiction. (Again, we've just arbitrarily supplied a contradiction—any contradiction would do.) Once a contradiction is derived, the rule of Indirect Proof permits the assertion of the conclusion, in this case *A:*

```
    7.  A                          3–6 IP
```

Line 7 is permitted in an Indirect Proof because the premise assumed (in line 3) is the negation of the conclusion, *A;* and use of that assumed premise (plus the original premises) led to a contradiction.

But line 7, or any line derived by **IP,** can be derived by **CP.** This is because *any* sentence can be derived from a proof that contains a contradiction. This is illustrated by the following argument:

```
    1.  B · ~ B                     /∴ X
    2.  B                           1 Simp
    3.  B ∨ X                       2 Add
    4.  ~ B                         1 Simp
    5.  X                           3,4 DS
```

Obviously, the conclusion *X* might have been *any* sentence whatever. Therefore, from the contradiction *B · ~ B*—indeed, from any contradiction—it is clear that *any* sentence whatever can be obtained.

Returning to our skeleton of an Indirect Proof, one sentence in particular that can be derived is the negation of our assumed premise, as follows:

```
    1.  ?
    2.  ?                           /∴ A
 →  3.  ~ A                         AP
    4.  ?
    5.  ?
    6.  B · ~ B                     4,5 Conj
    7.  B                           1 Simp
    8.  B ∨ A                       2 Add
    9.  ~ B                         1 Simp
   10.  A                           8,9 DS
```

The proof is not complete at this point, because we have not discharged the assumption. If we now discharge the assumption with **CP,** we get the following odd conditional:

```
   11.  ~ A ⊃ A                     3–10 CP
```

But from this point it is a simple matter to obtain *A*:

12.	$\sim\sim A \vee A$	11 **Impl**
13.	$A \vee A$	12 **DN**
14.	A	13 **Taut**

This example illustrates the fact that whenever the negation of the conclusion of an argument is taken as an assumed premise in a Conditional Proof and a contradiction is derived, then it must be possible to obtain the conclusion of the argument by the procedure just illustrated (so that the conclusion depends on the original premises but not on the assumed premise). But since this always can be done, there is little point in actually doing so in every case. Instead, we permit the use of the rule of Indirect Proof, which we now see is simply a shorter way of proving what could have been proved by Conditional Proof.

L⚙ Exercise 5-3

Prove the following arguments valid using **IP.**

(1)   1. $A \vee B$
       2. $A \vee \sim B$ /∴ A

(2)   1. $\sim A \supset B$
       2. $\sim (\sim A \cdot B)$ /∴ A

(3)   1. $A \supset (B \cdot C)$
       2. $\sim B$ /∴ $\sim A$

(4)   1. $A \vee (\sim B \cdot C)$
       2. $B \supset \sim A$ /∴ $\sim B$

(5)   1. $A \supset \sim B$
       2. $B \vee C$
       3. $A \vee C$ /∴ C

(6)   1. $(A \cdot B) \supset C$
       2. $\sim A \supset C$
       3. B /∴ C

(7)   1. $A \supset B$
       2. $C \supset D$
       3. $(B \vee D) \supset E$
       4. $\sim E$ /∴ $\sim (A \vee C)$

(8)   1. $A \supset (B \supset C)$
       2. $A \supset B$
       3. $\sim C \supset (A \vee D)$ /∴ $C \vee D$

(9)   1. $\sim A$
       2. $(A \vee B) \equiv C$
       3. $\sim B$ /∴ $\sim (C \cdot D)$

(10)   1. $C \supset [D \vee \sim (A \vee B)]$
       2. $\sim A \supset B$ /∴ $\sim D \supset \sim C$

L⚙ Exercise 5-4

Prove valid, first without using **IP** or **CP,** and then using **IP,** and compare the lengths and difficulty of the corresponding proofs.

(1)   1. $A \supset B$
       2. $C \supset A$
       3. $C \vee (B \cdot D)$ /∴ B

(2)   1. $H \supset (A \supset B)$
       2. $\sim C \supset (H \vee B)$
       3. $H \supset A$ /∴ $C \vee B$

(3)   1. $P \vee Q$
       2. $Q \supset (R \cdot S)$
       3. $(R \vee P) \supset T$ /∴ T

(4)   1. $(A \vee B) \supset (C \supset \sim D)$
       2. $(D \vee E) \supset (A \cdot C)$ /∴ $\sim D$

(5) 1. $A \supset \sim (B \vee C)$
    2. $\sim D \supset (\sim A \supset \sim E)$
    3. $\sim (\sim E \vee F)$
    4. $\sim F \supset (A \supset B) / \therefore D$

(6) 1. $(L \vee N) \supset (F \cdot P)$
    2. $F \supset (H \cdot K)$
    3. $H \supset (\sim L \cdot M) / \therefore \sim L$

(7) 1. $H \supset (A \cdot B)$
    2. $B \supset (M \vee \sim A)$
    3. $M \supset (\sim H \vee \sim B) / \therefore \sim H$

(8) 1. $(R \supset M) \supset L$
    2. $(N \vee S) \supset (M \cdot T)$
    3. $(P \supset R) \supset L$
    4. $(T \vee K) \supset \sim N / \therefore L$

3   *Strategy Hints for Using Conditional Proof and Indirect Proof*

The main point of strategy is that by prudent use of **CP** or **IP,** you can often make a difficult proof much easier to solve. Use **CP** routinely if your conclusion is a conditional. Even if it is not a conditional, if it is equivalent to a conditional use **CP** to derive *that* formula. Also, remember to check to see if it would be even more useful to assume the negation of the target conditional's consequent, derive the negation of the antecedent, use **CP,** and apply Contraposition to the result.*

Every proof can be solved using **IP.** So if all else fails, try using **IP.** (Note, however, that it isn't necessarily a good idea to routinely try **IP** first; sometimes solving with **IP** makes the proof more difficult.) When you use **IP,** you should try to break down complex formulas into simpler units. This is often the quickest way to find a contradiction. **IP** is particularly useful when the conclusion is either atomic or a negated atomic sentence. In this case **IP** is not just a last recourse—it's the preferred method. More often than not, short premises make for easier proofs, and short conclusions make for harder ones. Using **IP** on a proof that has a short conclusion gives you an additional useful short premise to work with, and you are no longer forced to derive the difficult short conclusion directly—*any* contradiction will do.

LC Exercise 5-5

Prove valid using **IP** or **CP.**

(1) 1. $\sim (P \cdot \sim Q)$
    2. $\sim Q \vee M$
    3. $R \supset \sim M / \therefore P \supset \sim (R \vee \sim M)$

(2) 1. $F \vee G$
    2. $H \cdot (I \supset F)$
    3. $H \supset \sim F / \therefore G \cdot \sim I$

(3) 1. $(A \cdot B) \vee C$
    2. $(A \cdot B) \supset (E \supset A)$
    3. $C \supset D / \therefore (E \supset A) \vee D$

(4) 1. $S \vee (T \supset R)$
    2. $S \supset T$
    3. $\sim (T \supset R) / \therefore T$

---

*For an example, see the discussion on pages 112–113.

(5)   1. $\sim (T \lor U)$
      2. S
      3. $R \equiv \sim S /\therefore \sim (U \lor R)$

(6)   1. $\sim A \supset (D \cdot C)$
      2. $\sim (B \cdot A) /\therefore \sim C \supset \sim B$

(7)   1. $A \supset (\sim D \supset C)$
      2. $\sim D \supset (C \supset B)$
      3. $\sim (D \cdot A) /\therefore A \supset B$

(8)   1. $A \lor (\sim B \lor \sim C)$
      2. $A \supset (D \supset E)$
      3. $\sim (\sim B \lor \sim D) /\therefore C \supset E$

(9)   1. $I \supset F$
      2. $G \supset (H \supset I)$
      3. $\sim (\sim H \lor F) /\therefore \sim G$

(10) 1. $S \lor (T \cdot R)$
      2. $S \supset T /\therefore T$

(11) 1. $(D \lor E) \supset C$
      2. $(A \lor B) \supset \sim C /\therefore D \supset \sim B$

(12) 1. $(H \lor K) \supset (L \lor K)$
      2. $M \supset [H \supset (N \cdot \sim L)]$
         $/\therefore (M \cdot H) \supset (N \cdot K)$

(13) 1. $C \equiv D$
      2. $B \supset (D \cdot E)$
      3. $\sim C \lor \sim D /\therefore \sim B$

(14) 1. $D \supset (E \supset F)$
      2. $H \supset (E \lor G)$
      3. $D \supset (G \supset \sim H)$
         $/\therefore \sim (\sim F \supset \sim H) \supset \sim D$

(15) 1. $N \supset (P \supset R)$
      2. $\sim (R \supset S) \supset \sim T$
      3. $(M \lor \sim T) \lor \sim (P \supset S)$
         $/\therefore \sim M \supset \sim (N \cdot T)$

4 Theorems

In all of the proofs you have seen so far, you are given premises at the beginning of the proof and these premises are never discharged (unlike assumed premises that must always be discharged before the proof is complete). A **theorem** is the conclusion of a proof that has no undischarged premises. Since the rules of our natural deduction system are complete, every sentence that is a tautology is also a theorem. Theorems are also known as *logical truths* or *truths of logic,* because they are truths provable (and hence knowable) without the aid of contingent information. They are, so to speak, truths knowable by the use of logic alone.

Since you are not provided with premises in proofs of theorems, you must use either **CP** or **IP** and begin the proof with an assumed premise. Suppose, for example, you want to prove the theorem $A \lor \sim A$. You can prove this theorem using **IP** as follows:

1. $\sim (A \lor \sim A)$ AP
2. $\sim A \cdot \sim \sim A$ 1 DeM
3. $A \lor \sim A$ 1–2 IP

Here is an example of a theorem that is proved with **CP**:

1. $\sim A$ AP
2. $\sim A \lor B$ 1 Add
3. $A \supset B$ 2 Impl
4. $\sim A \supset (A \supset B)$ 1–3 CP

LC Exercise 5-6

Prove that the following sentences are theorems.

(1) $A \supset (A \vee B)$

(2) $(A \cdot B) \supset A$

(3) $A \supset (\sim A \supset B)$

(4) $[A \supset (B \supset C)] \supset [(A \supset B) \supset (A \supset C)]$

(5) $(A \vee B) \supset [C \supset (A \vee B)]$

(6) $(A \vee B) \supset \{[(A \supset C) \cdot (B \supset C)] \supset C\}$

(7) $(A \vee B) \supset [(A \supset B) \vee (B \supset A)]$

(8) $(A \equiv B) \equiv (\sim A \equiv \sim B)$

5   *Proving Premises Inconsistent*

In general, logic alone cannot determine the truth-values of premises. But if the premises of an argument (taken as a unit) are inconsistent, then at least one of them must be false, and this fact can be proved by logic alone. Of course, we can use truth tables to show that a set of premises are inconsistent, but we can also show this by means of natural deduction. To prove that an argument has inconsistent premises, use the eighteen valid argument forms to derive a contradiction from the premises. (And, of course, to prove *any* set of statements inconsistent, use the same method.)

For example, consider an argument with the following premises:

1. $A \supset B$
2. $A \supset \sim B$
3. A

From these premises, we can derive a contradiction, as follows:

4. B 1,3 **MP**

5. $\sim B$ 2,3 **MP**

6. $B \cdot \sim B$ 4,5 **Conj**

Because line 6 is an explicit contradiction, it must be false. And if it is false, then at least one premise must be false, since line 6 follows from the premises. Thus, taken together, the premises form a false conjunction. But that conjunction is not contingently false, since its falsehood is proved by logic alone, so it must be false because it is *contradictory,* that is, inconsistent.

In Chapter 3, we used truth tables to explain why all arguments with inconsistent premises are valid. Now we are in position to see how this same result is borne out in natural deduction. If you can derive a contradiction from the premises alone, obviously you can prove any conclusion you like by means of the rule of Indirect Proof: Simply assume the negation of the desired conclusion and derive a contradiction. For example, consider the following proof:

1. A
2. $\sim A$ $/\therefore X$
→ 3. $\sim X$ **AP**
    4. $A \cdot \sim A$ 1,2 **Conj**
    5. X 3–4 **IP**

Obviously, we could prove *any* conclusion from these two premises, or from any other inconsistent premises.

LC Exercise 5-7

A. Prove that the following arguments all have inconsistent premises.

(1) 1. $B \supset (\sim C \cdot \sim D)$
    2. $C \vee D$
    3. $B /\therefore \sim D \supset C$

(2) 1. $\sim A \vee B$
    2. $\sim B \vee \sim A$
    3. $A /\therefore B$

(3) 1. $A \cdot \sim B$
    2. $B \supset A$
    3. $A \supset B /\therefore B$

(4) 1. $\sim R \cdot \sim S$
    2. $S \vee (\sim S \cdot T)$
    3. $\sim (R \vee S) \supset \sim (S \vee T) /\therefore R$

(5) 1. $A \supset (B \vee C)$
    2. $\sim (\sim A \vee C)$
    3. $\sim B /\therefore C$

(6) 1. $(H \vee \sim H) \supset (L \vee K)$
    2. $(L \vee K) \supset (H \vee \sim H)$
    3. $(H \cdot \sim H) \supset (L \vee K)$
    4. $(L \vee K) \supset (H \cdot \sim H)$
    $/\therefore (K \cdot \sim L) \supset H$

(7) 1. $K \supset (L \supset M)$
    2. $N \vee K$
    3. $\sim (\sim L \vee M)$
    4. $\sim N /\therefore K \supset (\sim M \vee L)$

(8) 1. $A \supset (C \supset B)$
    2. $(B \cdot C) \vee A$
    3. $C \vee (B \cdot A)$
    4. $B \supset \sim C$
    5. $D \vee B$
    6. $B \cdot \sim A /\therefore B \vee (A \supset D)$

(9) 1. $A \supset (C \supset D)$
    2. $\sim A \supset (D \supset C)$
    3. $(A \vee \sim A) \supset \sim D$
    4. $(A \cdot D) \vee (\sim A \cdot \sim D)$
    5. $(C \cdot D) \vee (\sim C \cdot \sim D)$
    6. $A /\therefore D$

(10) 1. $A \supset (B \supset C)$
    2. $\sim [\sim C \vee (A \vee \sim D)]$
    3. $\sim \{\sim A \vee [C \supset (B \cdot D)]\}$
    $/\therefore (A \vee C) \supset D$

B. You can know that all of these arguments are valid without proving any of them. Why? How?

6   *Adding Valid Argument Forms*

Once we have become familiar with the eighteen valid argument forms, once we have become *practiced* in their use, once all systematic errors in their use have been eliminated, it becomes convenient to simplify proofs by combining two or more rules into one step. Logical candidates are rules that are frequently used together; for example, **DeM** and **DN**, **DN** and **Impl**, and two uses of **DN**.

Here is a proof using the first two of these shortcuts:

1. $A \lor B$
2. $\sim (B \cdot \sim C)$ $/\therefore \sim A \supset C$
3. $\sim A \supset B$ 1 **DN, Impl**
4. $\sim B \lor C$ 2 **DeM, DN**
5. $B \supset C$ 4 **Impl**
6. $\sim A \supset C$ 3,5 **HS**

And here is one using Double Negation twice on one line:

1. $(F \cdot G) \supset H$
2. $\sim (\sim F \lor \sim G)$ $/\therefore H$
3. $\sim \sim F \cdot \sim \sim G$ 2 **DeM**
4. $F \cdot G$ 3 **DN** (twice)
5. H 1,4 **MP**

We could, of course, accomplish the same proof simplification by introducing new rules analogous to these rule combinations. For example, we could introduce a new rule allowing inferences of the form $p \lor q /\therefore \sim p \supset q$ and use it in going from line 1 to line 3 in the first proof above.

In fact, there is no reason why we could not add any reasonable number of valid rules to our list of eighteen (plus **CP** and **IP**) *provided* that any new rule added is proved to be valid, say, by truth table analysis. Here are a few candidates that may be useful in shortening proofs:

$p \equiv q$ $p \supset q /\therefore p \supset (p \cdot q)$
$p /\therefore q$

                                           $\sim (p \cdot \sim q) :: (p \supset q)$
$p \equiv q$
$\sim p /\therefore \sim q$ $\sim (p \supset q) :: (p \cdot \sim q)$

Exercise 5-8

Determine which of the following can and which cannot be added to our set of valid argument forms:

(1) $p \lor (q \lor r) :: r \lor (q \lor p)$
(2) $p \cdot (q \cdot r) :: r \cdot (p \cdot q)$
(3) $p \supset (q \supset r) :: r \supset (q \supset p)$
(4) $p \lor \sim q /\therefore p \supset \sim q$
(5) $p \supset q /\therefore \sim (\sim q \supset p)$
(6) $p \supset q, p \supset \sim q /\therefore \sim p$

7 *The Completeness of Sentential Logic*

Notice that we have produced two different conceptions of "logical truths"—tautologies and theorems. Tautologies have been defined in terms of truth tables, theorems in terms of proofs. Corresponding to this difference is a distinction drawn by logicians between the syntax and the semantics of a system of logic. The **semantics** of a formal system includes those aspects of the system having to do with meaning or truth. For example, the core of the semantics for sentential logic consists of the defining truth tables for each of the connectives.

The **syntax** of a system of logic, on the other hand, comprises those elements of the system having to do with matters of form or structure, which are independent of issues of meaning or truth. Questions about whether a sentence is well formed or whether a sentence is a substitution instance of a particular form are syntactic questions. In principle, we can address these questions without any notion whatsoever of what the symbols of our system actually mean. Likewise, even the question of whether something qualifies as a valid proof is a syntactic question because our rules are purposely stated solely by means of argument forms. Again, we could determine whether a proof is valid without knowing anything about the meaning of the connectives, since all this requires is that we determine whether each step of the proof is a substitution instance of one of a given set of argument forms.

Thus, we characterize logical truths in sentential logic semantically as tautologies, syntactically as theorems. Correspondingly, we have also explored validity both semantically, in Chapter 3, using truth tables, and syntactically in Chapters 4 and 5, using proofs. Semantically speaking, an argument is valid if and only if there is no interpretation on which the premises are true and the conclusion false. Syntactically, an argument is valid just in case it is possible to construct a proof of the conclusion from the premises.

Examples

Semantic Concepts	*Syntactic Concepts*
A sentence is a *tautology* if and only if it is true on every interpretation.	A sentence is a *theorem* if and only if it can be proved without any premises.
An argument is *valid* if and only if there is no interpretation on which the premises are all true and the conclusion false.	An argument is *valid* if and only if it is possible to construct a proof of the conclusion from the premises.
A group of sentences is *consistent* if and only if there is an interpretation on which all of the sentences are true.	A group of sentences is *consistent* if and only if it is not possible to prove a contradiction from them.

It is, of course, no coincidence that the same sentences are both tautologies and theorems and that arguments that are semantically valid are also syntactically valid. Our system of rules would be incomplete if there were arguments that could be shown to be valid with a truth table but that could not be proven. At the beginning of this chapter, we explained that our system of sentential logic without **CP** or **IP** is incomplete in this sense. We can say that a system of logic is **complete** if every argument that is semantically valid is syntactically valid. Sentential logic is complete in this sense if every tautology is a theorem.

Our system of sentential logic is not only complete, it is sound as well. A system of logic is **sound** if every argument that is syntactically valid is semantically valid. Sentential logic is sound if every theorem is a tautology. Our system of rules would be unsound if there were proofs for arguments that could be shown to be invalid with a truth table. Suppose, for example, we modified the rule of Simplification so that it applied to disjunctions as well as conjunctions, allowing arguments of the form *p* or *q,* therefore *p*. We could go on constructing "proofs" with such a system, but such proofs would be worthless, since they would permit us to deduce falsehoods from truths.

It can be rigorously proven that our system of sentential logic is both sound and complete. Such proofs are part of what is known as **metalogic,** or *metatheory,* because they are proofs *about* a logical system rather than proofs *within* a logical system. These proofs are complex and lie outside the scope of this book. We will, however, describe some of the more important metatheoretical results for each of the systems of logic we introduce.

8 Material Implication and Valid Argument Forms

In the discussion of material implication in Chapter 2, we pointed out that most implications used in daily life are not truth-functional. Nevertheless, we introduced the truth-functional implication, *material implication,* and gave reasons for defining it as we did.

Now we are able to provide another reason for translating implications by means of material implication and for using the particular truth table definition of material implication given in Chapter 2. The reason is that we want intuitively valid arguments and argument forms to remain valid when translated into our notation, and we want intuitively invalid arguments and argument forms to remain invalid. If we use any other truth table definition for implication, then we will be unable to attain this goal.

Consider the following four argument forms:

(1) 1. If *p* then *q*
2. $p / \therefore \sim q$

(2) 1. If *p* then *q*
2. $p / \therefore q$

(3) 1. If *p* then *q*
2. $\sim p / \therefore \sim q$

(4) 1. If *p* then *q*
2. $\sim p / \therefore q$

The first of these argument forms is obviously invalid. Symbolizing its first premise by means of material implication (defined as in Chapter 2), we can prove that argument form (1) is invalid by truth table analysis as follows:

1. $p \supset q$
    T T T

2. $p / \therefore \sim q$
    T   F T

Notice however, that if there were an **F** on the first line of the truth table for material implication, instead of a **T**, then we could not prove that argument form (1) is invalid. On the contrary, we could prove it valid as follows:

p q	↓ $p \supset q$	*p*	~ *q*
T T	T F T	T	F T
T F	T ? F	T	T F
F T	F ? T	F	F T
F F	F ? F	F	T F

(This truth table would prove that the argument form (1) is valid, because it would indicate that none of its substitution instances have true premises and a false conclusion, no matter how we fill in the rest of the table for $p \supset q$. Only the first line has both the second premise true and the conclusion false. By making $p \supset q$ false on this line, we ensure that it is impossible for the premises all to be true and the conclusion false.)

So we cannot place an **F** on the first line of the truth table for material implication. Instead, we must place a **T** on that line, to preserve the invalidity of certain intuitively invalid argument forms.

Now consider argument form (2) above. This argument form, Modus Ponens, obviously is valid. Indeed, if we allow symbolization of its first premise by means of material implication, then we have already proved that it is valid by truth table analysis. Of course, if there were a **T** on the second line of the truth table for material implication, instead of an **F,** then we could not prove Modus Ponens valid. Indeed, we could prove it *invalid* by truth table analysis, as follows:

1. $p \supset q$
    T T F

2. $p / \therefore q$
    T   F

So it is clear that we cannot allow a **T** on the second line of the truth table for material implication. Instead, we must place an **F** on that line, to preserve the validity of valid argument forms such as Modus Ponens.

Next, consider argument form (3) above. This form obviously is not valid. As noted in Chapter 4, its invalidity has been so infamous in the history of philosophy that reasoning having this form has acquired a special title, namely the fallacy of Denying the Antecedent. Symbolizing the first premise of (3) by material implication, defined as in Chapter 2, we can prove that (3) is invalid by truth table analysis, as follows:

1. $p \supset q$
    F T T

2. ~ $p / \therefore$ ~ q
    T F   F T

But if there were an **F** on the third line of the truth table for material implication, instead of a **T,** then we could not prove that (3) is invalid. On the contrary, we could prove it valid, as follows:

$p\,q$	$\downarrow$ $p \supset q$	$\sim p$	$\sim q$
T T	T ? T	F T	F T
T F	T ? F	F T	T F
F T	F F T	T F	F T
F F	F ? F	T F	T F

This truth table would prove the argument form in question valid, because it would indicate that none of its substitution instances have true premises and a false conclusion. The third line is the only interpretation on which the second premise is true and the conclusion is false. By making $p \supset q$ false on this line, we ensure that it is impossible for the premises all to be true and the conclusion false.

So it is clear that we cannot allow an **F** on the third line of the truth table for material implication. Instead, we must place a **T** on that line, to preserve the invalidity of certain intuitively invalid argument forms.

Finally, consider argument form (4) above. Clearly, this form also is not valid. Symbolizing its first premise using material implication defined as in Chapter 2, we can prove that (4) is invalid by truth table analysis, as follows:

1. $p \supset q$
    F T F

2. $\sim p /\therefore q$
    T F   F

But, if there were an **F** on the fourth line of the truth table for material implication, instead of a **T,** then we could not prove (4) invalid. On the contrary, we could prove it valid, as follows:

$p\,q$	$\downarrow$ $p \supset q$	$\sim p$	q
T T	T ? T	F T	T
T F	T ? F	F T	F
F T	F ? T	T F	T
F F	F F F	T F	F

Once again, for this form there is only one possible line where we could make the premises all true and the conclusion false—in this case the fourth line. It follows that we cannot allow an **F** on the fourth line of the truth table for material implication. We must place a **T** on that line to preserve the intuitive insight that this form is invalid.

The general conclusion to be drawn from the four examples above is that we must use material implication, as it was defined in Chapter 2, to ensure that our translations of certain invalid arguments and argument forms will be invalid. This discussion also illustrates the interplay between the semantics and syntax of sentential logic. Obviously, our choice of rules is constrained by the semantics of sentential logic. We need a system of rules that will render our natural deduction system both complete and sound. What is not so obvious, and what is illustrated here, is how the semantics of sentential logic is also constrained by our choice of rules. Given that of the four argument forms mentioned above we only want **MP** to be a valid inference rule, we must define the horseshoe as we did in Chapter 2.

Key terms

assumed premise: An assumption added to the given premises in an argument.

complete: A system of logic is complete if every argument that is semantically valid is syntactically valid as well. A system of sentential logic is complete in this sense if and only if every tautology is a theorem.

contradiction: A single sentence that is inconsistent. Examples: $A \cdot \sim A$, $\sim (A \vee \sim A)$, $\sim (B \supset C) \cdot \sim B$.

discharged premise: A premise has been discharged in the course of a proof once its truth is no longer being assumed. Every assumed premise must be discharged before a proof is complete.

explicit contradiction: A sentence that is a substitution instance of the form $p \cdot \sim p$. Examples: $A \cdot \sim A$, $\{C \equiv \sim (B \vee \sim D)] \cdot \sim [C \equiv \sim (B \vee \sim D)]\}$

indirect proof: (see *reductio ad absurdum proof*.)

metalogic: The study of the formal properties of logical systems. The proofs of metalogic are proofs about a logical system rather than proofs within a system. Examples of such proofs include proofs of the completeness or soundness of a system of logic.

reductio ad absurdum proof: The traditional name for an Indirect Proof. In an Indirect Proof, the assumed premise is reduced to absurdity by showing that an explicit contradiction can be validly inferred from it.

semantics: The semantics of a formal system includes those aspects of the system having to do with meaning or truth of its elements.

sound: A system of logic is sound if and only if every argument that is syntactically valid is semantically valid.

syntax: The syntax of a system of logic comprises those aspects of the system having to do with the form or structure of its elements.

theorem: The conclusion of an argument that has no undischarged premises.

Part Two

Chapter Six

Predicate Logic

Predicate Logic Symbolization

The sentential or propositional logic presented in the first five chapters deals with the internal structure of compound sentences but not with the internal structure of atomic sentences. Let's now examine what is called **predicate logic,** or quantifier logic, a logic concerned with the interior structure of both atomic and compound sentences.

Predicate logic gives us a way to prove the validity of many valid arguments that are invalid when symbolized in the notation of sentential logic. For example, the standard and ancient syllogism

1. All humans are mortal.
2. All Greeks are human. /∴ All Greeks are mortal.

must be symbolized in sentential logic in a way that makes it invalid, for instance, as

1. *A*
2. *B* /∴ *C*

Yet surely this syllogism is valid. Once we have introduced the machinery of predicate logic, we'll be able to prove its validity quite easily.

1   Individuals and Properties

Consider the sentence "Art is happy." This sentence asserts that some particular object or entity, Art, has a certain property, namely, the property of being happy. If we let the capital letter H denote the property of being happy, and the lowercase letter a name the individual, Art, we can symbolize this sentence as Ha. Similarly, the sentence "Betsy is happy" can be symbolized as Hb, the sentence "Art is friendly" as Fa, and the sentence "Betsy is friendly" as Fb. The sentences Fa, Fb, Ha, and Hb are alike in that they have the same general structure. In each of these sentences, a *property* is ascribed to some *individual entity*. This is one of the basic patterns of atomic sentences.

Examples

Here are a few more examples of this fundamental sentence structure, with symbolizations attached.

1. Elvis Presley was a rock star.   *Rp*
2. Alpha Centauri is a star.   *Sa*
3. Mike Tyson is headstrong.   *Ht*
4. Al Gore is environmentally correct.   *Cg*
5. Jeremiah was a bullfrog.   *Bj*

Another basic pattern is illustrated by the sentence "Art is taller than Betsy." This sentence asserts that there is a particular property (_____ being taller than _____) that holds *between* the two individual objects Art and Betsy. If we let *a* denote Art, *b* Betsy, and *T* the property of one thing being taller than another, we can symbolize the sentence "Art is taller than Betsy" as *Tab*. Similarly, we can symbolize the sentence "Betsy is taller than Art" as *Tba*. And if we let *F* denote the property of one thing being a friend of another (_____ is a friend of _____), then we can symbolize the sentence "Art is a friend of Betsy" as *Fab,* and so on.

Properties such as *is taller than* and *is a friend of,* which hold between two or more entities, are called **relational properties.** The particular properties in question are *two-place* relational properties because they hold between two entities. But we can also have three or four (or more) place properties. For instance, the property of being between two other objects (_____ is between _____ and . . . .) is a three-place relational property. Properties like *is happy* or *is wise,* which are ascribed to only one individual, are called *monadic properties.*

In some respects, the above analysis of the structure of atomic sentences is very much like those given in traditional grammar texts. For instance, a traditional grammar text would analyze the sentence "Art is human" as containing a subject, "Art," and a predicate, "is human." (Indeed, the term "predicate" is often used by logicians instead of the term "property." Hence, the name "predicate logic.") However, traditional grammars generally analyze all atomic sentences into this subject–predicate form. For instance, they construe the sentence "Art is taller than Betsy" as ascribing a predicate, being taller than Betsy, to a subject, Art. This is quite different from our analysis, for our analysis construes the sentence "Art is taller than Betsy" as concerning two subjects (or individual objects or entities), namely Art and Betsy, and construes this sentence as stating that a relational property holds between them. (Of course, we also can construe the sentence "Art is taller than Betsy" as ascribing the nonrelational property of being-taller-than-Betsy to Art, in which case that sentence will be symbolized as *Ta,* but to do so is to mask part of the structure of that sentence.)

To simplify matters, the next few chapters will deal entirely with predicate logic sentences that contain only monadic properties. We will then broaden our coverage of predicate logic to include relational predicates in Chapter 9.

Let's now be more specific about the two notational conventions introduced above. First, *capital letters* are used to denote properties, whether relational or nonrelational. And second, *lowercase letters* (up to and including the letter *t*) are used to denote individual objects, things, and entities, that is, any things that can have properties ascribed to them about which we wish to speak. Capital letters used to denote properties are called **property constants,** and lowercase letters (up to and including *t*) used to denote things, objects, and individual entities are called **individual constants.** Individual constants should never be used to designate groups of individuals, nor will we use these letters to designate properties. Systems that permit ascription of properties to properties encounter serious technical difficulties. (See, for instance, Chapter 11, Section 4.)

In addition, the lowercase letters *u* through *z* are used as **individual variables,** replaceable by individual constants. We will use individual variables when defining property constants. For example, instead of saying, "Let *M* denote the property of being a material object," we will say, "*Mx* = *x* is a material object." (The use of individual variables will be explained further on page 134.)

These notational conventions are to be used in addition to those previously introduced. We still allow the use of capital letters as sentence abbreviations, and the use of lowercase letters from *p* through *z* as sentence variables, just as in propositional logic.

Examples

Let *Px* = "*x* is president"; *Cx* = "*x* is charismatic"; *Tx* = "*x* is terribly disappointed"; *d* = "Dole"; *c* = "Clinton"; and *p* = "Perot." Then the expressions on the left symbolize the sentences on the right into the notation of predicate logic:

1.	Clinton is president.	1. *Pc*
2.	Dole is not president.	2. ~ *Pd*
3.	Clinton is president or Dole is president.	3. *Pc* ∨ *Pd*
4.	Either Clinton or Perot is charismatic.	4. *Cc* ∨ *Cp*
5.	Clinton is president but is not charismatic.	5. *Pc* · ~ *Cc*
6.	If Clinton is president, then neither Dole nor Perot is president.	6. *Pc* ⊃ (~ *Pd* · ~ *Pp*)
7.	It's not the case that Clinton is both president and charismatic.	7. ~ (*Pc* · *Cc*)
8.	If Clinton is president and Dole isn't, then although Perot is not president he is not terribly disappointed.	8. (*Pc* · ~ *Pd*) ⊃ (~ *Pp* · ~ *Tp*)

LC Exercise 6-1

Symbolize the following sentences, using the indicated letters.

1. Bo knows football. (*b* = "Bo"; *Fx* = "*x* knows football")
2. Bo knows baseball. (*Bx* = "*x* knows baseball")
3. Bo knows football and Bo knows baseball, but Bo doesn't know field hockey. (*Hx* = "*x* knows field hockey")

4. Neither Lou Holtz nor Bobby Knight is a mild-mannered coach. (*Mx* = "*x* is a mild-mannered coach"; *h* = "Lou Holtz"; *k* = "Bobby Knight")
5. Holtz and Knight both demand perfection. (*Dx* = "*x* demands perfection")
6. Not only is Bobby Knight a great basketball coach, he's a pretty good fly fisherman as well. (*Gx* = "*x* is a great basketball coach"; *Px* = "*x* is a pretty good fly fisherman")
7. Jon Bon Jovi is not the lead singer of Twisted Sister. (*Tx* = "*x* is the lead singer of Twisted Sister"; *j* = "Jon Bon Jovi")
8. If Bruce Willis is married, then so is Demi Moore. (*Mx* = "*x* is married"; *b* = "Bruce Willis"; *d* = "Demi Moore")

In developing a predicate logic, we do not abandon sentential logic. Instead, we include it within predicate logic. So mixed sentences are possible. An example is the sentence "Adam was foolish and Methuselah long-lived," symbolized as $A \cdot Lm$. Of course, we also can symbolize that sentence as $Fa \cdot Lm$ (so as to reveal the structure of the two atomic sentences "Adam was foolish" and "Methuselah was long-lived"). And we also can symbolize it as $Fa \cdot B$. (Of these three symbolizations the second is preferred because it reveals more logical structure.)

These uses of the capital letters *A* and *B* call attention to the fact that capital letters may serve more than one function. For instance, the letter *B* in this example serves in one place as a sentence constant and in another as a property constant. This ambiguity is harmless because it is clear in every case which function a letter serves: A property constant always occurs with a lowercase letter next to it, whereas a sentence constant never does.

The expression formed by combining a property constant and an individual constant is a sentence. The sentence *Pc* referred to above is an example. It has a truth-value, namely, the value **T** if Clinton is indeed president and **F** if he is not. But what about an expression formed by combining a property constant with an *individual variable*, say the form *Hx*? First, this form is not a sentence, since *x* is a variable. (Writing *Hx* is like writing *H* _____ , where the solid line serves as a place holder, to be filled in by an individual constant.) So the form *Hx* is neither true nor false. And second, since we can obtain a sentence from *Hx* by replacing the variable *x* with a lowercase letter denoting some object or entity, *Hx* is a *sentence form*. For instance, we can obtain the sentence *Ha* from *Hx* by replacing the variable *x* with the lowercase letter *a*.

Examples

The following are examples of sentence forms and some of their substitution instances.

Sentence Form	*Substitution Instances*
1. *Hy*	1. *Ha, Hb, Hc, . . .*
2. $Bx \supset Hy$	2. $Bb \supset Ha, Bb \supset Hb,$ $Ba \supset Hb, Ba \supset Ha, . . .$
3. $(Hx \cdot Bx) \supset Hy$	3. $(Hb \cdot Bb) \supset Ha,$ $(Ha \cdot Ba) \supset Hc, . . .$

2   *Quantifiers and Free Variables*

In sentential logic, to obtain a sentence from a sentence form, we have to replace all of the sentence variables in the sentence form by sentence constants. Thus, from the sentence form $p \supset q$, we obtain the sentence $A \supset B$, as well as many others. In predicate logic this also can be done, as was explained above. Thus, from the sentence form Hx, we obtain the sentences Ha, Hb, and so on. However, it is a fact of fundamental importance that in predicate logic a sentence can be obtained from a sentence form without replacing its individual variables by individual constants. For example, we can obtain a sentence from the sentence form Hx without specifying some particular entity that has the property H, by specifying instead how many entities have that property. This idea is familiar from its use in everyday English. For instance, in English we can form a sentence by ascribing the property of honesty to a particular man. The sentence "Art is honest" is an example. But we can also form a sentence by saying how many men are honest. The sentences "All men are honest" and "Some men are honest" are examples.

In predicate logic two symbols, called **quantifiers,** are used to state how many. The first is the **universal quantifier,** used to assert that *all* entities have some property or properties. The symbols (x), (y), and so on, that is, individual variables placed between parentheses, are used for this purpose. Thus to symbolize the sentence "Everything moves" or "All things move," start with the sentence form Mx and prefix the universal quantifier (x) to obtain the sentence $(x)(Mx)$, read as "For all x, Mx" or "Given any x, Mx."

The **existential quantifier** is used to assert that *some* individual or individuals have one or more properties. Here we use a symbol that looks like a backward letter E along with an individual variable, placing both symbols within parentheses, as in $(\exists x)$, $(\exists y)$, and so on. Thus to symbolize "Some things move," we again start with the sentence form Mx, but this time we prefix the existential quantifier $(\exists x)$ to obtain the sentence $(\exists x)(Mx)$, read as "there is an x, Mx" or "For some x, Mx" and so on.

In sentential logic, parentheses are used to remove ambiguity. For instance, the parentheses in the sentence $\sim (A \cdot B)$ indicate that the negation sign negates the whole compound sentence $A \cdot B$ and not just the atomic sentence A. The parentheses indicate the scope of the negation sign, that is, how much of the sentence the negation sign negates.

In predicate logic, parentheses serve a similar function. They indicate the **scope of a quantifier.** Take the sentence "Everything has mass and is extended." It is correctly symbolized as $(x)(Mx \cdot Ex)$ (where $Mx = $ "x has mass" and $Ex = $ "x is extended") and is read "For all x, x has mass and x is extended" or "Given any x, that x has mass and is extended." The parentheses around the expression $(Mx \cdot Ex)$ indicate that the scope of the (x) quantifier is the entire remaining part of the sentence, namely, $(Mx \cdot Ex)$, which is said to be within the scope of the (x) quantifier. Similarly, the brackets in $(x)[(Mx \cdot Ex) \supset Cx]$ indicate that the scope of this (x) quantifier is the entire remainder of that sentence.

However, when the scope of a quantifier extends just over the next minimal unit, parentheses may be omitted for the sake of simplicity. Thus, we may symbolize the sentence "Everything is heavy" either as $(x)(Hx)$ or as $(x)Hx$ (omitting parentheses of scope).

The expression $(x)(Mx \cdot Ex)$ is a sentence, but $(Mx \cdot Ex)$ is a sentence form, not a sentence. Is the expression $(x)(Mx) \cdot Ex$ a sentence? The answer is no, because it contains an individual variable that is not quantified, namely the x in Ex. Unquantified variables are called **free variables.** Quantified variables, such as the middle x in $(x)(Mx) \cdot Ex$, are said to be **bound variables.** An expression that contains one or more free variables is a sentence form, not a sentence.

Finally, it should be noted that merely being within the scope of a quantifier is not sufficient to make a variable a bound variable. To be bound, a variable must be within the scope of a quantifier using the same letter. Thus the y in $(x)(Fy \supset Gx)$ is within the scope of the (x) quantifier but is not bound by it, whereas the x in $(x)(Fy \supset Gx)$ is both within the scope of the (x) quantifier and bound by it.

LC Exercise 6-2

For each expression below, indicate (1) which variables are free and which are bound; (2) which letters serve as individual constants and which as property constants; (3) which free variables are within the scope of some quantifier or other and which individual constants are not within the scope of any quantifier.

1. $(x)(Fx \supset Ga)$
2. $(\exists x)\,(Fa \cdot Gx)$
3. $(x)[Fx \supset (Gy \vee Hx)]$
4. $(x)Fx \supset (\exists y)(Gy \vee Dx)$
5. $Fa \vee (x)[(Ga \vee Dx) \supset (\sim Ky \cdot Hb)]$
6. $(x)(Fa \supset Dx) \supset (y)[Fy \supset (\sim Gx \vee Fx)]$

3   *Universal Quantifiers*

When we use the universal quantifier (x), we are saying something about all of the individuals represented by the variable x in the quantifier. Just how many x's constitute *all* depends on how many things we want our language to be able to deal with. For instance, in some systems for arithmetic, we want the individual constants to denote numbers, so in such a system the number of x's will be infinite. The **domain of discourse** for a system for arithmetic is, so to speak, the world of numbers. Or, more specifically, it might be just, say, all of the positive integers. Usually, the domain of discourse is not explicitly specified but assumed to be "everything." Everything, obviously, includes quite a lot. It specifically includes all concrete (as opposed to abstract) things, such as people, trees, and logic books, but it also includes all of the numbers, as well as individual times and places. So to say, for example, $(x)Mx$ (with an unrestricted domain) is to say that the property designated by M applies to everything, including say, Hillary Rodham Clinton, the book you are presently reading, the number 5, and the city of Los Angeles. Obviously, few sentences will be correctly symbolized as $(x)Mx$ (with an unrestricted domain).

Now consider the sentence "All humans are mortal." It is correctly symbolized as $(x)(Hx \supset Mx)$ (where $Hx =$ "x is human" and $Mx =$ "x is mortal") and is read "For all x, if *x* is human, then *x* is mortal" or "Given any *x*, if *x* is human then *x* is mortal," which is roughly what the sentence "All humans are mortal" asserts.

Notice that "All humans are mortal" is not symbolized as $(x)(Hx \cdot Mx)$, for that says that given any *x*, it is both human and mortal, or, what amounts to the same thing, that all things are both human and mortal, and this is not what the sentence "All humans are mortal" means. (Note that "All humans are mortal" is true (alas!) whereas "All things are both human and mortal" is false.)

Remember, all material implications with false antecedents are true. So, given the truth conditions of "⊃", it *is* true of everything that *if* it is a human then it is mortal. This is true of humans, but it is also automatically true of all nonhumans as well. For example, it is true of one's desktop computer that if it is a human then it is mortal, because the antecedent of this material conditional is false—the computer is not a human. This conditional is true of the computer, it's true of any individual oak tree that exists, and its true of any number you care to pick out. So if we plug in, say, the individual constant *c* in place of the variable *x* in the formula $Hx \supset Mx$, where *c* designates a particular computer (or any other nonhuman), the resulting conditional $Hc \supset Mc$ will be true because its antecedent, *Hc*, is false.

We noted above that few ordinary true sentences would be correctly symbolized by the simple quantified formula $(x)Mx$, with an unrestricted domain. *Mx* would have to be a property that literally everything possesses (such as existence, perhaps). There are few properties that can be ascribed to just everything. One way to provisionally work around this would be to specify a more limited domain. So, for example, here are two equally accurate ways of symbolizing the sentence "All humans are mortal":

Domain: all humans   *Domain:* unrestricted
Symbolization: $(x) Mx$ *Symbolization:* $(x)(Hx \supset Mx)$

There are some important advantages to symbolizations with unrestricted domains, like the one on the right. Sometimes our ability to prove, say, that a particular argument is valid hinges upon displaying the logical structure that using an unrestricted domain makes possible. For example, in order to use a predicate logic proof (to be introduced in Chapter 8) to demonstrate the validity of the following obviously valid argument

1. All humans are mortal.
2. Not everything is mortal.
∴ Not everything is human.

it will be necessary to symbolize the first premise using an unrestricted quantifier.

So instead of restricting the domain and then producing a symbolization, we, in effect, place the restrictions within the sentence itself, as the antecedent of a conditional bound by a universal quantifier. This pattern is very common, so much so that if you produce a symbolization that is a universally quantified sentence, and the main connective of the sentence is not "⊃", you should suspect something may be wrong with your symbolization. There are exceptions, as some of the following examples illustrate, but the rule of thumb is that in symbolizing, the universal quantifier usually binds a sentence that has the horseshoe as its main connective.

Examples

Here are some English sentences and their correct symbolizations in predicate logic notation (using obvious abbreviations).

English Sentence	*Symbolization*
1. Everything is movable.	1. $(x)Mx$
2. Not everything is movable.	2. $\sim (x)Mx$
3. Nothing is movable.	3. $(x) \sim Mx$
4. Everything is immovable.	4. $(x) \sim Mx$

Notice that 3 and 4 are equivalent.

5. It's not true that everything is immovable.	5. $\sim (x) \sim Mx$
6. Sugar tastes sweet.	6. $(x)(Sx \supset Tx)$

In English, the quantifiers "all" and "some" often are omitted when context makes it clear what is intended.

7. If something is a piece of sugar, then it tastes sweet.	7. $(x)(Sx \supset Tx)$

Notice that 6 and 7 are equivalent.

8. Everything is either sweet or bitter.	8. $(x)(Sx \vee Bx)$
9. Either everything is sweet or else everything is bitter.	9. $(x)Sx \vee (x)Bx$

Notice that 8 and 9 are not equivalent.

10. Each person fears death.	10. $(x)(Px \supset Fx)$
11. Everyone fears death.	11. $(x)(Px \supset Fx)$

Notice that 10 and 11 are equivalent.

12. No one fears death.	12. $(x)(Px \supset \sim Fx)$
13. Not everyone fears death.	13. $\sim (x)(Px \supset Fx)$
14. All honest people fear death.	14. $(x)[(Px \cdot Hx) \supset Fx]$
15. Everyone who is honest fears death.	15. $(x)[(Px \cdot Hx) \supset Fx]$
16. Not all honest people fear death.	16. $\sim (x)[(Px \cdot Hx) \supset Fx]$
17. Anyone who doesn't fear death isn't honest.	17. $(x)[(Px \cdot \sim Fx) \supset \sim Hx)]$
18. Although all honest people fear death, Shirley MacLaine doesn't.	18. $(x)[(Px \cdot Hx) \supset Fx] \cdot \sim Fm$
19. Everyone either is honest or fears death.	19. $(x)[Px \supset (Hx \vee Fx)]$
20. It's false that no dishonest people fear death.	20. $\sim (x)[(Px \cdot \sim Hx) \supset \sim Fx]$

| 21. | Either all human beings are mortal or none are. | 21. | $(x)(Hx \supset Mx)$ $\lor (x)(Hx \supset \sim Mx)$ |
| 22. | If all human beings are mortal, then not to fear death indicates not being human. | 22. | $(x)(Hx \supset Mx) \supset$ $(x)(\sim Fx \supset \sim Hx)$ |

Of course, there is nothing sacred about the variable *x*. For instance, the sentence "Sugar tastes sweet" can be symbolized as $(y)(Sy \supset Ty)$ or $(z)(Sz \supset Tz)$, just as well as $(x)(Sx \supset Tx)$. All three of these sentences say the same thing. (In math we can write $(y + z) = (z + y)$ just as well as $(x + y) = (y + x)$; both of these formulas say the same thing.)

LG Exercise 6-3

Symbolize the following sentences, using the indicated letters.

1. All events have causes. (*Ex* = "*x* is an event"; *Cx* = "*x* has a cause")
2. Every event has a cause.
3. Not all events have causes.
4. No events have causes.
5. All natural events have causes. (*Nx* = "*x* is natural")
6. All events that have causes are natural.
7. No unnatural events have causes.
8. Anything that is caused is a natural event.
9. No natural events are uncaused.
10. Events are either natural or uncaused.
11. All miracles are unnatural events. (*Mx* = "*x* is a miracle")
12. Miracles have causes, but they aren't natural.
13. There are no uncaused events, but there are events that are miracles.
14. If there are no unnatural events, then there are no miracles.

LG Exercise 6-4

Symbolize the following sentences, letting *Px* = "*x* is (was) U.S. president"; *Ix* = "*x* is (was) well informed"; *r* = "Ronald Reagan"; and *b* = "George Bush."

1. All U.S. presidents have been well informed.
2. No U.S. presidents have been well informed.
3. Not all U.S. presidents have been well informed.
4. If Ronald Reagan wasn't well informed, then not all U.S. presidents have been well informed.
5. But not all U.S. presidents have been ill informed (not well informed) if George Bush was well informed.
6. Provided either Bush was well informed or Reagan not well informed, U.S. presidents have been neither all well informed nor all ill informed.

Now let Sx = "x is (was) a logic student"; Lx = "x is logical"; Px = "x is popular"; and a = "Art."

7. Logic students are logical.
8. No. Logic students definitely are not logical.
9. Well, not all logic students are logical.
10. Anyway, it's true that those who are logical are not popular.
11. So if all logic students are logical, none of them is popular.
12. But if not all of them are logical, then not all of them are unpopular.
13. Nor is it true that those who are unpopular all are illogical.
14. Now if those who are popular haven't studied logic, then if Art is illogical, he must have studied logic.
15. And if Art is illogical, it's false that logic students universally are logical or that the unpopular universally are logical.
16. Supposing Art is both unpopular and illogical, then logic students are neither all popular nor all logical.

4   *Existential Quantifiers*

As noted above, the existential quantifier, $(\exists x)$, is used to assert that some entities (at least one) have a given property. Thus, $(\exists x)Hx$ can be used to symbolize the sentence "Something is heavy" or the sentence "At least one thing is heavy," and is read "For some x, x is heavy," or "There is an x such that x is heavy," or "For some x, x is heavy." $(\exists x)Hx$ is as simple as an existentially quantified sentence can be. Other equally simple sentences are "Something is expensive," $(\exists x)Ex$, "Something is important," $(\exists x)Ix$, and so on. Adding negation increases complexity. For example, the expression $(\exists x) \sim Hx$ symbolizes the sentence "Something is not heavy," and the expression $\sim (\exists x)Hx$ the sentence "It's false that something is heavy." (Note that these two are not equivalent!)

More complicated symbolizations are obtained in other ways. Thus, to symbolize the sentence "Something is both heavy and expensive," conjoin Hx (for "x is heavy") with Ex (for "x is expensive") to get $(Hx \cdot Ex)$, and then add an existential quantifier to get $(\exists x)(Hx \cdot Ex)$. Similarly, to symbolize "Something is both sweet and fattening," conjoin Sx (for "x is sweet") with Fx (for "x is fattening") to get $(Sx \cdot Fx)$, and then add an existential quantifier to get $(\exists x)(Sx \cdot Fx)$.

Examples

Here are some other English sentences and their symbolizations using existential quantifiers (letting Px = "x is a person" and using other obvious abbreviations).

	English Sentence		*Symbolization*
1.	Some people are honest.	1.	$(\exists x)(Px \cdot Hx)$
2.	Some people are not honest.	2.	$(\exists x)(Px \cdot \sim Hx)$

3. Some honest people are mistreated.
4. Some people are liars and thieves.
5. It's not true that some people are honest.
6. Some people are neither honest nor truthful.
7. Some things are neither expensive nor worthwhile.
8. Some people are liars, and some are thieves.
9. Some thieving liars are caught, and some aren't.

3. $(\exists x)[(Px \cdot Hx) \cdot Mx]$
4. $(\exists x)[Px \cdot (Lx \cdot Tx)]$
5. $\sim (\exists x)(Px \cdot Hx)$
6. $(\exists x)[Px \cdot \sim (Hx \vee Tx)]$, or $(\exists x)[Px \cdot (\sim Hx \cdot \sim Tx)]$
7. $(\exists x) \sim (Ex \vee Wx)$, or $(\exists x)(\sim Ex \cdot \sim Wx)$
8. $(\exists x)(Px \cdot Lx) \cdot (\exists x)(Px \cdot Tx)$
9. $(\exists x)[(Tx \cdot Lx) \cdot Cx] \cdot (\exists x)[(Tx \cdot Lx) \cdot \sim Cx]$

LG Exercise 6-5

Symbolize the following sentences, using the indicated symbols as abbreviations.

1. Some athletes are overpaid. ($Ax =$ "x is an athlete"; $Ox =$ "x is overpaid")
2. Some athletes aren't overpaid.
3. It's not true that there are overpaid athletes.
4. Lots of elected officials are overpaid. ($Ex =$ "x is an elected official")
5. But somewhere there is at least one who is not overpaid.
6. There are PTA members who are parents and others who are teachers. ($Ax =$ "x is a PTA member"; $Px =$ "x is a parent"; and $Tx =$ "x is a teacher")
7. And some members are parents and teachers.
8. But teachers aren't all parents, by any means.
9. So the PTA has members who aren't parents and members who aren't teachers.
10. There are a few French restaurants that actually serve French fries. ($Rx =$ "x is a French restaurant"; $Sx =$ "x serves French fries")
11. Most of them serve Dijon mustard along with the fries. ($Dx =$ "x serves Dijon mustard with the fries")
12. But there are hardly any French restaurants anywhere that serve French's mustard with their fries. ($Fx =$ "x serves French's mustard with fries")
13. And, of course, French restaurants that serve Dijon don't serve French's.
14. From which it follows that the ones serving French's don't serve Dijon.
15. So, there're some French restaurants where you can get French fries and Dijon mustard, but not French's, a very few that serve French's mustard with their fries, but no Dijon, and a whole bunch that don't serve French fries at all.

5 *Basic Predicate Logic Symbolizations*

In sentential logic you learned to symbolize by learning how to deal with common patterns that frequently occur in English. For example, you learned that English sentences with the form "Neither A nor B" can be symbolized as $\sim A \cdot \sim B$, and sentences of the form "A, unless *B*" can be symbolized $\sim B \supset A$. You should approach predicate logic symbolization in the same way. Let's begin with four basic patterns we have already seen in previous sections.

All A's are B's

These sentences are ones where every individual of a certain kind is said to have some property or other. Such sentences commonly begin with words like "all," "every," or "any." Such sentences can be straightforwardly symbolized using the universal quantifier. Here are some more examples:

English sentence	**Symbolization**
1. All dogs have fleas.	$(x)(Dx \supset Fx)$
2. Every dog has fleas.	$(x)(Dx \supset Fx)$
3. Dogs have fleas.	$(x)(Dx \supset Fx)$

Some A's are B's

The sentences that follow are easily symbolized using the existential quantifier. These are sentences that ascribe a property to some but not all members of a group.

4. Some dogs have fleas.	$(\exists x)(Dx \cdot Fx)$
5. There are dogs that have fleas.	$(\exists x)(Dx \cdot Fx)$

No A's are B's (or equivalently, all A's are not B's)

Sentences that say that no individual of a certain kind has a property are equivalent to those that say all individuals of that kind lack the property. So both of these kinds of sentences can be symbolized either as negations of existentially quantified sentences or as universally quantified sentences with a negation sign before the consequent of the bound conditional. We provide both kinds of symbolizations for our examples:

6. No dogs have fleas.	$\sim (\exists x)(Dx \cdot Fx)$ or $(x)(Dx \supset \sim Fx)$
7. There aren't any dogs that have fleas.	$\sim (\exists x)(Dx \cdot Fx)$ or $(x)(Dx \supset \sim Fx)$
8. Dogs do not have fleas.	$\sim (\exists x)(Dx \cdot Fx)$ or $(x)(Dx \supset \sim Fx)$

Not all A's are B's (some A's are not B's)

Sentences having the pattern "Not all *A*'s are *B*'s" (for example, "Not all leopards have stripes") are logically equivalent to sentences having the pattern "Some *A*'s are not *B*'s" ("Some leopards do not have stripes"). You will probably find it most natural to symbolize the first of these sentences using a universal quantifier and the second using an existential. Either way of symbolizing is perfectly acceptable, so again we illustrate both:

9. Not all dogs have fleas. $\sim (x)(Dx \supset Fx)$ or
                                                $(\exists x)(Dx \cdot \sim Fx)$
10. Not every dog has fleas. $\sim (x)(Dx \supset Fx)$ or
                                                $(\exists x)(Dx \cdot \sim Fx)$
11. Some dogs don't have fleas. $\sim (x)(Dx \supset Fx)$ or
                                                $(\exists x)(Dx \cdot \sim Fx)$

Most of the sentences you will be asked to symbolize in this chapter are simply elabora-tions of these four basic sentence patterns. Complex sentences commonly just build on these patterns. So to symbolize "Wealthy people should pay more taxes and receive fewer Social Security benefits," the first step is to realize that this sentence is just a complex all A's are B's kind of sentence. This gives you the basic form $(x)(\underline{\hspace{1cm}} \supset \underline{\hspace{1cm}})$, and you simply fill in the blanks with the subject and the predicate. In this case both the subject and the predicate are compound, so we can fill in the blanks as follows: $(x)[(Wx \cdot Px) \supset (Tx \cdot Sx)]$.

6   *The Square of Opposition*

It is worth noting that any sentence that can be symbolized with a universal quantifier can be symbolized with an existential quantifier, and vice versa. For example, you can symbol-ize "All dogs have fleas" using the existential quantifier as $\sim (\exists x)(Dx \cdot \sim Fx)$ and "Some dogs have fleas" can be symbolized with the universal quantifier as $\sim (x)(Dx \supset \sim Fx)$. This means our symbols are redundant—we could dispense with one of the two quantifiers and still be able to symbolize just as accurately (though not as easily).

A traditional way of illustrating the relationship between the quantifiers is known as the **square of oppostion:**

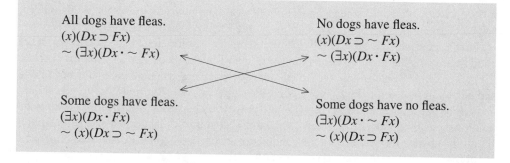

All dogs have fleas.
$(x)(Dx \supset Fx)$
$\sim (\exists x)(Dx \cdot \sim Fx)$

No dogs have fleas.
$(x)(Dx \supset \sim Fx)$
$\sim (\exists x)(Dx \cdot Fx)$

Some dogs have fleas.
$(\exists x)(Dx \cdot Fx)$
$\sim (x)(Dx \supset \sim Fx)$

Some dogs have no fleas.
$(\exists x)(Dx \cdot \sim Fx)$
$\sim (x)(Dx \supset Fx)$

Each of the four basic sentence patterns reviewed in the previous section are represented in the square. For each sentence, two equivalent symbolizations are provided, one with a universal quantifier and one with an existential quantifier. The sentences connected by the arrows contradict one another. (Notice that the second symbolization is simply the denial of the first symbolization at the other end of each arrow.)

A good way to gain additional practice at symbolizing is to use the other quantifier to produce a second, equivalent symbolization.

7   *Common Pitfalls in Symbolizing with Quantifiers*

Some English expressions that look like compound subjects or predicates should not be symbolized that way. "Some professional athletes excel in both football and baseball" can be symbolized (using the obvious abbreviations) as $(\exists x)[Px \cdot (Fx \cdot Bx)]$. You should not symbolize the "professional athletes" portion of this sentence as $Px \cdot Ax$ (where Px = "x is professional" and Ax = "x is an athlete") because one can be professional and an athlete without being a professional athlete.

Also be careful with sentences that contain the words "a" or "any." These particles sometimes operate logically just like the particle "all," but often they do not, as the following sentences illustrate:

1.	A barking dog never bites.	$(x)[(Dx \cdot Bx) \supset \sim Ix]$
2.	A barking dog is in the road.	$(\exists x)[(Dx \cdot Bx) \cdot Rx]$
3.	Anyone is welcome to enroll.	$(x)(Px \supset Wx)$
4.	There is not anyone here.	$\sim (\exists x)(Px \cdot Hx)$

So there is no general rule of thumb for how to symbolize these sentences.

Most other frequently occurring sentence patterns are fairly easy to symbolize. But a few are tricky. For instance, the sentence "Women and children are exempt from the draft" is correctly symbolized as $(x)[(Wx \lor Cx) \supset Ex]$, *not* as $(x)[(Wx \cdot Cx) \supset Ex]$. For the latter asserts that all things that are *both* women *and* children are exempt, whereas the original sentence states that all things that are *either* women *or* children are exempt.

In this case the "and" in the antecedent of the sentence misleads us into using the symbol "·" instead of "∨". However, there is a fairly straightforward symbolization of the sentence that contains the symbol "·", namely, $(x)(Wx \supset Ex) \cdot (x)(Cx \supset Ex)$. For to say that all women are exempt from the draft and all children are exempt from the draft is to say exactly that all women and children are exempt from the draft. And, indeed, $(x)(Wx \supset Ex) \cdot (x)(Cx \supset Ex)$ and $(x)[(Wx \lor Cx) \supset Ex]$ are logically equivalent.

Finally, consider the superficially similar sentence "Some dogs and cats do not make good house pets." Again, do not let the word "and" mislead you into a symbolization like $(\exists x)[(Dx \cdot Cx) \cdot \sim Gx]$ for this symbolization says that there is something that is both a dog and a cat and (not surprisingly) not a good house pet as well. But in this case, you should *not* symbolize this sentence as $(\exists x)[(Dx \lor Cx) \cdot \sim Gx]$ because on this symbolization the sentence would be true if, say, some dogs but no cats failed to be good house pets. So you should symbolize the sentence as the conjunction of two existentially quantified sentences, as follows: $(\exists x)(Dx \cdot \sim Gx) \cdot (\exists x)(Cx \cdot \sim Gx)$.

🚶 Walk-Through: Predicate Logic Symbolizations

A great many sentences simply predicate some property (simple or complex) of some or all individuals of a certain sort. A good way to symbolize these sentences is to first decide on the subject (who is the sentence about?), then supply the appropriate quantifier (is the sentence saying something about some or all of these individuals?), and finally fill in the predicate (what does it say about them?). For example, take the sentence "Some shifty-eyed lawyers are actually hard-working and honest." Obviously this sentence is about lawyers who have shifty eyes. This gives us

$Lx \cdot Sx$

We then supply the quantifier (and the connective that characteristically accompanies that quantifier).

$(\exists x) (Lx \cdot Sx) \cdot$

We complete our symbolization by filling in the predicate half of our sentence.

$(\exists x) [(Lx \cdot Sx) \cdot (Hx \cdot Wx)]$

Suppose our sentence is "Not all infomercials are about hair loss or psychic predictions." Who is this sentence about?

Ix

Some or all?

$\sim (x) Ix \supset$

What does it say about them?

$\sim (x)[Ix \supset (Hx \vee Px)]$

Examples

1.	All students who attend college are well educated.	$(x)[(Sx \cdot Cx) \supset Ex]$ or $\sim (\exists x)[(Sx \cdot Cx) \cdot \sim Ex]$
2.	All men and women are adults.	$(x)[(Mx \vee Wx) \supset Ax]$ or $\sim (\exists x)[(Mx \vee Wx) \cdot \sim Ax]$
3.	All lawyers are intelligent and shifty.	$(x)[Lx \supset (Ix \cdot Sx)]$ or $\sim (\exists x)[Lx \cdot \sim (Ix \cdot Sx)]$
4.	All doctors are intelligent or high-priced.	$(x)[Dx \supset (Ix \vee Hx)]$ or $\sim (\exists x)[Dx \cdot \sim (Ix \vee Hx)]$
5.	Not all doctors are money-grubbers.	$\sim (x)(Dx \supset Mx)$ or $(\exists x)(Dx \cdot \sim Mx)$
6.	No doctors are money-grubbers.	$(x)(Dx \supset \sim Mx)$ or $\sim (\exists x)(Dx \cdot Mx)$
7.	No one who attends college is ignorant.	$(x)[(Px \cdot Ax) \supset \sim Ix]$ or $\sim (\exists x)[(Px \cdot Ax) \cdot Ix]$
8.	There are no ignorant people who have attended college.	$(x)[(Ix \cdot Px) \supset \sim Ax]$ or $\sim (\exists x)[(Ix \cdot Px) \cdot Ax]$

LC Exercise 6-6

Symbolize the following so as to reveal as much logical structure as possible. Indicate the meanings of your abbreviations.

1. All marsupials have pouches.
2. Any animal that has a pouch is a marsupial.
3. Actually, not all marsupials have pouches.
4. Any animal without a pouch is no marsupial.
5. Kangaroos and opossums are both marsupials.
6. Wombats and bandicoots are marsupials that are not well known.
7. Koala bears are not really bears at all.
8. If all marsupials are cute and furry, then opossums are cute and furry.
9. Marsupials can be found in their natural habitats in both Australia and North America.
10. Neither aardvarks nor armadillos are marsupials.
11. Female marsupials have pouches, but males don't.
12. Armadillos are neither marsupials nor reptiles.
13. Any physician who is patient has plenty of patients.
14. There are physicians who are competent but lack tact.
15. Everyone who cheats feels guilty or should feel guilty.
16. Not every soldier who fought in Vietnam is a hero.
17. All Girl Scouts and Boy Scouts are to be congratulated by President Clinton.
18. Some Girl Scouts and Boy Scouts are to be congratulated by President Clinton.
19. The president will meet with dignitaries from China and Japan.
20. Neither all of the Democrats nor all of the Republicans supported the president's tax plan.

LC Exercise 6-7

Symbolize the following into English, being as colloquial as possible. Let Tx = "x is a TV newscaster"; Px = "x has a pleasant personality"; Ex = "x is a political expert"; b = "Barbara Walters"; r = "Dan Rather"; and m = "John Madden."

1. $(\exists x)(Tx \cdot Px)$
2. $(\exists x)(Tx \cdot \sim Ex)$
3. $\sim (\exists x)(Tx \cdot Ex)$
4. $(x)(Tx \supset \sim Ex)$
5. $\sim (x)(Tx \supset Ex)$
6. $(x)[(Ex \cdot \sim Px) \supset \sim Tx]$
7. $(\exists x)[Tx \cdot \sim (Px \cdot Ex)]$
8. $(\exists x)[Tx \cdot (Px \lor Ex)]$
9. $(x)(Tx \supset Ex) \supset \sim Tb$
10. $Tr \supset \sim (y)[(Ty \cdot Py) \supset Ey]$
11. $(Pm \cdot \sim Em) \supset \sim Tm$
12. $(x)[Tx \supset (Px \cdot Ex)] \supset \sim (Tr \lor Tb)$

8 *Expansions*

In the explanation above, we construed quantifiers as stating how many. But perhaps a more revealing way to think of them is as shorthand versions of much longer sentences of a certain kind.

Imagine a limited universe containing, say, only four individual entities. What would quantified sentences assert in such a universe? For instance, what would the sentence $(x)Fx$ assert? The answer (roughly) is that it would assert that *Fa* and *Fb* and *Fc* and *Fd*. (This is only roughly true because universally quantified sentences also assert that the items listed are all of the items there are [in the universe of discourse], and merely listing the items, even though all in fact are listed, does not say that all are listed.) In other words, it would assert that $(Fa \cdot Fb) \cdot (Fc \cdot Fd)$. Thus in this limited universe, the symbolization $(x)Fx$ would be shorthand for the expression $(Fa \cdot Fb) \cdot (Fc \cdot Fd)$, called the **expansion** of $(x)Fx$ with respect to that limited universe.

Of course our logic is applicable to the real universe, which contains many more than four individual entities. Can we construe quantified sentences in a universally applicable logic as a shorthand way of writing very long conjunctions? The answer is that we *could* construe them in this way if (1) there were only a finite number of entities in the real universe, and (2) we had a name in our language for every entity. But unfortunately we do not have a name for every entity in the real universe of discourse, and the number of entities we want to talk about frequently is not finite. For instance, in arithmetic, we want to be able to assert the sentence "Every even number is divisible by 2," that is, assert that 2 is divisible by 2, *and* 4 is divisible by 2, *and* 6 is divisible by 2, and so on. But since the number of numbers is infinite, we can't actually write down a conjunction listing each number that is equivalent to the sentence "Every even number is divisible by 2." Instead we can use a universal quantifier to symbolize that sentence. For instance, using obvious abbreviations, we can symbolize it as $(x)[(Nx \cdot Ex) \supset Dx]$. So we cannot say that a universally quantified sentence is *equivalent* to any very long conjunction that we might construct. Nevertheless, it is intuitively helpful to think of sentences such as $(x)Fx$ and $(x)(Hx \supset Mx)$ as shorthand for very long conjunctions.

Now consider a sentence containing an *existential* quantifier, say, the sentence $(\exists x)Fx$. In a limited universe containing only three objects, this sentence asserts not that *Fa* and *Fb* and *Fc*, since that is what is asserted by $(x)Fx$, but rather that *Fa* or *Fb* or *Fc*. So its expansion in this limited universe is $[(Fa \vee Fb) \vee Fc]$.

Examples

The following are expansions for a language containing three individual constants: *a, b,* and *c.*

1. *Symbolization:* $(\exists x) \sim Fx$
    Expansion: $\sim Fa \vee (\sim Fb \vee \sim Fc)$

2. *Symbolization:* $\sim (\exists x)Fx$
   Expansion: $\sim [Fa \vee (Fb \vee Fc)]$
3. *Symbolization:* $(x)(Fx \supset Gx)$
   Expansion: $(Fa \supset Ga) \cdot [(Fb \supset Gb) \cdot (Fc \supset Gc)]$
4. *Symbolization:* $(\exists x) \sim (Fx \cdot Gx)$
   Expansion: $\sim (Fa \cdot Ga) \vee [\sim (Fb \cdot Gb) \vee \sim (Fc \cdot Gc)]$
5. *Symbolization:* $(x)[(Fx \cdot Gx) \supset Hx]$
   Expansion: $[(Fa \cdot Ga) \supset Ha] \cdot \{[(Fb \cdot Gb) \supset Hb] \cdot [(Fc \cdot Gc) \supset Hc]\}$
6. *Symbolization:* $(\exists x)[(Fx \cdot Gx) \vee Hx]$
   Expansion: $[(Fa \cdot Ga) \vee Ha] \vee \{[(Fb \cdot Gb) \vee Hb] \vee [(Fc \cdot Gc) \vee Hc]\}$

LC Exercise 6-8

Construct expansions in a two-individual universe of discourse for the following sentences.

1. $(x)(Fx \cdot Gx)$
2. $(\exists x)(Fx \vee Gx)$
3. $(x)[Fx \supset (Gx \vee Hx)]$
4. $(\exists x)[Fx \cdot (Gx \vee Hx)]$
5. $(x) \sim (Fx \supset Gx)$
6. $(\exists x) \sim (Fx \vee Gx)$
7. $\sim (x)(Fx \supset Gx)$
8. $\sim (\exists x)(Fx \vee Gx)$
9. $(x)[Fx \supset (Gx \supset Hx)]$
10. $(x)(Fx \supset \sim (Gx \cdot Hx)]$
11. $(\exists x)[(Fx \cdot Gx) \vee (Hx \cdot Kx)]$
12. $(x)[(Fx \cdot Gx) \supset (Hx \cdot Kx)]$
13. $(\exists x) \sim [(Fx \supset Gx) \vee (Fx \supset Hx)]$
14. $\sim (x) \sim [(Fx \cdot Gx) \cdot \sim (Hx \cdot Kx)]$

Sentences of the form "Some _____ are _____," such as the sentence "Some humans are mortal," are often symbolized incorrectly by beginners. The correct symbolization is $(\exists x)(Hx \cdot Mx)$, because this sentence asserts that there is something, *x,* that is both human and mortal. The temptation is to symbolize it as $(\exists x)(Hx \supset Mx)$, by analogy with the symbolization of the sentence "All humans are mortal," which *is* correctly symbolized as $(x)(Hx \supset Mx)$. But in this case the similar grammatical structure of the two English sentences is misleading.

To see the difference between the sentence $(\exists x)(Hx \cdot Mx)$ and the sentence $(\exists x)(Hx \supset Mx)$, examine their expansions, namely, $[(Ha \cdot Ma) \vee (Hb \cdot Mb)] \vee \ldots$ and $[(Ha \supset Ma) \vee (Hb \supset Mb)] \vee \ldots$ (the dots are used in the sense of "and so on," or "etc." since we cannot completely write down an infinitely long conjunction or disjunction). The expansion $[(Ha \cdot Ma) \vee (Hb \cdot Mb)] \vee \ldots$ is true because there are some things that are both human and mortal, but the expansion $[(Ha \supset Ma) \vee (Hb \supset Mb)] \vee \ldots$ would be true even if there were no humans at all, mortal or immortal. The reason it would be true is this: Suppose *a* denotes some item that is not human. Then the disjunct $Ha \supset Ma$ is true, because its antecedent Ha is false. Therefore, because one of its disjuncts is true, the whole long disjunction $[(Ha \supset Ma) \vee (Hb \supset Mb)] \vee \ldots$ is true. Its truth has nothing to do with human mortality; it would be true even if there were no human beings. The reason symbolizations having the same form as $(\exists x)(Hx \supset Mx)$ are almost always incorrect is that such sentences will be trivially true so long as the property in the antecedent (Hx in this case) is not possessed by everything. But the expansion $[(Ha \cdot Ma) \vee (Hb \cdot Mb)] \vee \ldots$ would not be true if there were no human beings, because if that were the case, then all of its disjuncts would be false. (If there were no human beings in the universe, then $(Ha \cdot Ma)$ would be false, $(Hb \cdot Mb)$ would be false, $(Hc \cdot Mc)$ would be false, and indeed every disjunct of the infinitely long disjunction in question would be false, so that the infinitely long disjunction itself would be false.) So the correct symbolization for "Some humans are mortal" is $(\exists x)(Hx \cdot Mx)$ and not $(\exists x)(Hx \supset Mx)$.

9   *Symbolizing "Only," "None But," and "Unless"*

A good deal of care is needed in symbolizing sentences containing words or phrases such as "only," "none but," and "unless."

Consider a statement a professor might make in the classroom: (1) "Only those who study will pass the test." Restricting the universe of discourse to the professor's students, this sentence is correctly symbolized as $(x)(Px \supset Sx)$. It is tempting to symbolize it incorrectly as $(x)(Sx \supset Px)$, thus interpreting it to mean that all who study will pass. But to say that *only* those who study will pass does not (unfortunately) guarantee that *all* of those who do study will pass. Suppose it is a very difficult test and that some students who study pass and some do not, but no one who does not study passes. Then the sentence "All who study will pass the test" is false (since some who study do not pass), whereas the professor's sentence "Only those who study will pass the test" turns out to be true. Hence, the symbolization $(x)(Sx \supset Px)$ cannot be the correct symbolization of the professor's statement.

Another way to look at the problem is this: To say that only those who study will pass is to say that anyone who does not study will not pass. Since the sentence "All who do not study will not pass the test" is correctly symbolized as $(x)(\sim Sx \supset \sim Px)$, the equivalent sentence (1) "Only those who study will pass" also is correctly symbolized in this way. And since $(x)(\sim Sx \supset \sim Px)$ is equivalent to $(x)(Px \supset Sx)$ (by Contraposition), it follows that (1) is correctly symbolized as $(x)(Px \supset Sx)$.

Sentences containing the phrase "none but" are handled in a similar fashion. Thus, the sentences "Only the good die young" and "None but the good die young" are equivalent and can each be symbolized $(x)(Yx \supset Gx)$.

The phrase "none but" in a sentence of this kind means roughly the same thing as the phrase "none except." For instance, the sentence "None but the ignorant are happy" means the same thing as the sentence "None, except the ignorant, are happy." Therefore, both of these sentences are symbolized as $(x)(Hx \supset Ix)$.

English usage allows us to use the word "unless" to produce sentences that are equivalent to the ones we've just been discussing. For instance, instead of saying "Only those who study will pass" or "None but those who study will pass," we can say "No one will pass unless they study." (We use "they" here to avoid the masculine pronoun "he." Some object to this usage as ungrammatical. An alternative is "No one will pass unless he or she studies.") "Without" sometimes performs a similar function in English, as in "No one will pass without studying." All of these sentences say roughly the same thing and hence for our purposes can be symbolized in the same way, namely, $(x)(Px \supset Sx)$.

Remember that "unless" also often functions as a truth-functional connective, as explained in Chapter 2. So a sentence like "No one will get dessert unless everyone quiets down" should be symbolized $\sim (x)(Px \supset \sim Qx) \supset \sim (\exists x)(Px \cdot Dx)$. The word "if" has a similar dual usage. It can function as a truth-functional connective as in "If everyone in the class studies, no one in the class will fail" (symbolized $(x)(Cx \supset Sx) \supset \sim (\exists x)(Cx \cdot Fx)$) and can also be used to make generalizations, as in "If H$_2$O freezes it expands"— symbolized $(x)[(Hx \cdot Fx) \supset Ex]$.

Examples

1. Only celebrities can be elected president.
   $(x)(Ex \supset Cx)$ or $\sim (\exists x)(Ex \cdot \sim Cx)$
2. No one can be elected president unless he or she is a celebrity.
   $(x)(Ex \supset Cx)$ or $\sim (\exists x)(Ex \cdot \sim Cx)$
3. None but celebrities can be elected president.
   $(x)(Ex \supset Cx)$ or $\sim (\exists x)(Ex \cdot \sim Cx)$
4. Only glib politicians can be elected president.
   $(x)[Ex \supset (Gx \cdot Px)]$ or $\sim (\exists x)[Ex \cdot \sim (Gx \cdot Px)]$
5. None but glib politicians can be elected president.
   $(x)[Ex \supset (Gx \cdot Px)]$ or $\sim (\exists x)[Ex \cdot \sim (Gx \cdot Px)]$
6. No one can be elected president unless that person is a glib politician.
   $(x)[(Ex \supset (Gx \cdot Px)]$
7. No one can be elected president unless someone is nominated.
   $\sim (\exists x)(Px \cdot Nx) \supset (x)(Px \supset \sim Ex)$

L◖ Exercise 6-9

Symbolize the following and indicate your use of abbreviations.

1. Only those students who don't study regularly will flunk logic.
2. There won't be any students who flunk logic, except those who don't study regularly.
3. The gates of heaven shall open only to the poor.
4. None but the poor shall enter heaven.
5. No one will die of lung cancer unless they smoke tobacco.
6. Only those who smoke tobacco will die of lung cancer.
7. Unfortunately, it is not true that only those who smoke tobacco will die of lung cancer.
8. Unless John quits smoking, his entire family is at risk for lung cancer.
9. Unless all elephants are protected, all elephants are doomed.
10. If all elephants are not protected, all elephants are doomed.
11. If a rhinoceros feels threatened, it may charge.
12. A rhinoceros is a peaceful animal, unless threatened.

L◖ Exercise 6-10

Symbolize the following sayings so as to reveal as much of their structure as possible and indicate the meanings of the abbreviations you use.

1. There is no free lunch.—Al Smith(?)
2. All sin is a form of lying.—St. Augustine
3. If a thing is worth doing, it is worth doing badly.—G. K. Chesterton
4. All that glitters is not gold. (*Lx* = "*x* glitters"; *Gx* = "*x* is gold")
5. And all that is gold does not glitter.
6. Sometimes a cigar is just a cigar.—Sigmund Freud
7. He who can, does. He who cannot, teaches.—George Bernard Shaw (among others)
8. The only completely consistent people are the dead.—Aldous Huxley
9. You have to be over 30 to enjoy Proust.—Gore Vidal
10. No one but a blockhead writes except for money.—Samuel Johnson

Now symbolize the following sentences, letting *Px* = "*x* is a person"; *Bx* = "*x* is brilliant"; *Sx* = "*x* is a complete scoundrel"; *Cx* = "*x* is charismatic"; *Lx* = "*x* succeeds in life":

11. There are some brilliant people who are complete scoundrels.
12. And some of these scoundrels are quite charismatic.
13. Fortunately, most brilliant scoundrels aren't very charismatic.
14. And some of the charismatic ones aren't very bright.
15. Scoundrels who aren't either brilliant or charismatic always are failures (don't succeed) in life.
16. If plenty of scoundrels are failures, then at least a few people who aren't brilliant are scoundrels.
17. But in fact, no brilliant people are scoundrels, or failures in life for that matter.
18. Having every single scoundrel be brilliant would result in failed lives for the rest of us.
19. And having everyone be a scoundrel would result in life being "nasty, brutish, and short" (a complete failure) for everyone.
20. Of course, even if there were no scoundrels whatsoever, there would be people whose lives would be complete failures—along with those who would lead successful lives.

Key terms

bound variable: A variable within the scope of a relevant quantifier. For example, in the expression (*x*)*Fx* · *Gy*, the variable *x*, but not the variable *y*, is bound by the (*x*) quantifier.

domain of discourse: The items we want our statements to deal with. For instance, in arithmetic, the domain of discourse is the world of numbers. In daily life, the usual domain of discourse is implicitly taken to be everything.

existential quantifier: The symbols (∃*x*), (∃*y*), and so on, as used in sentences such as (∃*x*)(*Fx* · *Gx*) and (∃*y*)(*Fy* ∨ *Gy*). (∃*x*) can be read as "for some *x*," or "there is an *x* such that . . ."

expansion: A quantified sentence "spelled out" for a particular domain of individuals; for example, the expansion of the sentence

(*x*)(*Fx* ∨ *Gx*) for a domain of two individuals, *a* and *b*, is (*Fa* ∨ *Ga*) · (*Fb* ∨ *Gb*), and the expansion of the sentence (∃*x*)(*Fx* · *Gx*) for the same domain is (*Fa* · *Ga*) ∨ (*Fb* · *Gb*).

free variable: An unbound variable. A variable not within the scope of a relevant quantifier. For example, in the expression (*x*)*Fx* ⊃ (*Gx* ∨ *Dy*), the second *x* variable and the *y* variables are free.

individual constants: The small letters *a* through *t* used to denote particular individuals, as opposed to properties; for example, *a* may be used to designate the person Art.

individual variables: The small letters *u* through *z* used as variables replaceable by individual constants.

predicate logic: The logic that uses quantifiers, property constants, and individual constants and variables to symbolize the interior structure of atomic as well as compound sentences. Synonym: *quantifier logic.*

property constants: Capital letters used to denote particular properties, as opposed to individuals; for example, the *F* in (*x*)*Fx* used to denote the property, say, of being friendly.

quantifier: A symbol used (roughly) to state how many items (all or some) in the universe of discourse are being referred to. (See also *universal quantifier* and *existential quantifier.*)

relational property: A property that holds between two (or more) individual entities, for example, the property "_____ is next to _____ ," which can be symbolized as *Nxy.*

scope (of a quantifier): The extent of an expression quantified by a quantifier. For example, the scope of the (*x*) quantifier in $\sim$ (*x*) $\sim$ (*Fx* $\supset$ *Gx*) is $\sim$ (*Fx* $\supset$ *Gx*).

square of opposition: A diagram used to illustrate several of the inferential relationships (such as contradictoriness and contrariety) holding between categorical propositions.

universal quantifier: The expressions (*x*), (*y*), and so on, as used in sentences such as (*x*)(*Hx* $\supset$ *Mx*) and (*y*)*Fy.* (*x*) can be read as "for all *x*" or "for every *x*."

Chapter Seven

Predicate
Logic Invalidity

---

1   *Interpretations in Predicate Logic*

We used the idea of an **interpretation** to explain each fundamental concept as we explored the semantics of sentential logic. The good news is that all of these basic definitions remain the same in predicate logic. An argument is **valid** in predicate logic if and only if there is no interpretation on which the premises are true and the conclusion is false, sentences are **consistent** just in case there is some interpretation on which they are all true, two sentences are **logically equivalent** if and only if there is no interpretation on which one is true and the other false, and so on.

What is different is that more is involved in specifying an interpretation in predicate logic. In sentential logic we could typically list every one of a sentence's interpretations in short order. We used a truth table to do just this. But in predicate logic countless many interpretations are possible for any sentence. To provide an interpretation in predicate logic we must do three things in addition to assigning truth-values to any atomic sentential logic letters our sentence may contain. First we must specify a domain. Second, for each individual constant we must specify which individual in the domain it designates. Third, we must specify the meaning of each predicate constant so that it is clear which individuals in the domain have that property and which do not. In other words, an interpretation provides all of the information needed to determine a sentence's truth-value.

This sounds complicated, but a few examples should help to make the idea clear. Here are a number of different interpretations of the simple sentence $(x)(Ax \supset Bx)$:

Domain: unrestricted
Ax: x is an elephant
Bx: x has a trunk

On this interpretation, the sentence says that every elephant has a trunk. Here is another completely different interpretation, again using an unrestricted domain:

Domain: unrestricted
Ax: x is a professor
Bx: x is an astronaut

Here is another, this time with the domain restricted to the set of natural numbers:

Domain: natural numbers
Ax: x is an even number
Bx: x is divisible by 2

All of our examples so far have had infinitely large domains. But on other interpretations the domain can be much smaller, such as the following:

Domain: citrus fruits
Ax: x is orange
Bx: x contains vitamin C

Is this sentence true or false? Although in an unrestricted domain, it is false that all orange things contain vitamin C, the sentence is true on this interpretation because it is true that all orange citrus fruits contain vitamin C.

Finally, the domain can be very small indeed, as the following illustrates:

Domain: one yellow pencil, one green textbook
Ax: x is a pencil
Bx: x is yellow

Note that on this interpretation the sentence is true because it correctly states that all pencils (in this domain) are yellow.

Exercise 7-1

Provide three completely different interpretations for each of the following sentences. On one interpretation use an unrestricted domain, on the second let the domain be the positive integers $(1, 2, 3, \ldots)$, and on the third let the domain consist of just two objects (specify the two objects you choose). Provide at least one interpretation on which the sentence is true and at least one on which it is false.

1. $(\exists x)(Ax \cdot Bx)$
2. $(\exists x)(Ax \cdot \sim Bx)$
3. $(x)(Ax \supset \sim Bx)$
4. $\sim (x)(Ax \supset Bx)$
5. $(x)[(Ax \lor Bx) \supset Cx]$
6. $(\exists x)[(Ax \cdot Bx) \cdot \sim Cx]$
7. $(\exists x)Gx \supset \sim (x)(Bx \supset Gx)$
8. $(x)(Ax \supset Bx) \supset (\exists x)(Bx \cdot Cx)$

2   *Proving Invalidity*

As we pointed out when discussing sentential logic, failure to find a valid proof for an argument does not justify concluding that the argument is invalid (because we may lack sufficient ingenuity or simply have overlooked the proof). Nor can we prove an argument is not valid by deriving the negation of its conclusion from its premises (because if its premises are *inconsistent,* then we can validly infer both to the conclusion and its negation). Instead, to show that an argument is invalid we need only show that it is possible for the premises all to be true and the conclusion false. To do so we produce a counterexample, an *interpretation* that makes the premises all true and the conclusion false. Producing such an interpretation shows that the argument is invalid no matter what the actual truth-value of the premises or conclusion may be. It is the *possible* truth-values of the premises and conclusion that are important here, not the *actual* truth-values of these claims.

In sentential logic, finding a counterexample was relatively straightforward. For example, to show that

1. $(A \supset B) \supset C$
2. $\sim (B \cdot C) / \therefore \sim A$

is invalid, all that we need to do is to produce the interpretation on which A is true, B is false, and C is true. In predicate logic, we show that an argument is invalid by producing a counterexample, but it is not always so easy to produce one. We have already seen examples of the different kinds of interpretations that are possible for individual sentences. To find a counterexample, we need an interpretation for an entire argument, one that makes the premises all true and the conclusion false.

Often one can find counterexamples leaving the domain of discourse unrestricted. Take the argument:

1. $(x)(Ax \supset Bx)$
2. $(x)(Cx \supset Bx) / \therefore (x)(Ax \supset Cx)$

We can prove that this argument is invalid by producing an interpretation with an unrestricted domain where $Ax =$ "x is human"; $Bx =$ "x is mortal"; and $Cx =$ "x is a dog." This interpretation demonstrated that the argument is invalid (since we know that all humans are mortal and all dogs are mortal but all humans are *not* dogs).

We can also use a more limited domain. For example, restrict the domain of discourse to human beings and consider the argument

1. $(\exists x)(Ax \cdot Bx)$
2. $(\exists x)(Ax \cdot Cx) / \therefore (\exists x)(Bx \cdot Cx)$

We can prove this argument invalid with the interpretation on which $Ax =$ "x is an NFL football player"; $Bx =$ "x is a world-class sprinter"; and $Cx =$ "x weighs more than 350 pounds." There are football players who are world-class sprinters, and football players who weigh over 350 pounds, but no one who weighs more than 350 pounds is a world-class sprinter.

A particularly useful limited domain of discourse is the universe of numbers. Restricting the universe of discourse to numbers, we can prove that the argument

1. $(x)(Fx \supset Gx)$
2. $(x)(Hx \supset Gx) / \therefore (x)(Fx \supset Hx)$

is invalid with the following interpretation:

Domain: the numbers
$Fx =$ "x is greater than 6"
$Gx =$ "x is greater than 1"
$Hx =$ "x is greater than 10"

On this interpretation the argument has true premises and a false conclusion. We can be sure both of the premises of this argument are true because we know that all numbers greater than 6 are greater than 1 (which is what its first premise asserts). And we can be sure the conclusion of this argument is false because we know that *not* all numbers greater than 6 also are greater than 10 (contrary to the conclusion, which states that all numbers greater than 6 *are* greater than 10). So this argument is invalid.

Remember, *any* interpretation will do as long as it makes the premises all true and the conclusion false.

☍ Walk-Through: Invalidity in Predicate Logic

Admittedly, it is often not easy to come up with a counterexample in predicate logic. There are so many possible interpretations to choose from. Unless another interpretation suggests itself right away, it may help to use a mathematical interpretation. For example, if we restrict the domain to the positive integers, this gives us a ready supply of different sorts of predicates. If we need a predicate true of no individual in the domain, we can use "x is < 0" or "x is > 1 and < 2" and so on. If we need a predicate true of every individual, we can use "$x > 0$" or even "x is an integer." Finally, for predicates true of some individuals and false of others we have such predicates as "$x < 2$"; "x is even"; "x is odd"; "x is divisible by 4"; "x is prime," and so on.

Suppose our argument is

1. $(\exists x)(Fx \cdot Gx)$
2. $(x)(Fx \supset Hx) \, / \therefore \, \sim (\exists x)(Gx \cdot \sim Hx)$

Restricting the domain to the positive integers, we attempt to come up with a counterexample, that is, an interpretation on which both premises are true and the conclusion false. It is often useful to start with the conclusion. In this case our conclusion is a negation. To make this sentence false, we need an interpretation on which the negated sentence, $(\exists x)(Gx \cdot \sim Hx)$, is true. Thus we need to define Gx and Hx so that there is some individual that has the first property and lacks the second. Let's let $Gx = x > 1$ and $Hx = x > 2$. Moving to the first premise, given the way we have defined Gx, we need Fx to be a property possessed by an integer greater than 1. And to make the second premise true, every integer that has this property must also be greater than 2. Lots of predicates will do the trick. For example, we can let $Fx =$ "x is a multiple of 4." Here then is our completed interpretation:

Domain: the positive integers
$Fx = $ "x is a multiple of 4"
$Gx = $ "$x > 1$"
$Hx = $ "$x > 2$"

Clearly premise 1 is true (4 is a positive integer that is a multiple of 4 and is greater than 1), and premise 2 is true (every multiple of 4 is greater than 2), whereas the conclusion is not true. (There *is* a number that is greater than 1 and not greater than 2, namely, the number 2 itself.)

Exercise 7-2

Prove that the following arguments are invalid:

(1) 1. $(\exists x)(Ax \cdot Bx)$
    2. $(\exists x)(Bx \cdot Cx) / \therefore (\exists x)(Ax \cdot Cx)$

(2) 1. $(x)(Ax \supset Bx)$
    2. $(\exists x) \sim Ax / \therefore (x) \sim Bx$

(3) 1. $(\exists x)(Ax \cdot \sim Bx)$
    2. $(\exists x)(Ax \cdot \sim Cx)$
    3. $(\exists x)(\sim Bx \cdot Dx)$
    $/ \therefore (\exists x)[Ax \cdot (\sim Bx \cdot Dx)]$

(4) 1. $(x)(Fx \supset Gx)$
    2. $(x)(\sim Fx \supset Ex)$
    $/ \therefore (x)(\sim Gx \supset \sim Ex)$

(5) 1. $(\exists x)(Px \cdot \sim Qx)$
    2. $(x)(Rx \supset Px)$
    $/ \therefore (\exists x)(Rx \cdot \sim Qx)$

(6) 1. $(x)[(Px \cdot Qx) \supset Rx]$
    2. $(\exists x)(Qx \cdot \sim Rx)$
    3. $(\exists x)(Px \cdot \sim Rx)$
    $/ \therefore (\exists x)(\sim Px \cdot \sim Qx)$

(7) 1. $(x)(Px \supset Qx)$
    2. $(x)(Qx \supset Rx) / \therefore (\exists x)(Px \cdot Rx)$

(8) 1. $(x)[Mx \supset (Nx \supset Px)]$
    2. $(x)(\sim Qx \supset \sim Px)$
    $/ \therefore (x)[\sim Qx \supset (Mx \vee Nx)]$

(9) 1. $(\exists x)(Ax \cdot Bx)$
    2. $(x)(\sim Bx \vee \sim Cx)$
    $/ \therefore (x)(\sim Ax \vee \sim Cx)$

(10) 1. $(\exists x)(Ax \vee \sim Bx)$
    2. $(x)[(Ax \cdot \sim Bx) \supset Cx] / \therefore (\exists x)Cx$

3 *Using Expansions to Prove Invalidity*

So far we have shown arguments to be invalid using interpretations with quite large domains (the universal domain, the domain of humans, the domain of numbers). But one of the easiest ways to prove invalidity is to use an interpretation with a very small domain. For example, consider the following argument:

1. $\sim (\exists x) (\sim Ax \cdot Bx)$
2. $(\exists x) (Ax \cdot Cx) / \therefore \sim (x)(Cx \supset \sim Bx)$

To show that this argument is invalid we need only postulate a domain that contains just two individuals, let's call them John and Mary. In providing an interpretation we need only stipulate whether the properties *Ax, Bx,* and *Cx* apply to John or Mary so that it is possible to determine the truth-values of the premises and conclusion. To show that the argument is invalid, we need only do this in a way that makes the premises true and the conclusion false. Suppose we let $Ax =$ "*x* is friendly"; $Bx =$ "*x* is gigantic"; and $Cx =$ "*x* is happy" and let it be true that John and Mary are both friendly and happy but false that either one of them is gigantic. On this interpretation, the premises are both true (there is no one who is both not happy and gigantic and there is someone who is friendly and happy), but the conclusion is false (because the conclusion says that not all who are happy are not gigantic).

It actually doesn't matter which particular properties we choose so long as we have two individuals that make the premises all true and the conclusion false. We can simply stipulate whether it is true that an individual has a property. And the really nice thing is that we can find out how to assign these truth-values mechanically by using expansions. First, construct the expansion of the premises and conclusion for a two-individual domain:

1. $\sim [(\sim Aa \cdot Ba) \vee (\sim Ab \cdot Bb)]$
2. $(Aa \cdot Ca) \vee (Ab \cdot Cb) / \therefore \sim [(Ca \supset \sim Ba) \cdot (Cb \supset \sim Bb)]$

Next, we show this argument is invalid using the shortcut technique we used in sentential logic. Remember, we can assign truth-values any way we like, provided only that we do so *consistently*. All that it takes to show that the argument is invalid is some interpretation, *any* interpretation, that makes the premises true and the conclusion false. Here is one such interpretation:

1. $\sim [(\sim Aa \cdot Ba) \vee (\sim Ab \cdot Bb)]$
       T   F T F F   F F T F F

2. $(Aa \cdot Ca) \vee (Ab \cdot Cb) / \therefore \sim [(Ca \supset \sim Ba) \cdot (Cb \supset \sim Bb)]$
        T T T T T T T   F   T T T F T T T T F

This proves that in a domain that contains exactly two individuals, *a* and *b,* the premises, $\sim (\exists x) (\sim Ax \cdot Bx)$ and $(\exists x) (Ax \cdot Cx)$, both could be true whereas the conclusion, $\sim (x)$ $(Cx \supset \sim Bx)$, is false. Our expansion shows that this would be the case on an interpretation where both individuals possess the properties designated by *A* and *C,* but neither individual has property *B.*

This makes it much easier to find a counterexample. Simply produce an expansion and assign truth-values in a manner that makes the premises all true and the conclusion false. Unfortunately, not all invalid arguments can be shown to be invalid using a two-individual domain. Some may require expansions of three or even more individuals. On the other hand, as a practical rule of thumb two-individual expansions will usually do the trick for ordinary invalid arguments.

Example

Argument:

1. $(x) [(Ax \cdot Bx) \supset Cx] / \therefore (x) [(Ax \vee Bx) \supset Cx]$

Counterexample: Let the domain contain two individuals, *a* and *b.* In this domain the argument in question is equivalent to the expansion:

1. $[(Aa \cdot Ba) \supset Ca] \cdot [(Ab \cdot Bb) \supset Cb]$
/ $\therefore$ $[(Aa \vee Ba) \supset Ca] \cdot [(Ab \vee Bb) \supset Cb]$

and is proved invalid by assigning truth-values as follows:

1. $[(Aa \cdot Ba) \supset Ca] \cdot [(Ab \cdot Bb) \supset Cb]$
        T F F T F T   T T T T T

/ $\therefore$ $[(Aa \vee Ba) \supset Ca] \cdot [(Ab \vee Bb) \supset Cb]$
        T T F F F F   T T T T T

LC Exercise 7-3

Use the expansion method to prove that the arguments in Exercise 7-2 are invalid.

4   *Consistency in Predicate Logic*

Just as in sentential logic, in predicate logic the whole method for proving the consistency of the premises of an argument is basically part of the method used for proving invalidity. To show that an argument is invalid, we produce an interpretation on which the premises are true and the conclusion is false. To show that the premises are consistent, one needs only an interpretation on which all of the premises are true. Note that whenever one proves that an argument is invalid one also proves the premises are consistent, since, of course, any interpretation on which the premises are all true and the conclusion is false is an interpretation on which the premises are all true.

Example

We can prove that the argument

1. $(x)(Fx \supset Gx)$
2. $(x)(Gx \supset Hx)$
3. $(\exists x)Fx$ /∴ $(\exists x)Hx$

has consistent premises by finding an interpretation that makes these premises all true. (The truth-value of the conclusion is irrelevant to the consistency of the premises.) For instance, if the universe of discourse is restricted to numbers, and the predicate Fx = "x is greater than 10"; Gx = "x is greater than 5"; and Hx = "x is greater than 0," then the argument's premises are all true (every number greater than 10 is greater than 5; every number greater than 5 is greater than 0; there is some number greater than 10; hence these premises are consistent.

LC Exercise 7-4

Show that the following arguments have consistent premises.

(1)   1. $(x)[Ax \supset (Bx \cdot Cx)]$
2. $(\exists x)(Bx \cdot \sim Cx)$ /∴ $(\exists x)(Ax \cdot \sim Bx)$
(2)   1. $(\exists x)(Rx \lor Mx)$
2. $(x)(Mx \supset \sim Rx)$ /∴ $(\exists x)Mx$
(3)   1. $(x)[(Lx \cdot \sim Mx) \supset Nx]$
2. $(x)[(Lx \cdot Mx) \supset \sim Nx]$
3. $(\exists x)Mx$
4. $(\exists x) \sim Mx$ /∴ $(\exists x)(Lx \cdot \sim Nx)$
(4)   1. $(\exists x) \sim Bx$
2. $(\exists x)Bx$
3. $(\exists x) \sim Kx$
4. $(x)(\sim Kx \supset \sim Bx)$ /∴ $(x)Kx$

(5)   1. $(x)[Rx \supset \sim (Tx \cdot Sx)]$
    2. $(\exists x)(Rx \cdot Tx)$
    3. $(\exists x)(Rx \cdot Sx) / \therefore (\exists x)(Tx \cdot Sx)$
(6)   1. $\sim (x)[Dx \supset (\sim Fx \vee Gx)]$
    2. $[(\exists x)[Fx \cdot (Dx \vee \sim Gx)] / \therefore (\exists x)(Dx \cdot Fx)$
(7)   1. $(\exists x)Fx$
    2. $(x)[(Fx \vee Gx) \supset Dx]$
    3. $(x) \sim Gx / \therefore (\exists x)Dx$
(8)   1. $(x)(Fx \supset Gx)$
    2. $\sim (x)(Gx \supset Fx)$
    3. $(\exists x)(Fx \cdot Gx) / \therefore (\exists x) \sim Fx$

5   *Validity and Inconsistency in Predicate Logic*

So far we have demonstrated how to show that an argument is invalid or that a set of sentences is consistent. But what about validity and inconsistency? An argument is valid just in case among all of the argument's many interpretations there is not a single one in which the premises are true and the conclusion false. A set of sentences is inconsistent if and only if there is not a single interpretation on which all of the sentences are true. Unfortunately, we cannot do here as we did in sentential logic and survey all of an argument's interpretations. Hence to demonstrate validity or inconsistency in predicate logic we must either use a proof (as explained in the next chapter) or a truth tree (as explained in Chapter 12).

Key terms

consistent: A sentence or group of sentences is consistent in predicate logic if and only if there is an interpretation on which the sentences are all true.

interpretation: To provide an interpretation for a sentence or group of sentences in predicate logic we must specify (1) a domain, (2) an assignment for each individual constant, and (3) the extension of each predicate constant (a list of the individuals in the domain that have the property in question). We must also specify a truth-value for any atomic sentential logic sentences if any are present.

In other words, an interpretation provides all of the information needed to determine the sentences' truth-value.

logically equivalent: Two predicate logic sentences are logically equivalent if and only if there is no interpretation on which one is true and the other false.

valid: A predicate logic argument is valid if and only if there is no interpretation on which the premises are all true and the conclusion false.

Chapter Eight

Predicate
Logic Proofs

---

1   *Proving Validity*

The eighteen valid argument forms plus **CP** and **IP** that constitute the proof machinery of
sentential logic are incorporated intact into predicate logic. Here is a proof that illustrates
their use in predicate logic:

       p q
1. $Fa \supset Ga$

       p
2. Fa $/\therefore Ga$

       q
3. Ga 1,2 **MP**

    Notice that in this use of Modus Ponens the expressions *Fa* and *Ga* are treated as units,
just as we treated the capital letters *A, B,* and so on in propositional logic. Thus, the
expression on line 1 is taken to be a substitution instance of the sentence form $p \supset q$, where
the unit *Fa* is substituted for p and the unit *Ga* is substituted for q.
    Here is another example:

         p q
1. $(x) \sim (Fx \cdot Gx)$ $/\therefore (x)(\sim Fx \vee \sim Gx)$

         p q
2. $(x)(\sim Fx \vee \sim Gx)$ 1 **DeM**

    In this case, the application of DeMorgan's Theorem to line 1 does not involve the whole
of line 1. This is permissible because, as stated in Chapter 4, the ten equivalence forms
among the eighteen valid argument forms can be used on parts as well as wholes of
sentences and sentence forms.
    But the eight implicational forms cannot be used on parts of sentences (or sentence
forms). Their use is restricted to whole sentences, as in the previous example containing a
valid use of Modus Ponens. Here is a proof that is invalid because an implicational argument form (Modus Ponens) is used on part of a line:

1. $(x)(Fx \supset Gx)$
2. $(x)Fx$ $/\therefore (x)Gx$
3. $(x)Gx$ 1,2 **MP**

This proof is invalid because the whole of line 1 has the form $(x)(p \supset q)$ and not the form $p \supset q$. We cannot apply **MP** to part of a line.

In order to deal with arguments like the one just discussed, five new rules will be introduced into our system. The first four are implicational rules. The remaining rule is an equivalence rule we could actually do without, but this rule makes proof discovery and construction a good deal simpler.

The four implicational rules specify the conditions under which a quantifier may be dropped or added to a formula. Two rules, **UI** and **EI,** are for taking off each kind of quantifier; the other two, **UG** and **EG,** are for putting them back on. For example, here is how the proof discussed above can be completed using two of the four rules:

1. $(x)(Fx \supset Gx)$
2. $(x)Fx$ $/\therefore (x)Gx$
3. $Fx \supset Gx$ 1 **UI**
4. Fx 2 **UI**
5. Gx 3,4 **MP**
6. $(x)Gx$ 5 **UG**

This simple proof illustrates a three-step pattern typical of predicate logic proofs. (1) We use **UI** or **EI** to take the quantifiers in the premises off, so that, (2) we can apply sentential logic rules, and then, (3) use **UG** or **EG** to put the quantifiers back on. By and large the real work of the proof is done in the second step, the sentential logic portion of the proof— using the rules you already know. But, of course, you can't just take off and put back on quantifiers haphazardly. Thus mastery of predicate logic largely comes down to learning when you can, and when you can't, take off or add a quantifier.

The equivalence rule, **QN,** it turns out, is reasonably easy to understand and use, as we shall see. (It is introduced in the last section of this chapter.) But it has to be admitted that the four rules for adding and deleting quantifiers are a bit complicated and even, in some odd details, somewhat nonintuitive (although never counterintuitive!). Most students quickly grasp the fundamental idea on which these four rules are based but need more time (and effort) to fully comprehend some of the theoretically important (and, some of us think, fascinating) details. So let's make the task of mastering the four quantifier rules easier by breaking our discussion of this topic into three parts. In the first part we informally describe the way in which the four quantifier rules function, omitting complicated details; next we discuss the five primary restrictions that govern the use of these rules, and finally we will then introduce a precisely stated version of the four rules, with all the restrictions and provisos carefully spelled out.

2   *The Four Quantifier Rules*

We now introduce four quantifier rules used to add quantifiers to formulas or to delete them.

Universal Instantiation (UI)

Consider the argument

1. $(x)(Fx \supset Gx)$
2. $Fa \: / \therefore \: Ga$

Suppose $Fx =$ "x is friendly" and $Gx =$ "x is generous." Then line 1 asserts that for all x, if x is friendly, then x is generous, or that everything that is friendly is generous. Surely it follows from this that if a particular person, say Anna, is friendly, then she's also generous, because whatever is true of *everything* must be true of any *particular* thing. Hence it is legitimate to write as the next line in the proof

3. $Fa \supset Ga$ 1 **UI** (Universal Instantiation)

Then we can assert the conclusion

4. Ga 2,3 **MP**

  We call the rule of inference that permits the leap from line 1 to line 3 Universal Instantiation, because it yields an *instance, ($Fa \supset Ga$)*, of the *universal* generalization $(x)(Fx \supset Gx)$.

  It is important to note that a universal quantifier must quantify a *whole line* in a proof to be dropped by **UI.** Thus, **UI** cannot be applied to the line

1. $(x)Fx \supset (\exists x)Gy$

to obtain

2. $Fa \supset (\exists x)Gy$

because the (x) quantifier in line 1 does not quantify the whole of that line.
  Similarly, **UI** cannot be applied to the line

1. $\sim (x)(Fx \supset Gx)$

to obtain

2. $\sim (Fa \supset Ga)$

because the (x) quantifier in line 1 does not quantify the negation sign, and thus does not quantify the entire line.

  Perhaps a better intuitive understanding of the nature and general validity of **UI** can be obtained by again thinking of symbolizations containing quantifiers as a kind of shorthand for expanded expressions. Take the quantified expression $(x)(Fx \supset Gx)$. Its expansion is $[(Fa \supset Ga) \cdot (Fb \supset Gb)] \ldots$ If we take this expansion as a premise, rather than the expression itself, then we can infer to $Fa \supset Ga$ by Simplification (plus Association), without appealing to a new inference rule at all. Using rule **UI** to move from $(x)(Fx \supset Gx)$ to $Fa \supset Ga$ is like using Simplification to move from $[(Fa \supset Ga) \cdot (Fb \supset Gb)] \ldots$ to $Fa \supset Ga$.
  In our example, we use Universal Instantiation to replace the variables freed by dropping the universal quantifier with *constants*. But, as we will see, it is useful to permit their

replacement by individual variables also. For instance, we permit inferences by **UI** from $(x)(Fx \supset Gx)$ to $Fx \supset Gx$ and $Fy \supset Gy$, as well as to $Fa \supset Ga$ and $Fb \supset Gb$.

Examples

The following are examples of correct uses of **UI.**

(1) 1. $(x)[(Fx \cdot Gx) \supset Hx)]$
    2. $(Fy \cdot Gy) \supset Hy$ 1 **UI**
    3. $(Fa \cdot Ga) \supset Ha$ 1 **UI**
    4. $(Fx \cdot Gx) \supset Hx$ 1 **UI** (replacing each freed variable with itself)

(2) 1. $(x)[Fx \supset (Gx \supset Ha)]$
    2. $Fx \supset (Gx \supset Ha]$ 1 **UI**
    3. $Fy \supset (Gy \supset Ha)$ 1 **UI**
    4. $Fa \supset (Ga \supset Ha)$ 1 **UI**
    5. $Fb \supset (Gb \supset Ha)$ 1 **UI**

Universal Generalization (UG)

Now consider the proof

1. $(x)(Hx \supset Mx)$
2. $(x)(Gx \supset Hx)$ /∴ $(x)(Gx \supset Mx)$
3. $Hy \supset My$ 1 **UI**
4. $Gy \supset Hy$ 2 **UI**
5. $Gy \supset My$ 3,4 **HS**

Note once again that in order to use **HS** to derive line 5 we *must* first use **UI** to remove the quantifiers. This illustrates what is perhaps the most important function of our four quantifier rules: making it possible to use the eight implicational argument forms of sentential logic in predicate logic proofs. If we were not allowed to drop or add quantifiers, the eight implicational forms could not be used on quantified sentences, because these rules must be used on whole lines only.

Now, having dropped the quantifiers and derived line 5, we need to add a quantifier to obtain the conclusion:

6. $(x)(Gx \supset Mx)$ 5 **UG** (Universal Generalization)

We introduce the rule called Universal Generalization (**UG**) to permit valid steps like the one from line 5 to line 6. Subject to certain important restrictions to be discussed later, rule **UG** permits the addition of universal quantifiers *that quantify whole sentences.*

Note, by the way, that if we let Hx = "x is human"; Mx = "x is mortal"; and Gx = "x is Greek," then we have just proved the quintessential syllogism that we used as our example (on page 131) of a valid argument not provable in sentential logic. Now, we can prove arguments of this kind valid (if they are, of course).

The use of **UG** should be familiar to students of geometry. In geometry, a proof that a given triangle has a particular property is considered proof that all triangles have that property, provided the proof does not depend on something peculiar to the given triangle, which means provided the given triangle is arbitrarily selected. Similarly, **UG** is a valid step (with the exceptions to be noted in the next chapter) provided that it is applied in cases where the actual letters employed (in the above example the letter *y*) are arbitrarily selected, and any other letters could have been selected just as well.

Examples

Here are two typical proofs using rules **UI** and **UG**:

(1)   1. $(x)[(Fx \supset Gx) \cdot (Hx \supset Kx)]$ $/\therefore (x)(Fx \supset Gx)$
      2. $(Fx \supset Gx) \cdot (Hx \supset Kx)$ 1 **UI**
      3. $Fx \supset Gx$ 2 **Simp**
      4. $(x)(Fx \supset Gx)$ 3 **UG**

(2)   1. $(x)(Fx \supset Gx) \supset (x)(Hx \supset Fx)$
      2. $(x) \sim Fx$ $/\therefore (x) \sim Hx$
      3. $\sim Fy$ 2 **UI**
      4. $\sim Fy \vee Gy$ 3 **Add**
      5. $Fy \supset Gy$ 4 **Impl**
      6. $(x)(Fx \supset Gx)$ 5 **UG**
      7. $(x)(Hx \supset Fx)$ 1,6 **MP**
      8. $Hy \supset Fy$ 7 **UI**
      9. $\sim Hy$ 3,8 **MT**
     10. $(x) \sim Hx$ 9 **UG**

Existential Instantiation (EI)

Next, consider the proof

1. $(x)(Hx \supset Kx)$
2. $(\exists x)Hx$ $/\therefore (\exists x)Kx$
3. Hy 2 **EI** (Existential Instantiation)

In this proof, line 3 follows from line 2 by the inference rule called Existential Instantiation (**EI**).

Technically, we should not permit this step from line 2 to line 3, because *y* is a variable. Instead, we should introduce a new set of terms, construed not as variables, but rather as unknowns or ambiguous names. The difference between a variable and an unknown is illustrated by an example from algebra. In the algebraic theorem

$(a + b) = (b + a)$

a and *b* function as variables, because the theorem is true of all numbers. But in the algebraic problem

1. $x + 1 = 3$
2. $x = 2$

the x on line 1 functions not as a variable but as an unknown value, to be discovered, as it is on line 2, where it turns out to be the number 2. So also, in the step from

2. $(\exists x)Hx$

to

3. Hy

the letter y serves not as a variable but as an unknown, in the sense that if $(\exists x)Hx$ is true, then there is some value of x (exactly which value is unknown) that has the property H. In line 3 we call that unknown value y.

It is important to note that although the result of a **UI** or **EI** step may look just the same there is a significant difference. The free variable produced by **UI** we might call a universal name. It designates an arbitrarily selected individual. It could designate anyone, or anything in the domain. The free variable in an **EI** line is different. It is not a universal name, but rather a name we make up to designate a particular individual. This individual is not arbitrarily selected. For all we know, what an **EI** line says of this individual may be true of that individual only and no other.

Compare the difference between the made-up names "John Doe" and "Jack the Ripper." "John Doe" is commonly used to stand for just anyone. (This is sexist, of course. Perhaps we should take a page from "Saturday Night Live" and change the name to "Pat Doe.") "Jack the Ripper," on the other hand, designates a particular historical individual who committed a series of grisly murders in London in the 1800s. "Jack" isn't this person's real name. Someone ("Jack," in fact) just made this name up for the sake of convenience. We essentially do the same thing in an **EI** step. Because an existentially quantified sentence assures us that at least one individual of a certain kind exists, we introduce a free variable as a name for one such individual.

Existential Generalization (EG)

So far, the proof we have been constructing reads as follows:

1. $(x)(Hx \supset Kx)$
2. $(\exists x)Hx$ $/ \therefore (\exists x)Kx$
3. Hy 2 **EI**

Continuing,

4. $Hy \supset Ky$ 1 **UI**
5. Ky 3,4 **MP**
6. $(\exists x)Kx$ 5 **EG** (Existential Generalization)

The step from line 5 to line 6 is justified by the inference rule Existential Generalization (**EG**). This use of **EG** obviously is valid, since if the unknown individual designated by the free variable y has the property K, then there is something that has that property.

Examples

The following proofs contain examples of correct uses of **EI** and **EG.**

(1)   1. $(\exists x)(Fx \cdot Gx)$
      2. $(Fx \cdot Gx)$ 1 **EI**
      3. $(Fy \cdot Gy)$ 1 **EI**
      4. $(\exists x)(Fx \cdot Gx)$ 2 **EG** (or 3 **EG**)
      5. $(\exists z)(Fz \cdot Gz)$ 2 **EG** (or 3 **EG**)
(2)   1. $(\exists x)[Fx \cdot (y)Gy]$
      2. $Fx \cdot (y)Gy$ 1 **EI**
      3. $Fz \cdot (y)Gy$ 1 **EI**
      4. $(y)Gy$ 2 **Simp**
      5. Gz 4 **UI**
      6. $(\exists y)Gy$ 5 **EG**
      7. $(\exists x)Gx$ 5 **EG**
      8. $(\exists z)Gz$ 5 **EG**
      9. Fz 3 **Simp**
     10. $Fz \cdot Gz$ 5,9 **Conj**
     11. $(\exists x)Fx$ 9 **EG**
     12. $(\exists x)[Fx \cdot (y)Gy]$ 3 **EG**
     13. $(\exists x)Fx \cdot (\exists x)Gx$ 7,11 **Conj**
     14. $(\exists x)(Fx \cdot Gx)$ 10 **EG**

To summarize, we have introduced two instantiation rules for removing quantifiers, **UI** and **EI,** and two generalization rules for putting them back on, **UG** and **EG.** As noted above, we cannot just add and remove quantifiers haphazardly. In particular, there are important restrictions on the use of **EI** and **UG** that will be explained in the next section. On the other hand, you already have enough information to complete the following exercise, which involves only **UI** and **EG.** Remember, for **UI** you remove the quantifier and replace the variable that had been bound by that quantifier with a variable or constant. For **EG** you reverse the process, taking either a free variable or a constant and replacing it with a variable that is bound by an existential quantifier that is added to the front of the line. Remember also that these rules are implicational rules and thus cannot be used on parts of lines. You can only remove or add a quantifier if its scope includes the entire sentence.

LG Exercise 8-1

Complete the following proofs using the rules for adding and removing quantifiers where appropriate.

(1)   1. $(x) Fx \vee (x) \sim Gx$
      2. $\sim (x) Fx$
      3. $(x) (Dx \supset Gx) / \therefore (\exists x) \sim Dx$

(2) 1. $(x) [Ax \lor (Bx \cdot \sim Cx)]$
       2. $(x) Cx \, / \therefore \, (\exists x) (Dx \supset Ax)$
(3) 1. $(x) [Ax \supset (Bx \cdot Cx)]$
       2. $(x) [(Ax \cdot Cx) \supset Dx]$
       3. $(x) (Dx \supset \sim Cx) \, / \therefore \, \sim Aa$
(4) 1. $Ab \supset Bc$
       2. $(x)(Ax \supset Bx)$
       3. $(x) [(Ax \supset Bx) \supset Ax] \, / \therefore \, Bc$
(5) 1. $Ab \lor Bc$
       2. $(x) \sim Bx \, / \therefore \, (\exists x) Ax$
(6) 1. $(y)(Ry \supset \sim Gy)$
       2. $(z)(Bz \lor Gz)$
       3. $(y)Ry \, / \therefore \, (\exists y)By$
(7) 1. $(z)[Az \supset (\sim Bz \supset Cz)]$
       2. $\sim Ba \, / \therefore \, Aa \supset Ca$
(8) 1. $(x)[(Rx \cdot Ax) \supset Tx]$
       2. Ab
       3. $(x)Rx \, / \therefore \, Tb \cdot Rb$

3   *The Five Main Restrictions*

In the next section we will provide a precise version of the four quantifier rules. But let's anticipate a bit and discuss five of the simpler cases in which these rules must be restricted. *Understanding these five restrictions is the key to mastery of predicate logic proofs.*

The first two restrictions apply to uses of **EI.** Here, for instance, is an example of the first kind of case:

(1) 1. $(\exists x)Hx$
       2. Ha 1 **EI** (invalid)

Because some item or other has the property H, say of being honest, it doesn't follow that a particular item a, say Adolf Hitler, ever was associated with that quality. The precise version of the quantifier rules blocks this kind of invalid inference by requiring that when an existential quantifier is dropped by **EI,** the variables thus freed must be replaced by variables, never constants. Remember, constants are always names of specific individuals. *When we introduce a free variable into a proof using EI, we must use a new name.*

Now, here is an example of another kind of case concerning **EI:**

(2) 1. $(\exists x)Fx$
       2. $(\exists x)Gx$
       3. Fx 1 **EI**
       4. Gx 2 **EI** (invalid)

And this is what can happen when steps like 4 are permitted:

       5. $Fx \cdot Gx$ 3,4 **Conj**
       6. $(\exists x)(Fx \cdot Gx)$ 5 **EG**

Letting Fx = "x is a fox" and Gx = "x is a goose," this invalid inference moves from the true facts that there are foxes and there are geese to the silly conclusion that there exist items that are both foxes and geese. (It would have been all right to move from "$(\exists x)Gx$" to, say, Gy or to Gz, but not to Gx.) We're going to block this kind of invalid move in the next section by requiring that *a variable introduced free into a proof by rule* **EI** *must not have occurred free previously in the proof.*

The remaining three restrictions have to do with the rule **UG.** Here is an inference that is obviously invalid:

(3)   1. Fa
     2. $(x)Fx$ 1 **UG** (invalid)

Believing, say, that Adam was a fool (anyone who manages to get himself evicted from the Garden of Eden can't be too smart) doesn't justify believing that everyone is a fool. So the argument clearly is invalid. To block moves of this kind, we're going to restrict rule **UG** so that it forbids Universal Generalization on a constant.

Next, consider this example:

(4)   1. $(\exists x)Fx$
     2. Fx 1 **EI**
     3. $(x)Fx$ 2 **UG** (invalid)

Clearly, although there are plenty of foxes, not everything is a fox. So the argument is invalid. To block moves of this kind, we're going to restrict rule **UG** so that it forbids generalization on a variable that is free in a line that is justified by **EI.** The point of using **UG** is to generalize on arbitrarily selected letters. In the case at hand, we generalized on the variable x that was introduced free into the argument by rule **EI** and hence was not arbitrarily selected.

So before using **UG** we must check every previous line that is justified by **EI.** *If the variable is free in an* **EI** *line we cannot use* **UG** *to bind that variable.* Think of **EI** as poisoning, for the purposes of **UG,** every variable that is free in an **EI** line.

The last restriction applies only to proofs that have assumed premises. If an assumed premise has a free variable, we are not allowed to use **UG** to bind that variable.

    1. $\sim (x)Fx$
 → 2. Fx **AP**
    3. $(x)Fx$ 2 **UG** (invalid)
    4. $(x)Fx \cdot \sim (x)Fx$ 1,3 **Conj**
    5. $\sim Fx$ 2–4 **IP**
    6. $(x) \sim Fx$ 5 **UG**

We can't, for example, infer that everyone is not fat from the fact that not everyone is fat. Remember, we can only bind a variable using **UG** provided that the variable functions as a universal name for an arbitrarily selected individual. In making an assumption with a free variable, the variable does not name an arbitrary individual. Rather, it names an individual assumed to have a particular property. So, *we cannot bind that variable with* **UG** *as long as we are relying upon that assumption.*

However, once the assumption is discharged we are free to use **UG** to bind that variable, because we no longer are depending on an assumption about the individual designated by the variable. Unlike **EI,** an assumed premise poisons the variable only temporarily. So the following use of **UG** is legitimate:

1.	$(x) \sim Fx$	
→ 2.	Gx	**AP**
3.	$\sim Fx$	1 **UI**
4.	$Gx \supset \sim Fx$	2–3 **CP**
5.	$(x)(Gx \supset \sim Fx)$	4 **UG** (valid)

To summarize: The first two of our restrictions have to do with **EI,** the last three with **UG.** The two restrictions on **EI** both require that the free variable introduced by **EI** be a new name. You cannot use a constant, and you cannot use a variable that already occurs free earlier in the proof—those names are already taken. The three restrictions on **UG** are designed to ensure that when we add a universal quantifier we bind only a symbol that functions as a universal name designating an arbitrarily chosen individual. Obviously this is not true of a constant—but it is also not true of variables that are free in an **EI** line and variables that are free in an undischarged assumed premise.

Examples

The following contain examples of both valid and invalid uses of the four quantifier rules.

(1)
1.	$(Aa \cdot Bb) \supset Cc$	
2.	$(x)(Ax \cdot Bx)$	
3.	$Aa \cdot Bb$	2 **UI** (invalid, can't change a variable into two *different* constants with **UI**)
4.	Cc	1,3 **MP**
5.	$(x)Cx$	4 **UG** (invalid, can't bind a constant with **UG**)

(2)
1.	$(x)(\sim Gx \supset \sim Fx)$	
2.	$\sim Gc \supset \sim Fc$	1 **UI**
3.	$Fc \supset Gc$	2 **Contra**
4.	$(x)(Fx \supset Gx)$	3 **UG** (invalid, can't bind a constant with **UG**)
5.	$\sim Gx \supset \sim Fx$	1 **UI**
6.	$Fx \supset Gx$	5 **Contra**
7.	$(x)(Fx \supset Gx)$	6 **UG**

(3)
1.	$(x)(Fx \supset Gx)$	
2.	$(\exists y)(Gy \cdot Hy)$	
3.	$Fx \supset Gx$	1 **UI** (valid)
4.	$Gx \cdot Hx$	2 **EI** (invalid, x already occurs free)
5.	Gx	4 **Simp**
6.	$(x)Gx$	5 **UG** (invalid, x is free in an **EI** line)

(4)
1.	$Sb \cdot Cb$
2.	$(x)(Sx \cdot Cx) \supset \sim (\exists y)Fy$

3. $(Sb \cdot Cb) \supset \sim (\exists y)Fy$ 2 **UI** (invalid, can't use **UI** on part of a line)
4. $\sim (\exists y)Fy$ 1,3 **MP**
5. $\sim Fz$ 4 **EI** (invalid, this time **EI** on part of a line)
6. $(\exists x) \sim Fx$ 5 **EG**

(5)   1. $(x)[Fx \supset (\exists y)Gy]$
     2. $(\exists x)Fx$
     3. Fz 2 **EI**
     4. $Fz \supset (\exists y)Gy$ 1 **UI**
     5. $(\exists y)Gy$ 3,4 **MP**
     6. Gz 5 **EI** (invalid, z already occurs free)
     7. $Fz \cdot Gz$ 3,6 **Conj**
     8. $(x)(Fx \cdot Gx)$ 7 **UG** (invalid, z is free in line 3—an **EI** line)

(6)   1. $(x)(Fx \supset Gx)$
     2. Fx **AP**
     3. $Fx \supset Gx$ 1 **UI**
     4. Gx 2,3 **MP**
     5. $(x)Gx$ 4 **UG** (invalid, x is free in an undischarged assumption)
     6. $Fx \supset (x)Gx$ 2–5 **IP**
     7. $(x)Fx \supset (x)Gx$ 6 **UG** (invalid, **UG** on part of a line)

Exercise 8-2

Which lines in the following are not valid? Explain why in each case.

(1)   1. $(x)[(Hx \cdot Kx) \supset Mx]$ p
     2. $(\exists x)(Hx \cdot Kx)$ p
     3. $Hx \cdot Kx$ 2 **EI**
     4. Mx 1,3 **MP**
     5. $(\exists x)Mx$ 4 **EG**

(2)   1. $(x)(Fx \supset Gx) \supset Ma$ p
     2. $(x)(\sim Gx \supset \sim Mx)$ p
     3. $\sim Gx \supset \sim Mx$ 2 **UI**
     4. $(x)(\sim Gx \supset \sim Fx) \supset Ma$ 1 **Contra**
     5. $(\sim Gx \supset \sim Fx) \supset Ma$ 4 **UI**
     6. Ma 3,5 **MP**
     7. $(x)Mx$ 6 **UG**

(3)   1. $(x)[(Gx \vee Hx) \supset Mx]$ p
     2. $(\exists x)(Fx \cdot \sim Mx)$ p
     3. $(Gy \vee Hy) \supset My$ 2 **UI**
     4. $Fy \cdot \sim My$ 1 **EI**
     5. $\sim My$ 4 **Simp**
     6. $\sim (Gy \vee Hy)$ 3,5 **MT**
     7. $(\exists x) \sim (Gx \vee Hx)$ 6 **EG**

(4)   1. $(\exists x)(Px \cdot Qx)$ p
        2. $Py \cdot Qy$ 1 **EI**
        3. Qy 2 **Simp**
        4. $Qy \vee \sim Ry$ 3 **Add**
        5. $(x)(Qx \vee \sim Rx)$ 4 **UG**
        6. $(x)(\sim Rx \vee Qx)$ 5 **Comm**
        7. $(x)(Rx \supset Qx)$ 6 **Impl**

(5)   1. $(\exists x)[(Px \cdot Qx) \vee Rx]$ p
        2. $(x) \sim Rx$ p
        3. $(\exists x)(Px \vee Rx)$ 1 **Simp**
        4. $Px \vee Rx$ 3 **EI**
        5. $\sim Px$ 2,4 **DS**
        6. $(x) \sim Px$ 5 **UG**
        7. $\sim Py$ 6 **UI**
        8. $(z) \sim Pz$ 7 **UG**

(6)   1. $\sim (x)Fx$ p
        2. $(\exists x)Lx$ p
        3. $(x) \sim Fx$ p
        4. $\sim Fx$ 1 **UI**
        5. La 2 **EI**
        6. Lx 2 **EI**
        7. $Lx \cdot \sim Fx$ 4,6 **Conj**
        8. $(\exists x)(Lx \cdot \sim Fx)$ 7 **EG**
        9. $(x)Lx$ 5 **UG**

Precise Formulation of the Four Quantifier Rules

To state the quantifier rules precisely and economically, we need a way to refer to a great many expressions at once. For example, we want our precise statement of rule **UI** somehow to refer to, and permit, all of the following inferences:

(1)   1. $(x)Fx$
        2. Fy 1 **UI**

(2)   1. $(x)Fx$
        2. Fx 1 **UI**

(3)   1. $(x)Fx$
        2. Fa 1 **UI**

(4)   1. $(z)(Fz \supset Gz)$
        2. $Fy \supset Gy$ 1 **UI**

(5)   1. $(x)(Fx \supset Gx)$
        2. $Fx \supset Gx$ 1 **UI**

(6)   1. $(x)[Fx \supset (\exists y)Gy]$
        2. $Fz \supset (\exists y)Gy$ 1 **UI**

     In each of these examples, the move is from a universally quantified formula to one of its instances. The universal quantifier is dropped and the variables thus freed are replaced by instances of some variable or constant or other. Thus, in the first example, we dropped the (x) quantifier and replaced the one x variable thus freed by a free y variable, to get the conclusion Fy. In the fifth we dropped the (x) quantifier and replaced the x variables thus freed by themselves (it's perfectly all right to do this), to arrive at the conclusion $Fx \supset Gx$. And in the third, we dropped the (x) quantifier and replaced the x thus freed by the constant a, to arrive at the conclusion Fa.

Suppose that we use the letter u to refer to the variables that become free as a result of dropping a quantifier, and to the quantifier itself as (u). Then we can think of each of the premises in the six arguments above as having the form $(u)(\ldots u \ldots)$. For instance, the premise $(x)(Fx \supset Gx)$ of the fifth argument is clearly a substitution instance of this form, obtained from it by substituting (x) for (u) and $(Fx \supset Gx)$ for $(\ldots u \ldots)$. In fact, we can use the form $(u)(\ldots u \ldots)$ to represent the logical structure of any expression in which the initial universal quantifier, whether (x), (y), (z), or whatever, quantifies the whole remainder of the expression. And similarly, we can use, say, the expression $(\ldots w \ldots)$ to represent the structure of the expression that results when we drop a quantifier and replace the variables thus freed either with themselves or with some other letter.

Using this notation, we can say that each use of rule **UI** involves moving from an expression of the form

$(u)(\ldots u \ldots)$

to an expression of the form

$(\ldots w \ldots)$

where the expression $(\ldots w \ldots)$ resulted from replacing all occurrences of u free in $(\ldots u \ldots)$ by occurrences of w free in $(\ldots w \ldots)$.

All six of the examples introduced at the beginning of this section satisfy this form. They move from premise to conclusion by first dropping the quantifier that binds the remainder of the premise and then replacing the variables that become free in this process by instances of some variable or constant or other. Typical is (4), in which the universal quantifier (z) is dropped, freeing two z variables that are then replaced by two free y variables. (Of course, if we replace one of the z variables by a free y variable, we must replace the other z by a y.)

The schematic notation just introduced also is to be used in the formulation of rules **EI**, **UG**, **EG**. For instance, we shall characterize **UG** as a process in which we move from an expression $(\ldots u \ldots)$ to an expression $(w)(\ldots w \ldots)$, by replacing all free occurrences of u in $(\ldots u \ldots)$ by occurrences of w free in $(\ldots w \ldots)$. Of course, such occurrences of w will then be bound in the whole expression $(w)(\ldots w \ldots)$. The point is that they not be bound by a w quantifier occurring within $(\ldots w \ldots)$.

We now are ready to state our precise version of the quantifier rules.

Rule UI: $(u)(\ldots u \ldots) / \therefore (\ldots w \ldots)$ *Provided:*

1. $(\ldots w \ldots)$ results from replacing each occurrence of u free in $(\ldots u \ldots)$ with a w that is free in $(\ldots w \ldots)$ (making no other changes).

Rule EI: $(\exists u)(\ldots u \ldots)/\therefore (\ldots w \ldots)$ *Provided:*

1. w is not a constant.
2. w does not occur free previously in the proof.
3. $(\ldots w \ldots)$ results from replacing each occurrence of u free in $(\ldots u \ldots)$ with a w that is free in $(\ldots w \ldots)$ (making no other changes).

Rule UG: $(\ldots u \ldots)/\therefore (w)(\ldots w \ldots)$ *Provided:*

1. u is not a constant.
2. u does not occur free previously in a line obtained by **EI.**
3. u does not occur free previously in an assumed premise that has not yet been discharged.
4. $(\ldots w \ldots)$ results from replacing each occurrence of u free in $(\ldots u \ldots)$ with a w that is free in $(\ldots w \ldots)$ (making no other changes), and there are no additional occurrences of w already contained in $(\ldots w \ldots)$.

Rule EG: $(\ldots u \ldots)/\therefore (\exists w)(\ldots w \ldots)$ *Provided:*

1. $(\ldots w \ldots)$ results from replacing *at least one* occurrence of u free in $(\ldots u \ldots)$ with a w that is free in $(\ldots w \ldots)$ (making no other changes), and there are no additional occurrences of w already contained in $(\ldots w \ldots)$.

5   *Mastering the Four Quantifier Rules*

The task of mastering the four quantifier rules can be lightened a bit by concentration on the rules beginners are most tempted to violate. Most problems are associated with the five restrictions we have already discussed. But let's look briefly at the other restrictions contained in our rules. These restrictions rule out such peculiar inferences as:

1. $(x)(Fx \supset Gx)$
2. $Fa \cdot Gb$
3. $Fy \supset Gz$ 1 UI (invalid)
4. $Fx \supset Gz$ 1 UI (invalid)

5. $(\exists x)(Fx \cdot Gx)$ 2 **EG** (invalid)
6. $(x)(Fx \supset Gx)$ 4 **UG** (invalid)

Steps 3 and 4 of this proof amount to attempting to do two different things with the *x* variables that are bound in line 1. In line 3 the attempt is made to change these variables into a free *y* and a free *z,* and in line 4 they are changed into a free *x* and a free *y.* Likewise, lines 5 and 6 amount to attempting to bind two different variables at once. You shouldn't concern yourself too much with these restrictions at this stage. For the proofs you will encounter in this chapter, problems with these rules rarely arise. We will discuss them in greater detail in our coverage of relational predicate logic in Chapter 9, and Chapter 10 consists of an exhaustive list of every type of bad inference these rules are designed to prevent. Just remember not to try to do two things at once, that is, change bound *x*'s to free *x*'s and *y*'s, bind both an *x* and a *y* in one swoop, and so on.

Returning to our five major restrictions, even beginners are not likely to violate the two restrictions having to do with constants. Consider rule **EI**. Few will be tempted to infer, say, from $(\exists x)Hx$ to Ha. For that would be like arguing (invalidly) that since something or other has the property of being an axe murderer, a particular entity, say Mother Teresa, has that property. The same holds for the similar restriction on **UG**. In actual applications of **UG**, even beginners are not likely to attempt to infer from Fa to $(x)Fx$. For that would be like arguing (invalidly) that because the Hope diamond is valuable, everything is valuable.

So beginners should concentrate on the remaining three of the five major restrictions. These restrictions require that we check previous lines whenever we justify a line with **EI** or **UG**. When we **EI**, we must check to be sure the variable we are introducing does not occur free on any earlier line. When we **UG**, we must be sure that the variable we are binding is not free in an **EI** line or an undischarged assumed premise.

In particular, beginners should be on the lookout for invalid inferences such as the one from 5 to 6 in the proof

1. $(\exists x)Fx$
2. $(y)Gy$
3. Fx 1 **EI**
4. Gy 2 **UI**
5. $Fx \cdot Gy$ 3,4 **Conj**
6. $(x)(Fx \cdot Gy)$ 3 **UG** (invalid)

for this inference violates the second restriction on **UG**. Similarly, they should look out for invalid inferences like the one from 1 to 2 in the proof

  ⌐→ 1. $Fy \supset (x)Gx$ **AP**
       2. $(z)[Fz \supset (x)Gx]$ 1 **UG** (invalid)

for this inference violates the third restriction on **UG**.

Violations of the second restriction on **EI** are very common for beginners, but many are easily avoided. Remember: *if you must EI do so as soon as possible.* The following argument illustrates the point:

1. $(x)(Ax \supset Bx)$
2. $(\exists x)Ax$ $/\therefore (\exists x)Bx$

If we remove the universal quantifier first, there will be no way to complete the proof without violating the second restriction on **EI**.

3.	$Ax \supset Bx$	1 **UI**
4.	Ax	2 **EI** (invalid)
5.	Bx	3,4 **MP**
6.	$(\exists x)Bx$	5 **EG**

Instead, *when faced with such a choice, always **EI** first.*

3.	Ax	2 **EI**
4.	$Ax \supset Bx$	1 **UI**
5.	Bx	3,4 **MP**
6.	$(\exists x)Bx$	5 **EG**

If you follow this simple rule of thumb, you will minimize your chance of running afoul of this particular restriction.

To sum up, in using the four quantifier rules, students should pay special attention to the second and third restrictions on **UG** and the second restriction on **EI**. Most problems with the second restriction on **EI** will be avoided by using **EI** as soon as possible.

One last word: It must be remembered that these rules are to be applied to *whole lines of proofs only.* Inferences such as the one from 1 to 2 in the proof

1.	$\sim (x)Fx$	
2.	$\sim Fx$	1 **UI** (invalid)

are never valid. If they were valid, then in this case we could move to

3.	$(x) \sim Fx$	2 **UG**

thus inferring from, say, "It's not true that everything is friendly" to "Everything is not friendly," a clearly invalid inference.

𝕏 Walk-Through: Basic Predicate Logic Proofs

Here is a typical argument in predicate logic:

1.	$(y)(By \supset Ny)$	
2.	$(z)(\sim Bz \supset \sim Az)$	
3.	$(\exists x) Ax \ / \therefore \ (\exists x) (Ax \cdot Nx)$	

We remove the existential quantifier first, to avoid violating the second restriction on **EI**.

4.	Ax	3 **EI**

Now we remove the remaining quantifiers. As we remove the quantifiers, we change the bound variables so they are all free variables of the same kind. (We use the variable x here, but y or z or even w would work just as well.)

5.	$Bx \supset Nx$	1 UI
6.	$\sim Bx \supset \sim Ax$	2 UI

We complete the proof by using sentential logic and then binding the result with **EG.**

7.	$Ax \supset Bx$	6 **Contra**
8.	$Ax \supset Nx$	5,7 **HS**
9.	Nx	4,8 **MP**
10.	$Ax \cdot Nx$	4,9 **Conj**
11.	$(\exists x)(Ax \cdot Nx)$	10 **EG**

Examples

Here are two more examples:

(1)	1. $(x)\,(Ax \supset Bx)$		
	2. $(x)\,[Bx \supset (Ax \supset \sim Fx)]$		
	3. $(x)\,[(\sim Cx \cdot Dx) \supset Fx]$		$/\therefore (x)\,[Ax \supset (Cx \lor \sim Dx)]$
	4. Ax		**AP**
	5. $Ax \supset Bx$		1 **UI**
	6. $Bx \supset (Ax \supset \sim Fx)$		2 **UI**
	7. $(\sim Cx \cdot Dx) \supset Fx$		3 **UI**
	8. Bx		4,5 **MP**
	9. $(Bx \cdot Ax) \supset \sim Fx$		6 **Exp**
	10. $Bx \cdot Ax$		4,8 **Conj**
	11. $\sim Fx$		9,10 **MP**
	12. $\sim (\sim Cx \cdot Dx)$		7,11 **MT**
	13. $\sim \sim Cx \lor \sim Dx$		12 **DeM**
	14. $Cx \lor \sim Dx$		13 **DN**
	15. $Ax \supset (Cx \lor \sim Dx)$		4–14 **CP**
	16. $(x)\,[Ax \supset (Cx \lor \sim Dx)]$		15 **UG**

Note the use of **CP** in this proof. This is a very useful way to solve proofs that have universally quantified conclusions.

(2)	1. $(\exists x)\,Fx \supset (x)\,(Gx \supset Fx)$		
	2. $(\exists x)\,Hx \supset (x)(Fx \supset Hx)$		
	3. $(\exists x)\,(Fx \cdot Hx)$		$/\therefore (x)\,(Gx \supset Hx)$
	4. $Fx \cdot Hx$		3 **EI**
	5. Fx		4 **Simp**
	6. Hx		4 **Simp**
	7. $(\exists x)Fx$		5 **EG**
	8. $(\exists x)Hx$		6 **EG**
	9. $(x)\,(Gx \supset Fx)$		1,7 **MP**

10. $(x)(Fx \supset Hx)$ 2,8 **MP**
11. $Gy \supset Fy$ 9 **UI**
12. $Fy \supset Hy$ 10 **UI**
13. $Gy \supset Hy$ 11,12 **HS**
14. $(x)(Gx \supset Hx)$ 13 **UG**

Two things are notable about this example. First, we could not use **EI** on the first two premises. Second, in the last half of the proof we were forced to use some other free variable than x, because x was poisoned by **EI** in line 4.

LC Exercise 8-3

Prove valid:

(1)   1. $(x)(Rx \supset Bx)$
     2. $(\exists x) \sim Bx$ /∴ $(\exists x) \sim Rx$

(2)   1. $(x)(Fx \supset Gx)$
     2. $(y)(Gy \supset Hy)$ /∴ $(z)(\sim Hz \supset \sim Fz)$

(3)   1. Ka
     2. $(x)[Kx \supset (y)Hy]$ /∴ $(x)Hx$

(4)   1. $(x)(Fx \supset Gx)$
     2. $(x)(Ax \supset Fx)$
     3. $(\exists x) \sim Gx$ /∴ $(\exists x) \sim Ax$

(5)   1. $(x)(Mx \supset Sx)$
     2. $(x)(\sim Bx \vee Mx)$ /∴ $(x)(\sim Sx \supset \sim Bx)$

(6)   1. $(x)(Rx \supset Ox)$
     2. $(\exists y) \sim Oy$
     3. $(z)(\sim Rz \supset Pz)$ /∴ $(\exists z)Pz$

(7)   1. $(\exists x)(Ax \cdot Bx)$
     2. $(y)(Ay \supset Cy)$ /∴ $(\exists x)(Bx \cdot Cx)$

(8)   1. $(\exists x)Rx$
     2. $(x)(\sim Gx \supset \sim Rx)$
     3. $(x)Mx$ /∴ $(\exists x)Gx \cdot (\exists x)Mx$

(9)   1. $(x)[(Fx \vee Rx) \supset \sim Gx]$
     2. $(\exists x) \sim (\sim Fx \cdot \sim Rx)$ /∴ $(\exists y) \sim Gy$

(10)   1. $(x)(Kx \supset \sim Lx)$
      2. $(\exists x)(Mx \cdot Lx)$ /∴ $(\exists x)(Mx \cdot \sim Kx)$

(11)   1. $(x)(Fx \supset Gx)$
      2. $(y)(Ey \supset Fy)$
      3. $(z) \sim (Dz \cdot \sim Ez)$ /∴ $(x)(Dx \supset Gx)$

(12)   1. $(x)(Lx \supset \sim Kx)$
      2. $(\exists z)(Rz \cdot Kz)$
      3. $(y)[(\sim Ly \cdot Ry) \supset By]$ /∴ $(\exists x)Bx$

6 *Quantifier Negation (QN)*

The four other inference rules to be introduced into our predicate logic proof procedure all are referred to by the name **Quantifier Negation (QN).** Our proof system is complete without the addition of these four rules, but it is customary to include them because they are so useful in reducing the length and difficulty of a great many proofs.

To see how rule **QN** works, consider the following two statements:

1. $(x)(Wx)$ 　　　　　　　　　　Everything has weight.
2. $\sim (\exists x) \sim (Wx)$ 　　　　　　　　　There isn't anything that doesn't have weight.

Clearly, if everything has weight, then there isn't anything that doesn't have weight, and if there isn't anything that doesn't have weight, then everything must have weight. So statements 1 and 2 are logically equivalent statements. They say the same thing, only in different words. And so we ought to be able to substitute one for the other in any context, which is what the first of the four **QN** rules allows.

Of course, that rule does not concern just this one pair of sentences. Any two sentences related in the way that these two are fall under this rule. Here are several other examples:

1. From $\sim (\exists y) \sim (Fy \cdot Gy)$ we can derive $(y)(Fy \cdot Gy)$, and vice versa, from $(y)(Fy \cdot Gy)$ we can derive $\sim (\exists y) \sim (Fy \cdot Gy)$.
2. From $\sim (\exists z) \sim (\sim Rz \vee Lz)$ we can derive $(z)(\sim Rz \vee Lz)$, and vice versa.
3. From $(x)[Fx \supset \sim (Mx \supset \sim Nx)]$ we can derive $\sim (\exists x) \sim [Fx \supset \sim (Mx \supset \sim Nx)]$, and vice versa.

The point is that adding (x) to an expression does the same job as adding $\sim (\exists x) \sim$ to that expression, and similarly, adding $\sim (\exists x) \sim$ to an expression does the same job as adding (x) to it. And the first version of rule **QN** permits us to make inferences from one of these sorts of expressions to the other.

Now consider two proofs that illustrate the usefulness of this first version of rule **QN.** Here is the first proof:

1. $(y)(Wy) \supset (\exists x)(Hx)$
2. $\sim (\exists y) \sim (Wy) / \therefore (\exists x)(Hx)$

In this case, rule **QN** permits us to move from premise 2 to

3. $(y)(Wy)$ 　　　　　　　　　　　2 **QN**

And then we can complete the proof quite easily:

4. $(\exists x)(Hx)$ 　　　　　　　　　　1,3 **MP**

In this case, rule **QN** permitted us to replace the argument's second premise with an equivalent premise that permitted us then to use another rule of inference (**MP**) and successfully drive the argument's conclusion.

Now consider a second argument:

1. $\sim (\exists z) \sim (Wz \supset Hz)$
2. $Wa / \therefore Ha$

In order to construct this proof, we need to drop the ($\exists z$) quantifier from the first premise, but we can't use rule **EI** to do so, because the quantifier ($\exists z$) does not quantify the whole of the first line. Using rule **QN,** however, we can replace the first premise of this argument with the equivalent statement $(z)(Wz \supset Hz)$, obtained by replacing the expression $\sim (\exists z) \sim$ with (z):

3. $(z)(Wz \supset Hz)$ 1 **QN**

And then we can use rules **UI** and **MP** to obtain the argument's conclusion:

4. $Wa \supset Ha$ 3 **UI**
5. Ha 2,3 **MP**

What the first version of rule **QN** tells us is that if we have a statement quantified by a universal quantifier, we can replace that quantifier by an existential quantifier provided we place negation signs both to the right and the left of the existential quantifier. And, of course, the first version of **QN** also permits the reverse process, replacing an existential quantifier that has negation signs both right and left with a universal quantifier that has negation signs neither to the right nor to the left.

Examples

Here are several examples of correct uses of this first version of rule **QN:**

(1)   1. $(x)(Fx \supset Gx)$
        2. $\sim (\exists x) \sim (Fx \supset Gx)$ 1 **QN**
(2)   1. $\sim (\exists x) \sim (Fx \supset Gx)$
        2. $(x)(Fx \supset Gx)$ 1 **QN**
(3)   1. $(y)[Fy \supset (Ry \vee Hya)]$
        2. $\sim (\exists y) \sim [Fy \supset (Ry \vee Hya)]$ 1 **QN**
(4)   1. $\sim (\exists z) \sim [\sim Sz \vee \sim (\sim Tz \vee \sim Pz)]$
        2. $(z)[\sim Sz \vee \sim (\sim Tz \vee \sim Pz)]$ 1 **QN**

The other three varieties of rule **QN** are quite similar to the first one. Here is what all four of the **QN** rules say with respect to one set of substitution instances:

1. $(x)(Wx) :: \sim (\exists x) \sim (Wx)$
2. $(\exists x)(Wx) :: \sim (x) \sim (Wx)$
3. $(x) \sim (Wx) :: \sim (\exists x)(Wx)$
4. $(\exists x) \sim (Wx) :: \sim (x)(Wx)$

The first of these formulas tells us that we can move from "Everything has weight" to "There isn't anything that does not have weight," the second from "Something has weight" to "It's false that nothing has weight," the third from "Everything is such that it doesn't have weight" to "It's false that something has weight," and the fourth from "There is something that doesn't have any weight" to "It's false that everything has weight."

Examples

The **QN** rules permit an indefinite number of moves like the ones just given. For instance, it permits all of the following inferences:

1. $(\exists y)(\sim Fy \vee Gy)$
∴ 2. $\sim (y) \sim (\sim Fy \vee Gy)$
1. $\sim (\exists x)[\sim Rx \supset (\exists y)(Cy \vee \sim Dy)]$
∴ 2. $(x) \sim [\sim Rx \supset (\exists y)(Cy \vee \sim Dy)]$
1. $(z) \sim (Fz \supset Gz)$
∴ 2. $\sim (\exists z)(Fz \supset Gz)$
1. $\sim (x) \sim [Pxa \vee (Gx \supset \sim Fx)]$
∴ 2. $(\exists x)[Pxa \vee (Gx \supset \sim Fx)]$

The key to successful use of the four quantifier negation rules is to notice that they all require us to do exactly the same three things: (1) change the quantifier in question from an existential to a universal quantifier, or vice versa; (2) remove any negation signs there may be either to the left or to the right of that quantifier; and (3) put negation signs in whichever of these two places there may not have originally been one. Thus, in one of the examples above, we moved from $(x)(Fx)$ to $\sim (\exists x) \sim (Fx)$ by changing the quantifier from (x) to $(\exists x)$ and by adding negation signs both to the right and to the left of the quantifier (where there had been none before). And in moving from, say, $\sim (\exists y)(Fy \cdot \sim Gy)$ to $(y) \sim (Fy \cdot \sim Gy)$, we would change the existential quantifier to a universal, remove the negation sign from in front of the quantifier, and add a negation sign right after the quantifier.

The notation introduced to state the four quantifier rules in a precise manner also can be used to do the same for the four versions of the Quantifier Negation (**QN**) rule:

1. $(u)(\ldots u \ldots) :: \sim (\exists u) \sim (\ldots u \ldots)$
2. $(\exists u)(\ldots u \ldots) :: \sim (u) \sim (\ldots u \ldots)$
3. $(u) \sim (\ldots u \ldots) :: \sim (\exists u)(\ldots u \ldots)$
4. $(\exists u) \sim (\ldots u \ldots) :: \sim (u)(\ldots u \ldots)$

where the expression $(\ldots u \ldots)$ is some sentence or sentence form, generally (but not necessarily) containing at least one occurrence of u free in $(\ldots u \ldots)$. Rule **QN** permits the assertion of one side of these equivalence argument forms once the other side has been obtained in a proof.

L& Exercise 8-4

Which of the following are not correct uses of rule **QN**? For each incorrect use, provide an alternative sentence that can be correctly derived using this rule.

(1) 1. $(x) \sim Fx$
  $\therefore$ 2. $\sim (\exists x) \sim Fx$

(2) 1. $\sim (\exists x)Fx$
  $\therefore$ 2. $(x) \sim Fx$

(3) 1. $(x) \sim (\sim Fx \lor Gx)$
  $\therefore$ 2. $\sim (\exists x)(Fx \lor Gx)$

(4) 1. $\sim (\exists y) \sim (Ry \cdot \sim Ky)$
  $\therefore$ 2. $(y) \sim (Ry \cdot \sim Ky)$

(5) 1. $\sim (\exists y)(\sim Ry \cdot \sim Ky)$
  $\therefore$ 2. $(y)(Ry \cdot \sim Ky)$

(6) 1. $(z)(Fz \supset Gz)$
  $\therefore$ 2. $\sim (\exists z) \sim (Fz \supset Gz)$

(7) 1. $\sim (z) \sim [(Fz \supset Gz) \supset \sim Gz]$
  $\therefore$ 2. $(\exists z)[(Fz \supset Gz) \supset \sim Gz]$

(8) 1. $(y) \sim (Fy) \supset (\exists z)(Gz \cdot Hz)$
  $\therefore$ 2. $\sim (\exists y)[Fy \supset (\exists z)(Gz \cdot Hz)]$

(9) 1. $(y) \sim Fy \supset (\exists z)(Gz \cdot Hz)$
  $\therefore$ 2. $\sim (\exists y) \sim Fy \supset (\exists z)(Gz \cdot Hz)$

(10) 1. $(x) \sim (Fx \supset Gx)$
  $\therefore$ 2. $\sim (\exists x) \sim (Fx \supset Gx)$

⚹ Walk-Through: Predicate Logic Proofs with QN

Rule **QN** makes it possible to solve many proofs efficiently. Let's work through an example.

1. $\sim (\exists x) \sim (\sim Ax \lor Bx)$
2. $\sim (x) Bx$ $/ \therefore \sim (x)Ax$

We need to use **QN** on our premises to get them in shape for removing quantifiers.

3. $(x)(\sim Ax \lor Bx)$ 1 **QN**
4. $(\exists x) \sim Bx$ 2 **QN**

Now we can remove the quantifiers, remembering to **EI** first. Then we can use **DS**.

5. $\sim Bx$ 4 **EI**
6. $\sim Ax \lor Bx$ 3 **UI**
7. $\sim Ax$ 5,6 **DS**

In order to solve the proof, we need to recognize that the conclusion is equivalent to $(\exists x) \sim Ax$ (by **QN**). So we can complete the proof by adding on the *existential* quantifier and then applying **QN** to the result.

8. $(\exists x) \sim Ax$ 7 **EG**
9. $\sim (x)Ax$ 8 **QN**

L& Exercise 8-5

Prove valid:

(1) 1. $(\exists x)Fx \lor (\exists x)Gx$
  2. $(x) \sim Fx / \therefore (\exists x)Gx$

(2) 1. $(x)(Hx \supset \sim Kx)$
  /∴ $\sim (\exists y)(Hy \cdot Ky)$
(3) 1. $\sim (x)Ax$ /∴ $(\exists x)(Ax \supset Bx)$
(4) 1. $\sim (\exists x)Fx$ /∴ $Fa \supset Ga$
(5) 1. $(\exists x)Fx \supset (x) \sim Gx$
  2. $(\exists x)Ex \supset \sim (x) \sim Fx$
  /∴ $(\exists x)Ex \supset \sim (\exists x)Gx$
(6) 1. $(\exists x)(Ax \cdot Bx) \supset (y)Cy$
  2. $\sim Ca$ /∴ $(x)(Ax \supset \sim Bx)$
(7) 1. $(x)[(Fx \lor Hx) \supset (Gx \cdot Ax)]$
  2. $\sim (x)(Ax \cdot Gx)$ /∴ $(\exists x) \sim Hx$
(8) 1. $\sim (x)(Hx \lor Kx)$
  2. $(y)[(\sim Ky \lor Ly) \supset My]$ /∴ $(\exists z)Mz$
(9) 1. $(x)[(Fx \lor Gx) \supset Hx]$
  2. $(x)[(Hx \lor Kx) \supset Lx]$
  /∴ $(x)(Fx \supset Lx)$
(10) 1. $(\exists x)Rx \supset (\exists x)Sx$
  2. $(x)(Tx \supset Rx)$
  /∴ $(\exists x)Tx \supset (\exists x)Sx$
(11) 1. $(x)[(Ax \lor Bx) \supset Cx]$
  2. $\sim (\exists y)(Cy \lor Dy)$ /∴ $\sim (\exists x)Ax$
(12) 1. $(x)(Gx \supset Hx)$
  2. $(\exists x)(Ix \cdot \sim Hx)$
  3. $(x)(\sim Fx \lor Gx)$ /∴ $(\exists x)(Ix \cdot \sim Fx)$
(13) 1. $(x)[(Ax \cdot Bx) \supset Cx]$
  2. $\sim Cb$ /∴ $\sim (x)(Ax \cdot Bx)$
(14) 1. $\sim (x)(Fx \supset Gx)$
  2. $\sim (\exists x)(\sim Gx \cdot Hx)$ /∴ $(\exists x) \sim Hx$
(15) 1. $(x)(Hx \supset Kx)$
  2. $(\exists x)Hx \lor (\exists x)Kx$ /∴ $(\exists x)Kx$
(16) 1. $(x)[(Rx \lor Qx) \supset Sx]$
  2. $(\exists y)(\sim Qy \lor \sim Ry)$
  3. $(\exists z) \sim (Pz \lor \sim Qz)$ /∴ $(\exists w)Sw$
(17) 1. $\sim (x)(Ax \lor Bx)$
  2. $(\exists x) \sim Ax \supset (y)(Cy \supset By)$
  /∴ $\sim (x)Cx$
(18) 1. $(\exists x)Fx \supset (\exists x)(Gx \cdot Hx)$
  2. $(\exists x)(Hx \lor Kx) \supset (x)Lx$
  /∴ $(x)(Fx \supset Lx)$
(19) 1. $(x)[(Bx \cdot Ax) \supset Dx]$
  2. $(\exists x)(Qx \cdot Ax)$
  3. $(x)(\sim Bx \supset \sim Qx)$
  /∴ $(\exists x)(Dx \cdot Qx)$
(20) 1. $(x)[Px \supset (Ax \lor Bx)]$
  2. $(x)[(Bx \lor Cx) \supset Qx]$
  /∴ $(x)[(Px \cdot \sim Ax) \supset Qx]$

(21)   1. $(x)[Px \supset (Qx \vee Rx)]$
      2. $(x)[(Sx \cdot Px) \supset \sim Qx]$
      $/\therefore (x)(Sx \supset Px) \supset (x)(Sx \supset Rx)$
(22)   1. $(x)[(Ax \vee Bx) \supset (Cx \cdot Dx)]$
      $/\therefore (\exists x)(Ax \vee Cx) \supset (\exists x)Cx$

Key terms

The natural deduction rules introduced in this chapter can be found on pages 173 and 174. They are also reprinted inside the front cover.

Chapter Nine

Relational
Predicate Logic

---

1 *Relational Predicates*

We now broaden our coverage of predicate logic to include relational predicates. This allows us to symbolize sentences like "Kareem is taller than Mugsy" as *Tkm*. With relational predicates the order in which letters occur is significant. If we reverse the individual constants in the sentence just mentioned, giving us *Tmk*, the sentence now asserts that Mugsy is taller than Kareem.

Examples

Let *Dxy* denote the relational property of *x* having defeated *y*, *j* denote Joe Louis, *m* Max Schmeling, *r* Rocky Marciano, and *b* Billy Conn:

1. Joe Louis defeated Max Schmeling.   *Djm*
2. Schmeling also defeated Louis.   *Dmj*
3. Louis didn't defeat Rocky Marciano.   ~ *Djr*
4. But he did beat Billy Conn.   *Djb*
5. So Louis defeated Conn and Schmeling.   *Djb · Djm*
6. And he lost to Marciano and Schmeling.   *Drj · Dmj*

Here are several utterances translated using obvious abbreviations:

7. Mount Everest is taller than Mt. Godwin Austen (K2). *Teg*
8. Lake Huron is larger than Lake Erie.   *Lhe*
9. But it's smaller than Lake Superior.   *Lsh*
10. Hillary was sitting between Barbara and Nancy.   *Bhbn*

Simple sentences with relational predicates, like those above, are not particularly difficult to symbolize. Neither are sentences where a relational predicate is accompanied by a single quantifier. The three-step strategy we employed in Chapter 6 works well here also. For example, if our sentence is "Everyone likes Henry" we first ask who or what the sentence is about. In this case our subject is people—*Px*. Our sentence says something about all people; this gives us $(x)(Px \supset$ ____ $)$. And, finally, what it says about all people is that they like Henry, which we can symbolize using a relational predicate: $(x)(Px \supset Lxh)$.

Note that the subject we should use for symbolizations involving relational predicates is not always the grammatical subject of the sentence. For example, we can rephrase the sentence "Henry likes everyone" as "Everyone is liked by Henry," which can then be translated $(x)(Px \supset Lhx)$. Rephrasing like this gives us a subject that is coupled with a quantifier, so that the sentence as reformulated is predicating something of some or all individuals of a certain kind. Sentences often need to be reworked this way before it becomes obvious how they should be symbolized.

Examples

Let $Axy =$ "*x* is afraid of *y*"; $b =$ "Biff"; and $p =$ "Percy." For the sake of simplicity, we will restrict our domain of discourse to humans.

1.	Biff is afraid of no one.	$\sim (\exists x)Abx$
2.	Biff is afraid of everyone.	$(x)Abx$
3.	Everyone is afraid of Biff.	$(x)Axb$
4.	No one is afraid of Biff.	$\sim (\exists x)Axb$
5.	No one is afraid of Biff or Percy.	$\sim (\exists x)(Axb \lor Axp)$
6.	Everyone who is afraid of Biff is also afraid of Percy.	$(x)(Axb \supset Axp)$
7.	Biff is afraid of everyone who is not afraid of Percy.	$(x)(\sim Axp \supset Abx)$
8.	Biff is not afraid of anyone who is afraid of Percy.	$(x)(Axp \supset \sim Abx)$

LC Exercise 9-1

Symbolize the following sentences, using the indicated letters. (Restrict the domain of discourse to humans.)

1. Cybill Shepherd isn't married to Bruce Willis. ($Mxy =$ "*x* is married to *y*"; $c =$ "Cybill Shepherd"; $b =$ "Bruce Willis")
2. So, obviously, Willis isn't married to Shepherd.
3. But if Willis is married, it isn't to Jane Fonda. ($Mx =$ "*x* is married"; $j =$ "Jane Fonda")
4. In fact, Bruce Willis is married to Demi Moore. ($d =$ "Demi Moore")
5. So if Bruce Willis is married, it isn't to Cybill Shepherd or to Jane Fonda.
6. David Letterman is not married to anyone. ($d =$ "David Letterman")
7. David Letterman is not interested in anyone who breaks into his house. ($Ixy =$ "*x* is interested in *y*"; $Bxy =$ "*x* breaks into *y*'s house")

8. There is some woman who keeps breaking into Dave's house, but he is not interested in her. (*Wx* = "*x* is a woman")

9. If Beth can't pass the final, no one can. (*b* = "Beth"; *f* = "the final"; *Pxy* = "*x* can pass *y*"; *Px* = "*x* is a person")

10. If someone didn't pass the final, it was Jeff or Kate. (*j* = "Jeff"; *k* = "Kate")

11. If someone is sitting between Julia and Harry, then there must not be anyone between Alice and Bob. (*j* = "Julia"; *h* = "Harry"; *a* = "Alice"; *b* = "Bob"; *Sxyz* = "*x* is sitting between *y* and *z*")

12. If there is an empty chair, then no one is sitting between Elmer and Gertrude. (*Cx* = "*x* is a chair"; *Ex* = "*x* is empty"; *e* = "Elmer"; *g* = "Gertrude")

13. Harriet has read all of Shakespeare's works. (*h* = "Harriet"; *s* = "Shakespeare"; *Rxy* = "*x* has read *y*"; *Wxy* = "*x* is a work of *y*")

14. Laura doesn't like any of Woody Allen's movies (*l* = "Laura"; *Lxy* = "*x* likes *y*"; *Mxy* = "*x* is a movie directed by *y*"; *a* = "Woody Allen")

15. Melissa likes some of Woody's movies, but not others. (*m* = "Melissa")

16. If Paul likes *Manhattan,* then he likes at least one of Woody Allen's movies. (*m* = "Manhattan"; *p* = "Paul")

17. Some people think Clarence Thomas harassed Anita Hill, and some do not. (*c* = "Clarence Thomas"; *a* = "Anita Hill"; *Txyz* = "*x* thinks *y* harassed *z*"; *Px* = "*x* is a person")

18. If Thomas harassed Hill, then at least one Supreme Court judge is not qualified. (*Hxy* = "*x* harassed *y*"; *Sx* = "*x* is a Supreme Court judge"; *Qx* = "*x* is qualified")

19. If Thomas did not harass Hill, then some of the things said by Hill at the hearing are not true. (*h* = "the hearing"; *Sxyz* = "*x* is said by *y* at *z*"; *Tx* = "*x* is true")

20. If everything Hill said about Thomas at the hearing is true, then Thomas did sexually harass her. (*Swxyz* = "*w* is said by *y* about *x* at *z*")

2 *Symbolizations Containing Overlapping Quantifiers*

Symbolizations may contain quantifiers having overlapping scopes. An example is the sentence "Everything is different from everything," which in symbols becomes (*x*)(*y*)*Dxy*. This sentence is false, of course, because nothing can be different from itself. But it is meaningful, and so we want to have a way to symbolize it. (Notice that the false sentence "Everything is different from everything" is not the same as the true sentence "Everything is different from everything *else.*" To symbolize the latter, we need a symbol for identity, which will be introduced in Chapter 11.)

Examples

Here are some examples of multiply quantified sentences with overlapping quantifier scopes, along with their correct symbolizations (letting *Lxy* = "*x* loves *y*" and restricting the domain of discourse to human beings).

Sentence	Symbolization
1. Everyone loves everyone.	1. $(x)(y)Lxy$
2. Someone loves someone.	2. $(\exists x)(\exists y)Lxy$
3. Not everyone loves everyone.	3. $\sim (x)(y)Lxy$
4. No one loves anyone.	4. $(x)(y) \sim Lxy$ or
	$\sim (\exists x)(\exists y)Lxy$

The examples just considered all contain overlapping quantifiers of the same type. For instance, in sentence 1 above, both quantifiers are universal quantifiers; in sentence 2 both are existential quantifiers. In such cases, the order in which the quantifiers occur is not relevant to the meanings of the sentences. Thus, $(x)(y)Lxy$ says the same thing as $(y)(x)Lxy$.*

But when an existential and a universal quantifier are involved, order becomes crucial. Compare, for instance, the order of quantifiers in the two expressions $(x)(\exists y)Lxy$ and $(\exists y)(x)Lxy$. (In the former, the existential quantifier is within the scope of the universal quantifier, whereas in the latter it is the other way around.) If we let $Lxy =$ "x loves y" and restrict the domain of discourse to human beings, then $(x)(\exists y)Lxy$ says that every x (every person) loves some person or other, whereas $(\exists y)(x)Lxy$ says that some y (some person) is such that everyone loves that person. In other words, $(x)(\exists y)Lxy$ says that everyone loves someone or other, whereas $(\exists y)(x)Lxy$ says that there is someone who is loved by everyone, and these clearly are different.

3   Expansions and Overlapping Quantifiers

One way to better understand sentences of this kind is to become familiar with the *expansions* of various multiply quantified sentences. Take the sentence "Everyone loves everyone," in symbols $(x)(y)Lxy$, and consider its expansion in a universe containing just two individuals, a and b. To say that everyone loves everyone is to say that every x loves every y. Since there are exactly two x's in this universe, this says that the first x, namely a, loves every y (in symbols $(y)Lay$), and the second x, namely b, loves every y (in symbols $(y)Lby$). So a partial expansion of $(x)(y)Lxy$ is just the conjunction of $(y)Lay$ and $(y)Lby$, or $(y)Lay \cdot (y)Lby$. To obtain the complete expansion of $(x)(y)Lxy$, we also have to expand for the (y) quantifier. First, the left conjunct, $(y)Lay$, says that a loves every y, which in *this* two-individual universe means that $Laa \cdot Lab$. And second, the right conjunct, $(y)Lby$, says that b loves every y, which in this two-individual universe means that $Lba \cdot Lbb$. So the complete expansion of $(x)(y)Lxy$ is the conjunction $(Laa \cdot Lbb) \cdot (Lba \cdot Lbb)$.

---

*Of course, order is important when quantifiers have different scopes. For example, we can't reverse the positions of the universal quantifiers in $(x)(Fx \supset (y)Gxy)$ to get $(y)(Fx \supset (x)Gxy)$ because these two symbolizations clearly have different meanings (the second is not even a sentence, because the first x occurring in it is a free variable).

Now consider the sentence "Someone loves someone (or other)," in symbols $(\exists x)(\exists y)$ *Lxy*. To say that someone loves someone is to say that there is some *x* that loves some *y*. Since there are exactly two individuals in the universe in question, this is to say that either *a* loves some *y* (in symbols $(\exists y)Lay$) or *b* loves some *y* (in symbols $(\exists y)Lby$), in other words that $(\exists y)Lay \lor (\exists y)Lby$. The left disjunct, $(\exists y)Lay$, says that *a* loves either *a* or *b*, or in symbols that $Laa \lor Lab$. And the right disjunct, $(\exists y)Lby$, says that *b* loves either *a* or *b*, or in symbols that $Lba \lor Lbb$. So the complete expansion for $(\exists x)(\exists y)Lxy$ is the disjunction $(Laa \lor Lbb) \lor (Lba \lor Lbb)$. (Compare this with the expansion for $(x)(y)Lxy$.)

Examples

Here are more examples of multiply quantified sentences (including a few with mixed quantifiers), their correct symbolizations, and their expansions in a two-individual universe of discourse.

1. *Sentence:* No one loves anyone.
    Symbolization: $(x)(y) \sim Lxy$
    Expansion: $(\sim Laa \cdot \sim Lab) \cdot (\sim Lba \cdot \sim Lbb)$
2. *Sentence:* It's not true that someone loves some person (or other).
    Symbolization: $\sim (\exists x)(\exists y)Lxy$
    Expansion: $\sim [(Laa \lor Lab) \lor (Lba \lor Lbb)]$

Notice that this is just the expansion of the sentence "Someone loves someone (or other)" *negated.* (Notice also that the expansions of sentences 1 and 2 are logically equivalent.)

3. *Sentence:* There is somebody who doesn't love someone (or other).
    Symbolization: $(\exists x)(\exists y) \sim Lxy$
    Expansion: $(\sim Laa \lor \sim Lab) \lor (\sim Lba \lor \sim Lbb)$
4. *Sentence:* Not everyone loves everyone.
    Symbolization: $\sim (x)(y)Lxy$
    Expansion: $\sim [(Laa \cdot Lab) \cdot (Lba \cdot Lbb)]$

Notice that the expansion of sentence 4 is just the expansion of the sentence "Everyone loves everyone" *negated.* (Notice also that the expansions of sentences 3 and 4 are logically equivalent by DeMorgan's Theorem.)

5. *Sentence:* Everyone loves someone (or other).
    Symbolization: $(x)(\exists y)Lxy$
    Expansion: $(Laa \lor Lab) \cdot (Lba \lor Lbb)$

We arrive at this expansion by expanding first with respect to the universal quantifier to obtain the semi-expansion $(\exists y)Lay \cdot (\exists y)Lby$, then expanding the left conjunct to obtain $(Laa \lor Lab) \cdot (\exists y)Lby$, and finally the right conjunct to obtain $(Laa \lor Lab) \cdot (Lba \lor Lbb)$.

6. *Sentence:* Someone is such that everyone loves that person (or, more colloquially, someone is loved by everyone).
    Symbolization: (∃y)(x)Lxy
    Expansion: (Laa · Lba) ∨ (Lab · Lbb)

To arrive at this expansion, we can expand first with respect to the existential quantifier, to obtain the semi-expansion (x)Lxa ∨ (x)Lxb, then expanding the left disjunct to obtain (Laa · Lba) ∨ (x)Lxb, and finally the right disjunct to obtain (Laa · Lbb) ∨ (Lab · Lbb). (Sentences 5 and 6 are important because their expansions show that the order of mixed quantifiers *does* make a difference.)

7. *Sentence:* There is someone whom no one loves.
    Symbolization: (∃x)(y) ~ Lyx
    Expansion: (~ Laa · ~ Lba) ∨ (~ Lab · ~ Lbb)
8. *Sentence:* Everyone is such that someone (or other) does not love that person (or, more colloquially, everyone is unloved by someone (or other)).
    Symbolization: (x)(∃y) ~ Lyx
    Expansion: (~ Laa ∨ ~ Lba) · (~ Lab ∨ ~ Lbb)

LC Exercise 9-2

Symbolize the following sentences (letting *Sxy* = "*x* is smaller than *y*") and construct their expansions in a two-individual universe of discourse.

1. Everything is smaller than everything.
2. Something is smaller than something (or other).
3. There is something that is smaller than everything.
4. Everything is smaller than something (or other).
5. Not all things are smaller than something (or other).
6. There isn't anything that is smaller than everything.
7. Nothing is smaller than anything.
8. There is something such that everything is smaller than that thing.
9. It's false that nothing is smaller than anything.
10. It's an untruth that everything is smaller than something (or other).
11. Nothing is smaller than itself.
12. Anything that is smaller than everything is smaller than itself.

4   *Places and Times*

Mastering multiply quantified symbolizations generally just requires a bit of practice to get the hang of it. But the symbolizations of statements concerning places or times are particularly interesting and sometimes cause trouble.

Consider the statement "Somewhere, the streets are all paved with gold." This sentence asserts that there is someplace where all things that are streets are paved with gold. So it can be symbolized as $(\exists x)[(Px \cdot (y)(Syx \supset Gy)]$, where $Px = $ "x is a place"; $Sxy = $ "x is a street in y"; and $Gx = $ "x is paved with gold."

Similarly, the sentence "The sun never sets on the British empire" can be symbolized as $\sim (\exists x)(Tx \cdot Ssbx)$, where $Tx = $ "x is a time"; $b = $ "the British empire"; $s = $ "the sun"; and $Sxyz = $ "x sets on y at time z." This symbolization makes clear the idea that it is not the case that there is a time when the sun sets on the British empire. (This is what is called a dated example in the trade.)

And then there is the famous line "The poor will always be with us," which we can symbolize as $(x)[Tx \supset (\exists y)(Py \cdot Wyx)]$, where $Tx = $ "x is a time"; $Px = $ "x is poor"; and $Wxy = $ "x is with us at y." This symbolization expresses the idea that given any time whatsoever there is some poor person or other who is alive at that time. (This, unfortunately, is not a dated example.)

Finally, here is one that is somewhat more complicated: "If all industrial nations don't stop polluting the atmosphere, then every place on earth will be contaminated." Letting $Ix = $ "x is an industrial nation"; $Sx = $ "x stops polluting the atmosphere"; $Pxy = $ "x is a place on y"; $e = $ "earth"; and $Cx = $ "x is contaminated," we can symbolize this sentence as $\sim (x)(Ix \supset Sx) \supset (y)(Pye \supset Cy)$. Note that no quantifier quantifies the whole of this symbolization and that the major logical connective is the horseshoe.

🚶 Walk-Through: Symbolizations with Multiple Quantifiers

To symbolize with multiple quantifiers, we employ a slightly modified version of our standard three-step strategy. The first two steps are usually the same. We begin by determining the subject (not necessarily the grammatical subject) and the quantifier that goes with that subject. If our sentence is "Cheaters never prosper," we can construe this as making a claim about all cheaters. This gives us the first half of our symbolization: $(x)(Cx \supset \underline{\quad})$. The third step is just a bit trickier. What does this sentence say about all cheaters? It says there is no time at which they prosper. To complete our symbolization, we in effect translate as though our variable x were a constant. To see how this is so, consider how we would symbolize the sentence "Larry never prospers." We could symbolize the sentence this way: $\sim (\exists y)(Ty \cdot Ply)$. The second half of our more complex symbolization looks just like this, except instead of the constant l we have our variable x: $\sim (\exists y)(Ty \cdot Pxy)$. Here then is our complete symbolization: $(x)[Cx \supset \sim (\exists y)(Ty \cdot Pxy)]$

Here's another example.

Sentence: The only good test is one that some students will fail.
Subject: Good tests: Gx
Some or all? All: $(x)[Gx \supset$
What does it say about them? There is at least one student who fails the test: $(x)[Gx \supset (\exists y)(Sy \cdot Fyx)]$

Here is a sentence where the second quantifier is added in the first step.

Sentence: "Any test that everyone fails is a bad test."
Subject: Tests that are failed by everyone (that take them): $Tx \cdot (y)(Tyx \supset Fyx)$
Some or all? All: $(x)[Tx \cdot (y)(Tyx \supset Fyx)] \supset$
What does it say about them? They are bad tests: $(x)\{[Tx \cdot (y)(Tyx \supset Fyx)] \supset Bx\}$

LC Exercise 9-3

Symbolize the following, revealing as much structure as you can and indicating the meanings of the abbreviations that you use.

1. There are cheaters in some places.
2. But there aren't cheaters in every place.
3. Cheaters are everywhere.
4. There is no place more beautiful than Hawaii.
5. A person's work is never done.
6. There comes a time in every person's life when that person must face reality.
7. You can fool all of the people some of the time.
8. You can fool some of the people all of the time.
9. You can't fool all of the people all of the time.
10. It's never too late to reform.
11. A barking dog never bites.
12. Hillary Rodham Clinton always wears designer dresses.
13. There never was a time or place without sin.
14. But there also never was a time or place without honesty.
15. There is a sucker born every minute.—P. T. Barnum (?)

5   *Symbolizing "Someone," "Somewhere," "Sometime," and So On*

Finally, we need to consider a few somewhat different symbolizations. Take the sentence "If someone is too noisy, then everyone in the room will be annoyed." Restricting the universe of discourse to human beings, we can partially symbolize this sentence as

If $(\exists x) Nx$ then $(y)(Ry \supset Ay)$

and then complete the symbolization as

$(\exists x)Nx \supset (y)(Ry \supset Ay)$

But the grammatically similar sentence "If someone is too noisy, then everyone in the room will be annoyed *with that person*" must be symbolized somewhat differently. We cannot partially symbolize it as

If $(\exists x)\, Nx$ then $(y)(Ry \supset Ayx)$

and then complete the symbolization as

$(\exists x) Nx \supset (y)(Ry \supset Ayx)$

because the last x variable in this expression is a *free variable,* so that this expression is not a sentence.

    And we cannot rectify this error simply by extending the scope of the existential quantifier; that is, we cannot correctly symbolize the sentence as

$(\exists x)[Nx \supset (y)(Ry \supset Ayx)]$

Although this is a sentence, it is not equivalent to one we are trying to translate. This new sentence asserts that there is at least one person such that if that person is too noisy, then everyone in the room will be annoyed with that person. This would be true if everyone became annoyed when one person, say Smith, was too noisy, but not when some other person, say Jones, was too noisy. But the implication of our original sentence is that if *anyone* is too noisy, then everyone will be annoyed with that person. So the symbolization just suggested will not do.

    Instead, we can symbolize our sentence as

$(x)[Nx \supset (y)(Ry \supset Ayx)]$

using a *universal* quantifier.

    In this case, it is the word "someone" that is misleading. It sometimes functions as an existential quantifier and sometimes as a universal quantifier. The words "something," "somewhere," "sometime," and so on can be misleading in the same way. Hence it is wise to pay close attention to the precise meaning of a sentence in which any of these terms occurs before deciding whether its correct symbolization requires an existential or a universal quantifier.

    Even so, it still may seem strange that "If someone is too noisy, then everyone in the room will be annoyed" is correctly symbolized as $(\exists x)(Nx) \supset (y)(Ry \supset Ay)$, using an existential quantifier whose scope is restricted to the antecedent of the symbolization, whereas "If someone is too noisy, then everyone in the room will be annoyed with that person" is correctly symbolized as $(x)[Nx \supset (y)(Ry \supset Ayx)]$, using a universal quantifier whose scope is the entire symbolization. But perhaps this strangeness can be dispelled to some extent by pointing out that $(\exists x)(Nx) \supset (y)(Ry \supset Ay)$ *is equivalent to* $(x)[Nx \supset (y) (Ry \supset Ay)]$. In other words, there is a sense in which the term "something" functions as a universal quantifier in both sentences.

    Now consider the sentence "If someone is too noisy, then if everyone in the room is annoyed, someone will complain." Restricting the universe of discourse to human beings, we can partially symbolize this sentence as

If $(\exists x)(Nx)$ then $[$if $(y)(Ry \supset Ay)$ then $(\exists z)(Cz)]$

and complete the symbolization as

$(\exists x)(Nx) \supset [(y)(Ry \supset Ay) \supset (\exists z)(Cz)]$

But the grammatically similar sentence "If someone is too noisy, then if all of the people in the room are annoyed, they all will dislike *that person*" must be symbolized somewhat differently. We cannot partially symbolize *it* as

If $(\exists x)Nx$ then [if $(y)(Ry \supset Ay)$ then Dyx] and complete the symbolization as $(\exists x)[Nx \supset [(y)(Ry \supset Ay) \supset (z)(Dyx)]$

because the last *x* and *y* variables in this symbolization *are free variables,* so that this expression is not a sentence. Instead, the correct symbolization of our sentence is

$(x)\{Nx \supset [(y)(Ry \supset Ay) \supset (y)(Ry \supset Dyx)]\}$

Examples

1. Everyone knows somebody (or other).
   $(x)[Px \supset (\exists y)(Py \cdot Kxy)]$
2. Everyone knows everyone.
   $(x)[(Px \supset (y)(Py \supset Kxy)]$ or $\sim (\exists x)[Px \cdot (\exists y)(Py \cdot \sim Kxy)]$
3. Someone knows everyone.
   $(\exists x)[Px \cdot (y)(Py \supset Kxy)]$ or $(\exists x)[Px \cdot \sim (\exists y)(Py \cdot \sim Kxy)]$
4. Someone knows somebody (or other).
   $(\exists x)[Px \cdot (\exists y)(Py \cdot Kxy)]$
5. No one knows everybody.
   $(x)[Px \supset (\exists y)(Py \cdot \sim Kxy)]$ or $\sim (\exists x)[Px \cdot (y)(Py \supset Kxy)]$
6. No one knows anybody.
   $(x)[Px \supset \sim (\exists y)(Py \cdot Kxy)]$ or $\sim (\exists x)[Px \cdot (\exists y)(Py \cdot Kxy)]$
7. Some people don't know everybody.
   $(\exists x)[Px \cdot (\exists y)(Py \cdot \sim Kxy)]$
8. Some people don't know anybody.
   $(\exists x)[Px \cdot (y)(Py \supset \sim Kxy)]$
9. Honest candidates always get defeated by dishonest ones.
   $(x)\{(Cx \cdot Hx) \supset (\exists y)[(Cy \cdot \sim Hy) \cdot Dyx]\}$
10. Some honest candidates get defeated by dishonest ones.
    $(\exists x)\{(Cx \cdot Hx) \cdot (\exists y)[(Cy \cdot \sim Hy) \cdot Dyx]\}$
11. No honest candidates get defeated by dishonest ones.
    $\sim (\exists x)\{(Cx \cdot Hx) \cdot (\exists y)[(Cy \cdot \sim Hy) \cdot Dyx]\}$
12. All candidates who get defeated by honest candidates are themselves dishonest.
    $(x)\{\{Cx \cdot (\exists y)[(Cy \cdot Hy) \cdot Dyx]\} \supset \sim Hx\}$
13. All barbers who don't shave themselves don't shave any barbers.
    $(x)[(Bx \cdot \sim Sxx) \supset \sim (\exists y)(By \cdot Sxy)]$
14. Barbers who don't shave themselves are shaved by someone who is a barber.
    $(x)[(Bx \cdot \sim Sxx) \supset (\exists y)(By \cdot Syx)]$
15. Barbers shave all and only those who are barbers.
    $(x)[Bx \supset (y)(Sxy \equiv By)]$

16. If someone is a barber who does not shave himself, then someone does not get shaved by any barber.
    $(\exists x)(Bx \cdot \sim Sxx) \supset (\exists y)[Py \cdot (z)(Bz \supset \sim Szy)]$

17. If there is anyone who does not shave himself, then if no one is shaved by any barber, he (who does not shave himself) will not be shaved by any barber.
    $(x)\{(Px \cdot \sim Sxx) \supset \{(y)[Py \supset \sim (\exists z)(Bz \cdot Szy)] \supset \sim (\exists v)(Bv \cdot Svx)\}\}$

18. If there is someone who does not shave himself, then if no barber shaves anyone, there is someone who is not shaved by anyone.
    $(\exists x)(Px \cdot \sim Sxx) \supset \{(y)[By \supset (z)(Pz \supset \sim Syz)] \supset (\exists u)[Pu \cdot (w)(Pw \supset \sim Swu)]\}$

🔲 Exercise 9-4

Symbolize the following sayings, revealing as much of their internal structure as possible and indicating the intended meanings of your abbreviations.

1. A drama critic is a man who leaves no turn unstoned. —George Bernard Shaw
2. The one who laughs last laughs best.
3. What is a cynic? A man who knows the price of everything and the value of nothing. —Oscar Wilde
4. A cult is a religion with no political power. —Tom Wolfe
5. Where there's smoke, there's fire.
6. All governments are run by liars. —I. F. Stone
7. Let the one who is without sin cast the first stone. —Jesus Christ
8. Uneasy lies the head that wears the crown. —William Shakespeare
9. He jests at scars that has never felt a wound. —William Shakespeare
10. A good professional can outperform any amateur.
11. Anyone who consults a psychiatrist ought to have his head examined.
12. God only helps those who help themselves.
13. God helps those who help themselves.
14. No one learns anything unless he teaches it to himself.
15. Every major horror of history was committed in the name of an altruistic motive. —Ayn Rand (among others)
16. Virtue has never been as respectable as money. —Mark Twain
17. A lawyer who pleads his own case has a fool for a client.
18. No one ever went broke underestimating the intelligence of the American public. —H. L. Mencken
19. Whosoever sheddeth man's blood, by man shall his blood be shed. —Genesis 9:6
20. The good that I want to do, I do not; but the evil I don't want to do, I do. —Romans 7:19

🔲 Exercise 9-5

Follow the instructions for Exercise 9-4. (Some of these are difficult.)

1. If a company goes bankrupt, then it deserves to go out of business.
2. Any candidate who doesn't cater to all potential voters is going to lose.

3. If any frontrunners don't cater to all potential voters, then some longshots are going to win.
4. If any politicians engage in demagoguery, then all politicians have to.
5. Everyone who believes in God obeys all of His commandments.
6. Everyone who believes in God always obeys all of His commandments.
7. Everyone who has benefited from a scientific discovery owes money to some scientist or other.
8. There isn't a single person in the whole world who has not benefited at one time or another from some scientific discovery or other.
9. If everyone has benefited from some scientific discovery or other, then some people haven't paid all of their bills.
10. If everyone has benefited from the scientific discoveries of Isaac Newton, then lots of us owe a debt of gratitude to him.
11. There is no psychiatrist who can help anyone who acts on astrological advice.
12. If everybody owes some amount of money or other to somebody or other, then no one is debt-free.
13. If some of us owe money to Isaac Newton, then there will come a time when we should pay him what we owe.
14. Everyone who has not paid any money to some scientist or other looks down on anyone who has.
15. You can fool some of the people all of the time, and all of the people some of the time, but you can't fool all of the people all of the time. —Abraham Lincoln

LC Exercise 9-6

Translate the following into English, giving the predicate letters and individual constants their indicated meanings, making sure your translations are as close to colloquial English as you can make them.

Bxy = "x believes in y"
Dx = "x is disenfranchised"
Hxy = "x has y"
Mxy = "x is the master of y"
Px = "x is a person"
Rx = "x is a redeeming feature"
Vx = "x votes"
a = "Art"
g = "God"

1. $(x)(Px \supset Bxg)$
2. $(\exists x)(Px \cdot Bxg)$
3. $(\exists x)(Px \cdot \sim Gx)$
4. $\sim (x)(Px \supset Bxg)$
5. $\sim (\exists x)(Px \cdot Bxg)$
6. $(x)[(Px \cdot \sim Vx) \supset Dx]$
7. $(x)[(Px \cdot Dx) \supset \sim Mxx]$
8. $\sim (x)[(Px \cdot \sim Vx) \supset Dx]$

9. $(x)[Px \supset (\exists y)(Ry \cdot Hxy)]$
10. $(\exists x)[Px \cdot (y)(Ry \supset \sim Hxy)]$
11. $(\exists x)[Rx \cdot (y)(Py \supset Hyx)]$
12. $(x)[Rx \supset (\exists y)(Py \cdot \sim Hyx)]$
13. $\sim (\exists x)(\exists y)[(Px \cdot Ry) \cdot Hxy]$
14. $(x)[Px \supset (y)(Ry \cdot \sim Hxy)]$
15. $(x)\{Px \supset [(y)(Ry \supset Hxy) \supset Bxg]\}$
16. $\sim Va \supset \{(x)[(Px \cdot \sim Vx) \supset Dx] \supset Da\}$
17. $(x)\{(Px \cdot Vx) \supset (y)[(Py \cdot \sim Vy) \supset Mxy]\}$
18. $(x)\{(Px \cdot Vx) \supset (\exists y)[(Py \cdot \sim Vy) \cdot Mxy]\}$

6   *Invalidity and Consistency in Relational Predicate Logic*

We demonstrate invalidity and consistency in relational predicate logic using the same techniques we employed for monadic predicate logic. For invalidity we produce an interpretation that makes the premises all true and the conclusion false. For consistency we need only an interpretation that makes all of the sentences true. As in monadic predicate logic, we can provide a complete interpretation, or we can use the more mechanical method in which we replace the quantified sentences with their expansions. Consider, for example, the following invalid argument:

1. $(x) (\exists y) Fxy / \therefore (\exists x) (y) Fxy$

We can show this argument to be invalid by providing an interpretion such as the following:

Domain: the integers
Fxy: x is greater than y

On this interpretation the premise says that every integer is greater than some integer, which is true, whereas the conclusion makes the obviously false assertion that some integer is greater than all integers.

   We can also show this argument to be invalid by producing an expansion of the premise and conclusion, assigning truth-values so as to make the premise true and the conclusion false, as follows:

1. $(Faa \lor Fab) \cdot (Fba \lor Fbb)$
       F T T   T   F T   T
$\therefore$ $(Faa \cdot Fab) \lor (Fba \cdot Fbb)$
       F F T F   F F T

LC Exercise 9-7

Show that the following arguments are invalid.

(1)   1. $(\exists x)(y)Fxy / \therefore (x)(\exists y)Fxy$
(2)   1. $(x)(\exists y) \sim Fxy / \therefore (\exists x)(y) \sim Fxy$

(3)   1. $(\exists x)\,(\exists y)Fxy$
          2. $(\exists x)\,(\exists y)Gxy$ /∴ $(\exists x)\,(\exists y)\,(Fxy \cdot Gxy)$
(4)   1. $(x)(\exists y)(Fx \supset Gxy)$ /∴ $(\exists x)\,(y)\,(Fx \supset Gxy)$
(5)   1. $(\exists x)(y)\,Fxy$ /∴ Faa
(6)   1. $(x)(\exists y)(Fxy \supset Gxy)$
          2. $(x)(\exists y)(Gxy \supset Hxy)$ /∴ $(x)(\exists y)(Fxy \supset Hxy)$
(7)   1. $(x)(y)(\exists z)\,Fxyz$ /∴ $(\exists x)(y)\,(z)\,Fxyz$
(8)   1. $(\exists x)(y)(z)\,Fxyz$ /∴ $(x)(y)\,(\exists z)\,Fxyz$

7   *Relational Predicate Logic Proofs*

The rules for predicate logic proofs introduced in Chapter 8 were devised to handle the complexities of relational predicate logic as well. If you have a premise that has multiple quantifiers, simply take them off one at a time, left to right. Remember, you can only use **UI** or **EI** if the sentence begins with a quantifier that governs the entire sentence. If you need to deduce a conclusion that begins with multiple quantifiers, put them back on in reverse order. Again, when you add a quantifier with **EG** or **UG,** the scope of that quantifier must include the entire sentence. The following proof illustrates the process:

1.	$(x)(y)Lxy$	
2.	$(\exists x)(y)(Lxy \supset Gxy)$	/∴ $(\exists x)(y)(Gxy)$
3.	$(y)(Lxy \supset Gxy)$	2 **EI** (notice we **EI** first)
4.	$(y)Lxy$	1 **UI**
5.	$Lxy \supset Gxy$	3 **UI**
6.	Lxy	4 **UI**
7.	Gxy	5,6 **MP**
8.	$(y)(Gxy)$	7 **UG** (OK because y is not free in line 3)
9.	$(\exists x)(y)(Gxy)$	8 **EG**

   In Chapter 8 we applied **UI** or **EI** to lines that had only one quantifier and only one type of variable, for example,

1.	$(x)(Fx \supset Gx)$	
2.	$Fx \supset Gx$	1 **UI**

Relational predicate logic is more complex because here we encounter lines with more than one quantifier and more than one type of variable.

Examples

Here are some valid applications of **UI** and **EI.**

1.	$(\exists x)(y)(Fx \cdot Fxy)$	
2.	$(y)(Fx \cdot Fxy)$	1 **EI**

3. $(Fx \cdot Fxy)$ 2 **UI**
   ·
   ·
   ·

1. $(x)(\exists y)[(Fx \cdot Gy) \supset Hxy]$
2. $(\exists y)[(Fw \cdot Gy) \supset Hwy]$ 1 **UI**
3. $(Fw \cdot Gz) \supset Hwz$ 2 **EI**
   ·
   ·
   ·

The presence of more than one quantifier and more than one type of variable in the same line presents some new dangers. For example, consider the following proof:

1. $(\exists x)(\exists y)Hxy$
2. $(\exists y)Hyy$ 1 **EI** (invalid)

The problem with this proof is that no free variable is introduced in the **EI** step. Remember, when we use **EI** we drop an existential quantifier and replace the variables that were bound by that quantifier with *free* variables. In the invalid **EI** step above there are no free variables—instead the new variable is still bound by the remaining quantifier. We must not allow such steps to avoid invalid proofs. (That the above proof is invalid can be seen if we let Hxy = "x is heavier than y," since "Something is heavier than something" is true and "Something is heavier than itself" is false.)

The only rule for **UI** and the third rule for **EI** forbid such inferences. Here is **UI:**

Rule UI:

$(u) (\ldots u \ldots) / \therefore (\ldots w \ldots)$ *Provided:*

                                1. $(\ldots w \ldots)$ results from replacing each occurrence of u free in $(\ldots u \ldots)$ with a w that is free in $(\ldots w \ldots)$(making no other changes).

And here is the third restriction on **EI:**

Rule EI:

$(\exists u) (\ldots u \ldots) / \therefore (\ldots w \ldots)$ *Provided:*

                                3. $(\ldots w \ldots)$ results from replacing each occurrence of u free in $(\ldots u \ldots)$ with a w that is free in $(\ldots w \ldots)$(making no other changes).

In less formal terms, when you remove a quantifier you must replace *all* the variables that were bound by that quantifier with only one kind of *free* variable (or, in the case of **UI**, you may also replace the variables with constants).

It may help to picture the process of removing a quantifier like this: We begin with the original bound formula, for example,

1. $(x)(\exists y)[(Fx \cdot Gy) \supset Lxy]$

We then remove the left-most quantifier and all of the variables that were bound by that quantifier:

$(\exists y)[(F\_\_ \cdot Gy) \supset L\_\_y]$ (The blanks indicate the spots that were occupied by the variables.)

Finally, we fill in the blanks with a free variable (or with **UI** we can use a constant):

2. $(\exists y)[(Fw \cdot Gy) \supset Lwy]$ 1 UI
3. $(\exists y)[(Fa \cdot Gy) \supset Lay]$ 1 UI

We can use any kind of free variable we like. So all of the following can be validly derived from our original sentence:

3. $(\exists y)[(Fu \cdot Gy) \supset Luy]$ 1 UI
4. $(\exists y)[(Fx \cdot Gy) \supset Lxy]$ 1 UI
5. $(\exists y)[(Fz \cdot Gy) \supset Lzy]$ 1 UI

We cannot fill in the blanks with two *different* kinds of variables, as in

6. $(\exists y)[(Fw \cdot Gy) \supset Lxy]$ 1 UI (invalid)

And the new variables must all be *free*—so in this case we cannot fill in the blanks with the variable *y,* as in

7. $(\exists y)[(Fy \cdot Gy) \supset Lyy]$ 1 UI (invalid)

Similar problems can arise when adding on quantifiers. For example, we cannot permit the following inference:

.
.
.

4. $(x)Fxy$
5. $(\exists x)(x)Fxx$ 4 EG (invalid)
.
.
.

because here we would be replacing a free variable (*y*) with a variable (the second *x*) that is bound *twice.*

Our rules for adding quantifiers have restrictions that are carefully designed to prevent such inferences. The fourth restriction on **UG** reads as follows:

Rule UG:

$(\dots u \dots) / \therefore (w)(\dots w \dots)$ *Provided:*

> 4. $(\dots w \dots)$ results from replacing each oc-
> currence of u free in $(\dots u \dots)$ with a w that
> is free in $(\dots w \dots)$ (making no other
> changes), and there are no additional occur-
> rences of w already contained in $(\dots w \dots)$.

Less formally, we use **UG** to replace *all* of the occurrences of a particular kind of free variable with *variables that are bound by the newly introduced universal quantifier.*

Again, it may help to visualize this process graphically. We begin with a line that contains one or more free variables, such as

1. $(\exists y)[(Fw \cdot Gy) \supset Lwy]$

We then erase all of the free variables

$(\exists y)[(F\_\_ \cdot Gy) \supset L\_\_y]$

and we fill in these blanks with a new variable that is bound only by the universal quantifier we add to the front of the line:

2. $(x)(\exists y)[(Fx \cdot Gy) \supset Lxy]$ 1 **UG**

We cannot bind just *some* occurrences of the original free variable—so, in this case, we cannot infer

3. $(x)(\exists y)[(Fw \cdot Gy) \supset Lxy$ 1 **UG** (invalid)

We cannot fill in the blanks with two *different* kinds of variables, as in

4. $(w)(\exists y)[(Fw \cdot Gy) \supset Lxy$ 1 **UG** (invalid)

And the variable we use to fill in the blanks must not occur *elsewhere* in the line. So, in our case we cannot fill in the blanks using the variable y, as follows:

5. $(y)(\exists y)[(Fy \cdot Gy) \supset Lyy]$ 1 **UG** (invalid)

This inference is doubly problematic. First, the new variable is bound twice: by the new universal quantifier and the old existential quantifier. Second, not only is our new variable bound by the old quantifier, but the variable that was formerly bound by this quantifier gets bound again by the new quantifier. The quantifier we add must not bind any other variables besides those we've used to fill in the blanks. Remember, when filling in the blanks, you must use some other variable than those that remain in the proof. If our line is

1. $(Fz \cdot Gy) \supset (y)(Lyx \supset Rwz)$

and we want replace the free z with a bound variable, we cannot use y, x, or w because these variables are used elsewhere in the line. So from this line we can derive

2. $(z)[(Fz \cdot Gy) \supset (y)(Lyx \supset Rwz)]$ 1 **UG**

and

3. $(u)[(Fu \cdot Gy) \supset (y)Lyx \supset Rwu]$ 1 **UG**

but *not*

4. $(y)[(Fy \cdot Gy) \supset (y)Lyx \supset Rwy]$ 1 **UG** (invalid)

or

5. $(x)[(Fx \cdot Gy) \supset (y)Lyx \supset Rwx]$ 1 **UG** (invalid)

or

6. $(w)[(Fw \cdot Gy) \supset (y)Lyx \supset Rww]$ 1 **UG** (invalid).

Now let's look at the only restriction on **EG:**

Rule EG:

$(\dots u \dots) / \therefore (\exists w)(\dots w \dots)$ *Provided:*

1. $(\dots w \dots)$ results from replacing **at least one** occurrence of u free in $(\dots u \dots)$ with a w that is free in $(\dots w \dots)$ (making no other changes) and there are no additional occurrences of w already contained in $(\dots w \dots)$.

The boldface type indicates the crucial difference between **EG** and **UG.** With **EG** you are permitted to replace *some but not all* variables or constants of a particular kind with a bound variable.

To illustrate, suppose we wish to apply **EG** to the following line:

1. *Lhh*   *p*

Not only can we infer

2. $(\exists x)Lxx$ 1 **EG**

we can also infer

3. $(\exists x)Lxh$ 1 **EG**

or

4. $(\exists x)Lhx$ 1 **EG**

The reason for this exception is to permit obviously valid inferences to existentially quantified sentences. From "Henry loves himself" we can infer "Someone loves Henry" and "Henry loves someone" in addition to "Someone loves someone."

Other than this exception, applying **EG** is like applying **UG.** We take one or more occurrences of a free variable or constant, erase it, and fill in the blanks with a bound variable. We fill in the blanks with only one kind of variable, and that variable must not occur elsewhere in the line.

Examples

The following proofs contain examples of both valid and invalid uses of the four quantifier rules.

(1)
1. $(\exists x)(\exists y)(Fx \supset Gy)$
2. $(\exists y)(Fx \supset Gy)$ 1 **EI**
3. $Fx \supset Gy$ 2 **EI**
4. $Fx \supset Gx$ 2 **EI** (invalid, because x occurs free previously in the proof, namely on line 2)

5. $(\exists x)Fx \supset Gy$ 3 **EG** (invalid, because $(\exists x)$ does not quantify the whole of line 5)

6. $(\exists x)(Fx \supset Gy)$ 3 **EG**
7. $(z)(\exists x)(Fx \supset Gz)$ 6 **UG** (invalid, because y is free in a line obtained by **EI**)

(2)
1. $(\exists x)(y)[Fxy \supset (\exists z)(Gxz \supset Hy)]$
2. $(y)[Fxy \supset (\exists z)(Gxz \supset Hy)]$ 1 **EI**
3. $(y)[Fzy \supset (\exists z)(Gzz \supset Hy)]$ 1 **EI** (invalid, because every x free in $(y)[Fxy \supset (\exists z)(Gxz \supset Hy)]$ is not replaced by a z free in line 3)

4. $Fxx \supset (\exists z)(Gxz \supset Hx)$ 2 **UI**
5. $Fxx \supset (Gxz \supset Hx)$ 4 **EI** (invalid, because $(\exists z)$ does not quantify the whole of line 4)

6. Fxx **AP**
7. $(\exists z)(Gxz \supset Hx)$ 4,6 **MP**
8. $Gxu \supset Hx$ 7 **EI**
9. $(\exists y)(Gyu \supset Hx)$ 8 **EG** (valid)
10. $(\exists z)(\exists y)(Gyz \supset Hz)$ 9 **EG** (invalid, because to each z free in $(\exists y)(Gyz \supset Hz)$ there does not correspond an x free in $(\exists y)(Gyu \supset Hx)$

11. $(\exists y)(Gyu \supset Hy)$ 8 **EG**
12. $(\exists z)(\exists y)(Gyz \supset Hy)$ 11 **EG**
13. $Fxx \supset (\exists z)(\exists y)(Gyz \supset Hy)$ 6–12 **CP**
14. $(x)[Fxx \supset (\exists z)(\exists y)(Gyz \supset Hy)]$ 13 **UG** (invalid, because x was introduced into the proof free by **EI**)

15. $(\exists x)[Fxx \supset (\exists z)(\exists y)(Gyz \supset Hy)]$ 13 **EG**

Exercise 9-8

Indicate which (if any) of the inferences in the following proofs are invalid, and state why they are invalid.

(1)
1. $(\exists x)(y)Fxy$ *p*
2. $(y)Fxy$ 1 **EI**
3. Fxx 2 **UI**

	4. $(\exists y)Fyy$	3 **EG**
	5. $(x)(\exists y)Fyx$	4 **UG**
(2)	1. $(\exists x)Fx$	p
	2. $(\exists x)Gx$	p
	3. Fy	1 **EI**
	4. Gy	2 **EI**
	5. $Fy \cdot Gy$	3,4 **Conj**
	6. $(\exists y)(Fy \cdot Gx)$	5 **EG**
	7. $(\exists z)(\exists y)(Fy \cdot Gz)$	6 **EG**
(3)	1. $(x)(\exists y)(Fx \supset Gy)$	p
	2. $(\exists y)(Fx \supset Gy)$	1 **UI**
	3. $Fx \supset Gy$	2 **EI**
	4. $(x)(Fx \supset Gy)$	3 **UG**
	5. $(\exists y)(x)(Fx \supset Gy)$	4 **EG**

(4)

1. $(x)(\exists y)(Fx \supset Gy)$		p
2. Fx		**AP**
3. $(\exists y)(Fy \supset Gy)$		1 **UI**
4. $Fy \supset Gy$		3 **EI**
5. Gy		2,4 **MP**
6. $(\exists w)(Fw \supset Gy)$		4 **EG**
7. $Fw \supset Gy$		6 **EI**
8. $(\exists w)(Fw \supset Gw)$		7 **EG**
9. $(\exists w)[(Fw \supset Gw) \cdot Gy]$		5,8 **Conj**
10. $Fx \supset (\exists w)[(Fw \supset Gw) \cdot Gy]$		2–9 **CP**
11. $(x)\{Fx \supset (\exists w)[(Fw \supset Gw) \cdot Gy]\}$		10 **UG**

(5)

1. $(x)(y)[(z)Fzx \cdot (Gy \cdot Hd)]$		p
2. $(y)[(z)Fza \supset (Gy \cdot Hd)]$		1 **UI**
3. $(z)Fza \supset (Ga \cdot Hd)$		2 **UI**
4. $Fba \supset (Ga \cdot Hd)$		3 **UI**
5. $(\exists y)[Fby \supset (Gy \cdot Hd)]$		4 **EG**
6. Fby		**AP**
7. $Gy \cdot Hd$		5,6 **MP**
8. Hd		7 **Simp**
9. $(\exists x)Hx$		8 **EG**
10. Gy		7 **Simp**
11. $(x)Gx$		10 **UG**
12. $Fby \supset (x)Gx$		6–11 **CP**
13. $(y)Fby \supset (x)Gx$		12 **UG**

(6)

1. $(x)[(y)Fxy \supset Gx]$		p
2. $(y)Fay \supset Ga$		1 **UI**
3. $Fay \supset Ga$		2 **UI**
4. $\sim Ga$		**AP**
5. $\sim Fay$		3,4 **MT**
6. $(x)\sim Fax$		5 **UG**
7. $\sim Ga \supset (x)\sim Fax$		4–6 **CP**
8. $(\exists y)\sim Gy \supset (x)\sim Fyx$		7 **EG**

8

Strategy for Relational Predicate Logic Proofs

If a premise contains more than one quantifier, you may have no choice but to use **EI** after you have already used **UI**. Still, you should usually remove the existential quantifier as soon as possible, as illustrated in the following proof:

1. $(x)(y)(Fx \supset Gxy)$
2. $(x)(\exists y) \sim Gxy$
3. $(\exists y) \sim Gxy$ **2 UI**
4. $\sim Gxy$ **3 EI** (valid, because y is not free in an earlier line)
5. $(y)(Fx \supset Gxy)$ **1 UI**
6. $Fx \supset Gxy$ **5 UI**
7. $\sim Fx$ **4,6 MT**
8. $(\exists x) \sim Fx$ **7 EG**

Sometimes it helps when removing quantifiers to introduce entirely new variables, as in the following proof:

1. $(\exists x)(y)Fxy$
2. $(y)(x)(Fyx \supset Gxy)$
3. $(y)Fwy$ **1 EI**
4. Fwz **3 UI**
5. $(x)(Fwx \supset Gxw)$ **2 UI**
6. $Fwz \supset Gzw$ **5 UI**
7. Gzw **4,6 MT**
8. $(\exists x) Gzx$ **7 EG**
9. $(y)(\exists x) Gzx$ **8 UG**

Suppose we had used x and y when we removed the quantifiers from line 1, as follows:

1. $(\exists x)(y)Fxy$
2. $(y)(x)(Fyx \supset Gxy)$
3. $(y)Fxy$ **1 EI**
4. Fxy **3 UI**

The problem is that now we cannot drop the first universal quantifier from line 2 and substitute an x.

5. $(x)(Fxx \supset Gxx)$ **2 UI** (invalid, the new variable, x, is not free)

Introducing new variables avoids this problem entirely.

The last point of strategy is very important. There are some proofs that can only be solved using **IP**. Consider the following:

1. $(x)(\exists y)(Fx \cdot Gy)$ $/ \therefore (x)Fx$

If we proceed directly, we will have a problem at the end of the proof when we want to add the universal quantifier on using **UG**.

2. $(\exists y)(Fx \cdot Gy)$ 1 **UI**
3. $Fx \cdot Gy$ 2 **EI**
4. Fx 3 **Simp**
5. $(x)Fx$ 4 **UG** (invalid, x is free in an **EI** line)

Note that our rules do not permit line 5, even though x was not made free by the **EI** step. If x is free in an **EI** line, no matter how it became free, we cannot use **UG** to replace the x with a bound variable. The way around this difficulty is to use **IP**.

1. $(x)(\exists y)(Fx \cdot Gy)$ $/ \therefore (x)Fx$
2. $\sim (x)Fx$ **AP**
3. $(\exists x) \sim Fx$ 2 **QN**
4. $\sim Fx$ 3 **EI**
5. $(\exists y)(Fx \cdot Gy)$ 1 **UI**
6. $Fx \cdot Gy$ 5 **EI**
7. Fx 6 **Simp**
8. $Fx \cdot \sim Fx$ 4,7 **Conj**
9. $(x)Fx$ 2–8 **IP**

Using this strategy lets us dispense with having to use **UG**. Thus, the free x in the **EI** line presents no difficulty.

LG Exercise 9-9

Prove valid. Some of these are rather difficult.

(1)   1. $(\exists x)[Ax \cdot (y)(Qy \supset Lxy)]$
      2. $(x)[Ax \supset (y)(Ey \supset \sim Lxy)] / \therefore (x)(Qx \supset \sim Ex)$
(2)   1. $(\exists x)[Fx \cdot (y)(Gy \supset Hxy)] / \therefore (\exists x)[Fx \cdot (Ga \supset Hxa)]$
(3)   1. $(x)(\exists y)(\sim Fx \vee Gy) / \therefore (x)Fx \supset (\exists y)Gy$
(4)   1. $(x)(Ax \supset Hx)$
      2. $(\exists x)Ax \supset \sim (\exists y)Gy / \therefore (x)[(\exists y)Ay \supset \sim Gx]$
(5)   1. $(\exists x)Hx \supset (\exists y)Ky$
      2. $(\exists x)[Hx \cdot (y)(Ky \supset Lxy)] / \therefore (\exists x)(\exists y)Lxy$
(6)   1. $(x)(\exists y)Fxy \supset (x)(\exists y)Gxy$
      2. $(\exists x)(y) \sim Gxy / \therefore (\exists x)(y) \sim Fxy$
(7)   1. $(x)[(Fx \vee Gx) \supset (Hx \cdot Kx)]$
      2. $(x)\{(Hx \vee Lx) \supset [(Hx \cdot Nx) \supset Px]\} / \therefore (x)[Fx \supset (Nx \supset Px)]$
(8)   1. $(x)[Ax \supset (\exists y)(Ay \cdot Bxy)]$
      2. $(\exists x)\{Ax \cdot (y)[(Ay \cdot Bxy) \supset Cxy]\} / \therefore (\exists x)(\exists y)[(Ax \cdot Ay) \supset Cxy]$
(9)   1. $\sim (\exists x)(Axa \cdot \sim Bxb)$
      2. $\sim (\exists x)(Cxc \cdot Cbx)$
      3. $(x)(Bex \supset Cxf) / \therefore \sim (Aea \cdot Cfc)$
(10) 1. $(x)[Ax \supset (Bx \supset \sim Cx)]$
      2. $\sim (\exists x)(Cx \cdot Dx) \supset (x)(Dx \supset Ex)$
      $/ \therefore \sim (\exists x)[Dx \cdot (\sim Ax \vee \sim Bx)] \supset (x)(Dx \supset Ex)$

(11)   1. $(x)(Ex \lor Gx)$
     2. $(x)(y)[(\sim Lx \lor Mx) \supset Nyx]$
     $/ \therefore (x)[\sim (\exists y)(Gy \lor Lx) \supset (\exists z)(Ez \cdot Nzx)]$
(12)   1. $(x)[(\exists y)(Ay \cdot Bxy) \supset Cx]$
     2. $(\exists y)\{Dy \cdot (\exists x)[(Ex \cdot Fx) \cdot Byx]\}$
     3. $(x)(Fx \supset Ax) / \therefore (\exists x)(Cx \cdot Dx)$
(13)   1. $(x)(Ax \supset Bx)$
     $/ \therefore (x)[(\exists y)(Ay \cdot Cxy) \supset (\exists z)(Bz \cdot Cxz)]$
(14)   1. $(\exists x)(\exists y)(Axy \lor Bxy) \supset (\exists z)Cz$
     2. $(x)(y)(Cx \supset \sim Cy) / \therefore (x)(y) \sim Axy$
(15)   1. $(\exists x)Fx \supset (x)[Px \supset (\exists y)Qxy]$
     2. $(x)(y)(Qxy \supset Gx) / \therefore (x)[(Fx \cdot Px) \supset (\exists y)Gy]$

9   *Theorems and Inconsistency in Predicate Logic*

As explained in Chapter 5, the conclusion of a valid deduction in which there are no given premises is said to be a *theorem of logic.* Theorems are sometimes referred to as *logical truths,* or *truths of logic,* because they are truths provable without the aid of contingent information. They are, so to speak, truths knowable by the use of logic alone. All the tautologies of sentential logic are theorems of logic because they can be proved without using contingent premises.

But the tautologies of sentential logic also can be proved by truth table analysis. In this respect, they differ from most theorems of predicate logic, for we can prove by truth table analysis only those theorems of predicate logic that are substitution instances of tautologous sentence forms of sentential logic. The sentence $(x)Fx \lor \sim (x)Fx$ is an example because it is a substitution instance of the tautology $p \lor \sim p$ and a theorem of predicate logic provable by truth table analysis. But most theorems of predicate logic must be proved by the standard predicate logic proof method.

Examples

As in sentential logic, because there are no premises to prove that an expression is a theorem, we must use either **CP** or **IP**. Here is a fairly simple but otherwise typical proof of a theorem of predicate logic using **CP**:

To prove: $(x)Fx \supset (\exists x)Fx$

→ 1.	$(x)Fx$	**AP**
2.	Fx	1 **UI**
3.	$(\exists x)Fx$	2 **EG**
4.	$(x)Fx \supset (\exists x)Fx$	1–3 **CP**

In this proof, the assumed premise is the antecedent of the theorem to be proved (the conclusion of the proof). However, sometimes it is easier to assume the negation of the consequent of the desired conclusion, derive the negation of the antecedent, and then obtain the conclusion by Contraposition. This strategy is illustrated by the following proof:

To prove: $[(\exists x)Fx \lor (\exists x)Gx] \supset (\exists x)(Fx \lor Gx)$

→	1.	$\sim (\exists x)(Fx \lor Gx)$	**AP**
	2.	$(x)\sim (Fx \lor Gx)$	**1 QN**
	3.	$\sim (Fx \lor Gx)$	**2 UI**
	4.	$\sim Fx \cdot \sim Gx$	**3 DeM**
	5.	$\sim Fx$	**4 Simp**
	6.	$(x) \sim Fx$	**5 UG**
	7.	$\sim Gx$	**4 Simp**
	8.	$(x) \sim Gx$	**7 UG**
	9.	$\sim (\exists x)Fx$	**6 QN**
	10.	$\sim (\exists x)Gx$	**8 QN**
	11.	$\sim (\exists x)Fx \cdot \sim (\exists x)Gx$	**9,10 Conj**
	12.	$\sim [(\exists x)Fx \lor (\exists x)Gx]$	**11 DeM**
	13.	$\sim (\exists x)(Fx \lor Gx) \supset \sim [(\exists x)Fx \lor (\exists x)Gx]$	**1–12 CP**
	14.	$[(\exists x)Fx \lor (\exists x)Gx] \supset (\exists x)(Fx \lor Gx)$	**13 Contra**

Many theorems of logic are equivalences. In general, the easiest way to prove a theorem of logic that is an equivalence is to prove the two conditionals that together imply the equivalence, and then join them together by Conjunction:

To prove: $(\exists x)Fx \equiv \sim (x) \sim Fx$

→	1.	$(\exists x)Fx$	**AP**
	2.	$\sim (x) \sim Fx$	**1 QN**
	3.	$(\exists x)Fx \supset \sim (x) \sim Fx$	**1–2 CP**
→	4.	$\sim (x) \sim Fx$	**AP**
	5.	$(\exists x)Fx$	**4 QN**
	6.	$\sim (x) \sim Fx \supset (\exists x)Fx$	**4–5 CP**
	7.	$(\exists x)Fx \supset \sim (x) \sim Fx \cdot$	
		$\sim (x) \sim Fx \supset (\exists x)Fx$	**3,6 Conj**
	8.	$(\exists x)Fx \equiv \sim (x) \sim Fx$	**7 Equiv**

It is also possible to use a predicate logic proof to show that the premises of an argument are inconsistent. Just as we did in sentential logic we simply deduce a contradiction from the premises. A *logical contradiction,* or *logical falsehood,* is a single statement that can be proved false without the aid of contingent information, that is, proved false by logic alone. As in sentential logic, to show that a statement is a logical falsehood, we deduce a contradiction from it. (Note that the negation of a logical falsehood is a logical truth, and vice versa.)

Example

The following argument is shown to have inconsistent premises:

1.	$\sim (\exists x)Fx$	
2.	$\sim (x)(Fx \supset Gx)$	
3.	$(x) \sim Fx$	1 QN
4.	$(\exists x) \sim (Fx \supset Gx)$	2 QN
5.	$\sim (Fx \supset Gx)$	4 EI
6.	$\sim Fx$	3 UI
7.	$\sim (\sim Fx \vee Gx)$	5 Impl
8.	$\sim\sim Fx \cdot \sim Gx$	7 DeM
9.	$\sim\sim Fx$	8 Simp
10.	$\sim Fx \cdot \sim\sim Fx$	6, 9 Conj

LC Exercise 9-10

Prove that the following are theorems of logic.*

1. $(x)(y)Fxy \equiv (y)(x)Fxy$
2. $(x)(Gx \equiv Gx)$
3. $(\exists x)Gx \equiv (\exists y)Gy$
4. $(\exists x)(y)Fxy \supset (y)(\exists x)Fxy$ (but *not* vice versa)
5. $(x)(Fx \cdot Gx) \supset [(x)Fx \cdot (x)Gx]$
6. $[(x)Fx \vee (x)Gx] \supset (x)(Fx \vee Gx)$ (but *not* vice versa)
7. $(x)(Fx \supset Gx) \supset [(\exists x)Fx \supset (\exists x)Fx]$ (but *not* vice versa)
8. $(\exists x)(Fx \cdot Gx) \supset [(\exists x)Fx \cdot (\exists x)Gx]$ (but *not* vice versa)
9. $(\exists x)(Fx \vee Gx) \supset [(\exists x)Fx \vee (\exists x)Gx]$

In the following theorems, the letter P denotes any sentence that does not contain a free occurrence of the variable x. Thus in number 10, P might be Fa, Fy, $(y)(Fy \supset Gy)$, and so on.

10. $[(x)Fx \cdot P] \equiv (x)(Fx \cdot P)$
11. $(x)(Fx \vee P) \equiv [(x)Fx \vee P]$
12. $(x)(P \supset Fx) \equiv [P \supset (x)Fx]$
13. $(x)(Fx \supset P) \equiv [(\exists x)Fx \supset P]$
14. $(\exists x)(P \cdot Fx) \equiv [P \cdot (\exists x)Fx]$

---

*These theorems are extremely important. First, each one is a substitution instance of what might be called a *theorem schema*, and the proofs of the theorem schemas exactly parallel the proofs of their substitution instances. For example, the first theorem, $(x)(y)Fxy \equiv (y)(x)Fxy$, is a substitution instance of the general schema $(u)(w)(\ldots u, w \ldots) \equiv (w)(u)(\ldots u, w \ldots)$, and the proof of the schema exactly parallels the proof of its substitution instance. And second, these theorem schemas are very important in deriving what are known as *normal forms of formulas* (not discussed in this text, but useful when doing higher-level work in logic). In addition, it's useful to notice which of these are only one-way, or implicational, theorems so that we don't waste time trying to prove substitution instances of their reversals.

15. $(\exists x)(P \vee Fx) \equiv [P \vee (\exists x)Fx]$
16. $(\exists x)(Fx \supset P) \equiv [(x)Fx \supset P]$
17. $(\exists x)(P \supset Fx) \equiv [P \supset (\exists x)Fx]$

10   *A Simpler Set of Quantifier Rules*

The quantifier rules **UI**, **EI**, **UG**, **EG**, and **QN** (together with the eighteen valid argument forms—plus **CP** and **IP**) form a complete set of rules for quantifier logic. Sets of this kind have become standard because they allow inferences that fairly closely resemble a great many of those made in everyday life and, in particular, in certain technical fields (such as mathematics) and also because they permit relatively short proofs.

But there are simpler sets of quantifier rules. We now present a very simple set indeed, almost as simple as any set can be and still be complete. However, we pay a price for this simplicity of rules, namely, complexity of proofs, as well as an inability to parallel certain standard ways of reasoning.

First, let's adopt two of the four **QN** rules. Where u is any individual variable,

1. $(u) \sim (\ldots u \ldots) :: \sim (\exists u)(\ldots u \ldots)$
2. $(\exists u) \sim (\ldots u \ldots) :: \sim (u)(\ldots u \ldots)$

And now, let's restate and adopt rules **UI** and **EI**:

Rule UI:

$(u)(\ldots u \ldots) / \therefore (\ldots w \ldots)$ *Provided:*

1. $\ldots w \ldots$ results from replacing each occurrence of u free in $\ldots u \ldots$ with a w that is free in $\ldots w \ldots$ (making no other changes).

Rule EI:

$(\exists u)(\ldots u \ldots) / \therefore (\ldots w \ldots)$ *Provided:*

1. w is not a constant.
2. w does not occur free previously in the proof.
3. $\ldots w \ldots$ results from replacing each occurrence of u free in $\ldots u \ldots$ with a w that is free in $\ldots w \ldots$ (making no other changes).

It should be obvious from this formulation that every inference permitted by the simpler rules also is permitted by the standard rules, although the reverse is not true. So the alternative rules permit a subset of the inferences permitted by the standard rules. It follows that the standard rules contain features that are logically superfluous, although they are certainly not superfluous in other ways (chiefly in permitting proofs that more faithfully mirror everyday reasoning and the informal reasoning encountered in mathematics and logic).

The key to use of the simpler quantifier rules is that in most cases we must use **IP.*** Here is a simple example:

1.	$(x)(Fx \supset Gx)$	
2.	$(\exists x)Fx$	$/\therefore (\exists x)Gx$
3.	$\sim (\exists x)Gx$	**AP**
4.	$(x) \sim Gx$	3 **QN**
5.	Fx	2 **EI**
6.	$Fx \supset Gx$	1 **UI**
7.	Gx	5,6 **MP**
8.	$\sim Gx$	4 **UI**
9.	$Gx \cdot \sim Gx$	7,8 **Conj**
10.	$(\exists x)Gx$	3–9 **IP**

And here is a more complicated example:

1.	$(\exists y)(x)(Fx \supset Gy)$	$/\therefore (\exists x)Fx \supset (\exists x)Gx$
2.	$\sim [(\exists x)Fx \supset (\exists x)Gx]$	**AP**
3.	$(x)(Fx \supset Gy)$	1 **EI**
4.	$\sim [\sim (\exists x)Fx \lor (\exists x)Gx]$	2 **Impl**
5.	$\sim \sim (\exists x)Fx \cdot \sim (\exists x)Gx$	4 **DeM**
6.	$\sim \sim (\exists x)Fx$	5 **Simp**
7.	$(\exists x)Fx$	6 **DN**
8.	Fx	7 **EI**
9.	$Fx \supset Gy$	3 **UI**
10.	Gy	8,9 **MP**
11.	$\sim (\exists x)Gx$	5 **Simp**
12.	$(x) \sim Gx$	11 **QN**
13.	$\sim Gy$	12 **UI**
14.	$Gy \cdot \sim Gy$	10,13 **Conj**
15.	$(\exists x)Fx \supset (\exists x)Gx$	2–14 **IP**

LC Exercise 9-11

Using the simpler set of quantifier rules, prove that each of the following is valid.

(1) 1. $(\exists x)(Fx \cdot Gx) /\therefore (\exists x)Fx$
(2) 1. $\sim (\exists x)Fx /\therefore Fa \supset Ga$
(3) 1. $(x)(Hx \supset \sim Kx) /\therefore \sim (\exists y)(Hy \cdot Ky)$
(4) 1. $(y)[Fy \lor (\exists x)Gx]$
     2. $(x) \sim Fx /\therefore (\exists x)Gx$

---

*The reason is that we have no **UG** or **EG** at our disposal, and hence no way of deriving a conclusion that is either a Universal or an Existential Generalization.

(5)   1. $(x)[(Rx \cdot Ax) \supset Tx]$
      2. Ab
      3. $(x)Rx / \therefore Tb \cdot Rb$
(6)   1. Ka
      2. $(x)[Kx \supset (y)Hy] / \therefore (x)Hx$
(7)   1. $(x)(Fx \supset Gx)$
      2. $(\exists x) \sim Gx / \therefore (\exists x) \sim Fx$
(8)   1. $\sim (\exists x)Ax / \therefore (\exists x)(Ax \supset Gx)$
(9)   1. $(x)(Mx \supset Sx)$
      2. $(x)(\sim Bx \vee Mx) / \therefore (x)(\sim Sx \supset \sim Bx)$
(10) 1. $(\exists x)Rx$
      2. $(x)(\sim Gx \supset \sim Rx)$
      3. $(\exists x)Mx / \therefore (\exists x)Gx \cdot (\exists x)Mx$

LC Exercise 9-12

Using the simpler set of quantifier rules, prove that each of the following is valid. (The last two are rather difficult.)

(1)   1. $(x)(y)(Fxy \supset Gx)$
      2. $(\exists x)(\exists y)Fxy / \therefore (\exists x)Gx$
(2)   1. $(\exists y)(x)Fxy / \therefore (x)(\exists y)Fxy$
(3)   1. $(\exists x)[Fx \cdot (y)Hxy] / \therefore (\exists x)(Fx \cdot Hxa)$
(4)   1. $(x)[Fx \supset (\exists y)Gxy]$
      2. $(\exists x)Fx / \therefore (\exists x)(\exists y)Gxy$
(5)   1. $(\exists x)[Ax \cdot (y)(By \supset Cxy)] / \therefore (y)[By \supset (\exists x)(Ax \cdot Cxy)]$
(6)   1. $(\exists x)Ax \supset \sim (\exists y)Gy / \therefore (x)[(\exists y)Ay \supset \sim Gx]$
(7)   1. $(\exists x)Fx \supset (\exists x)Gx / \therefore (\exists y)(x)(Fx \supset Gy)$

Chapter Ten

Rationale Behind the Precise Formulation of the Four Quantifier Rules

Although the general idea behind the rules for dropping and adding quantifiers is fairly simple (and intuitive), the reason why these rules are so complicated is, as should be expected, rather complicated. There are eighteen kinds of cases that the four quantifier rules must handle correctly.

1   *Cases Involving the Five Major Restrictions*

The first case concerns uses of rule **EI** such as this one:

(1)   1. $(\exists x)Hx$
       2. Ha 1 **EI** (invalid)

Although it follows from line 1 that some entity or other has the property H, it doesn't follow that whatever is named by the individual constant a is that entity. Knowing that somebody or other is happy doesn't justify the belief that Abe Lincoln was happy. The moral of this example is that *when **EI** is used to drop an existential quantifier, the variables thus freed cannot validly be replaced by individual constants. Instead, they must be replaced by individual variables.*

Now consider the proof

(2)   1. $(\exists x)Fx$
       2. $(\exists x)Gx$ $/\therefore (\exists x)(Fx \cdot Gx)$
       3. Fx 1 **EI**
       4. Gx 2 **EI** (invalid)
       5. $Fx \cdot Gx$ 3,4 **Conj**
       6. $(\exists x)(Fx \cdot Gx)$ 5 **EG**

The trouble with line 4 is the use of the same free variable, x, that already had been used free (on line 3). This makes it possible to derive the unfortunate conclusion that there is some object or other with two incompatible properties, say of being both a fox and a goose. The moral this time is that *a variable introduced free into a proof by* **EI** *must not occur free previously in the proof.* (Of course, we could have used some variable other than x on 4. For instance, we could have used the variable y, to obtain Gy on that line, because y does not occur free previously in the proof.)

Now consider the use of **UG** in the following proof:

(3)   1. *Fa*
          2. $(x)Fx$ 1 **UG** (invalid)

That a particular item, say Adam, had a certain property, say of being foolhardy, hardly proves the universality of foolhardiness. The moral this time is that *we cannot use* **UG** *on a constant.*

Next, consider another invalid use of UG:

(4)   1. $(\exists x)Fx$ / $\therefore$ $(x)Fx$
          2. *Fy*   1 **EI**
          3. $(x)Fx$ 2 **UG** (invalid)

That there are foxes can't by itself justify the conclusion that everything is a fox (and a good thing it is too for all of us nonfoxes). To eliminate this bad kind of passage from "some" to "all," *we must forbid use of* **UG** *on a variable introduced free into a proof by* **EI.**

Now we have to consider a more difficult example.

(5)   1. $(x)(\exists y)Lyx$ / $\therefore$ $(\exists y)(x)Lyx$
          2. $(\exists y)Lyx$ 1 **UI**
          3. *Lyx*   2 **EI**
          4. $(x)Lyx$ 3 **UG** (invalid)
          5. $(\exists y)(x)Lyx$ 4 **EG**

Suppose Lxy = "y is larger than x," and the universe of discourse has been restricted to numbers only. Then premise 1 asserts the arithmetic truth that given any number x, there is some number y that is larger than x; that is, 1 asserts that whichever number we choose, there is some number larger than that number or that there is no largest number. So the premise of this argument is true.* But its conclusion, line 5, is false, because it asserts that there is some number y that is larger than all numbers. This must be false, because no number is larger than itself and because (as the premise of this argument asserts) there is no largest number. So in going from 1 to 5 we have passed from a true premise to a false conclusion.

---

*This assertion is a truth of arithmetic because the series of numbers has no end. We know intuitively that this must be true, because we know that we can always add 1 to any number, no matter how large, to obtain a larger number, then add 1 more to obtain an even larger number, and so on, indefinitely.

It is rather difficult to see what went wrong in this proof, and in particular what is wrong with the inference from line 3 to line 4. After all, the x free on 3, to which **UG** was applied, does not result from an application of **EI**, as in the previous invalid proof; rather it results from an application of **UI** to line 1, so that we seem to be simply dropping and then adding the same universal quantifier. This seems as harmless as the similar process in the proof:

1. $(x)Fx$
2. Fx 1 **UI**
3. $(x)Fx$ 2 **UG**

But the use of **UG** in proof (5) is not harmless by any means. The mere fact that x is free on line 3 of that proof, a line obtained by **EI**, is sufficient to make the application of **UG** to x invalid. It is as though (to use a metaphor) the "taint" of **EI** placed on the y variable in line 3 "rubbed off" the y variable onto the other variable, x, free on that line. The moral is that *we cannot use **UG** on a variable free in a line obtained by **EI**, whether that variable became free by using **EI** or not.* (Notice that by forbidding such applications of **UG** we eliminate not only the invalid use of **UG** in proof (5) but also the invalid use of **UG** in proof (4).)

This restriction on **UG** introduces a nonintuitive element into our discussion for the very first time, for taken in isolation it is neither intuitive nor counterintuitive. Its justification is that without it, or some similar restriction, we would be able to go from true premises to false conclusions, whereas with it we cannot do so.

Next consider the following proof:

(6) ┌→1. Fy **AP** $/ \therefore (z)[Fz \supset (x)Fx]$
    │   2. $(x)Fx$ 1 **UG** (invalid)
    │   3. $Fy \supset (x)Fx$ 1–2 **CP**
        4. $(z)[Fz \supset (x)Fx]$ 3 **UG**

Suppose Fy = "y is friendly." Then the conclusion, which depends on no premises whatever, asserts that if anything is friendly, then everything is friendly, an obviously false statement. The moral is that *within the scope of an assumed premise we cannot use **UG** on a variable free in that assumed premise.* This restriction rules out the use of **UG** on line 2 of the above proof, because it occurs within the scope of the assumed premise 1. But it does not rule out the valid use of **UG** that yields line 4, because 4 is outside the scope of that assumed premise.

To some extent, this restriction on **UG** may seem nonintuitive, just like the previous one. However, as explained in Chapter 8, the point of this restriction on **UG** is to make sure that the variable bound in a **UG** step names an arbitrary individual. It makes sense then that we cannot use **UG** to bind a variable so long as the individual designated by that variable is assumed to possess one or more properties. The bottom line is that without this restriction we could go from true premises to false conclusions.

Notice, however, that this restriction does not rule out all uses of **UG** within the scope of an assumed premise. It forbids only those uses where the Universal Generalization takes place on a variable free in the assumed premise itself. Thus, the restriction does not rule out the use of **UG** in the following proof:

	1.	$(x)(Fx \supset Gx)$	$/\therefore (x)Fx \supset (x)Gx$
→	2.	$(x)Fx$	**AP**
	3.	Fx	2 **UI**
	4.	$Fx \supset Gx$	1 **UI**
	5.	Gx	3,4 **MP**
	6.	$(x)Gx$	5 **UG** (valid)
	7.	$(x)Fx \supset (x)Gx$	2–6 **CP**

2   One-to-One Correspondence Matters

One might naively characterize a particular application of **EI** or **UI** as a process in which a quantifier is dropped and all of the variables thus freed are replaced by a particular varia-ble.* Thus, in the following use of **EI,**

1. $(\exists x)(Fx \cdot Gx)$
2. $(Fy \cdot Gy)$ 1 **EI**

the quantifier $(\exists x)$ is dropped, and each x thus freed is replaced by a free y. (Of course, we could just as well have replaced each x by itself.) The important point is that there is a *one-to-one correspondence* between the x's freed by dropping the $(\exists x)$ quantifier and the free y's that replaced them; that is, to each x freed by dropping the $(\exists x)$ quantifier in line 1, there corresponds a y free in line 2; and to each y free in line 2, there corresponds an x in line 1 that is freed by dropping the $(\exists x)$ quantifier.

The question naturally arises as to whether all valid uses of **UI, EI, UG,** and **EG** require one-to-one correspondences of this kind. Surprisingly, it turns out that there are two cases in which this one-to-one correspondence cannot be required, if our logic is to be complete.

The first case concerns **UI.** Consider the argument:

(7)	1.	$(\exists y)(x)Lyx$	$/\therefore (\exists x)Lxx$
	2.	$(x)Lyx$	1 **EI**
	3.	Lyy	2 **UI** (valid)
	4.	$(\exists x)Lxx$	3 **EG**

Suppose the domain of discourse is limited to human beings only, and suppose $Lyx =$ "y loves x." Then the premise of this argument asserts that there is someone who loves everyone, whereas its conclusion asserts that there is someone who loves himself. Now this premise may be true or it may be false. But if it is true, then surely the conclusion is true also, for if it is true that someone loves everyone, then it follows that that person loves himself. So we must have a way to infer from the premise of this argument to its conclusion, and the most intuitive way is to permit inferences like the one on line 3. Notice that there is not a one-to-one correspondence between free y variables on line 3 and bound x variables on line 2. Since we must allow the step from line 2 to line 3, it follows that *we*

---

*In the remaining example we will sometimes refer to the variables thus freed as x variables and their replacements in the resulting formulas as y variables. An analogous x and y notation will be used in discussing **UG** and **EG.**

cannot require a one-to-one correspondence between x *and* y *variables in the application of* **UI.**

The other case in which we cannot require a one-to-one correspondence concerns **EG.** Consider the argument:

· **(8)**   1. $(x)Fxx$ $/\therefore (x)(\exists y)Fxy$
2. Fxx 1 **UI**
3. $(\exists y)Fxy$ 2 **EG** (valid)
4. $(x)(\exists y)Fxy$ 3 **UG**

Suppose $Fxx =$ "x is identical with x." Then the premise of this argument asserts that everything is identical with itself, which is true, and its conclusion that given any x, there is something (y) identical with x, which is true also, because the y in question for any particular x is that x itself. Clearly, if 1 is true, and it is, then 4 must be true also. We must permit a step such as the one from 2 to 3 to enable us to draw the conclusion on line 4. So, in general, *we cannot require a one-to-one correspondence between* x *and* y *variables in the application of* **EG.**

The eight possibilities we have just considered comprise a catalogue of cases that might puzzle students, or concerning which they might incline toward error. Before going on to the more technical cases, let's summarize what the eight examples were designed to prove:

1. When **EI** is used to drop an existential quantifier, the variables thus freed cannot validly be replaced by individual constants.
2. A variable introduced free into a proof by **EI** must not occur free previously in the proof.
3. We cannot use **UG** on a constant.
4. We cannot use **UG** on a variable introduced free into a proof by **EI.**
5. We cannot use **UG** on a variable free in a line obtained by **EI.**
6. Within the scope of an assumed premise we cannot use **UG** on a variable free in that assumed premise.
7. We cannot require a one-to-one correspondence between x and y variables in the application of **UI.**
8. We cannot require a one-to-one correspondence between x and y variables in the application of **EG.**

Now let's look at a few cases that are a bit more obscure, but still related to this issue of one-to-one correspondence. When we add an existential quantifier, we want to quantify (bind) occurrences of one variable only, and not two. Thus we don't want to allow the use of **EG** in the following proof:

(9)   1. $(\exists y)(\exists x)Fxy$
2. $(\exists x)Fxy$ 1 **EI**
3. Fxy 2 **EI**
4. $(\exists y)Fyy$ 3 **EG** (invalid)

This time, let $Fxy =$ "x is the father of y" and restrict the domain of discourse to human beings. Then 1 asserts (truly) that someone is the father of someone (or other), whereas 4 asserts (falsely) that someone is the father of himself. The trouble is that the added existential quantifier on line 4 binds not only the *y* that replaces the free *x* on line 3, but also an extra *y* that just happens to be free on line 3.

Similarly, when we add a universal quantifier, we want to quantify occurrences of one variable only, and not two. The unhappy consequence of capturing occurrences of two different variables is illustrated by the following example:

(10)   1. $(\exists y)(x)Lyx$
2. $(x)Lyx$ 1 **EI**
3. Lyx 2 **UI**
4. $(y)Lyy$ 3 **UG** (invalid)

Suppose this time that Lyx = "*y* loves *x*" and the domain of discourse is restricted to persons. Then 1 asserts that someone loves every person, whereas 4 asserts that every person loves himself. Because 1 could be true when 4 is false, the proof is not valid. The trouble is that in generalizing on the *x* variable in 3, we also quantified the *y* variable that is free on that line. The moral of this and the previous example is that *in using* **EG** *or* **UG**, *the replacements for the occurrences of only one variable in the original formula are to be bound in the resulting formula by the newly introduced quantifier.*

We stated previously that when applying **UI** we cannot require a one-to-one correspondence between bound *x* variables in the original formula and free *y* variables in the resulting formula, because this would block perfectly valid inferences, such as the one in proof (7) from $(x)Lyx$ to Lyy. In that proof, one *x* variable was freed when we dropped the universal quantifier, and yet we ended up with two free *y* variables. So we ended up with more variables free than were bound in the original formula.

But what about the reverse process? What about dropping a quantifier by **UI** and replacing, say, only one of two variables thus freed by some other variable? The answer is that such a use of **UI** is invalid, as the following example illustrates:

(11)   1. $(x)(Ox \lor Ex)$
2. $Ox \lor Ey$ 1 **UI** (invalid)
3. $(y)(Ox \lor Ey)$ 2 **UG**
4. $(x)(y)(Ox \lor Ey)$ 3 **UG**

Suppose Ox = "*x* is odd" and Ex = "*x* is even," and the domain of discourse is restricted to positive whole numbers. Then 1 asserts (truly) that every number *x* is either odd or even, whereas 4 asserts (falsely) that given any two numbers, *x* and *y*, either *x* is odd or *y* is even. (That 4 is false can be seen by considering the substitution instance of 4 obtained by replacing *x* by 2 and *y* by 1, since this substitution instance asserts the falsehood that either 2 is odd or 1 is even.)

The moral this time is that *if one occurrence of some variable* x *is freed by* **UI** *and replaced by a free* y *variable, then all* x *variables freed by this application of* **UI** *must be replaced by free* y *variables.*

Whether a similar restriction must also be placed on **EI** depends on how the restrictions on **UG** have been worded. Consider the following example:

(12)   1. $(\exists x)Ixx$
2. Iyx 1 **EI** (?)

Should we allow the step from 1 to 2 by **EI,** even though only one of the x variables freed by dropping the existential quantifier from line 1 is replaced by a y variable? The answer is that it depends on how we have restricted **UG.** The essential thing is to forbid passage from 1 to

3. $(x)Iyx$ 2 UG

and then to

4. $(\exists y)(x)Iyx$ 3 EG

Let Iyx = "y is identical with x," and it becomes obvious that we must block the inference from 1 to 4, because 1 then asserts that something is identical with itself, whereas 4 says that something is identical with everything.

It turns out that we can block this inference either by putting a restriction on **UG,** forbidding the inference from 2 to 3, or on **EI,** forbidding the inference from 1 to 2. Most sets of quantifier rules place the restriction on **EI.** However, it happens that the set of rules presented in Chapter 8 places appropriate restrictions on both **EI** and **UG** (because to do otherwise would make the statement of the rules slightly more complicated).

We said above that we must permit uses of **UI** such as the one from $(x)Lyx$ to $Lyy.$ But what about similar uses of **EI,** such as the one inferring from $(\exists x)Fxy$ to Fyy? Should we allow these also? The answer is no; all such uses of **EI** are invalid. But it turns out that all cases in which such inferences might arise are forbidden by the restriction (already mentioned) that a free variable introduced into a proof by **EI** must not occur free previously in the proof. The following argument contains an example:

(13)   1. $(\exists y)(\exists x)Txy$
         2. $(\exists x)Txy$ 1 EI
         3. Tyy 2 EI (invalid)
         4. $(\exists x)Txx$ 3 EG

Suppose Txy = "x is taller than y" and the domain of discourse is restricted to persons. Then the premise of this argument, line 1, asserts that someone is taller than someone, which clearly is true, whereas its conclusion, line 4, asserts that someone is taller than himself (or herself), which obviously is false.

We also said above that we must permit uses of **EG** like the one from Fxx to $(\exists y)Fxy.$ But what about similar uses of **UG,** such as the one from Fxx to $(y)Fxy$? The answer is that such inferences are invalid, as the following example illustrates:

(14)   1. $(x)Ixx$
         2. Ixx 1 UI
         3. $(y)Ixy$ 2 UG (invalid)
         4. $(x)(y)Ixy$ 3 UG

Suppose Ixy = "x is identical with y." Then line 1 states the truth that everything is identical with itself, whereas line 4 states the falsehood that everything is identical with everything.

So our last moral on the issue of one-to-one correspondence is that *in the use of* **UG,** *if a free* x *in the original formula is replaced by a* y *that becomes bound in the resulting* *formula, then all free occurrences of* x *in the original formula must be replaced by bound* y *variables in the resulting formula.*

3   *Accidentally Bound Variables*

Now let's consider four remaining possibilities. These cases all involve the accidental binding of a free variable by an extraneous quantifier.

The primary aim in the use of **UI** and **EI** is to drop a quantifier and free the variables that it bound. Consequently, we must forbid uses of **UI** and **EI** in which the variable that is supposed to be freed ends up bound. The following is an example involving **UI**:

(15)   1. $(x)(\exists y)Lyx$
      2. $(\exists y)Lyy$ 1 **UI** (invalid)

Suppose $Lyx =$ "y is larger than x," and x and y range over numbers only. Then the premise of this argument asserts the true statement that given any number x, there is some number larger than x, whereas its conclusion asserts the falsehood that there is some number larger than itself. The trouble is that the x variable in 1, which the application of **UI** is supposed to free, is replaced in 2 by a bound y variable.

Similarly, the use of **EI** in the following proof is invalid:

(16)   1. $(\exists x)(y) \sim Dxy$
      2. $(y) \sim Dyy$ 1 **EI** (invalid)

Suppose $Dxy =$ "x dislikes y," and the domain of discourse is restricted to human beings. Then the premise of this argument asserts that there is someone who doesn't dislike anyone, which is true (surely there is a newborn baby somewhere who doesn't dislike anyone), whereas its conclusion asserts that no one dislikes himself, which (unfortunately) is false.

The moral of all this is that *when a quantifier is dropped by* **UI** *or* **EI**, *all the variables thus freed must be replaced by free variables (or, in the case of* **UI**, *by free variables or constants).*

Now let's consider a slightly different case concerning **UG** and **EG**. When we use **UG** or **EG**, we want the occurrences of the appropriate y variables to be bound by the newly introduced quantifier. We definitely do not want any of the occurrences of that variable to be bound by some other quantifier that just happens to occur in the resulting formula. For instance, we don't want to allow the following use of **UG**:

(17)   1. $(x)(\exists y)Lyx$
      2. $(\exists y)Lyx$ 1 **UI**
      3. $(y)(\exists y)Lyy$ 2 **UG** (invalid)

Suppose again that $Lyx =$ "y is larger than x," and the domain of discourse is restricted to numbers. Then 1 asserts the truth that given any number x, there is some number larger than x, whereas 3 asserts the falsehood that some number is larger than itself.*

The case is just the same for **EG,** as this example illustrates:

(18)   1. $(\exists x)(y)Dxy$
      2. $(y)Dxy$ 1 **EI**
      3. $(\exists y)(y)Dyy$ 2 **EG** (invalid)

This time, let Dxy = "x dislikes y," with the domain of discourse restricted to humans. Then 1 asserts that someone dislikes everyone, which may well be true, whereas 3 asserts that everyone dislikes everyone (again the initial quantifier is vacuous), which undoubtedly is false.

The moral is that *in using* **UG** *or* **EG,** *the variables to be quantified by the newly introduced quantifier must not be bound by some other quantifier.*

The above constitutes a catalogue of the kinds of inferences we must forbid (as well as two kinds we must permit). The four quantifier rules (**EI, UI, EG, UG**) were carefully spelled out (in Chapter 8) so as to forbid all of the kinds of inferences that we've just seen must be forbidden, whereas permitting the two kinds we've found must be permitted. Let's review. Here is a quick summary of the sixteen kinds of cases we have described in this chapter:

Cases involving the five main restrictions

(1)   1. $(\exists x)Hx$
      2. Ha 1 **EI** (invalid—when **EI** is used to drop an existential quantifier, the variables thus freed cannot validly be replaced by individual constants)

(2)   8. Fx
      9. Gx 7 **EI** (invalid—a variable introduced free into a proof by **EI** must not occur free previously in the proof)

(3)   1. Fa
      2. $(x)Fx$ 1 **UG** (invalid—we cannot use **UG** on a constant)

(4)   2. Fy 1 **EI**
      3. $(x)Fx$ 2 **UG** (invalid—we cannot use **UG** on a variable introduced free into a proof by **EI**)

(5)   1. $(x)(\exists y)Lyx$
      2. $(\exists y)Lyx$ 1 **UI**

---

*The universal quantifier on line 3 is said to be a *vacuous* quantifier, because the closer existential quantifier binds the y variables that follow it.

3. *Lyx*   2 **EI**

4. *(x)Lyx*   3 **UG** (invalid—we cannot use **UG** on a varia-
                                            ble free in a line obtained by **EI,** even if **EI** is
                                            not used to introduce the variable)

(6) 1. *Fx*   **AP**

2. *(x)Fx*   1 **UG** (invalid—within the scope of an assumed
                                            premise we cannot use **UG** on a variable free in
                                            that assumed premise)

The first kind of inference is forbidden by the first restriction on **EI;** the second by the
second restriction on **EI;** the third by the first restriction on **UG;** the fourth and fifth by the
second restriction on **UG;** and the sixth by the third restriction on **UG.**

One-to-one correspondence cases

(7) 2. *(x)Lxy*

3. *Lyy*   2 **UI** (valid—we are *permitted* to drop a quan-
                                           tifier with **UI** and replace the variable that was
                                           bound with one that already occurs free else-
                                           where in the formula)

(8) 2. *Lyy*

3. *(∃x)Lxy*   2 **EG** (valid—when we add a quantifier with
                                           EG we are *permitted* to choose not to bind all
                                           of the free variables of a certain sort)

(9) 3. *Lxy*

4. *(∃x)Lxx*   3 **EG** (invalid—we may not use **EG** to bind two
                                           different kinds of free variables at once)

(10) 3. *Lxy*

4. *(x)Lxx*   3 **UG** (invalid—we may not use **UG** to bind
                                           two different kinds of free variables at once)

(11) 1. *(x)Lxx*

2. *Lxy*   1 **UI** (invalid—we may not use **UI** to replace
                                           one kind of bound variable with two different
                                           kinds of free variables)

(12) 1. *(∃x)Lxx*

2. *Lyx*   1 **EI** (invalid—we may not use **EI** to replace
                                           one kind of bound variable with two different
                                           kinds of free variables)

(13) 2. *(∃x)Lxy*

3. *Lyy*   2 **EI** (invalid—unlike **UI** (see case 7), we may
                                           not drop a quantifier with **UI** and replace the
                                           variable that was bound with one that already
                                           occurs free elsewhere in the formula)

(14)   2. *Lyy*
      3. *(x)Lxy*   2 **UG** (invalid—unlike **EG** (see case 8), when we add a quantifier with **UG** we may *not* bind only some of the free variables of a certain sort)

Cases like (9), (10), (11), and (12) are forbidden by the precise wording used (respectively) in the only restriction on **EG,** the fourth restriction on **UG,** the only restriction on **EG,** and the third restriction on **EG.** Note, in particular, the phrase that is repeated in each of these very similar restrictions: "... making no other changes."

The way that cases like (7) are permitted but cases like (13) prohibited is the second restriction on **EI,** for which no analogue exists in the case of **UI.**

The way that cases like (8) are permitted but cases like (14) prohibited is that, whereas the fourth restriction on **UG** begins with "provided that ... *w* ... results from replacing *each* occurrence of *u* free in ... *u* ......," the only restriction for **EG** begins with "provided that ... *w* ... results from replacing *at least one* occurrence of *u* free in ... *u* ...."

Cases involving accidentally bound variables

(15)   1. *(x)(∃y)Lxy*
      2. *(∃y)Lyy*   1 **UI** (invalid—when we use **UI** to introduce a free variable, we must be sure that variable is not accidentally bound by another quantifier)

(16)   1. *(∃x)(y)Lxy*
      2. *(y)Lyy*   1 **EI** (invalid—when we use **EI** to introduce a free variable, we must be sure that variable is not accidentally bound by another quantifier)

(17)   2. *(∃y)Lxy*
      3. *(y)(∃y)Lyy*   2 **UG** (invalid—when we use **UG** to bind a free variable, we must be sure that we don't accidentally bind another free variable already contained in the proof)

(18)   2. *(y)Lxy*
      3. *(∃y)(y)Lyy*   2 **EG** (invalid—when we use **EG** to bind a free variable, we must be sure that variable is not accidentally bound by another quantifier as well)

The only restriction on **UI** and the third restriction on **EI** prevent cases like (15) and (16), with the phrase "with a *w* that is free in ... *w* ...." The fourth restriction on **UG** and the only restriction on **EG** use this same phrase to prohibit cases like (17) and (18).

There are, of course, many other ways to write the quantifier rules so that they correctly handle all eighteen of these cases. The formulation in this book was chosen for simplicity and relative ease of comprehension.

Exercise 10-1

Some of these questions are rather difficult. Don't get discouraged.

1.   Why can't we use **UG** on a variable introduced free into a proof by **EI**?

2. State which step in the following proof is invalid, and explain how the quantifier rules are designed to block steps of this kind:

    1. $(\exists x)[(Px \cdot (y)(Py \supset Lxy)]$
    2. $Px \cdot (y)(Py \supset Lxy)$ 1 **EI**
    3. $(y)(Py \supset Lxy)$ 2 **Simp**
    4. $Py \supset Lxy$ 3 **UI**
    5. $(x)(Px \supset Lxx)$ 4 **UG**

3. Why can't we require a one-to-one correspondence between variables freed when using **UI** and resulting free variables? That is, why shouldn't we say that the use of **UI** in the following proof is invalid on grounds that there is not such a one-to-one correspondence?

    1. $(\exists x)(y)(Fx \cdot Gxy)$
    2. $(y)(Fx \cdot Gxy)$ 1 **EI**
    3. $Fx \cdot Gxx$ 2 **UI**
    4. Gxx 3 **Simp**
    5. $(\exists x)Gxx$ 4 **EG**

4. When we drop a quantifier, it seems intuitively right that the variables thus freed not be captured by some other quantifier. Prove that our intuition on this is correct by violating it and deriving a false sentence from a true one. (Try to find an original example.)

5. Is the following use of **UG** valid or invalid? Explain why in either case, supporting what you say with an example.

    1. $(y)[Py \supset (\exists x)Rxy]$
    2. $Py \supset (\exists x)Rxy$ 1 **UI**
    3. $(x)[Px \supset (\exists x)Rxx]$ 2 **UG**

6. Explain why, to quote the text, "if one occurrence of some variable x is freed by **UI** and replaced by a free y variable, then all x variables freed by this application of **UI** must be replaced by free y variables." Support your answer with an example, original if possible.

7. Carefully explain the need for the fourth restriction on rule **UG,** the restriction that states "provided to each w free in (. . . w . . .) there corresponds a u free in (. . . u . . .)." Support your answer with an example, original if possible.

8. Carefully explain the need for this similar restriction on rule **EG.** Support your answer with an example, original if possible.

Chapter Eleven

Identity and Philosophical
Problems of Symbolic Logic

---

1   *Identity*

The verb "to be," in all its variations ("is," "was," and so on), is ambiguous. Take the following sentences:

John is tall.
Mark Twain is Samuel Clemens.

In the first sentence, the word "is" indicates that the property of being tall is a property of John. This is sometimes called the predicating function of the word "is." But in the second sentence, no property is predicated of Mark Twain. Instead, the word "is" indicates an identity between the person who is Mark Twain and the person who is Samuel Clemens. It would be correct to symbolize the first sentence as Tj, but incorrect to symbolize the second sentence as Ct (where t = "Mark Twain" and C = "Samuel Clemens").

We introduce the identity symbol "=" so that we can correctly translate statements of identity into our logical notation. Using this new symbol, we can symbolize the sentence "Mark Twain is Samuel Clemens" as $t = c$. Similarly, we can symbolize the sentence "United Brands is United Fruit" as $b = f$, the sentence "Archie Leach is Cary Grant" as $l = g$, and so on.

Now let's look at the following argument, in which the identity sign is used:

1. Wtf (Mark Twain wrote *Huckleberry Finn.*)
2. $t = c$ (Mark Twain is Samuel Clemens.)
∴ Wcf (Samuel Clemens wrote *Huckleberry Finn.*)

Clearly, this argument is valid. But so far, our system provides no justification for the conclusion. Let's now introduce such a justification, namely, the **rule of identity (ID)**, which states, in effect, that we may substitute identicals for identicals. The rule can be schematized as follows:

1. $(\ldots u \ldots)$
2. $u = w \mathbin{/} \therefore (\ldots w \ldots)$

Where u and w are any individual constants or individual variables, and where $(\ldots w \ldots)$ results from replacing one or more occurrences of u free in $(\ldots u \ldots)$ by occurrences of w free in $(\ldots w \ldots)$.

Further, since if $u = w$, then $w = u$, we allow the following variation on the rule of identity:

1. $(\ldots u \ldots)$
2. $w = u \mathbin{/} \therefore (\ldots w \ldots)$

Examples

The following examples illustrate the use of the identity sign and also the rule of identity (**ID**) in proofs.

(1) 1. $Fa \supset Ga$
     2. $\sim Ga$
     3. $a = b$ $\mathbin{/}\therefore \sim Fb$
     4. $\sim Fa$ 1,2 **MT**
     5. $\sim Fb$ 3,4 **ID** (rule of identity)

(2) 1. $(x)[(x = b) \supset Fx]$
     2. $a = b$
     3. $a = c$ $\mathbin{/}\therefore Fc$
     4. $(a = b) \supset Fa$ 1 **UI**
     5. Fa 2,4 **MP**
     6. Fc 3,5 **ID**

(3) 1. $Fa \supset Ga$
     2. $\sim (Fb \supset Gb)$ $\mathbin{/}\therefore \sim (a = b)$
     3. $\sim \sim (a = b)$ **AP**
     4. $a = b$ 3 **DN**
     5. $Fb \supset Gb$ 1,4 **ID**
     6. $(Fb \supset Gb) \cdot \sim (Fb \supset Gb)$ 2,5 **Conj**
     7. $\sim (a = b)$ 3,6 **IP**

Expressions such as $\sim (a = b)$ also can be written as $a \neq b$. Here is a proof using this notation:

(4) 1. $(x)[(x \neq b) \supset Fx]$
     2. $a \neq b$ $\mathbin{/}\therefore Fa$
     3. $(a \neq b) \supset Fa$ 1 **UI**
     4. Fa 2,3 **MP**

To make our system complete, we introduce a rule, let's call it **Identity Reflexivity, or IR,** allowing introduction of the formula $(x)(x = x)$ into a proof at any time.* Most valid arguments containing uses of the identity symbol can be proved without resorting to **IR,** but a few cannot. Here is an example:

1.	$(x)[(x = a) \supset Fx]$	$/\therefore Fa$
2.	$(a = a) \supset Fa$	1 UI
3.	$(x)(x = x)$	**IR**
4.	$a = a$	3 UI
5.	Fa	2,4 **MP**

L〔 Exercise 11-1

Prove valid:

(1)   1. $Fa \cdot (x)[Fx \supset (x = a)]$
      2. $(\exists x)(Fx \cdot Gx) / \therefore Ga$

(2)   1. $(x)(Px \supset Qx)$
      2. $(x)(Qx \supset Rx)$
      3. $Pa \cdot \sim Rb / \therefore \sim (a = b)$

(3)   1. $Hc \supset Kc$
      2. $Md \supset Nd$
      3. $Hc \cdot Md$
      4. $c = d / \therefore Kd \cdot Nc$

(4)   1. $(x)[Fx \supset (\exists y)Gyx]$
      2. Fa
      3. $(y) \sim Gyb / \therefore \sim (a = b)$

(5)   1. $(\exists x)\{\{Px \cdot (y)[Py \supset (y = x)]\} \cdot Qx\}$
      2. $\sim Qa / \therefore \sim Pa$

(6)   1. $(\exists x)(y)\{[\sim Fxy \supset (x = y)] \cdot Gx\}$
      $/\therefore (x)\{\sim Gx \supset (\exists y)[\sim (y = x) \cdot Fyx]\}$

(7)   1. $(\exists x)\{Px \cdot \{(y)[Py \supset (y = x)] \cdot Qx\}\}$
      2. $(\exists x) \sim (\sim Px \lor \sim Ex)$
      $/\therefore (\exists x)(Ex \cdot Qx)$

(8)   1. $(x)[Fx \supset (x = a)]$
      2. $(x)[Mx \supset (x = b)]$
      3. $(\exists x)(Fx \cdot Mx) / \therefore a = b$

(9)   1. $(x)(Gx \supset Fx)$
      2. $(x)(y)[(Fx \lor Fy) \supset (x = y)]$
      3. $Gb / \therefore a = c$

---

*In the history of logic, the idea that any given thing is identical with itself, called the law of identity (one of the basic principles believed in times past to be the fundamental laws of thought), has usually been expressed as "*a* is *a*." But the meaning of this formula is better expressed in our notation by $(x)(x = x)$. Why we have named this principle Identity Reflexivity will become apparent from the discussion of the property of reflexivity later in this chapter.

(10)   1. $\sim (x) \sim (Ax \cdot Bx)$
     2. $(y)[\sim (y = a) \supset \sim Ay]$
     3. $(z) \sim [(z \neq b) \cdot Bz] / \therefore a = b$

Once the identity sign is added to predicate logic, we can symbolize sentences stating quantities other than all, some, and none.

At least

We already know how to symbolize sentences containing the expression "at least one," namely, by means of the existential quantifier. Thus, the sentence "There is at least one student" can be symbolized as $(\exists x)Sx$.

But we cannot symbolize the sentence "There are at least two students" as $(\exists x)(\exists y)$ $(Sx \cdot Sy)$, because the x and y referred to might be the same entity. However, using the identity sign, we can correctly symbolize it as

$$(\exists x)(\exists y)[(Sx \cdot Sy) \cdot (x \neq y)]$$

This expression says that there is an x that is a student, and a y that is a student, and x is not identical to y, which is what the sentence "There are at least two students" states.

Similarly, we can symbolize the sentence "There are at least three students" as

$$(\exists x)(\exists y)(\exists z)\{[(Sx \cdot Sy) \cdot Sz] \cdot \{[(x \neq y) \cdot (x \neq z)] \cdot (y \neq z)\}\}$$

And in the same way, we can handle the phrases "at least four," "at least five," and so on.

At most

Next take the sentence "There is at most one student." It is correctly symbolized as

$$(x)\{Sx \supset (y)[Sy \supset (x = y)]\}$$

The reason for the universal quantifier is that this sentence asserts not that there are any students, but rather that there is not more than one student. It would be true if there were no students at all, as well as if there were exactly one.

Similarly, we can symbolize the sentence "There are at most two students" as

$$(x)(y)\{[(Sx \cdot Sy) \cdot (x \neq y)] \supset (z)\{Sz \supset [(z = x) \vee (z = y)]\}\}$$

And in the same way we can handle sentences containing the phrases "at most three," "at most four," and so on.

Exactly

Now consider the sentence "There is exactly one student." First, if there is exactly one student, then there is at least one. So part of the meaning of "exactly one" is captured by the phrase "at least one," and hence part of the meaning of the sentence "There is exactly one student" can be symbolized as $(\exists x)Sx$. And second, if there is exactly one student then there is at most one student. So the rest of the meaning of "exactly one" is captured by the phrase "at most one." Thus, "There is exactly one student" is correctly symbolized as

$(\exists x)\{Sx \cdot (y)[Sy \supset (x = y)]\}$

This asserts that there is at least one student, x, and given any allegedly other student, y, y is identical with x. That is, it asserts that there is at least one student and at most one student, which is what is said by "There is exactly one student."

Similarly, we can symbolize the sentence "There are exactly two students" as

$(\exists x)(\exists y)\{[(Sx \cdot Sy) \cdot (x \neq y)] \cdot (z)\{Sz \supset [(z = x) \vee (z = y)]\}\}$

And obviously, the same method can be applied in symbolizing the phrases "exactly three," "exactly four," and so on.

Addition of the identity sign to our vocabulary also enables us to symbolize several other kinds of statements we couldn't handle before, including the following two.

Only

Take the statement "Only George didn't pass the exam." We can't symbolize that statement simply as $\sim Pg$, because that says just that George didn't pass the exam, but not that only George didn't pass. Instead, we can symbolize it as

$\sim Pg \cdot (x)\{[Sx \cdot (x \neq g)] \supset Px\}$

This statement says that George didn't pass the exam but that all the other students did, which is what the original statement asserts.

Everyone but

Now consider the statement "Every student in this class but George passed the exam." Another way to say the same thing is to say that George didn't pass the exam, but every student in the class not identical with George passed, easily symbolized using identity (and obvious abbreviations) as

$\sim Pg \cdot (x)\{[Sx \cdot (x \neq g)] \supset Px\}$

Similarly, all sorts of other expressions can be captured once the identity sign is introduced. Perhaps the most important of these expressions are the definite descriptions discussed in the next section.

Examples

Here are a few more examples of symbolizations using the identity sign (restricting the universe of discourse to human beings).

1. Everyone loves exactly one person.
    $(x)(\exists y)\{Lxy \cdot (z)[Lxz \supset (z = y)]\}$
2. Everyone loves exactly one other person.
    $(x)(\exists y)\{[(x \neq y) \cdot Lxy] \cdot (z)[(Lxz \cdot (x \neq z)) \supset (z = y)]\}$

3. We all love only ourselves (interpreted to mean that we all love ourselves and no one else).
   $(x)\{Lxx \cdot (y)[(y \neq x) \supset \sim Lxy]\}$
4. At most, we all love only ourselves.
   $(x)(y)[Lxy \supset (x = y)]$
5. Someone loves someone.
   $(\exists x)(\exists y)Lxy$
6. Someone loves someone else.
   $(\exists x)(\exists y)[Lxy \cdot (x \neq y)]$
7. Some people love only other people.
   $(\exists x)(y)[Lxy \supset (x \neq y)]$
8. Some people love no one else.
   $(\exists x)(y)[(x \neq y) \supset \sim Lxy]$
9. Only Art loves Betsy (interpreted to imply that Art does love Betsy).
   $Lab \cdot (x)[Lxb \supset (x = a)]$
10. Every planet except the earth is uninhabitable.
    $(x)\{[Px \cdot (x \neq e)] \supset \sim Ix\} \cdot Ie$

LC Exercise 11-2

Symbolize the following, using the indicated letters.

1. Only George Washington was the first president of the United States. (g = "George Washington"; Fx = "x is the first U.S. president")
2. Only Ronald Reagan was president of the Screen Actors' Guild and also U.S. president. (r = "Ronald Reagan"; Px = "x is president of the United States"; Sx = "x is president of the Screen Actors' Guild")
3. At least one famous Hollywood actor was elected governor of California. (Fx = "x is a famous Hollywood actor"; Gx = "x was elected governor of California")
4. At most, two famous Hollywood actors ran for governor of California. (Rx = "x ran for governor of California")
5. Exactly three famous Hollywood actors have been president of the Screen Actors' Guild.
6. No president of the United States has also been president of the Screen Actors' Guild, except for Ronald Reagan.
7. Adolf Hitler hated every human being—except for himself, of course. (h = "Adolf Hitler"; Px = "x is a person"; Hxy = "x hated y")
8. Abe Lincoln was more compassionate than any other U.S. president. (a = "Abe Lincoln"; Cxy = "x is more compassionate than y")
9. All the other U.S. presidents have been less compassionate than Abraham Lincoln.
10. Darryl Zanuck knew every celebrity in Hollywood, not counting himself. (d = "Darryl Zanuck"; Cx = "x is a Hollywood celebrity"; Kxy = "x knew y")

2   *Definite Descriptions*

We can refer to a person or entity by name, for example, "Samuel Clemens," "Mount Everest," or by description, for example, "the author of *Huckleberry Finn*," "the tallest mountain in the world." A description of this kind is called a **definite description,** because it picks out or describes one definite entity. The identity sign is needed in order to symbolize sentences containing definite definitions.

Take the sentence "The president of the United States is religious." A person who utters this sentence asserts (in part) that there is one and only one person who is president of the United States, since it would be inappropriate to talk about the president of the United States if there were more than one such person. Therefore, this sentence can be symbolized by first symbolizing "There is exactly one president of the United States" and then adding that he is religious. So the sentence "The president of the United States is religious" is symbolized as

$$(\exists x)\{\{Px \cdot (y)[Py \supset (x = y)]\} \cdot Rx\}$$

The first conjunct asserts that some (at least one) entity is president of the United States, the second that at most one is, and the third that that entity is religious.*

Examples

Here are a few more sentences containing definite descriptions and their correct symbolizations (again restricting the universe of discourse to human beings).

1. Everyone admires the most intelligent person in the world.
   $$(\exists x)\{(y)[(x \neq y) \supset Ixy] \cdot (z)Azx\}$$
   (Ixy = "x is more intelligent than y"; Axy = "x admires y")
2. The most intelligent person in the world is also the most admired.
   $$(\exists x)(\exists y)\{\{(z)[(x \neq z) \supset Ixz] \cdot (w)[(y \neq w) \supset Ayw]\} \cdot (x = y)\}$$
   (Axy = "x is more admired than y")
3. The most intelligent person in the world admires only intelligent people.
   $$(\exists x)\{(y)[(y \neq x) \supset Ixy] \cdot (z)(Axz \supset Iz)\}$$
4. The person most admired by Art is also admired by Betsy.
   $$(\exists x)\{(y)[(x \neq y) \supset Aaxy] \cdot Abx\}$$
   ($Axyz$ = "x admires y more than z"; Axy = "x admires y"; a = "Art"; b = "Betsy")

---

*This analysis was first proposed by Bertrand Russell. See his "On Denoting," *Mind,* n.s., vol. 14 (1905), reprinted in Robert C. Marsh, ed., *Logic and Knowledge* (New York: Macmillan, 1956).

5. Art's father admires him.
    $(\exists x)\{\{Fxa \cdot (y)[Fya \supset (x = y)]\} \cdot Axa\}$
6. Art's father admires the most intelligent person in the world.
    $(\exists x)\{(y)[(x \neq y) \supset Ixy] \cdot (\exists z)\{Fza \cdot (w)[Fwa \supset (w = z)] \cdot Azx\}\}$
7. Everyone admires the most generous person.
    $(\exists x)\{(y)[(x \neq y) \supset Gxy] \cdot (z)Azx\}$
    $(Gxy = $ "x is more generous than y")

The same caution is necessary in symbolizing sentences containing phrases like "the Chairman" and "the tallest person in the world" as is necessary in symbolizing other complicated sentences. In particular, sentences of this kind frequently are ambiguous; before symbolizing them we must get clear as to which meaning we intend our symbolization to capture.

Take the sentence "The present king of France is not bald," which can mean either that there is one and only one present king of France and he is not bald, or that it is not the case that there is one (and only one) present king of France (who is bald). If the former is intended, then the sentence in question is correctly symbolized as

$(\exists x)\{\{Px \cdot (y)[Py \supset (x = y)]\} \cdot \sim Bx\}$

(where $Px = $ "x is, at present, king of France" and $Bx = $ "x is bald"). If the latter is intended, then it is correctly symbolized as

$\sim (\exists x)\{\{Px \cdot (y)[Py \supset (x = y)]\} \cdot Bx\}$

Caution also is necessary because phrases that usually function as definite descriptions occasionally do not. An example is the sentence "The next person who moves will get shot," snarled by a gunman during a holdup. Clearly, the gunman does not intend to assert that there is one and only one person who will get shot if he moves. Instead, he intends to say that *anyone* who moves will get shot. So his threat is correctly symbolized as

$(x)[(Px \cdot Mx) \supset Sx]$

Another example is the chauvinistic saying "The female of the species is vain," which means something like "All females are vain" or "Most females are vain" but surely does not say anything about the one and only female.

On the other hand, some uses of the phrase "the so and so" that may appear not to function as definite descriptions really do. For instance, when the presiding officer of the U.S. Senate recognizes "the senator from California," it may appear that that phrase cannot be functioning as a definite description, since there are two California senators. However, in this context the phrase "the senator from California" means the one who has requested the floor. But if, say, both California senators request the floor at the same time (and they're standing right next to each other), the presiding officer would use a phrase like "the junior senator from California" or "the senior senator from California," thus unambiguously selecting one definite person to have the floor.

LC Exercise 11-3

Symbolize the following sentences and indicate the meanings of the abbreviations you use.

1. Every student is more intelligent than some student (or other).
2. Bonny is more intelligent than any other student.
3. The hardest thing to put up with is a good example.
4. There are no rules other than this one that have no exceptions.
5. Bobby Fischer is the best chess player that ever lived.
6. Garri Kasparov is the current chess champion of the world.
7. Any current chess player who is better at the game than Anatoly Karpov must be one and the same as Garri Kasparov.
8. The two Maine senators like each other.
9. The two presidential candidates dislike each other.
10. If Carl Lewis isn't the best sprinter, then there is just one who is better than he is.

3   *Properties of Relations*

There are several interesting properties that relational properties themselves may possess.

Symmetry

All two-place relations (relations of the general form Fxy) are either *symmetrical, asymmetrical,* or *nonsymmetrical.* A relation is **symmetrical** if and only if when one thing bears that relation to a second, the second must* bear it to the first. So a relation designated by Fxy is a symmetrical relation if and only if it must be the case that

$$(x)(y)(Fxy \supset Fyx)$$

The relation "_____ is married to _____" is an example of a symmetrical relation. For given any x and y, if x is married to y, then y must be married to x.

An **asymmetrical relation** is just the opposite of a symmetrical relation. Thus, a relation is asymmetrical if and only if when one thing bears that relation to a second, the second thing cannot bear it to the first. So a relation designated by Fxy is asymmetrical if and only if it must be the case that

$$(x)(y)(Fxy \supset \sim Fyx)$$

---

*The sense of "must" involved here, indeed even the use of that term in characterizing relations of this kind, is in dispute. The same is true of the related term "cannot" used as a synonym for "it is not possible that."

The relation "_____ is the father of _____" is an example of an asymmetrical relation. For given any x and y, if x is the father of y, then it must be false that y is the father of x.

All relations that are neither symmetrical nor asymmetrical are **nonsymmetrical.** For example, the relation "_____ loves _____" is nonsymmetrical, since loving someone entails neither being loved by that person nor not being loved by that person.

Transitivity

All two-place relations are either *transitive, intransitive,* or *nontransitive.* A relation is **transitive** if and only if when one thing bears that relation to a second, and the second to a third, then the first must bear it to the third. Thus, a relation designated by Fxy is transitive if and only if it must be the case that

$$(x)(y)(z)[(Fxy \cdot Fyz) \supset Fxz]$$

The relation "_____ is taller than _____" is an example. For if a given person is taller than a second, and the second is taller than a third, then the first must be taller than the third.

It is interesting to note that the statement of a property of a relation often is required in order to present a valid proof for an otherwise invalid argument. For instance, the argument

1. *Tab* (Art is taller than Betsy.)
2. *Tbc* (Betsy is taller than Charles.)
∴ *Tac* (Art is taller than Charles.)

is invalid as it stands (using the machinery of predicate logic), but can be made valid by the introduction of a premise concerning the transitivity of the relation "taller than," as follows:

1. *Tab*
2. *Tbc*
3. $(x)(y)(z)[(Txy \cdot Tyz) \supset Txz]$ / ∴ *Tac*
4. $(y)(z)[(Tay \cdot Tyz) \supset Taz]$ 3 **UI**
5. $(z)[(Tab \cdot Tbz) \supset Taz]$ 4 **UI**
6. $(Tab \cdot Tbc) \supset Tac$ 5 **UI**
7. $(Tab \cdot Tbc)$ 1,2 **Conj**
8. *Tac*   6,7 **MP**

A relation is **intransitive** if and only if, when one thing bears that relation to a second, and the second to a third, then the first cannot bear it to the third. Thus a relation designated by Fxy is intransitive if and only if it must be the case that

$$(x)(y)(z)[(Fxy \cdot Fyz) \supset {\sim} Fxz]$$

The relation "_____ is the father of _____" is an example. For if one person is the father of a second, and the second of a third, then the first cannot be the father of the third.

All relations that are neither transitive nor intransitive are **nontransitive.** For example, the relation "_____ loves _____" is nontransitive, since if one person loves a second, and the second loves a third, it follows neither that the first person loves the third nor that the first person doesn't love the third.

Reflexivity

The situation with respect to reflexivity is more complex.

A relation is **totally reflexive** if and only if everything must bear that relation to itself. So a relation designated by Fxy is totally reflexive if and only if it must be the case that

$$(x)Fxx$$

The relation "_____ is identical with _____" is an example. For everything must be identical with itself.

Almost all interesting relations are *not* totally reflexive. There is no name in common use for relations that are not totally reflexive, but we can say that a relation designated by Fxy is *not totally reflexive* if and only if it is not necessarily the case that

$$(x)Fxx$$

The relation "_____ loves _____" (restricting the domain of discourse to human beings) is an example. For it is not necessarily true that all human beings love themselves.

A relation is said to be **reflexive** if and only if everything that bears that relation to anything must bear it to itself. That is, a relation designated by Fxy is reflexive if and only if it must be the case that

$$(x)(y)[Fxy \supset (Fxx \cdot Fyy)]$$

An example is the relation "_____ belongs to the same political party as _____," since if a given entity—say, Art—belongs to the same political party as anyone else—say, Betsy—then Art must belong to the same political party as himself, and so must Betsy.

Notice that "_____ belongs to the same political party as _____" is not totally reflexive, since everything does not belong to the same political party as itself. For example, a piece of chalk doesn't belong to any political party at all. So some reflexive relations are not totally reflexive. But all totally reflexive relations are reflexive.

A relation is **irreflexive** if and only if nothing can bear that relation to itself. Thus, a relation designated by Fxy is irreflexive if and only if it must be the case that

$$(x) \sim Fxx$$

The relation "_____ is taller than _____" is an example. For nothing can be taller than itself.

Finally, all relations that are neither reflexive nor irreflexive are **nonreflexive.** For example, the relation "_____ loves _____" is nonreflexive because (1) it is not reflexive (a person can love someone else but not love himself), and (2) it is not irreflexive (a person can love someone else and also love himself).

Exercise 11-4

A. Determine the status of the following relations with respect to symmetry, transitivity, and reflexivity:

1. _____ is ashamed of _____.
2. _____ is the mother of _____.
3. _____ is ≥ _____. (concerning numbers only)
4. _____ is north of _____.
5. _____ is at least one year younger than _____.
6. _____ is identical with _____.
7. _____ is the sister of _____.
8. _____ sees _____.

B. Prove that all asymmetrical relations are irreflexive.

4   *Higher-Order Logics*

The predicate logic discussed so far expressly forbids sentences that ascribe properties to properties themselves and restricts quantification to individual variables. A predicate logic restricted in this way is said to be a **first-order predicate logic.** We now will consider the bare bones of a higher-order predicate logic.

Quantifying over property variables

Just as we can have individual variables, so we can have **property variables.** Let's use the capital letters F, G, H, and K as property variables, for the time being forbidding their use as property constants. The expression Fa will then be a sentence form and not a sentence. But obviously, we can obtain a sentence from this expression by replacing the property variable F by a property constant. Thus, we can obtain the sentence Sa (where Sx = "x is smart") from the sentence form Fa. (Hence, Sa is a substitution instance of Fa.)

But we also can obtain a sentence from the sentence form Fa by quantifying the property variable F. Thus we can obtain the sentences $(F)(Fa)$, read "Art has every property," or "Given any property, F, Art has F," and $(\exists F)(Fa)$, read "Art has some property (or other)," or "There is some property F such that Art has F."

We also can have sentences that quantify both property variables and individual variables. An example would be the sentence "Everything has some property (or other)," symbolized as $(x)(\exists F)Fx$.

Examples

Some other examples of symbolizations containing quantified property variables are:

1.	$(x)(F)Fx$	Everything has every property.
2.	$(\exists x)(F)Fx$	Something has every property.
3.	$(\exists x)(\exists F)Fx$	Something has some property (or other).
4.	$(F)(\exists x)Fx$	Every property belongs to something (or other).
5.	$(\exists F)(x)Fx$	Some property belongs to everything.
6.	$\sim (\exists x)(F)Fx$	Nothing has all properties.
7.	$(F)\{Fa \supset \sim (\exists x)[(Px \cdot Fx) \cdot (x \neq a)]\}$	No one else has any property that Art has.
8.	$(\exists F)\{Fa \cdot (y)\{[Py \cdot (y \neq a)] \supset \sim Fy\}\}$	Art has some property no one else has.

Now that we have introduced property variables and the quantification of property variables, we can give a more precise definition of the identity symbol, for we can say that the expression $x = y$ means that necessarily $(F)(Fx \equiv Fy)$. It follows then that $(x)(y)[(x = y) \equiv (F)(Fx \equiv Fy)]$,* from which we can prove that the identity relation is transitive, symmetrical, and reflexive. (Recall that we labeled one of the identity rules of inference Identity Reflexivity.)

Higher-order properties

So far, we have considered only properties of individuals. But properties themselves can have properties. For instance, honesty is a rare property, whereas (unfortunately) dishonesty is quite common. Similarly, courage is an honorable property, cowardice dishonorable.

Let's use the symbols A_1, B_1, C_1, and so on, to refer to properties of properties. Then we can symbolize the sentence "Honesty is a rare property" as R_1H, and the sentence "Courage is a useful property" as U_1C. Similarly, we can symbolize the sentence "We all have useful properties" as $(x)[Px \supset (\exists F)(Fx \cdot U_1F)]$, and so on.

Examples

Some other examples of symbolizations containing properties of properties are:

1.	$(F)U_1F$	All properties are useful.
2.	$(\exists F)(U_1F \cdot R_1F)$	Some useful properties are rare.

---

* A variation on Leibniz's law.

3. $(\exists F)(G_1 F \cdot Fa)$ Art has some good properties
                                                                                   (qualities).
4. $(\exists F)[(G_1 F \cdot Fa) \cdot Fb]$ Art and Betsy share some good
                                                                                   qualities.
5. $(F)[(Fb \cdot G_1 F) \supset Fa]$ Art has all of Betsy's good qualities.
6. $(x)\{(\exists F)\{Fx \cdot (G)[Gx \supset (F = G)]\} \supset \sim$ Nothing that has only one property
      $(\exists H)(Hx \cdot G_1 H)\}$ has any good properties.

Unfortunately, higher-order logics involving properties of properties have encountered important difficulties, which have not yet been satisfactorily worked out. In contrast to first-order predicate logic, there is no system of inference rules for second-order logic that is both sound and complete.

5   *Limitations of Predicate Logic*

At the beginning of the discussion of predicate logic, we pointed out that certain kinds of valid arguments are invalid when symbolized in the notation of sentential logic. We then proceeded to develop predicate logic, which provides a method for symbolizing these arguments and for proving them valid.

The question naturally arises whether there are other arguments that, although invalid using the notation and proof technique of predicate logic, are valid in some wider (perhaps ideal) deductive system. The answer is that there seem to be such arguments.

Consider the argument

1. Art knows that he'll go either to the show or to the concert (but not to both).
2. Art knows that he won't go to the show.
∴. Art knows that he'll go to the concert.

Clearly this argument is valid in some sense or other. But there is no way to symbolize it in the standard predicate logic notation so that we can prove it is valid. For instance, if we symbolize the argument as

1. *Kaf*
2. *Kag*
∴. *Kah*

where $K =$ "knows that"; $f =$ "he'll go either to the show or the concert"; $g =$ "he won't go to the show"; and $h =$ "he'll go to the concert," then clearly we cannot prove that it is valid.

This is an example of an argument involving what are sometimes called **indirect contexts.** In this case, the clue that we are dealing with an indirect context is the phrase "knows that." Some other phrases that usually indicate indirect contexts are "believes that," "is looking for," "prays to," and "is necessary that."

So far, the logic of indirect contexts has not been worked out, at least not to the satisfaction of most philosophers. The whole area is one of extreme disagreement, and the predicate logic presented in this and other textbooks is not able to deal adequately with it.

There are other cases where it is claimed that the predicate logic presented here is inadequate. We present two that are the centers of interesting disputes.

The first is illustrated by the argument:

1. Art sang the Hamilton school song beautifully.
∴. Art sang the Hamilton school song.

Again, the argument is valid, and again it is claimed that we cannot prove that it is valid using the notation and proof technique of predicate logic.

Several solutions have been proposed for this problem. One is simply that there is a "missing premise." According to this solution, the argument in question is invalid as it stands, but can be made valid by supplying an obvious "missing premise," namely, the premise that if someone sang a particular song beautifully, then he sang that song. Once we add this missing premise, the argument can be proved quite easily in predicate logic.

Another dispute involves what we might call "semantically valid arguments." Suppose for the moment that the term "bachelor" means exactly the same thing as "unmarried adult male." Then it is clear that the argument

1. All bachelors are handsome.
∴. All unmarried adult males are handsome.

is valid in some sense or other. But again, it appears to be invalid in the predicate logic system developed in this text.

Several ways have been proposed to handle so-called semantically valid arguments. One is to introduce a rule permitting the substitution of terms *synonymous* with any terms occurring in an argument as stated.

Another way is to claim that these arguments are *enthymematic*—that they have "missing premises." In the example in question, the missing premise is that all bachelors are unmarried adult males.

And a third way is to deny that the argument in question is valid, on the grounds that truly synonymous expressions do not exist, at least not in natural languages.

Finally, note that predicate logic has trouble dealing with statements about *dispositional properties* and with *subjunctive statements,* in particular, *counterfactual conditionals.*

Dispositional properties are powers, potentials, or dispositions of objects. An example is the dispositional property of being flammable. Although dispositional properties cannot be experienced through the five senses, in some cases their observable "mates" can be. For instance, we can't see that a piece of dry wood is flammable (dispositional term), but when it is lighted, we can see it burn (observational property). Since dispositional properties can't be experienced directly, we must infer to their existence.

Obviously, dispositional properties such as being flammable or flexible are closely connected to their observational mates. Being flexible, for instance, is connected to the observational property of bending, for to say that something is flexible is to say that it has the power, potential, or disposition to bend, under certain conditions. Similarly, to say that something is flammable is to say that it has the power, disposition, or potential to burn. And so on for other dispositional properties.

The problem for logic has to do with the correct symbolization of statements about dispositional properties. What does it mean to say, for instance, that sugar is soluble (dispositional property) in water? What is a disposition, power, or potential?

The problem is easy to overlook in everyday life because an easy answer seems readily available. It seems natural to suppose, for instance, that when we say a particular lump of sugar has the dispositional property of being soluble in water, we mean simply that if we place the lump in water (under suitable conditions of temperature, water saturation, and so on) then it will dissolve. Similarly, if we say that a plastic tube is flexible, we mean that if suitable pressure is applied to it, then it will bend. And so on.

Therefore, it seems initially plausible to say that given a sentence containing a dispositional term, we can replace it by an "If _____ then _____" sentence containing not the dispositional term but rather its observational mate. For instance, we seem able to replace the dispositional sentence "Lump of sugar s is soluble" by the statement "If s is placed in water under suitable conditions, then s will dissolve" and replace the dispositional sentence "Piece of wood w is flammable" by the sentence "If oxygen and heat are applied to w under suitable conditions, then w will burn."

All of this seems reasonable until we try to put these sentences into the symbolic notation of predicate logic or into some other equally precise notation. Take the dispositional sentence "Lump of sugar s is soluble." It seems plausible to translate that sentence into the nondispositional sentence "If s is placed in water, then it will dissolve," symbolized as $Ws \supset Ds$ (omitting the qualification about suitable conditions for the moment). But does the sentence $Ws \supset Ds$ really mean the same thing as the dispositional sentence "Lump of sugar s is soluble"? Unfortunately, it does not.

To see that it does not, consider the false dispositional sentence "Piece of copper c is soluble" and its analogous translation to "If c is placed in water, then c will dissolve," symbolized as $Wc \supset Dc$. Suppose we never place c in water, so that the antecedent Wc is false. If so, then the whole sentence $Wc \supset Dc$ will be true, because all conditional statements with false antecedents are true. But if the sentence $Wc \supset Dc$ is true, it cannot possibly be a correct translation of the false sentence "Piece of copper c is soluble," since a sentence and its correct translation cannot have different truth-values.

Analogously, the translation of the sentence "Lump of sugar s is soluble" into $Ws \supset Ds$ also must be incorrect, even though in this case, luckily, both the sentence translated and the sentence it is translated into have the same truth-value. That this is a matter of luck becomes obvious when we realize that the analogous translation of the sentence "Lump of sugar s is not soluble" into "If s is placed in water then it will not dissolve" also is true if s is never placed in water. But surely, the two statements "s is soluble" and "s is not soluble" cannot both be true.

To put the difficulty another way, if we translate all dispositional sentences into nondispositional conditional sentences in the above way, then all of these conditionals with false antecedents will have to be judged to be true, even though many of the dispositional sentences they are intended to translate (for example, "Piece of copper c is soluble," "Lump of sugar s is not soluble") are false.

The conclusion we must draw is that dispositional sentences cannot be replaced by nondispositional material conditional sentences, or at least not in this simple way. The so-called problem of dispositionals is to find a satisfactory way to translate sentences of this type.

It has been suggested that the correct analysis of dispositional sentences is not into indicative conditionals but rather into **subjunctive** or **contrary-to-fact conditionals.** For instance, according to this view, the correct translation of "*s* is soluble" is not into the indicative conditional "If *s* is placed in water, then it will dissolve" but rather into the subjunctive conditional "If *s* were placed in water, then it would dissolve" or into the contrary-to-fact conditional "If *s* had been placed in water, then it would have dissolved."

The trouble with this analysis of dispositional sentences into subjunctive or contrary-to-fact (counterfactual) conditionals is that subjunctive and counterfactual sentences present a translation problem just as baffling as the one presented by dispositional sentences.

Take the counterfactual "If *s* had been placed in water, then it would have dissolved." Suppose we try to translate that sentence into the truth-functional notation of propositional or predicate logic.

The obvious starting point in such a translation procedure is to replace the "If _____ then _____" of the counterfactual by the "⊃" of truth-functional logic. If we do so, then the counterfactual in question translates into "(*s* had been placed in water) ⊃ (*s* would have dissolved)." The trouble with this translation is that its antecedent and consequent are not sentences, and so the whole conditional is not a sentence. To make it a sentence, we must replace the subjunctive antecedent and consequent with their corresponding "mates" in the indicative mood. For instance, we must replace the antecedent "*s* had been placed in water" by the indicative sentence "*s* is placed in water" (or by "*s* was placed in water") and replace the consequent "*s* would have dissolved" by the indicative sentence "*s* dissolves" (or by "*s* dissolved"). The result is the translation of the counterfactual "If *s* had been placed in water, then *s* would have dissolved" into the indicative conditional "If *s* is placed in water, then *s* will dissolve" (or "If *s* was placed in water, then *s* dissolved"), which in symbols is $Ps \supset Ds$. In a similar way, we can translate all other counterfactuals.

But once we actually translate in this way, it becomes obvious that such translations are unsatisfactory, because the end product of this translation procedure for counterfactual sentences is exactly the same, and just as inadequate, as the end product of the translation procedure for dispositional sentences discussed in the last section. So the suggested method of translating counterfactual sentences cannot be correct. Similar remarks apply to other kinds of subjunctive conditionals. The so-called problem of counterfactuals, really a problem concerning all kinds of subjunctive conditionals, is to find a way to symbolize subjunctives so that they can be handled by some sort of appropriate logical machinery. Until it is solved, the formal logic we have developed so far will not be able to handle all arguments about dispositions or arguments in the subjunctive mood (for example, contrary-to-fact conditionals).

6 *Philosophical Problems*

In addition to the problems discussed in the previous section, there are serious philosophical problems underlying the whole of sentential and predicate logic. Let's now briefly discuss a few of these problems.

Propositions versus sentences

One basic issue is whether logic deals with sentences or propositions. For instance, in using the argument form

If p then q
If q then r
$\therefore$ If p then r

the English equivalent of Hypothetical Syllogism, whatever is substituted for one p must be substituted for the other, and similarly for q and r. We must substitute *the very same thing* for both occurrences of p. But what is this same thing we must substitute? Some philosophers say we must substitute the same *sentence,* whereas others say that we must substitute sentences that express the same *proposition.*

We can think of a *sentence* as a series of ink marks on paper (or sounds in the air). Thus, as you read the sentence that precedes this one, you look at particular ink marks on a particular sheet of paper, and those ink marks may be said to *be* a particular sentence. But we would ordinarily say that someone else reading another copy of this book might read the *same* sentence. Thus, the everyday meaning of the word "sentence" is ambiguous. So let's resolve the ambiguity by saying that both of you looked at different **sentence tokens** of the same **sentence type.** Here is another sentence token of that sentence type:

We can think of a sentence as a series of ink marks on paper (or sounds in the air).

During the rest of this discussion, when we use the word "sentence," let's mean sentence type, because no one would argue that the same sentence token has to be substituted in two different places in an argument form (since that is impossible). Thus, no one would argue that the principal unit dealt with in logic is sentence tokens.

As for *propositions,* recall our earlier example. The expressions "Snow is white" and "*Der Schnee ist weiss*" are tokens of two different sentence types and thus of two different sentences. But they seem to have something in common; they seem to "express the same idea," "say the same thing," or "have the same meaning." Whatever they have in common, whether meaning or something else like it, we shall call a *proposition.* Then we can say that these two expressions, although different sentences, express the same proposition.

Of course, two sentences don't have to be in different languages to express the same proposition. For instance, the two different sentences "Snow is white" and "White is the snow" express the same proposition, as do "John loves Mary" and "Mary is loved by John."

Now the principal objection to saying that logic deals with propositions rather than sentences is simply that the very existence of propositions can be doubted. Sentences, or at least sentence tokens, can be *looked at* or *heard;* they are perceivable. But you can't perceive a proposition. (Nor is it exactly clear what a proposition is supposed to be.)

Well, if propositions are such doubtful entities, can we make sense of logic without them? There seem to be good reasons to answer no to that question.

In the first place, if logic deals with sentences and not propositions, then the rules of logic are at best much more restricted than is normally supposed. Take Simplification. We ordinarily suppose that the following argument is valid because it is an instance of Simplification:

(1)   1.   Art will get elected, and he'll serve well.
      ∴. He's going to get elected.

But if logic deals with sentences, this argument is not a valid instance of Simplification (or any other standard rule of inference). For Simplification has the form

p and q
∴ p

and if we substitute the sentence "Art will get elected" for the first p, we must substitute the same sentence for the second p. We can't substitute the sentence "He's going to get elected" for the second p, because that is a different *sentence* from "Art will get elected" (although it expresses the same proposition).

     The obvious thought is that in this case "Art will get elected" and "He's going to get elected" are *synonymous* (have the same meaning), and that all we have to do is allow synonymous sentences to replace one another whenever it is convenient to do so. The trouble is that those who reject propositions cannot appeal to sameness of meaning, for in the last analysis that amounts to a tacit appeal to propositions (or at least to abstract entities just as mysterious to those who reject propositions as propositions themselves).

     In addition, when propositions are rejected, problems arise because terms and sentences in natural languages tend to be *ambiguous*. For ambiguity also leads to trouble when substituting sentences into valid argument forms. Take the argument:

1.   Whales are fish.
2.   If whales are fish, then whales are cold-blooded.
∴ 3.   Whales are cold-blooded.   1,2 **MP**

Premise 1 of this argument is true if we construe the word "fish" in its everyday sense, and premise 2 is true if we construe that word in its scientific sense. And yet the conclusion clearly is false. So it seems that **MP** has let us down.

     The usual explanation, of course, is that the trouble arises because the word "fish" is being used ambiguously. If the word "fish" is used unambiguously throughout the proof, then the argument is valid, but one or the other of its premises is false (depending on what sense of that word we use). But if we use the word "fish" *equivocally,* meaning one thing in one premise and another thing in the other, then the argument is *invalid.* In either case, we have not validly proceeded from true premises to a false conclusion.

     But this explanation is not open to those who claim that logic deals with sentences and not propositions. For them, the form of **MP** is satisfied whenever the letters p and q are replaced respectively in each of their occurrences by the same *sentences.* And in the above example, each use of p is replaced by the same sentence, namely, "Whales are fish." Of course, that sentence is used ambiguously, but that is another matter.

     Another way to put the problem facing those who advocate sentences over propositions is just that those who reject propositions have a hard time separating uses of a sentence that have one meaning from those that have another. (For instance, they won't be able to say that in the above argument the sentence "Whales are fish" expresses one proposition when said truly and another proposition when said falsely.) Their problem, in other words, is to find some way to distinguish ambiguous uses of terms and sentences without appealing to propositions, a problem some of their opponents (including most definitely your authors) feel confident they cannot solve.

A third truth-value?

Sentential logic is a two-valued truth-functional logic. But are most natural language sentences two-valued? It has been argued that they are not.

Recall our discussion of definite descriptions (in Section 2 of this chapter), and consider the sentence "The present king of France is bald." According to the analysis in Section 2, asserting this sentence amounts to saying that (1) there is a present king of France; (2) there is only one present king of France; and (3) that person is bald.

But it has been argued that this analysis is incorrect, because it confuses *referring* to something with asserting that it exists. In saying that the present king of France is bald, according to this view, a speaker does not assert that a present king of France exists. Instead, *he presupposes* that the thing referred to, the present king of France, exists. But to presuppose that there is a present king of France is not to *assert* that there is a present king of France (nor—according to this view—does that presupposition *logically imply* the existence of a present king of France).

Now as a matter of fact there is no present king of France. So a person uttering the sentence "The present king of France is bald" will fail in his attempt to refer. Hence, it is claimed, that sentence, although meaningful, is neither true nor false, and thus literally has no truth-value. It follows then that it is incorrect to say that all sentences are either true or false.*

If correct, this is a very serious matter for logic, for we would have to change all of the truth table definitions of the sentence connectives and even have to give up the law of the excluded middle (that p or $\sim p$).

But the presupposition theory is not the only argument in favor of giving up two-valued logic. Another takes its cue from paradox-generating sentences such as "This very sentence is false."[†] Someone uttering this sentence intends to refer to that very sentence; and since the sentence does exist, there is no failure of reference. Nevertheless, it has been argued that, though meaningful, this sentence has no truth-value. For if it is true, then it is false, and if it is false, then it is true. Hence we must regard it as neither true nor false, even though meaningful, and therefore we must give up two-valued logic.[‡]

The status of sentence connectives in predicate logic

In sentential logic we explained the meaning of the logical connectives "$\sim$", "$\cdot$", "$\vee$", "$\supset$", and "$\equiv$", by means of truth tables, thus making them truth-functional connectives. But now consider their occurrences in quantified sentences, for instance, in the sentence $(x)(Fx \supset Gx)$. The expressions Fx and Gx are sentence forms and hence cannot have truth-

---

*This is roughly the view argued by P. F. Strawson. (More precisely, he argues that assertion of the sentence "The present king of France is bald" fails to make a true or false statement. But what it is to utter a statement other than asserting a proposition is not clear.) See Strawson's "On Referring," *Mind*, n.s., vol. 59 (1950), and Bertrand Russell's reply, "Mr. Strawson on Referring," in Russell, *My Philosophical Development* (London: Allen & Unwin, 1959), pp. 238–245.

†Discussed further in the last section of this chapter.

‡This is essentially the argument proposed in Frederick B. Fitch, *Symbolic Logic* (New York: The Ronald Press, 1952), p. 8.

values. Thus, there is no truth-value for the expression $Fx \supset Gx,$ and so the use of the horseshoe symbol " $\supset$ " in $(x)(Fx \supset Gx)$ does not appear to be truth-functional. But if it isn't truth-functional, how is it defined?

This problem is frequently overlooked, perhaps because an easy solution seems readily at hand. Recall that when we first discussed quantifiers, we said (in Chapter 6, Section 5) that it was convenient to regard quantified sentences as very long conjunctions (in the case of universally quantified sentences) or disjunctions (in the case of existentially quantified sentences). For instance, in a two-individual universe of discourse $(x)(Fx \supset Gx)$ amounts to the expansion $(Fa \supset Ga) \cdot (Fb \supset Gb),$ and $(\exists x)(Fx \supset Gx)$ amounts to the expansion $(Fa \supset Ga) \vee (Fb \supset Gb).$ Now, clearly, the horseshoe symbols occurring in these expansions are truth-functional. Hence, we can regard those occurring in the related quantified sentences as truth-functional.

The trouble with this, alluded to before, is that in some cases the domain of discourse is infinitely large (an example is the domain of positive integers), or even nondenumerably large (an example is the domain of real numbers). When dealing with domains of this size, we cannot replace quantified sentences with their expansions.

Nevertheless, some philosophers* regard quantified sentences as very long conjunctions or disjunctions, even though they cannot actually be written down, and thus feel justified in believing that the connectives occurring in quantified sentences are truth-functional. Perhaps, then, the issue is whether it makes a difference that we cannot actually write down an infinitely long conjunction or disjunction. If so, this dispute may be related to the dispute about propositions and sentences. For there are no infinitely long sentences, but assuming there are any propositions at all, there may be propositions that could be expressed by infinitely long conjunctions or disjunctions, if only we were able to write them down.

Whatever the solution to the above may be, there is another objection to the view that quantified sentences are shorthand for very long conjunctions or disjunctions. When we say, for instance, that $(x)Fx,$ we seem to say more than that $(Fa \cdot Fb) \cdot \ldots$. The sentence $(x)Fx$ seems to do more than merely list all the items, $a, b, c, \ldots$ and say they have the property $F.$ It also says that the items $a, b, c, \ldots$ in the expansion of $(x)Fx$ are in fact all the items there are (or all the items in the domain of discourse). The expansion doesn't say this, although the quantified sentence does. Hence, it can be argued that a quantified sentence and its expansion are not equivalent. If this argument is a good one, then the question of how to interpret the occurrences of connectives in quantified sentences remains unsolved.

Difficulties with truth-functional translations

When we introduced the sentence connective "$\supset$", we pointed out that it is a truth-functional connective and is to be used in translating everyday "If _____ then _____" sentences, even though most such sentences are not truth-functional. We justified this on several grounds, one of which was that such translations render valid arguments into valid arguments and invalid arguments into invalid arguments.

---

*See, for instance, Richard L. Purtill, *Logic for Philosophers* (New York: Harper & Row, 1971), pp. 226–227.

We saw in the previous section how this translation procedure failed when applied to subjunctive sentences. But some philosophers claim that it fails also for indicative sentences. Consider the following argument.[*]

(1) If this is gold, then it is not soluble in water.
   ∴ It's not the case that if this is gold, then it is soluble in water.

If we mechanically translate this argument as

(2) $G \supset \sim S$
   $\therefore \sim (G \supset S)$

we get into trouble, because (2) is invalid, whereas (1) is valid. And yet (2) seems to be the straightforward truth-functional translation of (1).

One way to solve this problem is to deny that the conclusion of (1) is correctly symbolized as $\sim (G \supset S)$. It might be claimed, for instance, that the placement of the negating expression in the conclusion deceives us into thinking that the whole remainder of the sentence is being negated, whereas only the consequent is being negated.

We already have precedent for the assumption that the placement of a negating expression doesn't always reflect its logical scope. Recall our discussion of the sentence "The present king of France is *not* bald," which in some contexts may mean that it is not the case that there is a present king of France, bald or otherwise. In examples of this kind, the negating term, although toward the end of the sentence, actually negates all the rest of the sentence. So in the gold example, the negating term, although at the beginning of the sentence, may negate just the second half of the sentence.

However, it isn't at all clear that this proposed solution to the problem is adequate.[†] And if it isn't, then we are faced with an extremely serious translation problem, standing in the way of the acceptance of any truth-functional logic as a device useful in dealing with real-life arguments.

The use of a truth-functional conditional also has been objected to on grounds that it generates so-called **paradoxes of material implication.** Thus, it is sometimes held to be paradoxical that a false sentence materially implies any sentence whatever (that is, paradoxical that if p is false, then $p \supset q$ is true, no matter what q happens to be) and paradoxical that a true sentence is materially implied by any sentence whatever (that is, paradoxical that if q is true, then $p \supset q$ is true, no matter what p happens to be).

But these alleged paradoxes are not truly paradoxical. They stem from a misunderstanding of the nature of material implication. Recall that material implication was introduced in earlier chapters to capture the part of their meaning that all implications share, namely the claim that it won't happen that their antecedents are true and their conclusions false. We said that a statement of the form $p \supset q$ is defined to be equivalent to the analogous statement of the form $\sim (p \cdot \sim q)$. And clearly, for any statement of this form, if p is false,

---

*Taken from Charles L. Stevenson, "If-iculties." *Philosophy of Science,* vol. 41 (1970), pp. 27–49.

†Most objections to it tend to be quite complicated, but one is fairly simple: In the gold example, if we symbolize as suggested, the argument becomes totally trivial, namely, $G \supset \sim S$ /∴ $G \supset \sim S$; yet the original argument seems to have more to it than that.

or if q is true, then $\sim (p \cdot \sim q)$ has to be true, as is easily proved by truth table analysis. So the alleged paradoxes of material implication aren't really paradoxical.

No doubt some of those who say that they are paradoxical simply mean to assert their objection to the translation of everyday non-truth-functional implications by means of a truth-function sentence connective such as "⊃". That is, they mean to say that the truth-functional implication of sentential logic cannot successfully translate everyday implications. And this is a point we've already encountered.

What is a deductively valid argument?

In Chapter 1, we stated that the fundamental property of a deductively valid argument is that, roughly speaking, if all of its premises are true, then its conclusion *must* be true also, so that it is *impossible* for all of its premises to be true and yet its conclusion be false. This characterization of deductive validity has been objected to on several grounds.

One objection stems from the ambiguity of the terms "must" and "impossible." What we mean by these terms can be specified more closely by the concept of *necessity*. If all premises of a deductively valid argument are true, then its conclusion *necessarily* will be true. The trouble is that the concept of necessity also is ambiguous, as the discussion to be presented in Chapter 16 will make clearer. We can, of course, remove the ambiguity by specifying that we have in mind here the idea of logical necessity, and indeed this is what is done in Chapter 16. But what is logical necessity, as opposed, say, to the physical necessity that is involved in the laws of nature? One way to answer this question is to say that logical necessity is what we have been discussing in the first ten chapters of this text (and what will be discussed in Chapter 16) and to provide examples, for instance, of the necessity that theorems of logic be true. But that, it can be argued, simply begs the question of what it is we have been discussing in those chapters.

Another way to answer the question is to appeal to the "spelling out" view of logical necessity that we used in explaining deductive validity in Chapter 1. On this view, it is necessary that the conclusion of a deductively valid argument be true if all of its premises are true because, as we said in Chapter 1, the conclusion of a valid deduction already is contained in its premises, although usually only implicitly, not explicitly. If the deductive process is one of drawing out all or part of what the premises of an argument assert, then this accounts for and explains the kind of necessity we have in mind when we speak of logical necessity.

But this just brings us to a second objection to our conception of deductive validity, for there are two important kinds of cases where it seems that logical necessity cannot be explained in this way. The first concerns certain arguments whose conclusions are theorems of logic or logical truths. Consider the following example:

(1)   1. Sugar tastes sweet.
     ∴2. All cats are cats.

This argument is without doubt deductively valid, at least it is according to the criterion of deductive validity we have provided in this text. But the spelling out view of deductive validity does not seem to account for its validity. After all, the premise of this argument is about sugar; it says absolutely nothing about cats. In what sense, then, does the conclusion of this argument spell out anything whatever that is in its premise?

There is no answer to this question that is, or can be, generally accepted by logicians and other philosophers. Indeed, how it is answered depends on all sorts of answers to related philosophical issues that are beyond the scope of an introductory text. But permit the authors of this text a brief explanation of their position on this matter.

Many philosophers who accept the general philosophical position called *empiricism* distinguish meanings into different kinds, one kind being what is sometimes called *factual meaning*. Roughly speaking, a sentence has this kind of meaning only if it makes a claim about the nature of the world, or about some of the entities in it. The sentence "All cats have hearts" thus has factual meaning because it makes a claim about cats, namely that they have hearts. Anyone who doubts this can check up on at least part of what this sentence asserts by a careful examination of some cats. But now consider argument (1) above whose conclusion is the logical truth that all cats are cats. We could, of course, check up on this statement by examining several cats and "discovering" that they all are cats, but that would be a waste of time. First, if we did so and discovered that one of the examined "cats" was, on closer inspection, not a cat, we would not count this as counterevidence to our statement that all cats are cats, but rather as evidence that the thing we thought was a cat in fact was not. The point is that the statement "All cats are cats" cannot be refuted by an investigation of the world and the things in it, which means that the statement does not have factual meaning—it tells us nothing about cats that might turn out to be false. Second, we can be quite sure that all cats are cats without examining any cats whatsoever, indeed without even knowing what counts as a cat. The reason for this, according to some empiricists, is that the spelling out of what the statement "All cats are cats" asserts leads to the conclusion that it says nothing *factual* about cats or about anything else. Its truth stems not from any facts about the world, or about cats, but from its structure, given that any sentence of the form "All _____ are _____" is true.

Well, then, how does this save the spelling-out view of deductive validity? It does so, on this view, because the factual claim made by the conclusion of an argument like the above argument (1), having no factual content whatever, is contained in every statement whatsoever. The premise of argument (1), namely that sugar tastes sweet, thus does indeed contain all of the zero factual content of the argument's conclusion that all cats are cats.

The second kind of case that seems to contradict the spelling-out view of logical necessity concerns arguments whose premises are contradictory. Consider the example:

(2) 1. Snow is white.
     2. It's false that snow is white.
∴3. All dogs have six tails.

Opponents of the spelling-out view would argue that it cannot account for the deductive validity of arguments like argument (2). Whether or not dogs have six tails does not seem to be part of the content of statements about snow being both white and not white.

But notice that, as we stated in Chapter 5, contradictory premises imply everything whatsoever. From a contradiction, we can derive any conclusion we care to. If a contradiction were true, per impossible, then everything would be true. So if snow were both white and not white, as, of course, it cannot be, then *everything* would be true, and so all dogs would indeed have six tails. (Of course, they would also not have six tails.) Thus, it seems reasonable to claim that the premises of argument (2) above, being contradictory, do indeed implicitly contain the factual claim made by the conclusion of that argument, since these contradictory premises implicitly make every factual claim whatsoever.

This brings us to a third objection to our view of the nature of a deductively valid argument. This objection is that the everyday use or sense of language is violated in calling argument (1) or argument (2) a deductively valid *argument*. (A similar objection can be made against our calling argument (1) a *sound* argument, and our saying that we have *proved* the conclusion of arguments (1) and (2).) And to this objection we have to plead guilty. Even though the concepts in question are both vague and ambiguous in everyday speech, our use of these terms does stretch matters beyond what would sound right in everyday conversation. Or rather it would do so without an explanation of how we are using these terms. But we have provided such an explanation, and we have a very good reason for using these terms in the way we have specified, for all of the cases we have called deductively valid arguments share an important characteristic: If their premises are true, then their conclusions must be true; or, to put it another way, the factual content of the conclusion of what we call a deductively valid argument is already contained, explicitly or implicitly, in its premises.

7   *Logical Paradoxes*

In addition to the problems just discussed that trouble first-order predicate logic, higher-order logics are plagued by the so-called **logical paradoxes,** some of which date back to the time of the early Greeks.

Syntactic paradoxes

In a first-order predicate logic there is no straightforward way to express the predication of properties to other properties. The usual way to express such predications is via the symbolism of a *second-order* (or higher) predicate logic. In Section 4 of this chapter, we very briefly discussed higher-order logics and in particular the predication of properties to other properties. (An example is the property of *honesty,* which seems itself to have the property of being *rare*—in that its extension is rather small.) But if we allow the predication of properties to properties, then certain alleged paradoxes called **syntactic paradoxes** can be generated.

If we can predicate properties of other properties, it seems reasonable to suppose that we can predicate properties of *themselves.* For example, it seems reasonable to suppose that the property of being *comprehensible* itself is comprehensible (in contrast to the property of being incomprehensible, which itself is not incomprehensible), and reasonable to suppose that the property of being *common* (as opposed to rare) is itself common. But sometimes the predication of a property to itself yields trouble. The most famous example is the so-called **impredicable paradox.**

Let's call any property that can be truly predicated of itself a *predicable property,* and any property that cannot be truly predicated of itself an *impredicable property.* Using this notation we can say that the property of being common is a predicable property, since being *common* is a common property, and that the property of being *rare* is an *im*predicable property, since being rare is *not* a rare property (because there are many kinds of rare things).

But what about the property of being *impredicable?* Can this property be truly predicated of itself? The unfortunate answer seems to be that if the property of being impredicable is predicated of itself, then it is *not* predicated of itself, and if it is *not* predicated of itself, then it is predicated of itself. Hence, the paradox.

To make this clear, let's symbolize the property of being predicable as P and the property of being impredicable as $\bar{P}$. Thus, to say a given property F is P is to say that FF, and to say that a given property F is $\bar{P}$ is to say that $\sim FF$.

To start with, either $\bar{P}$ is itself $\bar{P}$ or else $\bar{P}$ is P. Suppose $\bar{P}$ is $\bar{P}$. If $\bar{P}$ is $\bar{P}$, then $\bar{P}$ is predicated of itself, and hence $\bar{P}$ is P. So if $\bar{P}$ is $\bar{P}$, then $\bar{P}$ is P.

Now suppose $\bar{P}$ is P. If $\bar{P}$ is P, then $\bar{P}$ is not predicated of itself, and hence $\bar{P}$ is $\bar{P}$. So if $\bar{P}$ is P, then $\bar{P}$ is $\bar{P}$.

It follows that if $\bar{P}$ is $\bar{P}$, then it is P, and if $\bar{P}$ is P, then it is $\bar{P}$. Translating this back into plain English, what we have shown is that if the property of being impredicable is impredicable, then it is predicated of itself, and hence is predicable. And if the property of being impredicable is predicable, then it is not predicated of itself (impredicable would have to be impredicable to be predicated of itself), and hence is impredicable.

This contradictory result can be made even more explicit by writing down the definition of $\bar{P}$ and then constructing a simple argument, as follows:

1. $\bar{P}F = df \sim FF$

That is, to say that a property, F, is impredicable is to say that it is not the case that F is F. From which it follows that given any property F, F is $\bar{P}$ if and only if it is not the case that F is F. In other words,

2. $(F)(\bar{P}F \equiv \sim FF)$

Hence, substituting $\bar{P}$ for F, we get (by **UI**)

3. $\bar{P}\bar{P} \equiv \sim \bar{P}\bar{P}$

from which an explicit contradiction can be derived.

Several solutions to paradoxes of this kind have been proposed. One of them is the **simple theory of types.*** According to this theory, all entities divide into a hierarchy of types, starting with individual entities, moving to properties of individual entities, then to properties of properties of individual entities, and so on. For instance, Art is an individual entity; the property of being honest is a property Art may possess (hence honesty is a property of individuals); and the property of being rare is a property possessed by the property of being honest (hence rarity is a property of properties).

Having arranged entities in this way, the simple theory of types requires that the type of a property be higher than any property of which it can be predicated. For instance, if

---

*Proposed by Bertrand Russell. See *Principles of Mathematics* (Cambridge: Cambridge University Press, 1903), Appendix B.

being old is predicated of Art, then it cannot be predicated either of itself or any other property.

It is customary to mark the distinction between properties of individuals and properties of properties by some notational device, such as the use of standard type to denote properties of individuals and boldface type to denote properties of properties of individuals.

Using a notation of this kind, a sentence such as "Art is not old" will be symbolized as ~ *Oa,* and a sentence such as "Honesty is rare" will be symbolized as **R***H*.

Notice that the sentence "Honesty is rare" is correctly symbolized as **R***H,* and *not* as *R***H,** for according to the theory of types, the property of being rare, which is predicable of properties, is of a type one level higher than properties that are predicable of individuals.

To summarize, the simple theory of type requires, first, that we arrange entities into a hierarchy of categories or types, starting with individuals, moving to properties of individuals, and then to properties of properties, properties of properties of properties, and so on; and second, that the type of a property be one type higher than any property or entity of which it can be predicated.

An obvious consequence of the simple theory of types is that no property can be predicated of itself. And it is this consequence that solves the impredicable paradox, for if no property can be predicated of itself, then it becomes senseless to ask if the property of being impredicable is itself impredicable.

The simple theory of types has been objected to as both *ad hoc* and *counterintuitive.* For example, according to the simple theory of types, the rareness we can predicate of, say, a postage stamp is different from the rareness we can predicate of the property of being honest. But it seems intuitively clear that it is the very same property of rareness that is predicable of postage stamps and of honesty.

The counterintuitive nature of the simple theory of types is further illustrated by the fact that it forbids assertion of sentences such as "Some members of every type (in the hierarchy of types) are rare," a sentence that seems not only *meaningful,* but also *true.*

Indeed, it has been argued that the very statement of the simple theory of types presupposes a violation of the theory itself. For instance, the simple theory of types presupposes that all individuals, properties of individuals, properties of properties, and so on have the property of being *type classifiable* (that is, have the property of belonging to exactly one category in the hierarchy of types). But the property of being type classifiable is not permitted by the simple theory of types. Hence the theory presupposes what it will not permit.

Semantic paradoxes

Although adoption of the simple theory of types has its difficulties, it does solve syntactic paradoxes like the impredicable paradox. But unfortunately, it fails to solve the paradoxes usually referred to as **semantic paradoxes.**

The most famous semantic paradox is the so-called paradox of the liar, which was first posed by the ancient Greeks. Put into more modern dress, the paradox is this: It seems reasonable to suppose that every declarative sentence is either true or false. But consider the sentence

(1)   Sentence (1) is false.

Is sentence (1) true or is it false? The unfortunate answer seems to be that if sentence (1) is true, then it is false, and if it is false, then it is true.

Take the first possibility, namely, that sentence (1) is true. If (1) is true, and (1) asserts that (1) is false, then it follows that (1) is false. So if (1) is true, then (1) is false.

Now suppose (1) is false. If (1) is false, and (1) asserts that (1) is false, then it follows that it is false that (1) is false, and therefore follows that (1) is true. So if (1) is false, then (1) is true. Either way, we have a contradiction and hence a paradox.

An obvious thought is to solve the liar paradox by ruling out (as meaningless) any sentence that refers to itself. (Indeed the liar paradox often is conceived of—erroneously—as a paradox of self-reference.) But, unfortunately, the liar paradox can be generated without self-reference. For example, consider the following two sentences:

(2) Sentence (3) is false.
(3) Sentence (2) is true.

Sentence (2) refers to sentence (3), and sentence (3) refers to sentence (2), but neither (2) nor (3) refers to itself. So both of these sentences satisfy the requirement that sentences not be self-referential, and they seem to have the form required of legitimate declarative sentences.

But is sentence (2) true or is it false? Again, the unfortunate answer seems to be that if it is true, then it is false, and if it is false, then it is true.

Take the first possibility, namely that sentence (2) is true. If (2) is true, and (2) asserts that (3) is false, it follows that (3) is false. But if (3) is false, and (3) asserts that (2) is true, it follows that it is false that (2) is true and hence that (2) is false. So if (2) is true, then (2) is false.

Now suppose sentence (2) is false. If (2) is false, and (2) asserts that (3) is false, it follows that it is false that (3) is false and hence that (3) is true. But if (3) is true, and (3) asserts that (2) is true, it follows that (2) is true. So if (2) is false, then (2) is true. Again we have a contradiction, and hence again we have a paradox.

One way to solve the semantic paradoxes is to distinguish between **levels of language,** that is, between languages that are used to talk about nonlinguistic things and those used to talk about other languages. A language used to talk about some other language is considered to be on a higher level than the language talked about,* so that sentences asserting the truth or falsity of a given sentence must be placed in a language at least one level higher than the given sentence. For instance, the sentence "The sentence 'Art is tall' is true" must be placed in a language one level higher than the language in which the sentence "Art is tall" occurs.†

It is clear that adoption of the above machinery solves the liar paradox. In the first place, all self-referential sentences, such as sentence (1), will be rejected as meaningless. And in the second place, at least one of every pair of sentences like sentences (2) and (3) will be

---

*This division into higher and lower language levels is discussed in greater detail in Chapter 15, Section 4.

†This solution was first proposed by Bertrand Russell in his "Introduction" to Ludwig Wittgenstein's *Tractatus Logico-Philosophicus* (New York: Harcourt Brace, 1922), p. 23. See also Alfred Tarski, "Semantic Conception of Truth." *Philosophy and Phenomenological Research,* vol. 4 (1944), pp. 241–275.

rejected as meaningless. (For instance, if (2) occurs in a given language, and (3) in a language one level higher, then (2) will be rejected as meaningless—whatever the fate of (3)—because no sentence can be permitted to assert the truth or falsity of a sentence in the same or a higher level language.)

But not all philosophers accept the levels of language solution.* Perhaps the main reason is that it seems to be much too strong, eliminating as meaningless not only the troublesome sentence (1) but also many apparently meaningful sentences. For instance, it eliminates the sentence "Every language (including this one) permits the expression of at least one true sentence," which may be false, but does seem to be meaningful.

Exercise 11-5

Here are versions of several well-known logical paradoxes. Show how in each case a solution offered for one of the paradoxes in this chapter might plausibly be said to solve these puzzles.

1. BONNY: My teacher said in class today that all generalities are false. Do you think that's true?

   CHARLIE: Who knows? Maybe yes, maybe no.

   BONNY: I know. It's false. Look. Suppose it were true. Then the statement (A) "All generalities are false" would be true. But (A) itself is a generality. So if (A) is true, it's true that *all* generalities are false, so (A) must be false. So if (A) is true, then it's false. Well then, (A) must be false. Right?

   CHARLIE: Wrong! But I don't know why.

2. CHARLIE: What we need is a bibliography listing all bibliographies.

   BONNY: That would be nice. But how about a bibliography that lists all and only those bibliographies that do not list themselves?

   CHARLIE: Not terribly useful. But why not?

   BONNY: Here's why not. Such a bibliography either lists itself or it doesn't. Right? If it does list itself, then it violates the condition that it list *only* those bibliographies that don't list themselves. So it can't list itself. But if it doesn't list itself, then it violates the condition that it list *all* those bibliographies that do not list themselves. So either way the conditions of such a bibliography are violated. So there cannot be such a bibliography.

   CHARLIE: That's what's wrong with you philosophy majors—you think too much for your own good.

3. BONNY: Ready for another one?

   CHARLIE: No. But you'll go ahead anyway.

   BONNY: OK. Let's call a number *interesting* if we can say something special about that number that we can't say about any other number (not counting things such as being identical with themselves, or one greater than the next number, and things like that).

---

*For example, see Frederick B. Fitch, *Symbolic Logic* (New York: The Ronald Press, 1952), p. 111.

Every low number clearly is interesting: 1 is the lowest number; 2 is the lowest even number; 3 is the number of logic books on my shelf; 4 is the number of offensive backs in football, and so on. But when we get to extremely large numbers, the situation would seem to be different; for instance, there seems to be nothing interesting about $(10^{61} + 33)$. So some numbers are *not* interesting. Right?

CHARLIE: Right, . . . on your definition of interestingness.

BONNY: Wrong! I'm going to prove to you that there are no *un*interesting numbers. Imagine two huge bags, A and B, A containing all the interesting numbers, B the uninteresting ones. If there are no uninteresting numbers, bag B will be empty. So you think B will not be empty, because you think some numbers are uninteresting. But if there are *any* numbers in bag B, there must be a lowest one, right?

CHARLIE: Right.

BONNY: Well, if that's true, then we can say something about that number that we can't say about any other number, namely, that it is the lowest uninteresting number. Right?

CHARLIE: Right.

BONNY: Well, *isn't that interesting!*

CHARLIE: What?!?

BONNY: So there can't be a lowest uninteresting number, because that would be interesting. But if there is no lowest uninteresting number, then there aren't *any. Q.E.D.*

4. BONNY: Now I'm going to show you that your intuitions about classes are all wet. For instance, you believe that any items can form a class, don't you, and also that there is a universal class that contains everything?

CHARLIE: Sure, why not?

BONNY: Well, here's why not. If any items can form a class, then classes themselves can be items that form a class. So we can construct a class containing other classes as members (for example, the class of all classes containing exactly ten members), and even construct a class containing itself as a member (for example, the class consisting of itself and the class of states in the Union).

CHARLIE: That last is a weird class, but why not?

BONNY: Here's why not. Divide all classes into those that are a member of themselves (for example, the class containing all classes) and those that are not (for example, the class containing all football players and nothing else). Then the class containing all classes that are a member of themselves would seem to contain itself. But what about the class containing all classes that do not contain themselves? Is it a member of itself? Clearly not, since it is the class of all classes that are not members of themselves. Well, then, is it not a member of itself? Again, clearly not, for if it were not, then it would be a class that is not a member of itself, and hence would be a member of itself. So, if it is a member of itself, it isn't a member of itself, and if it isn't, it is. Clearly, there is no class containing just those classes that are not members of themselves. Hence, every bunch of items does not form a class, and, incidentally, it therefore can't be true that there is a universal class containing everything.

CHARLIE: Very clever, but I'll figure out what's wrong . . . later.

Exercise 11-6

1. Which of the following require an identity sign if we are to symbolize them so as to reveal the most possible internal structure?
   (1) The horse is an intelligent animal.
   (2) The horse that wins the derby wins a lot of money.
   (3) W. A. Mozart is the greatest composer in history.
   (4) Mozart is a better composer than anyone else.
   (5) No one had a higher grade-point average than Susan.
   (6) The graceful winner also is a graceful loser.
   (7) Susan had the highest grade-point average.
2. Explain the difference between the properties of being *symmetrical, asymmetrical,* and *nonsymmetrical.* (Include at least one original example of each.)
3. In Part One, we defined "⊃" *truth-functionally.* What objection is there to the use of this truth-functional definition of "⊃" in predicate logic when dealing with indicative sentences?
4. When using, say, Modus Ponens, $p \supset q, p / \therefore q,$ whatever is substituted for the first p must be substituted for the second. What is it that we must substitute? Is it sentence tokens, sentence types, propositions, or what? Defend your answer. If you don't know, explain what's troubling about each of the three alternatives mentioned.
5. True or false? Defend your answers.
   (1) To say that food has the disposition or power to nourish is to say that if we eat food, then we'll be nourished.
   (2) We can't solve the problem of dispositionals just by translating them into related counterfactuals, because the problems in symbolizing counterfactuals are pretty much the same as those encountered in symbolizing dispositionals.
   (3) The subjunctive conditional "If we were to make cigarettes illegal, then more people would smoke" is correctly symbolized as $C \supset S$, where $C =$ "we make cigarettes illegal" and $S =$ "more people will smoke."
6. Which of the following underlined words are used as dispositionals and which are not? Explain.
   (1) The sugar was <u>observed</u> to dissolve.
   (2) But no one has ever observed the <u>solubility</u> of sugar.
   (3) Since I was wearing sunglasses, I assumed the leaves were not as <u>green</u> as they looked.
   (4) None of her teachers teach Betsy, but she is <u>teachable</u>.
   (5) Tobacco is a more <u>dangerous</u> drug than marijuana.
   (6) Bonny is a very <u>dependable</u> person.
   (7) In fact, she has a sterling <u>character</u>.

Key terms

asymmetrical relation: A relation *Fxy* such that it must be the case that $(x)(y)(Fxy \supset \sim Fyx)$. The relation "_____ is the mother of _____" is asymmetrical.

contrary-to-fact conditional (counterfactual): A subjunctive conditional whose antecedent is a contrary to fact. The sentence "If Art had studied hard, then he would have become a great logician" is a contrary-to-fact conditional.

definite description: A descriptive phrase used to select or refer to a particular individual entity; for example, "the tallest man in the world," "the author of *Huckleberry Finn*," and "the chairman of the club."

dispositional property: An unobservable power or potential of an item. Example: the power of being soluble.

first-order predicate logic: The predicate logic that forbids sentences ascribing properties to properties themselves, but restricts quantification to individual variables. The logic presented in Part Two, prior to Section 4 of this chapter, is a first-order predicate logic.

impredicable paradox: The paradox concerning the predicate impredicable, namely that if impredicable is itself impredicable, then it is predicable, and if impredicable is not impredicable, then it is impredicable.

indirect context: A context involving believing, knowing, seeking, necessity, or possibility, and so on. Sentences containing indirect contexts generally contain phrases such as "believes that," "is looking for," or "it is necessary that," which introduce the indirect context. Some typical sentences containing indirect contexts are "Art is looking for Betsy," "Art believes that Betsy is tall," "It is possible that it will rain tomorrow."

intransitive relation: A relation Fxy such that it must be the case that when one thing bears that relation to a second, and the second to a third, then the first cannot bear it to the third. The relation "_____ is a mother of _____" is an example.

irreflexive relation: A relation Fxy such that it must be the case that $(x) \sim Fxx$. The relation "_____ is lighter than _____" is an example.

levels of language theory: The theory that certain parts of the semantic apparatus of a language, in particular the truth conditions of a language, must be contained not in the language itself but in the metalanguage, in order to get around the difficulties illustrated by paradoxes such as the liar paradox.

logical paradoxes: Paradoxes generated or clarified by the use of logic, for example, the syntactic and semantic paradoxes.

nonreflexive relation: A relation that is neither reflexive nor irreflexive. The relation "_____ understands _____" is an example.

nonsymmetrical relation: A relation that is neither symmetrical nor asymmetrical. The relation "_____ loves _____" is nonsymmetrical.

nontransitive relation: A relation that is neither transitive nor intransitive. The relation "_____ loves _____" is an example.

paradoxes of material implication: The allegedly paradoxical results that a sentence of the form $p \supset q$ is true if p is false or q is true, no matter what p and q happen to be.

property variable: A variable ranging over properties. (Property variables are admissible only in higher-order logics.) An example is the property F in the statement "Art has some property, F, or other."

reflexive relation: A relation Fxy such that it must be the case that $(x)(y)[Fxy \supset (Fxx \cdot Fyy)]$. The relation "_____ belongs to the same church as _____" is a reflexive relation.

semantic paradox: A paradox such that most philosophers would accept only a semantic solution to it. For example, the liar paradox is a semantic paradox. Most philosophers accept a semantic theory, the so-called levels of language theory, as a solution to this paradox.

sentence token: A series of marks on paper, or sounds in the air, used to make a sentence.

sentence type: The class of sentence tokens of the same sentence; for example, the two sentence tokens "Snow is white" and "Snow is white" are tokens of the same sentence type.

simple theory of types: The syntactic theory according to which all properties are categorized in a hierarchy of categories, starting with properties of things, properties of properties, properties of properties of properties, and so on. The theory was proposed as a solution to syntactic paradoxes such as the impredicable paradox.

subjunctive conditional: A conditional sentence in the subjunctive mood. The sentence "If Art were to study hard, then he would be a great logician" is a subjunctive conditional.

symmetrical relation: A relation Fxy such that it must be the case that $(x)(y)(Fxy \supset Fyx)$. The relation "_____ is divorced from _____" is an example.

syntactic paradox: A paradox such that most philosophers would accept only a syntactic solution to it. For instance, the impredicable paradox is a syntactic paradox.

totally reflexive relation: A relation *Fxy* such that it must be the case that (x)*Fxx*. Hardly any interesting relations are totally reflexive. The relation "_____ is identical with _____" is totally reflexive.

transitive relation: A relation *Fxy* such that it must be the case that (x)(y)(z)[(*Fxy* · *Fyz*) ⊃ *Fxz*]. The relation "_____ is shorter than _____" is an example.

Chapter Twelve

---

1   *The Sentential Logic Truth Tree Method*

As we have seen, truth tables can be used to test for validity and invalidity, as well as for consistency and inconsistency. The problem with truth tables is that they can be quite tedious. Testing sentences that contain as few as 6 different atomic letters requires us to construct a 64-line truth table. The shortcut method is by comparison admirably efficient, but it also has its shortcomings. Most importantly, although you can use the shortcut method to test for invalidity or consistency, the method doesn't lend itself to demonstrating validity or inconsistency. Likewise, natural deduction proofs can't be used for everything. You can use natural deduction to demonstrate validity and inconsistency but not invalidity and consistency. Proofs also require ingenuity. They are not mechanical, like truth tables. In this chapter we introduce the **truth tree method.** Truth trees have the virtues of truth tables but not their vices. They are quick and efficient, and in sentential logic they can tell us mechanically, without fail, whether any argument is valid or invalid, and whether any group of sentences is consistent or inconsistent.

    Truth trees are built by a process called **decomposition.** In decomposition, longer sentences are replaced by shorter sentences that are placed along a structure that looks like an upside-down tree. *These shorter sentences represent more simply what it takes to make the longer sentences true.* So the basic idea in constructing truth trees is that we decompose sentences into shorter and shorter units, arranging them along the branches of the tree in a way designed to make it obvious whether or not it is possble to make the original sentences true.

    The way to read a truth tree is to examine its branches. Each branch stemming downward from the trunk of the tree corresponds to an attempt to make the original sentences contained in the trunk true. Typically, some of these attempts fail, because they would require making both a sentence and its denial true. Whenever this happens we place an $\times$ at the bottom of the branch. Such a branch is said to be **closed** and is not developed further. If all of the branches of a tree close, this shows conclusively that it is impossible to make all of the original sentences true. In other words, the original set of sentences is shown to be *inconsistent.* On the other hand, if any branch remains **open** when the tree is completed, the original set of sentences is *consistent* and the short sentences arrayed along the open branch constitute a recipe for how to make the original sentences true.

Examples

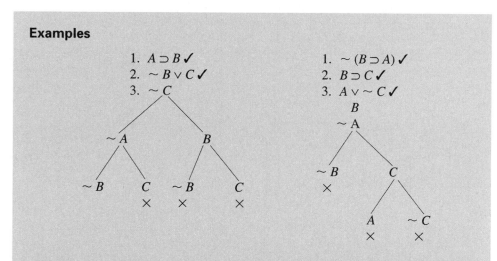

The tree on the left has one open branch. Therefore the original set of sentences is consistent. You can make these sentences true by making each unchecked sentence along the open branch true (in this case $\sim A$, $\sim B$, $\sim C$). The tree on the right has no open branches, therefore the original set is inconsistent. The tree demonstrates that there is no way to make all of these sentences true. Every attempt to do so results in a contradiction.

Because truth trees reveal whether groups of sentences are consistent, they can be used to determine whether any argument in sentential logic is valid. To do this we simply begin by adding the negation of the conclusion to the argument's premises. We then construct a tree. If there are any open branches on this tree, we've shown that it is possible to make the premises of the argument true and the conclusion false—so the argument is invalid. On the other hand, if there are no open branches, the argument is shown to be valid.

2 *The Truth Tree Rules*

To simplify matters, let's call atomic sentences (A, B, C, . . .) and negated atomic sentences ($\sim A$, $\sim B$, $\sim C$, . . .) **short sentences;** all others we will refer to as **long sentences.** Then we can say that *in decomposition we break down all long sentences until either every branch of the tree is closed or until no long sentences remain to be decomposed.* But what are the right ways to break long into short, and where on the tree are the appropriate places to put the short?

Let's begin with a simple argument

1. $A \vee B$
2. $\sim A$ $/\therefore B$

The first step in the tree method tells us to add the negation of the conclusion of this argument to the list of its premises, to form the trunk of a budding tree, like this:

1. $A \vee B$
2. $\sim A$ $/\therefore B$
   $\sim B$

And now the second step says that we should break the long formula $(A \vee B)$ into its two components, A and B, in this way:

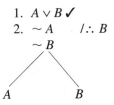

The short formulas, A and B, are each placed on a branch, and the long sentence, $(A \vee B)$, is checked to indicate that it has been decomposed.

The two branches represent two ways of making the original formula true. One way you can make $A \vee B$ true is to make A true. That alone would do it. If A is true, $A \vee B$ is true no matter what truth-value B has. Likewise, if we make B true, $A \vee B$ is guaranteed to be true. Finally, notice that if we are going to make this sentence true, we must at least do one of these two things. So the decomposition rule for disjunctions graphically displays these two ways of making the sentence true, as follows:

You might be tempted to think there is a third way to make disjunctions true, namely by making both disjuncts true. But we already have this possibility covered. Remember, we are trying to state only *the bare minimum* that it takes to make the sentence being decomposed true. If you can make a disjunction true by making both disjuncts true, obviously you can make it true by making one of the two disjuncts true. So our method, which puts each disjunct on a branch, guarantees that if there is a way to make the sentence true the tree will display one.

At this point, we have a tree with two paths: one running through the trunk of the tree and then branching to the left (containing ~ A, ~ B, and A) and the other running through the trunk and branching to the right (containing ~ A, ~ B, and B). The third step in the truth tree method requires that we examine every path in the tree and close those that contain a contradiction by marking them with an ✕. Doing so makes the tree in question look like this:

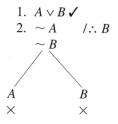

Having done all of this, we're ready for step 4 and the payoff. Step 4 requires that we declare an argument valid if and only if every one of its paths is closed and to declare it invalid if even one of its paths is open. In this case, every path is closed, and so the argument is valid.

Before proceeding, let's summarize what we did in carrying out the four tasks the tree method requires us to perform. First, we placed the premises of the argument one under the other to form a tree trunk and added the negation of the conclusion to the trunk. Second, we decomposed the one long sentence in the tree trunk (the disjunction A ∨ B) into its two component short sentences (A and B) and placed each of these short sentences in a separate branch of the truth tree, checking the long sentence to indicate that it has been decomposed. Third, we placed an ✕ at the bottom of the closed paths in the tree, that is, at the bottom of paths containing explicit contradictions. Having carried out these three tasks, we then were able to "read" the verdict from the resulting tree diagram that the argument is valid because all paths in the tree are closed.

Now consider a simple invalid argument, say, the argument

$$1.\ A \lor B$$
$$2.\ A \qquad /∴\ B$$

To construct its tree, we add the negation of the conclusion to the list of premises and then decompose the disjunction A ∨ B, to get this tree:

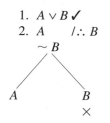

In this case, only the right path is closed; the left path does not contain a contradiction and so is open. Thus, the argument in question is not valid.

Now consider an argument containing a premise that is a conjunction, say the trivial argument

$$1. \ A \cdot B \qquad /\therefore A$$

First, we add the negation of its conclusion to its premise, forming a tree trunk that looks like this:

$$1. \ A \cdot B \qquad /\therefore A$$
$$\sim A$$

Then, we check the conjunctive premise, $A \cdot B$, and decompose it into its components, placed at the bottom of the column that forms the trunk of the tree:

$$1. \ A \cdot B \checkmark \qquad /\therefore A$$
$$\sim A$$
$$A$$
$$B$$
$$\times$$

Since the one path in this tree contains an explicit contradiction, indicated by placing an $\times$ at its end, the argument is valid.

Notice that we didn't place A and B into the tree by means of branches, as we did in the previous case. Branching is used to decompose disjunctions, and in this case we decomposed a conjunction. The rule for decomposing conjunctions is to place each conjunct into the tree trunk one under the other as we have done in this case. The reason we don't add branches is that there is only *one* way to make a conjunction true and that is to make each conjunct true. Thus the rule for decomposing conjunctions has the general form:

$$p \cdot q \checkmark$$
$$p$$
$$q$$

We can, of course, handle more complicated arguments containing, say, a conjunction and a disjunction. Here is an example:

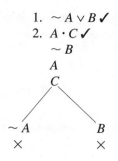

1. $\sim A \vee B$ ✓
2. $A \cdot C$ ✓
   $\sim B$
   A
   C

$\sim A$ B
$\times$ $\times$

Since both paths are closed, the argument is valid.

Now consider an example involving implication, say the argument

1. $A \supset B$
2. A $/ \therefore B$

After adding the negation of the conclusion to the trunk of its truth tree, we need to decompose the premise, $A \supset B$. And the key to how to do this is contained in the fact that the implication $(A \supset B)$ is logically equivalent to the disjunction, $\sim A \vee B$. We therefore can decompose this implication in the same way that we would decompose its analogous disjunction $\sim A \vee B$. So the truth tree for the argument in question will look like this:

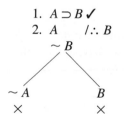

1. $A \supset B$ ✓
2. A $/ \therefore B$
   $\sim B$

$\sim A$ B
$\times$ $\times$

Since both paths of this tree are closed, the argument (a substitution instance of Modus Ponens) is valid (and a very good thing that it is, too).

This should make it clear that the general form of the process for decomposing a material conditional is this:

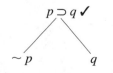

$p \supset q$ ✓

$\sim p$ q

So far we have covered the rules for disjunctions, conjunctions, and material condition-als. Now consider a case involving negation over a large unit:

1. *A*
2. *B*   /∴. *A* · *B*

Adding the negation of the argument's conclusion to the trunk of the tree, we get:

1. *A*
2. *B*   /∴. *A* · *B*
   ~ (*A* · *B*)

We now need to decompose the large compound ~ (*A* · *B*), and the key to how this is done lies in the fact that ~ (*A* · *B*) is logically equivalent (by DeMorgan's Theorem) to the disjunction ~ *A* ∨ ~ *B*, so that the two decompose in the same way. The completed tree for the argument in question thus looks like this:

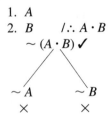

Again, since both branches are closed, the argument is valid.

It should be obvious that statements having the form ~ (*p* · *q*) are to be decomposed in this way:

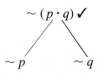

Likewise, a negated disjunction, like ~ (*A* ∨ *B*), is logically equivalent (again by DeMorgan's) to a conjunction, in this case ~ *A* · ~ *B*. So the decompostion rule for negated disjunctions is as follows:

~ (*p* ∨ *q*) ✓
  ~ *p*
  ~ *q*

A negated conditional, like $\sim (A \supset B)$, is equivalent (this time by Implication + DeMorgan's + Double Negation) to a conjunction, in this case, $\sim A \cdot B$. Perhaps the easiest way to see this is to think about the truth conditions for material conditionals. Making a negated material conditional true amounts to making the material conditional inside the parentheses false—and there is only one way to make a conditional false and that is to make the antecedent true and the consequent false. Hence, the general decomposition rule for negated conditionals is as follows:

$$\sim (p \supset q)\ \checkmark$$
$$p$$
$$\sim q$$

Next, let's consider the decomposition of a double negation, like $\sim \sim (A \vee B)$. It should be obvious that the general form of the procedure for decomposing double negations is this:

$$\sim \sim p\ \checkmark$$
$$p$$

The only rules that remain are the two rules involving biconditionals. These rules are straightforward if you keep the standard truth table for biconditionals in mind. Recall that biconditionals are true just in case the two component sentences have the same truth-value. Obviously there are two, and only two, ways of doing this: You can make the two component sentences true or you can make the two component sentences false. So the decomposition rule for biconditionals is as follows:

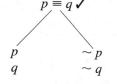

Likewise, a biconditional is false if and only if the two component sentences have different truth-values. So there are two ways of making negated biconditionals true: Make the first component of the biconditional true and the other false or vice versa. So here is the decomposition rule for negated biconditionals:

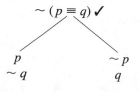

Here, now, is the complete set of decomposition rules for our sentential logic tree method:

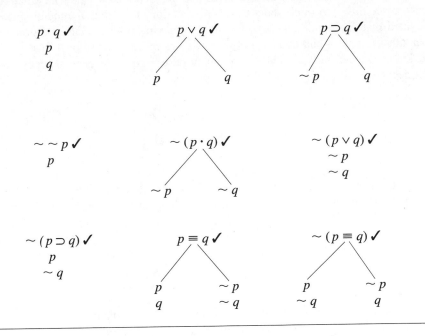

3   *Details of Tree Construction*

Once you have mastered each of the nine decomposition rules, all that is left is to see how to put a number of decomposition steps together so as to make a completed tree. After forming the trunk, we build trees as follows:

1. Find a long sentence along an open branch of the tree.
2. Decompose the sentence and place the results at the bottom of each open branch that stems downward from the sentence being decomposed.
3. Check to see if this results in any new closed branches. Place an × below any such branches.
4. Look to see if there are any more unchecked long sentences remaining along an open branch. (Ignore closed branches.) If so, repeat the process for this new sentence. If not, the tree is completed.

Let's construct a tree for the following argument:

1. $\sim A \vee B$
2. $\sim (B \cdot \sim C)$
3. $\sim \sim A$ $/\therefore C$

After adding the negation of the conclusion to the trunk of the tree, we begin by decomposing the first sentence. This sentence is a disjunction so we add a branch to the tree, as follows:

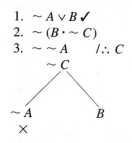

1. $\sim A \vee B$ ✓
2. $\sim (B \cdot \sim C)$
3. $\sim \sim A$ /∴ C
   $\sim C$

Since the left path already contains a contradiction, even without the information contained
in the premise $\sim (B \cdot \sim C)$, we close that path. And then we decompose $\sim (B \cdot \sim C)$ onto
the remaining open path, resulting in this lop-sided tree:

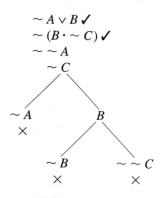

All three paths are closed, which proves that the original set of sentences are inconsistent.

Notice that it does not matter in what order sentences are decomposed. For example, we
could just as well have started with the second sentence in the example above, resulting in
the following tree:

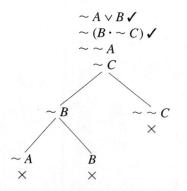

Finally, we should also take note of the fact that sentences sometimes have to be decomposed several times. Here is an example:

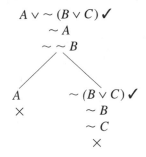

The point is that after we have decomposed the first sentence and placed its components onto the tree, we still need to decompose one of those components, $\sim (B \vee C)$, before we can determine the validity of the argument in question. (Once again it was unnecessary to decompose the formula $\sim \sim B$, although there would have been no harm in our doing so.) When decomposing a formula like this one, which occurs along a branch of the tree, the shorter sentences are placed only along those branches that stem downward from the sentence being decomposed.

Hints for efficient trees

Trees can consume a lot of paper. If you are not sure how long your tree is, leave yourself plenty of room. Start in the center of your page and begin with very wide branches. As we stated above, you can decompose the sentences on your tree in any order. The following three guidelines will help you produce less bushy, more efficient, trees.

1.   Always decompose sentences that do not branch first.
2.   When faced with a choice of branching decompositions, first decompose those sentences that will quickly lead to closed branches.
3.   When faced with a choice of branching decompositions, and you cannot tell which will result more quickly in closed branches, decompose the longest sentence.

🚶 Walk-Through: Truth Trees

As usual, we begin our tree by adding the negation of the conclusion below the argument's premises

1. $(D \supset G) \supset F$
2. $\sim [(\sim G \vee \sim B) \supset D]$
3. $\sim F \vee (B \cdot D)$
4. $\sim G \equiv \sim D$ $/ \therefore \sim (G \vee B)$
     $\sim \sim (G \vee B)$

Next we look for nonbranching decompositions. We can decompose our negated conclusion and the second line without branching:

1. $(D \supset G) \supset F$
2. $\sim [(\sim G \vee \sim B) \supset D]$ ✓
3. $\sim F \vee (B \cdot D)$
4. $\sim G \equiv \sim D$ $/ \therefore \sim (G \vee B)$
    $\sim \sim (G \vee B)$ ✓
    $(G \vee B)$
    $\sim G \vee \sim B$
    $\sim D$

It's not clear which line we should decompose next. Let's do the fourth line, since its decomposition is the most complicated, and since one of the branches will close right away:

1. $(D \supset G) \supset F$
2. $\sim [(\sim G \vee \sim B) \supset D]$ ✓
3. $\sim F \vee (B \cdot D)$
4. $\sim G \equiv \sim D$ ✓
    $\sim \sim (G \vee B)$
    $G \vee B$
    $\sim G \vee \sim B$
    $\sim D$

```
              ╱        ╲
          ~ G          ~ ~ G
          ~ D          ~ ~ D
                         ✕
```

Likewise, the decompositions for the third line, and for $G \vee B$, will produce branches that immediately close:

1. $(D \supset G) \supset F$
2. $\sim [(\sim G \vee \sim B) \supset D]$ ✓
3. $\sim F \vee (B \cdot D)$ ✓
4. $\sim G \equiv \sim D$ ✓
    $\sim \sim (G \vee B)$ ✓
    $G \vee B$ ✓
    $\sim G \vee \sim B$
    $\sim D$

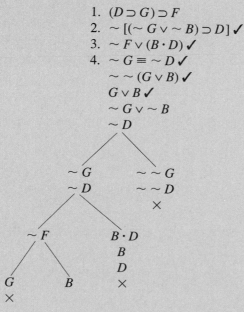

This leaves us with $\sim G \vee \sim B$ and the first premise as the only lines yet to be decomposed. The first premise will have to be decomposed twice:

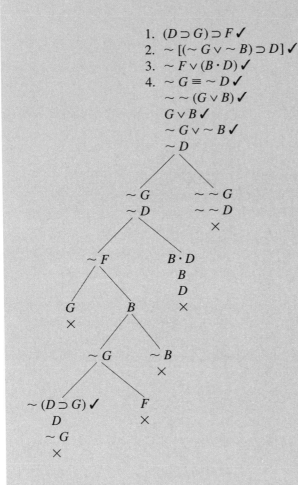

1. $(D \supset G) \supset F$ ✓
2. $\sim [(\sim G \vee \sim B) \supset D]$ ✓
3. $\sim F \vee (B \cdot D)$ ✓
4. $\sim G \equiv \sim D$ ✓
   $\sim \sim (G \vee B)$ ✓
   $G \vee B$ ✓
   $\sim G \vee \sim B$ ✓
   $\sim D$

All branches close, so our argument is valid.

Examples

Here are three more examples of sentential logic tree method proofs:

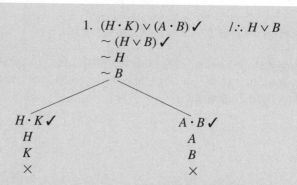

The argument is valid since all of the branches close. The left-hand branch is closed by the *H*, even though there is another sentence, *K*, below it:

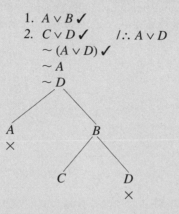

One branch remains open; therefore, the argument is invalid.

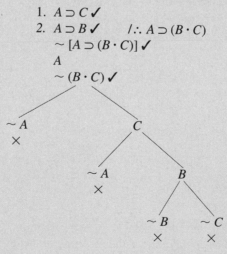

Valid. All branches close.

4   *Rationale Behind the Tree Method*

It is instructive to compare truth trees with the other methods we have used to show validity and invalidity. Let's look first at the short truth table technique for proving invalidity. Consider the following simple argument:

1. $A \supset B$
2. $\sim (B \vee D)$
3. $D \supset C$ $/\therefore \sim C$

With the short truth table method we begin by making each premise true and the conclusion false. With trees we add the negation of the conclusion to the premises:

<table>
<tr><td>

1. $A \supset B$
     T
2. $\sim (B \vee D)$
     T
3. $D \supset C$ $/\therefore \sim C$
     T   **F**

</td><td>

1. $A \supset B$
2. $\sim (B \vee D)$
3. $D \supset C$ $/\therefore \sim C$
     $\sim \sim C$

</td></tr>
</table>

Next for the short tabular method is to begin assigning truth-values where there is no choice. In this case we must make *C* true in order to make the conclusion false, and we must make both *B* and *D* false in order to make the second premise true. Likewise we begin our tree with decompositions that do not branch. Not coincidentally, we end up decomposing the same two lines—the conclusion and the second premise:

<table>
<tr><td>

1. $A \supset B$
     T F
2. $\sim (B \vee D)$
     T FFF
3. $D \supset C$ $/\therefore \sim C$
     F T T   **F T**

</td><td>

1. $A \supset B$
2. $\sim (B \vee D)$ ✓
3. $D \supset C$
     $\sim \sim C$ ✓
     C
     $\sim B$
     $\sim D$

</td></tr>
</table>

At this point we see that we must make *A* in the first premise false. Likewise if we decompose the first premise, only one of the resulting branches remains open—the one that contains $\sim A$. We complete our tree by decomposing the third premise:

1. $A \supset B$
    F T F
2. $\sim (B \lor D)$
    T FFF
3. $D \supset C$ $/\therefore \sim C$
    F T T   **F T**

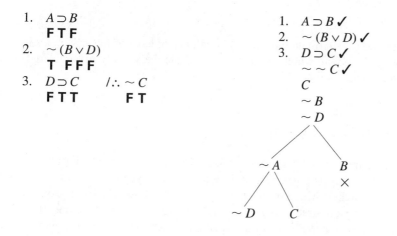

1. $A \supset B$ ✓
2. $\sim (B \lor D)$ ✓
3. $D \supset C$ ✓
    $\sim \sim C$ ✓
    C
    $\sim B$
    $\sim D$

The open branches on our completed tree show precisely what our short tabular method shows, and that is that this argument is invalid because it would have true premises and a false conclusion if A, B, and D were false and C were true.

Now let's compare trees to natural deduction. In particular, trees have some interesting affinities with the rule **IP.**

1. $\sim A \lor B$
2. $\sim B$ $/\therefore \sim A$
3. $\sim \sim A$ **AP**
4. B **1,3 DS**
5. $B \cdot \sim B$ **2,4 Conj**
6. A **3–5 IP**

1. $\sim A \lor B$ ✓
2. $\sim B$ $/\therefore \sim A$
    $\sim \sim A$
    $\sim A$ B
    ✗   ✗

Both begin by adding the negation of the conclusion to the argument's premises. And both conclude by showing that doing so leads to contradiction. The difference is that with **IP** we *infer* one particular contradiction, whereas with the tree we mechanically demonstrate that every attempt to make the premises true will result in contradiction. One last comparison is that the way we often go about completing proofs using **IP** is to break complex formulas down using rules like **DeM,** which, of course, is very similar to what we do in completing a tree.

Exercise 12-1

Use the truth tree method to determine the validity/invalidity of each of the arguments in Exercise 3-5.

LC Exercise 12-2

Use the truth tree method to determine the validity/invalidity of each of the arguments in Exercise 4-12. Note the ease with which you can demonstrate the validity of these arguments compared to completing a proof.

5   *Putting Truth Trees to Work*

So far we have used truth trees only for determining whether arguments are valid. But obviously we can use trees for other purposes as well. Indeed, anything you can do with a truth table you can do (much quicker) with a truth tree. Of course, to show whether a group of sentences is consistent simply construct a tree. The sentences are consistent if and only if the tree has an open branch. Less obviously, you can use a tree to determine whether sentences are tautologies, contradictions, or contingent. If a tree for a single sentence has no open branches, the sentence is a contradiction. A sentence is a tautology if and only if a tree of *the negation* of that sentence has no open branches. And to show that a sentence is contingent, you must construct *two* trees—one for the sentence and one for the negation of the sentence. If and only if both of these trees have open branches, the sentence is contingent. (To see why two trees are required, note that a tree for a tautology will have open branches.)

It is easy to fall into a mistake here and think that since contradictions have no open branches, tautologies are sentences that have all open branches, and contingent sentences are those sentences with some open branches and some closed. But, if you think about it, obviously there are many contingent sentences that have no closed branches. Consider, for example, atomic sentences, or basic compound sentences like $A \vee B$. Likewise, many tautologies will produce trees that have some closed branches, as the following tree illustrates:

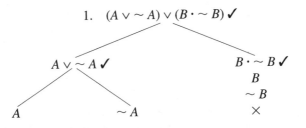

Finally, one can also use trees to determine whether sentences are logically equivalent or whether one sentence logically implies another. As we learned in Chapter 3, a sentence p is logically equivalent to a sentence q if and only if $p \equiv q$ is a tautology, and p logically implies q if and only if $p \supset q$ is a tautology. So p is logically equivalent to q if and only if the tree for $\sim (p \equiv q)$ has no open branches, and p logically implies q if and only if the tree for $\sim (p \supset q)$ has no open branches.

LC Exercise 12-3

Use the truth tree method to complete Exercise 3-3.

Before leaving the topic of the sentential logic truth tree method, it should be remarked that this method is a mechanical method (you just have to follow the rules); indeed, one that can be programmed into a computer quite easily. Further, it is a complete method in that there is no argument that can be formulated into the notation of sentential logic that it cannot deal with correctly. Every such argument that is valid can be proved valid using the sentential logic truth tree method, and every such argument that is invalid can be proved invalid. In these respects, incidentally, the sentential logic truth tree method is just like its cousin, the sentential logic truth table method. Not only are truth trees much quicker to construct than truth tables, we will also routinely be able to use the tree method (but not truth tables) to check predicate logic arguments for validity.

6 *The Predicate Logic Truth Tree Method*

Some of the arguments symbolized in the notation of predicate logic can be dealt with by means of the rules and procedures already introduced. An example is the argument

$$1.\ (x)Fx \lor (x)Gx$$
$$2.\ \sim (x)Fx \qquad /\therefore (x)Gx$$

This argument can be proved valid by the following truth tree:

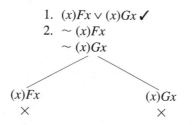

Since both paths are closed, the argument is valid.

But to deal with other sorts of cases, we need to introduce additional rules. We need a rule for breaking down sentences governed by each kind of quantifier, and we need a rule for decomposing negated quantified sentences of each type. Fortunately we can use some of the same rules we used in our system of predicate logic natural deduction. We will use **UI, EI,** and two of the four **QN** rules.*

---

*These rules were explained in Chapter 8.

Consider the following argument:

       1. $(x)(Fx \lor Gx)$
       2. $\sim Fa$ /∴ Ga

First, we add the negation of the conclusion to the premises, and then, in this case, use **UI** on the first premise:

       1. $(x)(Fx \lor Gx)$
       2. $\sim Fa$
       3. $\sim Ga$
       4. $Fa \lor Ga$ 1 **UI**

(Note that to make it easier to keep track of things, we have started to number lines in tree proofs that make use of predicate logic rules, such as **UI**, and to cite those rules in the proper place.)

Now, we check the disjunction, $Fa \lor Ga$, and decompose it as in the sentential logic procedure, closing all paths that contain a contradiction:

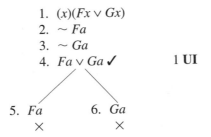

Since both paths are closed, the argument is valid.

Notice, however, that we didn't check the first line when we applied **UI** to it. The reason is that this use of **UI** extracts only part of the content of line 1. It ignores, for instance, the information $Fb \lor Gb$, $Fc \lor Gc$, and so on. In this case, we don't need any of this additional information, but in some other cases we do. Here is an example:

       1. $(x)(Fx \lor Gx)$
       2. $\sim Fa$
       3. $\sim Fb$ /∴ Gb

Its tree continues:

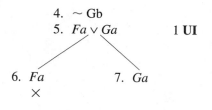

4. ~ Gb
5. *Fa* ∨ *Ga*   1 UI

6. *Fa*   7. *Ga*
  ✕

Suppose that after applying **UI** to line 1 we had checked off that line, making it unavailable for further use in the proof. Then we wouldn't have been able to close the right path of the tree and determine, correctly, that the argument in question is valid. Instead, we would have had to conclude, erroneously, that the argument is invalid. By not checking line 1 after applying **UI** to it, we leave open the possibility of applying **UI** to it again, and again, as often as we need to. In this case, we need to apply it once more, because another individual constant, *b*, appears in the proof in addition to *a*. So the next step in constructing a truth tree for this argument is to apply **UI** again to line 1, this time getting:

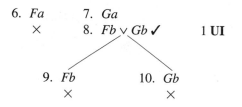

6. *Fa*   7. *Ga*
  ✕   8. *Fb* ∨ *Gb* ✓   1 UI

9. *Fb*   10. *Gb*
  ✕   ✕

All paths on this tree are closed, and so the argument is valid. (Notice we don't have to bother adding *Fb* ∨ *Gb* to the left path of the tree, since that path already was closed.)

Here is the truth tree for another argument, listing justifications to the right of each line:

1. (∃x)(y)*Fxy* ✓   /∴ (y)(∃x)*Fxy*
2. ~ (y)(∃x)*Fxy*
3. (∃y)(x) ~ *Fxy* ✓   2 QN (twice)
4. (y)*Fxy*   1 EI
5. (x) ~ *Fxy*   3 EI
6. *Fxy*   4 UI
7. ~ *Fxy*   5 UI
  ✕

Because the only path in this very sparse tree is closed, the argument is valid. (Notice that this nonbranching tree exactly parallels an ordinary indirect proof.)

Examples

(1)

1. $(x)(Fx \supset Gxx)$
2. $\sim (x)Gxx$ ✓   /∴ $\sim (x)Fx$
3. $(x)Fx$
4. $(\exists x) \sim Gxx$ ✓   2 **QN**
5. $\sim Gxx$ 4 **EI**
6. Fx 3 **UI**
7. $Fx \supset Gxx$ ✓   1 **UI**

8. $\sim Fx$ 9. Gxx
   ✕   ✕

Because both paths are closed, the argument is valid.

(2)

1. $(x)(Fx \supset Gxx)$
2. $\sim (x)Gxx$ /∴ $(\exists x)Fx$
3. $\sim (\exists x)Fx$
4. $(x) \sim Fx$ 3 **QN**
5. $(\exists x) \sim Gxx$ ✓   2 **QN**
6. $\sim Gxx$ 5 **EI**
7. $\sim Fx$ 4 **UI**
8. $Fx \supset Gxx$ ✓   1 **UI**

9. $\sim Fx$ 10. Gxx
                      ✕

Because one path is open, the argument is invalid.

(3)

1. $(x)[(\exists y)Lxy \supset (y)Lyx]$
2. Laa /∴ Lba
3. $\sim Lba$
4. $(\exists y)Lay \supset (y)Lya$ 1 **UI**

5. $\sim (\exists y)Lay$ 5 **QN**   6. $(y)Lya$
7. $(y) \sim Lay$ 7 **UI**   9. Lba 6 **UI**
8. $\sim Laa$ ✕
   ✕

Both paths are closed, and so the argument is valid.

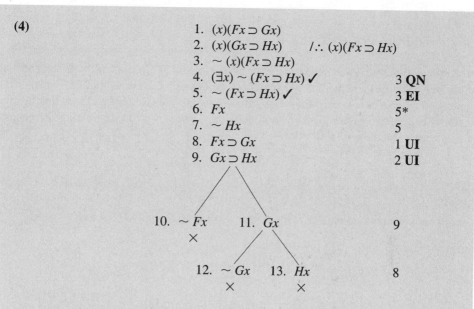

(4)

1. $(x)(Fx \supset Gx)$
2. $(x)(Gx \supset Hx)$ $/ \therefore (x)(Fx \supset Hx)$
3. $\sim (x)(Fx \supset Hx)$
4. $(\exists x) \sim (Fx \supset Hx)$ ✓   3 QN
5. $\sim (Fx \supset Hx)$ ✓   3 EI
6. Fx 5*
7. $\sim Hx$ 5
8. $Fx \supset Gx$ 1 UI
9. $Gx \supset Hx$ 2 UI

10. $\sim Fx$ 11. Gx 9
   ×

12. $\sim Gx$ 13. Hx 8
   ×   ×

All paths are closed, and so the argument is valid. (Note how much simpler an ordinary proof would be.)

(5)

1. $(x) \sim Fxx$
2. $\sim (x)Gx \supset (\exists y)Fyy$ ✓ $/ \therefore (\exists z)(Gz \cdot \sim Fzz)$
3. $\sim (\exists z)(Gz \cdot \sim Fzz)$ ✓
4. $(z) \sim (Gz \cdot \sim Fzz)$ 3 QN
5. $\sim (Gz \cdot \sim Fzz)$ ✓   4 UI

6. $\sim Gz$ 5   7. $\sim \sim Fzz$ 5
                          14. $\sim Fzz$ 1 UI
                                   ×

8. $\sim \sim (x)Gx$ ✓   2   9. $(\exists y)Fyy$ ✓   2
10. $(x)Gx$ 8   12. Fyy 9 EI
11. Gz 9 UI   13. $\sim Fyy$ 1 UI
   ×   ×

All paths are closed. So the argument is valid.

---

*Up to now we haven't been keeping track of the lines obtained by the sentential logic truth tree rules for decomposing sentences. But now it will be useful to cite sometimes the line from which the decomposed material has been obtained.

7   *Infinite Trees*

Unfortunately, some truth trees can never be completed. This possibility arises once we introduce relational predicate logic sentences. Suppose we want to find out whether the sentence $(x)(\exists y)Fxy$ is consistent or inconsistent. If its tree contains all closed paths, it is inconsistent, and if its tree contains an open path, it is consistent. Following the general procedure, we start the tree as follows:

1. $(x)(\exists y)Fxy$
2. $(\exists y)Fxy$ 1 **UI**
3. Fxz 2 **EI**

Since z now occurs free on line 3, it seems that we need to apply **UI** to line 1 again:

4. $(\exists y)Fzy$ 1 **UI**

And then apply **EI** again:

5. Fzw 4 **EI**

But doing so just introduces a new letter free into the proof; so we again have to apply **UI** and then **EI:**

6. $(\exists y)Fwy$ 1 **UI**
7. Fwv 6 **EI**

And so on, indefinitely.

A branch like the one just considered, supposing that in fact it never does close, is called a *nonterminating branch*. Unfortunately, there is no effective way to determine in every case whether a branch is nonterminating or will close at some later point. So the predicate logic truth tree method will not get us an answer in every case. (This point will be enlarged on later.) It so happens, however, that many trees containing an apparently nonterminating branch when constructed one way don't contain such a branch when constructed another way. The trick in these cases is to not spin our wheels concentrating on lines derived from one sentence, but to move back and forth from that sentence to others, as in this example:

1. $(x)(\exists y)Fxy \ /\therefore \ (\exists x)Fax$
2. $\sim (\exists x)Fax$

If we concentrate on line 1 and lines derived from line 1, we get an apparently never-ending tree, like this:

3. $(\exists y)Fay$ 1 **UI**
4. Faz 3 **EI**
5. $(\exists y)Fzy$ 1 **UI**
6. Fzw 5 **EI**
7. $(\exists y)Fwy$ 1 **UI**
8. Fwv 7 **EI**

And so on, indefinitely. But if we mix in lines following from line 2, we get a quickly closing tree:

3. $(\exists y)Fay$ 1 UI
4. Faz 3 EI
5. $(x) \sim Fax$ 2 QN
6. $\sim Faz$ 5 UI
        $\times$

LG Exercise 12-4

Use the truth tree method to determine which of the following arguments are valid and which invalid (noting the one argument whose tree is inconclusive):

(1)   1. $(x)(Fx \supset Gx)$
      2. $(\exists x) \sim Gx /\therefore (\exists x) \sim Fx$
(2)   1. $(x)[Fx \supset (y)Gy]$
      2. $Fa /\therefore (x)Gx$
(3)   1. $(x)(Ax \supset Bx)$
      2. $(x)(\sim Ax \supset Cx) /\therefore (x)(\sim Bx \supset \sim Cx)$
(4)   1. $(\exists x)Fx$
      2. $(x)(\sim Gx \supset \sim Fx)$
      3. $(x)Mx /\therefore (\exists x)Gx \cdot (\exists x)Mx$
(5)   1. $(\exists x)[Fx \cdot (y)(Gy \supset Lxy)]$
      2. $(x)[Fx \supset (y)(My \supset \sim Lxy)] /\therefore (x)(Gx \supset \sim Mx)$
(6)   1. $(x)(Ax \supset Fx)$
      2. $(\exists x)Fx \supset \sim (\exists y)Gy /\therefore (x)[(\exists y)Ay \supset \sim Gx]$
(7)   1. $(\exists x)(Ax \cdot \sim Bx)$
      2. $(\exists x)(Ax \cdot \sim Cx)$
      3. $(\exists x)(\sim Bx \cdot Dx) /\therefore (\exists x)[Ax \cdot (\sim Bx \cdot Dx)]$
(8)   1. $(x) \sim Fxx$
      2. $\sim (x)Gx \supset (\exists y)Fya /\therefore (\exists z)(Gz \cdot Fzz)$
(9)   1. $(\exists x)(Ax \vee \sim Bx)$
      2. $(x)[(Ax \cdot \sim Bx) \supset Cx] /\therefore (\exists x)Cx$
(10) 1. $(x)(\exists y)(Fx \cdot Gxy) /\therefore (\exists y)(x)(Fx \cdot Gxy)$

We mentioned above that the sentential logic truth tree method provides us with a mechanical proof procedure that works in every case we can cast into the notation of sentential logic. As we have seen in this section, similarly flattering things cannot quite be said for the predicate logic tree method.

Here are the details. If an argument cast into the notation of predicate logic is valid, then we can prove that it is valid using the machinery of the predicate logic truth tree method. Although most such proofs will be quite short, a few very unusual ones may be very long indeed. However, if an argument is invalid, then in most cases we will be able to prove invalidity, but in a few we will not.

So when applying the rules of the predicate logic tree method in a given case, any one of the following three things may happen:

1. All paths in the tree will close. If they do, then the argument is valid.
2. At least one path will remain open after everything required by the tree method rules has been done. If this happens, then the argument is invalid.
3. The truth tree may continue to grow in a seemingly endless way (recall the example on page 280). In this case, we can't tell whether the argument in question is or is not valid.

Key terms

closed branch: A path, or branch, of a truth tree that contains an explicit contradiction and that we have therefore marked with an ×. (See also *open branch.*)

decomposition: The process of dividing a long formula into short ones placed appropriately onto a truth tree.

long sentence: A sentence, or formula, that contains more elements than a short one. (Examples: $(A \lor B)$, $[(\sim A \supset B) \lor \sim C]$, and so on.) (See also *short sentence.*)

open branch: A branch of a truth tree that does not contain an explicit contradiction. (See also *closed branch.*)

short sentence (or short formula): An expression containing just an atomic sentence or sentence form, or the negation of same. (See also *long sentence.*)

truth tree method: A method for diagramming arguments to determine whether they are valid or invalid (also used to determine the consistency or inconsistency of argument premises).

Part Three

Chapter Thirteen

Other Systems of Logic

Syllogistic Logic

The logic discussed in Parts One and Two was first developed in the late nineteenth and early twentieth centuries. But it did not arise in a vacuum. The discipline of logic has existed for over 2,000 years, since the first system was developed by Aristotle. It has become customary to apply the term "symbolic" to systems like sentential and predicate logic, and the terms **traditional, Aristotelian,** and **syllogistic** to the earlier systems. Predicate logic is much more powerful than syllogistic logic. Every argument provable in syllogistic logic is provable in predicate logic, but not vice versa. Nevertheless, within its limits, syllogistic logic constitutes a useful and (for many) fascinating logical tool.

1 Categorical Propositions

Syllogistic logic is primarily concerned with *categorical propositions*. **Categorical propositions** assert or deny relationships between terms or classes. For instance, the sentence "All humans are mortal" is a categorical proposition and asserts (roughly) that all members of the class of humans are members of the class of mortals.

The term "humans," which designates the class of human beings, is said to be the **subject,** or **subject term,** and the term "mortal," which designates the class of mortals, is said to be the **predicate,** or **predicate term,** of the categorical proposition "All humans are mortal." Similarly, all categorical propositions contain a subject and a predicate, as well as some form of the verb "to be" ("is," "are," and so on) relating the subject and predicate.

There are four kinds of categorical propositions: (1) **universal affirmative,** having the general form "All S are P" (where S denotes some subject class and P some predicate class); (2) **universal negative,** having the general form "No S are P"; (3) **particular affirmative,** having the general form "Some S are P"; and (4) **particular negative,** having the general form "Some S are not P."

It is customary to use the capital letter A in symbolizing universal affirmative propositions. Similarly, it is customary to use E for universal negatives, I for particular affirmatives, and O for particular negatives. It also is customary to refer to universal affirmative propositions as A propositions, universal negative propositions as E propositions, and so on. According to tradition, these letters come from the Latin "Aff**I**rmo" (I affirm) and "n**E**g**O**" (I deny).

Notice that *A, E, I,* and *O* propositions differ with respect to two kinds of properties; namely, quality (being either affirmative or negative) and quantity (being either universal or particular). Thus, all *I* propositions are both *affirmative* (quality) and *particular* (quantity). For example, the *I* proposition "Some humans are mortal" is affirmative (quality), because it affirms that some humans are mortal, and particular (quantity), because it affirms that some (not necessarily all) humans are mortal. On the other hand, all *E* propositions are both *negative* (quality) and *universal* (quantity). For example, the *E* proposition "No humans are mortal" is negative (quality), because it denies that humans are mortal, and universal (quantity), because it denies of all humans that they are mortal.

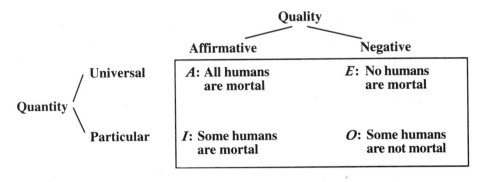

The English language, like all natural languages, permits a great deal of variety in the expression of propositions. Take St. Augustine's interesting thesis that all sin is a kind of lying, which can be put into *A* form as "All sins are lies." We can also express this thesis in English as "Sins are lies," "The one who sins, lies," "Sinning is lying," "To sin is to lie," "Anyone who sins, lies," "Whoever sins, lies," and so on. All of these therefore translate into *A* propositions.

Examples

Here are a few more sentences that translate into *A* propositions.

Men are naturally selfish.	(All men are naturally selfish.)
Anyone who is a woman is maternal.	(All women are maternal.)
Copper conducts electricity.	(All copper things are electrical conductors.)
Sugar tastes sweet.	(All things composed of sugar are sweet tasting.)
Vanity is a universal condition.	(All humans are vain.)
Those who live by the pen are called liars.	(All professional writers are liars.)
Whoever uses crack is foolish.	(All crack users are foolish.)
The gods have mercy.	(All gods are merciful.)

Show me an officer and I'll show you a dandy. | (All officers are dandies.)

And here are a few sentences that translate into *E* propositions.

Men are not selfish by nature.	(No men are naturally selfish.)
There aren't any women who are maternal.	(No women are maternal.)
Copper doesn't conduct electricity.	(No copper things are electrical conductors.)
Sugar doesn't taste sweet.	(No things made from sugar are sweet tasting.)
Vanity is unheard of among humans.	(No humans are vain.)
There has never been a professional writer who lies.	(No professional writers are liars.)
The gods have no mercy.	(No gods are merciful.)
No one who is an officer also is a dandy.	(No officers are dandies.)

Here are some sentences that translate into *I* propositions.

There are honest men.	(Some men are honest.)
A great many women are maternal.	(Some women are maternal.)
There exist some elements that are inert.	(Some elements are inert.)
There are active paraplegics.	(Some paraplegics are active.)
Lots of rivers have wide mouths.	(Some rivers are wide-mouthed.)
Musicians occasionally have tin ears.	(Some musicians are tin-eared.)
Killers frequently are paranoid.	(Some killers are paranoid.)
A few senators are against big business.	(Some senators are against big business.)
An occasional *Playboy* interview is with a presidential candidate.	(Some *Playboy* interviews are interviews with presidential candidates.)
Policemen have been known who will take bribes.	(Some policemen are bribable.)

And here are some sentences that translate into *O* propositions.

There are dishonest men.	(Some men are not honest.)
There are women who aren't maternal.	(Some women are not maternal.)
Most elements are not inert.	(Some elements are not inert.)
There are inactive paraplegics.	(Some paraplegics are not active.)
Many rivers don't have wide mouths.	(Some rivers are not wide-mouthed.)
Most musicians don't have a tin ear.	(Some musicians are not tin-eared.)
A few killers are not paranoid.	(Some killers are not paranoid.)
The majority of senators are not against big business.	(Some senators are not against big business.)
Most *Playboy* interviews are not with presidential candidates.	(Some *Playboy* interviews are not with presidential candidates.)
Policemen have been known who will not take bribes.	(Some policemen are not bribable.)

LC Exercise 13-1

Translate the following sentences into equivalent *A, E, I,* or *O* propositions.

1.   Whoever is rich is a sinner.
2.   The poor are lazy.
3.   Most children aren't naughty.
4.   Porno flicks aren't erotic.
5.   Albino crows are known to exist.
6.   Amateurs aren't professionals.
7.   There are plenty of immodest failures.
8.   Most prescription drugs are harmful.
9.   Human beings are omnivorous.
10. Most movie stars aren't happy.
11. Omnivores occasionally are vegetarians.
12. None who have dry wits drink.
13. Some drinkers have wet whistles.
14. Those who forget the past suffer from amnesia.
15. Omnivores usually are not vegetarians.

2   *Existential Import*

A proposition is said to have **existential import** if its subject and predicate are taken to refer to classes that are not empty. For instance, if we assume existential import for the *A* proposition "All angels are without moral blemish," then we are assuming that there are angels and also that there are things without moral blemish.

Syllogistic logic traditionally rested on the assumption that all the propositions to be dealt with do have existential import. In other words, syllogistic logic traditionally was restricted to categorical propositions whose terms all were taken to refer to nonempty classes.

Such a restriction severely limits the scope of syllogistic logic, since it often is quite important to reason about nonexistent entities—for one thing to make sure that they remain nonexistent. (We want to reason about World War III precisely to prevent such a disaster from occurring.) Yet if we are to retain several of its interesting and important features (and have them be valid), we must restrict the use of traditional logic to propositions that have existential import.

So let's assume for the moment that all of the categorical propositions to be dealt with do have existential import.

3   *The Square of Opposition*

The **square of opposition** illustrates some of the more interesting features of traditional logic:

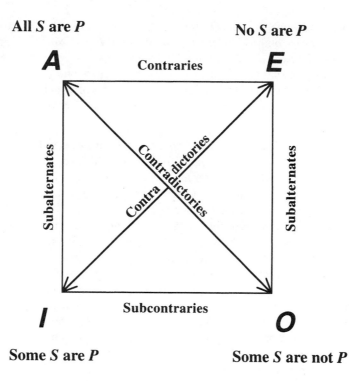

All *S* are *P*　　　　　　　　**No *S* are *P***

A　　　Contraries　　　*E*

Subalternates　　Contradictories　Contradictories　　Subalternates

I　　Subcontraries　　*O*

Some *S* are *P*　　　　　　**Some *S* are not *P***

1. *Corresponding A and O propositions are contradictories.* Two propositions are **contradictory propositions** *if both cannot be true and both cannot be false.* (So one must be true, the other false.) For instance, the *A* proposition "All humans are mortal" is true, whereas its contradictory "Some humans are not mortal," an *O* proposition, is false.

2. *Corresponding E and I propositions also are contradictories.* Hence, both cannot be true and both cannot be false. For example, the *I* proposition "Some humans are mortal" is true, and its contradictory, "No humans are mortal," an *E* proposition, is false.

3. *Corresponding A and E propositions are contraries.* Two propositions are **contrary propositions** *if both cannot be true but both may be false.* For instance, the *A* proposition, "All scientists are philosophers," is false, and its contrary, "No scientists are philosophers," an *E* proposition, also is false (since some scientists are philosophers and some aren't). This is an example of contraries both of which are false. And the *A* proposition, "All humans are mortal," is true, whereas its contrary, "No humans are mortal," an *E* proposition, is false. This is an example of contraries one of which is true, one false. (But we cannot give an example of contrary propositions both of which are true, because this case cannot occur.)

4. *Corresponding I and O propositions are subcontraries.* Two propositions are **subcontrary propositions** *if both cannot be false but both may be true.* For instance, the *I* proposition, "Some scientists are philosophers," is true, and its subcontrary, "Some

scientists are not philosophers," an *O* proposition, also is true. This proposition is an example of subcontraries both of which are true. And the *I* proposition, "Some humans are mortal," is true, whereas its subcontrary, "Some humans are not mortal," an *O* proposition, is false. This proposition is an example of subcontraries one of which is true, one false. (But we cannot give an example of subcontraries both of which are false, because this case cannot occur.)

5.   *Corresponding A and I propositions are subalternates.* **Subalternate propositions** are such that *if the universal member of the pair* (for instance, an *A* proposition) *is true, then so is the particular member of the pair* (for instance, the corresponding *I* proposition). The propositions, "All humans are mortal," a true *A* proposition, and "Some humans are mortal," a true *I* proposition, are subalternates.

Notice that if a particular *A* proposition is *false,* nothing can be inferred as to the truth-value of its subalternate; it may be true or it may be false. For instance, the false *A* proposition, "All scientists are philosophers," has as its subalternate the *true I* proposition, "Some scientists are philosophers," whereas the false *A* proposition, "All humans are immortal," has as its subalternate the *false I* proposition, "Some humans are immortal." Thus subalternation, conceived as a rule of inference, is *one-directional;* we can infer from the truth of an *A* proposition to the truth of its corresponding *I* proposition, but we cannot infer from the truth of an *I* proposition to the truth of its corresponding *A* proposition.

However, we can infer from the *falsity* of an *I* proposition to the *falsity* of the corresponding *A* proposition. For instance, if it is false that even *some* men are immortal, then it must be false that all men are immortal.

6.   Finally, *corresponding E and O propositions also are subalternates.* Hence, we can infer from the truth of an *E* proposition to the truth of its subalternate, the corresponding *O* proposition. For example, we can infer from the truth of the *E* proposition, "No humans are immortal," to the truth of its subalternate, "Some humans are not immortal." But again, we cannot infer from the falsehood of an *E* proposition to the falsehood of its corresponding *O* proposition, although we can infer from the falsity of an *O* proposition to the falsity of the corresponding *E* proposition. For instance, if it is false that even some men are not mortal, then it must be false that no men are mortal.

The information about inferences provided by the square of opposition can also be put in tabular form, as follows (blanks indicate no valid inference possible).

A true:	*E* false	*I* true	*O* false
A false:	*E* _____	*I* _____	*O* true
E true:	*A* false	*I* false	*O* true
E false:	*A* _____	*I* true	*O* _____
I true:	*A* _____	*E* false	*O* _____
I false:	*A* false	*E* true	*O* true
O true:	*A* false	*E* _____	*I* _____
O false:	*A* true	*E* false	*I* true

Examples

(1) On the assumption that the *A* proposition "All college students are intelligent" is true (whether in fact it is or not), we can infer that
1. "Some college students are intelligent" is true (by subalternation).
2. "Some college students are not intelligent" is false (because "All college students are intelligent" and "No college students are intelligent" are contradictories).
3. "No college students are intelligent" is false (because "All college students are intelligent" and "No college students are intelligent" are contraries).

(2) On the assumption that the *I* proposition "Some college students cheat on exams" is false, we can infer that
1. "No college students cheat on exams" is true (because "Some college students cheat on exams" and "No college students cheat on exams" are contradictories).
2. "Some college students do not cheat on exams" is true (because "Some college students cheat on exams" and "Some college students do not cheat on exams" are subcontraries).
3. "All college students cheat on exams" is false (because "No college students cheat on exams" and "All college students cheat on exams" are contraries).

(3) On the assumption that the *E* proposition "No college students cheat on exams" is true, we can infer that
1. "Some college students cheat on exams" is false (because "No college students cheat on exams" and "Some college students cheat on exams" are contradictories).
2. "All college students cheat on exams" is false (because "No college students cheat on exams" and "All college students cheat on exams" are contraries).
3. "Some college students do not cheat on exams" is true (by subalternation).

(4) On the assumption that the *O* proposition "Some college students do not cheat on exams" is true, we can infer only that "All college students cheat on exams" is false.

LC Exercise 13-2

(1) Suppose the categorical proposition "All wars are hellish" is true. Using the machinery provided by the square of opposition, what can be inferred about the truth-values of the following?
1. Some wars are hellish.
2. No wars are hellish.
3. Some wars are not hellish.

(2) Suppose "All wars are hellish" is false. Then what can be inferred about the truth-values of the above three propositions?

(3) Suppose "Some congressmen are sexual gluttons" is true. Then what can be inferred
about the truth-values of the following?
1. No congressmen are sexual gluttons.
2. Some congressmen are not sexual gluttons.
3. All congressmen are sexual gluttons.
(4) Suppose "Some congressmen are sexual gluttons" is false. Then what can be inferred
about the truth-values of the following?
1. No congressmen are sexual gluttons.
2. Some congressmen are not sexual gluttons.
3. All congressmen are sexual gluttons.

4   *Conversion, Obversion, Contraposition*

Conversion

In the process of **conversion,** we replace the subject of a proposition with its predicate and
its predicate with its subject. For instance, "All humans are mortals" converts to "All
mortals are humans," "No humans are mortals" converts to "No mortals are humans,"
"Some humans are not mortals" to "Some mortals are not humans," and so on.

But conversion is a valid process only if used on *E* or *I* propositions. We can validly
infer from "No humans are mortals" to "No mortals are humans," and from "Some
humans are mortals" to "Some mortals are humans," but not from "All humans are
mortals" to "All mortals are humans," and not from "Some humans are not mortals" to
"Some mortals are not humans."

Conversion by limitation

In the process of **conversion by limitation** we replace the subject term of an *A* proposition
with its predicate term and its predicate term with its subject term, and then change the
quantity of the proposition from *A* to *I*. For instance, we can infer by conversion by
limitation from the *A* proposition "All hogs are mammals" to the *I* proposition "Some
mammals are hogs." Conversion by limitation is always a valid process.

Obversion

In the process of **obversion,** we change the quality of a proposition (from affirmative to
negative or from negative to affirmative), and then replace its predicate with the negation
or **complement** of the predicate. We can obvert, say, the *E* proposition "No shadows are
entities" by first changing the quality of that proposition from negative to affirmative,

obtaining the proposition "All shadows are entities," and then replacing the predicate with its complement, obtaining the proposition "All shadows are nonentities." Thus, "No shadows are entities" obverts to "All shadows are nonentities." Similarly, "All shadows are entities" obverts to "No shadows are nonentities." The *I* proposition "Some shadows are entities" obverts to the *O* proposition, "Some shadows are not nonentities," and, likewise, "Some shadows are not entities" obverts to "Some shadows are nonentities." Obversion is *always* valid.

Contraposition

In the process of **contraposition,** we replace the subject of a proposition with the complement of its predicate and replace its predicate with the complement of its subject. Thus, the contrapositive of "All humans are mortals" is "All nonmortals are nonhumans," and the contrapositive of "Some humans are not mortals" is "Some nonmortals are humans." Contraposition is valid for *A* and *O* propositions, but not for *E* and *I* propositions. Hence, we can validly infer from, say, "All humans are mortals" to "All nonmortals are nonhumans" and from "Some humans are not mortals" to "Some nonmortals are humans," but not from "No humans are mortals" to "No nonmortals are nonhumans," and not from "Some humans are mortals" to "Some nonmortals are nonhumans."*

Contraposition by limitation

Finally, we can validly infer from a given *E* proposition to a particular related *O* proposition by the process called **contraposition by limitation.** For instance, we can validly infer from the *E* proposition "No hems are mended" to the *O* proposition "Some mended things are not hems" by contraposition by limitation.

Contraposition by limitation obviously is valid, since it is simply the combination of subalternation (of an *E* proposition) and contraposition (of the resulting *O* proposition).

Notice that conversion, obversion, and contraposition are, in effect, *equivalent inference rules;* that is, they work in both directions. For instance, we can infer from "All humans are mortals" to "All nonmortals are nonhumans" by contraposition and also from "All nonmortals are nonhumans" to "All humans are mortals." But conversion by limitation and contraposition by limitation are just *implicational inference rules;* that is, they work in only one direction. For instance, we can infer from "All humans are mortals" to "Some mortals are humans" by conversion by limitation, but *not* from "Some mortals are humans" to "All humans are mortals."

---

*Note the comparison between contraposition in syllogistic logic and what we called contraposition in our exposition of symbolic logic. The former has the structure $(x)(Fx \supset Gx) :: (x)(\sim Gx \supset \sim Fx)$, whereas the structure of the latter is $(p \supset q) :: (\sim q \supset \sim p)$. Contraposition in syllogistic logic is thus like a quantified version of the contraposition introduced into symbolic (sentential) logic.

Examples

On the assumption that the *A* proposition "All college students are intelligent" is true, we can infer that

1. "No college students are nonintelligent" is true (by obversion).
2. "All who are not intelligent are not college students" is true (by contraposition).
3. "None who are not intelligent are college students" is true (by obversion of "All who are not intelligent are not college students").
4. "Some who are intelligent are college students" is true (by conversion by limitation).
5. "Some college students are intelligent" is true (by conversion of "Some who are intelligent are college students").
6. "Some who are intelligent are college students" is true (by obversion of "Some who are intelligent are college students").
7. "Some college students are not nonintelligent" is true (by contraposition of "Some who are intelligent are not noncollege students").

Making use of the processes illustrated by the square of opposition, we also can infer from the truth of "All college students are intelligent" that

8. "Some college students are not intelligent" is false (because "All college students are intelligent" and "Some college students are not intelligent" are contradictories).
9. "Some who are not intelligent are not noncollege students" is false (by contraposition of "Some college students are unintelligent").
10. "Some college students are unintelligent" is false (by obversion of "Some college students are not intelligent").
11. "Some who are not intelligent are college students" is false (by obversion of "Some who are not intelligent are not noncollege students").
12. "None who are intelligent are college students" is false (because "Some who are intelligent are college students" and "None who are intelligent are college students" are contradictories).
13. "No college students are intelligent" is false (by conversion of "None who are intelligent are college students").
14. "All college students are unintelligent" is false (by obversion of "No college students are intelligent").
15. "All who are intelligent are not college students" is false (by contraposition of "All college students are unintelligent").

LC Exercise 13-3

What can be said about the truth-values of the sentences in the following sets, assuming that the first sentence in each set is true?

(1) 1. No quitters are winners.
     2. All winners are nonquitters.

   3. Some quitters are not winners.
   4. Some winners are quitters.
   5. Some winners are nonquitters.
(2) 1. All great lovers are highly sexed.
   2. Some great lovers are highly sexed.
   3. No great lovers are highly sexed.
   4. Some highly sexed people are great lovers.
   5. No highly sexed people are great lovers.
(3) 1. No monkey wrenches are left-handed.
   2. Some left-handed things are not monkey wrenches.
   3. No left-handed things are monkey wrenches.
   4. All money wrenches are left-handed.
   5. Some monkey wrenches are left-handed.
(4) 1. Some SS men were not involved in atrocities.
   2. Some who were involved in atrocities were SS men.
   3. No SS men were involved in atrocities.
   4. All SS men were involved in atrocities.
   5. Some who were not involved in atrocities were SS men.

5 Syllogistic Logic—Not Assuming Existential Import

The logic developed so far rests on a blanket assumption of existential import. But no such assumption is made in everyday life. For instance, someone uttering the proposition "Let him who is without sin cast the first stone" does not necessarily assume that there are any human beings free from sin. Similarly, a scientist who says "All objects cooled down to absolute zero will conduct electricity" does not intend to imply that anything ever will be cooled down to absolute zero.

   How much of the traditional logic just described is invalid if we do not make a blanket assumption of existential import? First of all, some of the inferences represented on the traditional square of opposition are no longer valid.

A and E propositions are not contraries

We said before that two propositions are contraries if both cannot be true, but both can be false, and that *A* and *E* propositions are contraries. However, if we allow the use of empty classes, then corresponding *A* and *E* propositions both can be true, and *A* and *E* propositions will not be contraries. For instance, if there are no Martians, then the *A* proposition "All Martians are immortal" and the *E* proposition "No Martians are immortal" both are true (vacuously). Hence, they are not contraries in the traditional sense.*

---

*However, some texts define contraries as pairs of universal propositions that differ only in quality. According to this definition, corresponding *A* and *E* propositions automatically become contraries.

I and O propositions are not subcontraries

We said before that two propositions are subcontraries if both cannot be false, but both can be true, and that *I* and *O* propositions are subcontraries. However, if we allow the use of empty classes, then both of two corresponding *I* and *O* propositions can be false, and so some *I* and *O* propositions will not be subcontraries. For example, if there are no Martians, then the *I* proposition "Some Martians are immortal" and the *O* proposition "Some Martians are not immortal" both are false. Hence, they are not subcontraries in the traditional sense.*

But corresponding *A* and *O* propositions remain contradictories, as do corresponding *E* and *I* propositions.

Here are some more consequences of dropping the assumption of existential import.

Subalternation is invalid

For instance, if there are no Martians, then the *A* proposition "All Martians are immortal" is true (vacuously, because all of the zero number of Martians are immortal), whereas its subalternate "Some Martians are immortal," is false because nothing is both a Martian and immortal. So we cannot allow subalternation from an *A* to an *I* proposition. The same is true of subalternation from an *E* to an *O* proposition.

Conversion by limitation and contraposition by limitation both are invalid

For instance, if there are no Martians, then the *A* proposition "All Martians are immortal" is true, whereas the *I* proposition obtained from it by conversion by limitation, namely the proposition "Some immortals are Martians," is false.

To sum up, if we allow the subject or predicate terms of propositions to refer to empty classes, then subalternation, conversion by limitation, and contraposition by limitation are all invalid, some corresponding *A* and *E* propositions are not contraries, and some corresponding *I* and *O* propositions are not subcontraries.

And conversion of *E* and *I* propositions, obversion, and contraposition of *A* and *O* propositions all remain valid.

In the sections that follow we will no longer assume existential import.

LC Exercise 13-4

In this exercise, do *not* assume existential import.

(1) If it is false that all existentialists are theists then what can be said about the truth-values of the following?

---

*However, some texts define subcontraries as pairs of particular propositions that differ only in quality. According to this definition, corresponding *I* and *O* propositions automatically become subcontraries.

   1. No existentialists are theists.
   2. No theists are existentialists.
   3. Some nontheists are existentialists.
   4. All nonexistentialists are nontheists.
   5. Some existentialists are nontheists.
   6. Some theists are existentialists.
(2) If it is true that no existentialists are theists, then what can be said about the truth-values of the above six propositions?
(3) If the proposition "All senators are promiscuous" is true, what can be inferred about the truth-values of the following?
   1. Some who are not promiscuous are senators.
   2. No senators are not promiscuous.
   3. Some senators are promiscuous.
   4. No nonpromiscuous people are senators.
   5. Some promiscuous people are senators.
   6. Some who are not promiscuous are not senators.
(4) If "No nonsenators are not promiscuous" is false, what can be inferred about the truth-values of the above six propositions?
(5) Suppose you know that the classes senators, promiscuous people, nonsenators, and nonpromiscuous people all are nonempty. And suppose you know that "No nonsenators are promiscuous." What else can you infer? (Justify your answer.)

6 *Venn Diagrams*

It is both useful and informative to use **Venn diagrams** to picture categorical propositions. First, let's represent the classes denoted by the subject and predicate terms by overlapping circles, as follows:

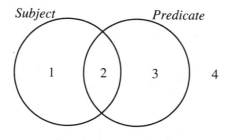

In this diagram, area 1 represents the class of things that are in the subject class but not the predicate, area 2 the class of things that are in both subject and predicate classes, area 3 the class of things that are in the predicate class but not subject, and area 4 the class of things that are in neither subject nor predicate classes.

Now consider the *A* proposition "All humans are mortals." This proposition asserts that the first class (things that are humans but not mortals) is empty. We can illustrate this using a Venn diagram *by shading out area 1* (shading an area indicates that the class represented by that area is empty), as follows:

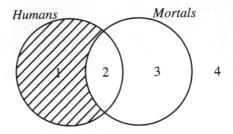

Next, consider the **E** proposition "No humans are mortal," which asserts that the class consisting of things that are both human and mortal is empty. We can diagram this proposition *by shading out area* 2 (to indicate that the class represented by this area is empty), as follows:

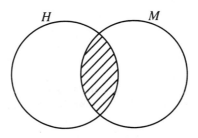

Now, consider the **I** proposition "Some humans are mortal," which asserts that the class consisting of things that are both human and mortal is *not* empty but has at least one member. We can diagram this proposition by *placing a mark (say the letter X) in area 2* (to indicate that the class represented by this area *is not* empty), as follows:

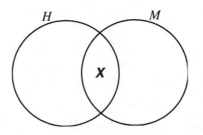

Finally, consider the **O** proposition "Some humans are not mortal," which asserts that the class consisting of things that are both human and not mortal is not empty, but has at least one member. We can diagram this proposition *by placing an X in area 1* (to indicate that the class represented by this area is not empty), as follows:

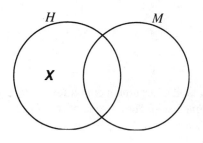

LC Exercise 13-5

Draw a Venn diagram for each proposition.

Example: All millionaires are crooks.

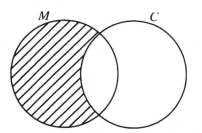

1. Most millionaires are crooks.
2. No crooks are paupers.
3. Some crooks are not millionaires.
4. No millionaires aren't crooks.
5. All environmentalists are a bit overzealous.
6. No environmentalists who tell the truth are taken seriously.
7. Some overzealous environmentalists are pretty unpopular.
8. Some mathematicians are not able to multiply.
9. No nonscientists are able to repair flush toilets.
10. Some questions are not answerable.
11. Non-football fans get pretty lonely in the fall.
12. Some who broadcast the news on TV are non-high school graduates.
13. Some Unitarians are believers in a deity.

14. And no agnostics are.
15. Yet there are plenty of Unitarians who are agnostics.
16. All Chicagoans are unafraid of frigid weather.
17. No comets are devoid of ice.
18. Some who believe in God are existentialists.

7 *Syllogisms*

A **syllogism** is a particular kind of argument containing three categorical propositions, two of them premises, one a conclusion. Here is one of the original examples (translated from the Greek and dechauvinized):

All humans are mortal.
All Greeks are humans.
∴ All Greeks are mortal.

The predicate of the conclusion, is said to be the **major term** of the syllogism; the subject of the conclusion, is said to be the **minor term;** and, finally, the **middle term** occurs once in each premise but not in the conclusion. In the argument just given, "mortal" is the major term, "Greeks" is the minor term, and "humans" is the middle term. Every syllogism has exactly three terms, each one repeated twice (but none repeated twice in the same proposition).

The **mood** of a syllogism is determined by the kind of propositions it contains. For instance, the above syllogism contains three *A* propositions, and so its mood is *AAA*. Similarly, the mood for the syllogism

All morticians are philosophical.
Some sadists are morticians.
∴ Some sadists are philosophical.

is *AII.*

The **figure** of a syllogism is determined by the position of the middle terms in its premises. There are four figures. These are easily remembered by noting the symmetrical arrangement of the middle terms. If we let *S* designate the subject of the conclusion (major term), *P* designate the predicate of the conclusion (minor term), and *M* designate the middle term, the four figures can be represented as follows:

I.		II.		III.		IV.	
M__P		*P__M*		*M__P*		*P__M*	
S__M		*S__M*		*M__S*		*M__S*	
∴ *S__P*		∴ *S__P*		∴ *S__P*		∴ *S__P*	

Notice that the order of premises is important in determining the mood or the figure of a syllogism. The rule is that the predicate of the conclusion, the major term, must occur in the first premise. A syllogism with its premises in the proper order (and, of course, containing only three terms, each one appearing twice) is said to be in **standard form.**

The **form** of a syllogism is simply the combination of mood and figure. For instance, the two syllogisms discussed above have the forms *AAA*-**I** and *AII*-**I,** respectively, and the syllogism

All Greeks are mortals.
No Greeks are humans.
∴ No humans are mortals.

has form *AEE*-**III.** (This syllogism happens to be invalid, but invalid syllogisms are still syllogisms.)

Examples

Here are more examples of syllogisms and their forms:

1. *IAO*-**III**
   Some Greeks are mortals.
   All Greeks are humans.
   ∴ Some humans are not mortals.
2. *AEE*-**IV**
   All mortals are Greeks.
   No Greeks are humans.
   ∴ No humans are mortals.
3. *EIO*-**II**
   No mortals are Greeks.
   Some humans are Greeks.
   ∴ Some humans are not mortals.
4. *AIE*-**I**
   All Greeks are mortals.
   Some humans are Greeks.
   ∴ No humans are mortals.
5. *EEE*-**III**
   No Greeks are mortals.
   No Greeks are humans.
   ∴ No humans are mortals.
6. *EIO*-**I**
   No Greeks are mortals.
   Some humans are Greeks.
   ∴ Some humans are not mortals.

LC Exercise 13-6

Using the *A, E, I, O* notation, symbolize the following arguments, put them into standard syllogistic form, and determine their mood and figure (and thus their form).

1. Some Beatles are musicians.
    All musicians are rhythmic.
    ∴ Some Beatles are rhythmic.
2. All things made out of grass are green.
    Some things made out of grass are cigarettes.
    ∴ Some cigarettes are green.
3. All homosexuals are gay.
    Some homosexuals are not happy people.
    ∴ Some happy people are not gay.
4. No Republicans are donkeys.
    Some politicians are not Republicans.
    ∴ Some politicians are donkeys.
5. All Democrats are donkeys.
    Some politicians are Democrats.
    ∴ Some donkeys are politicians.
6. No men not named after their fathers are juniors.
    Some college students are not men not named after their fathers.
    ∴ Some college students are not juniors.
7. All men whose sons are named after them are seniors.
    No coeds are men whose sons are named after them.
    ∴ No coeds are seniors.
8. No skiers are bathing lions.
    All bathing lions are cool cats.
    ∴ No cool cats are skiers.
9. All great chess players are geniuses.
    Some geniuses are completely overlooked.
    ∴ Some great chess players are completely overlooked.
10. No rules have exceptions.
    Some rules are exceptional.
    ∴ Some exceptional things are not exceptions.

8   *Determining Syllogism Validity*

A syllogism is **valid** if its form makes it impossible for the syllogism to have both premises true and its conclusion false. All other syllogisms are **invalid.** A valid syllogism guarantees the truth of its conclusion provided both of its premises are true. An invalid syllogism may have a false conclusion even though both of its premises are true. So an invalid syllogism obviously does not guarantee anything about its conclusion, which is why we say it is invalid.

If a syllogism having a given form is a valid syllogism, then all syllogisms having that form are valid, and if a syllogism having a given form is invalid, then all syllogisms having that form are invalid.*

9   *Venn Diagram Proofs of Validity or Invalidity*

Perhaps the most common way to determine the validity or invalidity of syllogisms and of what we might call "syllogism forms" is by using Venn diagrams.

To diagram a syllogism, three overlapping circles are required, one for each term. In overlapping the three circles, seven areas are formed (plus an eighth, outside the circles):

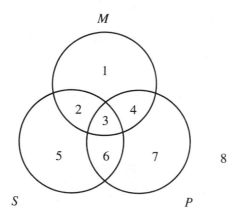

Area 1 represents the class things that are in class *M*, but not *S* or *P*; 2 the class of things that are in both *M* and *S* but not *P*; 3 the class of things that are in both *M*, *S*, and *P*; 4 the class of things in *M* and *P* but not *S*; and so on. The pair of areas 1 and 4, taken together, represent the class of things that are in *M* but not *S*; the pair 3 and 6 the class of things that are in both *S* and *P*; the pair 6 and 7, the class of things in *P* but not *M*; and so on. (We need two areas to represent these classes because in drawing a third overlapping circle we divide each of these areas in half.)

Now consider the syllogism:

All Greeks are mortals.
<u>All humans are Greeks.</u>
∴ All humans are mortals.

---

*Except for the cases considered in Section 14 of this chapter.

   In the Middle Ages, students determined the validity of a syllogistic form by reciting a chant containing a name for each of the valid moods in each figure. For instance, the name "bArbArA" occurs in the chant for the first figure, indicating that the form *AAA*-**I** is valid.

To diagram its first premise "All Greeks are mortals," we shade out areas 1 and 2 to indicate that they are empty:

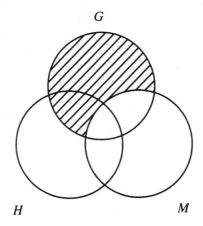

And to diagram its second premise "All humans are Greeks," we shade out areas, namely 5 and 6:

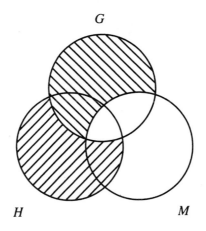

Were we now to diagram its conclusion "All humans are mortals," we would shade out areas 2 and 5. But in diagramming the two premises of this argument, we have already shaded out 2 and 5, and hence we have already diagrammed its conclusion. This indicates (speaking metaphorically) that the information contained in the conclusion already is contained in the premises. Hence, the syllogism, and any syllogism having the form *AAA*-**I,** is valid, since it cannot have true premises and a false conclusion.

Now consider the syllogism

All Greeks are mortals.
No humans are Greeks.
∴ No humans are mortals.

To diagram its first premise, we shade out areas 1 and 2, and to diagram its second premise, we shade out 2 and 3, to get:

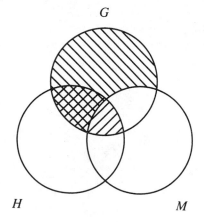

But to diagram its conclusion, we would have to shade out 3 and 6. It happens that we have shaded out 3, but we have not shaded out 6. So in diagramming the premises of this syllogism, we have not also diagrammed its conclusion. Hence, it is possible for its premises to be true and its conclusion false, and so the syllogism in question is invalid.

Examples

1. We can diagram the premises of the syllogism

   All Philadelphians are Metroliner fans.
   No Metroliner fans are frequent flyers.
   ∴ No Philadelphians are frequent flyers.

   as follows:

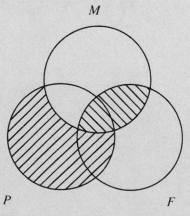

This proves that the syllogism is valid since in diagramming its premises we have also diagrammed its conclusion.

2.   We can diagram the premises of the syllogism

No doctors are in favor of smoking cigarettes.
Some cigarette smokers are doctors.
∴ Some cigarette smokers are not in favor of smoking cigarettes.

by shading out areas 3 and 4, then placing an *X* in area 2 to indicate that the class *CD* is not empty:

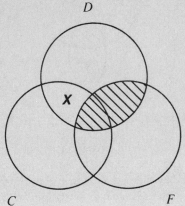

Although in diagramming the premises of this syllogism we have not quite dia-grammed its conclusion (as will become evident in the next few paragraphs), we still have proved that the syllogism is valid. The reason for this is that the conclusion "Some cigarette smokers are not in favor of smoking cigarettes" asserts that areas 2 and 3 are not both empty (that is, it asserts that either 2 or 3 has something in it), and in diagramming the premises we have placed an *X* in 2. So the premises of this argument already contain the information that is contained in the conclusion.

3.   We can diagram the premises of the syllogism

No shady characters are honest.
Some shady characters are highly respected.
∴ Some who are highly respected are honest.

as follows:

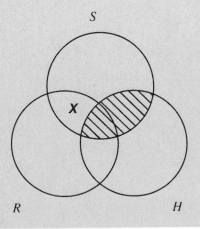

This proves that the syllogism is not valid, because in diagramming its premises we did not place an X in either 3 or 6, which (roughly) is what would be required to diagram its conclusion.

In diagramming the premises of a syllogism, sometimes an X can be placed in either one of two areas. This is the case for the syllogism

All Greeks are mortals.
Some humans are mortals.
∴ Some humans are Greeks.

We diagram the first premise as follows:

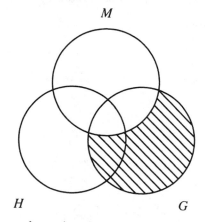

But in diagramming the second premise, the question arises as to whether to place an X in area 2 or in area 3. The answer is that we should not place an X in either area, since the premises assert only that one or the other (or perhaps both) of the classes represented by these areas has members, without indicating definitely either that the class represented by area 2 has members or that the class represented by area 3 has members. To indicate that the premises merely tell us that at least one of these classes has members, without telling us which one, we can place an X on the line between 2 and 3. And then, the diagram will look like this:

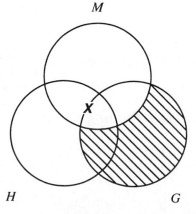

Is this syllogism valid? If it were, then in diagramming its premises, we would have placed an X either in 3 or in 4. Now clearly no X has been placed in 4. But no X has been placed in 3 either, for the X was placed on the line between 2 and 3. So we cannot guarantee the truth of the conclusion "Some humans are Greeks" on the basis of the evidence afforded by its premises, and hence the syllogism is invalid. (This is the only even mildly difficult case that can arise in proving validity or invalidity using Venn diagrams, so it is worthwhile to expend a little extra effort to understand it.)

In any event, cases of this kind present no problem in practice, since all syllogisms diagrammed by placing an X on a line are invalid. (Similarly, all syllogisms diagrammed by doubly shading out an area are invalid.)

Sometimes it becomes clear where to place the X after shading in for the other premise. Always represent premises involving shading (*A* and *E* propositions) before representing a premise that requires placing an X (*I* and *O* propositions). So, for the valid syllogism

Some professors are easy graders.
<u>All professors are teachers.</u>
∴ Some teachers are easy graders.

it becomes clear where to place the X for the first premise once we shade for the second premise, as follows:

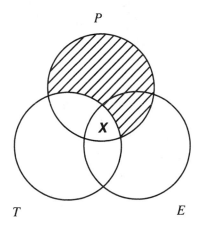

Exercise 13-7

Test the syllogisms in Exercise 13-6 for validity, using Venn diagrams as just discussed.

10   *Five Rules for Determining Validity or Invalidity*

An alternative (and much older) method for determining the validity or invalidity of syllogisms and syllogism forms is to use rules stating properties that all valid syllogisms must possess.

But before introducing a particular set of five rules of this kind, chosen from among several modestly similar sets, we must discuss the concept of **distribution.** In traditional logic texts, it is usually stated that a term in a proposition is *distributed* if (roughly) it says something about *all* members of the class designated by that term. For instance, the *A* proposition "All scientists are mathematicians" is said to distribute its subject term, since it says something about all scientists (namely that they are mathematicians), but not its predicate term, because it does not say something about all mathematicians. (It surely does not say, or imply, that all mathematicians are scientists.)

Traditional logic texts work out the distribution properties of all four kinds of categorical propositions. Letting *S* stand for subject terms and *P* for predicate terms, we can summarize the findings of the traditional logician as follows:

Table of distribution

1. *A* propositions distribute *S.*
2. *E* propositions distribute *S* and *P.*
3. *I* propositions distribute neither *S* nor *P.*
4. *O* propositions distribute *P.*

Most students readily accept the results summarized in the first three lines of this table. But they find the idea expressed on the fourth line, that *O* propositions distribute their predicate terms, rather counterintuitive. And yet there is a certain plausibility to this idea. For instance, it seems plausible to say that the *O* proposition "Some scientists are not philosophers" distributes its predicate term because it says of all philosophers that they are not some scientists (that is, that they are excluded from part of the class of scientists). In any event, we must say that *O* propositions distribute their predicates, or the five rules about to be presented will not function properly.*

According to these five rules for determining the validity or invalidity of syllogisms, all valid syllogisms must have:

1. A middle term that is distributed at least once.
2. No term distributed in the conclusion that is not distributed in a premise.
3. At least one affirmative (nonnegative) premise.
4. A negative conclusion if one of its premises is negative, and a negative premise if the conclusion is negative.
5. One particular premise if the conclusion is particular (that is, one *I* or *O* premise if the conclusion is an *I* or *O* proposition).

Any syllogism that does not have all five of these properties is invalid. (The fifth rule is required only if we allow propositions to refer to empty classes.)†

---

*Unfortunately, the traditional characterization of the concept of distribution is not satisfactory even for *A, E,* and *I* propositions. Take the *A* proposition "All bachelors are unmarried adult males" (let's assume that "bachelor" means "unmarried adult male"). Clearly this proposition "refers to" all bachelors, thus distributing its subject term, then it also "refers to" all unmarried adult males, thus distributing its predicate term. Hence, the traditional account of distribution is inadequate. There are ways of getting around this difficulty, but they require decisions on philosophical problems beyond the scope of this text and hence are omitted.

†A sixth rule, requiring that there be exactly three terms in a valid syllogism, often is added to these five. But this rule is unnecessary because an argument that does not have exactly three terms, each one repeated twice, is not a syllogism according to the generally accepted definition of that term.

Examples

1. The syllogism

    Some mathematicians are scientologists.
    All philosophers are mathematicians.
    ∴ Some scientologists are philosophers.

    violates the rule requiring that the middle term be distributed at least once and hence is invalid.

2. The syllogism

    All hats in hand are worth two in the closet.
    All bowlers in hand are hats in hand.
    ∴ All things worth two in the closet are bowlers.

    violates the rule requiring that no term be distributed in the conclusion that is not distributed in a premise and hence is invalid.

3. The syllogism

    Some umbrellas in hand are not worth two in the closet.
    No things worth two in the closet are better left there.
    ∴ Some umbrellas in hand are not better left there.

    violates the rule requiring at least one affirmative premise and hence is invalid.

4. The syllogism

    Some shrinks are not expensive.
    All who are expensive are expensive.
    ∴ Some shrinks are expensive.

    violates the rule requiring that the conclusion be negative, if a premise is negative, and hence is invalid. (This rule also requires that a premise be negative if the conclusion is negative.)

5. And the syllogism

    No expansive people are shrinks.
    All shrinks are expensive.
    ∴ Some expansive people are not expensive.

    violates the rule requiring that at least one premise be particular, if the conclusion is particular, and hence is invalid.

Ⓛ Ⓒ Exercise 13-8

Put the following arguments into standard syllogistic form, and test for validity, using either the five rules of valid syllogisms or Venn diagrams.

1. All sinners are punished in the next life. And all nonsinners are nonmurderers. So it follows that all murderers are punished in the next life.
2. Most sinners are not murderers, since most people punished in the next life are nonmurderers, and sinners are punished in the next life.
3. Eighteen-year-olds are permitted to vote. But not all who are permitted to vote in fact do vote. So there must be some 18-year-olds who don't exercise their right to vote.
4. Those who ignore relevant facts are likely to be mistaken. So the wise man is not likely to be mistaken, because he takes all known relevant facts into account.
5. Only the rich deserve the fair. So it follows that some who are handsome aren't nonrich, since some who deserve the fair aren't nonhandsome.
6. All logic classes are extremely interesting. So some classes that are harder than average are extremely interesting, since some logic classes are harder than average.
7. No logic classes are dreadfully boring, because no classes about good reasoning are boring, and all logic classes are about good reasoning.
8. All classes that are either interesting or difficult are uncrowded, due to the fact that all uncrowded classes are unexciting, and all interesting or difficult ones are exciting.
9. Salesmen will do whatever is most likely to sell their product. So salesmen often will tell lies, because telling the truth often is not the best way to sell a product.
10. Because Harry enjoys himself only when he has lots of money and because Harry always enjoys going out with Jane, it follows that Harry only goes out with Jane when he has lots of money.
11. He who lives by the sword dies by the sword. So all officers die with their boots on, since officers surely do live by the sword.
12. Some who live by the pen are called liars, and some are called sages. So there are people said to have great sagacity who have been referred to as frequent stretchers of the truth.
13. If to be human is to be vain, then everyone must be regularly looking in mirrors; everyone knows vanity tends to seek its own reflection.
14. We'll always have death and taxes. Right? And nobody ever gave in to either without a fight. Right? So that's why we're always fighting, fighting, fighting. Right!
15. Wet-whistled drunks all tend to be loud and shrill, which no doubt accounts for all the attention they get. Moral: Quiet people get ignored.

11   *Syllogistics Extended*

Several ways have been invented to extend the scope of syllogistic logic. Let's now consider some of these methods.

1. *Many arguments containing four, five, and even six terms can be reduced to three terms, and thus to syllogistic form, by eliminating negation signs or by replacing terms*

with their synonyms. For instance, we eliminate a negation sign and reduce the number of terms in the nonsyllogistic argument*

All dentists are sadists.
No MDs are nondentists.
∴ All MDs are sadists.

from four to three, by using obversion to replace its second premise with the equivalent proposition

All MDs are dentists.

thus obtaining the valid syllogism

All dentists are sadists.
All MDs are dentists.
∴ All MDs are sadists.

Similarly, we can reduce the number of terms in the nonsyllogistic argument

Some enclosed figures are squares.
All triangles are enclosed figures.
∴ Some three-sided enclosed figures are squares.

from four to three by replacing the phrase "three-sided enclosed figures" with its synonym "triangles," thus obtaining the syllogism

Some enclosed figures are squares.
All triangles are enclosed figures.
∴ Some triangles are squares.

2. *Many arguments that are not in syllogistic form because they contain propositions that are not categorical propositions can be translated into syllogistic form by translating the propositions they contain into categorical propositions.* Sometimes, this can be accomplished by a simple change in word order. For instance, the proposition "Gamblers are all broke" may be translated into categorical form as "All gamblers are broke."

Sometimes, simply adding a suppressed quantifier will suffice to translate a proposition into categorical form. Thus, an argument containing the proposition "Men are fickle" may be translated into categorical form as "All men are fickle." And, clearly, "Every woman is mortal" can be translated into the categorical proposition "All women are mortal" and "Most gamblers are broke" into "Some gamblers are broke."

3. *In addition, many other minor grammatical changes can be made.* For instance, we can translate the argument

---

*Sometimes it is said that an argument of this kind is a syllogism, but not a standard form syllogism, thus taking any set of three categorical propositions to constitute a syllogism, no matter how many terms it contains.

All Boy Scouts do good deeds.
Some Girl Scouts do good deeds.
∴ Some Girls Scouts are Boy Scouts.

into syllogistic form by replacing its first and second premises by the equivalent propositions "All Boy Scouts are doers of good deeds" and "Some Girl Scouts are doers of good
deeds," respectively, thus obtaining the (invalid) syllogism

All Boy Scouts are doers of good deeds.
Some Girl Scouts are doers of good deeds.
∴ Some Girls Scouts are Boy Scouts.

4. *All categorical propositions say something about classes.* Thus, technically, no *singular* proposition is a categorical proposition. Hence, no syllogism can contain a singular
proposition. (A **singular proposition** is a proposition one of whose terms refers to an
individual rather than to a class. Thus, "Socrates is mortal," "Ada is tall," and "This man
is short" all are singular propositions.)

But there are several standard ways to translate singular propositions into categorical
propositions. One is simply to replace the singular term in such a proposition by a class
term naming a class that can contain only one member (namely, the individual referred to
by the singular term). Thus, "Ada is tall" can be translated into "All members of the class
whose sole member is Ada are tall." (We can also translate "Ada is tall" into "All things
identical with Ada are tall" because only one thing, Ada, is identical with Ada.)

Using this method, we can translate the famous argument

All men are mortal.
Socrates is a man.
∴ Socrates is mortal.

into syllogistic form as follows:

All men are mortal.
All members of the class whose sole member is Socrates are men.
∴ All members of the class whose sole member is Socrates are mortal.

Indeed, since we can always replace singular statements with categorical equivalents, it
has become customary to treat singular propositions as categorical propositions, considering affirmative singular propositions, such as "Socrates is a man" as *A* propositions, and
negative singular propositions, such as "Socrates is not mortal" as *E* propositions, without
bothering to translate as we have done above. Thus the argument

All men are mortal.
Socrates is a man.
∴ Socrates is mortal.

is customarily treated as a syllogism, and in fact, a valid one.

5. *Sometimes a more radical translation procedure is required to translate propositions
into categorical form,* a procedure that involves the introduction of new classes. Take the
proposition "We always have death and taxes." We can translate this sentence into cate-

gorical form by using the class of *times* (suggested by the temporal term "always") to obtain the categorical proposition "All times are times in which we have death and taxes." (Notice that the subject class in this case is the class of times, and the predicate class is a *sub*class of the class of times, namely the class of times at which we have death and taxes.)

But, as usual, care must be used in translating. For instance, we don't want to translate the invalid argument

Every time Anne gets an A on a logic exam she is happy.
Anne always gets A's on logic exams.
∴ Anne is always happy.

as

All times at which Anne gets A's on logic exams are times at which Anne is happy.
All times are times at which Anne gets A's on logic exams.
∴ All times are times at which Anne is happy.

because the latter is a *valid* argument, and we don't want to translate invalid arguments into valid ones. The mistake was to translate the second premise "Anne always gets A's on logic exams" so as to have Anne taking logic exams at *all* times. Clearly, what we mean when we say "Anne always gets A's on logic exams" is more accurately rendered as "All times *at which Anne takes logic exams* are times at which she gets A's." And if we correctly symbolize this premise, then the resulting argument will not even be a syllogism, much less a valid one.

12 *Enthymemes*

Arguments in daily life often omit premises that everyone can be expected to know. For instance, someone might argue that Texas is larger than France, and, hence, that some state in the United States is larger than France, omitting as understood the fact that Texas is a state in the United States.

Sometimes the *conclusion* of an argument is omitted as obvious. And sometimes a premise *and* the conclusion are omitted. An example would be a mother who says, "Now son, it's eight o'clock, and all little boys have to go to bed at eight o'clock," thus omitting the premise that the son is a little boy, as well as the conclusion that the son has to go to bed.

An argument that omits a premise (or a conclusion) as "understood" is said to be an **enthymemic argument,** or simply an **enthymeme.**

Obviously, there is no point in declaring an argument in everyday life invalid when the addition of premises accepted by all concerned will render the argument valid. Life is short, and we have neither the time nor the inclination to be precise and complete about everything. So in determining the validity of arguments from everyday life, we should add any premises it is reasonable to assume all would concede, when such additions will make an argument in question valid.

Exercise 13-9

The following arguments are invalid as they stand. Supply a missing premise for each one that (perhaps with some arranging and synonym substitution) will turn it into a valid syllogism and prove that the resulting syllogism is indeed valid.

1.   No honest men are crooks. It follows then that no businessmen are honest.
2.   Abortion takes the life of a fetus. So abortion takes the life of a human being.
3.   Most adults are drug users, since caffeine and nicotine are drugs.
4.   Smith must be in pretty good shape. After all, she eats plenty of brown rice.
5.   Most American history textbooks conceal our theft of the American continent from the Indians. So most American history textbooks tell lies.
6.   Anyone who listens to television news programs listens to very superficial accounts of the news. So you waste your time if you watch TV news programs.
7.   Anyone whose primary interest is prestige or an easy life can't be a very good minister. So there must be some bishops who are pretty poor ministers.
8.   Plenty of high school dropouts are smarter than lots of college graduates. So there must be an awful lot of people who never finished high school who are not incapable of holding high-level management positions.
9.   Our Iranian policy was based on the judgment of some of America's best-known political scientists. So it wasn't a foolish policy.
10.   No one with a scrambled brain is likely to do much good in this world. So a lot of people who have taken LSD have had it so far as being part of an effective force for good is concerned.

13   *Sorites*

Consider the argument

All animals are life forms.
All insects are animals.
All bees are insects.
∴ All bees are life forms.

As it stands, it cannot count as a valid syllogism, since it contains four terms and three premises, and hence is not even a syllogism, much less a valid one. But clearly, it is a valid argument of some sort. In order to bring it into the syllogistic framework, we can consider it to be an enthymematic version of a chain of two valid syllogisms. For instance, we can take the first two propositions as the premises of the valid syllogism:

All animals are life forms.
All insects are animals.
∴ All insects are life forms.

and then use the conclusion of this syllogism and the third premise of our original argument as premises of the valid syllogism:

All insects are life forms.
All bees are insects.
∴ All bees are life forms.

Let's refer to any argument of the kind just considered that can be treated as a chain of enthymematic syllogisms as a **sorites.***

Sorites can have as many premises as you wish. Here is one with four premises:

All musicians are entertainers.
All bass players are musicians.
Some lead singers are bass players.
No rocket scientists are entertainers.
∴ Some lead singers are not rocket scientists.

This sorites breaks down into the following chain of valid syllogisms:

All musicians are entertainers.
All bass players are musicians.
∴ All bass players are entertainers.

All bass players are entertainers.
Some lead singers are bass players.
∴ Some lead singers are entertainers.

Some lead singers are entertainers.
No rocket scientists are entertainers.
∴ Some lead singers are not rocket scientists.

Since all three of these syllogisms are valid (which the reader may want to prove), the sorites as a whole is valid.

Exercise 13-10

Translate the following sorites into standard form and determine whether they are valid or invalid.

1. Men are fickle.
    No one is disliked who is good at logic.
    Fickle people are disliked.
    ∴ No men are good at logic.
2. No skiers are nonathletic.
    Some nutritionists are skiers.
    Athletes are not brawny.
    ∴ Some nutritionists are nonbrawny.

---

*Originally, the term "sorites" referred only to a special kind of enthymematic syllogism chain. But in recent years it has come to refer indiscriminately to all kinds.

3. Barbers are extroverts.
    No good barbers are nonbarbers.
    Some good barbers are high-strung.
    ∴ Some high-strung people are not extroverts.
4. No scientists are nonmathematicians.
    Geologists are friendly.
    No mathematicians are friendly.
    ∴ No geologists are scientists.
5. Occasionally one finds a genius in graduate school.
    No one can be admitted to grad school who isn't a college graduate.
    People in graduate school are not college graduates.
    ∴ Some geniuses cannot be admitted to graduate school.
6. No one whose soul is not sensitive can be a Don Juan.
    There are no profound scholars who are not great lovers of music.
    Only profound scholars can be dons at Oxford.
    No insensitive souls are great lovers of music.
    ∴ All Oxford dons are Don Juans.*

14   *Technical Restrictions and Limitations*

In Chapter 11, we pointed out that there are intuitively valid arguments that are not provable using predicate logic. One of the examples given there was the valid argument

Art knows that he'll go either to the show or to the concert (but not to both).
Art knows that he won't go to the show.
∴ Art knows that he'll go to the concert.

Unfortunately, traditional logic is even less complete than predicate logic; that is, there are arguments provable using predicate logic that are not provable using traditional logic, even as we have extended it in Section 11 above. Here is a famous example.†

All horses are animals.
∴ All heads of horses are heads of animals.

In recent years, much work has been done in an effort to extend the scope of syllogistic logic to make it equal to that of predicate logic. No one has proved that this effort cannot succeed, but so far it has not.

In addition to being less complete than predicate logic, traditional logic has other difficulties. In particular, it seems to break down when applied to certain odd kinds of arguments.‡ A typical example is the following:

---

*Taken from C. L. Dodgson (Lewis Carroll), *Symbolic Logic* (1896), a book that, as one would expect, contains lots of cute examples.

†Given by Bertrand Russell, an inventor of predicate logic.

‡See James W. Oliver, "Formal Fallacies and Other Invalid Arguments," *Mind*, n.s., vol. LXXVI (1967), pp. 463–478, for an excellent account of these difficulties.

All scientists are mathematicians.
Some brilliant scientists are not mathematicians.
∴ No scientists are brilliant scientists.

According to the five rules for valid syllogisms, this syllogism is invalid, since it contains a term (*B*) that is distributed in the conclusion but not in a premise. And according to the Venn diagram technique, the syllogism is invalid:

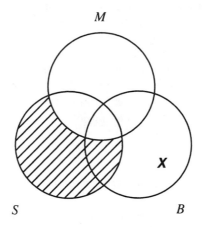

Nevertheless, this argument is valid, because its premises are contradictory,* and from contradictory statements we can prove whatever we wish. (Recall the discussion in Chapter 5, Section 4.)

Here is another argument that does not seem to be handled correctly either by the five rules of valid syllogisms or by Venn diagrams:

All philosophers are tall or nontall.
All philosophers are short or nonshort.
∴ Some tall-or-nontall things are short or nonshort.

---

*We can prove the validity of this argument using predicate logic machinery as follows:

1. $(x)(Sx \supset Mx)$
2. $(\exists x)[(Bx \cdot Sx) \cdot \sim Mx]$ $/ \therefore (x)\,[Sx \supset \sim (Sx \cdot Bx)]$
3. $(Bx \cdot Sx) \cdot \sim Mx$ 2 **EI**
4. $\sim Mx$ 3 **Simp**
5. $Bx \cdot Sx$ 3 **Simp**
6. Sx 5 **Simp**
7. $Sx \supset Mx$ 1 **UI**
8. Mx 6,7 **MP**
9. $Mx \lor (x)\,[Sx \supset \sim (Sx \cdot Bx)]$ 8 **Add**
10. $(x)[Sx \supset \sim (Sx \cdot Bx)]$ 4,9 **DS**

(Notice that lines 4 and 8 explicitly contradict each other, so that any conclusion whatsoever could have been derived.)

Again, using either Venn diagrams or the five rules of valid syllogism, we arrive at the incorrect conclusion that this syllogism is invalid. Nevertheless, the argument is valid, this time because *its conclusion is logically true.**

Obviously, something must be done to remedy the defects in syllogistic logic illustrated by these two examples. Two remedies come to mind. One is to say simply that as *syllogistic arguments* they are invalid, although they are valid in some wider system not yet worked out. Another way is to require that the premises of a syllogism, taken together, be consistent (that is, noncontradictory), and that its conclusion not be logically true.†

But remedies of this kind are not entirely satisfactory. More work must be done on these problems before the traditional syllogistic logic will be entirely acceptable.

Exercise 13-11

1. What is lost, if anything, by restricting syllogistic logic so that it deals only with propositions having existential import? Explain, including examples.
2. Which of the following are *equivalence* inference rules? Defend your answers.
   a. conversion
   b. contraposition by limitation
   c. obversion
   d. subalternation

---

*We can prove its validity using predicate logic as follows:

```
 1.   (x)[Px ⊃ (Tx ∨ ~ Tx)]
 2.   (x)[Px ⊃ (Sx ∨ ~ Sx)]          /∴ (∃x)[(Tx ∨ ~ Tx) · (Sx ∨ ~ Sx)]
 3.   ~ Tx                            AP
 4.   ~ Tx ∨ ~ Tx                     3 Add
 5.   ~ Tx                            4 Taut
 6.   ~ Tx ⊃ ~ Tx                     3–5 CP
 7.   Tx ∨ ~ Tx                       6 Impl, DN
 8.   ~ Sx                            AP
 9.   ~ Sx ∨ ~ Sx                     8 Add
10.   ~ Sx                            9 Taut
11.   ~ Sx ⊃ ~ Sx                     8–10 CP
12.   Sx ∨ ~ Sx                       11 Impl, DN
13.   (Tx ∨ ~ Tx) · (Sx ∨ ~ Sx)      7,12 Conj
14.   (∃x)[(Tx ∨ ~ Tx) · (Sx ∨ ~ Sx)]  3 EG
```

(Notice that the two given premises were not used in deriving the conclusion. We didn't have to use them because the conclusion (being logically true) follows from the null set of premises.)

†The problem for traditional logic posed by logically true and logically false categorical propositions is, in fact, even broader than we have indicated. For instance, it also occurs for the notions of contraries, subcontraries, and so on. Thus, logically true *A* propositions, such as "All bachelors are unmarried," cannot have contraries, even assuming existential import. And logically false *I* propositions cannot have subcontraries. For more on these difficulties, see David Sanford, "Contraries and Subcontraries," *Noûs,* vol. 2 (1969), pp. 95–96.

3. Which of the following become invalid or, in the case of (e) and (f), false once we remove the restriction to propositions that have existential import? Defend your answers.
    a. contraposition
    b. conversion by limitation
    c. subalternation
    d. obversion
    e. *A* and *O* propositions are contradictories
    f. *A* and *E* propositions are contraries

4. True or False: If in diagramming the premises of a syllogism using Venn diagrams we also have diagrammed its conclusion, then the syllogism is valid. Defend your answer.

5. True or False: Because the order of premises in part determines the figure of a syllogism, changing the order of its premises may change its validity. Defend your answer.

6. Carefully explain why *E* propositions distribute both their subject and predicate terms, and why *I* propositions distribute neither. Give examples.

7. When diagramming a syllogism to determine its validity, we sometimes have to place an × on the line between two slots. Carefully explain why. Give an example.

8. Are singular propositions such as "Ronald Reagan is an actor" also categorical propositions? Explain, with examples.

9. Figure out an original example (genuinely different from the one in the text) of a valid argument, provable using the machinery of predicate logic but not of syllogistic logic; prove the argument is valid; and explain why syllogistic machinery doesn't permit proof.

10. Figure out an original example of a valid argument that is invalid according to the five rules of valid syllogism and Venn diagram proof procedures; prove the argument valid; and then explain why syllogistic rules go wrong. This is a hard question.

Key terms

A proposition: (See *universal affirmative proposition.*)

Aristotelian logic: (See *syllogistic logic.*)

categorical proposition: A subject-predicate proposition that asserts, or denies, a relationship between two classes.

complement: The negation of a term. The *complement class* of a given class is the class of all things that are *not* members of the given class.

contradictory propositions: Two propositions such that if one of them is true, the other must be false, and vice versa. Corresponding *A* and *O* propositions, and *E* and *I* propositions, are contradictories.

contraposition: The rule permitting inference from a given proposition to a corresponding proposition in which the subject term has been replaced by the complement of the predicate term and the predicate term has been replaced by the complement of the subject term. For example, we can infer by contraposition from "All humans are mortals" to "All mortals are humans." Contraposition is valid only for *A* and *O* propositions.

contraposition by limitation: The rule permitting subalternation and contraposition (of the resulting proposition) to be performed on an *E* proposition, resulting in a particular *O* proposition. For example, using contraposition by limitation we can infer from the *E* proposition "No humans are mortals" to the *O* proposition "Some mortals are not humans." Contraposition by limitation is valid only on the assumption of existential import.

contrary propositions: Two propositions such that it is not possible for both of them to be true, although it is possible for both of them to be false. Assuming existential import, corresponding **A** and **E** propositions are contraries.

conversion: The rule permitting inference from a given proposition to another proposition just like the first one, except that its subject and predicate terms have been reversed. For example, the proposition "No humans are mortals" converts to "No mortals are humans." Conversion is valid only for **E** and **I** propositions.

conversion by limitation: The rule permitting inference from an **A** proposition to the converse of a corresponding **I** proposition. For example, we can infer from "All humans are mortals" to "Some mortals are humans" by conversion by limitation. However, conversion by limitation is valid only on the assumption of existential import.

distribution: A term in a syllogism is distributed if the proposition refers to all members of the class designated by that term.

enthymeme: An argument in which a premise, or premises, is omitted as understood. (Sometimes it is the conclusion that is omitted as understood.)

E proposition: (See *universal negative proposition.*)

existential import: A categorical proposition has existential import if it is assumed that its subject term and predicate term do not refer to empty classes.

figure: The property of a standard form syllogism determined by the positions of its major, minor, and middle terms in its premises.

form: The property of a syllogism determined by its mood and figure.

I proposition: (See *particular affirmative proposition.*)

invalid syllogism: A syllogism that is not valid.

O proposition: (See *particular negative proposition.*)

major term: The predicate term of the conclusion of a syllogism.

middle term: The term in a syllogism that occurs once in each premise but not in the conclusion.

minor term: The subject term of the conclusion of a syllogism.

mood: The property of a standard form syllogism determined by the quality of its three propositions. For example, the syllogism

All Greeks are mortals.
<u>Some humans are mortals.</u>
∴ Some humans are Greeks.

has the mood **AEE.**

obversion: The rule permitting inference from a given proposition to a corresponding proposition in which the quality has been changed and the predicate term replaced with its complement. For example, we can infer from "All humans are mortals" to "No humans are mortals" by obversion. Obversion always is valid.

particular affirmative proposition: A categorical proposition having the form "Some S are P," where S and P denote classes. Synonym: **I** *proposition.*

particular negative proposition: A categorical proposition having the form "Some S are not P," where S and P denote classes. Synonym: **O** *proposition.*

predicate (or predicate term) (of a categorical proposition): The term after the verb "to be," for instance, the word "hairsplitters" in "All logicians are hairsplitters."

quality (of a proposition): Every categorical proposition must have the quality either of being affirmative or of being negative.

quantity (of a proposition): Every categorical proposition must be either universal or particular.

singular proposition: A proposition one of whose terms refers to an individual entity rather than a class. For example, "Socrates is human" is a singular proposition.

sorites: An enthymemic version of a chain of syllogisms.

square of opposition: A diagram used to illustrate several of the inferential relationships (such as contradictoriness and contrariety) holding between categorical propositions.

standard form (of a syllogism): The form of a syllogism in which the premise placed first contains the predicate of the syllogism's conclusion.

subalternate proposition: The rule permitting inference from an **A** proposition to a corresponding **I** proposition, or from an **E** proposition to a corresponding **O** proposition. Subalternation is valid only on the assumption of existential import.

subcontrary propositions: Two propositions such that it is not possible for both of them to be false, although it is possible for both of them to be true. Assuming existential import, corresponding *I* and *O* propositions are subcontraries.

subject (or subject term) (of a categorical proposition): The term before the verb "to be" and after the term "all," "some," or "no"; for instance, the word "logician" in "All logicians are hairsplitters." (See also *predicate*.)

syllogism: An argument containing three categorical propositions, two of which are premises and one a conclusion, such that the three propositions taken as a group contain exactly three terms, each of which occurs twice (none occurring twice in a given proposition).

syllogistic logic: The traditional logic centering on and developed from the syllogistic theory of Aristotle. The term now is often used to distinguish the traditional logic from modern symbolic logic. Synonyms: *Aristotelian logic, traditional logic.*

traditional logic: (See *syllogistic logic.*)

universal affirmative proposition: A categorical proposition having the form "All *S* are *P*" where *S* and *P* denote classes. Synonym: *A proposition.*

universal negative proposition: A categorical proposition having the form "No *S* are *P*" where *S* and *P* denote classes. Synonym: *E proposition.*

valid syllogism: A syllogism whose conclusion must be true if all of its premises are true. It is impossible for a valid syllogism to have true premises and a false conclusion.

Venn diagrams: Overlapping circles, used to diagram categorical propositions and categorical syllogisms.

Chapter Fourteen

Inductive Logic

In Chapter 1, we divided correct arguments into two kinds: *deductively valid* arguments and *inductively strong* arguments. We now turn to an examination of inductive arguments and their role in scientific method.

However, a note of caution again is in order. Although it is true that literally nothing in philosophy is accepted by all philosophers, the material on symbolic logic presented in the first two parts of this text comes as close as anything to being generally accepted and noncontroversial. But almost all of the material to be presented now on induction and science is highly controversial, and the viewpoint expressed is just one of several.

1   *A Mistaken View of Induction and Deduction*

According to a common misconception about the distinction between deduction and induction, deductively valid reasoning involves inference from the general to the specific (particular) or from the more general to the less general, whereas inductively correct reasoning involves inference from the specific (particular) to the general, or from the less general to the more general. For example, the deductively valid argument

   1.   All who attain power are corrupted by it.
∴ 2.   If Jim and Tammy Bakker attained power, then they were corrupted by it.

proceeds from the general to the specific, and the inductively correct argument

   1.   So far, every intelligent student has done A work in logic.
∴ 2.   All intelligent students (past, present, and future) do A work in logic.

proceeds from the less general to the more general.

But only a moment's reflection is needed to see that this view of deductive and inductive reasoning is erroneous. First, deductively valid arguments do not always proceed from the general to the specific. For instance, they often proceed from the general to the equally general. An example is the argument

1. No police officers are corruptible.
∴ 2. Anyone who is corruptible is not a police officer.

And they often proceed from the specific to the specific. An example is the argument

1. If Dan Rather has attained power, then he has been corrupted by it.
2. Dan Rather has attained power.
∴ 3. He has been corrupted by it.

They sometimes even proceed from the specific to the general (or the less general to the more general), although cases of this kind tend to be a bit contrived. Here are two examples:

1. John is mortal.
∴ 2. All who know John know someone who is mortal.

1. John is mortal.
2. John is not mortal or all men are mortal.
∴ 3. All men are mortal.*

Further, inductively correct arguments do not always proceed from the specific to the general. For instance, they often proceed from the specific to the specific. An example is the analogical argument

1. In 1985 Garri Kasparov defeated Anatoly Karpov for the world chess championship.
2. He did so again in 1987.
∴ 3. He'll win again next time they play for the championship.

And they often proceed from the general to the equally general.

1. All NFL teams made tons of money this year.
∴ 2. All NFL teams will make tons of money next year.

Finally, here is one that moves from the general to the specific.

1. All NFL teams made tons of money this year.
∴ 2. The San Francisco 49ers NFL team will make tons of money next year.

These examples should make it clear that there is no truth to the view that deductively valid reasoning proceeds from the general to the specific, or from the more general to the less general, and inductively correct reasoning from the specific to the general, or the more specific to the less specific.

---

*This example is from Nelson Pole, "A Deductive Argument with a Specific Premise and a General Conclusion," *Notre Dame Journal of Formal Logic,* vol. XVI (1975), pp. 543–544. Pole points out that those who don't feel this argument moves from the less general to the more general (on grounds that premise 2 is as general as the conclusion) should consider the following deductively valid argument:

1. John is not mortal.
∴ 2. John is not mortal or all men are mortal.

See also Chapter 1 of Brian Skyrms, *Choice and Chance,* 3rd ed. (Belmont, CA: Wadsworth, 1985).

2 *Kinds of Inductive Arguments*

Recall that *pattern,* or *resemblance,* is the fundamental ingredient in inductive reasoning. We want our ideas about what this or that will be like in future to fit a pattern gleaned from what this or that was like in the past. (The problem, of course, is to find patterns or resemblances that fit, or take account of, everything we've experienced of the past.)

Inductive arguments can be divided into several different kinds.

Inductive generalization, categorical form

When we reason or argue from a premise or premises concerning particular instances, or from all examined cases of a certain kind, to a conclusion that is universal, or concerning all cases (examined or unexamined) of a certain kind, our reasoning has the form of a **categorical inductive generalization,** or **universal inductive generalization,** or simple **inductive generalization.** (These terms also apply to the conclusions of inductive generalizations.) An example is the argument

   1.   All examined copper things conduct electricity.
∴ 2.   All copper things (examined or as yet unexamined) conduct electricity.*

Categorical inductive generalizations all have the same general form, which can be put in either one of two ways. The first way is:

   1. $Fa \cdot Ga^\dagger$
   2. $Fb \cdot Gb$
   3. $Fc \cdot Gc$
              •
              •
              •
   N.   No F is known not to have G.
∴ $N + 1$. All F's are G's.

And the second (equivalent) way is:

   1.   All examined F's are G's.
∴ 2.   All F's are G's.

Translated into the notation of predicate logic, and letting Ex = "x is examined for the presence or absence of G," this reads:

---

*In this case, the premise of our inductive generalization is true. But the generalization would be just as inductively correct if its premise was false. The goodness of inductive reasoning depends on the connection between premises and conclusion, not on the truth of the premise. What makes an argument inductively strong is that if its premises were true, they would support acceptance of its conclusion.

†Because we are dealing with the form of categorical inductive generalizations, "F," "G," "a," "b," and "c" are being used as variables.

1. $(x)[(Fx \cdot Ex) \supset Gx]$
2. $(x)(Fx \supset Gx)$

Although there is much controversy over how to weigh the strength of a categorical inductive generalization, it is widely believed that the *probability,* or *degree of confirmation,* of a hypothesis, or the *evidential support* for a hypothesis, increases with each new confirming instance of it. For example, each newly examined instance of the hypothesis "All copper conducts electricity" increases the probability of that hypothesis. However, as the number of confirming instances mounts up, each new confirming instance counts less than the preceding instance. (Exactly how much less it counts is one of those things on which there is no general agreement.)

Even more controversial is the idea that the more important confirming cases are those that also disconfirm competing hypotheses. Looking out the window and finding yet another crow that's black doesn't do much, if anything, for the theory that all crows are black, given that we've already seen plenty of crows in similar circumstances. But hearing about black crows in some tropical area where crows had not previously been observed does count as good confirmation of the theory that all crows are black because, in this view, it disconfirms the competing theory that bird species in general, and thus crows in particular, vary in color from one sort of environment to another.

And some hold that the important confirmations of a theory are those that confirm consequences of the theory of a kind that hadn't been confirmed before. For example, successfully applying Newton's laws to determine the moon's gravitational force (as encountered by astronauts) tests a different consequence of Newton's laws than the usual ones about the moon's orbit or the trajectory of bullets on Earth.

Finally, some people say that there is no such thing as confirmation of an hypothesis, strictly speaking. What is often called confirmation on this view is better seen as the attempt to falsify an hypothesis; we speak (but shouldn't) about confirmation when attempts to falsify fail.

Many scientific hypotheses have the form of categorical inductive generalizations; for example, "All copper conducts electricity." But it is frequently held that the typical and important scientific hypotheses are not categorical inductive generalizations. The claim is that such categorical generalizations are characteristic of the early stages of a science, giving way fairly quickly to something more advanced and sophisticated. For example, some claim that even Galileo constructed more advanced hypotheses than the one above, since he constructed quantitative hypotheses. An example is the hypothesis (slightly simplified here) that the distance an object falls in free flight equals sixteen times the square of the time it falls, or in symbols $S = 16t^2$. Their claim is that the mathematical equation is the standard or at least most important form of scientific hypothesis.

There can be no doubt that many scientific hypotheses are constructed in the form of mathematical equations. But this fact does not constitute evidence against the importance of categorical inductive generalizations in science, because mathematical equations themselves can be stated as categorical generalizations. For example, we can translate the equation $S = 16t^2$ into the categorical generalization "All freely falling bodies are such that if S is the distance they fall, and t is the time it takes them to fall that distance, then $S = 16t^2$."

Inductive generalization, statistical form

When we reason or argue from a premise or premises concerning groups of instances to a conclusion that is statistical in form, our reasoning has the form of a **statistical inductive generalization.** An example is the argument

  1. Half of the tosses of this coin observed so far have landed heads up.
∴ 2. Half of all tosses of this coin (observed or otherwise) will land heads up.

  The general form of statistical generalizations can be stated as:

  1. *N* percent of all *F*'s tested for *G* have *G*.
∴ 2. *N* percent of all *F*'s (tested or otherwise) have *G*.

  Statistical generalizations play an important role in science. A great many of the hypotheses in the social sciences (economics, sociology, and others) are statistical, and many basic hypotheses of physics itself are statistical. Two important examples are the Second Law of Thermodynamics (the law of increasing entropy) and the gas laws. For example, the gas laws say nothing about the pressure of a gas at any given point on the surface of an enclosed container, but rather what the *average,* or *statistical,* pressure will be, calculated on the basis of the temperature and volume of the enclosed gas.

  But a statistical generalization is generally not as informative or useful as the corresponding universal generalization would be. Take the statistical generalization "One-fifth of all adult Americans who smoke an average of one or more packs of cigarettes per day will die of lung cancer within 25 years." Obviously, if true, this constitutes very valuable information, for it warns those who fall into the stated category (adult Americans who smoke at least one pack per day) of their "chances" of getting lung cancer if they persist in smoking so heavily.* But it doesn't tell them that they will get lung cancer merely because they are adult Americans who smoke at least one pack of cigarettes per day.

  However, suppose we discover that heavy cigarette smoking is only one of two factors leading to lung cancer, the other factor being, say, a particular abnormality in the surface tissue of the lung (let's call it "abnormality *A*"); that is, suppose we discover that every investigated case of heavy smoking in which abnormality *A* is present also is a case of lung cancer death. Then we could construct the following inductively strong argument:

  1. All heavy smokers who have been found to have abnormality *A* have died of lung cancer.
∴ 2. All heavy smokers who have abnormality *A* die of lung cancer.

  The conclusion of this argument is a categorical inductive generalization concerning the connection between smoking and death by lung cancer and would be much more informative and useful than the statistical generalization cited above. For if some person—say, Art—were found on examination to have abnormality *A*, then we could present him with an argument such as

---

*That their chances are one in five is significant because we know that hardly any people who don't smoke tobacco get lung cancer.

1. All heavy smokers who have abnormality A die of lung cancer.
2. Art has abnormality A.
∴ 3. If Art is (or becomes) a heavy smoker, then Art will die of lung cancer.

Surely this argument is more relevant to Art's decision about whether to smoke than the previous statistical argument linking heavy smoking and lung cancer. A corresponding statistical generalization, such as "One-fifth of all heavy smokers will die of lung cancer," which when combined with the information that Art is a heavy smoker, leads to the conclusion that the chance is one in five that Art will die of lung cancer, certainly is not so informative or useful as the conclusion that Art definitely will die of lung cancer if he becomes a heavy smoker.

In view of the above, the question naturally arises whether with sufficient knowledge we could not (at least theoretically) replace all statistical generalizations with categorical ones. It seems plausible to assume that this always can be accomplished by taking account of more and more relevant factors. For instance, knowledge that a given coin is symmetrical permits the conclusion that half of all random tosses with that coin will land heads up. But it seems plausible to assume that with better knowledge—that is, with knowledge of more relevant factors (such as the force of each toss, its starting position, wind velocity, and so on)—we could conclude that *all* tosses of a certain kind (tossed with a certain force or tossed from a certain starting position) will land heads up.

However, we cannot say ahead of time that all statistical generalizations are replaceable by categorical generalizations. In each case, we must examine the world to determine whether more relevant factors exist. (Of course, simply failing to find relevant factors does not prove that none exist. We may not have been sufficiently ingenious to discover them.) So the question of whether a given statistical generalization can be replaced by a corresponding categorical generalization can be answered only by accumulating more empirical evidence, to the extent that it can be answered at all.*

On the other hand, it is clear that we can regard a categorical inductive generalization as a special kind of statistical generalization, namely the kind in which the percentage of F's tested that turn out to be G's happens to be 100 percent. In other words, we can take the basic pattern of categorical inductive generalizations to be

1. 100 percent of all F's tested for G have G.
∴ 2. 100 percent of all F's (tested or otherwise) have G.

that clearly is just a special case of the general pattern for statistical generalization.

Analogies

When we infer from a premise or premises concerning particular instances (or all known instances) of a certain kind to a conclusion concerning some other particular instance

---

*Some claim that evidence discovered by twentieth-century physicists, in particular evidence supporting the Heisenberg Indeterminacy Principle, provides empirical reason for believing that at least some, and perhaps all, of the ultimate laws of physics are statistical and not categorical. See, for instance, Hans Reichenbach, *Rise of Scientific Philosophy* (Berkeley and Los Angeles: University of California Press, 1953), Chap. 10.

of that kind, we infer **analogically,** or by **analogy.** For example, we infer *analogically* when we reason from the premise that a course given last year by a particular teacher was interesting to the conclusion that the course the teacher is giving this year will be interesting.

Some analogies are *stronger* than others. Analogies differ in the degree to which they support their conclusions. For one thing, the greater the number of instances mentioned in the premises, the stronger the analogy. Thus, if we reason from the fact that both of two courses taken from a particular teacher were interesting to the conclusion that the next course we take from that teacher will be interesting, our analogy is better than if we reason on the basis of only one course taken from that instructor.

Analogies also are stronger if the instances they concern are alike in more relevant ways. Thus, if we reason from the fact that the two interesting courses taken previously from a particular teacher both were logic courses to the conclusion that the next logic course we take from that teacher will be interesting, our analogy is better than if the next course happens to be ethics.

However, only *relevant* ways in which the instances are alike count. For example, it might be irrelevant if the classes both happened to meet in the same room, or at the same time of day. But it is quite difficult to know in general, or even in a particular case, exactly which things are relevant and which are not. The room in which a course is to be taught may be relevant to how interesting it will be. (For example, it will be relevant if the teacher in question dislikes large, poorly lit rooms, and the next course that teacher teaches happens to be in such a room.)

It also is important to remember that the premises supporting an analogy may be more or less *probable.* The more probable they are, obviously, the stronger the analogy. For instance, having personally taken a course from a particular instructor, and having found it to be interesting and informative, should count more heavily than hearing these same opinions from the grapevine.

It follows from what has just been said that what is a strong analogy for one person, given what that person knows, may be quite weak for a second, given what that second person knows. For instance, one of your authors concluded by analogy that the Woody Allen flick *What's Up Tiger Lily?* would be funny, because the other Allen films he'd seen had been funny, but other Woody Allen fans stayed away in droves, having heard, as this writer had not, what kind of movie it was (klunko).

Analogies conveniently divide into two kinds, namely **categorical analogies** and **statistical analogies.**

Valid categorical analogies have the general form

1. All *F*'s tested or observed for *G* have *G*.
∴ 2. This particular *F*, untested as yet for *G*, has *G*.

The argument discussed above, about taking a class from a particular teacher, is an example of a categorical analogy.

Valid statistical analogies have the general form

1. *N* percent (or most, or almost all) of the *F*'s tested for *G* have *G*.
∴ 2. The probability is *N* percent (or the probability is high) that this particular *F*, as yet untested for *G*, has *G*.

Most analogies made in everyday life are statistical analogies. In daily life, we rarely encounter cases in which all of the known cases of a certain kind have some particular relevant property. For instance, even the best teachers are likely to teach an uninteresting class at least once, thus falsifying the premise of any *categorical* analogy whose conclusion is that their next course will be interesting, but not falsifying the premise of some *statistical* analogy whose conclusion is that their next course probably will be interesting.

It is sometimes held that analogical reasoning is not fundamental, in that any given analogy can be shown to be an enthymemic version of a categorical or statistical generalization. Take the analogy whose conclusion is that the next class taught by a particular teacher probably will be interesting. In this case, it is said, the complete form of our reasoning would be

    1.   Almost all classes taught so far by the teacher in question have been interesting.
∴ 2.   Almost all of the classes that teacher teaches are interesting.
    3.   This particular class will be taught by the teacher in question.
∴ 4.   This particular class will probably be interesting.

LC Exercise 14-1

Here are three analogical arguments, each one followed by a set of five additional premises. Some of these extra premises, if added to the original analogy, increase its strength; others decrease it. State which of the extra premises increase and which decrease the strength of the original analogy, and explain why you think so.

1.   The Carnegie Hall Cinema is playing Ingmar Bergman's flick *Scenes from a Marriage* tonight. This is a serious foreign film, and the last five foreign movies I saw seemed to me to be quite good. So I expect to like *Scenes from a Marriage.*
    a. Three of the other five were also Bergman films.
    b. All five were comedies.
    c. Liv Ullmann stars in *Scenes* but wasn't in any of the other five.
    d. I saw all five on a Wednesday evening. Today is Tuesday.
    e. All five were in black and white. *Scenes* is in color.

2.   They say that heart attacks run in families because of like habits and similar genes. Boy that makes me worried! My father died of a heart attack at age 55, my mother at 31, my grandfather (father's side) at 62, his wife at 58, my other grandmother at 63, and three aunts before age 65. I should be worried—all signs point to an early heart attack.
    a. I don't smoke cigarettes; my father and his father smoked over a pack a day for many years.
    b. All my close relatives ate the same sort of central European diet—lots of animal fats, pastries, highly seasoned foods; I'm a vegetarian and health nut.
    c. I'm a college graduate; my father dropped out after the eighth grade and my mother finished high school, but my grandparents never even started kindergarten.
    d. My father stood on his feet in a retail store for 55 to 60 hours per week for 25 years; my grandfather sat at a sewing machine. In contrast, I jog 2 to 5 miles every other day; I'm not sedentary as they were.

e. I remember that everyone in my family was always worried about money; we all ate well, but money for extras was very scarce. Looking back, they were all "type A" people—nervous, always in a hurry, late, tense. Now I'm a cool cat with the world's best occupation (for me)—good pay, job security, fun things to do, flexible hours, and lots of free time.

3. I recently started reading about countries that have medical care run primarily by government (socialized medicine). Finding at first that this is true in the former Soviet Union, its eastern European satellites, and China, and that medical care in all of these countries is extremely poor compared to that in the United States, I concluded tentatively that we don't want a medical system in the United States that is primarily run by government.

a. I then realized that none of the above countries where socialized medicine produces poor results have democratic governments—governments elected by the people in genuinely free elections.

b. Pursuing the matter further, I read that in Great Britain, which has both a democratically elected government and (primarily) socialized medicine, medical care on the whole seems to be a good deal poorer for most people than it is in the United States and several European countries that, like the United States, are democratic and have medical care that is mostly in nongovernmental hands.

c. Turning to other sources, I read that in democratic Canada, medicine is mostly in the hands of the government and seems to be on the whole better than in the United States (although hard to compare because medical attention in the United States is so uneven from rich to poor compared to in Canada).

d. Next, I read that in other countries there are all sorts of variations on the government/nongovernment theme (blends of the two kinds of systems—most not being pure one way or the other), and that the quality of medical care in these other countries on average varies more with respect to national wealth and how well in general things run in that country than with respect to what sorts of medical systems they happen to have (for example, Mexico, Sweden, Japan).

e. Finally, turning to a completely different set of sources, I found that there is a great deal of difference among authorities about much of what I had previously read. One highly respected libertarian source argued that medical attention in Canada in fact is not as good on the whole as in the United States, and that anyway lots of the problems in the United States are generated by govenment interference (Medicare, Medicaid, and so on) in the marketplace. But another respected source argued for a generally higher level of medical attention in Canada as well as several European countries where government plays a greater role in medicine than in the United States, citing statistics concerning greater longevity, lower infant mortality, and so on in these other countries than in the United States in support of that claim.

Exercise 14-2

Here are some arguments containing analogical reasoning. In each case state how strong you believe the analogy to be, given your background information, and explain your conclusion.

1. The Christians say, "Creatures are not bound with desires unless satisfaction for those desires exists." A baby feels hunger: well, there is such a thing as food. A duckling

wants to swim: well, there is such a thing as water. Men feel sexual desire: well, there is such a thing as sex. If I find in myself a desire which no experience in this world can satisfy, the most probable explanation is that I was made for another world. (C. S. Lewis, *Mere Christianity*)

2. That the aggressor, who puts himself into the state of war with another, and unjustly invades another man's right, can, by such an unjust war, never come to have a right over the conquered, will be easily agreed by all men, who will not think that robbers and pirates have a right of empire over whomsoever they have force enough to master, or that men are bound by promises which unlawful force extorts from them. Should a robber break into my house, and with a dagger at my throat, make me seal deed to convey my estate to him, would this give him any title? Just such a title by his sword has an unjust conqueror who forces me into submission. (John Locke, *Of Civil Government*)

3. If a single cell, under appropriate conditions, becomes a man in the space of a few years, there can surely be no difficulty in understanding how, under appropriate conditions, a cell may, in the course of untold millions of years, give origin to the human race. (Herbert Spencer, *Principles of Biology*)

4. "Do you think," said Candide, "that men have always massacred each other, as they do today, that they have always been false, cozening, faithless, ungrateful, thieving, weak, inconstant, mean-spirited, envious, greedy, drunken, miserly, ambitious, bloody, slanderous, debauched, fanatic, hypocritical, and stupid?"

   "Do you think," said Martin, "that hawks have always eaten pigeons when they could find them?"

   "Of course I do," said Candide.

   "Well," said Martin, "if hawks have always had the same character, why should you suppose that men have changed theirs?" (Voltaire, *Candide*)

5. We may observe a very great similitude between this earth which we inhabit and the other planets. . . . They all revolve around the sun as the earth does. . . . They borrow all their light from the sun, as the earth does. Several of them are known to revolve round their axis like the earth, and by that means, must have a like succession of night and day. . . . From all this similitude, it is not unreasonable to think that those planets may, like our earth, be the habitation of various orders of living creatures. (Thomas Reid, *Essays on the Intellectual Powers of Man*)

6. I am the father of two daughters. When I hear . . . that we can't protect freedom in Europe, in Asia, or in our own hemisphere, and still meet our domestic problems, I think it is a phony argument. It is just like saying that I can't take care of Luci because I have Lynda Bird. (President Lyndon B. Johnson, February 1968)

7. The philosopher Epicurus argued that the gods have bodies, because the gods are intelligent and all known intelligent entities (human beings) have bodies.

8. Suppose someone tells me that he has had a tooth extracted without an anesthetic, and I express my sympathy, and suppose I am then asked, "How do you know it hurt him?" I might reasonably reply, "Well, I know that it would hurt me. I have been to the dentist and know how painful it is to have a toothache stopped with an anesthetic, let alone taken out. And he has the same sort of nervous system as I have. I infer, therefore, that in these conditions he felt considerable pain, just as I should myself." (A. J. Ayer, "One's Knowledge of Other Minds," *Theorea,* 1953)

Inference from observed to unobservable

We have divided inductively correct inferences into three kinds, namely, categorical, statistical, and analogical. But there are other useful ways to divide them.

In particular, it is important to distinguish between reasoning from what is observed to what is as yet unobserved *but can be observed,* and reasoning from what is observed to what, even in principle, *cannot be observed.*

For instance, we reason from the observed to the *observable* when we infer from the fact that most autos of a certain kind have lasted a long time to the conclusion that a particular auto of this kind will last a long time. That an auto lasts a long time is something we can directly observe. But we reason or infer from the observed to that which even in principle *cannot be observed* when we infer from the fact that Smith's finger was pricked by a pin, followed by the rapid withdrawal of his hand, facial grimaces, exclamations of "ouch," and so on, to the conclusion that Smith is in pain. In this case, we cannot directly observe the thing inferred, namely Smith's pain, for it is impossible to experience or observe directly someone else's mental activity. In this case we must infer the unobservable pain from what we take to be causally related to the pain, namely the withdrawal of Smith's hand, his facial expression, his utterances, and so on.

Those things, like mental states, that cannot be observed directly are often called **theoretical entities,** to distinguish them from things that can be observed directly, called **observable entities.** But there is a great deal of controversy about which things are, in fact, directly observable.

In addition, it is useful to divide the entities commonly classed as theoretical into four kinds.

1. *Physical particles,* such as electrons that many scientists claim cannot be directly observed even in principle, constitute a kind of theoretical entity, for we must infer their existence.*

2. **Dispositional properties** (discussed briefly in Chapter 11) constitute another kind of theoretical entity. An example is the property of being *flammable.* We can observe that something *burns,* but not that it is *flammable.* Similarly, we can observe that something *bends,* but not that it is *flexible.* Burning and bending are *observable* properties; flammability and flexibility are *dispositional* properties. Since dispositional properties are not directly observable, we must *infer* their existence. They constitute a kind of theoretical entity.†

---

*Roughly, electrons are claimed to be unobservable because observing (in the sense of seeing) requires the use of entities (like light rays) that cannot interact appropriately with something so small as an electron.

†We omit discussion of entities like electromagnetic fields, in particular the question whether they can be analyzed as dispositional properties of particles or constitute a separate and different set of theoretical entity.

3.   *Mental events* or *mental experiences* constitute still another kind of theoretical entity. However, this kind of theoretical entity is different from all others in that every given entity of this kind can be experienced by someone or other (namely the person who "has" the mental experience), although it cannot be observed by anyone else. For instance, my pain can be (and is) experienced by me, but not by anyone else. And your pain can be (and is) experienced by you, but not by anyone else. From *your* point of view, *my* pain is theoretical, whereas from *my* point of view, *your* pain is theoretical. This is different from the case with respect to say, electrons, because (according to many scientists) no one can directly observe electrons. (It should be noted that according to one philosophical theory called the *neural identity* theory, consciousness is a brain process, and therefore is observable.)

4.   Finally, many philosophers consider all *physical objects, material objects,* or *material substance* to be theoretical entities. They believe that it is what they call *sense data* that we experience directly, and not the physical objects that may be causally related to them.* If we believe in the existence of physical objects in addition to the existence of sense data, and perhaps causally related to sense data, then this belief (if rationally founded) will be based on *inductive inferences* from what we experience, namely sense data, to their cause, namely physical objects.

We characterized theoretical entities as things that we cannot observe. But words such as "cannot," called *modal terms,* are notoriously tricky. In particular, the word "cannot" itself is *ambiguous.* When we say that electrons cannot be observed, we mean that it is impossible to observe them. Similarly, when we say that we cannot observe someone else's mental experiences, we mean that it is impossible for us to observe them. However, the senses of "impossible" are different in each case. In the first case, we mean that it is *physically impossible* to observe electrons directly; that is, we mean that the laws of nature (the way the world happens to be) precludes our observing electrons. Or, to put it another way, we mean that it is a *contingent fact* that we cannot observe electrons. But in the second case, we mean that it is *logically impossible* to observe someone else's experiences directly. We can have experiences that are just like someone else's experiences, but we cannot literally share the same experience.

So before we can say what kinds of things are theoretical entities (and thus cannot be observed), we must know what kind of impossibility is appropriate. It will come as no surprise that philosophers disagree on the matter.

---

*We cannot go into a detailed discussion concerning sense data at this point. But we can understand roughly what the philosopher who postulates the existence of sense data is talking about by thinking of a very vivid dream or hallucination concerning, say, seeing one's father, and comparing that experience with the experience of *really* seeing one's father. Taken alone, the dream or hallucination may be identical with the experience of really seeing one's father. Now, in the dream, the *experience of* seeing one's father is surely mental. So when really seeing one's father, the *experience* (as opposed perhaps to its cause) must also be mental, because taken alone (out of context) it is identical with the mental dream experience of seeing one's father. Roughly speaking, sense data philosophers merely attach the label "sense data" to the content of an experience, whether of the dream-hallucination kind or the "real" vision kind. And, of course, they attach that label to auditory experience, olfactory experience, and others, as well as to visual experience.

Exercise 14-3

In your opinion, which of the following underlined terms refer to theoretical entities and which to observable ones (or both)? Explain.

1. <u>George</u> picked up the <u>book</u> on the table and observed that it had an odd red cover.
2. Opening the book, he noticed that the first sentence was about Newton's law concerning <u>gravitational force</u>.
3. It was, strangely, the very same sentence that started the physics text he used last <u>year</u>, when he first took Physics I.
4. His <u>attention</u> wandered from Newton to what he knew would come sooner or later, twentieth-century physics, field theories, <u>neutrinos</u>, and all that sort of thing.
5. Vague <u>thoughts</u> of dropping out of <u>school</u> crossed his mind, especially when he realized he also was enrolled in Chemistry I this semester.
6. He walked into the next room and picked up his chemistry text—its cover looked <u>red</u>, but the light was poor, so he wasn't sure.

3   *Cause and Effect*

One of the chief uses of inductive reasoning is to establish the **causes** of different kinds of things and events. Having discovered that heating a gas in a balloon always makes it expand, a budding young Robert Boyle would be justified in concluding that heating *causes* gases to expand. But what does it mean to say that one thing is the *cause* of another, or that two things are *causally related?*

Just as in the case of many other concepts, the notion of causation is really a cluster of related concepts, mostly with blurred edges. Some writers, for instance, speak of the cause of a thing or event as simply the **sufficient condition** for bringing it about. In this sense, the cause of Marie Antoinette's death was being guillotined, because having one's head cut off is a sufficient condition of death.

On the other hand, some think of a cause as a **necessary condition** for bringing something about and of the sum total of all the necessary conditions required to produce it as its complete cause. The presence of oxygen can be thought of in this way as part of the cause of the lighting of a match, even though not a complete cause. It is part of what must occur for the effect—the lighting of the match—to occur.

Note also that we often speak of causation in a statistical or probabilistic sense in cases where it isn't true that producing the cause always produces the effect, but is true that it does so in a certain percentage of cases. We say, for instance, that cigarette smoking is a **probable cause** of most cases of lung cancer, even though we know that not all people who smoke heavily for years contract that dread disease and also know that nonsmokers occasionally do so.

There is also the notion of **causal connection,** or **causal relationship,** to consider, given in particular that so many scientific discoveries are of causal relationships. Gallileo's discovery of a causal connection between the time that a thing falls toward the earth and the distance it falls during that time is an example. (Note how odd it sounds to say that dropping a ball 64 feet *caused* it to fall for 2 seconds.)

Although all of the above senses of cause are common in everyday life as well as in the sciences, another sense is the most common in everyday life and is at least not uncommon in the sciences. Central to this way of looking at causation is the notion of *human agency* (or perhaps we should say *purposive agency* in this robotic space age). In this sense, the cause of a thing or event is whatever we would need to do or change so as to bring about that thing or event.

To see how this conception of causation works, consider a simple case from everyday life, say the lighting of a match. We know that the usual way to light a match is to strike it (on an abrasive surface), and so we would say in a given case that it was the striking of the match that caused it to light. And yet we know perfectly well that all struck matches do not light—wet matches and those struck in a vacuum being cases in point. Striking a match is therefore not a sufficient condition of its lighting. And we know that matches can easily be lit without striking them, say by heating them in an oven. Thus, striking a match is not a necessary condition of its lighting either. Even so, if asked what caused a particular match to light at a certain moment, it would be perfectly right to answer that striking the match caused it to light at that moment. The reason it would be right is that striking a match is the usual way in which we get matches to light.

It is because we attach this sense of agency to most everyday talk about causes that we reject certain kinds of sufficient conditions as causes. Take a simple case, say, one in which we know that striking (heating) a well-made match in the presence of oxygen is a sufficient condition of its lighting. Letting Mx = "x is a well-made match"; Hx = "x is heated to a sufficiently high temperature"; Px = "x is in the presence of oxygen"; and Lx = "x lights," we can symbolize the proposition that all well-made matches heated in the presence of oxygen will light as $(x)\{[(Mx \cdot Hx) \cdot Px] \supset Lx\}$. If asked why a particular match lit, we can say that it did so because it was struck (heated sufficiently) in the presence of oxygen (or say simply that it did so because it was struck—omitting reference to the presence of oxygen as understood). In other words, we can furnish an instance of the antecedent of the inductive generalization $(x)\{[(Mx \cdot Hx) \cdot Px] \supset Lx\}$ as the cause of the analogous instance of its consequent. (That is, we can furnish the instance $(Ma \cdot Ha) \cdot Pa$ of the antecedent of the generalization in question as the cause of the corresponding instance La of its consequent.)

However, we cannot do this in every case. For example, the inductive generalization just referred to, namely $(x)\{[(Mx \cdot Hx) \cdot Px] \supset Lx\}$, is logically equivalent to the generalization $(x)\{[(Mx \cdot Hx) \cdot \sim Lx] \supset \sim Px\}$. But usage does not permit us to say that an instance of the antecedent of this generalization can be taken to be the cause of the analogous instance of its consequent. For example, usage does not permit us to say that oxygen was not present $\sim Pa$, because the match didn't light when heated $(Ma \cdot Ha) \cdot \sim La$. This is true in spite of the fact that if the inductive generalization is true and an instance of its antecedent is true, then the analogous instance of its consequent must be true.

There must be an important difference, then, between the case where we say (correctly) that the match lit because it was heated in the presence of oxygen and where we say (incorrectly) that the match was not in the presence of oxygen because it was heated and didn't light. And that difference, as we stated before, is human agency. In everyday life, it's easy to make a match light by striking it (heating it), but we can't make a match not be in the presence of oxygen by striking it and having it not light.

In addition to all of the above, causes are frequently distinguished as proximate or as remote causes. Suppose that a truck jackknifes on an icy highway, blocking three of four lanes, and that an auto, call it auto *A,* in one of those lanes swerves into the fourth lane blocking that lane to still another vehicle, auto *B,* which then slams into *A* from the rear. The ice on the road would then be said to be the **proximate cause** of the truck's accident and a much more **remote cause** of the accident between cars *A* and *B.* In general, we refer to causes nearer to a given phenomenon as proximate and to causes more distant in the causal chain as remote, as we have done in this case.

And this suggests an important point—namely, that a given effect can be explained in terms of several different causes; which one we select usually depends on our particular interest in that effect. Thus, a philosopher may be interested in the conscious willing of Smith to raise his arm, a rather remote cause of that event, whereas a biologist's interests might gravitate to attending muscle contractions, a much more proximate cause of the raised arm.

Finally, it should be noted that a good deal of discussion has gone on in the history of philosophy concerning the nature of causation in general. When we say that *A* causes *B,* or that *A*-type cases cause *B*-type cases, do we mean to assert that the occurrence of *A* *necessitates* the occurrence of *B*? Are there things in the universe called *necessary connections* that we discover when we find out that a particular *A* causes a certain *B*? This is an important philosophical question that has received quite different answers from different philosophers over the years. A great many of the philosophers roughly classifiable as rationalists have claimed what is called "ontological status" to necessary connections, thus thinking of causal necessity as something that exists in addition to the events that are causally connected. Empiricists, on the other hand, tend to follow the lead of David Hume in thinking of causation in terms of constant conjunction between cause and effect. On the Humean analysis, the most we are justified in meaning when we say that *A* causes *B* is that whenever *A* occurs, *B* occurs. Or, to be more precise, what we mean is that whenever an *A*-like event occurs, a *B*-like event will occur (because events *A* and *B* are singular and thus cannot occur more than once). Thus, when we say that the cause of a particular well-made match's lighting is that it was struck (heated) in the presence of oxygen, most empiricists would say that this should be taken to mean that whenever a well-made match is struck in the presence of oxygen, it lights.

Note, however, that even staunch empiricists would want to qualify Hume's ideas about cause and effect somewhat. Not every constant conjunction indicates a causal connection. We don't think of night as the cause of day, or day of night, despite the (so far) constant conjunction between the two. We don't because, first, theories concerning higher-level constant conjunctions (for instance, those related to Newton's laws of motion) lead us to predict that someday the earth will stop rotating on its axis, so night will not be followed by day, and second, because we know how we could stop night from following day right now, if only we were able to exert sufficient power to stop the earth's rotation on its axis (for example, by setting off a great many very powerful atomic bombs in just the right way). Only those constant conjunctions not countermanded, so to speak, in this way by higher-level theories about much more general constant conjunctions are thought of as indicating causal connections.

4 *Mill's Methods*

The set of five methods for justifying conclusions about causes, called **Mill's Methods,*** were proposed as ways to both discover and justify conclusions about causal connections. We will briefly discuss three of the five methods that constitute the core of the system.

The method of agreement

The **method of agreement** is very much like inductive generalization. Here is Mill's characterization of this method (in his *System of Logic*):

> If two or more instances of the phenomenon under investigation have only one circumstance in common, the circumstance in which alone all the instances agree, is the cause (or the effect) of the given phenomenon.

In other words, if we find two or more instances in which a given phenomenon, P, occurs, and only one other phenomenon, Q, is present in each instance, then we can conclude that P and Q are causally connected (in other words, that P is the cause of Q, or Q of P). It should be noted that Mill intended us to consider only relevant circumstances—circumstances that might plausibly be the sought-after cause.

Mill's example is this:

> Instances in which bodies assume a crystalline structure are found to have been preceded by instances which have in common only one antecedent, namely, the process of solidification from a fluid state.

This antecedent, therefore, is the cause of the crystalline structure. In other words, all objects observed to have a crystalline structure (P) have been found to have one and only one other factor in common—namely, that they have solidified from a fluid state (Q). Using the method of agreement, Mill concluded that having solidified from a fluid state (Q) is the cause of their crystalline nature (P). (It can't be the effect, because their fluid state precedes their crystalline state.)

The method of agreement should be familiar from its frequent use in everyday life. An example is furnished by the State Department official who discovers the source of a series of leaks to the press by noticing that only one of the many people who were privy to some of the items leaked had access to all of them. This is very much like the examples invented

---

*After John Stuart Mill (1806–1873), who is chiefly responsible for their popularization, though not their initial formulation, for which much is owed to John Herschel, who in turn is fundamentally indebted to Francis Bacon and his *Novum Organon* (1620). For more on Mill's view of Mill's Methods, see his *A System of Logic* (1843).

by mystery writers who, imitating reality, sometimes have their detectives find the murderer by mentally going through a list of suspects and discovering that only one (not usually the butler) could have been present at each of the slayings.

The State Department example is a typical case of the method of agreement. Among the suspected causes (or perhaps we should say causers) of the leaks, only one had the opportunity in each case, and so that person must be the infernal leaker. The argument's structure is this (letting the capital letter P stand for the particular phenomenon under investigation, the other capital letters stand for possibly relevant circumstances, and supposing there were exactly three leaks):

Instance One: $A, B, C, D, \ldots P$
Instance Two: $A, L, C, Q, \ldots P$
Instance Three: $A, B, Q, D, \ldots P$
$\therefore A$ is the cause of P, or P of A.

Of course, as usual the greater the number of instances, the better the inference. Similarly, the greater the number of potential common circumstances investigated, the better the inference.

It should be obvious that Mill's method of agreement is very similar to the method of categorical inductive generalization. The form of the latter can be rendered this way:

1. All examined A's are P's.
$\therefore$ 2. All A's are P's.

This is more stringent than the method of agreement in requiring that all known cases be included in the premises of an argument, but it is less stringent in not requiring that there be no factor other than A that is always present when P is present. And, of course, it doesn't justify our concluding that A causes P, a point we will go into later.

The method of difference

Mill's rendition of his **method of difference** is this:

> If an instance in which the phenomenon under investigation occurs and an instance in which it does not occur, have every circumstance in common save one, that one occurring only in the former, the circumstance in which alone the two instances differ, is the effect, or the cause, or an indispensable part of the cause, of the phenomenon.

In other words, if there is some factor, Q, present in an instance when P is present and absent in an instance when P is absent, and the two instances are alike in every other (relevant) respect, then P is the cause of Q, or Q is the cause of P.

Mill's example is this:

> A man in the fullness of life is shot through the heart; he is wounded and dies. The wound is the only circumstance that is different; hence, his death is caused by the wound.

In other words, the circumstance of a man's being wounded (Q) is present in an instance when the man in question dies (P) and absent in an instance when the man is alive (nondead—absence of *P*), and the two instances—namely, his being wounded and dying (*Q* and *P*) and his being not wounded and not dying (absence of *Q* and absence of *P*)—are alike in every other (relevant) respect.

When used together, the methods of agreement and difference constitute a very much more powerful inductive tool than either one employed alone.* Take the example concerning the discovery of the identity of the leaker of confidential information. Using the method of agreement, it was concluded that the one person who had access to all of the leaked documents must have been the guilty party. This is a perfectly good induction of some strength. But its strength would have been increased had the State Department checked and found that the person in question, call him Smith, did not have access to any of the otherwise (relevantly) similar confidential State Department documents that were not leaked to the press. Here is a table that shows how someone in the State Department might have used both the method of agreement and of difference to conclude with a good deal of strength that Smith caused the leaks:

	Jones's Access	Perez's Access	Cohen's Access	Smith's Access	Leaked to Press
1.	absent	present	present	present	present
2.	absent	absent	present	present	present
3.	present	present	absent	present	present
4.	present	present	absent	absent	absent

The first three rows of this table indicate that of the possible relevant factors, only one, Smith having access to the leaked material, was present in every such case. The method of agreement tells us to conclude, therefore, that Smith was the cause of the leaks. The last two rows of the table picture the use of Mill's method of difference in this case, indicating that, although Smith had access in an instance when the material was leaked (the third row), he did not have access in an otherwise similar instance in which confidential material was not tipped off to the press (the fourth row).

It should be clear from the discussion so far that the method of agreement tells us to select as the cause of a phenomenon the one common factor in a number of otherwise different instances in which that phenomenon occurs. And the method of difference tells us to choose as the cause the one respect in which an instance where the phenomenon occurs differs from an otherwise relevantly similar instance where the phenomenon is absent.

In the cases discussed so far, Mill's methods were used to discover something *present* that caused the phenomenon in question. In the crystal case, for example, the factor present was the process of solidifying from a fluid state. But the cause of an event may be the *absence* of something or other. The discovery that lack of ascorbic acid (vitamin C) causes scurvy furnishes a good example. When scurvy was a serious problem, back in the pre-

---

*Using both methods together in this way very much resembles the method Mill called the *method of agreement and difference*.

steamboat days of sailing ships, anyone who tried to discover some factor that is always present when scurvy is present and absent when scurvy is absent was bound to have a hard time of it. But by thinking about what might cause scurvy by its absence, it was soon discovered that absence of the intake of something found in most fruits and vegetables, in particular citrus fruits (later identified as ascorbic acid), is the cause of scurvy.

It should be noted that in using Mill's methods in a *positive* way, to show that a particular factor is the cause of a particular kind of circumstance, we of necessity also use them in a *negative* way, showing that the other potential factors are not the cause of that kind of circumstance. Thus, in showing that Smith was the likely source of the leaked material, we of necessity showed that the other possible candidates in fact did not cause the leaks. And in the scurvy case, since an absence of ascorbic acid intake was determined to be the cause of scurvy, all sorts of other possible candidates, for instance, various kinds of germs, were eliminated as potential causes.

The method of concomitant variation

According to the **method of concomitant variation,** if a given phenomenon varies in amount or degree in some regular way with the amount or degree of some other phenomenon, then the two factors are causally related.

Take the relationship between cigarette smoking and lung cancer. Surveys show that there is a direct relationship between smoking cigarettes and dying from lung cancer—those who smoke more cigarettes get lung cancer more often. Hence we conclude that cigarette smoking is causally related to death by lung cancer. (Notice that we cannot say that cigarette smoking is the cause of death from lung cancer, since some people who do not smoke at all die of lung cancer, indicating that there must be other causes of that disease.)

Or take the causal relationship between air pressure and the height of a column of mercury in a barometer. In this case, there is a direct quantitative relationship between the two that is so close that we use the effect (the height of the column of mercury) to measure the cause (the amount of air pressure).

Objections to Mill's Methods

Many objections have been raised against the use of Mill's Methods. The most frequent is that Mill's Methods, even when correctly applied, may lead to erroneous, even absurd, consequences. One famous example concerns the drinker who drinks scotch and soda one night, bourbon and soda the next night, gin and soda the next, and Irish whiskey and soda on the last night, each drinking bout being followed by a severe hangover. Using Mill's Methods, the drinker concludes that soda, the one common factor present on each of the four occasions, must be the cause of the hangovers.

But objections of this kind are spurious. In the drinking example, either the drinker did know that another factor, namely, alcohol, was present in each case, or he did not. If he knew this, then he did not apply Mill's Methods correctly, because he knew that soda was not the only common factor. And if he did not know that alcohol was present in each case, then he was justified in applying Mill's Methods in spite of the fact that his conclusion is false and even appears ridiculous. The falsity of the conclusion is not evidence against

Mill's Methods because these methods are inductive, and it is the mark of inductive methods that they sometimes yield false conclusions.

In addition, the fact that the conclusion appears ridiculous to us also is not a mark against Mill's Methods, because we know that bourbon, scotch, gin, and Irish whiskey all contain alcohol, and we know that hangovers are caused by excessive intake of alcohol. But if we did not know this (and we assume the drinker did not), then the conclusion that hangovers are caused by soda consumption would appear to be quite reasonable. (Incidentally, once the drinker realizes that there is another common factor, alcohol, in every case in which he had a hangover, then he can use Mill's Methods to determine which of these factors causes hangovers, simply by trying a case in which soda is present, but not alcohol, and then a case in which alcohol is present, but not soda.)

Perhaps the most important objection to Mill's Methods is that the methods of agreement and difference require the instances of the phenomenon in question to have only one other characteristic in common. In reality, this is never the case. Take Mill's own example about crystals. The phenomenon whose cause needs to be discovered is the crystalline structure of certain bodies (P). Mill says that the only thing all crystals have in common, other than being crystals, is that they have solidified from a fluid state (Q) and concludes therefore that this Q is the cause of this particular P. But, in fact, there are indefinitely many other features present in every case in which P and Q are both present. For example, every crystal so far examined is smaller than a mountain, has been subjected to temperatures between zero and 100 degrees Celcius, and has been subjected to gravitational force. The fact is that we never can satisfy the method of agreement (or of difference either), as this example indicates.

Mill can be defended against this charge by pointing out that he intended us to consider only *relevant* common circumstances. None of the above bizarre circumstances count as relevant. But this only puts into sharper focus the underlying problem about how we are to decide which circumstances are relevant and which not in each case. Several solutions have been proposed, none of which have received anything like universal acceptance.* The point here is just that Mill's Methods themselves do not provide a solution.

Another objection to Mill's Methods is that the method of agreement is stated in such a way as to invite the fallacy of the *small sample,* or *hasty conclusion.* The reason this is so is that this method only requires us to investigate a minimum of two instances, which it does not require to be representative of the population from which they were drawn.

In this case, Mill can be partially defended by pointing out that his examples generally concern types of instances, not particular ones. Thus, in the crystal case, his evidence does in fact concern the many instances of the types being a crystal and being solidified from a fluid state.

Finally, it should be pointed out that Mill's Methods do not constitute a complete system for discovering causal connections. The method of concomitant variation, for instance,

---

*Perhaps the most plausible is that it is our background beliefs that determine relevance. Thus, we reject being smaller than mountains as a relevant factor because experience has never shown this to make a causal difference.

deals with cases in which we observe a continual variation in both the effect whose cause we seek and in the potential cause, as in the cigarette–cancer case above. But there are several other common, indeed perhaps more common, statistical patterns. Consider a typical experiment, say, in which we expose a group of laboratory mice to a suspected carcinogen but don't expose a control group of mice. A typical result in such a case is that there is a variation in the cancer rate between the two populations but only in the presence or the absence of the suspected carcinogen, not its variation. To cover cases like this one, we need to construct additional methods, such as the one called the *Split Method of Difference and Concomitant Variation,** which deals with cases in which the effect varies in some way with the total presence or absence of the suspected causal factor.

LC Exercise 14-4

Show for the following whether each contains a correct use of Mill's Methods, and if so which one(s).

1. If you heat a normally combustible item in a vacuum, or in water, or in any medium that lacks air, combustion will not take place. But if you heat such an object with air present, it will take place. So there is no question but that heating in the presence of air is the cause of combustion.

2. According to some economists, very large increases in an already huge national debt should fairly quickly lead to increases in the rate of inflation, because there should be a corresponding increase in the money supply. So the Reagan administration ran the biggest budget deficits in U.S. peacetime history. By 1985 the national debt was out of sight, and yet inflation was down several percentage points.

3. Smith reasoned that if strong labor unions demanding and getting high salaries are the primary cause of inflation, then less well-organized industries should have little or no price inflation. But on checking, he discovered that the industries studied did suffer from price inflation, although their prices rose more slowly than did those of industries having strong, well-organized unions.

4. Being told by a health enthusiast that my extreme lethargy might be caused by low blood sugar, I took his advice and stopped eating snacks high in carbohydrates and low in protein and almost immediately felt better.

5. Prison experience unquestionably boosts the chance that an offender will break the law again. In one experiment, conducted by the California Youth Authority, a group of convicted juvenile delinquents was given immediate parole and returned to their homes or foster homes, where they got intensive care from community parole officers. After five years, only 28 percent of this experimental group had had their paroles revoked, compared to 52 percent of a comparable group that was locked up after conviction. (*Time,* 24 March 1967)

6. I'm satisfied that smoking marijuana does not by itself lead one to try heroin. For one thing, I know quite a few people who have been smoking the stuff for years but have never tried heroin.

---

*By its inventor Thomas R. Grimes. See his article, "A Sixth Mill's Method," *Teaching Philosophy,* Vol. 10, pp. 123–127, June 1987.

7. Louis Pasteur's theory that vaccination with anthrax virus produces immunity to anthrax disease was confirmed by an interesting experiment. Over twenty farm animals were vaccinated with the virus, and then these animals, plus a like number not so vaccinated, were given a normally fatal dose of anthrax germs. None of the vaccinated animals contracted the disease; all those not vaccinated contracted it.

8. Mr. Joule of Manchester conclusively proved that friction is the cause of heat by expending exact quantities of force by rubbing one substance against another, and he showed that the heat produced was exactly greater or less in proportion as the force was greater or less. (W. S. Jevons)

9. If a man's destiny is caused by the star under which he is born, then all men born under that star should have the same fortune. However, masters and slaves and kings and beggars are born under the same star. (Pliny the Elder, *Natural History*)

10. It once was assumed that large brains (relative to body weight) are the cause of great intelligence, because the brains of several known geniuses had, after their deaths, turned out to be much larger than average. But when the brain of Anatole France was examined after his death, it was discovered to be quite small relative to his overall body size. However, his brain contained an unusually large number of deep furrows (resulting in a much larger than usual outer surface), as did the brains of several other geniuses when examined after their deaths. So rather than brain size, it would appear that it is the amount of outer brain surface that leads to genius in human beings.

11. All children up to fifth grade in a certain California elementary school were given a standard IQ test, which teachers were told was a test designed to predict the students who would have the largest intellectual growth in the following two years. After the test was administered, teachers were given the names of students selected at random (some had scored high and some low) but were told that these students had scored high on the test and therefore could be expected to "spurt" ahead academically in the following year. During the next two years, students were given follow-up IQ tests, and it was found that in some grades—especially the first and second—those designated as likely fast learners improved more than did those not so designated. Since the "spurters" were chosen at random, it was concluded that a teacher's expectations are a causal factor in improving student IQ. (From Robert Rosenthal and Lenore F. Jacobson, "Teacher Expectations for the Disadvantaged," *Scientific American,* April 1968)

12. I placed two silver dimes next to this bar, and they moved toward it. I then tried a few paper clips, a teaspoon, some nails, and a small pair of scissors, and they all moved toward it. So I tried a one-ounce liquor glass, a couple of envelopes, a half-gallon carton of milk, and a spool of thread; none moved toward the bar. Obviously, this wonderful bar attracts all metals, but nothing else.

13. A researcher noticed that several victims of keratitis (a kind of blindness) were deficient in riboflavin. So he examined others suffering from the disease, and they too were low on that nutrient. Finding no other likely cause for the disease, the researcher theorized that keratitis is caused by a lack of riboflavin and confirmed his hunch by giving keratitis victims large doses of riboflavin and observing that the keratitis was cured.

Exercise 14-5

True or false? Explain your answer.

1. An inductively strong argument can have true premises and a false conclusion.
2. Although false that induction goes from the particular to the general, whereas deduction goes the other way, still it's true that induction goes from the less general to the more general, whereas deduction goes just the other way.
3. There is no such thing as a correct statistical inductive generalization.
4. We can regard a categorical inductive generalization as a special kind of statistical generalization in which the ratio of examined F's that are G's is 100 percent.
5. The same hypothesis may be highly probable (highly confirmed) given one set of evidence while disconfirmed by another.
6. One way to state the pattern or form of correct categorical inductive generalizations is this:

    1. All examined F's are G's.
    ∴ 2. All F's are G's.

7. The greater the number of instances mentioned in the premises of an analogical argument, the higher their degree of support for its conclusion.
8. The greater the difference between items mentioned in the premises of an analogical argument, the lower their degree of support for the conclusion.
9. It has been claimed that analogies are just enthymematic versions of categorical or statistical inductions.
10. Theoretical entities are entities referred to in as yet unsupported scientific theories. After such a theory receives sufficient confirmation, its formerly theoretical entities are then considered to be existent, not theoretical, entities.
11. The property of being water soluble is a dispositional property, hence also a theoretical one.
12. The physically impossible violates at least one law of nature, whereas the logically impossible violates at least one law of logic.
13. What Mill's method of agreement requires is that we find at least two occurrences of some phenomenon, P, that are also occurrences of some phenomenon, Q; finding them, we're entitled to assert that P is (probably) the cause of Q.
14. The main problem with Mill's method of agreement is that all examined instances of a phenomenon never have only one other factor in common.
15. Mill's Methods can be used negatively to discover that one phenomenon, P, is not the cause of another, Q, by finding an instance of P that is not an instance of Q.

5   Inductive Probability

The premises of a strong inductive argument make its conclusion *probable*. Probabilities and sentences about probabilities play an important role both in everyday life and in science, as the following examples illustrate:

1.   The probability of getting a 7 with an honest pair of dice is 1/6.
2.   Art will probably beat Charles at squash this afternoon.
3.   We'll probably have rain tomorrow.
4.   The probability that a given U.S. male will die of lung cancer in the next year is 0.0008.
5.   The theory of relativity is more probable on today's evidence than on the evidence available in 1919.
6.   The probability that a given birth will be a male birth equals 0.51.

The variety of probability we are concerned with here is probability in the sense of *degree of support* or *degree of confirmation* and is commonly referred to as *inductive* or *logical probability.* An argument is inductively strong if and only if the conclusion of the argument is inductively probable given the argument's premises.

Unlike validity, inductive strength comes in degrees. The more probable an inductive argument's conclusion is relative to its premises, the stronger the argument. The probability here is conditional; the conclusion is probable relative to the argument's premises. Thus a conclusion that is probable relative to one set of premises may be improbable relative to a different set of premises. Stated formally, the expression $P(p/q)$ is shorthand for "the (inductive) probability of p, given q." If we let q represent the conjunction of an argument's premises and p the conclusion of the argument, then in order for an argument to be strong, $P(p/q)$ must be greater than .5. On the other hand to be inductively strong $P(p/q)$ must also be less than the maximum degree of probability, namely 1. If $P(p/q) = 1$ the argument is valid, not inductively strong, since in this case there is no possibility that the premises could be true and the conclusion false.

6 *The Probability Calculus*

Let's now consider how, given certain probabilities, other probabilities can be calculated from them. The **probability calculus** has been constructed to answer this question.

Some pairs of propositions are such that the truth of one of them has *an effect* on the probability of the other. For example, if it is true that I have already drawn an ace from a deck of cards (without putting it back into the deck), then the proposition that I will get an ace on the next draw is less likely to be true.

But other pairs of propositions have no bearing on each other. For example, the proposition that I have drawn an ace from a deck of cards and put the ace back into the deck has *no* effect on the proposition that I will get an ace on the next draw. (The cards don't "know" that an ace was picked on the first draw.) If two propositions are such that the truth of one has no effect on the probability of the second, they are said to be **independent events.**

In addition, some pairs of propositions are such that it is *logically* possible for both of them to be true. For example, it is logically possible for it to be true that a die will land with face six up on its first throw and also true that it will land with face six up on its second throw.

But other pairs of propositions are such that it is not logically possible for both to occur. For example, it is not logically possible for face five *and* face six to turn up on a single throw of a die. If two propositions are such that it is not logically possible for both to occur, they are said to be **mutually exclusive events.**

We can write the basic rules of the probability calculus, as follows:

1. Restricted conjunction rule

If p and q are independent propositions, then $P(p \cdot q) = P(p) \times P(q)$.

For instance, if the probability of getting a 6 on a given throw (p) = 1/6, and the probability of getting a 6 on some other throw (q) = 1/6, then since p and q are independent of each other, the probability of getting 6's on both throws equals the probability of getting a 6 on the first throw *times* the probability of getting a 6 on the second throw. Thus, the probability of getting 6s on both throws equals $1/6 \times 1/6$, or 1/36.

2. General conjunction rule

$P(p \cdot q) = P(p) \times P(q, \text{given } p)$.

For instance, if the probability of picking a spade on a second draw, *given that a spade was picked on the first draw* (and not replaced) = 12/51,* then the probability that spades will be drawn on both the first and second draws = $1/4 \times 12/51 = 1/17$.

Notice that if $P(q, \text{given } p) = P(q)$, then the two conjunction rules both yield the same result. In fact, this is the case in which p and q are independent of each other.

3. Restricted disjunction rule

If p and q are mutually exclusive propositions, then $P(p \vee q) = P(p) + P(q)$.

For example, if the probability of getting a 5 on a given throw of a die = 1/6, and the probability of getting a 6 on a given throw of that die = 1/6, then the probability of getting a 5 *or* a 6 on a given throw of the die = $1/6 + 1/6 = 2/6 = 1/3$.

4. General disjunction rule

$P(p \vee q) = P(p) + P(q) - P(p \cdot q)$.

For instance, if the probability of getting a 6 on any given throw of a die = 1/6, then the probability of getting at least one 6 out of two throws (that is, a 6 on the first throw or a 6 on the second) = $1/6 + 1/6 - (1/6 \times 1/6) = 2/6 - 1/36 = 11/36$.

Notice that if p and q are mutually exclusive, then $P(p \cdot q) = 0$, and then the two disjunction rules yield the same result.

In addition, it is customary to assume that the probability of a *contradiction* = 0, and the probability of a *logical truth* = 1. In symbols, this reads

*Because 12 spades remain out of 51 cards.

5. $P(p \cdot \sim p) = 0$

6. $P(p \vee \sim p) = 1$

It follows from this that the probability of $\sim p = 1 - P(p)$; that is,

7. $P(\sim p) = 1 - P(p)$

7 *Bayes' Theorem*

We have now, in effect, provided seven rules for calculating complicated probabilities from simpler ones. But one further kind of complicated probability needs mentioning, namely what is sometimes called an **inverse probability.**

Suppose we know that 90 percent of the families in a certain city own a television set, and that among these, 10 percent also own a computer. Suppose we also know that among the 10 percent who don't own a TV set, 20 percent do own a computer. What is the probability that a family owning a computer also owns a TV set?

To deal with this problem, let $P(p)$ = the probability that a given family owns a computer, and $P(q)$ = the probability that a given family owns a TV set. Then in our example,

$P(q) = 0.9$ $P(p, \text{given } q) = 0.1$
$P(\sim q) = 0.1$ $P(p, \text{given} \sim q) = 0.2$

(The probabilities on the left are sometimes called *prior probabilities* and those on the right *conditional probabilities*, or *forward probabilities*.) We want to calculate the probability that a given computer-owning family also owns a TV set, in symbols $P(q, \text{given } p)$, and for this purpose we can use a simplified version of **Bayes' Theorem,** namely,*

$$P(q, \text{given } p) = \frac{P(q) \times P(p, \text{given } q)}{[P(q) \times P(p, \text{given } q)] + [P(\sim q) \times P(p, \text{given} \sim q)]}$$

Plugging in values from the case at hand, we get,

$$P(q, \text{given } p) = \frac{0.9 \times 0.1}{(0.9 \times 0.1) + (0.1 \times 0.2)} = \frac{0.09}{0.11} = \frac{9}{11}$$

Bayes' Theorem is intuitively plausible. In our example, common sense says the probability that a computer family also is a television set family should depend on, first, the prior

---

*The general form of Bayes' Theorem is

$$P(q, \text{given } p) = \frac{P(q) \times P(p, \text{given } q)}{[P(q_1) \times P(p, \text{given } q_1)] + \ldots + [P(q_n) \times P(p, \text{given } q_n)]}$$

We use the general formula when there are more than two values for q to consider.

probability that a family owns a television set and, second, the conditional probability that a family owning a television set also owns a computer. And this is what Bayes' Theorem calculates.*

   Bayes' Theorem is clearly legitimate in cases, like the above, where the relevant prior probabilities are known (in our example, presumably known by statistical inductions from samples). But objections have been raised against the use of Bayes' Theorem when prior probabilities are not known (a common kind of case). Some answer such objections by saying that in the absence of reasons for preferring one value over another, all prior probabilities will be considered equal.
   In addition to questions about the applicability of Bayes' Theorem when prior probabilities are not known, questions have been raised as to the applicability of the probability calculus in general. An important argument often raised in support of the probability calculus is that using any other calculation rules leads to clearly unacceptable results, in particular making possible what is called a "Dutch book."
   The term comes from gambling. Gamblers who are sufficiently careless or ignorant in placing a series of bets may find that no matter what happens, the bookie must win. When this happens, they're said to have a **Dutch book** made against them. Obviously, any system of rules for calculating odds that might lead gamblers to allow a Dutch book to be made against them is not an acceptable system. It turns out that any system that deviates from the standard probability calculus is susceptible to a Dutch book (can have a Dutch book made against it). So many writers would say that only the standard calculus is acceptable as a measure of inductive probability.

LC Exercise 14-6

Use the probability calculus to determine the following probabilities, showing enough work to justify your answers.

1. What is the probability of getting (a) an even number face up on a given throw of a symmetrical die; (b) an odd number?
2. What is the probability of getting (a) two heads in a row with a symmetrical coin; (b) three heads in a row?

---

*We can prove Bayes' Thorem, in the sense that it can be derived from a few of the other rules for calculating probabilities. Here is a proof of the simplified version of Bayes' Theorem:

1. $P(q, \text{given } p) = \dfrac{P(p \cdot q)}{P(p)}$ from general conjunction rule

2. $P(q, \text{given } p) = \dfrac{P(p \cdot q)}{P[(p \cdot q) \vee (p \cdot \sim q)]}$ because p is logically equivalent to $(p \cdot q) \vee (p \cdot \sim q)$

3. $P(q, \text{given } p) = \dfrac{P(p \cdot q)}{P[(p \cdot q) + (p \cdot \sim q)]}$ from restricted disjunction rule

4. $P(q, \text{given } p) = \dfrac{P(q) \times P(p, \text{given } q)}{P(q) \times P(p, \text{given } q) + [P(\sim q) \times P(p, \text{given } \sim q)]}$ general conjunction rule

3. Suppose it's as likely that a person be born on one day as on another. Then what is the probability that two people chosen at random both were born on April 19? (Forget about leap year.)

4. What is the probability of getting an even number or a number less than 3 (or both) with a standard six-sided die on a single toss?

5. Using a pair of symmetrical dice, what is the probability of getting (a) two 7s on the first two tosses; (b) any combination of 7s and 11s on the first two tosses?

6. Alpha Alpha Alpha fraternity has a blind date affair each month with Phi Phi Phi sorority. The custom is to randomly pair ten members of each group with ten of the other. What is the probability that Babs, a member of Phi Phi Phi, will be paired with the same guy on the next two dates?

7. What is the probability of getting *at least* two heads out of three with a symmetrical coin?

8. What is the probability of getting exactly two heads out of three with a symmetrical coin?

9. Suppose you draw two cards from a standard deck, replacing the first one before drawing the second. What is the probability that you'll get (a) two aces; (b) at least one ace; (c) two spades; (d) at least one spade?

10. Suppose you draw two cards from a standard deck, not replacing the first one before drawing the second. What is the probability that you'll get (a) two aces; (b) at least one ace; (c) two spades; (d) two black aces?

8   *Induction Is Unjustified—The Old Riddle of Induction*

Recall that the characteristic mark of all inductive (nondeductive) reasoning is a "gap" between premises and conclusion. As soon as this gap was realized,* the question of *how any inductive argument can be justified* was raised; that is, the question was raised about the *rationality* of the acceptance of hypotheses on inductive grounds.

Unfortunately, a good answer to this question has been hard to come by. A great many solutions to the problem of induction have been proposed, most of which can be classified into four categories.

1. The most obvious thought is that we are justified in using induction because it "works." All of science is based on inductive conclusions of some sort or other, and everyone knows how successful science is. Everyone knows that scientific method, which uses induction, *works.*

Unfortunately, this obvious solution to the problem is not satisfactory. It simply isn't true that we know that induction works, or is successful. At best, what we know is that it *has worked,* or *has been successful. But* will it be successful in the future? We don't know.

---

*The philosopher David Hume was the first person to perceive it clearly and to try to bridge it. See *A Treatise of Human Nature,* Book I, Part IV, Section I, and *An Enquiry Concerning Human Understanding,* Section V.

Indeed, the problem seems to be that we haven't the slightest reason to think induction will be successful in the future.

It often is claimed that in fact we do have a very good reason for thinking that induction will be successful in the future, namely its success in the past. But only a little thought is needed to see that this reason will not do. For to argue that induction will be successful because it *has* been successful is to argue *inductively*. (The premise of such an argument is "Induction has been successful [on the whole] up to now," and its conclusion is "Induction always will be successful [on the whole]." Clearly, this argument itself is an inductive argument.) So when we argue this way, we use induction to justify itself, which means that we argue circularly, and hence fallaciously.

2.   Perhaps the most popular solutions to the problem of induction are those that use some principle concerning the *uniformity of nature,* such as the principle that *every event has a cause.*

For instance, if we assume that nature is uniform, then we can reason inductively from the fact that all examined pieces of copper are uniform with respect to conductivity to the conclusion that all pieces of copper (examined or as yet unexamined) are uniform with respect to the conducting of electricity.

But solutions of this kind are unsatisfactory. First, even if nature is uniform, there is no guarantee that the particular uniformities we have observed up to a given time will hold in the future; the true uniformities of nature may be more complex or subtle. And second, the assumption that every event has a cause, or that nature is uniform, itself can be challenged. Why assume that nature is uniform? Again, there seems to be no answer. (Remember that we cannot argue that the assumption that nature is uniform has been fruitful in the past, and hence is likely to be fruitful in the future, for such an argument would be an inductive argument, and we cannot use induction to justify a principle of uniformity and then use that principle to justify the use of induction.)

3.   Some philosophers have proposed justifications based on the so-called self-corrective nature of induction.* For example, suppose we conclude that half of 10,000 tosses of a coin will land heads up, on the basis of the evidence that half of the first 100 tosses of this coin landed heads up. Suppose this conclusion is false. Then we can "correct" it simply by observing larger and larger coin tossing samples, basing our conclusion about the relative frequency of heads in the total series of 10,000 tosses on the relative frequency of heads in the largest sample we have at any given time. If we continue the process long enough, at some point we must reach the correct value. Hence, it is claimed, we are justified in using inductive reasoning in such cases because the process is self-correcting; repeated applications must get us closer and closer to the truth.

Suppose, for instance, that one half of 10,000 tosses of a coin in fact will land heads up. If we get heads on exactly half of the first 5,000 tosses, then we know with deductive certainty that the relative frequency of heads compared to total tosses in the entire series of

---

*See, for example, Charles Peirce, "Induction as Experimental and Self-Correcting," *Collected Papers of Charles Sanders Peirce,* Vol. VI, Charles Hartshome and Paul Weiss, eds. (Cambridge, MA: Harvard University Press, 1935). Reprinted in Edward H. Madden, *The Structure of Scientific Thought* (Boston: Houghton Mifflin, 1960), pp: 296–298.

10,000 tosses must be somewhere between 1/4 and 3/4.* Hence our prediction that half of the 10,000 tosses will be heads cannot be off by more than ± 1/4.

Now suppose that after 8,000 tosses the observed relative frequency of heads is still 1/2. Then we know at this point that the relative frequency of heads in the total series of 10,000 tosses must be somewhere between 2/5 and 3/5.[†] Hence, at this point our prediction that half of the 10,000 tosses will be heads cannot be off by more than ± 1/10. So we are getting closer and closer to the correct value (no matter what that value happens to be), since the *largest possible error* in our predictions keeps getting smaller and smaller.

The trouble is that our predictions get closer and closer to the correct value because larger and larger portions of the series concern *past tosses* and are incorporated into our *evidence,* while smaller and smaller portions of the series concern *future tosses.* At no point do we have any guarantee that we are getting any closer to the actual relative frequency of heads among future (unexamined) tosses of the coin. But if the self-corrective claim is to have any force, it must apply to predictions about the future (or the as yet unexamined past).

The situation is even worse for infinitely long series, because the relative frequency of any given finite portion of an infinite series is compatible with any relative frequency whatever in the infinite series. For instance, even if every one of millions of tosses of a coin lands heads up, the *limit* of such an infinite series of tosses (assuming an infinite series of tosses is possible) still might equal zero. Hence, for an infinite series, inductive practices embody no self-corrective feature whatever.

We must conclude, then, that we cannot justify the use of induction on the grounds that it is self-correcting.

4.   Finally, there are the so-called "dissolutions" of the problem of induction, according to which the very problem itself is a pseudoproblem.[‡] We shall consider two of the many solutions of this kind. In the first, it is claimed that it is not rational to doubt the principles of inductive reasoning because these principles themselves *determine* (in part) what it means to be rational. In other words, if we doubt the rationality (the reasonableness) of the use of induction, then we simply don't know what it means to be rational.

Unfortunately, this argument is defective. Were we to find ourselves in a community in which it is considered rational to believe everything said by the oldest member of the community, it would be reasonable to inquire if it *really* is rational to do so. And if the reply were that what it *means* to be rational is to believe the oldest member of the community, then it would be perfectly proper to ask *why* we should be rational. Put into this context, the problem of induction is that we seem to have no answer to the question, Why be rational? either for the peculiar concept of rationality in the imaginary community just described or for the concept of rationality in the real community.

According to the second kind of "dissolution" of the problem, there is no problem of justifying the use of inductive principles because *no justification is possible,* and if none is

---

*If the 5,000 remaining tosses are all tails, then the relative frequency will be 1/4, and if they are all heads, then the relative frequency will be 3/4.

†If the 2,000 remaining tosses are all tails, then the relative frequency will be 2/5, and if they are all heads, then the relative frequency will be 3/5.

‡See, for instance, A. J. Ayer, *Language, Truth and Logic* (New York: Dover), pp. 49–50.

possible, then none can be required. Two kinds of arguments have been presented in support of this claim.

First, it has been argued that such a justification would have to be either *inductive* or *deductive*. An inductive justification would be circular, since it would use the very principles of reasoning we are trying to justify. And we could never construct a valid deductive justification, because it is impossible to prove deductively that nature is uniform, or that every event has a cause, or that the future will resemble the past.*

But this argument is defective. It is true that metaphysical assumptions, such as the uniformity of nature, cannot be proved deductively. But a deductive justification does not necessarily require that any such principle be proved. Perhaps other kinds of assumptions can be proved that will justify the use of induction.†

Second, it has been argued that just as the theorems in an axiom system cannot all be proved (without circularity or infinite regress), so also all principles of *reasoning* or *inferring* cannot be justified (without circularity or infinite regress). Hence, we should not be surprised that no justification of induction is possible.

Clearly, there is something to this last argument. It is true that we cannot justify every principle of reasoning any more than we can prove every theorem. And it may well be that the basic inductive principle will be among those that remain forever unjustified and hence remain forever as a kind of primitive inference rule. But the argument in question does not prove this. All that it proves is that some principle or other will remain unjustified. It does not prove induction is that principle.

On the other hand, recognition of the important fact that some principle or other must remain unjustified may make it more tolerable that as yet no one seems to have been able to justify the basic principle of induction.

9 *Not All Instances of Theories Confirm Them— The New Riddle of Induction*

Perhaps the most curious of the objections raised against our account of scientific method is the one posed by Nelson Goodman's so-called *new riddle of induction.*

The old riddle, you will recall, has to do with justifying induction and inductive inferences in general, and in particular with justifying the belief that generalizations are confirmed by their instances (as, say, the generalization "All dogs have tails" is confirmed by finding an instance of it, namely a dog with a tail). The new riddle, according to Goodmanites, has to do with distinguishing those generalizations that *are* confirmed by their instances from those that are not.

---

*What is often meant by such an argument is that metaphysical principles of this kind are not *theorems of logics,* or *deductively obtainable from the null set of premises,* or *knowable prior to any particular empirical observations.*

†For instance, the pragmatic justification presented by Hans Reichenbach in *The Theory of Probability* (Berkeley: University of California Press, 1949), pp. 469–482, is based on an attempt to prove deductively that if any method of predicting the future is successful, then the use of induction will be successful.

To see the difference between these two kinds of cases, consider the following example. Suppose 100 emeralds, all of them green, are observed for color. This would usually be considered good evidence for the hypothesis or generalization (H-1) "All emeralds are green." But now let's introduce a new color term, "grue," referring to all things examined for color *before* a particular time *t*, say January 1, 2001, that are green, and to other things just in case they are blue. Then emeralds, for instance, will be "grue" just in case they either are green and the time in question is *before* time *t* or are blue and the time in question is at *t* or after. An emerald examined now and found to be green would thus be "grue," but one examined in the twenty-first century and found to be green would not be "grue" (it would, however, be "bleen," that is, it would be either examined before time *t* and blue, or not so examined and green).

All of the 100 green emeralds observed in our hypothetical example are "grue," as well as green, since they're green and the time is prior to time *t*. So according to what has been said so far about confirmation, it would seem that the 100 observed "grue" emeralds constitute confirming instances of the hypothesis (H-2): "All emeralds are grue," just as these same emeralds, being green, confirm (H-1): "All emeralds are green." But (H-1) and (H-2) *conflict* with each other, because according to (H-1) emeralds observed after time *t* will be green whereas according to (H-2) they will be blue. In fact, of course, no one would accept (H-2) no matter how many confirming cases we find in its favor. Goodman's problem is to find some way to distinguish "grue-like" illegitimate predicates and hypotheses from legitimate green-like ones, so that hypotheses like (H-1) will be confirmed by their instances whereas those like (H-2) will not.

Most of the proposed solutions to this problem are seriously defective. Rudolf Camap, for example, argued that terms like "grue" are what he called "positional," meaning that they are terms whose definitions in part refer to individual objects, or to individual places or times. But Camap's solution is unsatisfactory, in particular because lots of "good" predicates are positional and in fact are used in acceptable generalizations all the time. Some examples given by Goodman are "Ming," "Arctic," and "Pleistocene." Generalizations like "All Ming vases are expensive" would usually be held to be confirmed by their instances (in this case, by particular Ming vases that are expensive).

The interesting thing about Goodman's riddle is that an obvious answer lies right at hand and was proposed soon after Goodman formulated the problem; indeed it must have occurred independently to countless readers of the literature since then. Take our two competing hypotheses (H-1) "All emeralds are green" and (H-2) "All emeralds are grue." The first contains the "good" term "green," the second the "bad" term "grue." What is good about the former but bad about the latter? The first thought many of us have is that all green things *resemble* each other in a certain way, namely by being green in color, whereas there is no such color resemblance uniting all grue things, since items that are grue prior to time *t* are green, whereas those that are grue after time *t* are blue. What the term "green" *means* requires all items referred to by that predicate to resemble each other in color— share a common color—namely green. But what the term "grue" means does not require this; prior to time *t* grue things are green, after time *t* they are blue. By simply saying that only those generalizations containing terms like "green" are confirmed by their instances, the problem would seem to be solved. That is, it seems as though we can quite easily solve the problem by rejecting all generalizations containing terms like "grue," which select classes of items that do not necessarily all resemble each other in some relevant way. One idea behind inductive reasoning is, after all, to find items that resemble each other in some specified way that also share some other common property. In the case of (H- 1) "All emeralds are green," we find stones that resemble each other in being beryl silicates (and thus emeralds)* and discover that they also share the common property of being green. In the case of (H-2) "All emeralds are grue," there also is a shared common property, namely that of being grue, but that is not a *resembling* property—all grue things do not resemble each other in the appropriate way.

Perhaps the main reason why this obvious solution to the grue problem has not settled the matter is that Goodman provided what most writers on the subject have accepted as a conclusive objection to it. Goodman argued that given any two things, however different they may seem, we can always invent a property they both share, as we did in fact in inventing the property of being grue. That is, he argued that all grue things do in fact share a common property, namely that of being grue, and thus do in fact resemble each other (since they all are grue). We've noticed that all emeralds have resembled each other by being green, perhaps, because "green" is a term we've become familiar with through long use—it has become well entrenched in our language. But we've failed to notice that all emeralds so far encountered have resembled each other by being grue, perhaps because we're not familiar with and haven't used the term "grue"—it hasn't become entrenched in our language.

Underlying Goodman's view on the grue question is an extreme version of a very old philosophical position, called *nominalism* (something some of the nonnominalistic writers on the subject seem to have overlooked). In its extreme form, nominalism says that "there is nothing common to a class of particulars called by the same name other than that they *are* called by the same name."[†] That is why Goodman says that just as green things resemble each other in being green so also grue things *equally* resemble each other in being grue.[‡]

But suppose we reject the nominalist's view and accept the commonsense, everyday idea of resemblance that makes it wrong to speak of "grue" things as resembling each other just as much as do green things. (This is in fact what the vast majority of philosophers have done over the ages.) Then the Goodman problem fails to get off the ground,[‡‡] and our account of the philosophy of science remains intact.

---

*Goodman's choice of example was unfortunate in that according to one common definition of *emerald* a non-green beryl silicate would not be an emerald.

[†]A. D. Woozley in his article "Universals," in the *Encyclopedia of Philosophy,* Paul Edwards, ed. (New York: Collier Macmillan, 1967). Woozley's article also contains an excellent rebuttal of this extreme form of nominalism (in the opinion of this writer).

[‡]Goodman's basic nominalistic principle is that there are individual things in the world, and sums of individual things, but no general properties. (See his article "A World of Individuals" in *The Problem of Universals* [Notre Dame, IN: Notre Dame University Press, 1956].) But he is quickly led to the version of nominalism Woozley discussed, and without doubt believes, that any two things (for example, any two grue emeralds) may resemble each other just as much as any other two things (for example, any two green emeralds).

[‡‡]There are, of course, some wrinkles to take care of. For example, Goodman argues that lots of acceptable terms, such as "electrical conductor," are not resembling terms in the everyday sense; we therefore have to show what the resemblances might be like in these cases. See co-author Howard Kahane's article "Pathological Predicates and Projections" (*American Philosophical Quarterly,* vol. 8 (1971), pp. 171–178), for more on this, and also for some other thoughts on the grue problem and how to solve it, as well as for a bibliography on the subject.

Key terms

analogical inference: An inductive inference from particular instances to a conclusion concerning some other particular instance. An example is the inference from the evidence that three English suits wore well to the conclusion that some other English suit will wear well.

Bayes' Theorem: The simplified version is

$P(q,$ given $p) =$
$$\frac{P(q) \times P(p, \text{given } q)}{[P(q) \times P(p, \text{given } q)] + [P(\bar{q}) \times P(q, \text{given } \bar{q})]}$$

The completely general version is

$P(q_1,$ given $p) =$
$$\frac{P(q_1) \times P(p, \text{given } q_1)}{[P(q_1) \times P(p, \text{given } q_1)] + \ldots + [P(q_n) \times P(p, \text{given } q_n)]}$$

categorical analogy: Inductive inference from the evidence that all tested F's are G's to the conclusion that some as yet untested F is a G.

categorical inductive generalization: An inductive inference from particular instances to a universal conclusion. An example is the inference from the evidence that all observed ravens are black to the categorical generalization that all ravens are black. Synonyms: *universal inductive generalization, inductive generalization.*

causal connection (or relationship): A certain kind of constant conjunction between two sorts of things (for instance, between putting sugar in coffee and having the coffee taste sweet).

cause (and effect): A kind of causal connection in which the earlier of a pair of causally connected items is said to be the cause and the latter the effect.

dispositional property: An unobservable property or power. An example is the property of being flexible.

Dutch book: A series of bets placed so that a gambler must lose, no matter what the outcomes of the individual bets.

general conjunction rule: The rule that $P(p \cdot q) = P(p) \times P(q, \text{given } p)$.

general disjunction rule: The rule that $P(p \vee q) = P(p) + P(q) - P(p \cdot q)$.

independent events: Events that are not logically or causally related. An example is the event of drawing an ace from a deck and the event of again drawing an ace from the deck when the first ace has been put back into the deck.

inductive generalization: (See *categorical inductive generalization.*)

inverse probabilities: Backward probabilities. Example: The inverse probability of p, given q is $P(q, \text{given } p)$.

method of agreement: One of Mill's Methods, namely the method of inferring that if P is the only factor present in every observed occurrence of Q, then P and Q are causally related.

method of concomitant variation: One of Mill's Methods, namely the method of inferring that if a given phenomenon varies in some regular way with some other phenomenon, then the two phenomena are causally related.

method of difference: One of Mill's Methods, namely the method of inferring that whatever is present when Q is present, and absent when Q is absent, is causally related to Q.

Mill's Methods: Methods for finding (or confirming) causal relationships, championed by the nineteenth-century philosopher John Stuart Mill.

mutually exclusive events: Events such that it is logically impossible for both to occur. An example is the event of picking an ace on a given draw and picking a deuce on the same draw.

necessary condition: A part of what is required in order to produce a thing or event (or, in some cases, all of what is required). Example: The presence of oxygen is a necessary condition for the lighting of a match. (See also *sufficient condition.*)

observable entity: That which can be experienced or observed directly. Antonym: *theoretical entity.*

probability calculus: A set of rules for calculating probabilities from initial probabilities. For instance, the restricted disjunction rule is a member of this set, and allows us to calculate, say, that the probability of getting a red jack or black queen with an ordinary card deck is $1/26 + 1/26 = 2/26 = 1/13$.

probable cause: Causation in the statistical sense, used when we have just a statistical connection between cause and effect. Example: Cigarette smoking is a probable cause of most cases of lung cancer among cigarette smokers.

proximate cause: A cause relatively close in a causal chain to an effect. Example: A muscle twitch that causes someone's arm to rise. (See also *remote cause.*)

remote cause: A cause relatively distant in a causal chain from an effect. Example: The willing that causes someone's arm to move. (See also *proximate cause.*)

restricted conjunction rule: The rule that if p and q are independent events, then $P(p \cdot q) = P(p) \times P(q)$.

restricted disjunction rule: The rule that if p and q are mutually exclusive events, then $P(p \vee q) = P(p) + P(q)$.

statistical analogy: Inductive inference from the evidence that N percent of the tested F's are G's to the conclusion that the probability is N percent that some as yet untested F is a G.

statistical inductive generalization: An inductive inference from particular instances to a statistical conclusion. An example is the inference from the evidence that half of all tosses with this coin so far landed heads up, to the statistical conclusion that half of all tosses with this coin will land heads up.

sufficient condition: Whatever is sufficient to bring about a particular event. Example: Chopping off Marie Antoinette's head was a sufficient condition to cause her death. (See also *necessary condition.*)

theoretical entity: Postulated entity that cannot be experienced or observed directly. Antonym: *observable entity.*

universal inductive generalization: (See *categorical inductive generalization.*)

Chapter Fifteen

Axiom Systems

One way to *systematize* a given area of knowledge is to use an axiom system.

1   *The Nature of an Axiom System*

An axiom system has three main elements: symbols (or words), formulas, and inference rules. Symbols divide into **defined symbols,** for which explicit definitions are presented, and **primitive (undefined) symbols,** for which no definitions are presented. For instance, in an axiom system for anthropology, we might introduce the terms "parent" and "male" as primitives and then define the term "father" to mean "male parent." Symbols also divide into **logical symbols,** such as "and," "not," and "some" and **extralogical** or **nonlogical symbols,** which vary depending on the area of knowledge to be systematized.

Formulas break down into sentences and sentence forms (or functions).* They also divide into **axioms,** for which no justification is provided within the system, and **theorems,** which can be derived from the axioms by means of the inference rules of the system. Indeed, one of the main reasons for constructing axiom systems is to derive theorems from axioms.

Formulas also can be divided into **well-formed formulas,** such as $p \supset q$ and $\sim [(A \vee B) \supset \sim C]$, and those that are not, such as $(pq \vee$ and $AB) \vee$. (This distinction will be explained in more detail later.) And finally, inference rules divide into **primitive inference rules,** for which no justification is provided within the system, and **derived inference rules,** for which a justification is provided.

Of course, every system need not have all of these elements. For instance, we can have an axiom system without defined symbols or derived rules. But to be complete, an axiom system must have symbols, formulas, and inference rules.

One of the primary motives for constructing axiom systems is *rigor.* We want symbols precisely defined, and theorems rigorously proved. Consequently, it might be supposed that

---

*This is not quite true for what are called *uninterpreted* systems, because it is inappropriate to speak of the formulas of such systems as sentences or sentence forms.

to include *undefined* symbols, *unproved* axioms, and *unjustified* inference rules is to settle for something less than the ideal. But this is an illusion. It is impossible to define all symbols, prove all sentences, or justify all inference rules within a given system, except either circularly or by an infinite (and useless) series of definitions or proofs. (For example, it would be useless to define "automobile" as "car" and then to define "car" as "automobile." And it would be useless to attempt to present an infinite series of definitions, because to understand it one would have to run through the entire series, something impossible to do.) So we must settle for at least some undefined symbols, unproved axioms, and unjustified inference rules.*

Of course, undefined symbols must be understood, and the axioms and inference rules must be acceptable. Clearly, some symbols will not do as primitives in a rigorous system. But the question of which symbols and which axioms and inference rules are acceptable as primitives is in dispute. For instance, some claim that the axioms of an axiom system for deductive logic must be *intuitively acceptable,* or *self-evidently true,* whereas others say that, theoretically, any theorems of logic can be axioms, the choice being made to obtain the smallest possible set of axioms from which all theorems can be derived. But all agree that (other things being equal) it is desirable to have very few axioms or primitive rules of inference and very few undefined symbols.

It should be noted that the undefinability *within a system* of all terms of that system does not entail the inherent *undefinability* of any terms of that system. It may be that no terms are undefinable.

Most of us are familiar with at least one axiom system, Euclidean geometry, although it is normally presented only in a semirigorous form. (For instance, usually only a partial list of inference rules is provided.) But it is clear how such a system can be made more rigorous, and so we can take Euclidean geometry as our model of an axiom system.

2 *Interpreted and Uninterpreted Systems*

An **uninterpreted axiom system** is one in which the primitive symbols not only are not defined *within* the system but are given no meaning or interpretation whatever. (Of course, those who construct uninterpreted axiom systems generally have particular interpretations in mind. For instance, anyone who constructs an uninterpreted axiom system for sentential logic obviously has sentential logic in mind; otherwise there would be no point in calling it an uninterpreted system *for sentential logic.*)

The point of an uninterpreted system is to enable us to concentrate on form or structure without being distracted by content and to make it less likely that we will tacitly use knowledge not contained in the axioms of the system. For example, dealing with an uninterpreted axiom system for geometry makes it less likely that we will tacitly appeal to geometric intuitions not explicitly stated in the axioms and inference rules of the system.

---

*It is sometimes possible to reduce the number of axioms to zero by increasing the number of primitive inference rules. But we can never reduce the number of axioms *and* primitive inference rules in a given system to zero.

(In fact, Euclid himself made tacit use of information about geometry not explicitly stated in his system.)

An **interpreted axiom system** is one for which all of the primitive terms are assigned a meaning or interpretation. In some axiom systems the formulas when interpreted are sentences, in others they are sentence forms.

Notice that it is one thing to define a term within a system and another to assign a meaning to a primitive term. A term defined within a system is defined by the primitive terms of the system (or other terms so defined). Primitive terms are assigned meanings in other ways. For example, in applied geometry the primitive term "straight line" may be taken to refer to the path of a light ray.

Although there is some dispute about which terms are usable as primitives, other things being equal, terms whose meanings we clearly understand (however we obtain this understanding) are preferable to those that are vague or figurative.

3   *Properties of Axiom Systems*

Good axiom systems themselves have several important properties, in particular *consistency* and *completeness*.

Consistency

The most important requirement for an acceptable axiom system is *consistency*. An axiom system is **consistent** if and only if (iff) contradictory formulas cannot be derived from its axioms by means of its rules of inference. An axiom system that fails to satisfy this requirement, so that a contradiction is derivable as a theorem, is said to be *inconsistent* and is obviously unsatisfactory.

Example

A system containing the two axioms

(A1) $p \supset {\sim} p$
(A2) p

plus the two inference rules

(R1)   If p and $p \supset q$, then we can infer q. (Modus Ponens)
(R2)   if p and q, then we can infer $p \cdot q$. (Conjunction)

is inconsistent, since we can derive a contradiction in such a system, as follows:

1. $p \supset {\sim} p$ **Axiom**
2. p **Axiom**
3. ${\sim} p$ 1,2 **MP**
4. $p \cdot {\sim} p$ 2,3 **Conj**

The general procedure for proving that an axiom system is *inconsistent* is the same as the one for proving a set of premises inconsistent, namely the derivation of an explicit contradiction. But failure to derive a contradiction does not prove that a given axiom system is consistent, for we may have failed through lack of ingenuity. Instead, the general procedure for proving that an axiom system is consistent is to prove that a formula exists that is not derivable as a theorem of that system. This proves that a given axiom system is consistent because inconsistent systems permit the derivation of any and every expressible formula (since a *contradiction* logically entails any and every expressible formula). Hence, if there is some formula that cannot be derived as a theorem, then no contradiction can be derived either, and the system must be consistent.*

Expressive completeness

An axiom system is **expressively complete** iff its language is rich enough to express everything that the system is intended to express. For example, the usual axiom systems for Euclidean geometry are expressively complete, because they permit every statement (true or false) concerning geometry. But an axiom system for Euclidean geometry would be expressively incomplete if, say, it contained no method for stating sentences about circles.

Completeness

There is another kind of completeness, more frequently discussed in the literature than expressive completeness and much more difficult to state. This kind concerns the *provability* or *derivability* of formulas. Perhaps the best criterion we can give for this kind of completeness is that an axiom system is **complete** in this sense iff all of the formulas we *desire* to prove as theorems of the system in fact are provable as theorems of that system.

Although it is quite difficult to state precisely what this kind of completeness consists of *in general,* it is less difficult to characterize it for several of the more important kinds of axiom systems:

1. An axiom system for sentential logic is complete if every tautologous sentence or sentence form expressible in the system is provable as a theorem of the system.

2. In Chapter 5, sentences that can be known to be true by means of logic alone were called *theorems of logic.* Adopting this terminology, we can say that an axiom system for predicate logic is complete iff every theorem of logic is provable as a theorem of that system. (Notice that we cannot use the same criterion of completeness for predicate logic that we used for sentential logic because many theorems of predicate logic are not tautologies.)

---

*This criterion of consistency, known as "Post's consistency criterion" after its inventor E. L. Post, works only for *complete* systems. Incomplete systems that also are inconsistent may be such that there are formulas expressible in the system that are not provable.

3.   An axiom system for *arithmetic* is complete iff every sentence expressible in the system is such that either it or its negation is a theorem of the system. To see that this criterion is adequate, consider several kinds of typical sentences of arithmetic.

First, consider *unquantified* sentences, such as $2 + 2 = 4, 7 + 1 = 3$, and so on. Clearly, every such sentence is either true, in which case it is a theorem of arithmetic, or false, in which case its negation is a theorem of arithmetic. (An example of the latter would be the sentence $\sim (7 + 1 = 3)$, which is a theorem of arithmetic.)

Next, consider quantified sentences, such as $(x)(y)[(x + y) = (y + x)]$, $\sim (x)(x = x)$, and so on. Once again, it is clear that every such sentence is either true, in which case it is a theorem of arithmetic, or false, in which case its negation is a theorem of arithmetic.

Notice that the kind of completeness required of an axiom system for arithmetic is stronger than that required for sentential or predicate logic. We cannot require such a strict kind of completeness for logic, because axiom systems for logic contain either *contingent sentences* or *contingent sentence forms,* and neither they nor their negations are theorems of logic.

Axiom independence

An axiom of a given system is **independent** of the other axioms iff it cannot be derived from them using the inference rules of that system. Otherwise, an axiom is dependent.

Example

We can prove that the axioms contained in the system discussed in the footnote on page 317 are not independent by showing, for instance, the dependence of the axiom $(p \supset q) \equiv (\sim q \supset \sim p)$. And we can show *this* by deriving it as a theorem of the system, as follows:

1.	$p \supset q$	AP
2.	$\sim p \lor q$	1 **Impl**
3.	$q \lor \sim p$	2 **Comm**
4.	$\sim \sim q \lor \sim p$	3 **DN**
5.	$\sim q \supset \sim p$	4 **Impl**
6.	$(p \supset q) \supset (\sim q \supset \sim p)$	1–5 **CP**
7.	$\sim q \supset \sim p$	AP
8.	$\sim \sim q \lor \sim p$	7 **Impl**
9.	$\sim p \lor \sim \sim q$	8 **Comm**
10.	$\sim p \lor q$	9 **DN**
11.	$p \supset q$	10 **Impl**
12.	$(\sim q \supset \sim p) \supset (p \supset q)$	7–11 **CP**
13.	$[(p \supset q) \supset (\sim q \supset \sim p)] \cdot$ $[(\sim q \supset \sim p) \supset (p \supset q)]$	6,12 **Conj**
14.	$(p \supset q) \equiv (\sim q \supset \sim p)$	13 **Equiv**

Naturally, the above proof does *not* use Contraposition, since that would make the proof viciously circular and hence useless.

We can prove that a given axiom is *dependent* by deriving it from the other axioms of a system. But failure to find such a proof does not constitute a proof that an axiom is independent; we may simply have overlooked the proof.

To prove that an axiom is *independent* of a given set of axioms, it suffices to show that there is some characteristic or property possessed by every axiom in the given set, and also possessed by every formula derivable from that set of axioms, which is not possessed by the axiom in question. This proves independence because any particular axiom that does not have a property possessed by every formula derivable from a given set of axioms itself cannot be derivable from that set and hence itself must be independent of that set.

Decision procedure

A **decision procedure** is a mechanical method for determining in a finite number of steps whether or not a given formula is a theorem of an axiom system. For example, truth table analysis is a decision procedure for sentential logic, since it enables us to determine in a finite number of steps whether or not a given formula is a tautology and hence a theorem of sentential logic.

The existence of a decision procedure for a given axiom system renders all questions about the theorems of that system *routinely* answerable, without the need for ingenuity in the construction of proofs. This has the advantage that all questions and disputes about whether a particular formula is a theorem of the system can be settled by the mere manipulation of symbols of the kind that computers can be programmed to perform.

Axiom systems for which there is no decision procedure are generally of more interest to logicians and mathematicians, since questions and disputes about alleged theorems of these systems, even if in principle soluble, require genius (or a good deal of luck) for their solution. Indeed many such questions may go unanswered forever.

4 *Outline of an Axiom System for Sentential Logic*

Object language—metalanguage

We now present the bare outline of an axiom system for sentential logic. However, to do so, we must *talk about* that system. Since there is a sense in which that axiom system itself constitutes a language, we need some other language to talk about it. And since the sentential logic axiom system, "SL" for short, is the *object* of discussion, we can refer to it as the **object language** and refer to the language used to talk about SL as the **metalanguage.**

The terms "object language" and "metalanguage" are relative. For instance, if we use German to talk about English, then German is the metalanguage. But if we use English to talk about German, then English is the metalanguage. Of course, the same language can be both object and metalanguage. For instance, in an English grammar class conducted in English, English is used to talk about itself and hence is both object and metalanguage. (However, problems arise when we use a language to talk about its own *semantic* properties. The liar paradox discussed in Chapter 11 is an example.)

Quotation marks often are used to distinguish between *talk about* (or *mention of*) a language and *use of* a language. For instance, we can use English sentences to talk about, or mention, the state of Kansas. But we also can talk about, or mention, the *words used* to talk about the state of Kansas. In talking about the state of Kansas, we use its English name without quotes; in talking about the word that is the name of the state, we put that word, "Kansas," in quotes. Thus, we can say that "Kansas" has six letters, whereas Kansas is a state roughly in the center of the continental United States. We can also go one step further and talk about the name of the name of Kansas. Thus, we can say that "'Kansas'" contains quotation marks, whereas Kansas does not, and that "Kansas" is the name of a state, whereas Kansas is not (since it *is* a state). In other words, the device of quotation marks provides a convenient and automatic way for generating names of linguistic entities.

Another device used for generating names of linguistic entities is boldface and lightface type. For instance, we can use the term *w* in the object language *SL* and **w** in the metalanguage when we wish to talk about "*w*."

From the point of view of logic, many other methods for naming words would do just as well as the above two. For instance, we might refer to the word "Kansas" by the name "Art." And then we could say (truthfully) that Art has six letters, the first one "K," the second "a," and so on. But such a notation would be inconvenient to say the least.

We shall adopt ordinary English (suitably fortified with special terms to refer to the symbols of SL) as the metalanguage both of SL and of itself. But in our informal exposition, we also shall refer to many terms and expressions of SL and its metalanguage simply by placing them in quotation marks.

Syntax, semantics, pragmatics

The **syntactic properties** of a language are its *structural* properties, that is, those properties it has in abstraction from the meanings of its terms (other than the logical terms). For instance, the English sentence "John is tall" has the syntactic property of containing ten letters. And the sentence "Art is handsome and Betsy is smart" has the syntactic property of being a *conjunction*.

The **semantic properties** of a language are those properties that it possesses by virtue of the meanings of its terms. For instance, English has the semantic property of containing sentences stating arithmetic truths, such as "2 plus 2 equals 4," a semantic property that SL lacks. And the sentence "Snow is white" has the semantic property of containing a color term, namely the term "white." (Notice that uninterpreted systems have no semantic properties whatever, because their symbols have no meanings.)

The **pragmatic properties** of a language are those that it has in relation to its speakers (or users). For example, the English sentence "Snow is white" has the pragmatic property of *being believed* by many English-speaking people. And English itself has the pragmatic property of being spoken by most citizens of the United States.

Another way to look at the difference between syntax, semantics, and pragmatics is to say that the syntax of a language concerns the relationships between the elements of the language (such as letters, words, sentences, and so on), semantics the relationships between the elements of a language and the things that the language can talk about, and pragmatics the relationships between the elements of a language, the things it talks about, and the users of the language.

Little will be said here about the pragmatic properties of SL. However, we should bear in mind that in considering only the syntax and semantics of a language we are abstracting from the total language-use situation, which by its very nature must include language users. A "language" that no one ever uses or understands is no language at all.

Similarly, we should bear in mind that in discussing the syntax of an interpreted system, we are abstracting not only from its pragmatic properties but also from its semantic properties.*

The symbols of SL

An axiom system for sentential logic can be either interpreted or uninterpreted.† The axiom system SL, to be outlined here, is an interpreted system. This means that although the primitive terms are not defined in the system, they are taken to have their usual meanings.

All of the symbols of SL are primitive symbols. Among these symbols we distinguish *logical primitives* and *extralogical primitives*. (But there is no indication *within* SL whether a symbol is a logical or extralogical primitive. This distinction is made in the metalanguage.)

SL contains exactly four logical primitives, namely "~", "⊃", "(" and ")", in boldface type (the last two to be used as left- and right-hand parentheses, respectively).

In addition, SL contains indefinitely many *sentence variables, p, q, r,* and so on, as extralogical primitives.

Notice that the usual logical connectives "·", "∨", and "≡" do not occur in SL. They are omitted to simplify the number of primitive symbols and the number of axioms. However, their counterparts will be introduced later as *defined* terms in the metalanguage.

Definition of WFF

Among all possible finite strings of terms of SL, some are *well formed*, such as $((p \supset q) \supset p)$, $(p \supset \sim q)$, and so on, and some not, such as $(pp \supset \sim)$, $)(((p,$ and others. Intuitively, it is clear that all of the well-formed formulas (WFF for short) of SL are sentence forms. So we could define "WFF of SL" to mean "sentence form of SL." This would be a *semantic* definition of WFF. But we cannot always provide semantic definitions of WFF. For instance, we cannot do so for uninterpreted axiom systems, since they do not have semantic properties. The definition of WFF for an uninterpreted system must therefore be *syntactic*. And since we want SL to serve as an example, we shall provide a purely syntactic definition of "WFF of SL."

Of course, the definition of WFF occurs in the metalanguage, not in SL itself. So we need to introduce certain terms into the metalanguage to talk about the formulas of the object language SL. For this purpose, we introduce into the metalanguage the symbols *P, Q, R* and so on as *formula variables,* that is, as symbols in the metalanguage for which formulas in the object language can be substituted. Thus, in a given use, a formula variable

---

*However, in syntactic analyses, we generally do not abstract from the meanings of the *logical* terms of a system. This fact is frequently overlooked.

†Although some would deny that it makes sense to speak of an uninterpreted axiom system for any given area.

denotes any formula of the object language (subject to the usual rule concerning the use of variables, which requires that in a single context every occurrence of a given variable must denote the same formula).

We also introduce the symbols "⊃", "~", "(" and ")" in lightface type and stipulate (roughly) that these symbols denote the boldface type symbols "**⊃**", "**~**", "**(**" and "**)**" of the object language. (We also have available in the metalanguage the lightface type symbols *p, q, r,* and so on, that is, symbols that name particular formulas of the object language. However, these symbols are not used in the definition of WFF.)

Finally, to facilitate talk about the object language, we introduce the symbols "∨", "~", and "≡" as *defined terms* of the metalanguage:

(D1): "$(P \vee Q)$" is defined as an abbreviation for "$(\sim P \supset Q)$."
(D2): "$(P \cdot Q)$" is defined as an abbreviation for "$\sim (\sim P \vee \sim Q)$."
(D3): "$(P \equiv Q)$" is defined as an abbreviation for "$(P \supset Q) \cdot (Q \supset P)$."

These defined terms are sometimes useful in talking about the WFF's of SL, but they are not used in the definition of "WFF of SL" itself.

We now are ready to define the term "WFF of SL":

1. All sentence variables of SL are WFF's of SL.
2. If a formula P is a WFF of SL, then so is $\sim P$.
3. If P and Q are WFF's of SL, then so is $(P \supset Q)$.

We further state that no formula is a WFF of SL unless it is according to lines 1 through 3 above.

This definition provides an effective mechanical procedure for recognizing the WFF's of SL. If a formula is a WFF of SL, repeated application of the above definition will reveal this fact.* An infinite number of formulas of SL are WFF's according to this definition.

To illustrate how this definition works, consider the formula $(\sim (p \supset p) \supset q)$. According to line 1 of the definition, *p* and *q* both are WFF's. Therefore, according to line 3, $(p \supset p)$ is a WFF; and according to line 2, $\sim (p \supset p)$ is a WFF. Consequently, according to line 3, $(\sim (p \supset p) \supset q)$ is a WFF.

The axioms and inference rules of SL†

We stipulate three WFF's as the axioms of SL:

(A1): $(p \supset (q \supset p))$
(A2): $((p \supset (q \supset r)) \supset ((p \supset q) \supset (p \supset r)))$
(A3): $((\sim q \supset \sim p) \supset ((\sim q \supset p) \supset q))$

We also stipulate two rules of inference for SL. However, these two rules are formulated in the metalanguage, not in SL itself:

---

*However, it does not provide an effective mechanical procedure for determining in general *whether* a formula is a WFF of SL; that is, it does not provide a method for determining that a non-WFF is not a WFF of SL. But such a procedure can be provided.

†For details of a system just like SL, see Eliot Mendelson, *Introduction to Mathematical Logic* (Princeton, NJ: Van Nostrand, 1964).

(Rl): If $(P \supset Q)$ and P are either axioms or theorems of SL, then Q may be inferred from them.

(R2): If P is an axiom or theorem of SL, then any WFF may be substituted for any variable in P, provided the substitution is made for every occurrence of that variable in P.

(RI) already is familiar, since it is simply Modus Ponens. (R2) also should be familiar, since it simply states *explicitly* the rule of substitution *used implicitly* in the sentential and predicate logics presented earlier. For instance, (R2) permits inferences from $(p \supset (q \supset p))$ to $(r \supset (q \supset r))$ and to $((s \supset t) \supset (q \supset (s \supset t)))$, and so on.

We now define a *proof of SL* as a sequence of WFF's, all of which are axioms of SL or are inferable from the axioms by repeated applications of (RI) and/or (R2). For example, all sequences of WFF's of the object language having the forms

$(P \supset (Q \supset P))$
$(\sim P \supset (Q \supset \sim P))$

are proofs of SL. An example would be the sequence of formulas

$(p \supset (q \supset p))$
$(\sim p \supset (q \supset \sim p))$

which constitutes a proof of SL because the second WFF follows from the first by an application of (R2), and the first is an axiom of SL.

Another example of a proof having this form is the following sequence of formulas:

$(p \supset (q \supset p))$
$(\sim (r \supset s) \supset (q \supset \sim (r \supset s)))$

which also constitutes a proof because the second WFF follows from the first by an application of (R2).

Proofs of SL tend to be quite long and very difficult to construct, which is the price we have to pay for having so few axioms and inference rules. The following is a more complex proof of SL:

$(p \supset (q \supset p))$
$(p \supset ((q \supset p) \supset p))$
$((p \supset (q \supset r)) \supset ((p \supset q) \supset (p \supset r)))$
$((p \supset ((q \supset p) \supset p)) \supset ((p \supset (q \supset p)) \supset (p \supset p)))$
$((p \supset (q \supset p)) \supset (p \supset p))$
$(p \supset p)$

This constitutes a proof of SL because the first and third lines are axioms of SL, the second line follows from the first by (R2), the fourth line from the third by (R2), the fifth line from the second and fourth by (RI), and the sixth line from the first and fifth by (RI).

We now define a *theorem of SL* as a WFF for which a proof can be given in SL. Thus, the WFF $(\sim p \supset (q \supset \sim p))$ is a theorem of SL, since it follows from the axiom $(p \supset (q \supset p))$ by an application of (R2), and consequently a proof for it can be given in SL. (Of course, the *fact* that it is a theorem of SL, and the *fact* that the two above formulas constitute a proof of SL, cannot be stated within SL itself, but must be stated in the metalanguage.)

Properties of SL

Earlier, we discussed the properties—completeness, consistency, expressive completeness, and so on—that we want axiom systems to possess. The question arises as to which of these properties are possessed by SL, and the answer is that SL possesses all of them.

It has been proved that SL is complete (in the sense that every tautology is a theorem of SL), consistent, and expressively complete. In addition, it has been proved that there is a decision procedure for SL (namely, truth table analysis) and that its axioms are independent.*

5 Axiom Systems for Predicate Logic

Axiom systems for first-order predicate logic are quite similar to those for sentential logic. (Indeed, to be complete a system for predicate logic must contain a system for sentential logic as a part.) Let's briefly examine a particular system of this kind, which we'll call "QL" (for quantifier logic).

The symbols of QL

The primitive symbols of QL will be those of SL plus a set of predicate symbols *F, G, H,* and so on, a set of variables *x, y, z,* and so on, and the symbol *U,* used to denote the *universal quantifier.*

In addition, we introduce the symbol U into the metalanguage to denote the symbol U of the object language, the symbol u as a metalanguage variable ranging over the object language variables *x, y, z,* and also the symbol "∃," which is introduced by means of the following definition:

"$(\exists u)P$" is defined as an abbreviation for "$\sim (Uu) \sim P.$"

Let's take infinitely many formulas as axioms of QL, and introduce five axiom patterns in the metalanguage, using the letters *P, Q,* and *R* as formula variables, as before, and the letters *u* and *w* as metalinguistic variables ranging over the object language individual variables *x, y, z,* and so on:

(A1): $(P \supset (Q \supset P))$
(A2): $((P \supset (Q \supset R)) \supset ((P \supset Q) \supset (P \supset R)))$
(A3): $((\sim Q \supset \sim P) \supset ((\sim Q \supset P) \supset Q))$
(A4): $(Uu)(P \supset Q) \supset (P \supset (Uu)Q)$, where P contains no free occurrence of the variable u.
(A5): $(Uu)P \supset Q$, where Q results from P by the replacement of all free occurrences of u in P by w, and w occurs free in Q at all places at which u occurs free in P.[†]

---

*It is possible to construct a simpler axiom system for sentential logic, but the cost is even lengthier proofs and formulas.

†(A5) corresponds to the rule **UI** introduced in Chapter 8.

The inference rules of QL

We introduce (into the metalanguage) two rules of inference for QL:

(Rl): If $(P \supset Q)$ and P are either axioms or theorems of QL, then Q may be inferred from them.

(R2): If P is an axiom or theorem of QL, then $(Uu)P$ may be inferred from P.*

Properties of QL

It has been proved that QL is complete (in the sense that all sentence forms expressible in QL that are theorems of logic are provable as theorems of QL), consistent, and expressively complete. In addition, it has been proved that the axioms of QL are independent. However, not only is there no known decision procedure for QL, but it has been proved that *there cannot be such a decision procedure.*[†] This fact is of vital importance, because the existence of a decision procedure for predicate logic would make possible the construction of a machine capable of answering all questions about predicate logic in a purely mechanical way.

6   *Other Kinds of Axiom Systems*

Some philosophers have held that axiom systems are the ideal way to systematize in the *sciences,* just as in logic or mathematics, although as a matter of fact very few axiom systems for science have been attempted.

1.   As stated previously, we want an axiom system for arithmetic to be complete in a different sense than is required for logic. The difference stems from the fact that (roughly) systems for logic can express *contingent* sentences whereas those for arithmetic cannot. And since they cannot, all of their well-formed formulas that are sentences will be either *truths of arithmetic* or *negations of truths of arithmetic.* Hence, to be complete, an axiom system for arithmetic must be such that every sentence expressible in the system is either a theorem of that system or the negation of a theorem of that system.

2.   There are axiom systems for sentential and predicate logic that have been proved to be complete. Unfortunately, not only has no completeness proof been discovered for arithmetic, but it has been proved that *there cannot be a complete axiom system for all of arithmetic.*[‡] No matter how many axioms and theorems such a system contains, we can

---

*(R2) of QL corresponds to the rule **UG** introduced in Chapter 8. Because QL contains infinitely many axioms, it doesn't have to contain a rule of inference similar to the (R2) of SL.

[†]The proof was first given by Alonzo Church. For details on this and related topics, see S. C. Kleene, *Introduction to Meta-Mathematics* (New York: Van Nostrand, 1952).

[‡]More precisely, what has been proved is that there cannot be a complete and consistent axiom system for arithmetic. Obviously, an inconsistent system could be constructed that would be complete, but such a system would be worthless. The proof that arithmetic is essentially incomplete is by Kurt Gödel. For details, see S. C. Kleene, *Introduction to Meta-Mathematics.*

always find some truth of arithmetic that is not a theorem of that system. Indeed, having found such a truth, it won't help matters to add it to the list of axioms of the system, for it has been proved that no matter how many times we do this, there will always be other truths of arithmetic discoverable that are still not axioms or theorems of the system.

The proof that we cannot have a complete axiom system for arithmetic is widely regarded as one of the most important proofs about arithmetic ever constructed.

3.   It also has been proved that *there can be no decision procedure for axiom systems for arithmetic.* Thus, just as in the case of predicate logic, we can never construct a computer that will solve all of the problems of arithmetic in a purely mechanical way.

4.   Perhaps there is some consolation in the fact that proofs of consistency have been constructed for axiom systems for certain parts of arithmetic, and that decision procedures also have been devised for portions of arithmetic.

7   *Objections to Axiom Systems*

Finally, let's note that some philosophers are less than enthusiastic concerning the construction of axiom systems. One reason for this lack of enthusiasm is that the construction of an axiom system (at least for logic) involves a certain amount of *vicious circularity.*

Take an axiom system for predicate logic. Suppose we want to prove that such a system is *consistent.* The trouble is that a proof of consistency (in the metalanguage) unavoidably uses the very "tools of reasoning" (such as Modus Ponens) that are taken as inference rules in the system itself. Now if these "tools of reasoning" themselves are consistent, then a proof that the object language system is consistent is worthwhile. However, if they are inconsistent, then such a proof is worthless. So no progress is made by constructing a consistency proof, since we have to believe ahead of time in the consistency of the very rules of inference that the consistency proof establishes as consistent.*

Key terms

axioms: Underived formulas for which no justification is provided within the system.

complete (axiom system): An axiom system is complete iff all of the formulas we *desire to* prove as theorems of the system in fact are provable as theorems of that system.

consistent (axiom system): An axiom system is consistent iff contradictory formulas cannot be derived from its axioms by means of its rules of inference.

decision procedure: A decision procedure is a mechanical method for determining in a finite number of steps whether or not a given formula is a theorem of an axiom system.

defined symbols: Symbols for which explicit definitions are presented.

derived inference rules: The rules of an axiom system for which a justification is provided using other rules in the system.

---

*The same is true for the *axioms* of the system. Indeed, to be precise, we should speak of the consistency of the rules of inference *and* axioms, taken as a unit.

expressively complete: An axiom system is expressively complete if its language is rich enough to express everything that the system is intended to express.

extralogical or nonlogical symbols: Symbols other than logical symbols. The meaning of these symbols will vary depending on the area of knowledge to be systematized.

independent (axiom system): An axiom of a given system is independent of the other axioms iff it cannot be derived from them using the inference rules of that system.

interpreted axiom system: An axiom system for which all of the primitive terms are assigned a meaning or interpretation.

logical symbols: Symbols that represent logical operators such as "and," "not," "some," and so on.

metalanguage: When talking about the properties of a particular language, the metalanguage is the language that is used to talk about the object language.

object language: When talking about the properties of a particular language, the object language is the language that is the object of discussion.

pragmatic properties: The pragmatic properties of a language are those that it has in relation to its speakers (or users). For example, the English sentence "Snow is white" has the pragmatic property of *being believed* by many English-speaking people. And English itself has the pragmatic property of being spoken by most citizens of the United States.

primitive (undefined) symbols: Symbols for which no definitions are presented.

primitive inference rules: Rules in an axiom system for which no justification is provided within the system.

semantic properties: The semantic properties of a language are those properties that it possesses by virtue of the *meanings* of its terms.

syntactic properties: The syntactic properties of a language are its *structural* properties, that is, those properties it has in abstraction from the meanings of its terms (other than the logical terms).

theorems: Formulas that can be derived from the axioms by means of the inference rules of the system.

uninterpreted axiom system: An axiom system in which the primitive symbols not only are not defined *within* the system, but are given no meaning or interpretation whatever.

well-formed formulas: A string of symbols that is properly put together according to the "grammatical" rules of a system. For example, strings such as $p \supset q$ and $\sim [(A \lor B) \supset \sim C]$ are well-formed formulas in sentential logic, whereas $(pq \lor$ and $AB) \lor$ are not.

Chapter Sixteen

Alternative Logics

The predicate logic developed earlier in this text, many claim, cannot adequately capture the logical structure of many valid arguments. To correct this deficiency alternative systems of logic have been devised. In this chapter we will briefly introduce three such systems: *modal logics, deontic logics,* and *epistemic logics.*

1   *Modal Logic*

Modal logic is designed to express the logic structure of sentences that contain **modal terms,** that is, terms like "possible," "necessary," and their variants.* To extend sentential logic to handle modal sentences, we must add at least one symbol denoting a modal term. Let's introduce the diamond symbol "◊" as the **possibility operator,** used to symbolize sentences expressing possibilities. For instance, using the possibility operator, we can symbolize "*A* is possible" as ◊ *A*.

Examples

Here are some basic sentences that can be symbolized using the possibility operator (letting *S* = "Snow is white"):

Symbolization	*English Sentence*
1. ◊ *S*	1. It's possible that snow is white.
2. ◊ ~ *S*	2. It's possible that snow isn't white.
3. ~ ◊ *S*	3. It's not possible that snow is white.
4. ~ ◊ ~ *S*	4. It's not possible that snow isn't white.

---

*For more details on modal logic than are presented in this book, see G. E. Hughes and M. J. Cresswell, *Introduction to Modal Logic* (London: Methuen, 1968), and (particularly for the so-called Lewis systems) C. I. Lewis and C. H. Langford, *Symbolic Logic,* 2nd ed. (New York: Dover, 1959).

After one modal symbol has been introduced, others can be defined in terms of it. For instance, we can define the **necessity operator** "□" by the following definition:

$\Box p = \mathrm{df} \sim \Diamond \sim p$*

To say, for instance, that it's not possible that snow *isn't* white, in symbols $\sim \Diamond \sim S$, is, after all, to say exactly that it's necessary that snow *is* white. □ S, then, has the same meaning as $\sim \Diamond \sim S$.

Similarly, to say that it's impossible that snow is white is to say that it's necessary that snow isn't white. So the formula $\sim \Diamond \ S$ is logically equivalent to □ $\sim S$.

In fact, as should be apparent from the above, the possibility and necessity operators are linked in exactly the same way as are the existential and universal quantifiers of predicate logic.

Examples

Here are four logical equivalences relating the existential and universal quantifiers and the analogous equivalences relating the possibility and necessity operators:

Quantifier Equivalences

1. $(x)p :: \sim (\exists x) \sim p$
2. $(\exists x)p :: \sim (x) \sim p$
3. $(x) \sim p :: \sim (\exists x)p$
4. $(\exists x) \sim p :: \sim (x)p$

Modal Equivalences

1. $\Box p :: \sim \Diamond \sim p$
2. $\Diamond p :: \sim \Box \sim p$
3. $\Box \sim p :: \sim \Diamond p$
4. $\Diamond \sim p :: \sim \Box p$

2　*Strict Implication*

There are different kinds of possibilities and necessities. For instance, we might mean by "necessarily p" that p is **logically necessary** (true because of the laws of logic) or that it is **physically necessary** (true because of the laws of nature). Modal logic systems have been developed to capture the ideas of logical necessity, logical possibility, and logical impossibility. In particular, a modal logic seems to be needed to capture the concepts of **logical entailment** (or **logical implication**) and **logical equivalence.**

Take the notion of logical implication, or entailment. If p logically implies q, we can't symbolize that fact as $p \supset q$, because $p \supset q$ is too weak. It might be true, for instance, simply because p is false and not because its truth logically implies the truth of q.

But by using modal operators, we can symbolize statements of logical implication quite easily. For *p logically implies q if, and only if, $p \supset q$ is a theorem of logic,* and thus

---

*We introduce the symbol "= df" to abbreviate "is defined as."

necessarily true.* Letting the symbol " $\Rightarrow$ " stand for logical implication, or as it is usually called, **strict implication,** we can introduce the following definition:

$$p \Rightarrow q = \mathrm{df} \,\square\, (p \supset q)$$

Examples

Here are some sentences and their correct symbolizations using first the necessity operator and then the symbol for strict implication:

1. $(A \cdot B)$ logically entails A.
   $\square\,[(A \cdot B) \supset A]$
   $(A \cdot B) \Rightarrow A$
2. $(B \supset C)$ logically implies $(\sim C \supset \sim B)$.
   $\square\,[(B \supset C) \supset (\sim C \supset \sim B)]$
   $(B \supset C) \Rightarrow (\sim C \supset \sim B)$
3. $[A \vee (B \cdot C)]$ entails $[(A \vee B) \cdot (A \vee C)]$.
   $\square\,\{[A \vee (B \cdot C)] \supset [(A \vee B) \cdot (A \vee C)]\}$
   $[A \vee (B \cdot C)] \Rightarrow [(A \vee B) \cdot (A \vee C)]$
4. $(A \supset B)$ logically implies $(B \supset A)$.
   $\square\,[(A \supset B) \supset (B \supset A)]$
   $(A \supset B) \Rightarrow (B \supset A)$

(Of course, this last sentence is false, but we must be able to symbolize false sentences, also.)

It is important that the difference between " $\Rightarrow$ " and " $\supset$ " be grasped quite clearly, and that it be understood why " $\supset$ " does not capture the sense of logical implication. Take the modal sentence " 'Anna is smart' logically implies 'Bob is bombastic.' " Letting $A =$ "Anna is smart" and $B =$ "Bob is bombastic," we can symbolize the sentence as " $A \Rightarrow B$." Now if A and B both are true, then $A \supset B$ will be true. But $A \Rightarrow B$ is false, no matter what the truth-values of A and B, since A does not logically imply B. That is, $A \Rightarrow B$ is false because " $A \,/\therefore\, B$ " is not a valid deductive argument (even if A and B both happen to be true).[†]

Now let's introduce a symbol for logical equivalence, bearing in mind that two sentences are *logically equivalent* if and only if they logically imply each other. Letting the symbol " $\Leftrightarrow$ " represent logical equivalence, we can introduce the following definition:

$$p \Leftrightarrow q = \mathrm{df}\, (p \Rightarrow q) \cdot (q \Rightarrow p)$$

---

*Or in the case of sentence forms, if and only if all of its substitution instances are true.

[†]This account of the logical necessity captured by the " $\Rightarrow$ " symbol avoids the controversy over semantic analytic truths. Most philosophers want the notion of logical implication to be wide enough to make, say, "(Art is a bachelor) $\Rightarrow$ (Art is unmarried)" a true modal statement, but some do not.

Examples

Here are some equivalences and their translations using the symbol for logical equivalence:

1. $(A \cdot B)$ is logically equivalent to $(B \cdot A)$.
    $(A \cdot B) \Leftrightarrow (B \cdot A)$
2. $(A \supset B)$ is logically equivalent to $(\sim B \supset \sim A)$.
    $(A \supset B) \Leftrightarrow (\sim B \supset \sim A)$
3. $(A \cdot B)$ is logically equivalent to A.
    $(A \cdot B) \Leftrightarrow A$

(Of course, this last sentence is false.)

3   *Modal Axioms*

The philosopher C. I. Lewis constructed the first axiom systems for sentential modal logic. Indeed, he constructed several nonequivalent modal systems.

The fact that *nonequivalent* systems have been proposed and argued about illustrates a difference in status between the ordinary truth-functional logic and non-truth-functional modal logic; modal logic is much more controversial than ordinary truth-functional logic. It is true that some argue against sentential or predicate logic on the grounds that they cannot adequately handle some of the non-truth-functional sentences of natural languages. But no one would argue that any of the axioms of an axiomatized sentential or predicate logic are *false.* Yet that is precisely the situation for modal logic. Modal axioms have been proposed whose very truth is in question.

Let's now examine the Lewis modal axioms (passing over the technical details of his systems). Here are thirteen of his axioms, the first eleven being used by Lewis in developing his modal systems S1 through S5 (along with their sentential logic analogues):*

Modal axiom	Sentential logic analogue	
(1) $(p \cdot q) \Rightarrow (q \cdot p)$	$(p \cdot q) \supset (q \cdot p)$	(Comm)
(2) $(p \cdot q) \Rightarrow p$	$(p \cdot q) \supset p$	(Simp)
(3) $p \Rightarrow (p \cdot p)$	$p \supset (p \cdot p)$	(Taut)
(4) $[(p \cdot q) \cdot r \Rightarrow [p \cdot (q \cdot r)]$	$[(p \cdot q) \cdot r \supset [p \cdot (q \cdot r)]$	(Assoc)
(5) $p \Rightarrow \sim \sim p$	$p \supset \sim \sim p$	(DN)
(6) $[(p \Rightarrow q) \cdot (q \Rightarrow r)] \Rightarrow (p \Rightarrow r)$	$[(p \supset q) \cdot (q \supset r)] \supset (p \supset r)$	(HS)
(7) $[p \cdot (p \Rightarrow q)] \Rightarrow q$	$[p \cdot (p \supset q)] \supset q$	(MP)

---

*With minor changes.

(8) $\Diamond\,(p \cdot q) \Rightarrow \Diamond\,p$
(9) $(p \Rightarrow q) \Rightarrow ({\sim}\,\Diamond\,q \Rightarrow {\sim}\,\Diamond\,p)$
(10) $\Box\,p \Rightarrow \Box\Box\,p$
(11) $\Diamond\,p \Rightarrow {\sim}\,\Diamond\,{\sim}\,\Diamond\,p$
(12) $p \Rightarrow {\sim}\,\Diamond\,{\sim}\,\Diamond\,p$
(13) $\Diamond\,\Diamond\,p$

The system S1 contains the first seven axioms (axiom (5) incidentally, can be derived from the others and is thus superfluous); S2 the first seven plus (8); S3 the first seven plus (9); S4 the first seven plus (10); and S5 the first seven plus (10). It has been proved that every theorem of S1 is a theorem of S2, every theorem of S2 a theorem of S3, and so on (but not vice versa). Thus, as you go up the Lewis modal ladder, the systems get stronger and stronger. (The problem is just how strong the *right* system should be.)

Axioms (10) and (13) are contraries. So on the assumption that there is at least one necessary proposition, we must reject either (10) or (13). This is unfortunate, because many have found both of these axioms, taken alone, to be intuitively plausible.

In addition, axiom (10) itself has generated a great deal of controversy. Take as an example the necessary sentence "Snow is white or it isn't." Clearly that sentence is necessary, since it is a logical truth. But is it *necessary* that it is necessary? Opinions seem to differ. (It should also be noted that adoption of S5 leads to the interesting consequence that all modal propositions will be either necessarily true or necessarily false, a consequence that some find unacceptable.)

4   *Modal Theorems*

There is a very close resemblance between the theorems (counting axioms as theorems) of modal logic and the theorems of sentential logic that correspond to the valid argument forms discussed in Part One. With three exceptions, these theorems parallel one another. For instance, corresponding to the theorem we might by extension call *Modus Ponens,* namely, $[p \cdot (p \supset q)] \supset q$, is the modal theorem $[p \cdot (p \Rightarrow q)] \Rightarrow q$. The three exceptions are *Implication, Exportation,* and one version of *Equivalence.* (In particular, $(p \Rightarrow q) \Leftrightarrow ({\sim}\,p \vee q)$, the modal parallel to *Implication,* is *not* a modal theorem.) However, for each of these there are slightly altered parallels. Thus for *Implication* there is $(p \Rightarrow q) \Rightarrow ({\sim}\,p \vee q)$, for *Exportation* there is $[(p \cdot q) \Rightarrow r] \Leftrightarrow [p \Rightarrow (q \supset r)]$, and for *Equivalence* there is $(p \Leftrightarrow q) \Rightarrow (p \cdot q) \vee ({\sim}\,p \cdot {\sim}\,q)]$.

Here are some other interesting theorems of modal logic, all provable in S5, although some are not provable in S4, S3, S2, or S1, and thus are controversial:

1. $(p \Rightarrow q) \Rightarrow (p \supset q)$
2. $(p \Leftrightarrow q) \Rightarrow (p \equiv q)$
3. $\Box\,(p \Leftrightarrow q) \Leftrightarrow (p \Leftrightarrow q)$
4. $(p \Rightarrow q) \supset (\Box\,p \Rightarrow \Box\,q)$
5. $\Diamond\,p \Rightarrow {\sim}\,\Diamond\,{\sim}\,\Diamond\,p$
6. $\Box\Box\,p \Rightarrow \Box\Box\Box\,p$
7. $\Diamond\,p \Rightarrow \Diamond\,\Diamond\,p$

8. $\Box\,(p\cdot q) \Leftrightarrow (\Box\,p\cdot\Box\,q)$
9. $\Diamond\,(p\vee q) \Leftrightarrow (\Diamond\,p\vee\Diamond\,q)$
10. $\Diamond\,(p\cdot q) \Rightarrow (\Diamond\,p\cdot\Diamond\,q)$ [but not vice versa]
11. $(\Diamond\,p\vee\Diamond\,q) \Rightarrow \Diamond\,(p\vee q)$ [but not vice versa]

5   *Modal Paradoxes*

When he developed his modal systems, Lewis pointed out that there are apparently paradoxical theorems in modal logic analogous to the alleged paradoxes of material implication.* One example is the theorem:

$$\sim\Diamond\,p \Rightarrow (p\Rightarrow q)$$

But Lewis felt that this theorem is acceptable, in spite of its apparent paradoxicality. For it merely states the principle behind the rule of *indirect proof* (*reductio ad absurdum*)—that what is contradictory (not possible) logically implies anything and everything.

    Another theorem that appears paradoxical is this one:

$$\Box\,p \Rightarrow (q\Rightarrow p)$$

Lewis felt this theorem also is acceptable, because it merely states the principle that we can deduce a tautology (necessarily true sentence) from any sentence whatever, which must be accepted since a tautology can be deduced even from the null set of premises.

6   *A Philosophical Problem*

At the beginning of this chapter, we introduced the topic of modal logic by saying that it is *claimed* by many that we need a special logic to deal with sentences containing modal terms. The word "claimed" was inserted because some deny that a special modal logic is needed at all.[†]
    One objection is that if " $\Box\,p$" *means* the same as "p is a theorem of logic" or "p is provable," then the statements of modal logic all become statements expressible in the *metalanguage* of any given system without the need to introduce special modal symbols.[‡] But lurking behind the dispute is the more serious question of exactly what necessity, possibility, and so on consist in. One view is that necessity is a purely linguistic concept. A theorem is provable, according to this view, precisely because of linguistic conventions. That is, a theorem is true just because of the meanings of its terms. (This theory is consis-

---

*Recall our brief discussion on pages 247–249.

[†]See, for instance, Gustav Bergmann, "The Philosophical Significance of Modal Logic," *Mind,* vol. 69 (1960), pp. 466–485.

[‡]Another is that in any event the term "modal *logic*" is a misnomer because the axioms of modal logic are not *logical* truths, containing as they do nonlogical constants such as "$\Box$" and "$\Diamond$".

tent with the view that theorems of logic and logical truths are provable from the null set of premises precisely because they are empty of factual content.)

On the other side are those who insist that necessity is more than merely linguistic, that necessities are real and independent of language conventions or even the existence of language users.

Those who hold the latter view tend to accept the principle that $\Box p \Rightarrow \Box \Box p$ (sometimes called the *axiom of reiterated necessity*). Those who hold the former view (that necessity is essentially linguistic) deny that principle, because if "$\Box p$" *means* the same as "*p* is a theorem of logic," then the axiom of reiteration would appear false. (For to be true it would have to be the case that the statement "*p* is a theorem of sentential logic" is itself a theorem of sentential logic, which it is not.)

7   *Modal Predicate Logic*

So far, we have been discussing modal extensions of sentential logic, a fairly controversial topic. Now let's very briefly discuss modal *predicate* systems, an even more controversial area.

There are two important problems with modal predicate logic systems, in addition to the ones it inherits from modal sentential logic. The first concerns the validity in modal logic of the four quantifier rules, as well as the rule of *identity* **(ID).***

Consider the following argument (where $a =$ "the number of planets"):

1. $(x)[(x = 9) \supset \Box (x > 7)]$ p
2. $a = 9$ $p\; /\therefore\; \Box (a > 7)$
3. $(a = 9) \supset \Box (a > 7)$ 1 **UI**
4. $\Box (a > 7)$ 2,3 **MP**

It appears that both premises are true and the conclusion false (since it isn't necessary that the number of planets be greater than seven). And yet the conclusion follows from the premises by the normal inference rules of predicate logic (in this case **UI** and **MP**).

Examples of this kind have elicited several different responses. One, of course, is simply to reject modal predicate logic entirely, as ill conceived. Another is to devise restrictions on the four quantifier rules (as well as the rule of identity, to handle related problems arising from the use of that rule). For instance, we seem able to block undesirable consequences of the kind just illustrated by placing a new restriction on the general schema for **UI:**†

$(u)(\ldots u \ldots .)$
$/\therefore (\ldots w \ldots) \ldots$

---

*See for instance, W. V. Quine, "Notes on Existence and Necessity," *The Journal of Philosophy,* Vol. 40 (1943), pp. 113–127.

†See Richard L. Purtill, *Logic for Philosophers* (New York: Harper & Row, 1971), pp. 289–291.

Proviso: No u free in ... u ... is within the scope of a necessity operator, unless (... w ...) is necessary (that is, unless $\Box$ (... w ...)).

This seems to eliminate the troublesome use of **UI** in the above example because the x in the phrase "$x > 7$" on line 1 is within the scope of a necessity operator. (But it doesn't rule out the legitimate use of **UI** in the inference from, say, $(x)[(x = 9) \supset \Box (x > 7)]$ to $(3^2 = 9) \supset \Box (3^2 > 7)$, because the latter is necessarily true.)

Finally, another way out of the problem is to argue that in spite of appearances, rule **UI** is universally valid in modal predicate logic. Take the example in question. Either a (the expression "the number of planets") designates the number 9, or it does not. If it does, then premise 2 is true. *But so is the argument's conclusion,* since the number 9 necessarily is greater than 7. So if a designates the number 9, the argument in question does not take us from true premises to a false conclusion, and we haven't proved the inference pattern invalid.

Now suppose that a does *not* designate the number 9. Then premise 2 is false, since it asserts that a is identical with the number 9, which must be false if a does not designate the number 9. (Obviously, only the number 9 is identical with the number 9, so if a does not designate that number what it does designate cannot be identical with the number 9.) So if a does not designate the number 9, one of the premises is false, we have not gone from true premises to a false conclusion, and thus have not proved that the argument schema is invalid in modal predicate logic. It may well be valid after all.

A second important problem for modal predicate logic is simply to decide which of the many plausible candidates should be accepted as *theorems* of modal predicate logic. Let's end our very brief discussion of modal logic by listing a few theorem candidates, then explaining why some of them are controversial (letting p and q be any well-formed formulas and "(u)" and "$(\exists u)$" be respectively any universal or existential quantifiers):

(A)	$(\exists u) \Box p \Rightarrow \Box (\exists u)p$
(B)	$\Diamond (u)p \Rightarrow (u) \Diamond p$
(C)	$(\exists u) \Diamond p \Leftrightarrow \Diamond (\exists u)p$
(D)	$\Box (u)p \Leftrightarrow (u) \Box p$
(E)	$\Box (u)(p \supset q) \supset \Box [(u)p \supset (u)q]$
(F)	$(u) \Box (p \supset q) \supset \Box [(u)p \supset (u)q]$

The first two of these formulas, although intuitively unobjectionable, are interesting because they generally are believed not to hold in the opposite direction. Take the reverse of (A), namely $\Box (\exists u)p \Rightarrow (\exists u) \Box p$, and consider the substitution instance $\Box (\exists x)Nx \Rightarrow (\exists x) \Box Nx$, where $Nx =$ "x is the number of planets." The antecedent of this expression states that necessarily some x is the number of planets, which is true, because even if there were no planets there still would of necessity be some number of planets (namely zero). But the consequent of this expression seems to be false, because there is no number that *necessarily* is the number of planets (since the actual number of planets is a contingent and not a necessary fact—logic does not dictate that there be exactly nine planets).

Now consider the reverse of (B), namely $(u) \Diamond p \Rightarrow \Diamond (u)p$, and consider the substitution instance $(x) \Diamond Nx \Rightarrow \Diamond (x)Nx$, where again $Nx =$ "x is the number of planets." The antecedent of this expression states that given any x, it is possible that x is the number of

planets, which is true because logic does not require that there be any certain number of
planets (instead of nine there might have been eight or seven or a million, so far as logic is
concerned). But the consequent of this expression is false because it is not possible that
every number be the actual number of planets.

Although (A) and (B), above, are generally accepted, and their reverses generally
rejected, (C) seems more problematic. Consider, for instance, the substitution instance
$(\exists x) \diamond Fx \Leftrightarrow \diamond (\exists x)Fx$, where $Fx =$ "*x* is on fire."* If we suppose that $(\exists x) \diamond Fx$
translates back into English as "There is something that may be on fire," and $\diamond (\exists x)Fx$ as
"There may be something on fire," then clearly the two do not strictly imply each other.
So if we want to accept (C) as a legitimate modal theorem, we must find some other
translation for the substitution instance in question.[†]

Theorem (D) above is also extremely controversial. Specifically, the controversy centers
on a particular consequence of (D), namely the formula $(u) \Box p \Rightarrow \Box (u)p$, called the
Barcan Formula.[‡]

At first glance, this formula seems acceptable. But consider one of its instances, say the
sentence $(x) \Box Tx \Rightarrow \Box (x)Tx$, where $Tx =$ "*x* is triangular." In the actual universe, the
antecedent of this statement is false, and hence the whole statement is true. But logical
principles have to be valid in all possible universes, not just the real one. So imagine a
universe containing nothing but trilaterals. Then, since all triangles are necessarily also
trilaterals, the left-hand side of the Barcan substitution instance, namely $(x) \Box Tx$, will be
true. But the right-hand side, namely $\Box (x)Tx$, appears to be false. For even though *in fact*
all *x*'s would be triangular in the world we have just imagined, it wouldn't be *necessary*
that all things in that universe be triangular; it *might* have contained some squares, circles,
or other nontriangles.

Hence, it is argued that the Barcan Formula is not acceptable. (Since the Barcan Formula
can be derived as a theorem in any modal predicate logic containing the Lewis system S5
as its sentential component, those who reject the Barcan Formula also have to reject S5.
Conversely, those who accept the Barcan Formula are almost certainly committed to accepting S5.)

8   *Epistemic Logic: The Logic of Knowledge and Belief*

In discussing the limitations of predicate logic (Chapter 10), we pointed out that it is not
clear whether predicate logic can adequately handle sentences containing so-called belief
contexts, such as the sentence "Art believes he'll go to the show." Attempts to develop a
logic of knowledge and belief, an **epistemic logic,** are intended to extend predicate logic
so that it can deal with such cases.

---

*The example is from W. Kneale and M. Kneale, *The Development of Logic* (London: Oxford University Press, 1962), p. 615.

[†]For instance, see Purtill, pp. 263–265.

[‡]After Ruth Barcan Marcus. See her article "A Functional Calculus of First Order Based on Strict Implication," *Journal of Symbolic Logic,* Vol. II (1946), p. 2.

The application of the standard rules of predicate logic to epistemic contexts is in doubt, just as is their application in modal contexts. Here is an example in which the rule of identity, **ID,** seems to fail when used in an epistemic context:

1. Art believes that Mark Twain wrote *Huckleberry Finn.*
2. Mark Twain = Samuel Clemens.
3. Art believes that Samuel Clemens wrote *Huckleberry Finn.* 1,2 **ID**

If we let Bxy = "x believes that y"; t = "Mark Twain"; c = "Samuel Clemens"; h = "Huckleberry Finn," a = "Art"; and Wxy = "x wrote y," then we can symbolize the above argument as:

1. $Ba\,(Wth)$
2. $t = c$
3. $Ba\,(Wch)$ 1,2 **ID**

The problem with this example is this. Suppose Art happens to be ignorant of the fact that Mark Twain and Samuel Clemens are the same person. Then it seems possible for premises 1 and 2 of this argument both to be true when the conclusion 3 is false. If so, then it is possible to go from true premises to a false conclusion by the rule of identity, something no valid system may permit.

Now let's look at an example where it is claimed that the quantifier rule **EG** gets us into trouble:*

1. Philip is unaware that Tully denounced Cataline.
2. Some x is such that Philip is unaware that x denounced Cataline.   1 **EG**

Letting Uxy = "x is unaware that y" and using other obvious abbreviations, we can symbolize this argument as:

1. $Up\,(Dtc)$
2. $(\exists x)Up(Dxc)$ 1 **EG**

Suppose we assume that Philip really is not aware that Tully denounced Cataline, but is aware that Cicero did, even though (unknown to Philip) Tully = Cicero. Then, it has been argued, although 1 is true, 2 is false. For who is the x who denounced Cataline without Philip learning of that fact? Tully, that is, Cicero? No, because this would conflict with the fact that the statement "Philip is unaware that Cicero denounced Cataline" is false. Hence, the inference from 1 to 2, it is claimed, is invalid.

Finally, consider one more example. Suppose it is true that some little child, say Virginia, believes that Santa Claus comes down her chimney every Christmas bringing toys. Then using rule **EG,** we can construct the following apparently invalid argument (letting Cx = "x comes down Virginia's chimney on Christmas"; g = "Virginia"; and c = "Santa Claus"):

---

*The example is from W. V. Quine, "Notes on Existence and Necessity," *Journal of Philosophy,* Vol. 40 (1943), pp. 117–118. Quine claims that this example shows rule **EG** must be restricted in epistemic contexts.

1. $Bg(Cc)$
2. $(\exists x)Bg(Cx)$ 1 **EG**

Again, we seem hard pressed to find an x that would make 2 a true statement. In particular, *Santa Claus* does not seem to be such an x, since, sad to relate, Virginia, there *is* no Santa Claus.

We can't go into all of the claims and counterclaims on this topic, but let's briefly look into a line of reasoning that parallels the defense (discussed on page 376) of the use of **UI** in modal contexts.

Consider again the argument.

1. $Ba(wth)$
2. $t = c$
3. $Ba\ (Wch)$ 1,2 **ID**

Either c designates the person Mark Twain or it does not. Suppose it does. (We're assuming, of course, that the term t designates the person Mark Twain.) Then if premise 1 is true (if Art believes the person Mark Twain wrote *Huckleberry Finn*), then so is the conclusion true (that Art believes the person Sam Clemens [also known as Mark Twain] wrote *Huckleberry Finn*). We thus will have moved from true premises to a true conclusion, and so the argument will be valid. Therefore this case can't be an example of the failure of **ID** in epistemic contexts.

Now suppose c does not designate the person Mark Twain. Then the second premise of this argument, which states that $t = c$, will be false (given that t does designate Mark Twain). We thus will not have moved from true premises to a false conclusion, and so this case can't be an example of the failure of **ID** in epistemic contexts.

In like manner, it is claimed, all of the varied examples alleged to illustrate the validity of rule **ID** in epistemic contexts can be successfully rebutted.*

It also is claimed that some (but not all) of the alleged counterexamples to the legitimacy of rule **EG** in epistemic contexts can be easily disposed of. Recall the one above about Philip being unaware that Tully denounced Cataline:

1. $Up\ (Dtc)$
2. $(\exists x)Up(Dxc)$ 1 **EG**

It was objected that although 1 is true, 2 is false, since there seems to be no x who denounced Cataline without Philip learning of that fact.

But surely, if there is no such x, then premise 1 is false (and so we will not have moved from true to false). After all, for Philip to be unaware that Tully was the denouncer, there must be an x, namely Tully, whose actions Philip is unaware of; if there is no such x, then Philip can't be unaware of his actions, and premise 1 will be false. (What is true, of course, is that Philip is unaware that the person he knows as *Cicero* also was known as *Tully*.)

---

*For a defense of his view, write to Professor Kahane for a copy of his unpublished "Quine and the Substitutivity of Identity."

9 *Epistemic Theorems*

A second problem for epistemic logic, again paralleling modal predicate logic, is the difficulty in deciding which epistemic statements we want to be theorems of epistemic logic. Here are a few of the obvious candidates (letting Kap = "*a* knows that *p*" and Bap = "*a* believes that *p*"):

1. $Kap \supset Bap$
2. $Ka \sim p \supset \sim Bap$
3. $\sim Kap \supset Ba \sim p$
4. $Kap \supset p$
5. $Bap \supset p$
6. $Kap \supset KaKap$
7. $Bap \supset BaBap$
8. $Bap \supset KaBap$
9. $Kap \supset BaKap$

Of these, (3) and (5) clearly are inadmissible. From the fact that Art doesn't know that Sophia is the capital of Bulgaria, it doesn't follow that he believes it isn't the capital of Bulgaria. So (3) must be rejected. And from the fact that Johnny believes Santa Claus comes down his chimney, it doesn't follow that Santa actually does so. So (5) must be rejected.

On the other hand, (1) clearly is acceptable; you can't know something without believing it. But all the others, however plausible they may initially appear, are open to doubt, or at least some have thought so.

Take (6), often called the **KK thesis,** according to which if you know something, it follows that you know you know that thing. One argument against the KK thesis is this:*
For a person *a* to know something, *a* must *understand* that thing. Hence, to know *p*, *a* has to understand *p*. But for *a* to know that *a* knows *p*, *a* must understand not only *p* but also the sentence "*Kap.*" It seems possible for *a* to understand *p*, but not understand "*Kap,*" and hence possible that *a* knows *p*, but does not know that *a* knows *p*.

Since similar remarks seem to apply to believing, formulas (7), (8), and (9) also appear to be fairly doubtful.

Now let's consider (2), which states that if *a* knows $\sim p$, then *a* doesn't believe *p*. If knowing *p* entails believing *p*, and if no one can believe contradictory propositions, then (2) has to be accepted. But there are those who claim that it is possible to believe contradictory propositions. And this is possible, then (2) must be rejected. For then someone might know $\sim p$ and still believe *p*.

Finally, there are a few who might reject even (4), which says that if you know *p*, then *p* must be the case. The idea behind this formula is that one cannot know something that is

---

*The argument is given by Arthur C. Danto in "On Knowing That We Know," in Avrum Stroll, ed., *Epistemology* (New York: Harper & Row, 1967), pp. 32–53.

false. But some pragmatists* have denied that one cannot know something that is false, because their pragmatic explication of the concept of knowledge does not make the truth of a sentence a necessary condition for knowing that sentence.

10 *Deontic Logic*

Predicate logic, modal logic, and epistemic logic all can be said to be **operator logics,** because they deal with operators (we called them quantifiers when we discussed predicate logic) that bind parts of expressions. Recently, attempts have been made to develop a similar system for another area of philosophy, namely certain kinds of reasoning in ethics. The result is **deontic logic,** which deals with the ethical notions of permission, obligation, and the like.

Several different deontic systems have been proposed. Most of them are fairly similar. To illustrate the problems and complexities they all face, let's concentrate on part of a typical system, namely the one proposed by Nicholas Rescher† (which we will refer to as RDL, for "Rescher's Deontic Logic").

RDL has seven axioms, written in the notation of modal predicate logic together with one new operator. The new operator is the **permission operator,** defined as:

$P(p/c) = $ df (action p is permitted in circumstance c)

Here are the axioms of RDL:

1. $P(p \vee \sim p/c)$
2. $P(p \vee q/c) \Rightarrow [P(p/c) \vee P(q/c)]$
3. $(p \Rightarrow q) \Rightarrow [P(p/c) \Rightarrow P(q/c)]$
4. $P(p \cdot q/c) \Rightarrow P(p/c \cdot q)$
5. $[P(p/c) \cdot P(q/c \cdot p)] \Rightarrow P(p \cdot q/c)$
6. $P(p/c \vee \sim c) \Rightarrow P(p/d)$
7. $P(p/d) \Rightarrow P(p/c \cdot \sim c)$

All of these axioms have an initial plausibility. The first says that tautologies are always permitted, which sounds fairly trivial but surely not fallacious; the second that $(p \vee q)$'s being permitted in some circumstance c is logically equivalent to either p's being permitted in that circumstance or q's being so permitted; the third that if p entails q, then that entails that p's being permitted in some circumstance c in turn entails that q is permitted in that circumstance; and so on.

---

*For instance, Robert J. Ackermann, who in effect argued against the validity of (4) in his paper "A Pragmatic Analysis of Knowledge," delivered to the American Philosophical Association, Western Division, May 1972. Ackermann argued along pragmatist lines that because we can never be sure a statement is true and hence (if truth is a component of knowledge) can never know that we know anything whatever, it is useless to make truth a component of knowledge. He thus advised that we adopt a conception of knowledge that has no truth component, using the word "true" to refer to very highly confirmed theories, making it possible to know x in some cases even though x later turns out to be false.

†In his article "An Axiom System for Deontic Logic," *Philosophical Studies,* vol. IX (1958), pp. 24–30.

From the axioms, many plausible permission theorems can be derived. For instance, here is a proof that $P(p/c) \vee P(\sim p/c)$, or in English that in any circumstance either p is permitted or $\sim p$ is permitted (important because it assures that in every circumstance there is *something* that you're permitted to do):

1.	$P(p \vee \sim p/c)$	**Axiom (1)**
2.	$P(p \vee \sim p/c) \Leftrightarrow P(p/c) \vee P(\sim p/c)]$	**Axiom (2)**
3.	$\{P(p \vee \sim p/c) \Rightarrow [P(p/c) \vee P(\sim p/c)]\} \cdot$	
	$\{[P(p/c) \vee P(\sim p/c)] \Rightarrow P(p \vee \sim p/c)\}$	2 **Strict Equiv.** *
4.	$P(p \vee \sim p/c) \Rightarrow [P(p/c) \vee P(\sim p/c)]$	3 **Simp**
5.	$P(p/c) \vee P(\sim p/c)$	1,4 **Strict MP** †

Here are some other plausible theorems:

8. $\sim P(p/c) \Rightarrow P(\sim p/c)$
9. $P(p \cdot q/c) \Rightarrow [P(p/c) \cdot P(q/c)]$
10. $P(p \cdot q/c) \Rightarrow [P(p/c) \cdot P(q/c \cdot p)]$
11. $P(p/c) \cdot P(q/c \cdot p)] \Rightarrow P(q/c)$
12. $P(p/c \cdot q) \Rightarrow P(p \vee \sim q/c)$
13. $[P(p/c) \cdot \sim P(q/c)] \Rightarrow P(p \cdot \sim q/c)$
14. $P(p/c) \Rightarrow [P(q/c) \vee P(p/c \cdot \sim q)]$

In addition, Rescher introduces several other deontic operators, defined in terms of the permission operator. For instance, he defines the **obligation operator** as:

$$O(p/c) = df \sim P(\sim p/c)$$

This says that "p is obligatory in circumstance c" means the same as "$\sim p$ is not permitted in circumstance c." Some theorems concerning this operator are:

15. $O(p/c) \Rightarrow P(p/c)$
16. $O(p \cdot q/c) \equiv [O(p/c) \cdot O(q/c)]$
17. $(p \Rightarrow q) \Rightarrow [O(p/c) \Rightarrow (q/c)]$
18. $[O(p/c) \vee O(q/c)] \Rightarrow O(p \vee q/c)$ [but not vice versa]

11 *Problems with Deontic Systems*

There is a great deal of controversy concerning most of the axioms proposed for deontic systems. For instance, one objection raised against RDL is that axioms three and five (plus appropriate rules and theorems of modal logic), yield the following theorem: ‡

$$[P(p/c) \cdot P(\sim p/c \cdot p)] \Rightarrow P(q/c)$$

---

*The modal equivalent of $(p \equiv q)$ ∷ $[(p \supset q) \cdot (q \supset p)]$.

†The modal equivalent of $p, p \supset q / \therefore q$.

‡For proof, see Alan Ross Anderson, "On the Logic of Commitment," *Philosophical Studies,* vol. (1959), pp. 23–27.

This theorem states that permission to do p in c and permission to do $\sim p$ in $c \cdot p$ entails permission to do any q whatever in c. Thus, if one is permitted to smoke and permitted to not smoke in the circumstance that one is smoking in a railroad smoking car, one is permitted to do anything (murder, for instance) in that smoking car.

Obviously, this theorem is not acceptable if it yields such results, so Rescher replaced axiom five with what he called "A5*":

A5* $\{[P(p/c) \cdot P(q/c \cdot p)] \cdot \Diamond (p \cdot q)\} \Rightarrow P(p \cdot q/c)$

Since $p \cdot \sim p$ is not possible, the counterexample just discussed cannot be derived in RDL when A5* replaces A5.

But other suspicious theorems can be derived. For example, from A5* plus A3 we can derive the theorem:*

$\{[P(p/c) \cdot P(q/c \cdot p)] \cdot \Diamond (p \cdot q)\} \Rightarrow [P(p/c) \cdot P(q/c)]$

But if c is, for instance, the circumstance of being in an honors program, p the action of taking Philosophy 1H, and q the action of taking Philosophy 2H, where 1H is a prerequisite for 2H, then this theorem yields an unacceptable result. For it says that if one is permitted to take Philosophy 1H, in the circumstance that one is in the honors program, and permitted to take Philosophy 2H, in the circumstance of being in the honors program and having taken Philosophy 1H, and if it is possible to take both 1H and 2H, then all of this entails that in the circumstance of being an honors student one is permitted to take 1H, and in the same circumstance (with or without the added circumstance of having taken 1H) one is permitted to take 2H. This is unacceptable of course since in the example only those honors students who take 1H are permitted to take 2H.

In addition to objections to its axioms, RDL has been objected to because one of its *definitions* seems to yield questionable consequences. The definition objected to[†] is the one defining the obligation operator:

$O(p/c) = \mathrm{df} \sim P(\sim p/c)$

For this definition (plus several RDL axioms), yields the following theorem:

$O(p/d) \Rightarrow O(p/c \vee \sim c)$

And this entails (using Castañeda's example, if women's liberationists will permit it) that if in the circumstance that you're married to Jane you ought to support her, then this entails that you ought to support her in any circumstance ($c \vee \sim c$). But surely we can't accept this result, and so we must reject either the definition of obligation (as Castañeda suggests) or else one of the axioms used in the proof.

---

*For more on this counterexample, see John Robison, "Further Difficulties for Conditional Permission in Deontic Logic," *Philosophical Studies,* vol. XVIII (1967), pp. 27–30.

†By Hector-Neri Castañeda, "The Logic of Obligation," *Philosophical Studies,* vol. X (1959), pp. 17–23.

Objections of the kind just discussed have led some to reject deontic logic, as some reject modal or epistemic logic. Some even claim, though for other reasons, that these operator systems, unlike predicate logic, are not real *logic* systems at all.

But whatever the merits of this last claim, this much seems certain. It would be very useful indeed if we had generally acceptable modal, epistemic, and deontic rules, so that when philosophers argued about ethics, or whatever, they could say (as Leibniz hoped we might some day be able to) "Come, let us calculate."

Key terms

Barcan Formula: The disputed modal theorem $(u) \Box p \Rightarrow \Box (u) p$.

deontic logic: A logic that deals with the ethical notions of obligation, permission, and so on.

epistemic logic: A logic designed to deal with statements containing epistemic contexts. Example: Enrique believes that now is the time to sell real estate.

KK thesis: The thesis that if someone knows some *x*, then that person knows that he or she knows *x*.

logical entailment: An implication that is a theorem of logic. Synonyms: *logical implication, strict implication*.

logical equivalence: An equivalence that is a theorem of logic.

logical implication: (See *logical entailment*.)

logical necessity: A statement that is true because of the laws of logic—a theorem of logic. Example: "It will rain or it won't."

modal logic: A logic designed to handle statements and arguments containing modal operators, such as "It is necessary that _____."

modal terms: Terms (operators) expressing necessity, possibility, and so on.

necessity operator: The symbol "$\Box$", used to express the concept of necessity.

obligation operator: The operator "*O*", used to express obligation.

operator logic: A logic dealing with operators that bind all or parts of expressions.

permission operator: The operator "*P*", used to express permission.

physical necessity: A statement that is true because of the laws of nature. Example: "All copper conducts electricity."

possibility operator: The symbol "$\Diamond$", used to express possibilities.

strict implication: (See *logical entailment*.) The symbol "$\Rightarrow$" is used to express strict implication.

Answers to Even-Numbered Exercise Items

Exercise 1-1

2. This is a *description* of how the speaker spent her summer vacation, not an argument.

4. At the present rate of consumption, the oil will be used up in 20–25 years (premise). And we're sure not going to reduce consumption in the near future (premise). So we'd better start developing solar power, windmills, and other "alternative energy sources" pretty soon (conclusion).

6. *Conjecture*, not an argument.

8. Don't be fooled by the "thus" in this passage. This is an explanation, not an argument.

10. To be sustained under the Eighth Amendment, the death penalty must "[comport] with the basic concept of human dignity at the core of the Amendment"; the objective in imposing it must be "[consistent] with our respect for the dignity of other men" (premise). [The death penalty] has as its very basis the total denial of the wrongdoer's dignity and worth (premise). The taking of life "because the wrongdoer deserves it" surely must fail (conclusion).

12. Every event must have a cause (premise). An infinite series of causes is impossible (premise). Or you can take their victory from them [commit suicide]. They will remember you (premise). [Therefore, commit suicide and be remembered] (implied conclusion).

Exercise 1-2

(2) 1. McDonald's serves lobster, or McDonald's serves hamburgers.

  2. It's not true that McDonald's serves lobster.

  ∴3. McDonald's serves hamburgers.

(4) 1. If McDonald's serves lobster, then McDonald's is a restaurant.

  2. It's not true that McDonald's sells auto parts.

  ∴3. McDonald's is a restaurant.

(6) 1. If McDonald's sells auto parts, then McDonald's is an auto parts store.

  2. It's not true that McDonald's sells auto parts.

  ∴3. McDonald's is an auto parts store.

Exercise 1-3

2. Yes, because the conclusion of such an argument makes a claim not contained in its premises.

4. Yes, if one or more of its premises are false.

6. No. A deductively valid argument with true premises guarantees the truth of its conclusion.

8. No, because a sound argument is one that is valid and has all true premises, and a valid argument containing all true premises must have a true conclusion.

10. Yes, so long as it is possible for them all to be true.

12. No.

14. Here are five—"Therefore," "Thus," "So," "Hence," and "Consequently."

Exercise 2-1

2, 4, 6, 10, and 12 are correctly symbolized by the dot. 8 is not.

Exercise 2-2

2. The horseshoe.

4. The first tilde.

6. The second horseshoe.

8. The tri-bar.

10. The tri-bar.

Exercise 2-3

2. $(J \vee A) \cdot \sim (J \cdot A)$ (J = "Michael Jordan is the greatest basketball player to ever play the game"; A = "Kareem Abdul-Jabbar is the greatest basketball player to ever play the game")

4. $C \vee N$ (C = "It's going to snow on Christmas eve"; N = "It's going to snow on New Year's eve")

6. $(T \vee F) \cdot \sim (T \cdot F)$ (T = "This sentence is true"; F = "This sentence is false") Arguably, a better translation would be $(T \vee \sim T) \cdot \sim (T \cdot \sim T)$.

8. $(A \vee C) \cdot \sim (A \cdot C)$ (A = "The A's are going to win the World Series this year"; C = "The Cleveland Indians are going to win the World Series this year")

10. $(A \vee L) \cdot \sim (A \cdot L)$ (A = "Anita Hill either told the truth about Clarence Thomas"; L = "The lie detector test is totally unreliable")

12. $I \vee S$ (I = "The gunman was insane", S = "The gunman was experiencing a severe emotional disturbance")

Exercise 2-4

2. $\sim (S \vee A)$, or $\sim S \cdot \sim A$

4. $\sim (H \vee P$, or $\sim H \cdot \sim P$

6. $\sim (E \vee C) \cdot \sim O$

8. $(M \vee D) \cdot \sim (M \cdot D)$

10. $\sim (D \vee H) \cdot (P \cdot C)$

12. $(U \cdot I) \vee C$

14. $(D \cdot I) \cdot \sim (S \vee B)$

Exercise 2-5

2. $\sim J \supset \sim H$, or $H \supset J$, or $\sim H \vee J$
4. $\sim (R \vee A)$, or $\sim R \cdot \sim A$
6. $R \supset A$, or $\sim A \supset \sim R$
8. $\sim P \supset \sim A$ or $A \supset P$
10. $A \supset \sim S$

Exercise 2-6

2. $\sim E \supset \sim B$
4. $B \supset (M \cdot S)$
6. $(M \vee B) \supset \sim E$
8. $\sim M \supset D$
10. $\sim G \supset \sim D$
12. $\sim (C \vee L)$
14. $(M \cdot \sim B) \cdot \sim F$
16. $(\sim M \cdot S) \supset \sim B$
18. $(\sim M \cdot \sim B) \supset \sim (\sim S \vee F)$
20. $B \cdot (\sim O \supset \sim W)$
22. $\sim (D \vee E) \supset G$
24. $\sim (D \vee E) \cdot \sim G$
26. $(T \cdot S) \vee \sim D$
28. $(T \cdot S) \supset (N \supset \sim D)$
30. $\sim [(R \vee S) \vee G]$ or $(\sim R \cdot \sim S) \cdot \sim G$

Exercise 2-7

2. Sheila likes neither Jay Leno nor David Letterman.
4. Sheila doesn't like Jay Leno, and she doesn't like David Letterman either. (Or you could use the answer from number 2.)
6. If Sheila likes "Ren N Stimpy," she's no pacifist.
8. If Sheila likes both "Ren N Stimpy" and "The Three Stooges," she's no pacifist.
10. If Sheila is a pacifist, then she doesn't like "Ren N Stimpy" or "The Three Stooges."
12. If Sheila likes either "Ren N Stimpy" or "The Three Stooges" and yet she's a pacifist, then she's got a twisted sense of humor.
14. If the economy is in a recession, then you shouldn't buy real estate or common stocks.
16. If demand is high and interest rates are low, then unless you are a knowledgeable investor, you should buy real estate.
18. You should buy stocks or bonds if and only if you are a knowledgeable investor (or a psychic) and the economy is not in a recession.
20. Unless you are a knowledgeable investor, you should not buy stocks or bonds; rather, you should invest in a mutual fund.
22. If you are not a knowledgeable investor, then you should not buy stocks or bonds, unless you are a psychic.
24. If the economy is in a recession and interest rates are low, and you are neither a knowledgeable investor nor a psychic, then you should invest in real estate.

Exercise 2-8

2. Inclusive: "Brenda jogs or pumps iron every day." Exclusive: "Either you're with me or you're against me."
4. "But," "however," and many others.

6. Compound. It is the negation of the atomic sentence "Archie Leach is a public figure."

8. Compound. It could be symbolized as $(\sim N \cdot \sim B) \cdot \sim W$.

Exercise 3-1

2. True: $A \equiv (C \vee B)$
         T T F T T
           ↓

4. True: $\sim [C \vee (D \vee E)]$
         T FF FFF
           ↓

6. False: $\sim [(A \cdot \sim B) \supset (C \cdot \sim D)]$
        F   TFFT T FFT F
               ↓

8. True: $\sim (C \cdot D) \vee \sim (\sim C \cdot \sim D)$
        T FFF TF TFTT F
         ↓

10. True: $A \supset [(B \supset C) \supset (D \supset E)]$
         T T TFF T FTF

12. False:
                      ↓
$[(A \supset \sim B) \vee (C \cdot \sim D)] \equiv [\sim (A \supset D) \vee (\sim C \vee E)]$
   TFFT F FFTF F T TFF T TFTF
                      ↓

14. False: $[A \supset (\sim A \vee A)] \cdot \sim [(A \cdot A) \supset (A \cdot A)]$
        T T FTTT FF TTT T TTT

Exercise 3-2

2. True. Because $\sim C$ is true, $Q \vee \sim C$ is also true.

4. False. A biconditional is true only if the two component sentences have the same truth value.

6. False. Because $\sim A$ is false, $\sim A \supset D$ is true. This tells us that $R \supset (\sim A \supset D)$ is true.

8. We can't tell in this case. We can tell that $C \supset Q$ is true, but that is all.

10. True. Because C is false, $\sim (C \cdot R)$ must be true. That's all we need to know to tell that the entire disjunction is true.

12. We can't tell in this case because we don't have enough information to tell whether the antecedent of this conditional is true or false.

Exercise 3-3

2. Tautology.

A	~ (A ≡ ~ A)
T	T TFFT
F	T FFTF

4. Tautology.

A B	A ⊃ (A ∨ B)
T T	TT TTT
T F	TT TTF
F T	FT FTT
F F	FT FFF

6. Contingent.

A B	A ≡ (B ∨ A)
T T	TT TTT
T F	TT FTT
F T	FF TTF
F F	FT FFF

8. Contingent.

A B	(B ⊃ A) ⊃ (A ⊃ B)
T T	TTT T TTT
T F	FTT F TFF
F T	TFF T FTT
F F	FTF T FTF

10. Contingent.

A B	(B ∨ A) ⊃ (A ⊃ B)
T T	TTT T TTT
T F	FTT F TFF
F T	TTF T FTT
F F	FFF T FTF

12. Contingent.

A B C	A ⊃ [B ⊃ (A ⊃ C)]
T T T	TT TT TTT
T T F	TF TF TFF
T F T	TT FT TTT
T F F	TT FT TFF
F T T	FT TT FTT
F T F	FT TT FTF
F F T	FT FT FTT
F F F	FT FT FTF

14. Tautology.

A B C D	{A ⊃ [(B ∨ C) ∨ (D ∨ ~ B)]} ∨ ~ A
T T T T	TT TTT T TTFT TFT
T T T F	TT TTT T FFFT TFT
T T F T	TT TTF T TTFT TFT
T T F F	TT TTF T FFFT TFT
T F T T	TT FTT T TTTF TFT
T F T F	TT FTT T FTTF TFT
T F F T	TT FFF T TTTF TFT
T F F F	TT FFF T FTTF TFT
F T T T	FT TTT T TTFT TTF
F T T F	FT TTT T FFFT TTF
F T F T	FT TTF T TTFT TTF
F T F F	FT TTF T FFFT TTF
F F T T	FT FTT T TTTF TTF
F F T F	FT FTT T FTTF TTF
F F F T	FT FFF T TTTF TTF
F F F F	FT FFF T FTTF TTF

Exercise 3-4

2. Not logically equivalent. *F* logically implies *F* ∨ *G*, but not vice versa.

	↓	
F G	F ∨ G	F
T T	T T T	T
T F	T T F	T
F T	F T T	F
F F	F F F	F

4. Not logically equivalent. *A* logically implies *A* ∨ ~ *A*, but not vice versa.

		↓
A	A	A ∨ ~ A
T	T	T T F T
F	F	F T T F

6. Logically equivalent.

	↓	↓
F	F · ~ F	F ≡ ~ F
T	T F F T	T F F T
F	F F T F	F F T F

8. Not logically equivalent. *A* · ~ *B* logically implies *A* ∨ ~ *B*, but not vice versa.

	↓	↓
A B	A ∨ ~ B	A · ~ B
T T	T T F T	T F F T
T F	T T T F	T T T F
F T	F F F T	F F F T
F F	F T T F	F F T F

10. Not logically equivalent. Neither sentence implies the other.

	↓	↓
L M	L ⊃ ~ M	L · M
T T	T F F T	T T T
T F	T T T F	T F F
F T	F T F T	F F T
F F	F T T F	F F F

12. Not logically equivalent. *A* ∨ *B* logically implies *A* ∨ (*B* ⊃ *B*), but not vice versa.

	↓	↓
A B	A ∨ B	A ∨ (B ⊃ B)
T T	T T T	T T T T T
T F	T T F	T T F T F
F T	F T T	F T T T T
F F	F F F	F T F T F

14. Not logically equivalent. *M* · *A* logically implies (*M* · ~ *A*) ⊃ (*M* · *A*), but not vice versa.

	↓	↓
M A	(M · ~ A) ⊃ (M · A)	M · A
T T	T F F T T T T T	T T T
T F	T T T F F T F F	T F F
F T	F F F T T F F T	F F T
F F	F F T F T F F F	F F F

16. Logically equivalent.

	↓	↓
A B	A ⊃ (B ⊃ A)	B ⊃ (A ⊃ B)
T T	T T T T T	T T T T T
T F	T T F T T	F T T F F
F T	F T T F F	T T F T T
F F	F T F T F	F T F T F

18. Not logically equivalent. $(H \cdot \sim K)$ logically implies $(\sim H \cdot \sim K) \vee (H \vee K)$, but not vice versa.

HK	$\sim (H \cdot \sim K)$	$(\sim H \cdot \sim K) \vee (H \vee K)$
T T	T TFF T	F TFF T T TTT
T F	F TTT F	F TFT F T TTF
F T	T FFF T	T FFF T T FTT
F F	T FFT F	T FTT F T FFF

↓ (over the first $\sim$ of $\sim (H \cdot \sim K)$) ↓ (over the $\vee$ of the second formula)

20. Not logically equivalent. Neither sentence logically implies the other.

HKL	$(H \cdot K) \vee (K \cdot L)$	$(\sim H \cdot \sim K) \vee (\sim K \cdot \sim L)$
T T T	TTT T TTT	F TFF T F FTF F T
T T F	TTT T TFF	F TFF T F FTF T F
T F T	TFF F FFT	F TFT F F TFF F T
T F F	TFF F FFF	F TFT F T TFT T F
F T T	FFT T TTT	T FFF T F FTF F T
F T F	FFT F TFF	T FFF T F FTF T F
F F T	FFF F FFT	T FTT F T TFF F T
F F F	FFF F FFF	T FTT F T TFT T F

↓ (over the first $\vee$) ↓ (over the main $\vee$)

Exercise 3-5

2. Valid. The first line is the only line where all of the premises are true, and on this line the conclusion is true as well.

ABC	$C \supset A$	$A \supset (B \cdot C)$	C	B
T T T	T T T	T T TTT	T	T
T T F	F T T	T F TFF	F	T
T F T	T T T	T F FFT	T	F
T F F	F T T	T F FFF	F	F
F T T	T F F	F T TTT	T	T
F T F	F T F	F T TFF	F	T
F F T	T F F	F T FFT	T	F
F F F	F T F	F T FFF	F	F

↓ (over $\supset$ of $C \supset A$) ↓ (over first $\supset$ of second formula)

4. Valid.

H K L	(H · K) ⊃ L	H	K ⊃ L
	↓		↓
T T T	T T T T T	T	T T T
T T F	T T T F F	T	T F F
T F T	T F F T T	T	F T T
T F F	T F F T F	T	F T F
F T T	F F T T T	F	T T T
F T F	F F T T F	F	T F F
F F T	F F F T T	F	F T T
F F F	F F F T F	F	F T F

6. Invalid. On the first line the premises are all true and the conclusion false.

A B C	A ⊃ B	~ (C · B)	C	~ A
	↓	↓		↓
T T T	T T T	F T T T	T	F T
T T F	T T T	T F F T	F	F T
T F T	T F F	T T F F	T	F T
T F F	T F F	T F F F	F	F T
F T T	F T T	F T T T	T	T F
F T F	F T T	T F F T	F	T F
F F T	F T F	T T F F	T	T F
F F F	F T F	T F F F	F	T F

8. Invalid. On the fifth line the premises are all true and the conclusion false.

L N R	L ∨ N	L ⊃ ~ R	R	~ N
	↓	↓		↓
T T T	T T T	T F F T	T	F T
T T F	T T T	T T T F	F	F T
T F T	T T F	T F F T	T	T F
T F F	T T F	T T T F	F	T F
F T T	F T T	F T F T	T	F T
F T F	F T T	F T T F	F	F T
F F T	F F F	F T F T	T	T F
F F F	F F F	F T T F	F	T F

10. Valid

A B C	(A · B) ∨ C	~ A	C
	↓	↓	
T T T	T T T T T	F T	T
T T F	T T T T F	F T	F
T F T	T F F T T	F T	T
T F F	T F F F F	F T	F
F T T	F F T T T	T F	T
F T F	F F T F F	T F	F
F F T	F F F T T	T F	T
F F F	F F F F F	T F	F

12. Valid.

A B C	(A · B) ∨ C	~ (A ∨ B)	C
	↓	↓	
T T T	T T T T T	F T T T	T
T T F	T T T T F	F T T T	F
T F T	T F F T T	F T T F	T
T F F	T F F F F	F T T F	F
F T T	F F T T T	F F T T	T
F T F	F F T F F	F F T T	F
F F T	F F F T T	T F F F	T
F F F	F F F F F	T F F F	F

14. Invalid. On the first two lines the premises are true and the conclusion false.

A B C	A ∨ (~ B · C)	B ⊃ ~ A	~ B
	↓	↓	↓
T T T	T T F T F T	T F F T	F T
T T F	T T F T F F	T F F T	F T
T F T	T T T F T T	F T F T	T F
T F F	T T T F F F	F T F T	T F
F T T	F F F T F T	T T T F	F T
F T F	F F F T F F	T T T F	F T
F F T	F T T F T T	F F F F	T F
F F F	F F T F F F	F F F F	T F

16. Invalid. On lines eleven and twelve the premises are true and the conclusion false.

A B C D	A ⊃ B	C ⊃ D	B ∨ D	A ∨ C
T T T T	T T T	T T T	T T T	T T T
T T T F	T T T	T F F	T T F	T T T
T T F T	T T T	F T T	T T T	T T F
T T F F	T T T	F T F	T T F	T T F
T F T T	T F F	T T T	F T T	T T T
T F T F	T F F	T F F	F F F	T T T
T F F T	T F F	F T T	F T T	T T F
T F F F	T F F	F T F	F F F	T T F
F T T T	F T T	T T T	T T T	F T T
F T T F	F T T	T F F	T T F	F T T
F T F T	F T T	F T T	T T T	F F F
F T F F	F T T	F T F	T T F	F F F
F F T T	F T F	T T T	F T T	F T T
F F T F	F T F	T F F	F F F	F T T
F F F T	F T F	F T T	F T T	F F F
F F F F	F T F	F T F	F F F	F F F

18. Invalid, as shown by line 12.

A B C D	A ⊃ B	C ⊃ D	B ∨ C	A ∨ D
T T T T	T T T	T T T	T T T	T T T
T T T F	T T T	T F F	T T T	T T F
T T F T	T T T	F T T	T T F	T T T
T T F F	T T T	F T F	T T F	T T F
T F T T	T F F	T T T	F T T	T T T
T F T F	T F F	T F F	F T T	T T F
T F F T	T F F	F T T	F F F	T T T
T F F F	T F F	F T F	F F F	T T F
F T T T	F T T	T T T	T T T	F T T
F T T F	F T T	T F F	T T T	F F F
F T F T	F T T	F T T	T T F	F T T
F T F F	F T T	F T F	T T F	F F F
F F T T	F T F	T T T	F T T	F T T
F F T F	F T F	T F F	F T T	F F F
F F F T	F T F	F T T	F F F	F T T
F F F F	F T F	F T F	F F F	F F F

20. Valid.

F G H K	F ⊃ (G ⊃ H)	(~ H · K) ⊃ (G ⊃ ~ F)
	↓	↓
T T T T	T T T T T	F T F T T T F F T
T T T F	T T T T T	F T F F T T F F T
T T F T	T F T F F	T F T T F T F F T
T T F F	T F T F F	T F F F T T F F T
F F T T	T T F T T	F T F T T F T F T
F F T F	T T F T T	F T F F T F T F T
F F F T	T T F T F	T F T T T F T F T
F F F F	T T F T F	T F F F T F T F T
T T T T	F T T T T	F T F T T T T T F
T T T F	F T T T T	F T F F T T T T F
T T F T	F T T F F	T F T T T T T T F
T T F F	F T T F F	T F F F T T T T F
F F T T	F T F T T	F T F T T F T T F
F F T F	F T F T T	F T F F T F T T F
F F F T	F T F T F	T F T T T F T T F
F F F F	F T F T F	T F F F T F T T F

Exercise 3-6

2. Inconsistent.

A B	A ≡ B	A ≡ ~ B
	↓	↓
T T	T T T	T F F T
T F	T F F	T T T F
F T	F F T	F T F T
F F	F T F	F F T F

4. Consistent, as shown by the seventh line.

A B C	A ⊃ B	~ B ∨ ~ C	C · ~ A
	↓	↓	↓
T T T	T T T	F T F F T	T F F T
T T F	T T T	F T T T F	F F F T
T F T	T F F	T F T F T	T F F T
T F F	T F F	T F T T F	F F F T
F T T	F T T	F T F F T	T T T F
F T F	F T T	F T T T F	F F T F
F F T	F T F	T F T F T	T T T F
F F F	F T F	T F T T F	F F T F

6. Consistent, as shown by the first, third, fifth, and seventh lines.

K L M	(K · L) ⊃ M	K ⊃ M	L ⊃ M
	↓	↓	↓
T T T	T TT T T	T T T	T T T
T T F	T TT F F	T F F	T F F
T F T	T FF T T	T T T	F T T
T F F	T FF T F	T F F	F T F
F T T	F FT T T	F T T	T T T
F T F	F FT T F	F T F	T F F
F F T	F FF T T	F T T	F T T
F F F	F FF T F	F T F	F T F

8. Inconsistent.

A B C	A ≡ ~ B	A	B ∨ C	~ C
	↓		↓	
T T T	T F F T	T	T T T	F T
T T F	T F F T	T	T T F	T F
T F T	T T T F	T	F T T	F T
T F F	T T T F	T	F F F	T F
F T T	F T F T	F	T T T	F T
F T F	F T F T	F	T T F	T F
F F T	F F T F	F	F T T	F T
F F F	F F T F	F	F F F	T F

10. Inconsistent.

H J K	(H ⊃ J) ∨ (H ⊃ K)	~ (J ∨ K)	H
	↓	↓	
T T T	T TT T TTT	F TTT	T
T T F	T TT T TFF	F TTF	T
T F T	T FF T TTT	F FTT	T
T F F	T FF F TFF	T FFF	T
F T T	F TT T FTT	F TTT	F
F T F	F TT T FTF	F TTF	F
F F T	F TF T FTT	F FTT	F
F F F	F TF T FTF	T FFF	F

Exercise 3-7

2. *A*—False; *B*—True

4. *N, R*—True; *L*—True or False

6. *A*—False; and either *B, C, D*—True; or *B, D*—True; *C*—False; or *B, C*—True; *D*—False; or *C, D*—True; *B*—False

8. *A*—False

10. *A, B, C*—True; *D*—False; or *A, B*—True; *C, D*—False; or *A, C*—True; *B, D*—False; or *B, D*—True; *A, C*—False; or *D*—True; *A, B, C*—False

12. *A, B, C*—True; *D*—False

14. *A, B, C, D*—False; *E, F*—True

16. *D, L, R*—False

18. *A, B, C, D*—True; *E, F*—False

20. *R, T*—True; *N, Q, S, W*—False; *P*—True or False

Exercise 3-8

2. *F*—True; *G, H*—False

4. *F, H*—False; *G*—True

6. *D*—True; *C*—False; and either *A*—True; *B*—True (or False); or *A*—False and *B*—True

8. *D*—True; *F*—False; *E*—True; *C*—False; *A*—True; *B*—True

Exercise 3-9

2. b, f

4. a, b, e, f

Exercise 3-10

2. a, d

4. a, c, m

6. a, d, f, k

8. a, d, j, l

10. a, d, f, k, o

12. a, d, f, k

14. a, b, h, i, q

Exercise 3-11

2. $p, p \supset q, \sim p \supset q, p \supset \sim q, \sim p \supset \sim q$

4. $p, \sim p, \sim (p \vee q)$

6. $p, p \equiv q, p \equiv \sim q, (p \cdot q) \equiv r, (p \cdot q) \equiv \sim r$

8. $p, p \supset q, \sim p \supset q, \sim (p \equiv q) \supset r$

10. $p, \sim p, \sim (p \supset q), \sim [(p \equiv q) \supset r]$

12. $p, \sim p, \sim (p \supset q), \sim [(p \cdot q) \supset r], \sim [p \supset (q \vee r)], \sim [(p \cdot q) \supset (r \vee s)]$

Exercise 3-12

2. Contingent

$$\downarrow$$

p	$\sim[p \supset (p \cdot \sim p)]$
T	T T F T F F T
F	F F F F F T F

4. Tautologous

$$\downarrow$$

$p\ q$	$p \vee (q \supset \sim p)$
T T	T T T F F T
T F	T T F T F T
F T	F T T T T F
F F	F T F T T F

6. Tautologous

$$\downarrow$$

$p\ q$	$(p \cdot \sim p) \supset q$
T T	T F F T T T
T F	T F F T T F
F T	F F T F T T
F F	F F T F T F

8. Tautologous

$$\downarrow$$

$p\ q$	$(p \vee q) \vee \sim (p \cdot q)$
T T	T T T T F T T T
T F	T T F T T T F F
F T	F T T T T F F T
F F	F F F T T F F F

10. Contingent

$$\downarrow$$

$p\ q\ r$	$\{[p \cdot (q \vee r)] \supset p\} \equiv q$
T T T	T T T T T T T T T
T T F	T T T T F T T T F
T F T	T T F T T T T F T
T F F	T F F F F T T F F
F T T	F F T T T T F T T
F T F	F F T T F T F T F
F F T	F F F T T T F F T
F F F	F F F F F T F F F

12. Contingent

$$\downarrow$$

$p\ q\ r$	$[(p \cdot q) \vee r] \equiv [(p \cdot q) \vee (p \cdot r)]$
T T T	T T T T T T T T T T T T T
T T F	T T T T F T T T T T T F F
T F T	T F F T T T T F F T T T T
T F F	T F F F F T T F F F T F F
F T T	F F T T T F F F T F F F T
F T F	F F T F F T F F T F F F F
F F T	F F F T T F F F F F F F T
F F F	F F F F F T F F F F F F F

14. Contingent

$$\downarrow$$

$p\ q\ r$	$p \supset [q \supset (p \supset r)]$
T T T	T T T T T T T
T T F	T F T F T F F
T F T	T T F T T T T
T F F	T T F T T F F
F T T	F T T T F T T
F T F	F T T T F T F
F F T	F T F T F T T
F F F	F T F T F T F

Exercise 3-13

2. Yes. Every compound sentence is a substitution instance of more than one form. For example, $A \vee B$ is a substitution instance of both p and $p \vee q$.

4. No.

6. The argument is valid. If one of the premises is a contradiction, it is not possible for all of the premises to be true—so, of course, it is impossible for all of the premises to be true and the conclusion false.

8. At least one of the premises must be false.

Exercise 4-1

(2)	4. 1,2 **HS**	(8)	6. 1,3 **HS**
	5. 3,4 **MT**		7. 5,6 **MP**
(4)	4. 2,3 **MP**		8. 2,4 **DS**
	5. 1,4 **MT**		9. 7,8 **MT**
(6)	5. 3,4 **HS**	(10)	6. 3,4 **HS**
	6. 2,5 **HS**		7. 5,6 **MP**
	7. 1,6 **MP**		8. 1,7 **MP**
			9. 2,8 **MP**

Exercise 4-2

(2)	3. R	1,2 **MP**	(12)	5. $\sim T$	1,4 **DS**
(4)	3. $L \supset (R \cdot W)$	1,2 **HS**		6. $\sim (L \vee M)$	3,5 **MP**
(6)	4. N	1,3 **DS**		7. R	2,6 **DS**
	5. G	2,4 **MP**	(14)	6. $P \cdot Q$	3,5 **MP**
(8)	4. $\sim H$	2,3 **DS**		7. $R \vee (T \cdot S)$	2,6 **MP**
	5. G	1,4 **DS**		8. R	4,7 **DS**
(10)	5. $\sim D$	2,4 **DS**			
	6. $A \supset B$	3,5 **MP**			
	7. C	1,6 **MP**			

Exercise 4-3

(2)	2. 1 **Simp**	(12)	5. 1,4 **HS**
(4)	4. 1,2,3 **CD**		6. 2 **Add**
(6)	4. 2,3 **DS**		7. 5,6 **MP**
	5. 1,4 **MP**		8. 3,7 **DS**
	6. 2,5 **MT**		9. 2,8 **Conj**
(8)	4. 2 **Simp**	(14)	5. 2 **Simp**
	5. 1,3 **HS**		6. 2 **Simp**
	6. 4,5 **MP**		7. 3,5 **DS**
	7. 2 **Simp**		8. 1,4,7 **CD**
	8. 6,7 **Conj**		9. 6,8 **DS**
(10)	4. 2 **Simp**		
	5. 1,4 **MT**		
	6. 3,5 **DS**		

Exercise 4-4

(2)	2. $(A \equiv B) \supset B$
(4)	2. $\sim C$
	3. $\sim B$
(6)	2. $A \vee D$
	4. A

(8)	1. $T \cdot S$
	2. $[(T \cdot S) \vee V] \supset \sim L$
	6. $\sim G$
	7. T

Exercise 4-5

(2)	3. $(R \vee S) \supset T$	2 Simp
	4. T	1,3 MP
	5. $T \vee L$	4 Add
(4)	3. B	1 Simp
	4. C	2,3 MP
(6)	3. A	2 Simp
	4. B	1,3 MP
	5. $B \vee D$	4 Add
(8)	5. $\sim B \cdot C$	1,4 MP
	6. C	5 Simp
	7. D	2,6 MP
	8. $\sim B$	5 Simp
	9. E	3,8 DS
	10. $D \cdot E$	7,9 Conj
(10)	4. $L \vee R$	1 Add
	5. $\sim T$	3,4 MP
	6. $\sim R$	2,5 DS
	7. $\sim R \vee B$	6 Add
(12)	4. $\sim (R \cdot A)$	2,3 MT
	5. E	1,4 DS
	6. $E \cdot \sim D$	3,5 Conj

(14)	3. $A \vee \sim D$	1 Add
	4. $R \cdot S$	2,3 MP
	5. $(R \cdot S) \vee B$	4 Add
(16)	5. $\sim R$	1,3 MT
	6. Z	4,5 DS
	7. $\sim M \cdot \sim N$	2,5 MP
	8. $(\sim M \cdot \sim N) \cdot Z$	6,7 Conj
(18)	5. B	1,4 DS
	6. $\sim C$	2,4 MT
	7. $B \cdot \sim C$	5,6 Conj
	8. $D \cdot \sim C$	3,7 MP
	9. D	8 Simp
(20)	6. $\sim (D \cdot E)$	2 Simp
	7. $\sim A$	4,6 DS
	8. $\sim A \cdot \sim (D \cdot E)$	6,7 Conj
	9. $B \supset \sim D$	1,8 MP
	10. $B \vee E$	5,6 MP
	11. $\sim D \vee F$	3,9,10 CD

Exercise 4-6

(2)	3. $\sim \sim T$	2 DN
	4. S	1,3 DS
(4)	3. $\sim F \vee \sim G$	1 DeM
	4. $\sim \sim F$	2 DN
	5. $\sim G$	3,4 DS
(6)	4. $\sim W \vee \sim \sim Z$	3 DeM
	5. $\sim \sim X$	2 DN
	6. $\sim \sim W$	1,5 MT
	7. $\sim \sim Z$	4,6 DS
	8. Z	8 DN

(8)	5. $\sim \sim A \vee \sim \sim B$	1 DeM
	6. $\sim C \vee \sim \sim D$	4 DeM
	7. $A \vee \sim \sim B$	5 DN
	8. $\sim \sim B$	3,7 DS
	9. B	8 DN
	10. C	2,9 MP
	11. $\sim \sim C$	10 DN
	12. $\sim \sim D$	6,11 DS
	13. D	12 DN

Exercise 4-7

(2) 4. 1 **DN**
     5. 3 **Comm**
     6. 4,5 **MT**
     7. 2 **DeM**
     8. 6,7 **DS**

(4) 3. 1 **Assoc**
     4. 2 **Dist**
     5. 4 **Simp**
     6. 4 **Simp**
     7. 3,5 **DS**
     8. 7 **Comm**
     9. 6,8 **Conj**
    10. 9 **Dist**

(6) 3. 1 **Equiv**
     4. 2 **DeM**
     5. 4 **Add**
     6. 5 **Impl**
     7. 2 **Impl**
     8. 6,7 **HS**
     9. 8 **Exp**
    10. 9 **Impl**
    11. 10 **Taut**

(8) 3. 2 **Comm**
     4. 3 **Assoc**
     5. 4 **Impl**
     6. 1 **Contra**
     7. 5,6 **HS**
     8. 7 **Impl**
     9. 8 **Assoc**
    10. 9 **Comm**
    11. 10 **DN**
    12. 11 **Impl**
    13. 12 **Impl**

(10) 3. 1 **Equiv**
     4. 3 **Impl**
     5. 4 **DeM**
     6. 5 **Impl** (*twice*)
     7. 6 **DN**
     8. 7 **DeM** (*twice*)
     9. 8 **DN**
    10. 9 **Assoc**
    11. 2 **DeM**
    12. 10,11 **DS**
    13. 12 **Comm**
    14. 13 **Dist**
    15. 14 **Simp**
    16. 15 **Taut**

Exercise 4-8

(2) 3. $\sim (R \cdot S)$ 1 **DeM**
     4. $\sim A$ 2,3 **MT**

(4) 3. $\sim B \lor \sim \sim C$ 2 **DeM**
     4. $\sim B \lor C$ 3 **DN**
     5. $B \supset C$ 4 **Impl**
     6. $A \supset C$ 1,5 **HS**

(6) 4. $\sim H \lor \sim G$ 2 **DeM**
     5. $\sim \sim H$ 3 **DN**
     6. $\sim G$ 4,5 **DS**
     7. $\sim F$ 1,6 **MT**

(8) 2. $(M \supset N) \cdot (N \supset M)$ 1 **Equiv**
     3. $N \supset M$ 2 **Simp**
     4. $\sim N \lor M$ 3 **Impl**

(10) 3. $\sim R \lor S$ 1 **Impl**
     4. $\sim R \lor T$ 2 **Impl**
     5. $(\sim R \lor S) \cdot (\sim R \lor T)$ 3,4 **Conj**
     6. $\sim R \lor (S \cdot T)$ 5 **Dist**
     7. $R \supset (S \cdot T)$ 6 **Impl**

(12)
3. $\sim C \vee \sim A$ — 2 DeM
4. A — 1 Simp
5. $\sim \sim A$ — 4 DN
6. $\sim C$ — 3,5 DS
7. $B \supset C$ — 1 Simp
8. $\sim B$ — 6,7 MT

(14)
4. $\sim A$ — 1,3 DS
5. $\sim A \vee \sim \sim B$ — 4 Add
6. $\sim (A \cdot \sim B)$ — 5 DeM
7. $\sim C$ — 2,6 MP

Exercise 4-9

(2)
2. $\sim \sim A \vee B$ — 1 DN
3. $\sim A \supset B$ — 2 Imp

(4)
2. $\sim A \vee \sim B$ — 1 Add
3. $\sim (A \cdot B)$ — 2 DeM

(6)
2. $\sim A \vee \sim B$ — 1 DeM
3. $A \supset \sim B$ — 2 Imp

(8)
2. $\sim (\sim A \vee B)$ — 1 Imp
3. $\sim \sim A \cdot \sim B$ — 2 DeM
4. $\sim B$ — 3 Simp

(10)
2. $A \vee \sim \{\sim [L \vee (\sim M \equiv R)]\}$ — 1 Add
3. $\sim \{\sim [L \vee (\sim M \equiv R)]\} \vee A$ — 2 Comm

(12)
2. $\sim \sim B \supset \sim A$ — 1 Contra
3. $B \supset \sim A$ — 3 Imp

(14)
2. $(A \cdot B) \supset C$ — 1 Exp
3. $(B \cdot A) \supset C$ — 2 Comm
4. $B \supset (A \supset C)$ — 3 Exp

(16)
2. $A \cdot (B \vee C)$ — 1 Dist
3. $B \vee C$ — 2 Simp

(18)
2. $C \vee (A \cdot B)$ — 1 Comm
3. $(C \vee A) \cdot (C \vee B)$ — 2 Dist
4. $C \vee A$ — 3 Simp

(20)
2. $\sim A \vee \sim A$ — 1 Imp
3. $\sim A$ — 2 Taut

Exercise 4-10

(2)
3. $A \vee (B \vee C)$ — 1 Assoc
4. $\sim A$ — 2,3 DS

(4)
3. $[(A \cdot B) \vee C] \cdot [(A \cdot B) \vee D]$ — 1 Dist
4. $(A \cdot B) \vee C$ — 3 Simp
5. $A \cdot B$ — 2,4 DS
6. A — 5 Simp

(6)
2. $[(A \cdot B) \vee C] \cdot [(A \cdot B) \vee D]$ — 1 Dist
3. $(A \cdot B) \vee D$ — 2 Simp
4. $D \vee (A \cdot B)$ — 3 Comm
5. $(D \vee A) \cdot (D \vee B)$ — 4 Dist
6. $D \vee A$ — 5 Simp

(8)
3. $C \cdot (A \vee B)$ — 1 Assoc
4. $(C \cdot A) \vee (C \cdot B)$ — 3 Dist
5. $\sim C \vee \sim A$ — 2 Comm
6. $\sim (C \cdot A)$ — 5 DeM
7. $C \cdot B$ — 4,6 DS

(10)
2. $(\sim R \cdot A) \vee \sim (R \vee Q)$ — 1 Assoc
3. $(\sim R \cdot A) \vee (\sim R \cdot \sim Q)$ — 2 DeM
4. $\sim R \cdot (A \vee \sim Q)$ — 3 Dist
5. $\sim R$ — 4 Simp

(12)
3. $[(D \cdot F) \vee (A \cdot B)] \vee (B \cdot C)$ — 1 Comm
4. $(D \cdot F) \vee [(A \cdot B) \vee (B \cdot C)]$ — 3 Assoc
5. $(A \cdot B) \vee (B \cdot C)$ — 2,4 DS
6. $(B \cdot A) \vee (B \cdot C)$ — 5 Comm
7. $B \cdot (A \vee C)$ — 6 Dist
8. B — 7 Simp

Exercise 4-11

(2)   4. $[(A \lor B) \supset C] \cdot$
        $[C \supset (A \lor B)]$ 2 Equiv
       5. $C \supset (A \lor B)$ 4 Simp
       6. $\sim A \cdot \sim B$ 1,3 Conj
       7. $\sim (A \lor B)$ 6 DeM
       8. $\sim C$ 5,7 MT
       9. $\sim C \lor \sim D$ 8 Add
      10. $\sim (C \cdot D)$ 9 DeM

(4)   3. $(S \lor \sim R) \cdot (S \lor T)$ 1 Dist
       4. $S \lor \sim R$ 3 Simp
       5. $\sim \sim S \lor \sim R$ 4 DN
       6. $\sim S \supset \sim R$ 5 Impl
       7. $R \supset \sim R$ 2,6 HS
       8. $\sim R \lor \sim R$ 7 Impl
       9. $\sim R$ 8 Taut

(6)   5. $\sim (B \lor D)$ 3, 4 MT
       6. $\sim B \cdot \sim D$ 5 DeM
       7. $\sim B$ 6 Simp
       8. $\sim A$ 1,7 MT
       9. $\sim D$ 6 Simp
      10. $\sim C$ 2,9 MT
      11. $\sim A \cdot \sim C$ 8,10 Conj
      12. $\sim (A \lor C)$ 11 DeM

(8)   3. $\sim C \cdot \sim \sim A$ 2 DeM
       4. $\sim C$ 3 Simp
       5. $[(A \cdot B) \supset C] \cdot$
        $[C \supset (A \cdot B)]$ 1 Equiv
       6. $(A \cdot B) \supset C$ 5 Simp
       7. $\sim (A \cdot B)$ 4,6 MT
       8. $\sim A \lor \sim B$ 7 DeM
       9. $\sim \sim A$ 3 Simp
      10. $\sim B$ 8,9 DS

(10)   4. $(W \cdot Y) \lor$
        $(\sim W \cdot \sim Y)$ 1 Equiv
       5. $\sim (W \cdot Y)$ 2 DeM
       6. $\sim W \cdot \sim Y$ 4,5 DS
       7. $\sim Y$ 6 Simp
       8. $\sim Y \lor \sim Z$ 7 Add
       9. $\sim (Y \cdot Z)$ 8 DeM
      10. $\sim X$ 3,9 MT

(12)   2. $\sim R \supset \sim P$ 1 Contra
       3. $\sim R \supset (\sim R \supset S)$ 1,2 HS
       4. $(\sim R \cdot \sim R) \supset S$ 3 Exp
       5. $\sim R \supset S$ 4 Taut
       6. $\sim \sim R \lor S$ 5 Impl
       7. $R \lor S$ 6 DN

(14)   3. $\sim (A \lor C)$ 1 Comm
       4. $\sim (\sim \sim A \lor C)$ 3 DN
       5. $\sim (\sim A \supset C)$ 4 Impl
       6. $\sim B$ 2,5 MT

Exercise 4-12

(2)	3. $(S \lor \sim R) \cdot (S \lor T)$	1 Dist
	4. $S \lor \sim R$	3 Simp
	5. $\sim R \lor S$	4 Comm
	6. $R \supset S$	5 Impl
	7. $\sim S \supset \sim R$	6 Contra
	8. $R \supset \sim R$	2,7 HS
	9. $\sim R \lor \sim R$	8 Imp
	10. $\sim R$	9 Taut
(4)	4. $D \supset C$	3 Contra
	5. $B \lor C$	1,2,4 CD
	6. $\sim \sim B \lor C$	5 DN
	7. $\sim B \supset C$	6 Impl
	8. $\sim B \supset B$	2,7 HS
	9. $\sim \sim B \lor B$	8 Impl
	10. $B \lor B$	9 DN
	11. B	10 Taut
(6)	4. $(D \cdot B) \supset W$	2 Exp
	5. $(B \cdot D) \supset W$	4 Comm
	6. $B \supset (D \supset W)$	5 Exp
	7. $D \supset (D \supset W)$	1,6 HS
	8. $(D \cdot D) \supset W$	7 Exp
	9. $D \supset W$	8 Taut
	10. $D \supset (W \supset S)$	1,3 HS
	11. $(D \cdot W) \supset S$	10 Exp
	12. $(W \cdot D) \supset S$	11 Comm
	13. $W \supset (D \supset S)$	12 Exp
	14. $D \supset (D \supset S)$	9,13 HS
	15. $(D \cdot D) \supset S$	14 Exp
	16. $D \supset S$	15 Taut

(8)	3. $\sim (R \lor S) \lor T$	2 Impl
	4. $(\sim R \cdot \sim S) \lor T$	3 DeM
	5. $T \lor (\sim R \cdot \sim S)$	4 Comm
	6. $(T \lor \sim R) \cdot$ $(T \lor \sim S)$	5 Dist
	7. $T \lor \sim R$	6 Simp
	8. $\sim R \lor T$	7 Comm
	9. $R \supset T$	8 Impl
	10. $[K \cdot (L \lor M)] \supset R$	1 Exp
	11. $[(L \lor M) \cdot K] \supset R$	10 Comm
	12. $(L \lor M) \supset (K \supset R)$	11 Exp
	13. $\sim (L \lor M) \lor$ $(K \supset R)$	12 Impl
	14. $(\sim L \cdot \sim M) \lor$ $(K \supset R)$	13 DeM
	15. $(K \supset R) \lor$ $(\sim L \cdot \sim M)$	14 Comm
	16. $[(K \supset R) \lor \sim L] \cdot$ $[(K \supset R) \lor \sim M]$	15 Dist
	17. $(K \supset R) \lor \sim M$	16 Simp
	18. $\sim M \lor (K \supset R)$	17 Comm
	19. $M \supset (K \supset R)$	18 Impl
	20. $(M \cdot K) \supset R$	19 Exp
	21. $(M \cdot K) \supset T$	9,20 HS
	22. $(K \cdot M) \supset T$	21 Comm
	23. $K \supset (M \supset T)$	22 Exp
(10)	5. $C \lor A$	2 Comm
	6. $\sim \sim C \lor A$	5 DN
	7. $\sim C \supset A$	6 Impl
	8. $\sim C \supset B$	1,7 HS
	9. $\sim C \lor D$	4 Comm
	10. $C \supset D$	9 Impl
	11. $C \supset B$	3,10 HS
	12. $B \lor B$	1,5,11 CD
	13. B	12 Taut

(12) 2. $(\sim A \vee A) \supset$
       $(\sim\sim A \vee \sim A)$ 1 **Impl** (*twice*)

    3. $\sim(\sim A \vee A) \vee$
       $(\sim\sim A \vee \sim A)$ 2 **Impl**

    4. $(\sim\sim A \cdot \sim A) \vee$
       $(\sim\sim A \vee \sim A)$ 3 **DeM**

    5. $(A \cdot \sim A) \vee$
       $(A \vee \sim A)$ 4 **DN** (*twice*)

    6. $(A \vee \sim A) \vee (A \cdot \sim A)$ 5 **Comm**

    7. $[(A \vee \sim A) \vee A] \cdot$
       $[(A \vee \sim A) \vee \sim A]$ 6 **Dist**

    8. $(A \vee \sim A) \vee \sim A$ 7 **Simp**

    9. $A \vee (\sim A \vee \sim A)$ 8 **Assoc**

   10. $A \vee \sim A$ 9 **Taut**

(14) 3. $\sim A \vee B$ 1 **Impl**

    4. $(\sim A \vee B) \vee D$ 3 **Add**

    5. $\sim A \vee (B \vee D)$ 4 **Assoc**

    6. $(B \vee D) \vee \sim A$ 5 **Comm**

    7. $\sim C \vee D$ 2 **Impl**

    8. $(\sim C \vee D) \vee B$ 7 **Add**

    9. $\sim C \vee (D \vee B)$ 8 **Assoc**

   10. $\sim C \vee (B \vee D)$ 9 **Comm**

   11. $(B \vee D) \vee \sim C$ 10 **Comm**

   12. $[(B \vee D) \vee \sim A] \cdot$
      $[(B \vee D) \vee \sim C]$ 6,11 **Conj**

   13. $(B \vee D) \vee$
      $(\sim A \cdot \sim C)$ 12 **Dist**

   14. $(\sim A \cdot \sim C) \vee$
      $(B \vee D)$ 13 **Comm**

   15. $\sim(A \vee C) \vee$
      $(B \vee D)$ 14 **DeM**

   16. $(A \vee C) \supset (B \vee D)$ 15 **Impl**

Exercise 4-13

   2. Equivalence argument forms may be used on parts of lines because in doing so we replace part of a line with another formula having the same truth value, so that the truth value of the whole line remains the same.

   4. Because some substitution instances of some invalid argument forms are valid, since they also are substitution instances of some valid argument form or other. Example: The valid argument $A \supset B$, A /∴ B, a substitution instance of the invalid form p, q /∴ r, also is a substitution instance of the valid argument form Modus Ponens.

Exercise 5-1

(2)   → 2. A **AP**
       3. $B \cdot C$ 1,2 **MP**
       4. C 3 **Simp**
       5. $A \supset C$ 2-4 **CP**

(4)   → 3. A **AP**
       4. $B \supset C$ 1,3 **MP**
       5. $\sim B$ 2,4 **MT**
       6. $A \supset \sim B$ 3-5 **CP**

(6)   → 3. A **AP**
       4. B 2,3 **MP**
       5. $B \supset C$ 1,3 **MP**
       6. C 4,5 **MP**
       7. $A \supset C$ 3-6 **CP**

(8)   → 3. $A \cdot B$ **AP**
       4. C 1,3 **MP**
       5. B 3 **Simp**
       6. $B \cdot C$ 4,5 **Conj**
       7. D 2,6 **MP**
       8. $(A \cdot B) \supset D$ 3-7 **CP**

(10) → 3. A **AP**
       4. $B \supset C$ 1,3 **MP**
       5. $B \supset D$ 2,4 **HS**
       6. $A \supset (B \supset D)$ 3-5 **CP**

(12)   4. $(B \cdot C) \vee (E \cdot F)$ 1,2,3 **CD**
      5. $[(B \cdot C) \vee E] \cdot$
        $[(B \cdot C) \vee F]$ 4 **Dist**
      6. $(B \cdot C) \vee F$ 5 **Simp**
      7. $F \vee (B \cdot C)$ 6 **Comm**
      8. $(F \vee B) \cdot (F \vee C)$ 7 **Dist**
      9. $F \vee B$ 8 **Simp**
    10. $B \vee F$ 9 **Comm**

(14)   2. D **AP**
      3. G 1,2 **MP**
      4. $D \cdot G$ 2,3 **Conj**
      5. $D \supset (D \cdot G)$ 2-4 **CP**
      6. $D \cdot G$ **AP**
      7. D 6 **Simp**
      8. $(D \cdot G) \supset D$ 6-7 **CP**
      9. $[D \supset (D \cdot G)] \cdot$
        $[(D \cdot G) \supset D]$ 5,8 **Conj**
    10. $(D \cdot G) \equiv D$ 9 **Equiv**

Exercise 5-2

(6)   4. D **AP**
      5. $B \supset W$ 2,4 **MP**
      6. B 1,4 **MP**
      7. $W \supset S$ 3,6 **MP**
      8. W 5,6 **MP**
      9. S 7,8 **MP**
    10. $D \supset S$ 4-9 **CP**

(8)   3. K **AP**
      4. M **AP**
      5. $(L \vee M) \supset R$ 1,3 **MP**
      6. $M \vee L$ 4 **Add**
      7. $L \vee M$ 6 **Comm**
      8. R 5,7 **MP**
      9. $R \vee S$ 8 **Add**
    10. T 2,9 **MP**
    11. $M \supset T$ 4-10 **CP**
    12. $K \supset (M \supset T)$ 3-11 **CP**

(14)   3. $A \vee C$ **AP**
      4. $B \vee D$ 1,2,3 **CD**
      5. $(A \vee C) \supset (B \vee D)$ 3-4 **CP**

Exercise 5-3

(2)   3. $\sim A$ **AP**
      4. B 1,3 **MP**
      5. $\sim \sim A \vee \sim B$ 2 **DeM**
      6. $A \vee \sim B$ 5 **DN**
      7. $\sim B$ 3,6 **DS**
      8. $B \cdot \sim B$ 4,7 **Conj**
      9. A 3-8 **IP**

(4)   3. B **AP**
      4. $\sim A$ 2,3 **MP**
      5. $\sim B \cdot C$ 1,4 **DS**
      6. $\sim B$ 5 **Simp**
      7. $B \cdot \sim B$ 3,6 **Conj**
      8. $\sim B$ 3-7 **IP**

(6)

→ 4.	~ C	AP
5.	~ ~ A	2,4 MT
6.	A	5 DN
7.	A · B	3,6 Conj
8.	C	1,7 MP
9.	C · ~ C	4,8 Conj
10.	C	4-9 IP

(8)

→ 4.	~ (C ∨ D)	AP
5.	~ C · ~ D	4 DeM
6.	~ C	5 Simp
7.	A ∨ D	3,6 MP
8.	~ D	5 Simp
9.	A	7,8 DS
10.	B	2,9 MP
11.	B ⊃ C	1,9 MP
12.	C	10,11 MP
13.	C · ~ C	6,12 Conj
14.	C ∨ D	4-13 IP

(10)

→ 3.	~ (~ D ⊃ ~ C)	AP
4.	~ (~ ~ D ∨ ~ C)	3 Impl
5.	(~ ~ ~ D · ~ ~ C)	4 DeM
6.	~ D · C	5 DN (*twice*)
7.	C	6 Simp
8.	D ∨ ~ (A ∨ B)	1,7 MP
9.	~ D	6 Simp
10.	~ (A ∨ B)	8,9 DS
11.	~ A · ~ B	10 DeM
12.	~ A	11 Simp
13.	B	2,12 MP
14.	~ B	11 Simp
15.	B · ~ B	13,14 Conj
16.	~ D ⊃ ~ C	3-15 IP

Exercise 5-4

(2) *Without* **IP**:

4.	(H · A) ⊃ B	1 Exp
5.	(A · H) ⊃ B	4 Comm
6.	A ⊃ (H ⊃ B)	5 Exp
7.	H ⊃ (H ⊃ B)	3,6 HS
8.	(H · H) ⊃ B	7 Exp
9.	H ⊃ B	8 Taut
10.	~ C ⊃ (B ∨ H)	2 Comm
11.	~ C ⊃ (~ ~ B ∨ H)	10 DN
12.	~ C ⊃ (~ B ⊃ H)	11 Impl
13.	(~ C · ~ B) ⊃ H	12 Exp
14.	(~ C · ~ B) ⊃ B	9,13 HS
15.	~ C ⊃ (~ B ⊃ B)	14 Exp
16.	~ C ⊃ (~ ~ B ∨ B)	15 Impl
17.	~ C ⊃ (B ∨ B)	16 DN
18.	~ C ⊃ B	17 Taut
19.	~ ~ C ∨ B	18 Impl
20.	C ∨ B	19 DN

(2) *With* **IP**:

→ 4.	~ (C ∨ B)	AP
5.	~ C · ~ B	4 DeM
6.	~ C	5 Simp
7.	H ∨ B	2,6 MP
8.	~ B	5 Simp
9.	H	7,8 DS
10.	A	3,9 MP
11.	A ⊃ B	1,9 MP
12.	B	10,11 MP
13.	B · ~ B	8,12 Conj
14.	C ∨ B	4-13 IP

(4)   *Without* **IP**:

3.	$\sim (D \lor E) \lor (A \cdot C)$	2 **Impl**
4.	$(\sim D \cdot \sim E) \lor (A \cdot C)$	3 **DeM**
5.	$(A \cdot C) \lor (\sim D \cdot \sim E)$	4 **Comm**
6.	$[(A \cdot C) \lor \sim D] \cdot$ $[(A \cdot C) \lor \sim E]$	5 **Dist**
7.	$(A \cdot C) \lor \sim D$	6 **Simp**
8.	$\sim D \lor (A \cdot C)$	7 **Comm**
9.	$(\sim D \lor A) \cdot (\sim D \lor C)$	8 **Dist**
10.	$\sim D \lor A$	9 **Simp**
11.	$(\sim D \lor A) \lor B$	10 **Add**
12.	$\sim D \lor (A \lor B)$	11 **Assoc**
13.	$D \supset (A \lor B)$	12 **Impl**
14.	$D \supset (C \supset \sim D)$	1,13 **HS**
15.	$(D \cdot C) \supset \sim D$	14 **Exp**
16.	$(C \cdot D) \supset \sim D$	15 **Comm**
17.	$C \supset (D \supset \sim D)$	16 **Exp**
18.	$\sim D \lor C$	9 **Simp**
19.	$D \supset C$	18 **Impl**
20.	$D \supset (D \supset \sim D)$	17,19 **HS**
21.	$(D \cdot D) \supset \sim D$	20 **Exp**
22.	$D \supset \sim D$	21 **Taut**
23.	$\sim D \lor \sim D$	22 **Impl**
24.	$\sim D$	23 **Taut**

(4)   *With* **IP**:

→ 3.	$\sim \sim D$	**AP**
4.	D	3 **DN**
5.	$D \lor E$	4 **Add**
6.	$A \cdot C$	2,5 **MP**
7.	A	6 **Simp**
8.	$A \lor B$	7 **Add**
9.	$C \supset \sim D$	1,8 **MP**
10.	C	6 **Simp**
11.	$\sim D$	9,10 **MP**
12.	$D \cdot \sim D$	4,11 **Conj**
13.	$\sim D$	3-12 **IP**

(6) *Without* **IP**:

4. $\sim (L \vee N) \vee (F \cdot P)$ 1 **Impl**

5. $[\sim (L \vee N) \vee F] \cdot$
   $[\sim (L \vee N) \vee P]$ 4 **Dist**

6. $\sim (L \vee N) \vee F$ 5 **Simp**

7. $F \vee \sim (L \vee N)$ 6 **Comm**

8. $F \vee (\sim L \cdot \sim N)$ 7 **DeM**

9. $(F \vee \sim L) \cdot (F \vee \sim N)$ 8 **Dist**

10. $F \vee \sim L$ 9 **Simp**

11. $\sim L \vee F$ 10 **Comm**

12. $L \supset F$ 11 **Impl**

13. $L \supset (H \cdot K)$ 2,12 **HS**

14. $\sim L \vee (H \cdot K)$ 13 **Impl**

15. $(\sim L \vee H) \cdot (\sim L \vee K)$ 14 **Dist**

16. $\sim L \vee H$ 15 **Simp**

17. $L \supset H$ 16 **Impl**

18. $L \supset (\sim L \cdot M)$ 3,17 **HS**

19. $\sim L \vee (\sim L \cdot M)$ 18 **Impl**

20. $(\sim L \vee \sim L) \cdot$
    $(\sim L \vee M)$ 19 **Dist**

21. $\sim L \vee \sim L$ 20 **Simp**

22. $\sim L$ 1 **Taut**

(6) *With* **IP**:

4. L **AP**

5. $L \vee N$ 4 **Add**

6. $F \cdot P$ 1,5 **MP**

7. F 6 **Simp**

8. $H \cdot K$ 2,7 **MP**

9. H 8 **Simp**

10. $\sim L \cdot M$ 3,9 **MP**

11. $\sim L$ 10 **Simp**

12. $L \cdot \sim L$ 4,11 **Conj**

13. $\sim L$ 4-12 **IP**

(8) *Without* **IP**:

5. ~ $(R \supset M) \lor L$	1 **Impl**
6. ~ $(\sim R \lor M) \lor L$	5 **Impl**
7. $(\sim \sim R \cdot \sim M) \lor L$	6 **DeM**
8. $L \lor (\sim \sim R \cdot \sim M)$	7 **Comm**
9. $(L \lor \sim \sim R) \cdot$ $(L \lor \sim M)$	8 **Dist**
10. $L \lor \sim \sim R$	9 **Simp**
11. ~ $(P \supset R) \lor L$	3 **Impl**
12. $L \lor \sim (P \supset R)$	11 **Comm**
13. $L \lor \sim (\sim P \lor R)$	12 **Impl**
14. $L \lor (\sim \sim P \cdot \sim R)$	13 **DeM**
15. $(L \lor \sim \sim P) \cdot$ $(L \lor \sim R)$	14 **Dist**
16. $L \lor \sim R$	15 **Simp**
17. $\sim \sim L \lor \sim R$	16 **DN**
18. ~ $L \supset \sim R$	17 **Impl**
19. $\sim \sim R \lor L$	10 **Comm**
20. ~ $R \supset L$	19 **Impl**
21. ~ $L \supset L$	18,20 **HS**
22. $\sim \sim L \lor L$	21 **Impl**
23. $L \lor L$	22 **DN**
24. L	23 **Taut**

(8) *With* **IP**:

→ 5. ~ L	**AP**
6. ~ $(R \supset M)$	1,5 **MT**
7. ~ $(\sim R \lor M)$	6 **Impl**
8. $\sim \sim R \cdot \sim M$	7 **DeM**
9. $\sim \sim R$	8 **Simp**
10. ~ $(P \supset R)$	3,5 **MT**
11. ~ $(\sim P \lor R)$	10 **Impl**
12. $\sim \sim P \cdot \sim R$	11 **DeM**
13. ~ R	12 **Simp**
14. ~ $R \cdot \sim \sim R$	9,13 **Conj**
15. L	5-14 **IP**

Exercise 5-5

(2)

→ 4. ~ $(G \cdot \sim I)$	**AP**
5. ~ $G \lor \sim \sim I$	4 **DeM**
6. H	2 **Simp**
7. $I \supset F$	2 **Simp**
8. ~ F	3,6 **MP**
9. G	1,8 **DS**
10. ~ I	7,8 **MT**
11. ~ $G \lor I$	5 **DN**
12. ~ G	10,11 **DS**
13. $G \cdot \sim G$	9,12 **Conj**
14. $G \cdot \sim I$	4-13 **IP**

(4)

→ 4. ~ T	**AP**
5. ~ S	2,4 **MT**
6. $T \supset R$	1,5 **DS**
7. $(T \supset R) \cdot \sim (T \supset R)$	3,6 **Conj**
8. T	4-7 **IP**

(6)

→ 3. B	**AP**
4. ~ $B \lor \sim A$	2 **DeM**
5. $\sim \sim B$	3 **DN**
6. ~ A	4,5 **DS**
7. $D \cdot C$	1,6 **MP**
8. C	7 **Simp**
9. $B \supset C$	3-8 **CP**
10. ~ $C \supset \sim B$	9 **Contra**

(8)

→ 4.	C		AP
5.	$(A \vee \sim B) \vee \sim C$		1 **Assoc**
6.	$\sim C \vee (A \vee \sim B)$		5 **Comm**
7.	$\sim \sim C$		4 **DN**
8.	$A \vee \sim B$		6,7 **DS**
9.	$\sim \sim B \cdot \sim \sim D$		3 **DeM**
10.	$\sim \sim B$		9 **Simp**
11.	A		8,10 **DS**
12.	$D \supset E$		2,11 **MP**
13.	$\sim \sim D$		9 **Simp**
14.	D		13 **DN**
15.	E		12,14 **MP**
16.	$C \supset E$		4-15 **CP**

(10)

→ 3.	$\sim T$		AP
4.	$\sim S$		2 **MT**
5.	$T \cdot R$		1,4 **DS**
6.	T		5 **Simp**
7.	$T \cdot \sim T$		3,6 **Conj**
8.	T		3-7 **IP**

(12)

→ 4.	$M \cdot H$		AP
5.	$(M \cdot H) \supset (N \cdot \sim L)$		2 **Exp**
6.	$N \cdot \sim L$		4,5 **MP**
7.	N		6 **Simp**
8.	$\sim L$		6 **Simp**
9.	H		4 **Simp**
10.	$H \vee K$		9 **Add**
11.	$L \vee K$		1,10 **MP**
12.	K		8,12 **DS**
13.	$N \cdot K$		7,12 **Conj**
14.	$(M \cdot H) \supset (N \cdot K)$		4-12 **CP**

(14)

→ 4.	$D \cdot H$		AP
5.	D		4 **Simp**
6.	$E \supset F$		1,5 **MP**
7.	$G \supset \sim H$		3,5 **MP**
8.	H		4 **Simp**
9.	$E \vee G$		2, 8 **MP**
10.	$F \vee \sim H$		6,7,9 **CD**
11.	$\sim \sim H$		8 **DN**
12.	F		10,11 **DS**
13.	$(D \cdot H) \supset F$		4-12 **CP**
14.	$D \supset (H \supset F)$		13 **Exp**
15.	$\sim (H \supset F) \supset \sim D$		14 **Contra**
16.	$\sim (\sim F \supset \sim H) \supset \sim D$		15 **Contra**

Exercise 5-6

(2)

→ 1.	$A \cdot B$		AP
2.	A		1 **Simp**
3.	$(A \cdot B) \supset A$		1-2 **CP**

(4)

→ 1.	$A \supset (B \supset C)$		AP
→ 2.	$A \supset B$		AP
→ 3.	A		AP
4.	B		2,3 **MP**
5.	$B \supset C$		1,3 **MP**
6.	C		4,5 **MP**
7.	$A \supset C$		3-6 **CP**
8.	$(A \supset B) \supset (A \supset C)$		2-7 **CP**
9.	$[A \supset (B \supset C)] \supset$ $[(A \supset B) \supset (A \supset C)]$		1-8 **CP**

(6)

→ 1.	$A \vee B$		AP
→ 2.	$(A \supset C) \cdot (B \supset C)$		AP
3.	$A \supset C$		2 **Simp**
4.	$B \supset C$		2 **Simp**
5.	$C \vee C$		1,3,4 **CD**
6.	C		5 **Taut**
7.	$[(A \supset C) \cdot (B \supset C)] \supset C$		2-6 **CP**
8.	$(A \vee B) \supset \{[(A \supset C) \cdot (B \supset C)] \supset C\}$		1-7 **CP**

(8)   → 1. $A \equiv B$ **AP**

       2. $(A \supset B) \cdot (B \supset A)$ **1 Equiv**

       3. $A \supset B$ **2 Simp**

       4. $B \supset A$ **2 Simp**

       5. $\sim B \supset \sim A$ **3 Contra**

       6. $\sim A \supset \sim B$ **4 Contra**

       7. $(\sim A \supset \sim B) \cdot$
           $(\sim B \supset \sim A)$ **5,6 Conj**

       8. $\sim A \equiv \sim B$ **7 Equiv**

       9. $(A \equiv B) \supset (\sim A \equiv \sim B)$ **1-8 CP**

  →10. $\sim A \equiv \sim B$ **AP**

     11. $(\sim A \supset \sim B) \cdot$
         $(\sim B \supset \sim A)$ **10 Equiv**

     12. $\sim A \supset \sim B$ **11 Simp**

     13. $\sim B \supset \sim A$ **12 Simp**

     14. $B \supset A$ **12 Contra**

     15. $A \supset B$ **13 Contra**

     16. $(A \supset B) \cdot (B \supset A)$ **14,15 Conj**

     17. $A \equiv B$ **16 Equiv**

     18. $(\sim A \equiv \sim B) \supset (A \equiv B)$ **10-17 CP**

     19. $(A \equiv B) \supset (\sim A \equiv \sim B) \cdot$
         $(\sim A \equiv \sim B) \supset (A \equiv B)$ **9,18 Conj**

     20. $(A \equiv B) \equiv (\sim A \equiv \sim B)$ **19 Equiv**

Exercise 5-7

(2)   4. $\sim \sim A$ **3 DN**

           5. B **1,4 DS**

           6. $\sim B$ **2,4 DS**

           7. $B \cdot \sim B$ **5,6 Conj**

(4)   4. $\sim (R \vee S)$ **1 DeM**

           5. $\sim (S \vee T)$ **3,4 MP**

           6. $\sim S \cdot \sim T$ **5 DeM**

           7. $\sim S$ **6 Simp**

           8. $\sim S \cdot T$ **2,7 DS**

           9. T **8 Simp**

         10. $\sim T$ **6 Simp**

         11. $T \cdot \sim T$ **9,10 Conj**

(6)   5. $(H \vee \sim H) \supset (H \cdot \sim H)$ **1,4 HS**

           6. $\sim (H \vee \sim H) \vee (H \cdot \sim H)$ **5 Impl**

           7. $(\sim H \cdot \sim \sim H) \vee$
             $(H \cdot \sim H)$ **6 DeM**

           8. $(\sim H \cdot H) \vee (H \cdot \sim H)$ **7 DN**

           9. $(H \cdot \sim H) \vee (H \cdot \sim H)$ **8 Comm**

         10. $H \cdot \sim H$ **9 Taut**

(8)	7.	*B*	6 **Simp**	(10)	4.	$\sim \sim A \cdot \sim [C \supset (B \cdot D)]$	3 **DeM**
	8.	$\sim C$	4,7 **MP**		5.	$\sim \sim A$	4 **Simp**
	9.	$B \cdot A$	3,8 **DS**		6.	$\sim \sim C \cdot \sim (A \vee \sim D)$	2 **DeM**
	10.	*A*	9 **Simp**		7.	$\sim (A \vee \sim D)$	6 **Simp**
	11.	$\sim A$	6 **Simp**		8.	$\sim A \cdot \sim \sim D$	7 **DeM**
	12.	$A \cdot \sim A$	10,11 **Conj**		9.	$\sim A$	8 **Simp**
					10.	$\sim A \cdot \sim \sim A$	5,9 **Conj**

Exercise 5-8

2 and 6 are valid argument forms, 4 is not.

Exercise 6-1

2. *Bb*

4. $\sim Mh \cdot \sim Mk$ or $\sim (Mh \vee Mk)$

6. $Gk \cdot Pk$

8. $Mb \supset Md$

Exercise 6-2

2. (1) *x* is bound.

(2) *a* is an individual constant; *F* and *G* are property constants.

(3) No free variables; *a* is within the scope of the (*x*) quantifier.

4. (1) *y* and the first *x* variable (not counting the *x* that is part of the quantifier) are bound; the second *x* variable is free.

(2) No individual constants; *F* and *G* are property constants.

(3) Free *x* variable is within the scope of the (*y*) quantifier.

6. (1) The *y* variable and the first *x* variable are bound. The last two *x* variables are free.

(2) *F* and *G* serve as property constants; *a* is an individual constant.

(3) The two free *x* variables are within the scope of the (*y*) quantifier. The individual constant, *a*, is within the scope of the (*x*) quantifier.

Exercise 6-3

2. $(x)(Ex \supset Cx)$

4. $(x)(Ex \supset \sim Cx)$

6. $(x)[(Ex \cdot Cx) \supset Nx]$

8. $(x)[Cx \supset (Nx \cdot Ex)]$

10. $(x)[Ex \supset (Nx \vee \sim Cx)]$

12. $(x)[Mx \supset (Cx \cdot \sim Nx)]$

14. $(x)(Ex \supset Nx) \supset (x) \sim Mx$

Exercise 6-4

2. $(x)(Px \supset \sim Ix)$

4. $\sim Ir \supset \sim (x)(Px \supset Ix)$

6. $(Ib \vee \sim Ir) \supset [\sim (x)(Px \supset \sim Ix) \cdot \sim (x)(Px \supset Ix)]$

8. $(x)(Sx \supset \sim Lx)$

10. $(x)(Lx \supset \sim Px)$

12. $\sim (x)(Sx \supset Lx) \supset \sim (x)(Sx \supset \sim Px)$

14. $(x)(Px \supset \sim Sx) \supset (\sim La \supset Sa)$

16. $(\sim Pa \cdot \sim La) \supset [\sim (x)(Sx \supset Px) \cdot \sim (x)(Sx \supset Lx)]$

Exercise 6-5

2. $(\exists x)(Ax \cdot \sim Ox)$

4. $(\exists x)(Ex \cdot Ox)$

6. $(\exists x)(Ax \cdot Px) \cdot (\exists x)(Ax \cdot Tx)$

8. $(\exists x)(Tx \cdot \sim Px)$

10. $(\exists x)(Rx \cdot Sx)$

12. $(\exists x)(Rx \cdot Fx)$

14. $(x)[(Rx \cdot Fx) \supset \sim Dx]$

Exercise 6-6

2. $(x)[(Ax \cdot Px) \supset Mx]$ ($Ax = x$ is an animal; $Px = x$ has a pouch; $Mx = x$ is a marsupial)

4. $(x)[(Ax \cdot \sim Px) \supset \sim Mx]$

6. $(x)[(Wx \cdot \sim Bx) \supset (Mx \cdot \sim Wx)]$ ($Wx = x$ is a wombat; $Bx = x$ is a bandicoot; $Wx = x$ is well known)

8. $(x)[Mx \supset (Cx \cdot Fx)] \supset (x)$ $[Ox \supset (Cx \cdot Fx)]$ ($Ox = x$ is an opposum)

10. $(x)[(Ax \vee Rx) \supset \sim Mx]$ ($Ax = x$ is an aardvark; $Rx = x$ is an armadillo)

12. $(x)[Ax \supset (\sim Mx \cdot \sim Rx)$ ($Rx = x$ is a reptile)

14. $(\exists x)[(Px \cdot Cx) \cdot \sim Tx]$ ($Px = x$ is a physician; $Cx = x$ is competent; $Tx = x$ has tact)

16. $\sim (x)[(Sx \cdot Fx) \supset Hx]$ ($Sx = x$ is a soldier; $Fx = x$ fought in Vietnam; $Hx = x$ is a hero)

18. $(\exists x)(Gx \cdot Cx) \cdot (\exists x)(Bx \cdot Cx)$ ($Gx = x$ is a girl scout; $Bx = x$ is a boy scout; $Cx = x$ is to be congratulated by President Clinton)

20. $\sim (x)(Dx \supset Sx) \cdot \sim (x)(Rx \supset Sx)$ ($Dx = x$ is a Democrat; $Rx = x$ is a Republican; $Sx = x$ supported the President's tax plan)

Exercise 6-7

2. Some TV newscasters are not political experts.

4. All TV newscasters are not political experts. Or, No TV newscasters are political experts.

6. Anyone who is a political expert but doesn't have a pleasant personality is not a TV newscaster. Or, No political expert lacking a pleasant personality is a TV newscaster.

8. Some TV newscasters either have pleasant personalities or are political experts.

10. If Dan Rather is a TV newscaster, then not all TV newscasters with pleasant personalities are political experts.

12. If all TV newscasters have pleasant personalities and are political experts, then it's not true that either Dan Rather or Barbara Walters are TV newscasters.

Exercise 6-8

2. $(Fa \vee Ga) \vee (Fb \vee Gb)$

4. $[Fa \cdot (Ga \vee Ha)] \vee [Fb \cdot (Gb \vee Hb)]$

6. $\sim (Fa \vee Ga) \vee \sim (Fb \vee Gb)$

8. $\sim [(Fa \vee Ga) \vee (Fb \vee Gb)]$

10. $[Fa \supset \sim (Ga \cdot Ha)] \cdot [Fb \supset \sim (Gb \cdot Hb)]$

12. $[(Fa \cdot Ga) \supset (Ha \cdot Ka)] \cdot [(Fb \cdot Gb) \supset (Hb \cdot Kb)]$

14. $\sim \{\sim [(Fa \cdot Ga) \cdot \sim (Ha \cdot Ka)] \cdot \sim [(Fb \cdot Gb) \cdot \sim (Hb \cdot Kb)]\}$

Exercise 6-9

2. $(x)[(Sx \cdot Fx) \supset \sim Rx]$

4. $(x)(Hx \supset Px)$

6. $(x)(Dx \supset Sx)$

8. $\sim Qj \supset (x)(Fx \supset Rx)$

10. $\sim (x)(Ex \supset Px) \supset (x)(Ex \supset Dx)$

12. $(x)[Rx \supset (\sim Tx \supset Px)]$

Exercise 6-10

(Using obvious abbreviations, except where noted otherwise.)

2. $(x)(Sx \supset Lx)$

4. $\sim (x)(Lx \supset Gx)$ or $(\exists x)(Lx \cdot \sim Gx)$
   (Lx = "x glitters"; Gs = "x is gold")

6. $(\exists x)(Cx \cdot Sx)$ (Cx = "x is a cigar";
   Sx = "x is significant"—the import
   of Freud's remark)

8. $(x)(Cx \supset Dx)$

10. $(x)[(Wx \cdot \sim Mx) \supset Bx]$

12. $(\exists x)[(Bx \cdot Sx) \cdot (Cx)]$

14. $(\exists x)[(Sx \cdot (Cx) \cdot \sim Bx]$

16. $(\exists x)(Sx \cdot \sim Lx) \supset (\exists x)[(Px \cdot \sim Bx) \cdot Sx]$

18. $(x)(Sx \supset Bx) \supset (x)[(Px \cdot \sim Sx) \supset \sim Lx]$

20. $\sim (\exists x) \, Sx \supset [(\exists x)(Px \cdot \sim Lx) \cdot (\exists x)(Px \cdot Lx)$

Exercise 7-1

2. True:
   Ax = x is an NBA basketball player
   Bx = x is more than 6 feet tall

   False:
   Ax = $x > 4$
   Bx = $x > 3$

   True:
   Domain: Amber, a Labrador Retriever,
   and Brutus, a guinea pig.
   Ax = x barks
   Bx = x squeaks

4. True:
   Ax = x is a bachelor
   Bx = x wants to marry

   True:
   Ax = x is a prime number
   Bx = x is odd

   False:
   Domain: Amber, a Labrador Retriever,
   and Brutus, a guinea pig.
   Ax = x barks
   Bx = x is a dog

6. False:
   Ax = x is an argument
   Bx = x has inconsistent premises
   Cx = x is valid

   True:
   Ax = $x > 2$
   Bx = $x > 3$
   Cx = $x > 5$

   True:
   Domain: Amber, a Labrador Retriever,
   and Brutus, a guinea pig.
   Ax = x wags its tail
   Bx = x catches frisbees
   Cx = x is a rodent

8. True:
   Ax = x is a whale
   Bx = x is a mammal
   Cx = x lives in the sea

   True:
   Ax = $x < 0$
   Bx = x is odd
   Cx = x is even

   False:
   Domain: Amber, a Labrador Retriever,
   and Brutus, a guinea pig.
   Ax = x barks
   Bx = x is a dog
   Cx = x is a rodent

Exercise 7-2

(Assume the domain of discourse to be positive integers.)

2. $Ax = x$ is an even number   8. $Mx = x > 25$

   $Bx = x$ is an integer $Nx = x > 20$

4. $Fx = x > 3$ $Px = x > 15$

   $Gx = x > 2$ $Qx = x > 10$

   $Ex = x > 0$ 10. $Ax = x > 10$

6. $Px = x$ is prime $Bx = x > 10$

   $Qx = x > 2$ $Cx = x > x$

   $Rx = x$ is odd

Exercise 7-3

(2)   1. $(Aa \lor Ba) \cdot (Ab \lor Bb)$

        F T T T T T T

    2. $\sim Aa \lor \sim Ab /\therefore \sim Ba \lor \sim Bb$

      T F T F T   F T F F T

(4)   1. $(Fa \supset Ga) \cdot (Fb \supset Gb)$

        F T F T T T T

    2. $(\sim Fa \supset Ea) \cdot (\sim Fb \supset Eb)$

      T F T T T F T T T

    $/\therefore (\sim Ga \supset \sim Ea) \cdot (\sim Gb \supset \sim Eb)$

      T F F F T F F T T F T

(6)   1. $[(Pa \cdot Qa) \supset Ra] \cdot [(Pb \cdot Qb) \supset Rb]$

       F F T T F T T F F T F

    2. $(Qa \cdot \sim Ra) \lor (Qb \cdot \sim Rb)$

      T T T F T F F T F

    3. $(Pa \cdot \sim Ra) \lor (Pb \cdot \sim Rb)$

       F F T F T T T T F

    $/\therefore (\sim Pa \cdot \sim Qa) \lor (\sim Pb \cdot \sim Qb)$

      T F F F T F F T F T F

(8)   1. $[Ma \supset (Na \supset Pa)] \cdot [Mb \supset (Nb \supset Pb)]$

       F T F T F T F T T T T

    2. $(\sim Qa \supset \sim Pa) \cdot (\sim Qb \supset \sim Pb)$

      T F T T F T F T T F T

    $/\therefore [\sim Qa \supset (Ma \lor Na)] \cdot [\sim Qb \supset (Mb \lor Nb)]$

      T F F F F F F F T T F T T

(10)   1. $(Aa \lor \sim Ba) \lor (Ab \lor \sim Bb)$

      T T F T T T T F T

    2. $[(Aa \cdot \sim Ba) \supset Ca] \cdot [(Ab \cdot \sim Bb) \supset Cb] /\therefore Ca \lor Cb$

      T F F T T F T T F F T T F   F F F

Exercise 7-4

(For our answers, assume the domain of discourse to be positive integers.)

2. $Rx = x$ is even

   $Mx = x$ is odd

4. $Bx = x$ is divisible by 4

   $Kx = x$ is even

6. $Dx = x$ is even

   $Fx = x$ is prime

   $Gx = x$ is odd

8. $Fx = x$ is divisible by 4

   $Gx = x$ is even

Exercise 8-1

(2)			(6)		
3. $Ax \lor (Bx \cdot \sim Cx)$	1 **UI**		4. $Rx \supset \sim Gx$	1 **UI**
4. Cx	2 **UI**		5. $Bx \lor Gx$	2 **UI**
5. Dx	3 **AP**		6. Rx	3 **UI**
6. $Cx \lor \sim Bx$	4 **Add**		7. $\sim Gx$	4,6 **MP**
7. $\sim Bx \lor Cx$	6 **Comm**		8. Bx	5,7 **DS**
8. $\sim Bx \lor \sim \sim Cx$	7 **DN**		9. $(\exists y)By$	8 **EG**
9. $\sim (Bx \cdot \sim Cx)$	8 **DeM**	(8)	4. $(Rb \cdot Ab) \supset Tb$	1 **UI**
10. Ax	3,9 **DS**		5. Rb	3 **UI**
11. $Dx \supset Ax$	5-10 **CP**		6. $Rb \cdot Ab$	2,5 **Conj**
(4) 4. $Ab \supset Bb$	2 **UI**		7. Tb	4,6 **MP**
5. $(Ab \supset Bb) \supset Ab$	3 **UI**		8. $Tb \cdot Rb$	5,7 **Conj**
6. Ab	4,5 **MP**			
7. Bc	1,6 **MP**			

Exercise 8-2

(2) 5. Invalid. The (x) quantifier did not quantify the whole line.

6. Invalid. Antecedent of line 5 does not match line 3.

7. Invalid. Can't universally generalize from a constant.

(4) 5. Invalid. Can't use **UG** to bind a variable that is free in a line that is justified by **EI**. In this case y is free in line 2.

(6) 4. Invalid. The (x) quantifier does not quantify the whole line.

5. Invalid. Can't replace a variable with a constant when using **EI**.

6. Invalid. Violates second restriction on **EI** because the x freed already is free on line 4.

9. Invalid. Can't universally generalize from a constant.

Exercise 8-3

(2) 3. $Fx \supset Gx$ 1 **UI**
     4. $Gx \supset Hx$ 2 **UI**
     5. $Fx \supset Hx$ 3,4 **HS**
     6. $\sim Hx \supset \sim Fx$ 5 **Contra**
     7. $(z)(\sim Hz \supset \sim Fz)$ 6 **UG**

(4) 4. $\sim Gx$ 3 **EI**
     5. $Ax \supset Fx$ 2 **UI**
     6. $Fx \supset Gx$ 1 **UI**
     7. $Ax \supset Gx$ 5,6 **HS**
     8. $\sim Ax$ 4,7 **MT**
     9. $(\exists x) \sim Ax$ 8 **EG**

(6) 4. $\sim Ox$ 2 **UI**
     5. $Rx \supset Ox$ 1 **UI**
     6. $\sim Rx \supset Px$ 3 **UI**
     7. $\sim Rx$ 4,5 **MT**
     8. Px 6,7 **MP**
     9. $(\exists z)Pz$ 8 **EG**

(8) 4. Rx 1 **EI**
     5. $\sim Gx \supset \sim Rx$ 2 **UI**
     6. Mx 3 **UI**
     7. $Rx \supset Gx$ 5 **Contra**
     8. Gx 4,7 **MP**
     9. $(\exists x)Gx$ 8 **EG**
     10. $(\exists x)Mx$ 6 **EG**
     11. $(\exists x)Gx \cdot (\exists x)Mx$ 9,10 **Conj**

(10) 3. $Mx \cdot Lx$ 2 **EI**
     4. $Kx \supset \sim Lx$ 1 **UI**
     5. Lx 3 **Simp**
     6. $\sim \sim Lx$ 5 **DN**
     7. $\sim Kx$ 4,6 **MT**
     8. Mx 3 **Simp**
     9. $Mx \cdot \sim Kx$ 7,8 **Conj**
     10. $(\exists x)(Mx \cdot \sim Kx)$ 9 **EG**

(12) 4. $Rx \cdot Kx$ 2 **EI**
     5. $Lx \supset \sim Kx$ 1 **UI**
     6. $(\sim Lx \cdot Rx) \supset Bx$ 3 **UI**
     7. Kx 4 **Simp**
     8. $\sim \sim Kx$ 7 **DN**
     9. $\sim Lx$ 5,8 **MT**
     10. Rx 4 **Simp**
     11. $\sim Lx \cdot Rx$ 9,10 **Conj**
     12. Bx 6,11 **MP**
     13. $(\exists x)Bx$ 12 **EG**

Exercise 8-4

2. Correct.

4. Incorrect. (Correct use would result in $(y)(Ry \cdot \sim Ky)$.)

6. Correct.

8. Incorrect. (Correct use would result in $\sim (\exists y)Fy \supset (\exists z)(Gz \cdot Hz)$

10. Incorrect. (Correct use would result in $\sim (\exists x)(Fx \supset Gx)$.)

Exercise 8-5

(2) 2. $Hx \supset \sim Kx$ 1 **UI**
     3. $\sim Hx \vee \sim Kx$ 2 **Impl**
     4. $\sim (Hx \cdot Kx)$ 3 **DeM**
     5. $(y) \sim (Hy \cdot Ky)$ 4 **UG**
     6. $\sim (\exists y)(Hy \cdot Ky)$ 5 **QN**

(4) 2. $(x) \sim Fx$ 1 **QN**
     3. $\sim Fa$ 2 **UI**
     4. $\sim Fa \vee Ga$ 3 **Add**
     5. $Fa \supset Ga$ 4 **Impl**

(6) 3. $(\exists y) \sim Cy$ — 2 **EG**
4. $\sim (y)Cy$ — 3 **QN**
5. $\sim (\exists x)(Ax \cdot Bx)$ — 1,4 **MT**
6. $(x) \sim (Ax \cdot Bx)$ — 5 **QN**
7. $(x)(\sim Ax \lor \sim Bx)$ — 6 **DeM**
8. $(x)(Ax \supset \sim Bx)$ — 7 **Impl**

(8) 3. $(\exists x) \sim (Hx \lor Kx)$ — 1 **QN**
4. $\sim (Hx \lor Kx)$ — 3 **EI**
5. $\sim Hx \cdot \sim Kx$ — 4 **DeM**
6. $\sim Kx$ — 5 **Simp**
7. $(\sim Kx \lor Lx) \supset Mx$ — 2 **UI**
8. $\sim Kx \lor Lx$ — 6 **Add**
9. Mx — 7,8 **MP**
10. $(\exists z)Mz$ — 9 **EG**

(10) ┌→ 3. $\sim (\exists x)Sx$ — **AP**
4. $\sim (\exists x)Rx$ — 1,3 **MT**
5. $(x) \sim Rx$ — 4 **QN**
6. $\sim Rx$ — 5 **UI**
7. $Tx \supset Rx$ — 2 **UI**
8. $\sim Tx$ — 6,7 **MT**
9. $(x) \sim Tx$ — 8 **UG**
└ 10. $\sim (\exists x)Tx$ — 9 **QN**
11. $\sim (\exists x)Sx \supset \sim (\exists x)Tx$ — 3-10 **CP**
12. $(\exists x)Tx \supset (\exists x)Sx$ — 11 **Contra**

(12) 4. $Ix \cdot \sim Hx$ — 2 **EI**
5. $\sim Fx \lor Gx$ — 3 **UI**
6. $Gx \supset Hx$ — 1 **UI**
7. $Fx \supset Gx$ — 5 **Impl**
8. $Fx \supset Hx$ — 6,7 **HS**
9. $\sim Hx$ — 4 **Simp**
10. $\sim Fx$ — 8,9 **MT**
11. Ix — 4 **Simp**
12. $Ix \cdot \sim Fx$ — 10,11 **Conj**
13. $(\exists x)(Ix \cdot \sim Fx)$ — 12 **EG**

(14) 3. $(\exists x) \sim (Fx \supset Gx)$ — 1 **QN**
4. $\sim (Fx \supset Gx)$ — 3 **EI**
5. $\sim (\sim Fx \lor Gx)$ — 4 **Impl**
6. $\sim \sim Fx \cdot \sim Gx$ — 5 **DeM**
7. $\sim Gx$ — 6 **Simp**
8. $(x) \sim (\sim Gx \cdot Hx)$ — 2 **QN**
9. $\sim (\sim Gx \cdot Hx)$ — 8 **UI**
10. $\sim \sim Gx \lor \sim Hx$ — 9 **DeM**
11. $Gx \lor \sim Hx$ — 10 **DN**
12. $\sim Hx$ — 7,11 **DS**
13. $(\exists x) \sim Hx$ — 12 **EG**

(16) 4. $\sim (Px \lor \sim Qx)$ — 3 **EI**
5. $\sim Px \cdot \sim \sim Qx$ — 4 **DeM**
6. $\sim \sim Qx$ — 5 **Simp**
7. Qx — 6 **DN**
8. $Qx \lor Rx$ — 7 **Add**
9. $Rx \lor Qx$ — 8 **Comm**
10. $(Rx \lor Qx) \supset Sx$ — 1 **UI**
11. Sx — 9,10 **MP**
12. $(\exists w)Sw$ — 11 **EG**

(18) ┌→ 3. Fx — **AP**
4. $(\exists x)Fx$ — 3 **EG**
5. $(\exists x)(Gx \cdot Hx)$ — 1,4 **MP**
6. $Gy \cdot Hy$ — 5 **EI**
7. Hy — 6 **Simp**
8. $Hy \lor Ky$ — 7 **Add**
9. $(\exists x)(Hx \lor Kx)$ — 8 **EG**
10. $(x)Lx$ — 2,9 **MP**
└ 11. Lx — 10 **UI**
12. $Fx \supset Lx$ — 3-11 **CP**
13. $(x)(Fx \supset Lx)$ — 12 **UG**

(20)

3.	$Px \supset (Ax \lor Bx)$	1 **UI**
4.	$(Bx \lor Cx) \supset Qx$	2 **UI**
→ 5.	$Px \cdot \sim Ax$	**AP**
6.	Px	5 **Simp**
7.	$Ax \lor Bx$	3,6 **MP**
8.	$\sim Ax$	5 **Simp**
9.	Bx	7,8 **DS**
10.	$Bx \lor Cx$	9 **Add**
11.	Qx	4,10 **MP**
12.	$(Px \cdot \sim Ax) \supset Qx$	5-11 **CP**
13.	$(x)[(Px \cdot \sim Ax) \supset Qx]$	12 **UG**

(22)

2.	$\sim (\exists x) Cx$	**AP**
3.	$(x) \sim Cx$	2 **QN**
→ 4.	$\sim Cx$	3 **UI**
5.	$(Ax \lor Bx) \supset (Cx \cdot Dx)$	1 **UI**
6.	$\sim (Ax \lor Bx) \lor (Cx \cdot Dx)$	5 **Impl**
7.	$(\sim Ax \cdot \sim Bx) \lor (Cx \cdot Dx)$	6 **DeM**
8.	$[(\sim Ax \cdot \sim Bx) \lor Cx] \cdot [(\sim Ax \cdot \sim Bx) \lor Dx]$	6 **Dist**
9.	$(\sim Ax \cdot \sim Bx) \lor Cx$	8 **Simp**
10.	$\sim Ax \cdot \sim Bx$	4,9 **DS**
11.	$\sim Ax$	10 **Simp**
12.	$\sim Ax \cdot \sim Cx$	4,11 **Conj**
13.	$(x)(\sim Ax \cdot \sim Cx)$	12 **UG**
14.	$(x) \sim (Ax \lor Cx)$	13 **DeM**
15.	$\sim (\exists x)(Ax \lor Cx)$	14 **QN**
16.	$\sim (\exists x) Cx \supset \sim (\exists x)(Ax \lor Cx)$	2-15 **CP**
17.	$(\exists x)(Ax \lor Cx) \supset (\exists x) Cx$	16 **Contra**

Exercise 9-1

2. $\sim Mbc$

4. Mbd

6. $(x) \sim Mdx$ (or $\sim (\exists x) Mdx$)

8. $(\exists x)[(Wx \cdot Bxd) \cdot \sim Idx]$

10. $(\exists x) \sim Pxf \supset (\sim Pjf \lor \sim Pkf)$

12. $(\exists x)(Cx \cdot Ex) \supset \sim (\exists x) Sxeg$

14. $\sim (\exists x)(Mxa \cdot Llx)$

16. $Lpm \supset (\exists x)(Mxa \cdot Lpx)$

18. $Hca \supset (\exists x)(Sx \cdot \sim Qx)$

20. $(x)(Sxach \supset Tx) \supset Hca$

Exercise 9-2

2. $(\exists x)(\exists y) Sxy$

   $(Saa \lor Sab) \lor (Sba \lor Sbb)$

4. $(x)(\exists y) Sxy$

   $(Saa \lor Sab) \cdot (Sba \lor Sbb)$

6. $\sim (\exists x)(y) Sxy$

   $\sim [(Saa \cdot Sab) \lor (Sba \cdot Sbb)]$

8. $(\exists x)(y) Syx$

   $(Saa \cdot Sba) \lor (Sab \cdot Sbb)$

10. $\sim (x)(\exists y) Sxy$

    $\sim [(Saa \lor Sab) \cdot (Sba \lor Sbb)]$

12. $(x)[(y) Sxy \supset Sxx]$

    $[(Saa \cdot Sab) \supset Saa] \cdot [(Sba \cdot Sbb) \supset Sbb]$

Exercise 9-3

2. $\sim (x)(\exists y)[(Px \cdot Cy) \supset Ayx]$ or $(\exists x)[Px \cdot (y)(Cy \supset \sim Ayx)]$ (Px = "x is a place"; Cx = "x is a cheater"; Axy = "x is at y")

4. $\sim (\exists x)(Px \cdot Mxh)$ (Px = "x is a place"; Mxy = "x is more beautiful than y"; h = "Hawaii")

6. $(x)\{Px \supset (\exists y)[(Ty \cdot Axy) \cdot Fxy]\}$ $(Px = x$ is a person; $Tx = x$ is a time; $Axy = x$ is alive at y; $Fxy = x$ must face reality at y)

8. $(x)[Tx \supset (\exists y)(Py \cdot Fyx)]$ or $(\exists x)(Px \cdot (y)(Ty \supset Fxy))$ (the sentence is ambiguous) $(Tx = "x$ is a time"; $Px = "x$ is a person"; $Fxy = "$you can fool x at $y")$

10. $\sim (\exists x)(Tx \cdot (\exists y)(Py \cdot \sim Ryx))$ $(Tx = "x$ is a time"; $Px = "x$ is a person"; $Rxy = "x$ can still reform at $y")$

12. $(x)[Tx \supset (\exists y)(Dy \cdot Wryx)]$ $(Tx = "x$ is a time"; $Dx = "x$ is a designer dress"; $Wxyz = "x$ wears y at z"; $r =$ Hillary Rodham Clinton)

14. $\sim (\exists x)[(Tx \vee Px) \cdot \sim (\exists y)(Hy \cdot Ayx)]$ $(Tx$ "x is a time"; $Px = "x$ is a place"; $Hx = "x$ is honesty"; $Axy = "x$ is at y") (But see Chapter Nine, Section 4, for a discussion of second order predicate logic and properties of items such as honesty.)

Exercise 9-4

2. $(x)(y)\{[(Px \cdot Py) \cdot \sim Iyx] \supset (Lxy \supset Bxy)\}(Px = "x$ is a person"; $Ixy = "x$ is identical with y"; $Lxy = "x$ laughs after y"; $Bxy = "x$ laughs better than y")

4. $(x)\{Cx \supset [Rx \cdot (y)(Py \supset \sim Hxy)]\}$ $(Cx = "x$ is a cult"; $Rx = "x$ is a religion"; $Px = "x$ is power"; $Hxy = "x$ has y)

6. $(x)[Gx \supset (y)(Ryx \supset Ly)]$ $(Gx = "x$ is a government"; $Rxy = "x$ runs y"; $Lx = "x$ is a liar")

8. $(x)\{[Px \cdot (\exists y)(Cy \cdot Wxy)] \supset (\exists z)(Hzx \cdot Lz)\}$ $(Px = "x$ is a person"; $Cx = "x$ is a crown"; $Wxy = "x$ wears y"; $Hxy = "x$ is the head of y"; $Lx = "x$ lies uneasily")

10. $(x)(y)[(Px \cdot Ay) \supset Oxy]$ $(Px = "x$ is a good professional"; $Ax = "x$ is an amateur"; $Oxy = "x$ can outperform y")

12. $(x)[(Px \cdot Hgx) \supset Hxx]$ $(g = "$God"; $Px = "x$ is a person"; $Hxy = "x$ helps y")

14. $(x)[Px \supset (y)(Lxy \supset Txyz)]$ $(Px = "x$ is a person"; $Lxy = "x$ learns y"; $Txyz = "x$ teaches y to z")

16. $(x)(y)[(Vx \cdot My) \supset (z)(Tz \supset Rxyz)]$ $(Vx = "x$ is virtue"; $Mx = "x$ is money"; $Tx = "x$ is a time; $Rxyz = "x$ is more respectable than y at z")

18. $(x)[Px \supset \sim (\exists y)(Ty \cdot Bxya)]$ $(Px = "x$ is a person"; $Tx = "x$ is a time"; $a = "$the American public"; $Bxyz = "x$ went broke at y underestimating z")

20. $(x)[(Gx \cdot Wsx) \supset \sim Dsx] \cdot (x)[(Ex \cdot \sim Wsx) \supset Dsx]$ or, perhaps $(\exists x)[(Gx \cdot Wsx) \cdot \sim Dsx] \cdot (\exists x)[(Ex \cdot \sim Wsx) \cdot Dsx]$ $(s = "$the speaker"; $Gx = "x$ is good"; $Ex = "x$ is evil"; $Wxy = "x$ wants to do y"; $Dxy = "x$ does y")

Exercise 9-5

2. $(x)\{[Cx \cdot (\exists y)(Vy \cdot \sim Cxy)] \supset Lx\}$ $(Cx = "x$ is a candidate"; $Vx = "x$ is a voter"; $Cxy = "x$ caters to y"; $Lx = "x$ will lose")

4. $(\exists x)(\exists y)[(Px \cdot Dy) \cdot Exy] \supset (x)[Px \supset (\exists y)(Dy \cdot Hxy)]$ $(Px = "x$ is a politician"; $Dx = "x$ is demogoguery"; $Exy = "x$ engages in y"; $Hxy = "x$ has to engage in y")

6. $(x)\{(Px \cdot Bxg) \supset (y)(z)[(Cyg \cdot Tz) \supset Oxyz]\}$ $(Px = "x$ is a person"; $Bxy = "x$ believes in y"; $Cxy = "x$ is a commandment of y"; $Tx = "x$ is a time"; $Oxyz = "x$ obeys y at z"; $g = "$God")

8. $(x)(Px \supset (\exists y)(\exists z)((Dy \cdot Tz) \cdot Bxyz))$, or $\sim (\exists x)(Px \cdot (y)(z)((Dy \cdot Tz) \supset \sim Bxyz))$ $(Px = "x$ is a person"; $Dx = "x$ is a scientific discovery"; $Tx = "x$ is a time"; $Bxyz = "x$ has benefited from y at z")

10. $(x)(Px \supset (\exists y)(Dyn \cdot Bxy)) \supset (\exists x)(\exists y) ((Px \cdot Gy) \cdot Oxyn)$ $(Px = "x$ is a person"; $Dxy = "x$ is a discovery of y"; $Bxy = "x$ has benefited from y"; $Gx = "x$ is a debt of gratitude"; $Oxyz = "x$ owes y to z"; $n = "$Newton")

12. $(x)\{Px \supset (\exists y)(\exists z)[(Py \cdot Mz) \cdot Oxzy]\} \supset \sim (\exists x)[Px \cdot (y)(Dy \supset Fxy)]$ (Px = "x is a person"; Mx = "x is money"; $Oxyz$ = "x owes y to z"; Dx = "x is a debt"; Fxy = "x is free of y")

14. $(x)[Px \cdot \sim (\exists y)(\exists z)[(My \cdot Sz) \cdot Pxyz] \supset (y) \{Py \cdot (\exists z)(\exists u)[(Mz \cdot Su) \cdot Pyzu] \supset Lxy]$ (Px = "x is a person"; Mx = "x is money"; Sx = "x is a scientist"; $Pxyz$ = "x pays y to z"; Lxy = "x looks down on y")

Exercise 9-6

2. Some people believe in God.

4. Not everyone believes in God.

6. Anyone who doesn't vote is disenfranchised.

8. Not all nonvoters are disenfranchised.

10. Some people don't have any redeeming features.

12. All redeeming features are lacked by somebody (or other).

14. No one has any redeeming features.

16. If Art doesn't vote, then if everyone who doesn't vote is disenfranchised, then Art is disenfranchised.

18. Anyone who votes is the master of someone who doesn't vote.

Exercise 9-7

(2) 1. $(\sim Faa \vee \sim Fab) \cdot (\sim Fba \vee \sim Fbb)$

        T F TF T T T F TF T

    $/\therefore (\sim Faa \cdot \sim Fab) \vee (\sim Fba \cdot \sim Fbb)$

        T F FF T F T F FF T

(4) 1. $[(Fa \supset Gaa) \vee (Fa \supset Gab)] \cdot [(Fb \supset Gba) \vee (Fb \supset Gbb)]$

        T T T T T F F T T F F T T T T

    $/\therefore [(Fa \supset Gaa) \cdot (Fa \supset Gab)] \vee [(Fb \supset Gba) \cdot (Fb \supset Gbb)]$

        T T T F T F F F T F F F T T T

(6) 1. $[(Faa \supset Gaa) \vee (Fab \supset Gab)] \cdot [(Fba \supset Gba) \vee (Fbb \supset Gbb)]$

        T T T T T F F T T T T T T F F

    2. $[(Gaa \supset Haa) \vee (Gab \supset Hab)] \cdot [(Gba \supset Hba) \vee (Gbb \supset Hbb)]$

        T F F T F T F T T F F T F T F

    $/\therefore [(Faa \supset Haa) \vee (Fab \supset Hab)] \cdot [(Fba \supset Hba) \vee (Fbb \supset Hbb)]$

        T F F F T F F F T F F F T F F

(8) 1. $[(Faaa \cdot Faab) \cdot (Faba \cdot Fabb)] \vee [(Fbaa \cdot Fbab) \cdot (Fbba \cdot Fbbb)]$

        T T T T T T T T F F F F F F F

    $/\therefore [(Faaa \vee Faab) \cdot (Faba \vee Fabb)] \cdot [(Fbaa \vee Fbab) \cdot (Fbba \vee Fbbb)]$

        T T T T T T T F F F F F F F F

Exercise 9-8

(2) 1. Inference to line 4 violates the second restriction on **EI**.

2. Inference to line 6 is invalid, because the *x* on line 6, supposedly obtained by **EG**, is in fact free.

(4) 1. Inference to line 3 is invalid because the *y* on line 3 that replaces the *x* on line 1 is not free.

2. Inference to line 5 is invalid because if *Fy* is substituted for *p* in a given use of **MP** we cannot also substitute *Fx* for *p* in that same use.

3. Inference to line 8 violates the restriction on **EG**, because there are not two *y* variables free in line 7 corresponding to the two *w* variables free in (*Fw* ⊃ *Gw*).

4. Inference to line 9 is invalid because the scope of the (∃*w*) quantifier has been extended to cover *Gy*.

(6) 1. Inference to line 3 is invalid because the (*y*) quantifier dropped by **UI** does not quantify the whole line.

2. Assuming that line 3 had been obtained by a valid use of **UI**, line 6 would be valid because the use of **UG** on that line quantifies the *y* variable introduced free by **UI** and not the *a* constant free in the assumed premise (line 4) within whose scope this use of **UG** lies.

3. Line 8 is invalid: the scope of "(∃*y*)" is not the whole of line 7.

Exercise 9-9

(2) 2. *Fx* · (*y*)(*Gy* ⊃ *Hxy*)   1 **EI**

3. *Fx*   2 **Simp**

4. (*y*)(*Gy* ⊃ *Hxy*)   2 **Simp**

5. *Ga* ⊃ *Hxa*   4 **UI**

6. *Fx* · (*Ga* ⊃ *Hxa*)   3,5 **Conj**

7. (∃*x*)[*Fx* · (*Ga* ⊃ *Hxa*)]   6 **EG**

(4) 3. (∃*y*)*Ay*   **AP**

4. *Ay*   3 **EI**

5. (∃*x*)*Ax*   4 **EG**

6. ~ (∃*y*)*Gy*   2,5 **MP**

7. (*y*) ~ *Gy*   6 **QN**

8. ~ *Gx*   7 **UI**

9. (∃*y*)*Ay* ⊃ ~ *Gx*   3-8 **CP**

10. (*x*)[(∃*y*)*Ay* ⊃ ~ *Gx*]   9 **UG**

(6)   3. $\sim (\exists x)(y) \sim Fxy$ AP
  4. $(x) \sim (y) \sim Fxy$ 3 **QN**
  5. $(x)(\exists y)Fxy$ 4 **QN**
  6. $(x)(\exists y)Gxy$ 1,5 **MP**
  7. $(y) \sim Gxy$ 2 **EI**
  8. $(\exists y)Gxy$ 6 **UI**
  9. Gxy 8 **EI**
  10. $\sim Gxy$ 7 **UI**
  11. $Gxy \cdot \sim Gxy$ 9,10 **Conj**
  12. $(\exists x)(y) \sim Fxy$ 3-11 **IP**

(8)   3. $Ax \cdot (y)[(Ay \cdot Bxy) \supset Cxy]$ 2, **EI**
  4. $Ax \supset (\exists y)(Ay \cdot Bxy)$ 1, **UI**
  5. Ax 3, **Simp**
  6. $(\exists y)(Ay \cdot Bxy)$ 4,5 **MP**
  7. $(Ay \cdot Bxy)$ 6, **EI**
  8. $(y)[(Ay \cdot Bxy) \supset Cxy]$ 3, **Simp**
  9. $(Ay \cdot Bxy) \supset Cxy$ 8, **UI**
  10. $Ax \cdot Ay$ AP
  11. Cxy 7,9 **MP**
  12. $(Ax \cdot Ay) \supset Cxy$ 10-11 **CP**
  13. $(\exists y)[(Ax \cdot Ay) \supset Cxy]$ 12, **EG**
  14. $(\exists x)(\exists y)[(Ax \cdot Ay) \supset Cxy]$ 13, **EG**

(10) 3. $\sim (x)(Dx \supset Ex)$ AP
  4. $\sim \sim (\exists x)(Cx \cdot Dx)$ 2,3 **MT**
  5. $(\exists x)(Cx \cdot Dx)$ 4 **DN**
  6. $Cx \cdot Dx$ 5 **EI**
  7. $Ax \supset (Bx \supset \sim Cx)$ 1 **UI**
  8. Cx 6 **Simp**
  9. $\sim \sim Cx$ 8 **DN**
  10. $(Ax \cdot Bx) \supset \sim Cx$ 7 **Exp**
  11. $\sim (Ax \cdot Bx)$ 9,10 **MT**
  12. $\sim Ax \vee \sim Bx$ 11 **DeM**
  13. Dx 6 **Simp**
  14. $Dx \cdot (\sim Ax \vee \sim Bx)$ 12,13 **Conj**
  15. $(\exists x)[Dx \cdot (\sim Ax \vee \sim Bx)]$ 14 **EG**
  16. $\sim \sim (\exists x)[Dx \cdot$
   $(\sim Ax \vee \sim Bx)]$ 15 **DN**
  17. $\sim (x)(Dx \supset Ex) \supset \sim \sim$
   $(\exists x)[Dx \cdot (\sim Ax \vee \sim Bx)]$ 3-16 **CP**
  18. $\sim (\exists x)[Dx \cdot (\sim Ax \vee \sim Bx)]$
   $\supset (x)(Dx \supset Ex)$ 17 **Contra**

(12)   4. $Dz \cdot (\exists x)[(Ex \cdot Fx) \cdot Bzx]$ 2 **EI**

    5. $(\exists x)[(Ex \cdot Fx) \cdot Bzx]$ 4 **Simp**

    6. $(Ew \cdot Fw) \cdot Bzw$ 5 **EI**

    7. $Ew \cdot Fw$ 6 **Simp**

    8. Fw 7 **Simp**

    9. $Fw \supset Aw$ 3 **UI**

    10. Aw 8,9 **MP**

    11. $(\exists y)(Ay \cdot Bzy) \supset Cz$ 1 **UI**

    12. Bzw 6 **Simp**

    13. $Aw \cdot Bzw$ 10,12 **Conj**

    14. $(\exists y)(Ay \cdot Bzy)$ 13 **EG**

    15. Cz 11,14 **MP**

    16. Dz 4 **Simp**

    17. $Cz \cdot Dz$ 15,16 **Conj**

    18. $(\exists x)(Cx \cdot Dx)$ 17 **EG**

(14)   3. $\sim (x)(y) \sim Axy$ **AP**

    4. $(\exists x) \sim (y) \sim Axy$ 3 **QN**

    5. $(\exists x)(\exists y)Axy$ 4 **QN**

    6. $(\exists y)Axy$ 5 **EI**

    7. Axy 6 **EI**

    8. $Axy \lor Bxy$ 7 **Add**

    9. $(\exists y)(Axy \lor Bxy)$ 8 **EG**

    10. $(\exists x)(\exists y)(Axy \lor Bxy)$ 9 **EG**

    11. $(\exists z)Cz$ 1,10 **MP**

    12. Cz 11 **EI**

    13. $(y)(Cz \supset \sim Cy)$ 2 **UI**

    14. $Cz \supset \sim Cz$ 13 **UI**

    15. $\sim Cz \lor \sim Cz$ 14 **Impl**

    16. $\sim Cz$ 15 **Taut**

    17. $Cz \cdot \sim Cz$ 12,16 **Conj**

    18. $(x)(y) \sim Axy$ 3-17 **IP**

Exercise 9-10

(2)
1. $\sim (x)(Gx \equiv Gx)$ — AP
2. $(\exists x) \sim (Gx \equiv Gx)$ — 1, QN
3. $\sim (Gx \equiv Gx)$ — 2, EI
4. $\sim [(Gx \cdot Gx) \vee (\sim Gx \cdot \sim Gx)]$ — 3, Equiv
5. $\sim (Gx \vee \sim Gx)$ — 4, Taut (2x)
6. $\sim Gx \cdot \sim \sim \sim Gx$ — 5, Dem
7. $(x)(Gx \equiv Gx)$ — 1-6 IP

(4)
1. $(\exists x)(y)Fxy$ — AP
2. $(y)Fxy$ — 1 EI
3. Fxy — 2 UI
4. $(\exists x)Fxy$ — 3 EG
5. $(y)(\exists x)Fxy$ — 4 UG
6. $(\exists x)(y)Fxy \supset (y)(\exists x)Fxy$ — 1-5 CP

(6)
1. $(x)Fx \vee (x)Gx$ — AP
2. $\sim Fx$ — AP
3. $(\exists x) \sim Fx$ — 2 EG
4. $\sim (x)Fx$ — 3 QN
5. $(x)Gx$ — 1,4 DS
6. Gx — 5 UI
7. $\sim Fx \supset Gx$ — 2-6 CP
8. $\sim \sim Fx \vee Gx$ — 7 Impl
9. $Fx \vee Gx$ — 8 DN
10. $(x)(Fx \vee Gx)$ — 9 UG
11. $[(x)Fx \vee (x)Gx] \supset [(x)(Fx \vee Gx)]$ — 1-10 CP

(8)
1. $(\exists x)(Fx \cdot Gx)$ — AP
2. $Fx \cdot Gx$ — 1 EI
3. Fx — 2 Simp
4. $(\exists x)Fx$ — 3 EG
5. Gx — 2 Simp
6. $(\exists x)Gx$ — 5 EG
7. $(\exists x)Fx \cdot (\exists x)Gx$ — 4,6 Conj
8. $(\exists x)(Fx \cdot Gx) \supset [(\exists x)Fx \cdot (\exists x)Gx]$ — 1-7 CP

(10)
1. $(x)Fx \cdot P$ — AP
2. $(x)Fx$ — 1 Simp
3. Fx — 2 UI
4. P — 1 Simp
5. $Fx \cdot P$ — 3,4 Conj
6. $(x)(Fx \cdot P)$ — 5 UG
7. $[(x)Fx \cdot P] \supset (x)(Fx \cdot P)$ — 1-6 CP
8. $(x)(Fx \cdot P)$ — AP
9. $Fx \cdot P$ — 8 UI
10. Fx — 9 Simp
11. $(x)Fx$ — 10 UG
12. P — 9 Simp
13. $(x)Fx \cdot P$ — 11,12 Conj
14. $(x)(Fx \cdot P) \supset [(x)Fx \cdot P]$ — 8-13 CP
15. $7 \cdot 14$ — 7,14 Conj
16. $[(x)Fx \cdot P] \equiv (x)(Fx \cdot P)$ — 15 Equiv

(12)
1. $(x)(P \supset Fx)$ — AP
2. P — AP
3. $P \supset Fx$ — 1 UI
4. Fx — 2,3 MP
5. $(x)Fx$ — 4 UG
6. $P \supset (x)Fx$ — 2-5 CP
7. $(x)(P \supset Fx) \supset (P \supset (x)Fx)$ — 1-6 CP
8. $P \supset (x)Fx$ — AP
9. P — AP
10. $(x)Fx$ — 8,9 MP
11. Fx — 10 UI
12. $P \supset Fx$ — 9-11 CP
13. $(x)(P \supset Fx)$ — 12 UG
14. $[P \supset (x)Fx] \supset (x)(P \supset Fx)$ — 8-13 CP
15. $7 \cdot 14$ — 7,14 Conj
16. $(x)(P \supset Fx) \equiv [P \supset (x)Fx]$ — 15 Equiv

(14)

→ 1.	$(\exists x)(P \cdot Fx)$	**AP**
2.	$P \cdot Fx$	1 **EI**
3.	P	2 **Simp**
4.	Fx	2 **Simp**
5.	$(\exists x)Fx$	4 **EG**
6.	$P \cdot (\exists x)Fx$	3,5 **Conj**
7.	$(\exists x)(P \cdot Fx) \supset$ $[P \cdot (\exists x)Fx]$	1-6 **CP**
→ 8.	$P \cdot (\exists x)Fx$	**AP**
9.	P	8 **Simp**
10.	$(\exists x)Fx$	8 **Simp**
11.	Fy	10 **EI**
12.	$P \cdot Fy$	9,11 **Conj**
13.	$(\exists x)(P \cdot Fx)$	12 **EG**
14.	$[P \cdot (\exists x)Fx] \supset$ $(\exists x)(P \cdot Fx)$	8-13 **CP**
15.	$(\exists x)(P \cdot Fx) \supset$ $[P \cdot (\exists x)Fx] \cdot$ $[P \cdot (\exists x)Fx] \supset$ $(\exists x)(P \cdot Fx)$	7,14 **Conj**
16.	$(\exists x)(P \cdot Fx) \equiv$ $[P \cdot (\exists x)Fx]$	15 **Equiv**

(16)

→ 1.	$(\exists x)(Fx \supset P)$	**AP**
→ 2.	$(x)Fx$	**AP**
3.	$Fx \supset P$	1 **EI**
4.	Fx	2 **UI**
5.	P	3,4 **MP**
6.	$(x)Fx \supset P$	2-5 **CP**
7.	$(\exists x)(Fx \supset P) \supset$ $[(x)Fx \supset P]$	1-6 **CP**
→ 8.	$\sim (\exists x)(Fx \supset P)$	**AP**
9.	$(x) \sim (Fx \supset P)$	8 **QN**
10.	$\sim (Fy \supset P)$	9 **UI**
11.	$\sim (\sim Fy \vee P)$	10 **Impl**
12.	$\sim \sim Fy \cdot \sim P$	11 **DeM**
13.	$Fy \cdot \sim P$	12 **DN**
14.	Fy	13 **Simp**
15.	$(x)Fx$	14 **UG**
16.	$\sim P$	13 **Simp**
17.	$(x)Fx \cdot \sim P$	15,16 **Conj**
18.	$\sim \sim (x)Fx \cdot \sim P$	17 **DN**
19.	$\sim [\sim (x)Fx \vee P]$	18 **DeM**
20.	$\sim [(x)Fx \supset P]$	19 **Impl**
21.	$\sim (\exists x)(Fx \supset P) \supset$ $\sim [(x)Fx \supset P]$	8-20 **CP**
22.	$[(x)Fx \supset P] \supset$ $(\exists x)(Fx \supset P)$	21 **Contra**
23.	$(\exists x)(Fx \supset P) \supset$ $[(x)Fx \supset P] \cdot$ $[(x)Fx \supset P] \supset$ $(\exists x)(Fx \supset P)$	7,22 **Conj**
24.	$(\exists x)(Fx \supset P) \equiv$ $[(x)Fx \supset P]$	23 **Equiv**

Exercise 9-11

(2)

2.	$(x) \sim Fx$	1 **QN**
3.	$\sim Fa$	2 **UI**
4.	$\sim Fa \vee Ga$	3 **Add**
5.	$Fa \supset Ga$	4 **Impl**

(4)

3.	$Fy \vee (\exists x)Gx$	1 **UI**
4.	$\sim Fy$	2 **UI**
5.	$(\exists x)Gx$	3,4 **DS**

(6)

→ 3.	$\sim (x)Hx$	**AP**
4.	$(\exists x) \sim Hx$	3 **QN**
5.	$\sim Hx$	4 **EI**
6.	$Ka \supset (y)Hy$	2 **UI**
7.	$(y)Hy$	1,6 **MP**
8.	Hx	7 **UI**
9.	$Hx \cdot \sim Hx$	8,5 **Conj**
10.	$(x)Hx$	3-9 **IP**

(8)   2. ~ (∃x)(Ax ⊃ Gx)   **AP**

       3. (x) ~ (Ax ⊃ Gx)   2 **QN**

       4. (x) ~ Ax   1 **QN**

       5. ~ Ax   4 **UI**

       6. ~ (Ax ⊃ Gx)   3 **UI**

       7. ~ (~ Ax ∨ Gx)   6 **Impl**

       8. ~ ~ Ax · ~ Gx   7 **DeM**

       9. ~ ~ Ax   8 **Simp**

     10. ~ Ax · ~ ~ ~ Ax 5,9 **Conj**

     11. (∃x)(Ax ⊃ Gx)   2-10 **IP**

(10)   4. ~ [(∃x)Gx · (∃x)Mx]   **AP**

       5. ~ (∃x)Gx ∨ ~ (∃x)Mx 4 **DeM**

       6. Rx   1 **EI**

       7. ~ Gx ⊃ ~ Rx   2 **UI**

       8. ~ ~ Rx   6 **DN**

       9. ~ ~ Gx   7,8 **MT**

     10. ~ ~ (∃x)Mx   3 **DN**

     11. ~ (∃x)Gx   5,10 **DS**

     12. (x) ~ Gx   11 **QN**

     13. ~ Gx   12 **UI**

     14. ~ Gx · ~ ~ Gx   13,9 **Conj**

     15. (∃x)Gx · (∃x)Mx   4-14 **IP**

Exercise 9-12

(2)   2. ~ (x)(∃y)Fxy   **AP**

       3. (∃x)(y) ~ Fxy   2 **QN** (*twice*)

       4. (y) ~ Fxy   3 **EI**

       5. (x)Fxy   1 **EI**

       6. Fxy   5 **UI**

       7. ~ Fxy   4 **UI**

       8. Fxy · ~ Fxy   6,7 **Conj**

       9. (x)(∃y)Fxy   2-8 **IP**

(4)   3. ~ (∃x)(∃y)Gxy   **AP**

       4. (x)(y) ~ Gxy   3 **QN** (*twice*)

       5. Fx   2 **EI**

       6. Fx ⊃ (∃y)Gxy   1 **UI**

       7. (∃y)Gxy   5,6 **MP**

       8. Gxy   7 **EI**

       9. ~ Gxy   4 **UI** (*twice*)

     10. Gxy · ~ Gxy   8,9 **Conj**

     11. (∃x)(∃y)Gxy   3-10 **IP**

(6)   2. ~ (x)[(∃y)Ay ⊃ ~ Gx] **AP**

       3. (∃x) ~ [(∃y)Ay ⊃ ~ Gx] 2 **QN**

       4. ~ [(∃y)Ay ⊃ ~ Gx]   3 **EI**

       5. ~ [~ (∃y)Ay ∨ ~ Gx]   4 **Impl**

       6. (∃y)Ay · Gx   5 **DeM DN**

       7. (∃y)Ay   6 **Simp**

       8. Ay   7 **EI**

       9. ~ (∃x)Ax   **AP**

     10. (x) ~ Ax   9 **QN**

     11. ~ Ay   10 **UI**

     12. Ay · ~ Ay   8,11 **Conj**

     13. (∃x)Ax   9,12 **IP**

     14. ~ (∃y)Gy   1,13 **MP**

     15. (y) ~ Gy   14 **QN**

     16. ~ Gx   15 **UI**

     17. Gx   6 **Simp**

     18. Gx · ~ Gx   16,17 **Conj**

     19. (x)[(∃y)Ay ⊃ ~ Gx] 2,18 **IP**

Exercise 10-1

    2. The inference to line 5 is invalid, because it violates the fourth restriction on **UG**; to each x free in (Px ⊃ Lxx) there does not correspond a y free in Py ⊃ Lxy.

    (No answers are provided for the other items in this exercise set because the importance of the questions lies in the way students explain and defend their answers.)

Exercise 11-1

(2)

4. $\sim\sim(a=b)$	**AP**	
5. $a=b$	4 **DN**	
6. $Pa \supset Qa$	1 **UI**	
7. $Qa \supset Ra$	2 **UI**	
8. $Pa \supset Ra$	6,7 **HS**	
9. Pa	3 **Simp**	
10. Ra	8,9 **MP**	
11. $\sim Rb$	3 **Simp**	
12. $\sim Ra$	5,11 **ID**	
13. $Ra \cdot \sim Ra$	10,12 **Conj**	
14. $\sim(a=b)$	4-13 **IP**	

(4)

4. $a=b$	**AP**
5. $Fa \supset (\exists y)Gya$	1 **UI**
6. $(\exists y)Gya$	2,4 **MP**
7. Gya	6 **EI**
8. $\sim Gyb$	3 **UI**
9. $\sim Gya$	4,8 **ID**
10. $Gya \cdot \sim Gya$	7,9 **Conj**
11. $\sim(a=b)$	4-10 **IP**

(6)

2. $\sim(\exists y)[\sim(y=z) \cdot Fyz]$	**AP**
3. $(y)\sim[\sim(y=z) \cdot Fyz]$	2 **QN**
4. $(y)\{[\sim Fwy \supset$ $(w=y)] \cdot Gw\}$	1 **EI**
5. $[\sim Fwz \supset (w=z)] \cdot Gw$	4 **UI**
6. $\sim[\sim(w=z) \cdot Fwz]$	3 **UI**
7. $(w=z) \vee \sim Fwz$	6 **DeM, DN**
8. $\sim(w=z) \supset \sim Fwz$	7 **DN, Impl**
9. $\sim Fwz \supset (w=z)$	5 **Simp**
10. $\sim(w=z) \supset (w=z)$	8,9 **HS**
11. $(w=z) \vee (w=z)$	10 **Impl, DN**
12. $w=z$	11 **Taut**
13. Gw	5 **Simp**
14. Gz	12,13 **ID**
15. $\sim\sim Gz$	14 **DN**
16. $\sim(\exists y)[\sim(y=z) \cdot Fyz] \supset$ $\sim\sim Gz$	2-15 **CP**
17. $\sim Gz \supset$ $(\exists y)[\sim(y=z) \cdot Fyz]$	16 **Contra**
18. $(x)\{\sim Gx \supset$ $(\exists y)[\sim(y=x) \cdot Fyx]\}$	17 **UG**

(8)

4. $Fx \cdot Mx$	3 **EI**
5. $Fx \supset (x=a)$	1 **UI**
6. Fx	4 **Simp**
7. $x=a$	5,6 **MP**
8. $Mx \supset (x=b)$	2 **UI**
9. Mx	4 **Simp**
10. $x=b$	8,9 **MP**
11. $a=b$	7,10 **ID**

(10)

4. $(\exists x)(Ax \cdot Bx)$	1 **QN**
5. $Ax \cdot Bx$	4 **EI**
6. $(x \neq a) \supset \sim Ax$	2 **UI**
7. Ax	5 **Simp**
8. $\sim\sim Ax$	7 **DN**
9. $\sim\sim(x=a)$	6,8 **MT**
10. $x=a$	9 **DN**
11. $\sim[(x \neq b) \cdot Bx]$	3 **UI**
12. $\sim(x \neq b) \vee \sim Bx$	11 **DeM**
13. Bx	5 **Simp**
14. $\sim\sim Bx$	13 **DN**
15. $\sim(x \neq b)$	12,14 **DS**
16. $x=b$	15 **DN**
17. $a=b$	10,16 **ID**

Exercise 11-2

2. $(x)[(Sx \cdot Px) \supset (x = r)]$

4. $(x)(y)[\{[(Fx \cdot Rx) \cdot (Fy \cdot Ry)] \cdot (x \neq y)\} \supset (z)\{(Fz \cdot Rz) \supset [(z = x) \vee (z = y)]\}]$

6. $(Pr \cdot Sr) \cdot (x)[(Px \cdot Sx) \supset (x = r)]$

8. $(x)\{[Px \cdot (x \neq a)] \supset Cax\}$

10. $(x)\{[Cx \cdot (x \neq d)] \supset Kdx\}$

Exercise 11-3

2. $Sb \cdot (x)\{[Sx \cdot (x \neq b)] \supset Ibx\}$ ($Sx =$ "x is a student"; $Ixy =$ "x is more intelligent than y"; $b =$ "Bonny")

4. $\sim (\exists x)\{[(Rx \cdot (x \neq r)] \cdot \sim Ex\}$ ($Rx =$ "x is a rule"; $Ex =$ "x has an exception"; $r =$ "this rule")

6. $Ck \cdot (x)[Cx \supset (x = k)]$ ($Cx =$ "x is currently world chess champion"; $k =$ "Gary Kasparov")

8. $(\exists x)(\exists y)\{\{[(Mx \cdot My) \cdot (x \neq y)] \cdot (Lxy \cdot Lyx)\} \cdot (z)\{Mz \supset [(x = z) \vee (y = z)]\}\}$ ($Mx =$ "x is a Maine senator"; $Lxy =$ "x likes y")

10. $\sim (x)(Sx \supset Bcx) \supset (\exists y)\{(Sy \cdot Byc) \cdot (z)[(Sz \cdot Bzc) \supset (z = y)]\}$ ($Sx =$ "x is a sprinter"; $Bxy =$ "x is a better sprinter than y"; $c =$ "Carl Lewis")

Exercise 11-4

2. Asymmetrical, intransitive, irreflexive

4. Asymmetrical, transitive, irreflexive

6. Symmetrical, transitive, totally reflexive

8. Nonsymmetrical, nontransitive, nonreflexive

Exercise 11-5

2. Some say that the levels of language theory solve this paradox. For we can think of a bibliography as a very long conjunction, each entry in the bibliography being a conjunct of that conjunction. Suppose (N) is a bibliography of this kind. Then, on the levels of language theory, no conjunct in (N) can refer to itself—to talk of (N) itself we need to go one flight up, to a higher-level language, where we can have a bibliography listing all bibliographies on a lower level. So on the levels of language theory, there cannot be a bibliography that lists all bibliographies that do not list themselves, nor indeed a bibliography that does list itself.

4. Some claim the simple theory of types solves this paradox. For on that theory, a class must be of a higher type than its members; thus there is neither a class of all classes that are members of themselves, nor of all classes that are not.

Exercise 11-6

2. (Not appropriate to answer.)

4. (Not appropriate to answer.)

6. (1) Observed—manifest
   (2) Solubility—dispositional
   (3) Green—both
   (4) Teach—manifest: teachable—dispositional

(5) Dangerous—dispositional
(6) Dependable—dispositional
(7) Character—dispositional

Exercise 12-1

(2)

1. $C \supset A$ ✓
2. $A \supset (B \cdot C)$ ✓
3. C

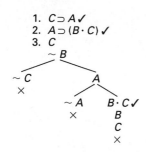

(Valid because all paths are closed.)

(4)

1. $(H \cdot K) \supset L$ ✓
2. H
   $\sim (K \supset L)$ ✓
   K
   $\sim L$

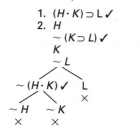

(Valid because all paths are closed.)

(6)

1. $A \supset B$ ✓
2. $\sim (C \cdot B)$ ✓
3. C
   $\sim \sim A$

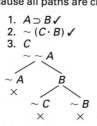

(Valid because all paths are closed.)

(8)

1. $L \vee N$ ✓
2. $L \supset \sim R$ ✓
3. R
   $\sim \sim N$

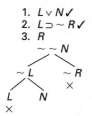

(Invalid because one path is open.)

(10)

1. $(A \cdot B) \vee C$ ✓
2. $\sim A$
   $\sim C$

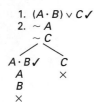

(Valid because all paths are closed.)

(12)

1. $(A \cdot B) \vee C$ ✓
2. $\sim (A \vee B)$ ✓
   $\sim C$
   $\sim A$
   $\sim B$

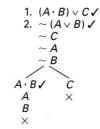

(Valid because all paths are closed.)

(14)

1. $A \vee (\sim B \cdot C)$ ✓
2. $B \supset \sim A$ ✓
   $\sim \sim B$

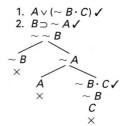

(Valid because all paths are closed.)

(16)

1. $A \supset B$ ✓
2. $C \supset D$ ✓
3. $B \vee D$ ✓
   $\sim (A \vee C)$ ✓
   $\sim A$
   $\sim C$

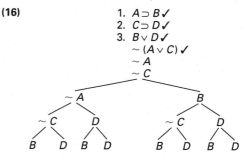

(Invalid because paths remain open.)

(18)

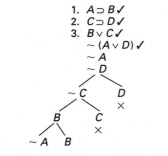

1. $A \supset B$ ✓
2. $C \supset D$ ✓
3. $B \lor C$ ✓
    $\sim (A \lor D)$ ✓
    $\sim A$
    $\sim D$

(Invalid because paths remain open.)

(20)

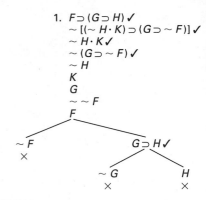

1. $F \supset (G \supset H)$ ✓
    $\sim [(\sim H \cdot K) \supset (G \supset \sim F)]$ ✓
    $\sim H \cdot K$ ✓
    $\sim (G \supset \sim F)$ ✓
    $\sim H$
    K
    G
    $\sim \sim F$
    F

(Valid.)

Exercise 12-2

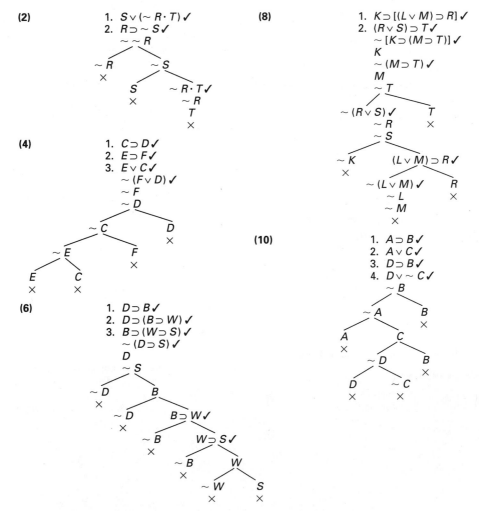

(2)

1. $S \lor (\sim R \cdot T)$ ✓
2. $R \supset \sim S$ ✓
    $\sim \sim R$

(4)

1. $C \supset D$ ✓
2. $E \supset F$ ✓
3. $E \lor C$ ✓
    $\sim (F \lor D)$ ✓
    $\sim F$
    $\sim D$

(6)

1. $D \supset B$ ✓
2. $D \supset (B \supset W)$ ✓
3. $B \supset (W \supset S)$ ✓
    $\sim (D \supset S)$ ✓
    D
    $\sim S$

(8)

1. $K \supset [(L \lor M) \supset R]$ ✓
2. $(R \lor S) \supset T$ ✓
    $\sim [K \supset (M \supset T)]$ ✓
    K
    $\sim (M \supset T)$ ✓
    M
    $\sim T$

(10)

1. $A \supset B$ ✓
2. $A \lor C$ ✓
3. $D \supset B$ ✓
4. $D \lor \sim C$ ✓
    $\sim B$

(12)   1. $(A \supset A) \supset (\sim A \supset \sim A)$ ✓
        $\sim (A \vee \sim A)$ ✓
        $\sim A$
        $\sim \sim A$
        $\times$

(14)

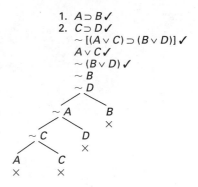

Exercise 12-3

(2)

(A tautology, because the negation of the sentence has no open branches.)

(4)

$\sim [A \supset (A \vee B)]$ ✓
A
$\sim (A \vee B)$ ✓
$\sim A$
$\sim B$
$\times$

(A tautology, because the negation of the sentence has no open branches.)

(6)

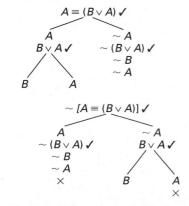

(Contingent, because both the sentence and its negation have open branches.)

(8)

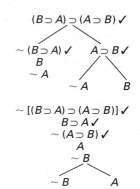

Contingent, because both the sentence and its negation have open branches.)

(10)

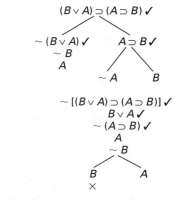

(Contingent, because both the sentence and its negation have open branches.)

(12) $A \supset [B \supset (A \supset C)] \checkmark$

$\sim A$ $B \supset (A \supset C) \checkmark$

$\sim B$ $A \supset C \checkmark$

$\sim A$ C

$\sim \{A \supset [B \supset (A \supset C)]\} \checkmark$
A
$\sim [B \supset (A \supset C)] \checkmark$
B
$\sim (A \supset C) \checkmark$
A
$\sim C$

(Contingent, because both the sentence and its negation have open branches.)

(14) $\sim (\{A \supset [(B \vee C) \vee (D \vee \sim B)]\} \vee \sim A) \checkmark$
$\sim \{A \supset [(B \vee C) \vee (D \vee \sim B)]\} \checkmark$
$\sim \sim A$
A
A
$\sim [(B \vee C) \vee (D \vee \sim B)] \checkmark$
$\sim (B \vee C) \checkmark$
$\sim (D \vee \sim B) \checkmark$
$\sim B$
$\sim C$
$\sim D$
$\sim \sim B$
$\times$

(A tautology, because the negation of the sentence has no open branches.)

Exercise 12-4

(2)
1. $(x)[Fx \supset (y)Gy]$
2. Fa
3. $\sim (x)Gx$
4. $(\exists x) \sim Gx$ — 3 QN
5. $[Fa \supset (y)Gy] \checkmark$ — 1 UI
6. $(\exists x) \sim Gx \checkmark$ — 3 QN
7. $\sim Gz$ — 6 EI
8. $\sim Fa$ 9. $(y)Gy$ — 5
$\times$
10. Gz — 8 UI
$\times$

(Valid, because all paths are closed.)

(4)
1. $(\exists x)Fx \checkmark$
2. $(x)(\sim Gx \supset \sim Fx)$
3. $(x)Mx$
4. $\sim [(\exists x)Gx \cdot (\exists x)Mx]$
5. Fx — 1 EI
6. Mx — 3 UI
7. $(\sim Gx \supset \sim Fx)$
8. $\sim \sim Gx$ $\sim Fx$
$\times$ $\times$

(Valid, because all paths are closed.)

(6)   1. $(x)(Ax \supset Fx)$

     2. $[(\exists x)Fx \supset \sim (\exists y)Gy]$ ✓

     3. $\sim (x)[(\exists y)Ay \supset \sim Gx]$ ✓

     4. $(\exists x) \sim [(\exists y)Ay \supset \sim Gx]$ 3 **QN**

     5. $\sim [(\exists y)Ay \supset \sim Gx]$ ✓   4 **EI**

     6. $(\exists y)Ay$

                Gx 5

     7. Ay 6 **EI**

     8. $\sim (\exists x)Fx$ $\sim (\exists y)Gy$ 2

     9. $(x) \sim Fx$ $(y) \sim Gy$ 8 **QN** (twice)

   10. $\sim Fx$ $\sim Gx$ 9 **UI** (twice)

                        ×

   11. $\sim Fy$ 9 **UI**

   12. $(Ax \supset Fx)$ ✓   1 **UI**

   13. $\sim Ax$ Fx 12

                 ×

   14. $(Ay \supset Fy)$ 1 **UI**

   15. $\sim Ay$ Fy 14

       ×   ×

     (Valid, because all paths are closed.)

(8)   1. $(x) \sim Fxx$

     2. $[\sim (x)Gx \supset (\exists y)Fya]$ ✓

     3. $\sim (\exists z)(Gz \cdot Fzz)$

     4. $(z) \sim (Gz \cdot Fzz)$ 3 **QN**

     5. $\sim (Ga \cdot Faa)$ ✓   4 **UI**

     6. $\sim Faa$ 1 **UI**

     7. $(x)Gx$ $(\exists y)Fya$ 2 (and **DN**)

     8. Ga Fza 7 **UI, EI**

     9. $\sim Ga$ $\sim Faa$ $\sim Ga$ $\sim Faa$ 5

        × | | |

             Fzz $\sim Fzz$ $\sim Fzz$ 1 **UI**

     (Invalid, because some paths are open.)

(10)   1. $(x)(\exists y)(Fx \cdot Gxy)$

2. $\sim (\exists y)(x)(Fx \cdot Gxy)$

3. $(y)(\exists x) \sim (Fx \cdot Gxy)$ 2 **QN** (*twice*)

4. $(\exists x) \sim (Fx \cdot Gxy)$ 3 **UI**

5. $\sim (Fx \cdot Gxy)$ 4 **EI**

6. $(\exists y)(Fx \cdot Gxy)$ 1 **UI**

7. $(Fx \cdot Gxz)$ 6 **EI**

8. Fx 7

                          Gxz 7

9. $\sim Fx$ $\sim Gxy$ 5

10. $\times$ $(\exists y)(Fz \cdot Gxy)$ ✓   1 **UI**

11. $(Fz \cdot Gzw)$ ✓   10 **EI**

12. Fz 11

                          Gzw 11

13. $(\exists y)(Fw \cdot Gwy)$ ✓   1 **UI**

14. $(Fw \cdot Gwu)$ ✓   13 **EI**

15. Fw 14

                          Gwu 14

                            .

                            .

                            .

(Inconclusive truth tree.)

Exercise 13-1

2. All poor are lazy.

4. No porno flicks are erotic.

6. No amateurs are professionals.

8. Some prescription drugs are harmful.

10. Some movie stars are not happy.

12. No persons who have dry wits are drinkers.

14. All persons who forget the past are sufferers from amnesia.

Exercise 13-2

(2)   1. Can't infer to the truth value of "No wars are hellish."

2. "Some wars are hellish" could be either true or false (because if one of two contraries is false, the other sometimes is true, sometimes false).

3. "Some wars are not hellish" is true (because "All wars are hellish" and "Some wars are not hellish" are contradictories).

(4) 1. "No congressmen are sexual gluttons" is true (because "Some congressmen are sexual gluttons" and "No congressmen are sexual gluttons" are contradictories).

2. "Some congressmen are not sexual gluttons" is true (because "Some congressmen are sexual gluttons" and "Some congressmen are not sexual gluttons" are subcontraries).

3. "All congressmen are sexual gluttons" is false (because its subalternate, "No congressmen are sexual gluttons," is false).

Exercise 13-3

(2) 2, 4—True; 3, 5—False

(4) 1-5—Indeterminate; 6—True

Exercise 13-4

(2) 1, 2—True; 3, 4, 5—Indeterminate; 6—False

(4) 1–5—Indeterminate; 6—True

Exercise 13-5

2.

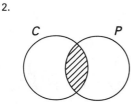

4.

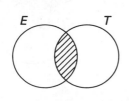

6.

8.

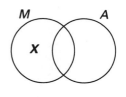

10.

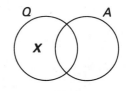

12.

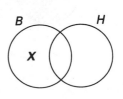

14.

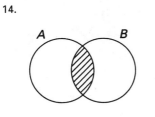

16.

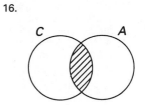

18.

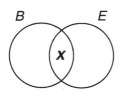

Exercise 13-6

2. *AII-III*

4. *EOI-I*

6. *EOO-I*

8. *EAE-IV*

10. *EIO-III*

Exercise 13-7

2. Valid

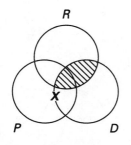

6. Invalid

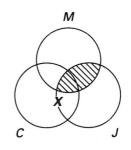

4. Invalid

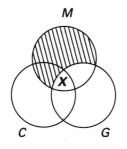

8. Invalid

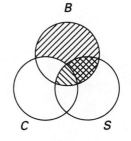

10. Valid

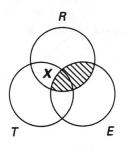

Exercise 13-8

(2) 1. Some people punished in the next life are not murderers.

2. All sinners are punished in the next life.

∴3. Some sinners are not murders.

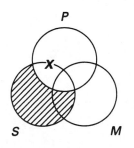

Invalid. Violates rule 1.

(4) 1. All who ignore the facts are likely to be mistaken.

2. All who are wise are not those who ignore the facts.

∴3. All who are wise are not likely to be mistaken.

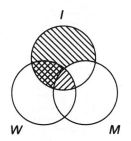

Invalid. Violates rule 2.

(6)   1. All logic classes are extremely interesting.

2. Some logic classes are harder than average.

∴3. Some classes that are harder than average are extremely interesting.

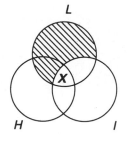

Valid.

(8)   1. All classes that are exciting are crowded.

2. All classes that are interesting or difficult are exciting.

∴3. No classes that are interesting or difficult are crowded.

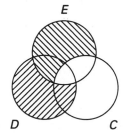

Invalid. Violates rules 2 and 4.

(10)   1. All times that Harry enjoys himself are times when Harry has lots of money.

2. All times Harry goes out with Jane are times that Harry enjoys himself.

∴3. All times Harry goes out with Jane are times when Harry has lots of money.

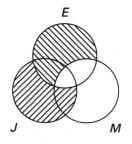

Valid.

(12)   1. Some who live by the pen are called liars.

2. Some who live by the pen are called sages.

∴3. Some who are called sages are called liars.

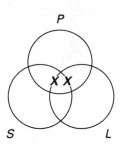

Invalid. Violates rule 1.

(14) 1. All times are times when we have death and taxes.

2. All times when we have death and taxes are times when we fight.

∴3. All times are times when we fight.

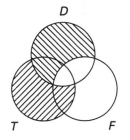

Valid.

Exercise 13-9

(2) 1. Abortion takes the life of a fetus.

2. Anything that takes the life of a fetus takes the life of a human being.

∴3. Abortion takes the life of a human being.

(4) 1. Smith eats plenty of brown rice.

2. Anyone who eats plenty of brown rice is in pretty good shape.

∴3. Smith is in pretty good shape.

(6) 1. Anyone who listens to television news programs listens to very superficial accounts of the news.

2. Anyone who listens to very superficial accounts of the news wastes their time.

∴3. Anyone who listens to television news programs wastes their time.

(8) 1. Some high school dropouts are smarter than lots of college grads.

2. Anyone who's smarter than lots of college grads is capable of holding a high-level management position.

∴3. Some high school dropouts are capable of holding a high-level management position.

(10) 1. Some who've taken LSD have scrambled brains.

2. No one with a scrambled brain is likely to do good in this world.

∴3. Some who've taken LSD are not likely to do good in this world.

Exercise 13-10

(2)   1. All skiers are athletes.
       2. Some nutritionists are skiers.
    ∴3. Some nutritionists are athletes.

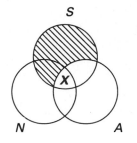

    Valid.
    1. Some nutritionists are athletes.
    2. No athletes are brawny.
 ∴3. Some nutritionists are not brawny.

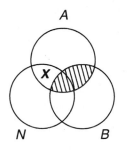

    Valid.

(4)   1. All scientists are mathematicians.
       2. No mathematicians are friendly.
    ∴3. No scientists are friendly.

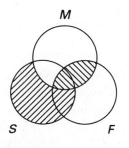

    Valid.
    1. No scientists are friendly.
    2. All geologists are friendly.
 ∴3. No geologists are scientists.

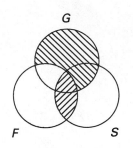

Valid.

(6) 1. All profound scholars are great lovers of music.

2. All Oxford dons are profound scholars.

∴3. All Oxford dons are great lovers of music.

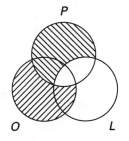

Valid.

1. No insensitive souls are great lovers of music.

2. All Oxford dons are great lovers of music.

∴3. No Oxford dons are insensitive souls.

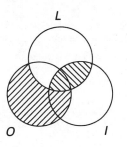

Valid.

1. No insensitive souls are Don Juans.

2. No Oxford dons are insensitive souls.

∴3. All Oxford dons are Don Juans.

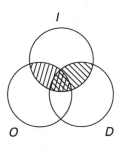

Invalid: *OD* slot is not completely shaded out. Violates rules 3 and 4.
(There are other possibilities, all invalid. A complete proof would cover all these
possibilities. But it is clear the sorites is invalid because one of its premises is
negative, and yet its conclusion is affirmative.)

Exercise 13-11

2. a and c, because they work in both directions.

4. False. The order of the premises makes no difference to validity.

6. Because sometimes a premise tells us that one of the two classes is nonempty, but
    does not tell us which one.

8. Yes, they can be interpreted as categorical propositions where the subject-class has
    only one member. "Bill Clinton jogs" can be translated into "All members of the
    class whose sole member is Bill Clinton jog."

10. Inappropriate to answer.

Exercise 14-1

2. Neutral: *c*; Decrease: *a, b, d, e.*

Exercise 14-2

2. **Strong analogy:** It calls our attention to a feature of military conquest we might
    otherwise overlook, and the one analogical instance it presents is convincing.

4. Although weak in itself because it has only one analogical instance, it is still very
    strong because it is enthymematic for an analogy that mentions the constant nature
    of as many animals as we wish, because all are constant.

6. **Weak analogy:** LBJ taking care of daughters and the U.S. government protecting
    freedom everywhere are two vastly different undertakings, depending on totally
    different factors, namely, Johnson's economic position and the power of the U.S.
    relative to its enemies.

8. Although weak in itself, because it has only one analogical instance, it still is very
    strong because it is enthymematic for an analogy that mentions lots of cases where
    we note a correlation between our inner sensations and overt appearance and
    behavior. However, this argument from analogy to the existence of other streams of
    consciousness notoriously differs from most cases in that we can never check up
    directly to see if our conclusion is correct, because we cannot experience another
    person's experience (behaviorists and others obviously disagree in one way or
    another). (This last point is also relevant to question 7.)

Exercise 14-3

2. Theoretical.

4. Attention—theoretical; neutrinos—probably theoretical.

6. Both: ". . . looked red"—observable; ". . . he wasn't sure" that it was red—theoretical.

Exercise 14-4

2. Concomitant variation (negative).

4. Difference.

6. Agreement (negative).

8. Concomitant variation.

10. Agreement (negative) and agreement (positive).

12. Agreement and difference.

Exercise 14-5

2. False.

4. True.

6. True.

8. True.

10. False.

12. True.

14. True.

Exercise 14-6

2. (a) $p = 1/2 \times 1/2 = 1/4$
   (b) $p = 1/2 \times 1/2 \times 1/2 = 1/8$

4. Probability of even number = 3/6
   Probability of number less than 3 = 2/6
   Probability of even number less than 3 = $3/6 \times 2/6 = 1/6$
   Probability of either even number or number less than 3 (or both) =
   $3/6 + 2/6 - 1/6 = 4/6 = 2/3$

6. $P(p \cdot q) = P(p) \times P(q) = \dfrac{1}{10} \times \dfrac{1}{10} = \dfrac{1}{100}$ or $P(p \cdot q) = \dfrac{1}{10}$

   (This item is ambiguous.)

8. Probability of *HHT* or (*HTH* or *THH*) = $1/2 \times 1/2 \times 1/2 = 1/8$
   Probability of exactly two heads out of three = $1/8 + 1/8 + 1/8 = 3/8$

10. (a) Probability of ace on first draw = 1/13
       Probability of ace on second draw = 3/51
       Probability of two aces in a row = $1/13 \times 3/51 = 1/221$
    (b) Probability of at least one ace = $1/13 + 3/51 - 1/221 = 29/221$
    (c) Probability of first spade = 1/4
       Probability of second spade = 12/51
       Probability of two spades = $1/4 \times 12/51 = 1/17$
    (d) Probability of first black ace = 1/26
       Probability of second black ace = 1/51
       Probability of two black aces = $1/26 \times 1/51 = 1/1326$

Bibliography

The following is a selected list of books and articles dealing with material covered in this book. Starred items are mentioned in the body of the text.

Parts One and Two

Bochenski, I. M. *A History of Formal Logic.* Translated and edited by Ivo Thomas. New York: Chelsea, 1970.

*Church, Alonzo. *Introduction to Mathematical Logic.* Princeton, N.J.: Princeton University Press, 1956.

*Copi, Irving. *Symbolic Logic,* Seventh Edition. New York: Macmillan, 1986.

*Fitch, Frederick B. *Symbolic Logic.* New York: The Ronald Press, 1952.

Jeffrey, Richard. *Formal Logic: Its Scope and Limit.* Second Edition. New York: McGraw-Hill, 1981.

Kleene, Stephen C. *Mathematical Logic.* New York: John Wiley, 1967.

Kneale, W., and M. Kneale. *The Development of Logic.* Oxford: Clarendon Press, 1962.

Lemmon, E. J. *Beginning Logic.* Revised by G. N. D. Barry. Indianapolis: Hackett, 1978. London: Thomas Nelson, 1965.

*Purtill, Richard L. *Logic for Philosophers.* New York: Harper & Row, 1971.

Reichenbach, Hans. *Elements of Symbolic Logic.* New York: Macmillan, 1947. Reprinted in a Dover edition.

*Russell, Bertrand. *Principles of Mathematics.* Cambridge, England: Cambridge University Press, 1903.

*_____. "On Denoting." *Mind*, n.s., vol. 14 (1905). Reprinted in *Logic and Knowledge*, edited by Robert C. Marsh. New York: Macmillan, 1956.

*_____. "Mr. Strawson on Referring." In *My Philosophical Development.* London: Allen and Unwin, 1959.

*Strawson, P. F. "On Referring." *Mind*, n.s., vol. 59 (1950).

*Suppes, Patrick. *Introduction to Logic.* Princeton, N.J.: Van Nostrand, 1957.

*Tarski, Alfred. "Semantic Conception of Truth." *Philosophy and Phenomenological Research*, vol. 4 (1944).

*Wittgenstein, Ludwig. *Tractatus Logico Philosophicus.* New York: Harcourt Brace, 1922.

Part Three

*Anderson, Allan Ross. "On the Logic of Commitment." *Philosophical Studies*, vol. X (1959).

*Ayer, A. J. *Language, Truth and Logic.* New York: Dover.

*Barcan Marcus, Ruth. "A Functional Calculus of First Order Based on Strict Implication." *Journal of Symbolic Logic*, vol. II (1946).

*Barker, Stephen. *Elements of Logic.* Fifth Edition. New York: McGraw-Hill, 1989.

*Baum, Robert. *Logic.* Second Edition. New York: Holt, Rinehart and Winston, 1981.

*Bergmann, Gustav. "The Philosophical Significance of Modal Logic." *Mind*, n.s., vol. 69 (1960).

Bird, Otto. *Syllogistics and Its Extensions.* Englewood Cliffs, N.J.: Prentice-Hall, 1964.

*Blair, J. Anthony, and Ralph H. Johnson, *Informal Logic: The First International Symposium.* Inverness, Calif.: Edgepress, 1980.

*Cadwallader, Eva H. "Christine Ladd-Franklin's Antilogism." *Newsletter on the Teaching of Philosophy*, Fall 1980.

*Carnap, Rudolf. "On the Application of Inductive Logic." *Philosophy and Phenomenological Research*, vol. 8 (1947).

*_____. *The Continuum of Inductive Methods.* Chicago: University of Chicago Press, 1952.

*_____. *Logical Foundations of Probability.* Second Edition. Chicago: University of Chicago Press, 1962.

*Carroll, Lewis. *Symbolic Logic and the Game of Logic.* New York: Dover, 1958.

*Castañeda, Hector-Neri. "The Logic of Obligation." *Philosophical Studies*, vol. 10 (1959).

Church, Alonzo. *Introduction to Mathematical Logic.* Princeton, N.J.: Princeton University Press, 1956.

Cohen, Morris R., and Ernest Nagel. *An Introduction to Logic.* New York: Harcourt, 1962.

Copi, Irving. *Symbolic Logic.* Sixth Edition. New York: Macmillan, 1982.

*_____. *Introduction to Logic.* Seventh Edition. New York: Macmillan, 1986.

*Danto, Arthur C. "On Knowing That We Know." In *Epistemology*, edited by Avrum Stroll. New York: Harper & Row, 1967.

*Dodgson, C. L. (Lewis Carroll). *Symbolic Logic.* 1896.

Eaton, Ralph M. *General Logic.* New York: Charles Scribner's Sons, 1931.

*Gensler, Harry. "Star Test." *Notre Dame Journal of Formal Logic*, vol. 14 (1973).

*Gierre, Ronald. *Understanding Scientific Reasoning.* Second Edition. New York: Holt, Rinehart and Winston, 1984.

*Goodman, Nelson. *Fact, Fiction, and Forecast.* Third Edition. Indianapolis: Bobbs-Merrill, 1973.

*Hempel, Carl. "Studies in the Logic of Confirmation." *Mind*, n.s., vol. 54 (1945).

*_____. *Philosophy of Natural Science.* Englewood Cliffs, N.J.: Prentice-Hall, 1966.

*Hume, David. *A Treatise of Human Nature.*

_____. *An Enquiry Concerning Human Understanding.*

*Kahane, Howard. "Baumer on the Confirmation Paradoxes." *British Journal for the Philosophy of Science*, vol. 18 (1967).

*_____. "Eliminative Confirmation and Paradoxes." *British Journal for the Philosophy of Science*, vol. 20 (1969).

*_____. "Pathological Predicates and Projection." *American Philosophical Quarterly*, vol. 8 (1971).

*_____. *Logic and Contemporary Rhetoric.* Eighth Edition. Belmont, Calif.: Wadsworth, 1998.

*_____. "Hempel and Goodman on the Ravens." (Private paper)

*Kleene, S. C. *Introduction to Meta-Mathematics.* New York: Van Nostrand, 1964.

*Mendelson, Elliot. *Introduction to Mathematical Logic.* Second Edition. Princeton, N.J.: Van Nostrand, 1979.

*Mill, John Stuart. *Systems of Logic.*

Nagel, Ernest. *The Structure of Science.* New York: Harcourt, 1961.

*Oliver, James W. "Formal Fallacies and Other Invalid Arguments." *Mind*, n.s., vol. 76 (1967).

Orwell, George. "Politics and the English Language." In *Shooting an Elephant and Other Essays.* New York: Harcourt Brace, 1945.

*Peirce, Charles. "Induction as Experimental and Self-Correcting." *Collected Papers of Charles Sanders Peirce*, vol. VI. Edited by Charles Hartshorne and Paul Weiss. Cambridge: Harvard University Press, 1935.

*Pole, Nelson. "A Deductive Argument with a Specific Premise and a General Conclusion." *Notre Dame Journal of Formal Logic*, vol. XVI (1975).

*Popper, Karl. *The Logic of Scientific Discovery.* New York: Basic Books, 1959.

*Quine, Willard V. "Notes on Existence and Necessity." *Journal of Philosophy*, vol. 40 (1943).

*_____. *From a Logical Point of View.* Cambridge: Harvard University Press, 1953.

*Ramsey, Frank. *The Foundations of Mathematics.* London: Routledge & Kegan Paul, 1931.

*Reichenbach, Hans. *The Theory of Probability.* Berkeley: University of California Press, 1949.

*_____. *Rise of Scientific Philosophy.* Berkeley: University of California Press, 1951.

*_____. *Nomological Statements and Admissible Operations.* Amsterdam: North Holland Publishing, 1954.

Reichman, William J. *Use and Abuse of Statistics.* New York: Oxford University Press, 1962.

*Rescher, Nicholas. "An Axiom System for Deontic Logic." *Philosophical Studies*, vol. IX (1958).

*Robison, John. "Further Difficulties for Conditional Permission in Deontic Logic." *Philosophical Studies*, vol. XVIII (1967).

*Ruby, Lionel. *The Art of Making Sense.* Second Edition. New York: J. B. Lippincott, 1954.

Salmon, Wesley C. *Scientific Explanation and the Causal Structure of the World.*

_____. *The Foundations of Scientific Inference.* Pittsburgh: University of Pittsburgh Press, 1967.

*Sanford, David. "Contraries and Subcontraries." *Nous*, vol. 2 (1968).

*Skyrms, Brian. *Choice and Chance.* Third Edition. Belmont, Calif.: Wadsworth, 1985.

*Suppes, Patrick. *Introduction to Logic.* Princeton, N.J.: Van Nostrand, 1957.

*von Wright, G. H. *Logical Problems of Induction.* Second Revised Edition. New York: Barnes & Noble, 1965.

*Woozley, A. D. "Universals." *Encyclopedia of Philosophy.* Edited by Paul Edwards. New York: Collier Macmillan, 1967.

Special Symbols

Index

Five Rules for Valid Syllogisms

All valid syllogisms must have

1. A middle term which is distributed at least once.

2. No term distributed in its conclusion which is not distributed in a premise.

3. At least one affirmative (nonnegative) premise.

4. A negative conclusion if and only if one of its premises is negative.

5. One particular premise if the conclusion is particular.

Antilogism Rules for Valid Syllogisms

1. Construct the antilogism by replacing the syllogism's conclusion by its negation.

2. The syllogism is valid if and only if its antilogism meets the following conditions:
   a. Exactly one of its three statements is an inequality.
   b. One of the two equalities has a term negated in the other equality.
   c. Each of the two terms in the inequality is either negated in both of its occurrences or in neither.

Truth Tables for Sentence Connectives

p	$\sim p$
T	F
F	T

p	q	$p \vee q$
T	T	T
T	F	T
F	T	T
F	F	F

p	q	$p \cdot q$
T	T	T
T	F	F
F	T	F
F	F	F

p	q	$p \supset q$
T	T	T
T	F	F
F	T	T
F	F	T

p	q	$p \equiv q$
T	T	T
T	F	F
F	T	F
F	F	T

Rules for Sentential Logic Truth Trees

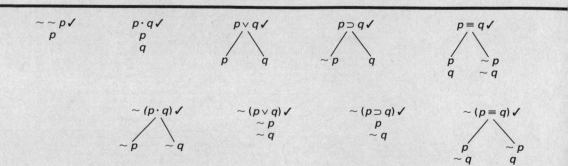

Rules of the Probability Calculus

1.	**Restricted Conjunction Rule:**	If p and q are independent events, then $P(p \cdot q) = P(p) \times P(q)$
2.	**General Conjunction Rule:**	$P(p \cdot q) = P(p) \times P(q, \text{if } p)$
3.	**Restricted Disjunction Rule:**	If p and q are mutually exclusive events, then $P(p \vee q) = P(p) + P(q)$
4.	**General Disjunction Rule:**	$P(p \vee q) = P(p) + P(q) - P(p \cdot q)$
5.	**Probability of a Contradiction:**	$P(p \cdot \sim p) = 0$
6.	**Probability of a Tautology:**	$P(p \vee \sim p) = 1$

7. **Bayes' Theorem (simplified form):**

$$P(q, \text{given } p) = \frac{P(q) \times P(p, \text{given } q)}{[P(q) \times P(p, \text{given } q)] + [P(\sim q) \times P(p, \text{given} \sim q)]}$$

8. **Bayes' Theorem (general form):**

$$P(q_1, \text{given } p) = \frac{P(q_1) \times P(p, \text{given } q_1)}{[P(q_1) \times P(p, \text{given } q_1)] + \ldots + [P(q_n) \times P(p, \text{given } q_n)]}$$

Basic Patterns of Inductive Generalization

Categorical Form:

1.	$Fa \cdot Ga$
2.	$Fb \cdot Gb$
3.	$Fc \cdot Gc$
	.
	.
	.
N.	No F is known not to have G.
$/\therefore N + 1.$	All F's are G's $(x)(Fx \supset Gx)$

Statistical Form:

1.	$N\%$ of all F's tested for G have G.
$/\therefore$ 2.	$N\%$ of all F's (tested or otherwise) have G.

Categorical Analogical Form:

1.	All F's tested (or observed) for G have G.
$/\therefore$ 2.	This particular F has G.

Statistical Analogical Form:

1.	$N\%$ of the F's tested for G have G.
$/\therefore$ 2.	The probability is $N\%$ that this F has G.

Mill's Methods:

The Method of Agreement: If we find two or more instances in which P occurs an only one other phenomenon, Q, is present in each instance, then P is the cause of Q, or Q of P.

The Method of Difference: If an instance in which P occurs and an instance in whi P does not occur are alike in every respect except one, Q, and Q occurs only wher P occurs, then P is the cause of Q, or Q of P.

The Method of Concomitant Variation: If P varies in amount or degree in some regular way with Q, then P and Q are causally related.